45⁰⁰
34²⁵

?53

GLOBAL MARKETING

PERSPECTIVES AND CASES

GLOBAL MARKETING

PERSPECTIVES AND CASES

SALAH S. HASSAN

The George Washington University

ROGER D. BLACKWELL

The Ohio State University

THE DRYDEN PRESS

HARCOURT BRACE COLLEGE PUBLISHERS

*Fort Worth   Philadelphia   San Diego   New York   Orlando   Austin   San Antonio
Toronto   Montreal   London   Sydney   Tokyo*

*With special appreciation to
Salem Hassan for the aesthetic
input that led to the artistic
concept that lends elegance
to this book.*

Acquisitions Editor:	Lyn Keeney Hastert
Production Manager:	Trisha Dianne
Manager of Production:	Diane Southworth
Manager of Art and Design:	Melinda Huff
Text Design:	Lewis Glaser
Cover and Part Opener Illustrations:	Lamberto Alvarez/Lamberto Alvarez, III
Project Management:	Ruth Cottrell
Compositor:	G & S Typesetters, Inc.

ISBN 0-03-098107-7

Library of Congress Catalog Card Number: 93-73016

Printed in the United States of America

4   5   6   7   8   9   0   1   2   3   090   9   8   7   6   5   4   3   2   1

ABOUT THE AUTHORS

SALAH S. HASSAN is an Associate Professor of Marketing at The George Washington University. He received his Ph.D. in 1984 from The Ohio State University. He is recognized for his research on global marketing, new product marketing, and international market segmentation. His work has been cited in leading publications such as *Advertising Age*, *AdWEEK*, and *Marketing News*.

Dr. Hassan is widely published in trade and academic journals, and this is his second book on global marketing. Dr. Hassan serves on the editorial boards of several journals such as the *Journal of Global Marketing* and as a guest editor for the *Journal of International Consumer Marketing*. Recent publications have appeared in refereed journals, including the *Journal of Euromarketing*, *Journal of International Consumer Marketing*, and the *International Journal of Bank Marketing*.

Dr. Hassan has consulted for marketing and research projects for several organizations in diverse industries, including travel and tourism, information services, packaged goods, and manufacturing. He has also conducted executive training programs for international business managers under the auspices of the U.S. Agency for International Development, American University in Cairo, Westinghouse Electric Corporation, Price Waterhouse, and ARAMCO.

ROGER D. BLACKWELL is a Professor of Marketing and Consumer Behavior at The Ohio State University. He is also president of Roger Blackwell Associates, Inc., a consulting firm in Columbus, Ohio, through which he has worked with many corporations throughout the world. He received a Ph.D. from Northwestern University and B.S. and M.S. degrees from the University of Missouri.

Dr. Blackwell was named "Outstanding Marketing Educator in America" by Sales and Marketing Executives International and received the "Alumni Distinguished Teaching Award," the highest award given by Ohio State. Having lectured around the world, he is often quoted in such publications as *Business Week*, *International Herald Tribune*, and *The Wall Street Journal* and has appeared on numerous television programs including *CBS This Morning*.

Dr. Blackwell is co-author of *Consumer Behavior* and *Contemporary Cases in Consumer Behavior,* used by schools throughout North America, Europe, Asia, and Africa. He has also published articles in *Journal of Marketing Research, Journal of Advertising Research, Journal of International Consumer Marketing,* and other journals. At The Ohio State University, he teaches courses in marketing, consumer behavior, and global marketing strategy.

Contributors

LYN S. AMINE, Associate Professor of Marketing and International Business, School of Business Administration, Saint Louis University, St. Louis, Missouri.

BEVERLEE B. ANDERSON, Professor of Marketing and Dean, College of Business Administration, California State University San Marcos, San Marcos, California.

RENA BARTOS, author and consultant on communications and consumer issues, formerly senior vice president and director of communication development at the J. Walter Thompson Company, New York, New York.

ANN C. BROWN, Adjunct Professor, School of Human Ecology, Virginia State University, Ettrick, Virginia.

MARY K. ERICKSEN, Associate Professor of Marketing, Bloomsburg University, Bloomsburg, Pennsylvania.

DHRUV GREWAL, Assistant Professor of Marketing, University of Miami, Coral Gables, Florida.

CURTIS P. HAUGTVEDT, Assistant Professor of Marketing, The Ohio State University, Columbus, Ohio.

JOHN S. HILL, Professor of International Business and Marketing, University of Alabama, Tuscaloosa, Alabama.

C. L. HUNG, Associate Professor, Faculty of Management, The University of Calgary, Calgary, Canada.

YOUNGHO LEE, Professor of Business Administration, School of Business, Howard University, Washington, D.C.

GARRY McCAIN, Professor of Marketing, Boise State University, Boise, Idaho.

JANE McNEILL, research assistant at the Roy E. Crummer Graduate School of Business, Rollins College, Winter Park, Florida.

MICHAEL MINOR, Associate Professor of Marketing and International Business, University of Texas-Pan American, Edinburg, Texas.

AMY S. MOBLEY, market analyst, McDonald and Company Securities Inc., Cleveland, Ohio.

SAK ONKVISIT, Professor of Marketing, College of Business, San Jose State University, San Jose, California.

NINA M. RAY, Associate Professor of Marketing, Boise State University, Boise, Idaho.

MARY ELLEN RYDER, Assistant Professor of Linguistics, Boise State University, Boise, Idaho.

A. COSKUN SAMLI, Research Professor of Marketing and International Business, College of Business Administration, University of North Florida, Jacksonville, Florida.

PAUL L. SAUER, Associate Professor of Marketing, Canisius College, Buffalo, New York.

STANLEY V. SCOTT, Associate Professor of Marketing, School of Business, University of Alaska Anchorage, Anchorage, Alaska.

JOHN J. SHAW, Professor of Marketing, Providence College, Providence, Rhode Island.

AHMED A. SOLIMAN, Associate Professor of Business Administration, College of Administrative Sciences, King Saud University, Riyadh, Saudi Arabia. Formerly on the faculties of Baruch College, Fairleigh Dickinson University, and University of North Carolina.

H. RAO UNNAVA, Assstant Professor of Marketing, The Ohio State University, Columbus, Ohio.

SANDRA VANDERMERWE, Professor of International Marketing and Services, The International Institute for Management Development, Lausanne, Switzerland.

M. VENKATESAN, Professor of Marketing, University of Rhode Island, Kingston, Rhode Island.

JULIAN W. VINCZE, Professor of Marketing, the Roy E. Crummer Graduate School of Business, Rollins College, Winter Park, Florida. Held Visiting Professor appointments at both Nijenrode University and the University of Twente, The Netherlands.

MURRAY W. YOUNG, Lecturer of International Business, Chinese University of Hong Kong, Shatin, Hong Kong. Formerly on the faculty of the University of Denver.

PREFACE

Teaching marketing and business courses today is a little like what Magellan, Columbus, and other early voyagers must have felt as they left familiar domestic waters for the uncharted areas of the new world. The rest of the world was always in existence, of course, but it was unknown and uncharted for the early "discoverers."

To teach or write about marketing from a global perspective is much the same process. The markets of the world were already in existence, of course. They were simply unknown and uncharted.

The purpose of this book is much like the maps of old. The book is designed to describe some of the changing landscapes of the global business world. The emphasis is on uncharted areas—new perspectives of global markets. Like the voyagers of old, we have relied on the best knowledge of other voyagers from around the world—the authors who contributed their original work to this new book.

TARGET AUDIENCE

This book is designed to provide the reader with cutting edge knowledge and know-how about global marketing. Specifically, it is designed to be used in marketing management, consumer behavior, and other courses where instructors want to go beyond the domestic market approach of standard books by adding global perspectives and cases. We believe it can be used as a supplementary text in many executive seminars as well as MBA and senior-level courses.

Many textbooks on international or global marketing spend so many of their pages on basic marketing concepts and principles that they have little time or space available for more advanced concepts and principles that apply specifically to global markets. This book fills that need. It should coordinate nicely with most of the existing textbooks used in international business, international marketing, and global marketing strategy courses.

This book can also be used as a core textbook in courses on globalized consumer markets. Recent professional meetings have defined the need for new courses on global consumer behavior and global advertising. We designed this book to be the core for such courses.

OUTLINE

In Part I we present strategic global marketing perspectives. In the first chapter, we try to give an emphasis on global thinking by looking at global business from the Dutch perspective—a perspective that has been global and profitable for several millennia. Global thinking implies corporate philosophy and skill that is based on understanding markets beyond one's own country-of-origin with respect to sources of demand, sources of supply, and methods of effective management and marketing. It is in this section of the book that we raise the strategic relevance of understandng the differences between international, global, and multinational approaches, as well as the questions of standardization versus localization.

Part II stresses the importance of global market segmentation. This concept is key to competitive global marketing decisions. Should firms focus on segments within markets (intramarket segmentation), or should they focus on segments across national boundaries (intermarket segmentation)? This part of the the book contains rich examples of the concept, including segmentation based on teenage consumers, "green" consumers, female consumers, and upscale consumers.

Part III focuses on consumer behavior in the global marketplace. Consumer behavior textbooks contain some materials on global behavior, of course, but in this section we go further by examining consumer behavior cross-culturally. Some of these topics include temporal dimensions across cultures, the effects of country-of-origin, and related information processing.

Part IV focuses on global advertising. In this section, the chapters examine the topic of cross-cultural communications, the impact of EC initiatives on global advertising, a cross-cultural analysis of automobile advertising in various countries, and the effective use of multilingual advertising.

Part V raises some very important macromarketing issues. Communism, to some extent, is rapidly being replaced by capitalism. But what kind of capitalism? And what is the role of marketing in market-driven communistic economies? These and other issues are provocative predictors of these and other consumption issues.

Part VI presents key global cases for discussion and analysis. This is where the "rubber meets the road." The cases were chosen to include a variety of problems, industries, countries-of-origin, and types of organization. We believe that many readers will be fascinated by the practical and philosophical problems of nonprofit marketing at the World Wildlife Fund. Plenty of problems will occupy students who choose to deal with the global marketing issues in the Reebok and Center Parcs cases. Japan Airlines, Wendy's International, Xerox, and Singapore Airlines are companies that are well known and are attempting, in a variety of ways, to survive and prosper in the global marketplace. We think readers will also be fascinated by the Kintetsu case and the insights this case brings to understanding the Japanese marketing environment.

ACKNOWLEDGMENTS

A book of this type is unique. Although we have taken the initiative in designing it and putting it together, the contributing authors of each chapter are the real "discoverers." Although we have tried to put the pieces of the map together in a meaningful framework and have done some editing, it is they who are pushing forward the map of knowledge about global marketing perspectives. We are grateful for their original contributions as well as grateful to the reviewers who helped us in the selections and the refinement of these contributions. Acknowledgment with appreciation is due to members of this book's editorial review board:

Philip R. Cateora, University of Colorado at Boulder
Michael R. Czinkota, Georgetown University
George Fisk, Emory University
Subhash Jain, University of Connecticut
Pradeep Rau, The George Washington University
David Ricks, American Graduate School of Int'l. Management
Jagdish N. Sheth, Emory University
James Sood, The American University
Attila Yaprak, Wayne State University
Ugur Yavas, East Tennessee State University

Many other colleagues gave assistance and invaluable advice throughout this book. Specifically, we appreciate the useful insights and suggestions provided by Kristina Blackwell, C.D.I.; Tevfik Dalgic, Henley Management College, The Netherlands; Adel I. El-Ansary, University of North Florida; Abdalla Hanafy, St. Cloud State University; Ibrahim A. Hegazy, The American University in Cairo, Egypt; Lea Prevel Katsanis, Concordia University, Canada; Erdener Kaynak, Pennsylvania State University at Harrisburg; Jonathan S. Kim, International University of Japan; Lynda Maddox, The George Washington University; Gillian Rice, American Graduate School of International Management; Fernando Robles, The George Washington University; A. Coskun Samli, University of North Florida; Stanley V. Scott, University of Alaska Anchorage; W. Wayne Talarzyk, The Ohio State University; and Sandra Vandermerwe, International Institute for Management Development, Switzerland.

We also gratefully acknowledge the help of Lyn Keeney Hastert, acquisitions editor at HBJ/Dryden Press, Trisha Dianne, Melinda Huff, and Ruth Cottrell, whose copyediting assistance was invaluable.

Finally, we dedicate this book to the very special people whose emotional support gave us an endless supply of energy to complete this voyage—our families.

Salah S. Hassan   Roger D. Blackwell
Washington, D.C.   Columbus, Ohio

CONTENTS IN BRIEF

CONTENTS

PART I

STRATEGIC GLOBAL MARKETING PERSPECTIVES

CHAPTER 1

GLOBAL MARKETING:
PERSPECTIVES AND ISSUES *

Roger D. Blackwell

Salah S. Hassan

Perhaps you are a person who believes that a museum or a history book is the best way to learn how to be a winner in today's highly competitive global economy. Or perhaps you are not. But museums can be a great place to start learning about the world. Consider the museums in modern-day Netherlands. Think about what you will find if you walk through a museum in Amsterdam or if you read about Holland's history.

As you walk through an Amsterdam museum, you see that many of the great Dutch paintings are small, in contrast to the massive paintings that are found in other European museums. Why? Because many of the Dutch masterpieces were commissioned for the comfortable but modest homes of Dutch business families and guildhouses. In the rest of Europe, the only people who could afford expensive art were Kings and the Church. Consequently, the great works of art were usually sizes that were suited to castles and cathedrals.

The culture of the Netherlands encouraged trading on a global basis, and this facilitated the rise of the great Dutch trading companies. These companies massed much wealth, not only for the companies but for the families who worked in and for the trading companies. The people of the Netherlands had a global business perspective centuries ago when many of their peers had a perspective limited to gold, colonization, and military

*The authors want to acknowledge Kristina Blackwell's useful insights and suggestions throughout this chapter.

conquest. Although the effects of the Dutch global perspective were felt from Manhattan to Cape Town to Jakarta, they were felt just as much in the prosperity of Dutch homes and families.

The early history of the Netherlands also provides a managerial perspective for business people who seek prosperity and competitive survival today. To control flooding, the Dutch needed to dam the Amstel River, but to do so would have created a problem for the many boats using the river for commerce. The Dutch could have ignored the concerns of their neighboring trading partners, but wisely they didn't want to make trouble. Instead, the industrious Dutch proposed a solution. They would provide the service of taking boats out of the river and carrying them around the dam. Furthermore, the proposed fee was so modest and the service so good that the boat owners agreed to the Dutch service fee. The Dutch could have taken the "It's not our problem" approach, or they could have taken advantage of their monopoly power, as many firms try to do today with patents, software, location, or other advantages. If the Dutch had done so in this instance, others, such as the powerful Germans, might have destroyed the dam and with it the Dutch. Then neither the dam nor the Dutch would have survived or prospered.

But the Dutch did survive and prosper, and so do firms that are built on the same principles. Provide a needed service, do it well, and charge low prices. The Dutch did it so well that they dominated much of the world's trade for centuries with their tiny resource base and without much military power. Consider the fact that, until recently, the Dutch owned more of the United States than any another country except the U.K. Or consider the fact that tiny Netherlands exports more value in agricultural products than Canada. Or consider the fact that such massive firms as KLM, Unilever, and Shell are based in such a small country. The Dutch mastered a basic principle of marketing that still works today: Make a little on a lot.

The Dutch principle of make a little on a lot is not only a way to make a fortune; it is also the way to dominate competitors from any country. If you consider the strategy for entering global markets used by many Japanese firms, you can see a lot of similarities to the Dutch approach. You also see it in the strategies of the emerging giant corporations of Korea, as well as in emerging economies of the world. Growing up Dutch is no guarantee of success for individuals or companies. But it does provide a perspective about business. In the case of the Dutch, it is definitely a global perspective.

Providing global perspectives about business is the purpose of this book. Having a global perspective is no guarantee of success for you individually or for your company. But it is an indispensable edge for survival and prosperity in today's globalized economy. Global perspectives provide an added advantage in all areas of marketing from advertising to product development, from operations to logistics management, and in many other areas of business strategy and tactics.

You can gain "global perspectives" on many areas of marketing and business strategy from the following chapters. These perspectives were prepared by some of the leading scholars and observers of global business from locations throughout the world. Learning these perspectives may give you an edge over business people who lack such global perspectives, whether your interest be product development, segmentation, promotion and communications, or other areas of marketing. These perspectives are not a replacement for the basic principles that must be learned in courses and textbooks on such topics. The methods of segmentation or advertising programs are fundamentally the same, regardless of geographic location. Rather, the concepts in this book are presented from global perspectives to enhance the effectiveness of the basic functions of marketing; they are the "extra edge" to help you compete in a changing global economy.

Ability to Think Globally

Global perspectives on marketing can be either general or specific. General perspectives might include understanding the process of inter-market segmentation—defining and delighting groups of consumers on a global basis. Specific perspectives include understanding how to profile and reach global teenage segments, global green segments, or affluent segments.

One of the most important perspectives that can be developed in future managers is the ability to think globally. Perhaps no person should be promoted to a position of major responsibility in a contemporary organization if that individual cannot "think globally."

The ability to think globally is not limited to the personal level. It also implies corporate philosophy and skill. In either case, it is increasingly a key to prosperity for individuals and organizations seeking to survive in contemporary, globalized economies. Thus the ability to think globally is the foundation for many of the general and specific managerial perspectives and issues advanced in the following pages.

Global thinking can be defined as the ability to understand markets beyond one's own country-of-origin with respect to (1) sources of demand, (2) sources of supply, and (3) methods of effective management and marketing. These are the key dimensions of global thinking that have produced practical results for world-class organizations.

GLOBAL THINKING

Dimensions	Practical Results
1. Understanding demand	How to market to worldwide buyers
2. Understanding sources of supply	How to source more efficiently
3. Understanding management and marketing methods	How to manufacture and market more effectively

Practical examples may help you understand the concept of global thinking and its three major dimensions. Using this concept of global thinking, Exhibit 1-1 examines three different companies and how they think globally in their business practices.

Global thinking is important in the study of both macromarketing and micromarketing issues. The standard of living and therefore the marketing environment of a country, the subject of macromarketing analysis, are very much influenced by the ability to think globally, as you observed in the opening paragraphs of this chapter about the Netherlands. Many more examples would be possible.

What country has the highest per capita dollar income, decade after decade? The highest income varies a bit from year to year, depending on currency fluctuation, but Switzerland is often at the top of the list. Japan also ranks high, sometimes in second place. Some of the greatest gains in recent decades have been in Singapore, often called the "Economic Miracle of the East."

Why is one country prosperous and another country not prosperous?

EXHIBIT 1-1
GOING GLOBAL:
DIFFERENT STROKES
FOR DIFFERENT FOLKS
SOURCE: REPRINTED
FROM JAMES F.
ENGEL, ROGER D.
BLACKWELL, AND PAUL
MINIARD, CONSUMER
BEHAVIOR, SEVENTH
EDITION (FORT
WORTH: DRYDEN
PRESS, 1993).

GLOBAL SOURCES OF DEMAND: Toys Я Us Sells to World Markets   In January 1992 Toys Я Us opened its second store in Kashihara, Japan after three years of planning and negotiating with the Japanese government. Building on its success in Europe, Toys Я Us has come to symbolize the heroic efforts often needed to open retail stores in the protected markets of Japan. President Bush was present for the opening and commented on how Toys Я Us has helped pave the way for other U.S. retailers to do the same.

Toys Я Us chairman and chief executive officer, Charles Lazarus, saw firsthand how the opportunities in the $6 billion Japanese toy market far outweighed the obstacles Toys Я Us faced. Approximately 160,000 shoppers filed through the doors of the Japanese outlet that day. Japanese con-

sumers, who place a high value on their children, were pleased with the
great selection and the relatively low prices. The independent Japanese toy
store owners that the government was trying to protect, however,
probably did not react as enthusiastically to the presence of the U.S. toy
powerhouse.

EXHIBIT 1-1
CONTINUED

GLOBAL SOURCES OF SUPPLY: The Limited Sources the World   One
of the world's most successful retailers of apparel, The Limited, achieved
its status because of its ability to think globally. With all of its retail outlets
located inside the United States, it can be described as a global company
because of its global sourcing practices.

   The process of getting its products on the store shelves begins with
the inception of the product design and ends with the shipment of the
garments to the individual stores, which at The Limited takes only approximately 60 days. Other retailers wait six to nine months for their
products. Besides superior logistics, one reason for the efficiency and
economy of this cycle is global sourcing. The designs are conceived in Italy
and other European countries, the garments are produced in Asian and
other countries by local manufacturers, and the garments shipped over
global logistics networks to Columbus, Ohio, where they are distributed
to the 3,600 retail outlets of The Limited, Express, Victoria's Secret, Aber-
crombie and Fitch, Lerner, Lane Bryant, and Henri Bendel.

GLOBAL MANAGEMENT AND MARKETING: Honeywell, Inc. Employs the
World   As companies become global in scope, managers face increased
responsibility for marketing to foreign countries and managing adaptation to cultural differences. European expansion often requires a "Euro-
manager" who can manage cultural diversity, understand foreign markets,
and travel or take temporary assignments in other countries to increase
his/her understanding of a foreign market. Firms such as Honeywell are
recognizing the increased need for hiring and promoting managers for
such services.

   Companies such as 3M are experimenting with international project
teams as an alternative to relocating its young managers to gain international experience. But Honeywell believes strongly in the value gained by
the company and the individual when managers work abroad. Honeywell
Europe offers an increased likelihood of promotion as an incentive for
temporary relocation. This incentive is supported by the fact that twelve
of the thirteen top positions at Honeywell Europe are held by non-Ameri-
cans, and Mr. Rosso, a Frenchman, heads the operation. His hope is that
a European executive will soon sit on the board of Honeywell in the
United States.

Some persons may naively answer, "natural resources." Yet Switzerland, Japan, and Singapore have no oil, few minerals, and little land (and most of the land in both Switzerland and Japan is covered with mountains). In contrast, Russia, Nigeria, and Brazil are examples of countries rich in natural resources but not rich in consumers' standard of living.

Why one country prospers and another does not is increasingly answered by the values of each country. The key is how people in the country have been acculturated to think about global markets and global marketing and management methods. The ability to function in a global economy is apparent in the cultures of both Japan and Switzerland.

The ability of Singapore to function as a globalized economy may not be as well known, but it is just as apparent if you have visited Singapore. It is a country with little poverty, little crime, little dirt, and one of the highest levels of computer literacy in the world. Much of the prosperity can be traced to the global perspectives found everywhere in Singapore.

More than 250 ships enter the Singapore harbor each day to be received by perhaps the most sophisticated loading and unloading system in the world. The same efficiency is true at the airport; there is no more efficient international facilitating institution than Changi Airport in Singapore. Changi also serves as the base for Singapore Airlines, the most consistently top ranked airline in the world even though it is based in a country of only about 3 million people! Walk through the shops of Singapore and you will see thousands of family-owned firms which, with the help of their suppliers, distribute goods from all parts of the world. Even the languages of the country—English and Mandarin—were chosen because they would aid the country in world trade, even though the choice meant abandoning Cantonese, the previous language of many of the citizens. Lee Kuan Yew, former prime minister, explains the process so anyone can understand the prosperity of this global thinking country: "We are a nation of immigrants; our values must be those required for stability, survival and success."

Global thinking provides many perspectives for understanding macroeconomic and macromarketing issues. In spite of the importance of macromarketing issues and the reality that they are critical elements in understanding the environment for marketing strategies, the focus of this book is on micromarketing issues. There are some instances, especially in Part V, in which macromarketing issues share more of the spotlight, but the overriding concern after this first chapter is on micromarketing issues—managerial perspectives and issues that will give you and your firm the ability to compete with and beat firms that lack the ability to be global thinkers.

What does it mean to say that a firm is a global firm? One way of answering this question is to examine a firm that is successful on a global basis. Such an example can be found in an industrial marketer called Liebert International, a division of Emerson Electric. Emerson Electric is a $7.7 billion corporation, regarded as one of the best managed in the United States because of the excellence of its strategic planning process (Knight 1992) and its record of increasing earnings and dividends every year for 35 consecutive years.

Exhibit 1-2 presents a minicase that describes how Liebert manifests all three dimensions of global thinking. Take time to study the Liebert minicase and you will see concrete examples of how a company has developed the ability to market to global buyers, the ability to source globally, and the ability to adopt global management and marketing methods. As you read through Exhibit 1-2, you should be able to see all three of these dimensions and consider how they might be applied to other business firms, whether those firms be large or small. Studying this minicase will also provide a structure and managerial perspectives that you may find helpful when analyzing the much longer cases in Part VI of this book.

Prosperity for firms and individuals is increasingly based on the ability to think globally. An interview with Karsten Boerger, president of Liebert International, illustrates the type of global thinking needed to survive and prosper in a global economy.

Liebert is the leading global producer of computer support systems for environmental control and site monitoring and the world's leading supplier of precise power distribution, power protection, and voltage regulation equipment for computer, industrial, and telecommunications applications.

"If we were not a global thinker, we would be a much smaller company," said Boerger at Liebert's headquarters in Columbus, Ohio. As CEO of Liebert International, Boerger has seen export sales grow in the past 10 years from $5 million to about $50 million. Global operations are much larger and now account for close to 50 percent of total Liebert sales.

Global thinking is so important to Liebert—and increasingly to all types of firms—that many of the jobs simply would not be available without the ability to compete in global markets. Boerger explains, "Liebert Associates know that international business is important to their job, so they go the extra mile for global exports." That sometimes means that they produce products in 10 days for export to China instead of taking more time, which is acceptable for domestic markets that have shorter shipping times. Boerger adds, "Our employees have not seen the recession our competitors have, because of our ability to compete in international markets."

EXHIBIT 1-2

HOW LIEBERT GROWS BY THINKING GLOBALLY

SOURCE: BASED ON MATERIALS ORIGINALLY PUBLISHED IN ROGER BLACKWELL, "LIEBERT GROWS BY THINKING GLOBALLY," COLUMBUS CEO (MARCH 1993), 16.

EXHIBIT 1-2
CONTINUED

What can other present and future managers learn from Liebert's success! First, effective managers must be able to lead firms into changing so they can be effective in global marketing. When Boerger arrived in 1983, Liebert was selling through distributors around the world as many competitors still do. Liebert had to lobby for the time and interest of its distributors. Today Liebert sells directly in most parts of the world.

The Hong Kong office provides an example of the results. In 1987, the distributor relationship was replaced by Liebert Hong King Limited. A local executive, Roger Chen, who is U.S. educated and Liebert trained, became managing director. The office soared from $600,000 sales in 1987 to $19.5 million in 1992 with a staff of nearly 50 people in Hong Kong. This office supports and coordinates with offices in Beijing, Shanghai, Chengdu, Guangzhou, Seoul, Taipei, and other cities. This is consistent with a major strategy for increasing commitment to Asia/Pacific markets by Liebert's parent, Emerson Electric.

Liebert gives its global offices a lot of freedom to make decisions based on local situations. Liebert does not send Americans to run offices in Hong Kong, Singapore, Germany, the U.K., or other Liebert locations. It recruits outstanding people from local offices, places a great deal of trust in them, and supports them with the rest of its global manufacturing and service force.

Boerger points out that Liebert is different from firms that try to have a standardized approach around the globe. Liebert International is run with few rules because every country has different ways of doing things: different power requirements, different shipping methods, and so forth. Instead of trying to sell standard American products to other countries, Liebert designs products that fit the special requirements of each country. U.S. product engineers, for example, go to Japan to be sure that U.S.-made products have the correct Japanese legends or gauges. This may be one of the most important principles a manager or future manager can learn from the Liebert approach to global thinking.

Boerger does have one rule for running an international company, however. Go to extremes to keep people happy in order to minimize turnover. Liebert's approach is to invest in good people rather than a rule book.

A second requirement for global thinking is the ability to source globally. Liebert manufactures products in several countries, including Italy, the U.K., and Ireland. "If you are not manufacturing in the European

Community, you are out of business," Boerger observes. European manufacturers will have increasing difficulty in selling to other countries, however, because of high wages, heavy social welfare costs, 6-week vacations, and 37-1/2 hour work weeks. Manufacturing in Liebert's U.S. plant is so efficient that it might not be necessary to have plants in other countries if it were not for fluctuations in the dollar and local-content requirements.

Liebert's sourcing is truly global, however. Liebert's U.K. manager gets help from Liebert's Taiwan purchasing person to buy components that are cheaper and better than European components. Liebert's sourcing includes working with an Indian firm that has developed such sophistication in design engineering and computer software that it can provide designs for Liebert products better and far more quickly than California suppliers.

3 The third lesson in global thinking that can be observed at Liebert is the ability to absorb the best in management and marketing methods, process engineering, and product improvements from around the world. When Liebert personnel compete with the best manufacturers and marketers in every part of the world, it helps Liebert be the best in the United States. Liebert is strong in Japan, so it knows about the latest Japanese advances in products and processes, something a nonglobal firm would find difficult. Boerger observes, "We benefit greatly by adopting the best from the best competitors throughout the world."

There is one important caveat in this process, however. Boerger points out that a global competitor must be careful not to add every feature from every part of the world. "To do so would price us out of the market. . . . there is no such thing as a global product for our firm. Maybe for a TV or radio but not in our company, or even in cars. We must produce the right product specifically for each country."

Karsten Boerger is himself a global person. Born in Germany, raised part of his life in South America, graduated from a Milwaukee high school, and a graduate in electrical engineering from a Wisconsin university, Boerger has perspectives that can benefit everyone.

Knowing foreign languages is essential, Boerger believes. When customers call from foreign countries, they find Liebert employees fluent in Spanish, Chinese, German, French, Portuguese, and other languages. Being bilingual is essential when a new secretary is recruited. Boerger believes U.S. students should learn a foreign language no later than the fourth or fifth grade. He also recommends students spend some time working overseas, if they want to be successful in business.

EXHIBIT 1-2
CONTINUED

THE CRITICALITY OF GLOBAL THINKING

Global thinking is a critical perspective for managers in firms of all sizes. Many industry analysts may think that global marketing strategies exist only among huge multinational enterprises (MNEs). Certainly globalization is a critical dimension in the survival potential of corporations such as General Motors, IBM, Xerox, Sony, Phillips, Nestlé, DeBeers, Ikea, McDonald's, and many other firms whose sales and number of employees outside their country of domicile often exceed 50 percent.

The effects of globalization are not limited to large corporations. Because of their size, small firms tend to be flexible and can adapt well to local markets—often better than large firms (Blackwell and Stephan 1991). Small, relatively obscure companies with specialized "niches" that transcend national boundaries are some of the most successful with global marketing programs. In fact 80 percent of the 100,000 U.S. companies that export are small businesses (*The Wall Street Journal* 1990). The perspectives on market segmentation, presented in Part II of this book, are just as relevant or more so for small firms than for large firms.

The globalization of marketing requires managers of all types, but especially those dealing with marketing, to understand the broad forces that characterize contemporary markets. The necessity of developing global perspectives can be accounted for by understanding some of the forces affecting the globalization of markets and international competition. These forces were identified by Porter (1986) to include the following:

1. Growing similarity of countries in terms of available infrastructure, distribution channels, and marketing approaches.
2. Fluid global capital markets. National capital markets are growing into global capital markets because of the large flow of funds between countries.
3. Technological restructuring—the reshaping of competition globally as a result of technological revolutions such as those in microelectronics.
4. The integrating role of technology. Reduced cost and increased impact of products have made them accessible to more global consumers.
5. New global competitors—a shift in competitors from traditional country competitors to emerging global competitors.

FALL OF THE WALL

The fall of the Berlin Wall may well have been the pivotal point in U.S. thinking about global management and education. Perhaps no single event sparked an interest in global markets and broke the bubble of eth-nocentricity as did the announcement that the Berlin Wall would be torn down. Ethnocentricity is a disease that has infected many American cor-porations for decades. Focusing only on one's own way of doing things with little sensitivity or interest in the ways of the rest of the world is a common symptom of this disease.

The fall of the wall provided a symbolic surrender in the Cold War that preoccupied Americans for close to a half century. Americans were raised in a culture that taught that communism was the mortal enemy of capitalism. Almost every aspect of national policy was dominated by the Cold War. Much of the industrial complex of the nation—especially re-search and development investment—was concentrated on supporting the "war against communism." Foreign policy decisions were dominated by a process that placed countries into one of two categories—allies or enemies. And the process was usually viewed in a military context, rarely as economic or trading allies or enemies.

For Japan and Germany, the globalization perspective was much dif-ferent. For the most part, the Japanese were prohibited from fighting the Cold War as a military power. Because the Germans might need to fight the Soviet Union, West Germany adopted a more military role than Ja-pan, but it was still a diminished role compared to that of the United States. With the military Cold War concentrated between the U.S. and the U.S.S.R., other countries began to rebuild their economic resources to be ready for a more globalized economy.

With the fall of the Berlin Wall, an astute observer might have para-phrased the ancient philosophy of monarchies by commenting, "The Cold War is over. Long live the Cold War." But the new cold war will be fought on economic principles with business strategies. Companies and countries that win this war will not be those with the most military re-sources, nor even with the most physical and natural resources. The new cold war is thoroughly globalized and will be won by individuals and or-ganizations with the most effective perspectives on global marketing and management.

The Berlin Wall did not come down because of debate about Marxist–Leninist philosophy. The wall came down because of empiricism. East Germans looked across the wall figuratively—and with the aid of televi-sion, literally—and saw that the market system produced ample numbers of telephones and cars whereas communism did not. Hardly anyone ex-pected the fall would be so abrupt. Nor did people expect the reverbera-tions to come so soon and to be so strong. No longer is the war between communism and capitalism (despite vestiges that remain); today the war is between various forms of capitalism that might loosely be called the American, the Japanese, and the German versions.

Lester Thurow, in his book *Head to Head* (1992), looked at the more than 340 million consumers in the European market and concluded that as the largest market in the world, Europe will do what the country with the largest market historically does. The dominant country will establish the economic and marketing rules for the rest of the world. The General Agreement on Tariffs and Trade (GATT) has fallen apart for precisely this reason; the United States can no longer set the rules. In the nineteenth century, the British dominated the world and established the rules for the global economy. In the twentieth century, the United States dominated the rules that managers had to learn if they operated globally. In the twenty-first century management and marketing will be dominated, if Thurow is correct in his analysis, by the Europeans, who will be dominated by the large and economically powerful, reunified Germany.

CAPITALISTIC DIVERSITY

The environment for global business today is one of capitalistic diversity. There is no longer a monolithic concept of capitalism. In addition to the Japanese, American, and European versions, there are variations that are distinctively Dutch, Singaporian, Korean, South African, Middle Eastern, and reflections of other countries.

Variations of the new blended economies are also found from the remnants of communism. China and the U.S.S.R. took different paths toward a market economy. The U.S.S.R. changed its political system before changing its economic system. China is changing its economic system before changing its political system. The world is watching to see which process is best. But both countries depend on global business to move ahead, and both countries provide opportunities in the future for globalized firms that understand the changes in China, the former U.S.S.R., and countries such as Cuba and North Korea.

A MANAGERIAL PERSPECTIVE ON GLOBAL OPPORTUNITIES

Enhancing shareholder value is the foundation of corporate strategy. Long-term, sustainable growth is the watchword for what the financial community expects a firm's senior management to be able to accomplish. Senior management, in turn, expects marketing managers to be able to deliver growth. Among both large and small firms, achieving the goal of long-term growth increasingly requires a globalized approach to competitive strategy.

At least two reasons exist for the new emphasis on globalized marketing strategies in large, successful firms that formerly depended on the domestic economy to provide growth opportunities. One reason is the declining rate of growth of population and the accompanying saturation of domestic markets in affluent countries. The other reason for the increasing search for global growth is the declining need for human workers in industrialized economies.

Saturated Domestic Markets in Affluent Countries

Growth-oriented firms, striving for enhanced shareholder value (ESV), need to find growth markets to grow profits. This often requires a global perspective to determine where the growth markets are—and are not—focusing on the variables of population and ability to buy.

Birth Dearth   The ability to buy has been concentrated historically in North America, Europe, and Japan. However, these affluent countries are expecting a decline or small increase in population in the next decade. Industrialized countries (North America, Europe, Israel, Japan, Australia) are projected to decline from 15 percent of the world's population in 1985 to barely 5 percent in the year 2100 (Wattenberg 1987).

European populations in Germany, the Scandinavian countries, and most of the other European countries have been flat or declining for several years—one of the reasons for the European Single Market Initiative that took effect on December 31, 1992.

The United States population is so large and, until recently, so rapidly growing that U.S. firms rarely faced saturation of domestic markets. Now, with the declining growth rate of population in the United States, many U.S. firms have a new impetus to search for success in the same segments they dominated in the past—but the same segments are now located in other countries. It is no accident that some of the most successful globalized companies are domiciled in countries such as Switzerland, Netherlands, and Japan. These countries—small in size and with slow-growth, aging populations—require globalized strategies to increase ESV in companies.

Growth Opportunities   Some countries are projected to grow rapidly. The fastest-growing country in the world is India. If current trends continue, India will surpass China as the largest country in the world in the next century. Kenya is one of the fastest-growing countries by percentage increase, rising at the rate of 4.2 percent annually. Another fast-growing country is Bangladesh, the eighth most populous nation in the world and growing rapidly. Between 1983 and 2000, 52 million people are projected to be added to Bangladesh's population. That is roughly equivalent to a country with the population of France being added to a state the size of Georgia.

The difference between growth rates of developed and developing countries is dramatically changing global marketing strategies. In 1950, only 8 of the top 15 most populous countries were developing countries. Currently the number is 10, and by 2050, it is projected to rise to 13 (Bureau of the Census 1987).

The changing rank of developing countries produces some dramatic changes over the next few decades. By 2025, Iran and Ethiopia will join the list of the 15 largest countries, whereas Japan is expected to drop from 7th to 20th. Perhaps the greatest changes for consumer analysts to monitor are countries such as Nigeria and Pakistan, which were 13th and 14th in 1950 but which are expected to move to 3rd and 4th place by the year 2050. Among Latin American countries, Brazil is expected to retain its rank as one of the 10 largest countries in the future.

The firm that lacks an adequate global perspective is limited in its ability to participate in much of the world's growth, especially for basic products such as food, energy, construction materials, capital goods, car and other consumer durables, and the many industrial products required to produce the goods and services demanded by newly industrialized, rapid growth countries. From an economic perspective, the greatest challenge for the "rich" countries that hope to have growing markets for their products in the future may be to assist the "poor" countries in developing themselves to a point where they also are rich enough to be economically strong markets.

The most attractive markets are countries that are growing both in population and in economic resources. The search for both population growth and ability to buy increasingly takes consumer analysts to the Pacific rim. Hong Kong, Singapore, Malaysia, and South Korea have much faster population growth than Europe and relatively high incomes. China and India currently have low per capita GNP, but they attract the interest of world marketers because of the size of the population bases and the rapidity of their growth. In Part V of this book, attention is focused on some of these countries and the need for managerial perspectives that will help in developing marketing strategies for interaction with these markets.

PERSONAL PROSPERITY AND THE DECLINING ECONOMIC NEED FOR HUMAN WORKERS

The key to a good career opportunity is to make a personal contribution to a growing firm. An individual who works for a growing firm but makes little personal contribution might have been tolerated by some firms in the past. In today's competitive environment, such individuals are usually eliminated from the work place. An individual who is personally productive but works for a firm that is declining in the marketplace also has no job security. Thus the key to future personal prosperity for most individuals is knowing how to make a significant personal contribution in a growing firm.

The problem that faces many college graduates and others worried about careers is that the economy needs fewer and fewer human workers. The process that occurred in agriculture a century ago has also occurred in manufacturing and is now occurring in white-collar and middle-management careers. In agrarian societies, the majority of the population needed to live and work on farms to feed the rest of the population. With the industrialization of agriculture, only 3 people are needed to work on a farm to raise the food required by 1,000 people.

The declining economic need for human workers also occurred in manufacturing. In the United States, it is estimated that manufacturing firms have about 20 percent more employees than they need and that some industries such as steel and autos have 50 percent more. Demand for most manufactured products can grow dramatically, yet manufacturing firms need to hire few if any additional workers. When labor is a major component, however, the labor that is required among surviving manufacturing firms will be shifted primarily to low-wage countries. This process has caused many large, successful firms to see their domestic markets decrease and their future growth opportunities linked to global marketing strategies.

The same process that occurred in agriculture and manufacturing is occurring in "white-collar" or managerial jobs. To a lesser extent, and perhaps more in the future, the process is even occurring in retailing and service jobs. Xerox recently experienced a 20 percent growth in sales due to a massive rise in market share (from 10 percent to 30 percent). Yet Xerox did not have to hire new employees to handle the dramatic sales increase. Another major firm in North America experienced a 30 percent sales gain over the previous year and was able to eliminate 1,200 jobs in the process.

In his book, *Liberation Management,* Tom Peters describes the very successful Swedish/Swiss firm Asea Brown Boveri (ABB), whose CEO insists that two-thirds of Europe's giant companies will fail in the wake of European economic integration. With nearly $30 billion revenue in 140 countries, the CEO is determined that ABB will not be one of them. To make sure, he recently cut white-collar, middle-management staff of the company from 2,000 to 200 in its Swedish headquarters. At the German headquarters of ABB, there were 1,600 people in 1988 and he cut the number to 100 (Peters 1992).

Companies such as IBM and General Motors are making cuts that number in the tens of thousands of human workers—often with the result of improved service and customer responsiveness. AT&T's cuts were made earlier, during the 1980s, and now the firm is positioned for rapid growth, much of it global in nature. AT&T has centralized global strategies and structures under the supervision of the vice chairman of the company, and it expects to grow to a sales level of $200 billion, at least half of it from global strategies (Blackwell, Blackwell, and Talarzyk 1993). One telecommunications firm eliminated two levels of management, saving the costs of employing more than 1,700 people.

What is the result of such changes? Almost universally, customer satisfaction with the company increases! To employ thousands of college graduates in multiple levels of management is increasingly seen as about as productive as putting the same people on farms and expecting them to grow food. But with fewer and fewer humans needed in agriculture, manufacturing, and management of major corporations, the firms that formerly employed these people must seek new markets and new strategies to grow or even to survive. Such companies are increasingly dependent for success, therefore, on individuals who have the ability to think globally and develop global marketing strategies.

Cultural Analysis of Global Markets

Strategic planning involves committing corporate resources to the most promising areas of the world. This process requires accurate projections of world population trends over the next few decades. A managerial perspective on global strategy requires more than forecasting and quantitative analysis, however. It also requires what might be called "cultural empathy."

A perspective that is essential to the development of global marketing strategies, *cultural empathy*, is defined as the ability to understand the inner logic and coherence of other ways of life. Cultural empathy includes restraint; one should not judge the value of other ways of life. In a given nation, consumer analysis must focus on consumers' "meaning systems," which are intelligible within the cultural context of that country.

One of the most important concepts in developing global marketing strategies is cross-cultural analysis. Cross-cultural analysis is the systematic comparison of similarities and differences in the behavioral and physical aspects of cultures. Cross-cultural analysis provides an approach to understanding market segments both across national boundaries and among groups within a society. The process of analyzing markets on a cross-cultural basis is particularly helpful in deciding which elements of a marketing program can be standardized in multiple nations and which elements must be localized.

Global strategies need to be adapted to meaning systems of markets rather than attempting to change the markets to the customary marketing programs of the firm. For example, firms in the United States typically spend about 3 percent of sales on advertising. In nations such as Australia, the advertising/sales ratio is typically between 7 and 8 percent, in Sweden about 5 percent, in Mexico a little over 5 percent, and in Canada between 4 and 5 percent (Keown et al. 1987). A U.S. company entering Australia might underestimate budget needs for advertising unless it developed a global perspective about local practices.

The need to localize or standardize and many related issues are discussed later in Part I of this book. An alternative perspective to identifying global market growth opportunities and segmentation options is presented in Part II. Perspectives that are useful in understanding consumer behavior globally and developing cultural empathy with diverse markets is the topic of Part III of this book. In this section you will be exposed to important dimensions of global consumer behavior, including varying concepts of time across cultures and the effects of country-of-origin on product choices. Perspectives needed to use this information in the development of communication and other marketing strategies is the topic of Part IV of this book. The chapters in Part V discuss special issues on consumerism and worldwide consumption.

The marketplace is changing rapidly. Global marketers find it useful to track global trends to predict and better understand how consumers in various parts of the world will change. This is a never ending process. This book focuses on some of the latest and potentially most useful perspectives. Keep in mind that such perspectives do not replace the basic principles and practices of marketing that you have studied in textbooks that focused mostly on domestic concepts and strategies. Nor does it obviate the years of successful experience an executive has accumulated in domestic marketing programs. In fact, it is just the opposite.

The best of the domestic experiences are the ones to build on in developing global strategies. This book is not intended to replace those experiences or textbooks about basic principles that are essential to effective marketing programs. This chapter, and the rest of the book, has as its purpose the development of some of the additional perspectives of a global nature that will be helpful in developing long-term sustainable growth for firms that will delight their customers as well as contribute to the general prosperity of the economy and the personal prosperity of the employees.

SUMMARY STATEMENT ON GLOBAL MARKETING PERSPECTIVES

Business without borders will not be the reality of the future, but global relationships among multinational enterprises will be the norm, at least for firms that experience enhanced shareholder value through long-term sustainable growth strategies. The managers who support and lead these organizations, whether the firms be large or small, need to understand the issues involved in global marketing as well as general and specific perspectives required for developing effective global strategies.

An important concept that cuts across all areas of global strategy is the ability to think globally: the ability to understand markets beyond one's own country-of-origin, with respect to sources of demand, sources of supply, and methods of effective management and marketing. Perhaps the most important aspect of global thinking is not knowledge of how to sell in other countries or how to source in other countries. Those factors are very important, but even more important is the ability to understand marketing and management globally, to adopt the best methods from around the globe, and to avoid the worst.

REFERENCES

Blackwell, R., K. Blackwell, and W. Talarzyk (1993). *Contemporary Cases in Consumer Behavior,* Fourth Edition, Fort Worth: Dryden Press.

Blackwell, R., and K. Stephan (1990). "Growing Profits for Small Business through Global Expansion," *Small Business Forum* (Winter), 41–56.

Bureau of the Census, World Population Profile, 1987 (Washington, DC: U.S. Department of Commerce, 1987).

Keown, C. F., N. Synodinos, L. Jacobs, and R. Worthley (1987). "Can International Advertising Be Standardized?" Barcelona: World Congress of the Academy of Marketing Sciences.

Knight, C. F. (1992). "Emerson Electric: Consistent Profits, Consistently," *Harvard Business Review* (January–February), 57–70.

Peters, T. (1992). *Liberation Management,* New York: Alfred A. Knopf.

Porter, M. E., ed. (1986). *Competition in Global Industries,* Cambridge, MA: Harvard Business School Press.

Thurow, L. (1992). *Head to Head,* New York: William Morrow.

The Wall Street Journal (1990). "Three Small Businesses Profit by Taking on the World," November 8, B2.

Wattenberg, B. J. (1987). *Birth Dearth,* New York: Pharos Books.

CHAPTER 2

STRATEGIC APPROACHES TO INTERNATIONAL MARKETS — GLOBAL, MULTINATIONAL, OR WHAT?

John S. Hill

I nternational marketing strategy has always been an area of controversy. In the early days, Buzzell (1968), Bartels (1968), and Keegan
(1969) highlighted the importance of environmental/national differences in formulating coherent strategies for overseas markets. Marketers
who ignored national differences did so at their own peril (Ricks 1983).
To be successful, marketers had only to follow their cause célèbre of adapting products and services to customer needs and all would be well. In the
international arena, this meant customizing offerings to the national market needs—a multinational marketing strategy.

    MULTIDOMESTIC APPROACH

    Then came Levitt's (1983) article on "The Globalization of Markets."
He posited that through technology transfers and advances in world communication, consumers were becoming more and more like each other.
Companies, he argued, should not waste corporate time and resources
adapting products to all market and customer idiosyncrasies. A better
strategy in Levitt's eyes was to standardize products and to capitalize on
the cost and quality advantages of long production runs. This was the
essence of global marketing.

    Of course, neither multinational nor global strategies are perfect. If
multinational marketers custom-built all of their foreign lines or adapted
products completely to local tastes, their marketing efforts would be similar to those of local competitors (except where superior market research
methods resulted in better products). They would also waste the many
products, services, and technologies that have genuine multimarket or
global appeals.

Likewise, there have been all too many reports of international product and promotion blunders for global marketers to be confident about totally standardizing their marketing mixes (Ricks 1983, Kotler 1986). Additionally, not responding to customer differences would take some of the marketing out of marketing managers' job descriptions and would confuse executives of companies whose reputations are based on being sensitive to customer needs.

To the marketing profession's surprise, global marketing methods caught on, with the Japanese in particular demonstrating their effectiveness (Kotler et al. 1985). Certainly standardized offerings do not occur by accident. Wind (1986) estimated that the odds against such occurrences were 256 to 1. But companies can make standardization happen even in the promotions field (Peebles 1989, Hill and James 1989). Clearly there are times when standardized global strategies are effective. There are also occasions when localized strategies are desirable. But which one should be used—and when?

....

Back to Marketing Basics

Marketers would be problem-free if they could deliver tailored products to customers at low prices. Unfortunately this is rarely feasible. Custom-built products command premium prices because their manufacturing costs are high. Similarly, the long production runs that yield competitive prices usually preclude extensive customizing of goods. Companies decide early on whether low prices or customized output has the most profit potential.

Once an initial decision has been made to compete either on low price and high quality (a global-type strategy) or on customized output (a multilocal orientation), there remains the task of determining the marketing tactics necessary to gain a unique market position. That is, companies with standardized price-competitive goods need to find ways of differentiating their market position from other firms in their class by adding a local touch. Similarly, firms that customize outputs must be able to gain international synergies to contain their worldwide marketing costs. The ways companies manipulate their international marketing mixes to achieve these objectives account not only for the global and multilocal marketing philosophies but also for the many different versions/degrees of them in order to gain a competitive advantage in the international marketplace. Table 1 illustrates these options with their varying degrees of global or local orientations.

Strategic Options	Global Strategies	Multinational Strategies	Multilocal Strategies	TABLE 2-1 INTERNATIONAL MARKETING STRATEGY OPTIONS
Total	Globally integrated marketing program			
↑	"Act Global, Be Local" (mandatory product changes and/or tailoring of promotions, prices, and distribution)	International products (locally produced with mandatory adaptations)		
Degree of Standardization		Heavily adapted product transfers		
↓		Locally conceived and built products	Totally local creation of product lines	
None				

Global Marketing—Standardize First, Adapt Later

Global marketers base their strategies on Levitt-style customer similarities using large-scale manufacturing methods to produce high-quality standardized products and services. Their leverage is the low cost that accrues to global operations (Porter 1986). There are four situations that particularly favor the use of global marketing strategies. These are:

1. *Similar customer needs worldwide*: Many industrial and consumer products meet similar needs in all their markets. Soft drinks, pharmaceuticals, cosmetics, medical equipment, and automobiles are typical examples.

2. *Luxury products with home-market manufacturing advantages*: The reputations of some products center around their home-market manufacturing advantages. French champagne, Italian Chianti, Swedish furniture, Scottish tartans, and Belgian and Swiss chocolates would all lose some of their allure if they were manufactured outside their country of origin. For example, Stetson cowboy hats, made in Hong Kong, would not command premium prices. Neither would Scotch whisky if it were produced anywhere but Scotland.

3. *Standardized technologies and intensely price-competitive markets*: These factors make global philosophies essential for products such as television sets, radios, VCRs, CDs, and stereos. If consumer electronics were customized, their costs would probably be exorbitant.

4. *Technology-intensive products with high research-and-development (R&D) costs*: Such products must be standardized globally to recoup sky-high start-up costs. Commercial aircraft, supercomputers, and pharmaceutical products have ever-escalating R&D costs. New drugs used to cost $16 million to develop over five years. Today, the price tag is $250 million over twelve years (Main 1989).

In most cases globally marketed products need worldwide distribution to keep costs down. However, once manufacturing scale economies are obtained and prices are competitive, companies differentiate their offerings through local appeals. These are "think local" strategies.

How Global Marketers Localize Their Offerings: "Act Global, Think Local" Strategies

Global marketers tailor strategies in two ways. First, although long production runs are necessary for competitive costs, mandatory adaptations are necessary to enter many markets. These include changing voltage levels for consumer electronics products (e.g., switching between 110 V and 220 V); substituting right-hand drives for autos in some countries; and alternating watch facings between orthodox Western numbers and characters suitable for the Arabic, Chinese, or Japanese markets. Without such adaptations, products are unacceptable to foreign customers.

The second way to localize global marketing strategies is to adapt nonproduct elements of marketing mixes. Pricing strategies may be changed, with higher or lower prices, different credit arrangements, varied discounts to customer groups, and so on. Warranties may be altered, and different promotions or media may be used. New segments may be attacked through message adaptations (e.g., Honda creating the recreational motorcycle segment). Heavier emphases may be placed on after-sales service (e.g., Caterpillar). Through such efforts, marketers give largely or completely standardized products local appeal.

MULTINATIONAL MARKETING—ADAPT FIRST, STANDARDIZE LATER

Some industries (such as food and drink) thrive on localized approaches (Kotler 1986). Multinational marketers start with the assumption that offerings must be adapted to customer and market differences. For this reason, on-site manufacturing is often desirable. This is made easier because in contrast to global products, gaining scale economies to maintain competitive costs is not essential. Food, drink, cosmetics, and general consumer-goods strategies cost little to produce and tend to compete on nonprice elements such as brand image, distinctive appeals, and creative promotions. Hence, multinational marketers start by ensuring that their offerings have local appeal.

However, such strategies are expensive. To execute them cost-effectively on a worldwide basis, multinationals must obtain some economies of scale in their international operations. Similarly, companies wishing to acquire international reputations must have some consistencies in their product offerings from market to market.

How Multinational Marketers Gain International Scale Economies

To gain needed synergies from their international operations, marketers transfer product ideas among country-markets. Hill and James (1991) found that U.S. multinational corporations' (MNCs) subsidiaries averaged 57 percent U.S. products in their foreign lines. Once transferred though, a product's fortunes may go in one of two directions. For some products which MNCs believe have universal appeal, brand identities are maintained as far as possible. These are their *international products.* Coca-Cola, Pepsi, Canada Dry mixers, Colgate toothpaste, Lever Brothers' margarines, and Chesebrough Pond's cold cream are used in similar fashions by consumers in most foreign markets. Their presence in most or all subsidiaries is also not coincidental, as they give MNCs continuity in their international marketing operations. Often such goods are locally produced, making mandatory adaptations such as labelling, measurement units, and perhaps pack sizes easy to make. For the most part though, managers make special efforts to maintain these products in their original forms (Hill and Still 1984, Porter 1986).

For other product transfers, maintaining original brand identities is less essential or not feasible within certain markets, and local managers are given complete freedom in customizing them to market needs (Hill and Still 1984, Porter 1986). But MNCs still gain financially. Leroy (1976) found that transferring and adapting products was still six times cheaper than creating completely new ones. These *localized product transfers* undergo partial or complete overhauls to ensure that they conform not only to local market conditions but also to customer needs. This often entails new package designs, colors, sales features, and new brand names.

Finally, not all MNC-marketed products are transfers from other countries. Inevitably, as MNC affiliates evaluate their markets, they find opportunities for *custom-made products.* Oftentimes these needs are unique to individual countries. Hill and James (1991) found these to average 26 percent of U.S. foreign affiliate lines in the consumer nondurable industry. Colgate-Palmolive reformulates its periodontal toothpastes in many markets. Likewise, Canada Dry reconstitutes its orange and non-mixer drinks. Gillette invented a tub-packaged shaving creme, Presto-barba ("Quick-Shave") for Mexican consumers (Wessell 1986). Such products give multinationals significant local orientations.

MULTILOCAL MARKETING—ADAPT FIRST AND LAST

MNCs derive considerable synergies from transferring products between markets and applying company-developed technologies to create locally tailored goods. But in some cases (especially in services such as distribution, insurance, and consumer financing), there are few or no product-service carryovers among markets. Then firms must custom-build lines in each country. For example, Karter (1989) noted that pollution liability in the business insurance field was highly individualized by country in Western Europe, but that some standardization was likely with the 1992 economic unification.

Multilocal strategies also occur when companies acquire foreign interests outside of their corporate domains and little or no international leverage can be applied. In such cases everything is localized. The only multinational linkages between head offices and affiliates are one-time technology transfers to set up administrative procedures and organizations. After that, apart from administrative ties, they operate purely as local firms. For example, Sony's U.S. investments include interests in the restaurant and construction business where synergies from their consumer electronics activities are not likely to be applicable (Kotler et al. 1985).

EFFECTIVE STRATEGY FORMULATION: COMBINING GLOBAL, MULTINATIONAL, AND MULTILOCAL ORIENTATIONS

Marketing strategy would be easy if all companies had to do was to select an orientation and then implement it. In practice, of course, firms use whatever strategy is prudent for particular markets. Some industries use predominantly one strategy. Autos, steel, consumer electronics, computers, high-profile consumer goods (e.g., Scotch whisky or Japanese sake) benefit from using global marketing methods. However, this does not stop companies like NCR or IBM from custom-building products when they feel localized strategies are necessary. Nor do companies in the same industry follow identical strategies. Porter (1986) noted that Toyota's global approach to auto marketing contrasted vividly with its arch rival, General Motors, which has historically allowed its foreign affiliates considerable autonomy in strategy formulation.

Similarly, consumer-packaged goods corporations are globally oriented when the need arises. They can (and often do) service multiple countries from single manufacturing locations. For example, Procter & Gamble's Geneva operation directs products all over the world from relatively few production locations. Colgate-Palmolive has more than forty manufacturing plants worldwide—yet it services well over one hundred markets. Clearly scale economies are important and where country demand does not justify local manufacturing, export-oriented global marketing is the answer.

Finally, both global and multinational marketers acquire multilocal dimensions when they locate profitable market opportunities outside of their corporate domains. The purchase of local real estate, investing in businesses, or taking advantage of national resources are all ways MNCs gain multilocal dimensions. Japanese businesses, for example, had invested more than $18 billion in U.S. real estate by 1989 (U.S. Department of Commerce 1990). Similarly, Coca-Cola's Japanese operation entered the local juice and potato chip markets where the company discovered plentiful supplies of local oranges and potatoes (Wilson 1986).

Conclusions—Reinterpreting Levitt?

The international marketing field has been so enamored with standardization-adaptation issues that everything in the area has been interpreted within that context. For example, globalized strategies have been equated with standardized products (e.g., Douglas and Wind 1987). Yet Levitt admits the existence of barriers that effectively prevent uniformity in marketing strategies. What marketers are seeking then, are not so much *identical* tastes (although there are many examples of them) but *similar* tastes that can be catered to with product transfers, suitably adapted.

Levitt admits this. He notes (p. 94) "the most effective world competitors . . . sell in all national markets the same kind of products sold at home or in their largest export market." *Product-mix* standardization is in itself an indicator of how similar customers are to those in other markets. Product transfers among markets give MNCs international synergies, and global similarities among customers make this possible. Certainly adaptations to product transfers are usually required, just as they are when regional tastes dictate changes within national markets. But the transfer of products and ideas among countries occurs because there are similarities among customers, not differences. In this sense, the high percentages of product transfers in multinational lines suggest that customer similarities dominate multinational product strategies.

But the multinational-global debate may soon be passé. Revolutions in manufacturing technology are enabling companies to tailor-make goods at relatively modest costs. By the twenty-first century, low-priced customized products will probably be commonplace. This will be made possible through increasing use of computer-aided manufacturing and design, which has transformed corporate thinking about personalized manufacturing. Soon customers' individual product needs will be programmed into the computer or faxed to a low-cost, offshore facility. The product will be fabricated and shipped back to the customer within hours. Matsushita currently custom-builds any one of eleven million versions of a bicycle in three hours. The company still makes customers wait two weeks for the finished product to ensure that they appreciate its uniqueness (Moffat 1990). With such advances, the old "customized versus standardized" controversy will become irrelevant for many products.

References

Bartels, R. (1968). "Are Domestic and International Marketing Dissimilar?" *Journal of Marketing*, 32, 3, 56–61.

Buzzell, R. D. (1968). "Can You Standardize Multinational Marketing?" *Harvard Business Review*, 46, 6, 102–113.

Douglas, S. M., and Y. Wind (1987). "The Myth of Globalization," *Columbia Journal of World Business*, 22, 4 (Winter), 19–29.

Hill, J. S. (1991). "Product and Promotion Transfers in Consumer Goods Multinationals," *International Marketing Review*, 8, 2, 6–17.

———, and R. R. Still (1984). "Adapting Products to LDC Tastes," *Harvard Business Review*, 62, 2, 92–102.

———, and W. L. James (1989). "Effects of Selected Environmental International Advertising Strategy: An Exploratory Study," *Current Issues and Research in Advertising*, 12, 1, 135–153.

Karter, J. (1989). "Pollution Liability: E.C., European Governments Considering Tougher Regulations," *Business Insurance*, January 2, p. 25.

Keegan, W. J. (1969). "Multinational Product Planning: Strategic Alternatives," *Journal of Marketing*, 33, 1, 58–62.

Kotler, P. (1986). "Global Standardization—Courting Danger," *Journal of Consumer Marketing*, 3, 2 (Spring), 13–15.

———, Liam Fahey, and S. Jatusripatak (1985). *The New Competition*, Englewood Cliffs, NJ: Prentice-Hall Inc.

Leroy, G. P. (1976). *Multinational Product Strategies: A Typology for Analysis of Worldwide Product Innovation Diffusion*, New York: Praeger Publishers.

Levitt, T. (1983). "The Globalization of Markets," *Harvard Business Review*, 61, 2, 92–102.

Main, J. (1989). "How to Go Global—and Why," *Fortune*, August 28, 70–76.

Moffat, S. (1990). "Japan's New Personalized Production," *Fortune*, October 22, 132, 134.

Peebles, D. M. (1989). "Don't Write Off Global Advertising," *International Marketing Review*, 6, 1, 73–78.

Porter, M. E. (1986). "The Strategic Role of International Marketing," *Journal of Consumer Marketing*, 3, 2 (Spring), 17–21.

Ricks, D. (1983). *Big Business Blunders: Mistakes in Multinational Marketing*, Homewood, IL: Dow-Jones-Irwin.

U.S. Department of Commerce Bureau of Economic Analysis (1990). *Survey of Current Business*, 70, 8 (August), 35–38.

Wessell, D. (1986). "Gillette Keys Sales to Third World Tastes," *Wall Street Journal*, January 23, 35.

Wilson, I. R. (1986). "American Success Story: Coca-Cola in Japan," in *International Marketing: Managerial Perspectives*, ed. Subhash Jain, Lewis R. Tucker, Jr., Boston, MA.: Kent Publishing, 184–192.

Wind, Y. (1986). "The Myth of Globalization," *Journal of Consumer Marketing*, 3, 2 (Spring), 23–26.

CHAPTER 3

STANDARDIZATION VERSUS LOCALIZATION: THE NEED FOR THE COMPROMISING PERSPECTIVE

Sak Onkvisit

John J. Shaw

D ue to the interdependence of nations as well as markets, it is not surprising that governments, scholars, corporations, and consumers have shown increasing interest in international marketing issues and practices. One issue that has emerged at the forefront of academic and corporate discussion is the globalization of markets. A number of prominent scholars (e.g., Levitt 1983), advertising agencies (e.g., Saatchi & Saatchi), and international marketers have claimed that the world is witnessing emerging commonalities in consumption patterns and the growing significance of global marketing campaigns.

The purpose of this chapter is to examine international marketing-mix strategies in general and international product and advertising strategies in particular. Regarding product and advertising decisions, there are generally four strategic options:

1. Standardized product-standardized advertising
2. Standardized product-localized advertising
3. Localized product-standardized advertising
4. Localized product-localized advertising

A discussion involving these strategic options necessitates making a distinction among such concepts as globalization, standardization, and localization. The validity of these concepts can be measured in terms of theoretical and empirical evidence. The assumptions related to market homogeneity and heterogeneity, as well as the practices of centralization and decentralization, also will be discussed. Finally, the market segmentation strategy is covered as a decision-making framework in order to determine whether a multinational corporation's international marketing mix should be globalized, standardized, or localized.

International Marketing Mix Decisions

An essential part of a marketer's market planning is the selection of an appropriate and effective marketing mix. While the mix consists of product, place, promotion, and pricing, this chapter focuses on only two of the four P's of marketing. The two elements of interest within the marketing mix are product and promotion.

In the case of a multinational firm, one important decision is whether to use the same marketing mix in more than one country. If so, how many countries should share a common strategy? If not, how many different variations across countries are needed? To put it another way, when and how should the international marketing mix be standardized, localized, or globalized?

Standardization is the controversial practice of marketing a particular product worldwide in the same way. Localization, in contrast, requires a firm to customize its marketing strategy for each individual market. The term "multidomestic" industry is essentially the same as localization. A company in a multidomestic industry "pursues separate strategies in each of its foreign markets" (Hout, Porter, and Rudden 1982). It should be apparent that the concepts of standardization and localization are two competing perspectives. Not so apparent is how these two opposing concepts are related to the concept of globalization.

Unfortunately, confusion abounds as different terminologies are used to express the same concept, and the same term is often used to describe different ideas. Frequently, globalization is confused with standardization because both terms are sometimes used loosely and carelessly to imply the same idea. One may question whether any particular differences between the two concepts are significant. The differences are more than just semantic because the concepts represent ideas that are distinctly different.

As explained by Hout, Porter, and Rudden (1982), a "global" company's strategies in various countries are highly interdependent in terms of operations and strategy as it "seeks to respond to particular local market needs, while avoiding a compromise of efficiency of the overall global system." Whereas a global firm's strategy is a centralized one, the various aspects of the operations may or may not be. Apparently, a global strategy is not necessarily a standardized one. It is thus necessary to differentiate among these three related but different strategies.

A Matter of Degree

While it is unlikely that a multinational corporation would completely standardize *or* localize its marketing mix, and because standardization and localization occupy different points on the same scale, it is important to define standardization. There is no uniform agreement on exactly what standardization is (Onkvisit and Shaw 1987). Originally, proponents of standardization defined it as a marketing strategy that presented basically the same product and communication message when a product designed for a given local market was exported to other countries. Allowing virtually no change in the product or message, this definition permits only cosmetic changes (i.e., translation of words). As stated by Levitt (1983), "a successful global marketing strategy consists of having a common brand name, packaging and communications." This definition is bold and exact. However, the rigidity imposed by this traditional definition makes it easy for opponents to criticize flaws within the standardization approach.

To make their position more defensible, a new breed of advocates of standardization has relaxed its position. According to them, a product (or advertisement) is a standardized one as long as only "minor" modification is involved. What is considered minor, however, is unclear. For example, Mercedes Benz, Volvo, and BMW equip their cars with left-hand steering for the U.S. market but switch the steering wheel to the right-hand side of the automobile for many Asian and European markets. Is this type of modification a minor adjustment, and are these automobiles standardized products?

In the case of advertising, the new advocates of standardization state that, as long as the same advertising *theme* is maintained, a standardized advertisement can have changes in its copy or illustration (e.g., a photograph of a foreign model in an overseas version). This newer, broader, and more subjective definition is imprecise since it fails to specify the extent of permissible change or the degree of flexibility allowed. The new interpretation makes it unclear when an advertisement loses its standardized identity and should be classified instead as a localized advertisement.

A vague definition precludes a systematic and scientific investigation of the validity of a concept. Testability/falsifiability must of course depend in part on the degree of measurability of a concept through an operational definition. The following sections, on the other hand, use other concepts to identify certain dimensions of the concept of standardization and suggest how the concept can be defined.

Three Kinds of Orientation

To differentiate among globalization, standardization, and localization, it is desirable to tie these concepts to the three kinds of orientation: ethnocentricity, polycentricity, and geocentricity.

Whereas ethnocentricity involves a strong orientation toward the home country, polycentricity is exactly the opposite in that it involves a strong orientation toward the host (i.e., foreign) country to which the strategy is aimed. The ethnocentric view, also sometimes called "national myopia," assumes that "foreign" markets and consumers are either insignificant or inferior. Therefore, production and marketing decisions should be centralized at the home base. Polycentricity, on the other hand, emphasizes the uniqueness of each market, and this perspective leads to a significant degree of decentralized decision making.

Geocentricity, the global orientation, is an orientation that considers the entire world as the target market. A geocentric firm takes the view that countries can be similar in some aspects and different in others. The firm thus adopts a loose-tight approach by developing a broad framework of its total strategy, which permits certain parts of its marketing program to be adapted, if and when necessary, to meet local needs. As an example, because Northern Europeans prefer large refrigerators with freezer compartments on the bottom whereas their Southern European counterparts prefer small refrigerators with freezers on top, Electrolux attempts to standardize production in its six European factories by producing component combinations that can be incorporated in standard refrigerator shells (Echickson 1990). In this particular case, the firm's effort represents an attempt to have partial standardization while satisfying local needs at the same time.

Proponents of standardization often use the two terms (standardization and globalization) indiscriminately and interchangeably, probably hoping that the positive implication of globalization will make the idea of standardization less objectionable. Whereas a global product (or advertisement) is a product designed for the international market, a standardized product (or advertisement) is simply a product (or advertisement) designed for one national market and exported virtually unchanged to other markets.

The standardization strategy is primarily ethnocentric as it seeks to export unchanged a product, an advertising campaign, and/or other components of the marketing mix. Unfortunately, many major U.S. firms are ethnocentric, and their performance problems can be traced to their ethnocentricity. In contrast, the localization strategy, which stresses the need to be sensitive to differences among countries, is polycentric and requires the development of a specific marketing program for each market. In the case of a global strategy, this strategy appears to reflect the geocentric view since it attempts to combine the other two approaches to create a world-oriented marketing mix. Some authors have discussed the emerging concept of "be global, act local" (Wills, Samli, and Jacobs 1991), and it can be argued that geocentricity is the basis for this practice.

Homogeneity and Heterogeneity

Economists have long assumed that markets are homogeneous on both the supply and demand sides. On the supply side, marketers are assumed to offer essentially identical products (i.e., commodities). As such, although carrying different brand names (which may contribute to products being physically different in terms of appearance), manufacturers' offerings are understood to be undifferentiated from an engineering or chemical standpoint. In other words, at the same grade, the offerings of one supplier cannot be distinguished from those of another.

On the demand side, consumers are presumed to be alike in terms of their desires and behavior. As a result, consumers maximize their satisfaction by purchasing suitable products at the lowest possible cost.

Consumer homogeneity can be classified in two basic ways—(1) by national boundaries and (2) by consumer characteristics. In the latter classification, consumers may be alike in terms of age, income, attitudes, and behavior, among other characteristics. It should also be pointed out that consumers may be homogeneous demographically but not behaviorally. On the other hand, consumers may exhibit similar behavior without being demographically alike.

Consumer characteristics are sometimes uniform across nations as well. Based on national boundaries, homogeneity can be categorized as vertical (i.e., homogeneous within the same country) or horizontal (i.e., homogeneous across countries). Two countries, while not vertically homogeneous within their borders, may still be horizontally homogeneous when a particular segment in one country is similar to an equivalent segment in another country. For instance, young consumers, although different from older consumers in the same market, may be similar to young consumers in another country.

The marketing discipline, an outgrowth of both economics and behavioral sciences, was founded on the principle of heterogeneity. Heterogeneity on the consumer side is highly evident because what consumers eat and wear clearly differs greatly in such characteristics as style, size, color, and quality. The variations in demand, without question, reflect different customs and user needs.

To judge diversity in supply, all one has to do is to observe the lack of close similarity among individual firms' products. While it is true that brands are sometimes physically similar (as assumed by economists), brands can be psychologically different. After all, marketers use promotional activities as a differentiating technique to endow their products with a distinct image.

The localization approach clearly reflects the heterogeneity assumption. Equally clear is the fact that a standardization strategy is based on the assumption of market homogeneity. If consumers across countries are homogeneous, standardization is the preferred strategy, and other strategies become irrelevant.

The homogeneity assumption, however, is improbable because it expects consumers to be "clones" of each other in terms of their attitudes and behavior—a virtual impossibility. The results of a literature review of management responses, consumer characteristics, and consumer responses indicate that there is no theoretical or empirical evidence to support the wholesale assumption of homogeneity in its present form (Onkvisit and Shaw 1987). However, standardization may now and then be appropriate on a modest scale. On a limited basis, therefore, a few countries may conceivably share *some* common characteristics—demographically and/or behaviorally.

Both the standardization strategy and the homogeneity assumption are prescriptive in that they describe events as they should be—not as they are. As a source-based but not audience-based strategy, standardization is based on management's view of the existence of a marketplace consisting of homogeneous consumers. The perception may have been realistic at one time in the past when life was simple, supply was limited, and most or all products were essentially commodities. These conditions may still exist to some extent in some lesser developed countries and planned economies. One U.S. commercial has portrayed this market situation in a tongue-in-cheek fashion by showing a plump Soviet model on stage, first with her "morningwear" and then later with her "eveningwear," the same identical shapeless dress but with a flashlight.

Centralization and Decentralization

The standardization-localization controversy is highly related to the centralization-decentralization controversy (Onkvisit and Shaw 1990). Standardization requires a high degree of centralization, which increases efficiency and uniformity while stifling local or lower-level initiative, decision making, and responsibility. It can be expected that ethnocentric firms are prone to adopt the centralization system.

Localization, in contrast, requires a high degree of decentralized decision making, which promotes flexibility and adaptability on the positive side and duplication and inefficiency on the negative side. Polycentricity encourages a significant degree of decentralization and allows host-country managers to have a great deal of latitude in making marketing decisions. This type of orientation, however, may result in duplication of effort among overseas subsidiaries, thus preventing the development of efficient and uniform strategies.

Geocentricity attempts to combine aspects of centralization and decentralization in a synthesis that allows some degree of uniformity as well as some degree of flexibility. A geocentric firm thus plans to offer a global marketing mix by making a coordinated effort to standardize certain marketing elements while localizing others.

The Perspective of Standardization

The standardization school of thought, sometimes called the "universal," "internationalized," "common," or "uniform," approach, questions the necessity of changing the marketing mix across markets. Its basic premise is that, because of education, travel, technology, and communication, there is a homogenization of culture, language, tastes, ideas, religious beliefs, and living conditions. Consumers are thus assumed to be homogeneous—if not economically or demographically, at least in their psychological needs.

One of the early proponents of the standardization approach is Elin-

Advantages of Standardization	Advantages of Localization	TABLE 3-1
decision simplification	possibility of larger market share	STANDARDIZATION VERSUS LOCALIZATION
ease of execution	better chance for repeat sales	
uniform physical product	legal necessity	
uniform worldwide brand image	price flexibility	
consistency in customer service	production flexibility (allowance of quality/ quantity variations across markets)	
better quality control		
better inventory control	more meaningful product	
lack of duplication	more meaningful communication	
good for culture-free products	avoidance of taxation on international brand/ad	
good for products for travelers	good for culture-bound products	
elimination of fragmentation	maximum effectiveness	
elimination of confusion among employees, dealers, and consumers	utilization of market segmentation technique	
operational efficiency due to economies of scale (lower legal/production/marketing costs)		
convenient identification for travel-related products		

der (1961) who stated: ". . . to begin marketing with a local appeal which changes from country to country is about as sensible as stopping a factory's machinery producing a product and setting up production in a number of small national factories—these producing their own national products in short series after their own recipe." More recently, Levitt (1983) has been successful in convincing a number of scholars and practitioners to consider standardization. According to Levitt, "the modern global corporation contrasts powerfully with the superficial corporation. Instead of adapting to superficial and even entrenched differences with and between nations, it will seek sensibly to force suitably standardized products and practices on the entire globe."

Standardization offers a number of advantages (see Table 3-1). The main reasons for adopting a standardization strategy are efficiency, uniformity, and simplicity. When there is virtually no change in the marketing mix, it is easy to see that the production, distribution, and promotion of the product are greatly simplified. Simplicity results in cost efficiency as economies of scale in production and advertising are achieved.

Standardization is desirable when a consistent company or product image is desired. McDonald's, for example, stresses consistent product quality and service. Regardless of where they are sold, hamburger meat, buns, french fries, and fruit pies must meet the firm's strict uniform specifications. Insisting on a particular quality hamburger bun that was unavailable in England, McDonald's ended up building its own plant in England to produce these buns.

It may be impractical to modify certain products. Artistic items (e.g., musical recordings, paintings, books, and motion pictures) tend to be subjective in value, and thus it is not easy to judge when or where they will be successful. Films and songs that are not successful at home are sometimes in high demand elsewhere. While Julio Iglesias has re-recorded certain songs in English exclusively for the U.S. market, it is difficult to envision Michael Jackson re-recording his hit songs in Spanish or Japanese for overseas fans.

Some products do transcend cultural and national boundaries because they are associated with certain cultural universals. In a number of cases, consumers of different countries share the same need, and a standardized product may appropriately satisfy all consumers. Watches and diamonds are examples of culture-free products. Cadbury's chocolate, with its stronger milk chocolate flavor, which is popular in Europe, has recently been gaining popularity in the United States as well.

Certain circumstances may favor a standardization strategy. An international marketer should standardize its marketing mix if:

1. It desires a simple marketing process.
2. It wants to achieve economies of scale.
3. It plans to have a consistent company or product image.
4. The product cannot be easily modified.
5. There is a product-market fit due to cultural universals.

According to one review, while "total uniformity" policies are rare, the propensity of firms for adopting standardization seems most likely within international product policy (Walters 1986). In one study, Boddewyn, Soehl, and Picard (1986) found that advertising is more resistant to standardization than are product and brand. Among the different aspects of a product, the likelihood of standardizing the brand aspect is very high—82.5 percent among U.S. consumer good manufacturers (Rosen, Boddewyn, and Louis 1989). Of course, having a standardized brand does not necessarily mean that the product itself is also standardized. With regard to message components, one study found that, in one out of five print campaigns, portions of the message content were standardized (Mueller 1990).

Standardization, while minimizing costs, does not necessarily guarantee improved profits. A standardized product/advertisement, by its nature, can perhaps never adequately satisfy *all* consumers and their needs. What may be suitable in one market is thus often unsuitable in another market. It should also be evident that cost control and profit maximization are two distinct entities. In some situations, these entities may converge when they complement each other. It is not uncommon, however, for these two competing goals to be highly divergent.

The problem with cost reduction for the purpose of efficiency, if carried to an extreme, is that a company can be penny wise but pound foolish. It would be unwise for an advertising agency to suggest the following steps to Philip Morris to increase efficiency in the United States and worldwide.

First, Philip Morris should not concern itself with different Marlboro advertisements for blacks and Hispanics since they would cost too much money. Second, there is no need to have different advertisements for Marlboro's various product forms (Marlboro, Marlboro Lights, Marlboro Medium, and Marlboro 100s). Third, it should use the Marlboro advertisements for the low-tar Merit brand (one cigarette is like all other cigarettes anyway) and the Virginia Slims brand for women (men and women are alike because they are human beings). Fourth, to save money, the same advertisement should be used for Philip Morris' subsidiaries and their products (e.g., General Foods' Maxwell House Coffee and Kraft's Philadelphia Cream Cheese). Next, to achieve further cost efficiencies and standardization, Philip Morris should continue using the same advertising since even occasional changes add new expenses. Finally, the firm may as well stop advertising altogether since advertising, after all, costs money. Clearly, a preoccupation with only cost reduction and standardization may make the operation successful even though the patient does not survive.

Standardization is the process of treating multimarkets as a single homogeneous market. The technique emphasizes the search for intermarket similarities while overlooking differences. Standardization is a first-rate strategy—as long as it is what consumers want. Undeniably, a standardized product designed for one market may in many situations fit other markets as well. Foreign consumers, for instance, may prefer U.S. products solely because these products are American. While some may consider VISA and American Express credit cards to be world products, they actually have domestic origins, being originally intended for local home markets before becoming a worldwide success, perhaps by accident (van Mesdag 1987). This type of success is in many cases nothing more than a fortunate random occurrence.

THE PERSPECTIVE OF LOCALIZATION

The localization strategy is also known as "nonstandardization," "individualization," "adaptation," "modification," "specificity," or "customization." Contradicting the homogeneity assumption, Lenormand (1964) states that "problems arise due to the diversity of mentalities, religious beliefs, customs, standards of living, legislations, advertising media, advertising agency structures and resources, etc." Reed (1967) echoes the same sentiment: ". . . it is true that all people are motivated by the same basic instincts, sense, affections, passions and aspirations, but the different manner of expressing these motivations and aspirations can wreck marketing plans and advertising campaigns, as can customs and many other differences." As a result, though a few common values may exist, this does not nullify other differences.

Though shared values may exist, this fact does not necessarily mean shared or identical behavior. The manner of expressing culturally universal traits still varies within as well as across countries. Although music is a cultural universal, it is obvious that younger and older individuals prefer different kinds of music. Moreover, while consumers may share common tastes even when they do not share a common culture, common tastes need not be behaviorally manifested in the same way.

It is fairly difficult to create a product or advertising message that appeals to all consumers in the same country because the consumers are of different age groups, races, income groups, and so on. To repeat the same process on a worldwide scale would dilute the effectiveness even more. A standardized product/message should be designed to appeal to the lowest common denominator so the product/message will be relevant to everyone. People are alike in the sense that they are human, but human beings are also different with regard to age, sex, culture, nationality, and other psychological factors that require the development of different appeals to satisfy such different characteristics.

Many U.S. firms are reluctant to develop a custom-made marketing mix for each individual market. The unwillingness to modify the marketing mix to suit overseas customers' needs can be attributed in part to the "big-car" and "left-hand-drive" syndrome—both of which find their origin in the automobile industry (Onkvisit and Shaw 1991).

The big-car syndrome reflects U.S. automakers' success in conditioning U.S. drivers to accept the idea that big cars are superior in terms of comfort, power, and safety. The reason that automakers want to encourage large purchases is simple: Big cars offer larger profit margins because the costs of manufacturing a big car are approximately the same as those of producing a small one. Armed with such success, U.S. automakers as well as other U.S. manufacturers have come to believe that U.S. tastes are superior and that foreign consumers should prefer the same kinds of products, not realizing that their assumptions are really self-serving.

The left-hand-drive syndrome reflects the driving practice in the United States where Americans are accustomed to having the steering wheel on the left side of the automobile in order to drive on the right side of the road. Although the U.S. automakers have long recognized that half of the world's drivers drive on the left side of the road, they reason that overseas sales are too small to justify manufacturing an automobile with a right-hand drive. Citing the fact that they have always done poorly abroad, U.S. automakers have failed to realize that their poor sales performance reflects their attitude toward (or contempt for) overseas markets. Making no conscientious attempt to cultivate "small" markets and seeing the markets remain "small" have resulted in a self-fulfilling prophecy and an unyielding attitude that shows no concern for overseas consumers' driving safety.

It is unsound to resist localization based on the logic (or illogic) of the big-car and left-hand-drive syndrome. For example, multinational corporations that understand when and where to modify their products can compete well even against very strong Japanese markets. Sprite became a best seller in the clear soft drink category when the Company took out the lime taste after realizing that Japanese consumers preferred a lemon flavor (Christopher 1986). On average, multinational corporations make four changes per product in less developed countries (Hill and Still 1984). Only one out of ten products is transferred to developing countries without modification.

Product/promotion modification is often mandatory because of government regulations that set product standards, systems, and other requirements. Dow Corning International, for example, had to make 96 packaging changes within a six-month period to meet various European regulations (Roth 1982, p. 132). Australia does not allow TV commercials filmed by outside producers to be shown there (Peebles and Ryans 1984). A television set designed for the U.S. NTSC broadcast system cannot receive signals broadcast through the PAL system that has been adopted by most nations. Because of differences in electrical current standards (phase, cycle, and voltage), a standardized product may function poorly or may not function at all in certain countries. Products manufactured for the U.S. 110–120-volt electrical standards are a safety hazard and will be damaged in markets where the electrical voltages are twice as high.

The lack of commonality in the modern world is well demonstrated by the diversity of measurement standards, some of which are both inferior and needlessly complicated. As in the case of the old but since abolished British currency system, a British pound once had 20 shillings, a shilling was equal to 12 pennies, and a penny consisted of 4 farthings. The United States, on the other hand, has a simple currency system (i.e., a U.S. dollar is equal to 100 cents). Inexplicably, the United States has stubbornly adhered to the outdated imperial system of liquid (a gallon = 4 quarts, 1 quart = 2 pints, 1 pint = 16 ounces) and linear (1 mile = 1,760 yards, 1 yard = 3 feet, 1 foot = 12 inches) measures. Because the metric system is simpler, more consistent, and superior, it makes little sense for Americans to have to divide by 12 or 16 to figure out the distance traveled or the amount of gasoline consumed. To make matters worse for the United States, the European Community countries do not permit nonmetric products to be sold there. Interestingly, the nonmetric United States requires liquor products (but not other liquid products) to be bottled in standard metric sizes.

While localization is mandatory for market entry, many multinational firms also use optional/discretionary modification to make their products/messages more suitable for overseas consumers. They may carry out this process for pricing purposes because higher-quality products designed for consumers in developed countries may be too costly in less developed countries. Therefore, product contents and nonessential parts (frills) are often reduced or removed. Furthermore, because it is tempting for a distributor in a high-priced country to import popular products from nearby countries that restrict prices, manufacturers may thus deliberately vary packaging, product characteristics, coloring, and brand names in order to discourage grey marketing (i.e., unauthorized import of the product).

A product/advertising message may also have to be modified due to local-use conditions. Such conditions include: weather conditions (gasoline requires a higher flash point in hot climates), space constraints (U.S. refrigerators are too bulky and noisy for the compact Japanese home), consumers' physical specifications (U.S. men's slacks that are based on U.S. tailoring patterns are too large and long for Asian customers), users' habits/local customs (the standard U.S. plywood dimensions of 4 by 8 ft differ from the Japanese standard of 3 by 6 ft), culture (Tokyo Disneyland replaced the Main Street USA park entrance—a concept that the Japanese do not understand—with a World Bazaar), religious beliefs (Halal-killed chickens are required for Middle East countries and Kosher foods for Jews), and other environmental characteristics (Totino's pizza reduced its size from the U.S. 12-ounce size to the Japanese 6.5-ounce size to fit into smaller Japanese ovens).

It must be explicitly stated that because of its cost, localization for its own sake may not always be a practical strategy. Not everyone can afford a private tailor, and many consumers willingly settle for mass-produced, standardized apparel. Without mass production and standardization, the automobile industry could not exist and society would not receive many of the benefits it has received through the automobile. Therefore, regardless of market differences, the benefits of standardization can sometimes outweigh the benefits of localization.

The Perspective of the Compromise

Between the two extreme schools of thought is the compromise school. A stubborn insistence on standardization can result in lost sales and opportunities. In contrast, adapting a product for each market can be costly. Instead, designing a world product may provide a solution as well as minimize both problems. For instance, a German subsidiary of ITT produces a "world chassis" that can accommodate all three existing TV systems (PAL, NTSC, and SECAM) in the world without changing the circuitry on the various modules. Norelco electric shavers and Sony portable stereo radios, likewise, have a universal-voltage feature. This is not unlike having a telephone that can be operated regardless of whether the system in use is rotary or touch tone.

According to Wind (1986), the following conditions are necessary for standardization to function properly.

1. Homogenization of the world's wants
2. Buyers' willingness to sacrifice preferred product features in favor of lower price and higher quality
3. Economies of scale
4. Preference of a number of global market segments for a uniform physical product and brand image
5. Absence of external constraints
6. Absence of internal constraints
7. Presence of positive synergy from multicountry operations

Since it is difficult to satisfy all conditions, an international marketer should "think globally, act locally."

Unlike standardization, which is a campaign developed for one market but exported to other markets regardless of justification, a geocentric campaign requires the development of a product and an advertisement for worldwide customers at the very outset. This approach attempts to address shared intercountry denominators while allowing for some modification to suit each market, thus achieving the cost-efficiency advantages of standardization and the communication-effectiveness advantages of localization. The geocentric approach represents a proper balance of consistency and economy on the one hand and a regional or local relevance on the other hand. A true geocentric campaign thus carefully examines the extent and conditions that allow a compromise between commonality and flexibility.

A multipurpose or multicultural product does not have to be more expensive than a local or standardized product. The geocentric strategy simplifies inventory control (in terms of parts and finished products) while eliminating costly downtime in production (i.e., eliminating the need to adjust equipment to produce different national versions). A world product, however, cannot succeed without corporate commitment. This approach requires executives to be outwardly oriented rather than inwardly inclined.

The middle-of-the-road school, while recognizing local differences, holds that some degree of standardization may be both possible and desirable under certain conditions. Jain (1989), for example, hypothesizes that standardization is possible when markets are similar in terms of: economy, a firm's competitive position, consumer behavior and lifestyle, cultural compatibility of the product, political and legal environments, marketing infrastructure, and so on.

The applicability of standardization is a function of two conditions—whether it is "feasible" and "desirable" to implement standardization. Many marketers have found that, even when they want to adopt the standardization approach, it may not be feasible to do so. The problem has to do with local regulations, media and agency availability, literacy, and other factors. Interestingly, several well-known U.S. movie stars (including Sylvester Stallone) appear in Japanese commercials, but these stars prohibit such commercials from being shown in the United States. The degree of feasibility, of course, varies from country to country. The applicability of standardization is thus very situation-specific (Walters 1986).

Assuming that it is feasible to implement standardization, international marketers still need to question whether it is desirable to do so. A standardized international marketing mix is desirable if and only if it offers significant cost savings and if consumers are homogeneous. To answer this question, it is useful to consider the concept of market segmentation, which is discussed next.

Market Segmentation

Market segmentation is a strategy of "divide and satisfy"—dividing a total heterogeneous market into meaningful and homogeneous segments of customers and devising a distinct marketing mix for each segment. Because of consumer heterogeneity, the use of a single marketing mix represents an attempt to be all things to all people by having a little bit of something for everyone. The consequence is that no one gets much of anything. As a result of this approach, a standardized product or advertising message inevitably ends up being vague, bland, and perhaps not very meaningful by design.

Market segmentation, by adjusting the mix across segments (i.e., multiple mixes for multiple segments), is instead an attempt to be something to some but not all consumers. Instead of trying to satisfy the total market or all individuals rather well, a segmentation strategy aims at satisfying part of the market or some consumers very well. It should be apparent that localization and market segmentation share the same premises.

While market segmentation inevitably results in smaller submarkets, the objective of market segmentation is not to operate in a small submarket but rather to seek a segment that is attractive and profitable regardless of whether this submarket is small or large. Profit can be maximized by a precise marketing effort to meet the customer requirements of the selected segment. This strategy, of course, is more costly than standardization. Nevertheless, the more meaningful offerings should increase sales to the most brand loyal customers. The goal is to gain a differential advantage by customizing the marketing mix for a particular segment in order to maximize marketing effectiveness in terms of response and sales. As an example, Gannett Company's *USA Today*, a national newspaper, represents the standardization approach, whereas local newspapers clearly rely on localization and market segmentation. *USA Today* attempts to be all things to all people by offering a little bit of news about each of the fifty states. Yet Gannett understands very well that *USA Today* can never replace local newspapers and thus promotes itself as a "second read" to supplement a local paper.

While market segmentation requires an adjustment of the marketing mix across segments (if multiple segments are chosen), it does not necessarily require modifying product form for each segment. Product, as one component of the marketing mix, may sometimes remain constant across segments as other components such as advertising are adjusted to achieve a more meaningful mix. While some firms segment the market by having multiple brands within the same product category, others use different advertisements for the same brand to appeal to different consumer groups.

As shown in Figure 3-1, market segmentation provides a practical framework for decision-making purposes (Onkvisit and Shaw 1987). A market should be segmented when the following five requirements are met: *identification, accessibility/selectivity, differential response, segment size*, and *cost/profit*. The identification criterion addresses the issue of whether consumers are demographically homogeneous within as well as across countries. The accessibility/selectivity criterion is concerned with

FIGURE 3-1
A DECISION-MAKING
FRAMEWORK FOR
STANDARDIZATION/
LOCALIZATION
*SOURCE: SAK
ONKVISIT AND JOHN J.
SHAW (1987).
"STANDARDIZED
INTERNATIONAL
ADVERTISING: A
REVIEW AND CRITICAL
EVALUATION OF
THE THEORETICAL
AND EMPIRICAL
EVIDENCE," COLUMBIA
JOURNAL OF WORLD
BUSINESS, 22
(FALL), 53.*

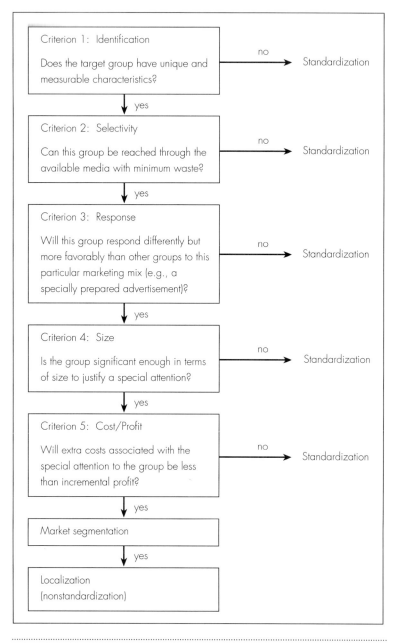

media waste and availability. The differential response criterion, on the other hand, focuses on the attitudinal/behavioral homogeneity. The segment size criterion measures the significance of a particular market segment since the segment must be sufficiently large and profitable to warrant a unique marketing mix.

Finally, the cost/profit criterion determines whether it is worthwhile to segment a market. An international marketer should compare incremental profits against the incremental costs associated with product/promotion adaptation to determine whether localization is desirable. Future earnings and costs in terms of the long run should be used in making this analysis.

When all the segmentation criteria are met, market segmentation is applicable and standardization is not. A country would be a distinct segment if:

1. The marketer can identify the residents' unique demographic characteristics.
2. These potential customers are accessible through available selective advertising media with minimum promotion waste.
3. Their responses to a unique marketing mix will be favorably different from those of other countries/segments.
4. The segment's size is large enough to justify a specially designed marketing program.
5. Incremental cost as a result of the segmentation is less than incremental profit.

It is common practice for most multinational corporations to treat the United States as a distinct segment because it easily satisfies all five requirements. As a rule, the United States is such a significant market that it requires special attention and a unique marketing mix. On the other hand, certain African or island countries are sometimes lumped together, either because they are somewhat alike or because they are too small to warrant individual attention. In such cases, a limited degree of standardization can be utilized regionally—but not globally. Therefore, the value of segmentation is to facilitate decision making by determining whether localization or standardized is a preferred strategy.

CONCLUSION

Marketing a product globally is not the same thing as marketing a global product. Marketing a standardized product globally does not make that product a global product. This chapter has shown how a number of concepts are related. First, standardization, globalization, and localization are a matter of degree, and they differ in degree rather than in kind. It is difficult to find a multinational firm that completely standardizes or localizes its marketing mix. Second, whereas a globalization strategy represents geocentricity, it is apparent that standardization is largely ethnocentric and that localization is basically polycentric. Third, whereas standardization is based on the homogeneity assumption, localization represents the perspective of heterogeneity. Finally, standardization and centralization are highly related, while decentralization encourages the utilization of localization.

Whether a glass is half-full or half-empty depends on one's perspective. Likewise, a partially localized product/advertisement is also a partially standardized product/advertisement and vice versa. Both standardization and localization should be viewed as occurring along a continuum on a bipolar scale (called the commonality-diversity or homogeneity-heterogeneity scale). If the world market could be treated like one total market of homogeneous consumers, a uniform marketing mix could be used in all countries. If this were truly the case, there would be no need for the existence of international marketing and international business texts. When a company is unwilling to suitably modify a product or advertisement, its management may be insensitive to cultural differences in foreign markets.

On the other hand, when preferential variations are significant, the value of a localization strategy is enhanced and a custom-made marketing mix for each segment is necessary. Any meaningful continent, region, or country may be considered a viable segment. In many cases, it is possible for a country to have multiple submarkets or segments as well. This submarket strategy, however, increases costs, some of which may be avoidable.

Multinational marketers should not be preoccupied with the artificiality of the standardization-localization issue. It is unsound to standardize (or localize) the international marketing mix just for the sake of standardization (or localization). Instead, a multinational organization's main goal should be to find the most effective and efficient way to satisfy both customer and corporate needs.

International marketing, like domestic marketing, should be guided by the marketing concept. The marketing concept requires the development of an integrated and customer-oriented marketing program to satisfy consumer and organizational goals simultaneously. Market segmentation reinforces this kind of orientation. Standardization, however, reflects only managements' needs while ignoring consumers' concerns. Instead of forcing customers to adjust their needs to fit what firms decide to offer, firms should sensibly adjust their marketing mix to fit market preferences. Any product or advertisement, whether standardized or not, should be tested for suitability for the intended target market before being introduced to the marketplace.

REFERENCES

Boddewyn, J. J., R. Soehl, and J. Picard (1986). "Standardization in International Marketing: Is Ted Levitt in Fact Right?" *Business Horizons*, 29 (November/December), 69–75.

Christopher, R. C. (1986). *Second to None: American Companies in Japan*, New York: Crown.

Echickson, W. (1990). "Electrolux's Brand of European Unity," *Wall Street Journal*, August 20, B4C.

Elinder, E. (1961). "International Advertisers Must Devise Universal Ads, Dump Separate National Ones, Swedish Adman Avers," *Advertising Age*, November 29, 91.

Hill, J. S., and R. R. Still (1984). "Adapting Products to LDC Tastes," *Harvard Business Review*, 62 (March–April), 92–101.

Hout, T., M. E. Porter, and E. Rudden (1982). "How Global Companies Win Out," *Harvard Business Review*, 60 (September–October), 98–108.

Jain, S. C. (1989). "Standardization of International Marketing Strategy: Some Research Hypotheses," *Journal of Marketing*, 53 (January), 70–79.

Lenormand, J. M. (1964). "Is Europe Ripe for the Integration of Advertising?" *The International Advertiser*, 5 (March), 14.

Levitt, T. (1983). "The Globalization of Markets," *Harvard Business Review*, 61 (May–June), 92–102.

Mueller, B. (1990). "Degrees of Globalization: An Analysis of the Standardization of Message Elements in Multinational Advertising," in *Current Issues & Research in Advertising*, J. H. Leigh and C. R. Martin, Jr., eds., Ann Arbor, MI: University of Michigan Press.

Onkvisit, S., and J. J. Shaw (1991). "Myopic Management: The Hollow Strength of American Competitiveness," *Business Horizons*, 34 (January–February), 13–19.

——— (1990). "Global Advertising: Revolution or Myopia?" *Journal of International Consumer Marketing*, 2 (3), 97–112.

——— (1987). "Standardized International Advertising: A Review and Critical Evaluation of the Theoretical and Empirical Evidence," *Columbia Journal of World Business*, 22 (Fall), 43–55.

Peebles, D. M., and J. K. Ryans, Jr. (1984). *Management of International Advertising: A Marketing Approach*, Boston: Allyn and Bacon.

Reed, V. D. (1967). "The International Consumer," in *Managerial Mar-*

keting, 3d ed., E. J. Kelly and W. Lazer, eds., Homewood, IL: Richard D. Irwin, 586–600.

Rosen, B. N., J. J. Boddewyn, and E. A. Louis (1989). "US Brands Abroad: An Empirical Study of Global Branding," *International Marketing Review*, 6 (1), 5–17.

Roth, R. F. (1982). *International Marketing Communications*, Chicago: Crain Books, 132.

van Mesdag, V. (1987). "Winging It in Foreign Markets," *Harvard Business Review* (January–February), 71–74.

Walters, P. G. P. (1986). "International Marketing Policy: A Discussion of the Standardization Construct and Its Relevance for Corporate Policy," *Journal of International Business Studies*, 17 (Summer), 55–69.

Wills, J., C. Samli, and L. Jacobs (1991). "Developing Global Products and Marketing Strategies: A Construct and a Research Agenda," *Journal of the Academy of Marketing Science*, 19 (Winter), 1–10.

Wind, Y. (1986). "The Strategic Role of International Marketing," *Journal of Consumer Marketing*, 3 (Spring), 23–26.

PART II

GLOBAL MARKET SEGMENTATION

CHAPTER 4

COMPETITIVE GLOBAL MARKET
SEGMENTATION

Salah S. Hassan

Roger D. Blackwell

S ome firms grow. Some firms stagnate and eventually die. The difference in these outcomes increasingly lies in the firms' understanding of and abilities in global marketing. Among those firms that achieve enviable growth rates, we sometimes find a strategic focus involving intermarket segmentation to be the reason for their competitiveness.

Segmentation is defined as the process of dividing the total market into subgroups for which a marketing mix that has special appeal to the most attractive (profitable) of the market segments can be developed. Segments historically have been regarded as *intra*market divisions, or subdivisions of the total market. Global firms, however, increasingly find it profitable to focus on *inter*market segments.

Intermarket segments are groups of customers who transcend traditionally defined markets. A market is traditionally defined as an aggregate of people with needs and the ability to buy, along with the willingness and authority to do so. In the past, the "aggregate of people" was often defined by geographic boundaries such as nations or regions of the world.

As firms grew, they often marketed their products across national boundaries. It was appropriate to describe such firms as international marketers. It was not unusual for international firms to analyze and to market on a regional basis. Thus the segment of the market for which they developed marketing mixes with special appeal might be Europe, Eastern Europe, Germany, or some other geographic basis of segmentation.

A primary difference between calling a firm international and global involves intermarket segmentation. An international firm is one with business transactions across few national boundaries. A global firm is one that views all areas of the globe as part of its total market and develops strategies to reach the most profitable segments of the market, wherever they are in the world. While such firms also cross national boundaries in the execution of their strategies, the market targets are people who have similar patterns of behavior regardless of national boundaries.

Global segmentation can be explained by an analogy to domestic segmentation. A firm in a country such as the United States can discover differences in behavior between states. Certainly language and other attributes vary between Michigan and Alabama, but most of the time it is more effective for firms to segment the market on variables other than states or other geographic jurisdictions. Most domestic firms use age, income, education, psychographics, or variables that are more closely related to buying behavior than are geographic boundaries.

The same is true in developing segmentation strategies for global markets. It is often more effective to segment the market on characteristics found among subgroups of people defined on some basis other than geographic boundaries. Thus the concept of intermarket segmentation has evolved to imply global segments defined on variables other than national boundaries. Intermarket segmentation refers to *ways of describing and reaching market segments that transcend national boundaries or that cut across geographically defined markets.*

In Chapter 5 you will have an opportunity to study in more depth the concept of intermarket segmentation and the methods of implementing the concept. In Chapters 6, 7, and 8, you will find examples of such intermarket segments. In this chapter, our objective is to explain how intermarket segmentation relates to strategic focus.

Global Segmentation as a Strategic Focus

Strategy involves the commitment of resources to a basic course of action. A new approach for many firms is to make sure their commitment of resources is closely related to global market segments. Firms are considered to have a *strategic focus involving intermarket segmentation when their strategies focus on similar customer behavior wherever it is found in the world rather than on national boundaries as definitions of markets.*

Global Vision

The practical application of intermarket segmentation as a corporate strategic focus can be observed in successful firms. One such example is the Avon Corporation. After two years of research and examination of its basic businesses, the company brought together 60 managers from around the world to define its mission and develop global strategies. The company's mission statement provides the basis for its strategies. "Our Vision: To be the company that best understands and satisfies the product, service and self-fulfillment needs of women—globally."

Avon has developed an intermarket segmentation strategy that is also intertemporal. The traditional Avon approach to segmentation works very well in developing countries. By appealing to segments in developing countries in ways that were previously effective for segments in the United States, Avon has entered new markets, added new products, and experienced growth in developing nations to an amount equal to 27 percent of its total sales volume. But in the United States and other developed industrial nations, the old system cannot prosper without major change. For segments of the population in these countries, Avon has developed new methods involving direct marketing programs that enable customers to buy Avon whenever, wherever, and however they want rather than relying only on Avon representatives. In developing markets, Avon's direct selling method is the primary distribution method. In China, women were so eager for Avon's products that the company sold its projected six-month inventory of lotion in only two weeks. Similarly, in Poland Avon customers are offered access to cosmetics and personal care items never available to them. In both China and Poland, the segments are similar, and they find Avon's offering so attractive that customers are willing to spend a considerable portion of their discretionary income on Avon products (Avon 1993).

A strategic focus on women and beauty implies much more than just a distribution system varied by segments. Meeting the subtleties and intricacies of customer demand around the world means Avon's business will vary from country to country and market to market, yet it is based on the commonality of beauty and a commitment to sell products to, for, and through women based on a thorough understanding of their needs and preferences.

Avon markets its products throughout much of the world. The company divides sales reporting into various countries and regions of the world. Cutting across these boundaries, however, are the products, distribution and sales methods, image and positioning programs, and pricing methods. These can be developed for specific segments that cut across many boundaries. The process has worked well, allowing the company to reverse the decline that occurred when it was primarily a domestic company focusing on diverse segments of the U.S. domestic market (such as home health care). Today, it is a market-driven, customer-oriented, intermarket focused company with 1992 sales of $1.41 billion in the United States and $2.25 billion outside the United States.

To say that a company has a strategic focus involving intermarket segmentation implies more than marketing variables. Production, human resources, and financial management are just a few of the variables necessary to carry out a strategic focus on a global intermarket segmentation basis. At Avon, the process extends to all levels of the firm from its front-line representatives, who are nearly all female, to the boardroom. At Avon, the traditional corporate males are found on the board of directors, but there are also women such as Dr. Cecily Selby, a distinguished scientist and trustee of both Radcliffe College and the Massachusetts Institute of Technology, who has been a member of the board since 1972. Other members of the board include Ernest Procope, chief executive officer of the country's largest minority-owned insurance brokerage firm and a board member since 1974, Remedios Diaz Oliver, chief executive officer of All American Containers, Inc. and a member of the Advisory Board–Trade Policy and Negotiations for the president of the United States, and Ann Moore, publisher of *People Magazine*.

Intermarket Segmentation and Market Dominance

One of the most important reasons for understanding and applying intermarket segmentation is the possibility the concept offers for achieving marketing dominance on a worldwide basis. Some of the best examples of global dominance by intermarket segmentation are found in Germany where they are known as the *Mittelstand.*

Many *Mittelstand* companies achieve world market shares in the range of 70 percent to 90 percent. Even when their market shares are smaller, it is not unusual for such companies to have four to ten times the market share of their nearest competitor. While many of these firms produce industrial products sold in business-to-business markets, some are consumer products. For example, Stihl sells high-quality power equipment to consumers and commands the highest market share, and often the highest prices, by relentless pursuit of the quality market segment, whether that segment is in Europe, North America, or other parts of the globe. Another German firm, TetraWerke, produces food for tropical fish at a relative market strength five times its nearest competitor.

The underlying factors associated with the strategies of such successful "niche" or intermarket segmentation firms were identified in a study by Simon (1992). Characteristics that are associated with the champions of intermarket segmentation success include the following:

1. Combine strategic focus with geographic diversity.
2. Emphasize factors like customer value.
3. Blend technology and closeness to customers.
4. Rely on their own technical competence.

5.   Create mutual interdependence between the company and its employees (Simon 1992).

On a worldwide basis, the markets for these niche-oriented strategies are increasingly linked or homogenized by a number of macro forces. These forces include increases in exports as a percent of world GNP, growth in industrialization and urbanization among developing countries, increases in share of manufactured exports by newly industrialized countries, advances in communications systems, expansion in transportation and world travel, and rapid increases in education throughout the globe.

GLOBAL POSITIONING

These macro forces influence consumption in a variety of ways that make it possible to develop a global positioning strategy. As a result, many consumer products can be segmented by variables that cut across national and cultural boundaries and yield to a unified marketing strategy on a global basis. Examples are found in consumer electronics, home appliances, automobiles, and apparel as well as many other products.

Boss and Eskada illustrate well how two German companies accomplish intermarket segmentation in the apparel industry. Both appeal to affluent, design-conscious people who are concerned about their appearance and constitute a basis for segmentation on a global basis. Whereas Boss provides clothing for men and Eskada provides clothing for women, both have similar product quality and positioning. The man who buys Boss can be found in the same type of stores, reading the same type of advertisements in globally distributed magazines, expecting the same type of fit and service, who is willing and able to buy at the same price points, whether that man lives in Munich, London, New York, Mexico City, or Hong Kong. Furthermore, the behavioral differences between a man in New York buying Boss and a man in New York buying a Sears suit are probably greater than behavioral differences between a man buying Boss in New York and a man buying Boss in Hong Kong.

Similarly, women who appreciate the design qualities of Eskada and are willing and able to afford Eskada prices are similar enough that they constitute an intermarket segment. That segment is targeted with a unified marketing strategy whether women in the segment live in Munich, New York, Mexico City, or Hong Kong. Eskada has successful stores in all of those cities. If a marketing analyst could look into the motivation and lifestyles of Eskada customers around the world, the analyst would probably find more similarity in the women's behavior than the traditional differences observed in the languages and local characteristics of women from each country.

THINK GLOBALLY, LINK LOCALLY

The challenge facing marketing managers is to design global marketing programs that are based on identifying and targeting intermarkets with appropriate goods and services. Understanding cultural subtleties is essential, however, for the incorporation of unique market needs that may require modifications in the offerings of a global marketing program to appeal to localized market needs (Engel, Blackwell, and Miniard 1990; Friedman 1986; and McCracken 1988).

For example, the Coca-Cola Company was able to become global in both vision and scale of operations, yet it has managed to stay close to local markets. With business operations in 160 countries and commanding a 47 percent share of soft drinks consumed on a worldwide basis, it is one of the most dominant brands in the world. Yet the Coca-Cola Company still manages to offer Indonesian and Filipino teenagers soda pop with local flavors (*The Wall Street Journal* 1989).

Consumer marketers should think globally and link locally. This perspective of "linking markets globally" is based on determining similarities across national and cultural boundaries while assessing domestic (within-country) differences. When this notion is accepted, *the question is not whether to globalize but how to identify and target intermarket links based on an understanding of the changing global environment.*

LINKING MARKETS GLOBALLY

Global marketing strategies depend on the ability to integrate and coordinate marketing programs worldwide. For those global strategies to be effective, however, they must be linked closely to local realities of the marketplace.

The development of effective global strategies can be achieved when a firm recognizes that the process of globalization includes two basic steps:

1. Configuration of the firm's activities in many nations in order to serve markets on a global scale.
2. Coordination among the dispersed activities in order to gain a competitive advantage (Porter 1990).

The ability to accomplish these steps may vary depending on the degree of globalization in the industry. Some industries such as consumer electronics, automobiles, fashion, and home appliances have achieved high degrees of globalization.

Another factor that may affect a firm's ability to configure and coordinate its activities on a global basis is the globalization of competition

(Sheth 1986). In today's global business environment, rivals end up buying firms instead of competing with them. Recently, Japan's Bridgestone Corporation bought most of Firestone's tire business. Consequently, the industry is global to the extent that there are intermarket links which require firms to target consumers on a worldwide basis.

Among families, one segment of the market buys infant formula rather than using mother's milk, soy milk, or cow's milk. To target this worldwide segment, Nestlé, which is a dominant player in many countries of the world, entered the U.S. market by purchasing Carnation Dairy Products. In this way it attacked industry leaders Ross Laboratories (Similac) and Mead-Johnson (Enfamil). Thus Similac and Enfamil, which were mostly domestic brands, suddenly found themselves in a competitive situation in which globalization is a major reality. And Nestlé, which dominates the world in many food-related products, was forced to link itself to the local realities of the U.S. infant formula market which it entered by acquisition while still pursuing an intermarket segmentation strategy with its own brand in other countries.

There are sizeable world markets where similar consumer segments are emerging across cultural and national boundaries. The challenge is to identify and profile these segments on an intermarket basis and to develop strategies to reach them via standardized marketing programs. The solution is to use intermarket segmentation as a framework to evaluate markets on a worldwide basis and to identify attributes suitable to the implementation of standardized marketing programs (Hassan 1991, and Kreutzer 1988).

Market Competitiveness in a Global Industry: A Strategic Framework

Competitiveness in the global marketplace is most likely to be achieved when it is based on a firm foundation of understanding the globalization process. Such a foundation is shown in Figure 4-1, which provides a strategic framework for configuring a global firm's intermarket segmentation strategy and coordinating the firm's marketing program on a global basis.

The strategic framework for understanding competitiveness shown in Figure 4-1 focuses on four main factors that are instrumental in developing a firm's global marketing strategies. The four factors are:

1. Demand structure
2. Strategic focus
3. Economies of scale
4. Scope of globalization

Demand Structure

First, global marketing managers must be able to analyze and respond to *demand structure.* As with domestic markets, the essential variables of demand structure involve people and their ability to buy. The number of people within geographic boundaries, their ages, and their incomes are the starting points of demand analysis.

The analysis of intermarket segmentation requires even more attention to demand components other than demographic variables. Global market analysts must understand core values and needs of consumers on a cross-cultural basis. Cross-cultural analysis is the systematic comparison of similarities and differences in the material and behavioral aspects of cultures. Global firms can win competitive battles when they are armed with superior strategies that are based on consumer orientation (Kilts 1990, Particelli 1990). Managers of global consumer markets use such knowledge to enable them to "think of global similarities and link with local markets."

Demand structure analyzed on a cross-cultural basis involves a number of elements. After a comprehensive demographic review, the cross-

FIGURE 4-1   DETERMINANTS OF MARKET COMPETITIVENESS IN THE GLOBALIZING INDUSTRY

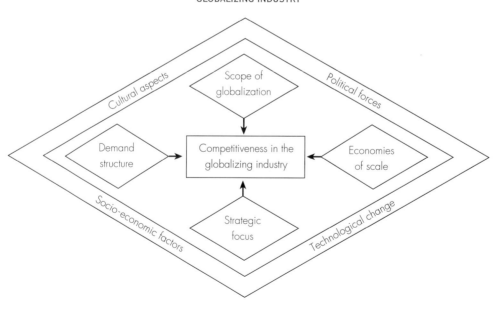

FIGURE 4-1 CONTINUED

Demand structure

- Competitiveness in the globalizing consumer markets will not be achieved without carefully understanding and responding to the core values and needs of the consumer.

- Managers of global consumer markets will win competitive battles if they are able to "think of global similarities and adapt to local differences."

- Get close to the consumer and build competitive strategies based on commonalities and differences.

Scope of globalization

- The globalization scope achieved in a particular industry in which the firm is trying to gain global competitive advantage dictates the degree of standardization of the marketing program and process.
- The standardized marketing program is defined in terms of: the various aspects of the marketing mix, target market, market position, and environmental elements.
- The standardized process implies the use of tools that assist in the development and implementation of global programs (Jain 1989).

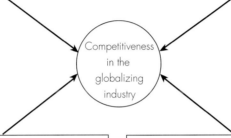

Competitiveness in the globalizing industry

Strategic focus
- Global marketing strategy needs to be an integral part of the overall global strategic focus of the firm.
- The role of marketing in the overall strategy of the firm is three-dimensional (Porter 1986). It involves
  - the geographic concentration of certain marketing activities
  - the coordination of dispersed marketing activities
  - the use of marketing strategy to gain competitive advantage
- The identification of target market segments within countries (country groups and buyers within countries) and physical product configurations would both assist in the determination of global marketing strategy (Porter 1986).
- The importance of segmentation to the global strategy is consistent with two key trends: the emergence of specific global segments, and the usefulness of segmentation to global strategy (Porter 1986; Douglas and Wind 1987; and Jain 1989).

Economies of scale
- Global competitiveness is demonstrated via the ability to standardize research and development, product design, manufacturing, assembly, and packaging procedures.

- Global sourcing for labor can serve as an example of how companies cut down on manufacturing costs as a result of shifting production from the United States and Europe to low-wage Asia and Latin America.

- Porter (1990) identifies a global approach to statgey that is based on competitive advantage via:

  - Configuration of the firm's activities in many nations in order to serve markets on a global scale.
  - Coordination among dispersed activities.

cultural analysis should focus on relevant motivations for using the product or service and characteristic behavior patterns that can be observed among markets or across markets. Demand analysis for intermarket segmentation should determine broad cultural values that may be relevant to this product, as well as characteristic forms of decision making within the segment.

Cross-cultural analysis of demand can help in determining the marketing processes that will be appropriate to reach intermarket segments. Demand analysis of this type can also help define promotion methods that are likely to be effective in reaching intermarket segments.

The overall goal in demand analysis is to define intermarket segments whose buying behavior can be clustered in such a way to minimize within group variance and maximize between group variance. This form of demand analysis differs from the historical approach in international marketing when markets frequently were defined by national or other geographic boundaries. The basic problem with defining markets on a national basis rather than an intermarket basis is that market segmentation on a geographic basis is more likely to yield market segments with high within-group variance and low between-group variance.

STRATEGIC FOCUS

Second, the emergence of globalized market segments across national boundaries can provide a basis for the *strategic focus* of the firm. Determining the strategic focus of a firm on a global basis involves the proper defining of key intermarket segments to be served. After the key segments are defined, the second stage is a decisive allocation of the firm's resources toward the development of marketing programs that delight the customers in these intermarket segments. In the Avon example described earlier, this process can be observed in the firm's product development, positioning activities, and distribution channels. The firm's clear definition of customer segments on a global basis provides the strategic focus for allocating resources to marketing activities.

The existence of intermarket segments is a key condition for success in any global marketing strategy. Focusing on consumer segments that transcend key markets in the context of the competitive strategy of a firm is linked to developing and managing standardized marketing programs. Developing and assessing the most competitive standardized marketing programs to target consumer segments that are highly receptive to global products are major challenges facing today's world-class firms. But a clear understanding of a segment, its motivations, and its behavior can provide a basis for dynamic, perhaps dramatic, competitive action that may have been lacking in the past as a result of a "myopia" in market segmentation. An example of dramatic positioning with its marketing programs is provided in Exhibit 4-1, illustrating how Benetton has built its global strategy based on its strategic focus on intermarket or global market segments.

Benetton was able to identify youthful market segments on a global scale based on converging wants, needs, and consumption patterns. Benetton recognized that on a global scale the emerging "teenage culture" shares a youthful life-style that values growth and learning with an appreciation for trendy and colorful fashion. Teenagers are very self-conscious about the way they look, and role models play an important influence on their choices (Guber 1987). In recognition of the growing demand among teenagers for colorful designer fashions, regardless of nationality, Benetton launched its global advertising campaign "The United Colors of Benetton." In one of its ads, the cross-cultural process is especially evident. In clothes and skin color, kids vary around the world, but the ad shows a behavior that is similar among kids around the world—the desire to stick out their tongues at other people. And when they do, another universal trait is revealed; regardless of skin color, all children have pink tongues!

A growing number of international marketers exhibit a strategic focus on the global youth or teenage market segment. In addition to Benetton, such firms include Coca-Cola, Pepsi-Cola, Levi Strauss, Gillette, and Swatch International. These firms, in varying degrees, achieve strategic focus in their firms by acting on the belief that there is one generic type of teenager in most parts of the world (Feinberg 1989).

Other global firms such as Sony have recognized a desire for novelty and trendier designs and images among intermarket teenage segments. Sony responded to this intermarket segment of consumers by introducing the "My First Sony" line of audio products. Also, teenagers often have aloof attitudes and tend to respond to brands and fads which reflect that behavior. Based on an understanding of these behavioral patterns, Swatch International targeted teens on a worldwide basis with trendy watches that make a fashion statement. The existence of such segments has provided the basis for the strategic focus of successful firms and their global marketing programs.

ECONOMIES OF SCALE

The third strategic factor for competitiveness in a global consumer market is *economies of scale*. Certain firms have demonstrated global competitiveness via their ability to standardize research and development, product design, manufacturing, assembly, and packaging procedures. Also, global sourcing for labor has helped companies to cut down on manufacturing costs by shifting production and assembly from high-wage to low-wage countries. Enormous economies of scale have been achieved by companies that acted globally on sourcing decisions and streamlining operations. To-

EXHIBIT 4-1

BENETTON: STRATEGIC
FOCUS ON THE
GLOBAL YOUTH
MARKET

SOURCE: EXCERPTED
FROM R. BLACKWELL,
K. BLACKWELL, AND
W. TALARZYK. (1993).
CONTEMPORARY
CASES IN CONSUMER
BEHAVIOR, 4TH
EDITION, FORT WORTH:
DRYDEN PRESS.

Benetton is a global apparel manufacturer with approximately 6,500 licensed retail stores in almost 100 countries on 6 continents. Founded in 1965 by the Benetton family in Treviso, Italy, where it is headquartered today, the company quickly created and filled a niche in the market for the colorful fashion-forward knitwear and sportswear that has become Benetton's signature around the world.

The Benetton family, Luciano, Giuliana, Gilberto and Carolo, began their entrepreneurial venture in 1965 with the establishment of their first factory at Ponzano Veneto, near Treviso. Today the Group has more than 3,000 employees in 14 factories in Italy, France, Spain, the United States, and Brazil. Benetton owns 50 percent of the shares of Linz Co., Ltd. of the Seibu/Saison Group in Japan. It also has a joint venture company, Ajas-Benetton, with its headquarters and a plant in Armenia to produce and distribute cotton clothing in the former U.S.S.R.

The success of the company's collections is based on color, design, and the quality of its raw materials. Careful attention is paid to fashion trends and the desires of the marketplace. Twice a year Benetton presents its rich range of styles, totalling about 5,000 annually. The system of production is flexible and highly decentralized, utilizing a network of outside

suppliers. The system relies heavily on advanced technology, such as electronic knitting machines (programmed to produce complex designs) and automated cloth-cutting machinery.

Distribution is handled by a network of 80 representatives, each one of whom is responsible for a precise geographic area, and to the 6,500 independent stores that agree to sell Benetton products exclusively. Orders are fed through a computerized network that enables the representatives to link up to the central system in Ponzano.

Part of the Group's marketing strategy is to allow the customer to experience a direct relationship with the merchandise. So in all Benetton stores, products are visible and can be handled. Stores' furniture and layouts have been designed with this objective in mind. All stores are light and airy, conveying youth and energy as well as accentuating the color of the clothes.

Benetton attributes much of its success to its unique and highly automated design, production, and warehouse and distribution facilities. All Benetton products are marketed under the *United Colors of Benetton* logo. The company has demonstrated its ability to tackle world markets, exporting not only its products but also its creativity, technology, and production know-how. The most recent examples have been in China, Turkey, Egypt, and India, where joint ventures with local companies have been set up to produce and distribute clothing and other products under the Benetton name. The company invests about 4.7 percent of total revenues in communications and advertising that provides a unifying element for all Benetton marketing. The universitality of Benetton's appeal as a strategic focus of the firm is reinforced by its theme: United Colors of Benetton.

Benetton has pursued a campaign of public communication based on a few key concepts that contain the essence of the company's philosophy. These concepts are: To create a long-term, homogeneous, international image that focuses on the ethos of the product. The campaign intends to capture the infinite variety and use of colors and the fact that the Benetton label is accessible and affordable to everyone.

In one of its ads, a photo of three children—Black, Caucasian, and Oriental—sticking out their tongues (the point of which is that all tongues are the same color)—serves to illustrate the universality of Benetton advertising. Even so, it sometimes encounters unforeseen cultural barriers. This image was deemed an inappropriate act of defiance and subsequently withdrawn from display in Arab countries, where it is impolite for children to defy their elders. Yet the same photo won several awards in Europe.

EXHIBIT 4-1
CONTINUED

day, firms are compelled to standardize in order to maximize their competitive advantage.

For example, Benetton's growth and success as a global player, described in Exhibit 4-1, can be attributed partly to its achievement of global economies of scale. These include the strong relationship between the company and its network of agents, standardized manufacturing procedures, advanced electronic communications technology, and unified overall store image and advertising theme.

Standardization of manufacturing procedures began in 1972 when Benetton started dying assembled garments rather than dying the yarns before assembly. This procedure led to significant growth in the number of garments produced, with more than 74 million garments produced today for distribution through 6,500 retail outlets in 100 countries (*United Colors of Benetton* 1991). A worldwide electronic data interchange system was developed to expedite orders and to maintain control over the shipping of raw materials. Additionally, Benetton's maintenance of strong relationships with its network of agents helped in the implementation throughout the world of a rigid store policy that is responsible for significant economies of scale in the design, construction, and operation of retail facilities (Rossant 1990). Other consumer industries such as consumer electronics, automobiles, and watches are achieving high degrees of standardization that are associated with global economies of scale.

SCOPE OF GLOBALIZATION

The fourth strategic factor is *scope of globalization,* and it refers to the degree of standardization that can be achieved on a worldwide basis in the development of a firm's strategies and programs. Key industries are globalizing to create a more competitive position in certain world markets via the employment of standardized marketing strategies and programs.

A standardized marketing program is defined in terms of the various aspects of the marketing mix: product, promotion, price, and place. Scope of standardization may also include other aspects of the marketing program such as target markets, market position, and environmental and organizational elements. For many global firms, some aspects of a marketing program (i.e., product design) may have greater standardization potential than others. The matrix shown in Figure 4-2 illustrates this point. The vertical axis represents various degrees of market receptivity, and the horizontal axis shows standardization versus adaptation. In this case markets with high receptivity to standardized programs can be plotted and clustered as part of intermarket segments. The circles in Figure 4-2 represent the scope of segmentation. Therefore, different clusters/intermarket segments can be identified as a function of customer receptivity, and they are dependent on the extent of commonalties in consumption patterns across cultural and national boundaries.

TARGETING THE "GLOBAL TEENAGER" MARKET   An example of an increasingly globalized industry is provided by the global teenager market. On a global scale, particularly in industrial societies, teenagers are being homogenized because of their intense exposure to television and frequent travel (Feinberg 1989).

Global teens from New York, Tokyo, Seoul, Hong Kong, Paris, London, and Rome share memorable experiences that are reflected in their consumption. Young consumers, whose cultural norms have not become

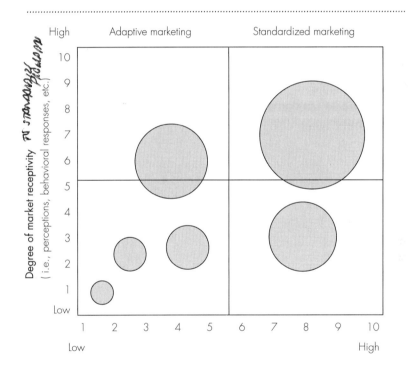

FIGURE 4-2
MATRIX FOR PLOTTING INTERMARKET SEGMENTS

Degree of standardization in the marketing program
(i.e., product mix, standardization in packaging, branding, etc.)

 Circle size illustrates scope of segmentation

ingrained, and who can share universal needs and fantasies, are influenced effectively by standardized marketing programs. Some of the variables that might be analyzed to appeal to the intermarket teenage market are shown in Figure 4-3.

U.S. marketers complain about closed Japanese markets; however, some companies that have targeted young Japanese consumers have done very well. Japanese youth are called *shinjinrui,* which means new human being. One example of a firm that appeals to this market is Tower Records of Sacramento, California, which exports records from the United States and markets them for prices that are 30 to 40 percent lower than those of its Japanese competitors. In 1987, the company did $12 million of business in Japan.

Other global firms such as Benetton focus their global strategy on this segment for several strategic reasons. A new demographic reality in Western Europe, Japan, and the United States indicates that the population is growing older. The baby boom era of 1946–1964 produced a population structure that currently represents the largest portion of the market (Vandermerwe 1990). Figure 4-4 illustrates this reality by indicating that 15–24-year-old consumers are projected to grow nearly 15 percent between 1985 and 2000, but the painful reality for industrialized countries such as the United States and Germany is that there will be a large decline in num-

	Attributes	Global teenagers
FIGURE 4-3 PORTRAIT OF AN EMERGING "GLOBAL CONSUMER" SEGMENT *SOURCE: ADAPTED FROM S. HASSAN AND K. KATSANIS (1990). "IDENTIFICATION OF GLOBAL CONSUMER SEGMENTS: A BEHAVIORAL FRAMEWORK," JOURNAL OF INTERNATIONAL CONSUMER MARKETING, VOL. 3., NO. 2. 11–28.*	Shared values	Growth, change, future, learning, play
	Key product benefits sought	Novelty, trendy image, fashion statement, name brands/novelty
	Demographics	Age: 12–19, well traveled, high media exposure
	Media communication	Teen magazines, MTV, radio, video, peers, role models
	Distribution channels	General retailers with name brands
	Price range	Affordable
	Targeted by global firms such as	Coca-Cola Co., Benetton, Swatch International, Sony, PepsiCo, Inc.
	Related micro-segments/clusters	Pre-adolescents, female teens, male teens, adolescents
	Factors influencing the emergence of the segment	Television media, international education

bers. Elsewhere in the world (i.e., Eastern Europe, Asia, Africa, and Latin America) the teenager population is growing at staggering rates (Vandermerwe 1990). For example, in Poland the teenager population (15–19 years of age) will increase 36 percent, and the youth population (20–24 years of age) will increase 17 percent. The youth market will also increase in other countries like Bulgaria (10 percent) and Hungary (31 percent).

These demographic realities leave companies such as Benetton with three strategic options. First, they can champion regional expansion strategies in an already saturated Western European market. This strategy was first adopted by Benetton during the early 1970s as the firm exploited opportunities outside its domestic market of Italy. Second, they can adopt a globalized strategy to exploit opportunities in other non-Western countries. During the early 1990s Benetton started looking for marketing opportunities on a global scale and championed the idea of interracial harmony to win the hearts of global teenagers. Third, they can experiment with a differentiation strategy. For example, Benetton decided to intro-

FIGURE 4-4   WORLD GROWTH TRENDS IN EUROPE, THE UNITED STATES, AND JAPAN FOR 15–TO 24–YEAR-OLDS, 1985–2000

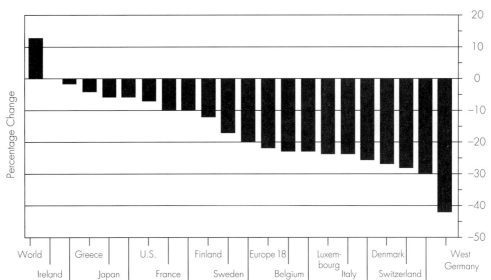

SOURCE: THE WORLD BANK, 1987/1988: ADAPTED FROM S. VANDERMERWE (1990). "YOUTH CONSUMERS: GROWING PAINS," BUSINESS HORIZONS, MAY/JUNE.

duce lines of business attire appealing to the baby-boom generation. The company targeted this growth segment during the late 1980s and early 1990s with a serious image of being concerned about the world we live in. Based on the strategic focus described earlier and illustrated in Exhibit 4-1, the firm launched a global marketing program that set it apart from other competitors in an industry where the scope of the industry is highly globalized.

Managerial Implications of Intermarket Segmentation

Segmentation is one of the most important factors to be considered in the marketing programs of any company, whether the firm is involved in domestic or global markets. The identification of international market segments (i.e., country groups and within-country segments) with product/ marketing configurations has been recognized in the past to be important in determining global marketing strategy (Porter 1986). In the new globalized markets, global marketing strategy using an intermarket segmentation approach needs to be integrated in the overall global strategy of the firm. In this final part of the chapter, we describe an approach to assist in developing managerial decisions and actions in the global management process.

Strategic Attractiveness of Intermarket Segments

The existence of global segments is a key condition for the success of any global marketing strategy (Douglas and Wind 1987; Hassan and Katsanis 1991). Clearly, determining the strategic attractiveness of any intermarket segment is a prerequisite for the successful deployment of global marketing programs. Determination of the strategic attractiveness of any intermarket segment should be based on criteria such as measurability, reachability, profitability, and receptivity to a given standardized marketing program.

The issue of focusing on strategically attractive intermarket segments in the context of the competitive strategy of the firm is linked to developing and managing standardized marketing programs and processes. For a segment to be attractive across markets, the behavior of customers must be similar enough across markets to permit similar marketing programs across markets. Assessing and developing standardized marketing programs for intermarket segments is a major challenge because these intermarket programs must be more effective than the domestic segmentation programs that may be used by competitors.

In spite of the desire to develop standardized marketing programs for intermarket segments, recent evidence points out the need to exercise care in the execution of standardized marketing programs. For example, certain standardized strategies were fatal to firms in the toy and automobile industries (Kashani 1989). Five pitfalls were identified in developing global marketing programs. These pitfalls include lack of formal research, tendency to overstandardize, inadequate followup, narrow scope of coordination, and lack of flexibility in execution (Kashani 1989).

Steps to Effective Intermarket Segmentation

Selecting attractive intermarket segments is only a portion of the problem. It is but one step or stage in a total process. The stage of identifying market segments is not easy in a domestic firm; it is even more difficult in a global firm in which the goal is intermarket segmentation. But these are the skills expected of effective marketing practitioners. Their skills will not manifest themselves in success, however, if the rest of the managerial process is not accomplished with an equal level of ability.

Strategic focus on market segments is the underlying reason for implementing such a process. The Japanese company Pioneer provides an excellent example of a firm that has achieved success for decades employing many of the elements of the process described in this chapter. In the case of Pioneer, the choice of an English name for a new Japanese company occurred in 1936. Seija Matsumoto, the founder, was impressed with the spirit of pioneers. He felt the concept and the name represented a type of customer who would accept innovative technology for high-quality audio reproduction. And he felt that this type of customer could be found in many countries, not just in Japan. It was several years before his concept of a type of customer who would exhibit similar behavior in the purchase of audio equipment on a global basis would be described as an intermarket segment. Yet his approach was not unlike the concept of intermarket segmentation described in this chapter.

At Pioneer, the founder selected a logo composed of two symbols. One symbol is a tuning fork, which represents clarity of musical tones. The other symbol is the Greek symbol ohm, which communicates electrical technology. It is fascinating to realize that Matsumoto selected this logo in 1937 because it would transcend national boundaries and languages and be a truly global symbol, with special appeal to the same segment of the population wherever those people were in the world. From that beginning more than a half century ago, Pioneer has refined its strategic focus to include a corporate vision for bringing entertainment to the world. Using a total managerial approach as its strategic focus, Pioneer describes itself

FIGURE 4-5
AN ORGANIZATIONAL
DECISION PROCESS
FOR INTERMARKET

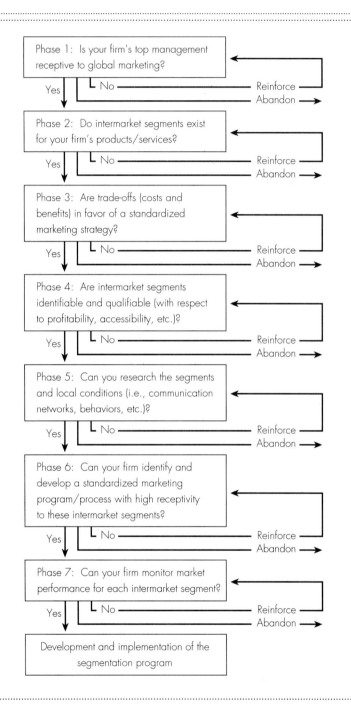

Phase 1: Is your firm's top management receptive to global marketing?
Yes   └ No ──────────────── Reinforce ──┘
                                  Abandon ──→

Phase 2: Do intermarket segments exist for your firm's products/services?
Yes   └ No ──────────────── Reinforce ──┘
                                  Abandon ──→

Phase 3: Are trade-offs (costs and benefits) in favor of a standardized marketing strategy?
Yes   └ No ──────────────── Reinforce ──┘
                                  Abandon ──→

Phase 4: Are intermarket segments identifiable and qualifiable (with respect to profitability, accessibility, etc.)?
Yes   └ No ──────────────── Reinforce ──┘
                                  Abandon ──→

Phase 5: Can you research the segments and local conditions (i.e., communication networks, behaviors, etc.)?
Yes   └ No ──────────────── Reinforce ──┘
                                  Abandon ──→

Phase 6: Can your firm identify and develop a standardized marketing program/process with high receptivity to these intermarket segments?
Yes   └ No ──────────────── Reinforce ──┘
                                  Abandon ──→

Phase 7: Can your firm monitor market performance for each intermarket segment?
Yes   └ No ──────────────── Reinforce ──┘
                                  Abandon ──→

Development and implementation of the segmentation program

as "a family of international enterprises" dedicated to entertainment segments globally.

Placing intermarket segmentation in the context of the total decision making of an organization offers the best chance of making intermarket segmentation approaches successful. Figure 4-5 provides a framework or checklist for understanding and implementing an organizational decision process for intermarket segmentation. This flowchart presents a practical framework for deciding on an effective intermarket segmentation program that may help to avoid some of the pitfalls. In this framework, the effectiveness of intermarket segmentation decisions is the key to the development and implementation of a successful standardized marketing program and process.

A standardized marketing program is defined in terms of various aspects of the marketing mix: product, promotion, price, and place. On the other hand, the standardized *process* implies the use of tools that assist in the development and implementation of a given global marketing program. In this context, standardization of the marketing program incorporates other factors in addition to the marketing mix, such as target markets, market position, and organizational/environmental elements like management receptivity and flexibility. The framework presented in Figure 4-5 is basic. It needs to be adapted and detailed to the industry in which a given firm competes. The effectiveness of this strategic framework also depends on other factors such as a firm's ability to succeed in the implementation process.

....

SUMMARY

Effective development and execution of intermarket segmentation programs can give a company a significant competitive edge. In this chapter, such an edge can be observed in companies from many countries. Avon is a U.S. example; Boss and Eskada are German examples; Nestlé is Swiss; Benetton is Italian and Pioneer is Japanese. Key trends in the global marketplace are increasing the importance of the intermarket segmentation effort in nearly every firm, regardless of its country of domicile.

Market segments have often been regarded as *intra*market divisions, or subdivisions of the total market. Global firms, however, find it increasingly profitable to focus on *inter*market segments. Intermarket segments are groups of customers that transcend national boundaries but exist on a global basis. An international firm is one with business transactions across national boundaries. A global firm is one that views all areas of the globe as part of the total market and develops strategies to reach the most profitable segments of the market, wherever they are in the world. The effectiveness of a firm in using intermarket segmentation depends on demand structure, strategic focus, economies of scale, and the scope of globalization.

A new approach for many firms is to make sure their commitment of resources is closely related to global market segments. Firms are considered to have a *strategic focus involving intermarket segmentation when their strategies focus on similar customer behavior wherever it is found in the world rather than relying on national boundaries to define markets.*

Effective managers need to take a systematic approach toward identifying and reaching their markets on a worldwide basis. An analysis of the key environmental conditions facing the firm, an assessment of the trade-offs associated with standardization, a careful definition of intermarket segments, and sophisticated market research should be part of this systematic approach to global strategy. The rethinking of conventional segmentation models should guide managers of consumer markets toward the formulation of global strategies that can be executed for competitive advantage.

References

Avon, 1992 Annual Report (1993). New York: Avon Corporation, February.

Douglas, S., and J. Wind (1987). "The Myth of Globalization," *Columbia Journal of World Business* (Winter), 19–30.

Engel, J., R. Blackwell, and P. Miniard (1990). *Consumer Behavior,* Fort Worth: 733.

Feinberg, A. (1989). "The First Global Generation," *Adweek,* February 6, 18–27.

Freidman, R. (1986). "Psychological Meaning of Products: A Simplification of the Standardization vs. Adaptation Debate," *Columbia Journal of World Business* (Summer).

Guber, S. (1987). "The Teenage Mind," *American Demographics* (August), 42–44.

Hassan, S. S. (1991). "A Strategic Framework for Identifying and Reaching Intermarket Segments," in K. D. Frankenberger, et al. (eds.), *World Marketing Congress,* Vol. V, Coral Gables, FL: Academy of Marketing Science, 34–37.

Hassan, S. S., and L. Katsanis (1991). "Identification of Global Consumer Segments: A Behavioral Framework," *Journal of International Consumer Marketing,* Vol. 3, No. 2, 11–28.

Jain, S. (1989). "Standardization of International Marketing Strategy: Some Research Hypotheses," *Journal Marketing* (January), 70–79.

Kashani, K. (1989). "Beware the Pitfalls of Global Marketing," *Harvard Business Review* (September/October), 91–98.

Kilts, J. M. (1990). "Adaptive Marketing," *Journal of Consumer Marketing* (Summer), Vol. 7, No. 3, 39–45.

Knowlton, C. (1988). "The New Export Entrepreneurs," *Fortune,* June 6, 87–102.

Kreutzer, R. T. (1988). "Marketing Mix Standardization: An Integrated Approach in Global Marketing," *European Journal of Marketing,* Vol. 22, No. 10, 19–30.

Levitt, T. "The Globalization of Markets," *Harvard Business Review* (May/June), 92–102.

McCracken, G. (1988). *Culture and Consumption,* Bloomington: Indiana State University Press.

Particelli, M. C. (1990). "A Global Arena," *Journal of Consumer Marketing* (Fall), Vol. 7, No. 4, 43–52.

Porter, M. E. (1986). "The Strategic Role of International Marketing," *Journal of Consumer Marketing* (Spring), 3 (2), 17–21.

Porter, M. E. (1990). *The Competitive Advantage of Nations,* New York: Free Press.

Rossant, J. (1990). "Benetton Strips Back Down to Sports Wear," *Business Week,* March 5, 42.

Sheth, J. (1986). "Global Markets or Global Competition?" *Journal of Consumer Marketing* (Spring), Vol. 3, No. 2, 9–11.

Simon, H. (1992). "Lessons from Germany's Midsize Giants," *Harvard Business Review* (March–April), 115–123.

The Wall Street Journal (1989). "The Real Thing: Tough and Consistent, Coke Excels at Global Marketing and Keeps an Eye on Youth," December 19, A1 and A6.

United Colors of Benetton (1991). "The Benetton Group," New York: Benetton Services Corp., 1.

Vandermerwe, S. (1990). "Youth Consumers: Growing Pains," *Business Horizons,* May/June, 30–36.

CHAPTER 5

THE NEW FRONTIERS OF
INTERMARKET SEGMENTATION

Salah S. Hassan

A. Coskun Samli

A new market reality points in the direction of emerging inter-market segments that transcend national boundaries. Segments such as teenagers, green consumers, yuppies, and elite consumers are converging in certain world markets. Consumers belonging to these segments are buying global products such as electronics, automobiles, designer fashions, home appliances, and beverages. The challenge facing global marketers is to identify these intermarket segments that are receptive to standardized marketing programs.

In a dramatically changing business environment, firms must develop and carefully target marketing programs on a global scale to maintain their competitive edge. There is a need to pay more attention to segmentation as an integral part of any competitive marketing strategy (Porter 1986). The usefulness of segmentation to global marketing strategy has been well supported in the literature (Douglas and Wind 1987, Jain 1989). Currently, the key issue in global marketing is the need to identify inter-market segments that are reachable with a global marketing strategy. It is also important to note that identifying intermarket segments by conventional methods is not adequate for successful international marketing. Therefore, this chapter pays special attention to these basic issues by exploring ways to segment global markets as well as some of the new frameworks and methods for segmentation.

CRITERIA FOR INTERMARKET SEGMENTATION

In the past, international marketers based their segmentation decisions on geopolitical, socioeconomic, demographic, and cultural factors. In other words, segmentation was done by grouping countries on the basis of macro-level characteristics. This conventional approach has potential inadequacies. Conventional segmentation factors and methods are not adequate for the new global market realities (see Table 5-1). In this case, country-by-country segmentation ignores the fact that world markets go beyond political boundaries. For instance, southern France and northern Italy have more in common than northern and southern Italy or northern and southern France. Similarly, northwestern Turkey has more in common with Europe than the southeastern part of Turkey, which is closer to certain Arab cultures. The existence of certain segments that transcend national boundaries is in fact a market reality. Thus conventional segmentation factors need to be re-examined. The following section examines international segmentation criteria and methods.

Conventional Wisdom	Unconventional Wisdom	
1. It assumes heterogeneity between countries.	1. It assumes the emergence of segments that transcend national boundaries.	**TABLE 5-1** CONVENTIONAL VERSUS UNCONVENTIONAL WISDOM IN INTERNATIONAL SEGMENTATION
2. It assumes homogeneity within any given country.	2. It acknowledges the existence of within-country differences.	
3. It is based on macro-criteria of segmentation (i.e. geopolitical, socioeconomic, demographic, cultural, etc.).	3. It focuses on "hybrid" or totally unusual criteria for segmentation.	
4. It focuses heavily on cultural differences.	4. It gives equal attention to differences as well as commonalities in values, patterns of consumption, and expectations.	
5. Methods of segmentation are based on discriminant analysis.	5. Methods of segmentation are based on the clustering of markets across national and regional boundaries.	
6. Micro- or within-country segments are given secondary priority.	6. Micro- or within-country segments are given primary priority.	
7. Countrywide market considerations are given higher priority.	7. Countrywide market considerations are given lower priority.	

Macro-Level Criteria for Segmentation

Macro-level criteria have traditionally been key bases for international segmentation. In addition to macro-level criteria, Table 5-2 illustrates some possible measurements with examples. The six macro-level criteria presented here are: (1) economy, (2) demography, (3) technology, (4) industrial structure, (5) geographic location, and (6) political factors.

(1) *Economy:* Economic development level can be a critical variable for international market segmentation. Marketing electric dishwashers and washers/dryers requires a certain level of per-capita income. Sri Lanka may *not* be an attractive market for these products. However, these products are almost a basic necessity in Scandinavian countries. Certain specific consumption patterns emerge on the basis of the level of economic development. Societies with high personal income spend more time and

	Criteria Levels	Measurements	Examples
TABLE 5-2 ILLUSTRATION OF MACRO-LEVEL AND MICRO-LEVEL CRITERIA FOR SEGMENTATION	*Macro-level*		
	Economy	Level of economic development	Per-capita income
	Demography	Population characteristics	Number of elderly or young
	Technology	Degree of technological advancement	Number of mainframe computers or personal computers
	Industrial structure	Characteristics of business organization	The type and number of existing retailers and wholesalers
	Geographic location	Where the market is located	Particular needs for air conditioning in Saudi Arabia
	Political	Degree of the power of central government	Legal constraints on retailers
	Micro-level		
	Personality	General temper of the people	Tendency to haggle
	Cultural characteristics	The role of housewife	The Swiss housewives' devotion to domestic duties
	Lifestyles	Food consumption habits	Tendency to eat spicy foods
	Attitudes, tastes, or predispositions	Status symbols	Identifying with American western heroes

more money on services, education, and recreation. Thus it may be possible to cluster certain income groups from different countries into certain segments. However, it is important to realize here that specific consumption patterns based on levels of economic development are the key criteria for segmentation.

(2) *Demography:* Demographic factors are critical bases for segmentation. Because they are key for segmentation, population characteristics must be analyzed in terms of the proportion of the elderly and/or the young in the total population. For instance, Geritol is a recognized tonic for the elderly. If Geritol were to go international, it would not consider a society where the longevity is 50 years as opposed to the U.S. average of about 74. Similarly, if a country's population is growing older and the number of infants per thousand population is declining, which is the case in some European and Scandinavian countries, then Gerber Baby Foods Co. would not consider that region as an attractive market. In Europe birthrates are tumbling and life spans lengthening. Baby-based industries, from toys to foods and diapers, face sharp contraction. Consumer electronics, housing, and other crucial industries are expected to be influenced (Templeman et al. 1989).

(3) *Technology:* The degree and characteristics of a country's technological status should be considered for international segmentation. The degree of technological advancement (i.e., the level of technological hardware) may easily be considered the basis for segmentation. As Table 5-2 illustrates, the number of telephone lines or the number of a certain type of mainframe computer may be the actual segmentation criterion. A software company planning to enter international markets may want to segment the markets on the basis of the number of PCs per thousand of population. It may not be worthwhile for such a company to enter markets below a certain number of PCs per thousand population. The company may find that Pakistan, Iran, certain Arab countries, all of Africa, and all of Eastern Europe are clustered markets with less-than-satisfactory conditions for entry.

The U.N. estimates that only 50 of every 1,000 people who will be added to the world's population in the next 20 years will be from industrialized countries. Thus exporters or international manufacturers of highly sophisticated consumer products may have to revise their plans and re-examine their international market segments. In fact, corporate planners at the Dutch electronics giant Phillips are already brainstorming about these changes in its markets and how to tailor its businesses in consumer electronics, lighting, and medical equipment to Europe's graying markets (Templeman et al. 1989).

(4) *Industrial structure:* A country's industrial structure is depicted by the characteristics of its business organizations, activities, and relationships. One country may have many small retailers, and another country

may rely on a large number of department stores for retail distribution. One country may thrive on small manufacturers and cottage industries, which implies manufacturing at home. Yet another may have very concentrated and large-scale manufacturing activity. The type of competition that exists at the wholesale level may be the critical specific factor to be used to cluster international markets. The international marketer may wish to work with a series of strong wholesalers; thus it may prefer countries in the Middle East and some African countries where strong wholesalers dominate the overall marketing process.

(5) *Geographic location:* Graphic proximity of world markets is a traditional criterion for segmentation. Countries may be clustered not only for their geographic proximity but also for other factors. For instance, air-conditioning needs in some Arab countries or electric appliance needs in Scandinavian countries have prompted a U.S. manufacturer to consider these regions as specific clusters. Therefore, combining consumer behavior factors with geographic clustering can become a more effective method of segmentation.

(6) *Political factors:* Countries can be grouped and world markets can be segmented based on broad political characteristics. Until recently the Iron Curtain and the Bamboo Curtain were commonly used for political segmentation. In these cases, the degree of power wielded by the central government may be the general criterion that is used for segmentation. For instance, it is possible that a company producing certain chemicals might consider closed markets too difficult to enter because of central government regulations. Table 5-2 indicates that both the degree of power that a central government has and how this power is used in different sectors are important. If a company plans to distribute its products through retail chains in different countries but is concerned about government regulations, then this company may segment world markets on the basis of the ease of legal constraints on retailing.

As seen in Table 5-2, these six macro-level criteria are described in terms of their conceptual and measurement characteristics and are then used to illustrate ways to segment the world markets. In fact, most of these criteria for segmentation, as depicted in Table 5-2, are rooted in the conventional wisdom approach presented in Table 5-1. It must be reiterated that international market segmentation can be based on one, two, or more of these or other criteria.

MICRO-LEVEL CRITERIA FOR SEGMENTATION

Although macro-level criteria can enable companies to segment world markets and cluster them according to international objectives, additional segmentation is possible. In fact, in some cases it is necessary to use other more subjective micro-level criteria. Table 5-2 identifies four such criteria: (1) personality, (2) cultural characteristics, (3) life-styles, and (4) attitudes, tastes, or predispositions.

(1) *Personality:* Personality reflects certain types of behavior. Certain personality characteristics such as temper and haggling may be considered a basis for segmentation. For example, Latin American and Mediterranean peoples are known to have certain personality traits, and those traits may be suitable for segmentation. In Table 5-2, one of the specific characteristics mentioned is the tendency to haggle. In pricing, for instance, an international firm has to allow a substantial degree of flexibility. However, the specific tendency to haggle may be a desirable criterion for a company to use to segment world markets and to decide how to market its products in these markets. Haggling in countries such as Egypt and Turkey is almost a national pastime. In the bazaars of Cairo and Istanbul, vendors are almost offended if a customer accepts the first asking price.

(2) *Cultural characteristics:* The cultural characteristics of a market may play a significant role in segmenting world markets. Table 5-2 gives the role of housewife as a general criterion. In this context, the role of Swiss housewives may be a specific characteristic to consider. For example, a manufacturer of dishwashers was unsuccessful in appealing to this group with the theme of "having more time for yourself." This campaign offended Swiss housewives. It gave them the impression that they were neglecting their families. The manufacturer changed its appeal to "you will have your dishes cleaned in a more sanitary manner," and the new campaign was very successful. Many dishwashers were sold in that market. Similar cultural characteristics can be used to segment markets and design international marketing plans.

(3) *Life-styles:* Life-style research is rather widespread in the domestic U.S. marketing scene. Typically activity, interest, and opinion (A.I.O.) research is the tool used for marketing consumer goods and services. However, such a research tool has not been developed for international purposes. Perhaps certain consumption habits or practices can be used as an indicator of the life-style that is being studied. Table 5-2 shows that a particular food consumption habit is one such general indicator. Types of foods eaten and tastes can easily indicate life-styles that should be considered by an international food company. Specifically, the tendency to eat spicy food is mentioned as a specific characteristic. Hot Indian-style curries are not likely to be popular in countries such as Germany with rather bland cooking. Hot Arab dishes are not likely to be popular in parts of western Europe.

(4) *Attitudes, tastes, or predispositions:* Attitudes, tastes, or predispositions are complicated concepts. Without entering into a deep philosophical discussion, it is reasonable to say that they can be utilized as subjective

measures for segmentation. In Table 5-2, status symbols are used as general criteria indicating attitudes, tastes, or predispositions. Status symbols indicate what some people in a given culture consider important aspects for enhancing their own self-concept and how they are perceived by others in their society. The specific example given in the table is identifying with American western heroes. Knowing that the Japanese identify themselves with American western heroes, Levi Strauss developed carefully designed commercials and successfully marketed blue jeans to the Japanese youth market.

These are only a few of the micro-level criteria that are commonly used. Certainly, there may be a need to develop more descriptive and measurable factors. The success of international marketers depends on their ability to identify micro- and macro-level criteria in order to segment world markets and perhaps cluster them on the basis of their similarities. The more global the firm, the more ready it may be to observe the similarities of world markets. On the other hand, the more multilocal the international firm is, the more closely it may observe differences among world markets.

Although the information presented in Table 5-2 does not deal exclusively with stereotypes, many parts of the table do not make enough distinction between segmenting based on consumer characteristics versus segmenting based on national stereotypes. Thus, in attempting to segment and cluster world markets, two points made in this chapter need to be reemphasized. First, in segmenting world markets, it is not necessary to emphasize nation-markets or worse yet multination markets. Second, in segmenting world markets, the global marketer is likely to be successful if the focus is on *consumer characteristics* rather than *national stereotypes* (Kale and Sudharshan 1987). Therefore, it may be necessary to use multiple/hybrid criteria for international segmentation. It is important for the international marketer to understand the numerous alternatives that exist in this area.

"HYBRID" CRITERIA FOR SEGMENTATION

Successful segmentation can be based on both macro-level and micro-level criteria. It may be more realistic to use "hybrid" or integrated criteria to segment consumers across the world. Some of these criteria may be particular to the company or the product in question and may not have been used before. Segmenting world markets and perhaps clustering them based on hybrid criteria provide a sound focus for formulating marketing strategies by global firms. The basis for this thinking is articulated in the following section.

Consider, for instance, a group of educationally elite readers who read *Scientific American, Time, Newsweek, The Financial Times,* and *The Economist.* There are at least 6,400,000 of these people who live in many parts of Europe, North America, Asia, Africa, and Australia. These people are likely to have more in common with each other rather than with their fellow countrymen.

A growing number of international marketers are starting to act as if a "global elite" segment is emerging. Among these are Mercedes Benz, Perrier, American Express, and Ralph Lauren's Polo. They are beginning to behave as if there is one generic type of elite consumer in certain parts of the world. Consumers aspiring to an "elite life-style" are profiled in Table 5-3 as an example of another growth segment on a global scale. The growth of this intermarket segment has been attributed to increased wealth and widespread travel, which stimulated a desire to own universally recognizable products. Global marketers may identify several micro-

Name of Intermarket Segment	Global Elites
Related micro-segments/clusters	Affluent men and women, top executives, highly educated professionals, professional athletes
Factors influencing the emergence of the segment	Incresed wealth, widespread travel, global communication technology, and mass media
Shared values	Wealth, success, status
Key products: benefits sought	Universally recognizable high-quality name brands with prestigious images
Demographics	Very high income, social status and class, well traveled, well educated
Media/communication	Upscale magazines, social selective channels (i.e., cliques), direct marketing, global telemarketing
Distribution channels	Selective (i.e., upscale retailers)
Price range	Premium
Targeted by global firms such as	Mercedes Benz Perrier American Express Ralph Lauren's Polo

TABLE 5-3
PORTRAITS OF EMERGING INTERMARKET SEGMENTS

SOURCE: ADAPTED FROM S. HASSAN AND L. KATSANSIS (1993). "GLOBAL MARKET SEGMENTATION STRATEGIES AND TRENDS," IN S. HASSAN AND E. KAYNAK (EDS.), GLOBALIZATION OF CONSUMER MARKETS: STRUCTURES AND STRATEGIES. BINGHAMTON, NY: THE HAWORTH PRESS.

level segments within this universal population of elite consumers. These consumers often differentiate themselves from mainstream consumers through buying and using products with prestige images (Hassan and Katsanis 1991). Such prestige products can be targeted globally to elite segments that desire exclusivity, premium quality, and status, in the same way they are currently targeted in their home markets (Quelch 1987).

Similarly, another intermarket segment may be called international yuppies. There have been studies indicating that not only are there yuppies in many parts of the world but also that these young upwardly mobile people throughout the world have much in common. In fact, yuppies throughout the world share more consumption patterns with other yuppies than they share with their fellow countrymen. Griffith Frost is an American who went to Japan as a student and stayed there. He has a license to manufacture and sell Soloflex exercise equipment. In his first full year of business (1986), Frost's sales reached $4 million (Katayama 1987).

In these situations, key clusters of consumers in different parts of the world are converging into intermarket segments that transcend national boundaries. These clusters of consumers located in different countries may respond similarly to standardized marketing strategies if they are properly grouped into a segment. For instance, while the mass Indian market might not respond favorably, a number of young Indians who are qualified to be called yuppies may be familiar with recent developments in modern American music and may know all the details of the most recent models of luxury automobiles.

CONVENTIONAL METHODS AND MODELS OF INTERNATIONAL SEGMENTATION

Perhaps the two best-known studies about classifying nation-markets into larger multiple-nation-markets are by Rostow and Dichter.

Rostow (1960) grouped countries on the basis of their economic growth and their readiness to develop economically. He classified countries as follows: traditional societies, societies that are developing as a precondition for takeoff, societies that are taking off, societies on their way to maturity, and societies with high mass consumption. His somewhat arbitrary and simplistic approach created an awareness of economic growth and its relationship to international markets (see Table 5-4).

Dichter, on the other hand, based his grouping on the size and development of the middle class in a country. He grouped societies as follows: almost classless societies, affluent countries, countries in transition, revolutionary countries, primitive countries, and new class societies. Dichter's

TABLE 5-4 SELECTIVE EXAMPLES OF CONVENTIONAL METHODS
AND MODELS OF INTERNATIONAL SEGMENTATION

Reference	Criteria	Method	Sophistication	Categories	Outcomes
Rostow	Economic growth	Arbitrary	Simple	From traditional to high mass consumption	Awareness of economic growth and markets
Dichter	Size and development of the middle class in a country	Arbitrary	Simple	From almost classless revolutionary country	Consumption to patterns and market opportunities
Liander et al.	Degree of economic and demographic mobilization	Two-dimensional direct-score	Somewhat complex	Classifying countries on two-dimensional graph	Assessment of market opportunities
Sethi and Holton	56 micro and macro variables	Cluster analysis	Complex	Country clusters	Better basis for analysis
Frank, Massy, and Wind	National market characteristcs	The hierarchy of segments	Somewhat complex	Different international segments	Better understanding of marketing
Goodnow and Hansz	59 variables	Hierarchical grouping cluster analysis	Complex	"Hot," "moderate," "cold" classification	An analysis of high- and low-risk markets
Kotler	Type of industrial structure/national income	Arbitrary	Simple	Industrial categories from subsistence to industrial economies: consumer categories from very low family income to mostly medium family income countries	A classification to analyze world markets more systematically

SOURCE: A. C. SAMLI AND S. HASSAN (1992). "INTERNATIONAL SEGMENTATION OPTIONS: GETTING AWAY FROM CONVENTIONAL WISDOM," IN V. CRITTENDEN (ED.), DEVELOPMENTS IN MARKETING SCIENCE, VOL. XV, CORAL GABLES, FL: ACADEMY OF MARKETING SCIENCE, 185–188.

approach was also arbitrary and simplistic. The outcome of his analysis was more closely related to consumption patterns that may be related to market opportunities (Dichter 1962).

Other studies analyzed and grouped world markets on the basis of two criteria: (1) the degree of economic and demographic activity and (2) domestic stability and cohesion. On the basis of these two criteria different countries have been assigned certain scores, and their positions have been determined on a two-dimensional graph (Liander et al. 1967). This somewhat complex method has led to assessment of international market opportunities.

Liander et al. clustered 88 countries based on approximate degrees of similarity. By this procedure they established five groups: (1) most highly developed, (2) developed, (3) semi-developed, (4) underdeveloped, and (5) very underdeveloped. These groups appear to be predetermined, and data to examine the usefulness of this scheme are lacking.

Sethi and Holton used 56 micro and macro variables dealing with a number of different socio-economic and political indicators. A sophisticated cluster analysis was used to perform a two-step procedure. First, a large number of variables were transformed into smaller groups of clusters. These groups were coined "variable clusters." These variable clusters were used to cluster the countries. Four variable clusters were established: (1) aggregate production and transportation, (2) personal consumption, (3) trade, (4) health and education. Aggregate production and transportation variables include, among others, number of air passengers, amount of air cargo, and number of newspapers. Personal consumption variables include, among others, per capita income, TV sets per capita, and number of hospital beds. Trade variables include, among others, imports as a percent of GNP and exports as a percent of GNP. Finally, health and education variables include, among others, illiteracy among adults, life expectancy, and political stability. These variable clusters are used to further cluster the countries. The outcome of this complex activity offers a better basis for analyzing international markets. Various clusters may be studied to determine which would be important for exporting manual sewing machines versus personal computers (Sethi and Holton 1969).

Frank, Massy, William, and Wind (1972) developed a hierarchy of segments based on national market characteristics and consumer characteristics. These are country markets. The analysis of this particular hierarchy is somewhat complex. This effort paved the way for analyzing international market segments and better understanding of marketing process in these country markets.

Hansz and Goodnow (1972) used 59 variables and developed a hierarchical grouping of world countries. This type of sophisticated and complex cluster analysis has led to the development of a cluster classification of "hot," "moderate," and "cold" markets. Hot countries are the ones that display the best potential for international marketing. By the same token the cold countries are the least desirable for investment or exporting. This complex technique has facilitated a better understanding of high- and low-risk markets.

Other relatively simple approaches were based on analyzing the type of industrial structure and the national incomes of countries, and they provided a systematic base for segmentation. On the basis of industrial structure, Kotler (1987) classified countries as (1) subsistence economies, (2) raw-material exporting economies, (3) industrializing economies, and (4) industrial economies. On the basis of national income, he classified countries into five categories: (1) very low family income economies, (2) mostly low family income economies, (3) very low very high family income economies, (4) low medium high family income economies, (5) mostly medium family income countries.

As we can see, early attempts took the direction of grouping countries. Although these attempts were important and encouraged international marketers to think along the lines of different markets and their attractiveness, they were not adequate. First, they did not take certain micro-level criteria into account and, second, they did not take noncountry segmentation possibilities into consideration. It is important to explore both of these points.

....

UNCONVENTIONAL METHODS AND MODELS OF INTERMARKET SEGMENTATION

The globalization of key industries such as retailing and electronics has led to an increase in the size of global consumer markets. Some global marketers view consumers as if they will eventually be homogenized into one large global market segment, where demand for products and services will be the same everywhere (Levitt 1983). Although this is not a realistic view of today's marketplace, there are sizeable markets where similar consumer segments are emerging across national boundaries. Douglas and Wind (1987) argued for the existence of global segments as a prerequisite for the successful deployment of any standardized marketing efforts.

Kreutzer (1988) proposed a two-stage segmentation approach in evaluating global markets. This approach includes grouping countries in terms of their suitability to implement the global marketing concept based on environmental indicators (such as technology, culture, ecology, and law). As a second stage in this segmentation model, Kreutzer (1988) recommended a within-country segmentation method based on behavioral attributes (such as consumption patterns, information processing, and brand name loyalty). Such an intermarket segmentation program must be conducted in the context of a total standardization strategy. Any standardized strategic framework must take into consideration such factors as culture, economy, customer perceptions, market position, nature of the product, and organizational factors (Jain 1989).

Hybrid Models of Intermarket Segmentation

As stated earlier in this chapter, attempts to develop frameworks for the identification of segments that transcend national and cultural boundaries are of critical importance to competitive global marketing. The process of identifying such intermarket segments occurs at three levels. The first level suggested in this model is the identification of global market trends, opportunities, and behavioral attributes of market segments that transcend cultures. In this case countries with a significant local market of the intermarket segments are identified and evaluated. The second level is the selection of country clusters and the analysis of the receptivity of consumers in these intermarket segments to this approach. This stage also serves to rank and select countries in terms of their strategic attractiveness and size. At the third and final level, the analysis concentrates on the selection of a family of products and services, within the general category of the business of the firm, that can be marketed effectively to consumers of these intermarket segments with a determined degree of standardization.

Figure 5-1 illustrates each of the three levels in this hybrid model of intermarket segmentation. The actual execution of this behavioral approach in terms of reaching these intermarket segments is discussed in the context of the global retailing industry.

Phase 1: Identification of Global Market Trends and Opportunities

The convergence of today's world markets has led to dramatic changes in consumption. It is essential to analyze commonalities and differences in consumption patterns as keys to the identification of emerging global segments. This is, in fact, the essence of intermarket segmentation. This approach enables the global marketer to determine similarities across national boundaries that may be blurred by domestic (within-country) differences. For example, U.S. companies targeting young Japanese consumers have done very well in penetrating Japan's restricted market. Japanese youth are called *Shinjinrui*, which means new human being. In appealing to this segment, Tower Records of Sacramento, California has priced records for 30 to 40 percent less than its Japanese competitors. In 1987 the company did $12 million of business in Japan.

Another example on a global scale is composed of consumers aspiring to an "elite life-style." As discussed earlier in Table 5-3, the emergence of this segment has been attributed to increased wealth and widespread travel; these factors, along with other influencing criteria, have stimulated a desire to own universally recognizable products (Hassan and Katsanis 1993). Products with prestige images that fit the expectation of global recognition are considered universal in nature. Global marketers may identify commonality in certain prestige segments and target them accordingly.

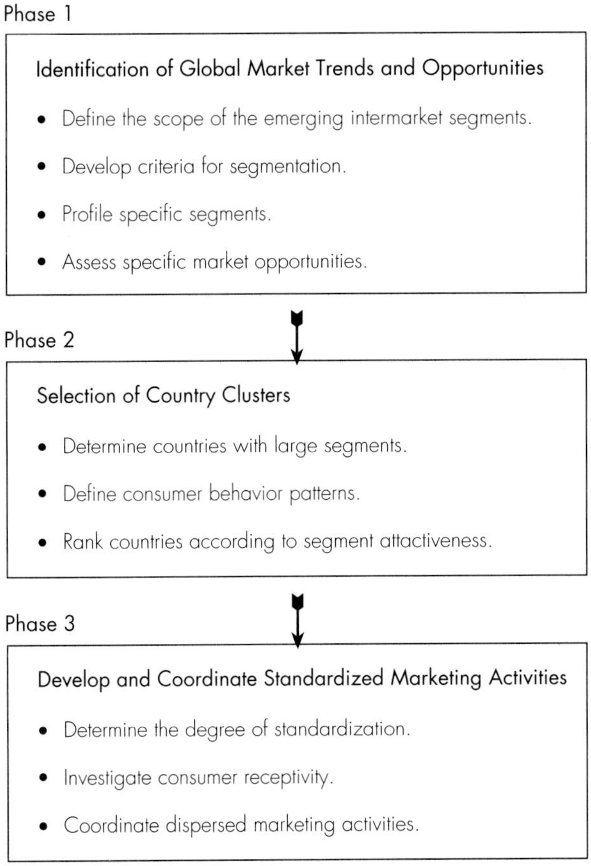

Phase 1

Identification of Global Market Trends and Opportunities

- Define the scope of the emerging intermarket segments.
- Develop criteria for segmentation.
- Profile specific segments.
- Assess specific market opportunities.

Phase 2

Selection of Country Clusters

- Determine countries with large segments.
- Define consumer behavior patterns.
- Rank countries according to segment attactiveness.

Phase 3

Develop and Coordinate Standardized Marketing Activities

- Determine the degree of standardization.
- Investigate consumer receptivity.
- Coordinate dispersed marketing activities.

FIGURE 5-1

A HYBRID MODEL FOR INTERMARKET SEGMENTATION
SOURCE: S. HASSAN (1991). "A STRATEGIC FRAMEWORK FOR IDENTIFYING AND REACHING INTERMARKET SEGMENTS," IN K. D. FRANKENBERGER ET AL., (EDS.), WORLD MARKETING CONGRESS, VOL. V, COPENHAGEN: ACADEMY OF MARKETING SCIENCE, 34–37.

Premium products can be targeted globally to certain consumer segments that aspire to the images of leadership, exclusivity, high quality, and status, in the same way they are currently targeted in their home market (Quelch 1987). Elite consumers often differentiate themselves through buying and using products that are distinguished from those purchased by mainstream consumers. Identification of behavioral factors related to media, product selection, information processing, acquisition, and purchasing decisions can be essential to successful global marketing efforts. For example, the marketing mix should be managed in a way that will target this segment with high-quality and high-priced products that are promoted and distributed through selective channels to build and maintain the image of exclusivity.

PHASE 2: SELECTION OF COUNTRY CLUSTERS

When the scope and profile of the intermarket segments have been defined, marketers need to formulate marketing approaches to these segments. The specific aspects of the marketing programs in this formulation are not included here. What is provided is a conceptualization of the general approach. One example is the use of direct response advertising to reach global markets (Robles, Hassan and Liebrenz-Himes 1993). This approach is successfully used by global retail catalogers such as The Sharper Image and Lands' End in reaching markets in Canada, Europe, and Japan.

Other global retailers such as Harrods, Ferragamo, and Galleries Lafayette targeted consumers in intermarket segments directly with standardized telemarketing/catalog and retailing strategies. Today, global telemarketing is changing dramatically; for example, AT&T International 800 services are now available in 41 countries (Butkus 1989). Toll-free calls are now available and being accepted from international consumers. In developing such global telemarketing programs, a company may have to introduce adjustments to the marketing strategy in response to language differences and calling-time zones.

Perhaps the most difficult task is the analysis of specific behavioral attributes that reveal receptivity to the standardized marketing program in a given intermarket segment. The careful selection and profiling of emerging intermarket segments are key to the formulation of an effective standardized marketing strategy.

PHASE 3: DEVELOP AND COORDINATE STANDARDIZED MARKETING ACTIVITIES

Perhaps the most important analysis at this stage is the identification of product attributes and characteristics that tend to be standardized and can be marketed to a given intermarket segment. These two conditions are key to the success of global marketing. For example, the marketing mix should be managed in a way that will target the "elite consumer" segments with high-quality products that are promoted and distributed through global retailers (i.e., prestige catalogs) in order to build and maintain the image of exclusivity.

PRACTICAL APPLICATIONS

Practical applications of the hybrid models were developed by leading global advertising agencies. Backer Spielvogel Bates (BSB) Worldwide, Inc. applied life-style segmentation methods to the identification of intermarket segments across eighteen countries. This comprehensive life-style segmentation research is called Global Scan © and is based on measuring and tracking consumer activities, interests, opinions, values, product usage, and behavior on an ongoing basis (Backer Spielvogel Bates 1991). Five major segments were identified among adults of the researched countries. These intermarket segments are:

- *Strivers* (24 percent). These are young people with median age of 31 years. They have busy schedules and demanding lives. They push themselves hard to obtain success in the future; the stress and time pressure are great because they have not yet made it. They are likely to be starting families—which is yet another demand on them. They demand products that fit their fast-paced life-styles.
- *Achievers* (20 percent). They are prototypical baby boomers, leaning to the upscale and professional/managerial. They have already achieved much of what the strivers are still working hard to attain. Health, nutrition, and fitness are important to them. They are stylish and lead mass market opinion. They go for quality and sophistication, whether it be a California wine or a German car.
- *Pressured* (16 percent). Largely women from every age group, they are caught in a relatively low station in life. They feel the pressure of living from many directions at once, from their role as women, from economic concerns, from broken families, from aging, etc. This pressure steals the joy from their lives. While nutrition is important to them, they also splurge. Convenience products can fit into their lives.
- *Traditional* (19 percent). A conservative group, these people are unwilling to accept changes around them. They stick to the tried and the true, the old fashioned ways of thinking, eating, and run-

ning their lives. Three key attitudes that define this group are: the man is boss; the woman stays at home; and the pet is an animal. Clearly, everything has its place. They embody the oldest values of their countries and cultures.

• *Adapters* (19 percent). They are the older consumers who are hardly shocked by the new. Adapters are making a comfortable adjustment to the 1990s. They accept modern mainstream values without rejecting their own traditional views. And they are ready to take up whatever activities will enrich their golden years.*

The Global Scan data are based on an ongoing survey of 15,000 consumers representing seventeen countries and eleven languages in North and South America, Europe, and throughout Asia and the Pacific basin. In this yearly survey, consumers are profiled based on 250 measures of values, attitudes, and behaviors. Half of these measures are based on global values, and the other half are based on characteristics that are unique to the consumers' local market. For the advertisers, targeting segments such as the strivers or achievers on a worldwide basis will require adjusting the global message to the local audience and local competition as well (Backer Spielvogel Bates Worldwide 1989).

Another study prepared by D'Arcy Masius Benton & Bowles (DMB&B) produced a similar life-style segmentation profile of Russian consumers. Five life-style segments of Russian consumers were identified by the DMB&B study for several firms including Mars and Procter & Gamble (*Harper's Magazine* 1992). In targeting the Russian consumers, marketers need to consider the following segments:

• *Kuptsi* (30 percent of Russian men; 45 percent of Russian women). *Kuptsi* are traditional, narrow-minded consumers, with an agrarian and highly Russian-oriented background. Their buying decisions are based on products' reliability, practicality, and proven quality. Western products and Western life-styles don't fit their outlook. This does not rule out their purchase of Western products, but it does rule out Western images and appeals.

• *Cossacks* (10 percent of men; 10 percent of women). They are fiercely Russian and they reject anything that is interpreted as anti-Russian. However, they are attracted to status symbols and public recognition. They use Western products that are unique and expensive as a way to gain status in the changing Russian society.

---

*Source: Adopted from Backer Spielvogel Bates, 1991. Data are based on global average.

- *Students* (10 percent of men; 5 percent of women). They are worldly and they have a cosmopolitan view of the world. They are very idealistic with societal commitment to welfare and quality-of-life standards. Their purchase of Western products simplifies their commitment to better life.
- *Businessmen* (25 percent of men; 10 percent of women). They have a Western outlook with a commitment to making money. They are very energetic, busy, and successful. Due to their limited time to shop around, products appealing to them have to be convenient and functional with a Western image.
- *Russian Souls* (25 percent of men; 30 percent of women). They are market followers. This group of Russian consumers has very low material status. They are vulnerable and follow the lead of other consumers. They always feel deceived in any buying situation, whether related to Russian-made or foreign products.*

These two examples are based on leading advertising agencies' research that illustrates the utility of hybrid models to track intermarket segments. Hybrid models offer valuable tools to obtaining information about global market trends and opportunities. It gives the marketer a forward-thinking approach to assessing emerging global marketing trends. Heinz, with its ketchup and Weight Watcher products, is appealing to world-class consumers who fit the modern profile and are receptive to global media (O'Reilly 1991). The new television technology complemented with satellite and cable communication will offer forward-thinking firms the means to produce global advertisements with multilingual dubbing features that will reach these consumers on worldwide bases. Eurosport utilized this technology in broadcasting athletic events in six languages (O'Reilly 1991).

Strategically Equivalent Segmentation

The process of identifying strategically equivalent segments (SES) begins with establishing the qualifying dimensions (Kale and Sudharshan 1987). These dimensions determine if it will be worthwhile for a firm to expand into other countries. Consider, for instance, India and Kuwait. The aver-

---

*Source: Adapted from "Targeting the Russian Consumer," *Harper's Magazine*, June, 1992, pp. 21–22.

age per capita income of Kuwait is about a hundred times greater than that of India. However, India's total GNP is about ten times that of Kuwait, and India's population is about 700 times that of Kuwait. Thus only 5 percent of Indians are in the same income category as an average Kuwaiti. The Indian market might be considered more attractive than the Kuwaiti market because of its population base. Thus IBM, Toshiba, Zenith, or Mercedes Benz might find it attractive to market selectively in India because of the size of the market. Thus strategically equivalent segmentation can be very effective. The success of SES, however, will depend on how companies market their products selectively in India's upper-income markets, along with other similar markets of the world.

Once a firm manages to narrow down the list to a number of countries as qualified markets, it can take one of two approaches. In the first, it can determine target segments within each qualified country and then cluster them across the qualified countries based on their similarities or their differences. In the second, it can aggregate the qualified countries together without paying attention to microsegments such as the yuppies, or the rich in India. Typically (as seen in the first half of this chapter) segmenting by countries on the basis of certain stereotypes has been the general practice in international segmentation. It must be reiterated here that the first approach is purported to be the better of the two.

Segmentation dimensions are determined on the basis of demographic variables, socioeconomic variables, personality and life-style variables, benefit segmentation variables, or situation-specific factors such as whether consumers are heavy users or light users of the product, loyal to certain brands, etc. The outcome of this process is reflected as step 3 in Figure 5-2. The end result of this step is the development of a series of microsegments in each of the qualified countries.

Step 4 is the final activity in the SES procedure. At this point the international marketer has to look at the similarities across microsegments in those countries which are to be considered after step 3 analysis. This step indicates a two-phase analysis. The first is the analytical focus. Microsegments can be rated on certain strategic action areas in terms of their potential, possible response to the firm's marketing efforts, and in terms of their desirability by using the factor analysis technique. A factor analysis rating of microsegments may indicate, for instance, that certain segments in India, Pakistan, Afghanistan, Iran, Bangladesh, Sri Lanka, and Nepal may react to marketing refrigerators in the same way. They may react to the product features, the price, and the commercials in the same way.

Now we need the second stage of the analysis in step 4. Once the microsegments in these countries have been scored, the clustering stage begins. Even though the countries originally qualified and there are pockets of certain groups of people that are suited for the international company, not all of them necessarily belong in the same cluster. For instance, although the microsegments of Sri Lanka, Nepal, and Iran are basically desirable and qualify to be clustered with the others, it may be prudent to leave them out because of the cost-benefit analysis. This may be the case because the microsegments in these three countries are basically much smaller than they are in others. Furthermore, transportation and distribution costs in Sri Lanka, Nepal, and Iran, for the specific product in question, may be a lot higher than the other countries. Thus the last portion of step 4 of the SES analysis indicates that, from a cost-benefit analysis perspective, the company may not wish to include these micromarkets with the rest. In this case, the company may wish to emphasize micromarkets of India, Pakistan, Afghanistan, and Bangladesh and leave Sri Lanka, Nepal, and Iran micromarkets for future reconsideration.

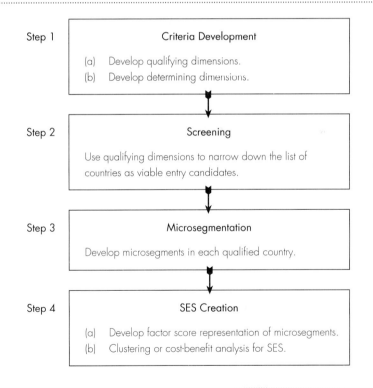

FIGURE 5-2

STEPS IN DEVELOPING STRATEGICALLY EQUIVALENT SEGMENTATION

SOURCE: SUDHIR H. KALE AND D. SUDHARSHAN (1987). "INTERNATIONAL SEGMENTATION," INTERNATIONAL MARKETING REVIEW, SUMMER, 62.

THE YUMMI YOGURT CASE*

Let us describe a hypothetical case that illustrates the SES procedure. A management team from a company named Yummi Yogurt is investigating international marketing opportunities for frozen yogurt. The company's management team determines four qualifying dimensions. First, only non-Communist countries are to be considered for entry. Using only this qualifying dimension, approximately 145 countries are qualified. Second, only those countries permitting repatriation of earnings to the home country are to be considered for entry. This qualifying dimension reduces the number of countries to about 25. Third, only those countries that have an affinity toward yogurt are to be considered. That further reduces the number of countries down to about 20. Finally, only countries with heavy ice cream consumption in *relatively* warm climates are to be considered. This may reduce the number of qualified countries down to, say, eight.

Now the microsegments need to be first identified and then scored. Let three microsegments be identified in each of eight qualified countries. In identifying the microsegments, assume that frozen yogurt will become a major substitute for ice cream or that it is a major food and dessert supplement. In country A the three microsegments might be heavy-user men, prospective heavy-user women, and prospective light-user large families. In country B the three microsegments might be heavy-user athletes, heavy-user teenagers, and heavy-user foreign-brand product purchasers. This process will result in 24 microsegments. These microsegments are next rated on a number of variables that have strategic importance. Examples of these variables are: media viewing habits, shopping habits, desirability of product characteristics, price sensitivity, consumption patterns, and information seeking habits. These variables and their ratings as they relate to each of the 24 microsegments are then analyzed on the basis of past experience, including discussions with local marketing consultants and national managers and conducting consumer focus groups and local surveys. Once again the ratings will be factor analyzed.

Let us assume the results of ratings will show the size and quality of the market. The size is expressed in terms of number of people qualifying in the microsegment. Quality is expressed in terms of the expected behavior of the microsegments. High quality therefore means a higher probability that the microsegment will purchase frozen yogurt. A clustering

---

*This section is based on Sudhir H. Kale, and D. Sudharshan (1987). "A Strategic Approach to International Segmentation," *International Marketing Review,* Summer, 62.

process will show how these markets might look based on these two
dimensions.

Figure 5-3 illustrates such an exercise. Twenty-four microsegments
have been reduced to five international market segments by employing
SES procedures. (The eight countries are represented by the letters A
through H, and the microsegments are identified as A1, A2, A3, etc.) As
can be seen the most attractive segment is numbered 1, the second most
attractive 2, etc. Only one segment is composed of three microsegments
from the same country. All other segments are composed of microsegments located in two or more countries. Some of the microsegments did
not cluster closely with other microsegments and are left alone. The worst

SEGMENTS

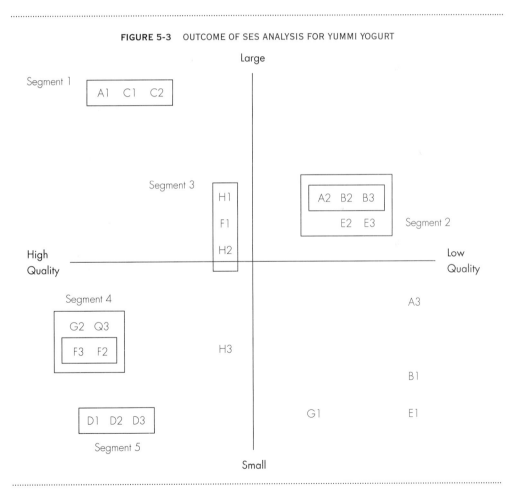

FIGURE 5-3   OUTCOME OF SES ANALYSIS FOR YUMMI YOGURT

microsegment in Figure 5-3 is the first microsegment of country E, or E1. The best one is the first microsegment of country A, or A1. Thus Yummi Yogurt will first cultivate segment 1 with one marketing strategy. The company's second target is segment 2. Although one marketing strategy will be used for all the microsegments in segment 2, this strategy may be different from the one used for segment 1. Thus strategically equivalent segmentation indicates the minimum amount of variation within the segment and some degree of variation among segments.

SUMMARY

The first section of this chapter focuses on the criteria for segmentation of world markets. Macro- and micro-level criteria are discussed to give insight into the basis for international segmentation. Also, the chapter emphasizes the need to segment world markets based on a hybrid/multicriteria approach.

Conventional methods to segment world markets have been based on stereotypical country characteristics. The second section of the chapter identifies country-by-country segmentation methods. Each method is evaluated on the basis of criteria, measurement, level of sophistication, and outcome.

Because markets are becoming more global, it is necessary to look at unconventional methods of intermarket segmentation. This unconventional orientation is currently neglected. In the final part of the chapter, two models identify market segments that transcend national boundaries. These two methods integrate behavioral and strategic aspects of intermarket segmentation.

REFERENCES

Backer Spielvogel Bates Worldwide (1991). "Global Scan: What It Is," (August) New York.

Backer Spielvogel Bates Worldwide (1989). "Global Scan Presentation," Press Conference, July 19, New York.

Butkus, R. (1989). "Global Telemarketing," *Export Today,* (December), 5–7.

Dichter, Ernest (1962). "The World Customer," *Harvard Business Review,* July–August, pp. 119–121.

Douglas, S. P., and Y. Wind (1987). "The Myth of Globalization," *Columbia Journal of World Business,* (Winter), 19–30.

Frank, R., E. Massy, F. William, and Y. Wind (1972). *Market Segments,* Englewood Cliffs, NJ: Prentice Hall.

Hansz, J. E., and J. Goodnow (1972). "A Multivariate Classification of Overseas Country Market Environments," in B. W. Becker and H. Becker (eds.), *Combined Proceedings,* Chicago: American Marketing Association, 191–198.

Harper's Magazine (1992). "Targeting the Russian Consumer," (June), 21–22.

Hassan, S. (1991). "A Strategic Framework for Identifying and Reaching Intermarket Segments," in K. D. Frankenberger, et al. (eds.), World Marketing Congress, Vol. V, Copenhagen: Academy of Marketing Science, 34–37.

———, and L. Katsansis (1993). "Global Market Segmentation Strategies and Trends," in S. Hassan and E. Kaynak (eds.), *Globalization of Consumer Markets: Structures and Strategies,* Binghamton, New York: The Haworth Press.

———, and L. Katsanis (1991). "Identification of Global Consumer Segments: A Behavioral Framework," *Journal of International Consumer Marketing,* 3 (2), 11–28.

Jain, S. C. (1989). "Standardization of International Marketing Strategy: Some Research Hypotheses," *Journal of Marketing,* (January), 53, 70–79.

Kale, H., and D. Sudharshan (1987). "A Strategic Approach to International Segmentation," *International Marketing Review* (Summer), 60–71.

Katayama, F. (1987). "Japan's Prodigal Young Are Dippy about Imports," *Fortune,* May 11, 18.

Kotler, P. (1987). *Marketing Management,* Englewood Cliffs, NJ: Prentice Hall.

Kreutzer, R. T. (1988). "Marketing Mix Standardization: An Integrated Approach in Global Marketing," *European Journal of Marketing,* 22 (10), 19–30.

Levitt, T. (1983). "The Globalization of Markets," *Harvard Business Review,* 61 (May–June), 92–102.

O'Reilly, A. J. F. (1991). "The Emergence of the Global Consumer," *Directors and Boards,* (Winter), 9–13.

Porter, M. E. (1986). "The Strategic Role of International Marketing," *Journal of Consumer Marketing,* (Spring), 3 (2), 17–21.

Quelch, J. (1987). "Marketing the Premium Product," *Business Horizons,* (May/June), 38–45.

Robles, F., S. Hassan, and M. Liebrenz-Himes (1993). "International Direct Marketing: Strategies of European and U.S.-Based Firms," *Journal of Euromarketing,* 2 (2), 105–130.

Rostow, W. W. (1960). *The Stages of Economic Growth,* New York: Cambridge University Press.

Samli, A. C., and S. Hassan (1992). "International Segmentation Options: Getting Away from Conventional Wisdom," in V. Crittenden (ed.), *Developments in Marketing Science,* vol. xv, Coral Gables, FL: Academy of Marketing Science, 185–188.

Templeman, J., D. Wise, E. Lask, and R. Evans (1989). "Grappling with the Graying of Europe," *Business Week,* March 13, 54.

CHAPTER 6

A GLOBAL VIEW OF
"GREEN" MARKETING

Salah S. Hassan

Sandra Vandermerwe

Environmentalists were once considered the only people concerned about the depletion of natural resources, waste accumulation, and pollution. Environmental groups such as Earth Day were created and driven by people who had deeply rooted concerns for the environment. The first Earth Day was held in 1970. Now this organization and others around the world are becoming global in scope and scale of operations. Their scope is to educate and to increase people's awareness about importance of environmental preservation on a global scale and how the lack of it will have a harmful effect on our universe. Global awareness about the environment is also being aroused by media reports on ecological disasters such as Chernobyl, the Exxon Valdez oil spill, acid rain, and the global warming trend.

The scientific community asserts that atmospheric pollution is having a damaging effect on the ozone layer. Two major factors influencing the depletion of the ozone layer are the use of aerosol sprays and the manufacture of certain types of plastic and foam insulation (Ivey 1990).

Because ecological grassroots campaigns (i.e., Earth Day) gain widespread recognition and support, and because global media networks (i.e., CNN) continue to report on environmental issues and disasters, today's consumer is becoming environmentally conscious. Various polls and surveys reveal that many consumers are taking environmental issues into consideration as they buy, consume, and dispose of products. Recent research points to a direct connection between a company's ability to attract and keep consumers and its ability to develop and execute environmentally sound strategies (Vandermerwe and Oliff 1990).

Some companies are managing to develop and market "green" products. Alberto-Culver Company, for example, has developed "ozone-friendly" Alberto VO-5 hairspray, which does not contain chlorofluoro-carbons (CFCs), propellants that harm the ozone layer. Guerlain, Inc. has introduced a new product, Whisper Spray, with spray-on-face powder that contains 142B, which is environmentally safe. These are just two examples of companies that are no longer simply reacting reluctantly to regulatory dicta but are preceding and even preempting the legislators by proactively defining environmental marketing profiles.

Several retailers have also committed themselves to marketing green products. For example, Loblaw Companies Limited, a Canadian-based food processor and retailer, is committed to producing a complete line of green products that are safe for the body and the environment and to obliging its suppliers to follow packaging initiatives that minimize if not avoid waste once the products have been sold and used. The London-based Body Shop, now comprised of more than 500 stores in 35 countries, offers minimally packaged, natural-ingredient products that have not been tested on animals. The company's continued growth record has made it one of the most internationally successful British franchises in years.

Portraits of "Green" Consumers

Understanding consumer trends and expectations is key to competitive marketing on a worldwide basis. Evidence supports the significance of understanding and responding to trends related to the greening of consumer values and attitudes. It is becoming essential for global marketers to correctly identify and thoroughly understand the motivations of green consumers. Based on Elkington, Hailes, and Makower (1990), a portrait of the purchasing behavior of a typical green consumer would look like this:

- Looks for products packaged in recyclable materials such as cardboard or glass or recycled/recyclable plastics.
- Does not buy products that are excessively packaged or wrapped.
- Is attracted to products and/or brands perceived as environmentally friendly.
- Looks for products made from recycled paper, aluminum, and other reusable materials.
- Chooses products that do not contain bleaches, dyes, or other toxic materials.
- Avoids buying anything packaged in foam or similar flexible foam materials.

The degree of greenness of this consumer portrait may vary among environmentally conscious consumer groups (see Table 6-1). According

Shades of Green

Aspects of Green Marketing	*Light Greens* "Followers"	*Evergreens* "Leaders"
Shared values	Environmentally aware, limited involvement, half-the-time green, economic motives	Environmentally concerned, high involvement, green-at-heart, not less than green, health and safety
Product benefits sought	Green packaging, reusable containers, less-safe packaging, eco-labeling	Green manufacturing and packaging, recyclable material, safe to use and dispose, green ingredients/labeling
Demographics	Lower-middle-income groups, conservative, mature	High-income group, young, baby boomers, well educated
Eco-positioning	Green-image, believable claims, financial incentive	Greener image, credible image, not too aggressive
Media/communications	Pamphlets, newspapers, TV ads, point-of-purchase displays, catalogs	Green societies/action groups, concerts, TV ads, magazines, catalogs
Price range	Affordable	Willing to pay more
Examples of green firms	McDonald, Amway, Wal-Mart stores, Procter & Gamble, Amoco, Sainsbury	Procter & Gamble, Loblaw, 3M, Apple Computer, Body Shop, Mercedes Benz
Micro-segments	Household products/cleaning products, energy-efficient products, safe seafood	Organic foods, safe seafood, natural cleaners, organic gardening products, fuel-safe products, green gifts, green services
Factors influencing the emergence of green consumers	Environmental education, media, ecological disasters/problems	Environmental groups, media, ecological disasters/problems, travel and education

TABLE 6-1
PROFILES OF TWO "GREEN" SEGMENTS

to a study by The Hazelton Group, the green consumer market is segmented into two distinct groups: green leaders and green followers. The green consumer leaders understand the trade-offs in accepting products that are environmentally sound. They perceive that it is for the good of the environment; therefore they are willing to pay for it.

The Hazelton Group study also reported that 26 percent of Americans are green followers. This group takes the environment into consideration in some purchasing situations but not in others. Another study conducted by The Roper Organization (1990) for S. C. Johnson & Son, Inc. concluded that 11 percent of Americans are "more likely to be involved in a wide range of pro-environmental activities." This study also reports that another 11 percent are willing to spend money, but not time, on environmental activities. In Europe, as well, the green consumer movement is large and growing, and certain countries can be considered leaders and standard setters in green awareness. Eighty percent of German consumers, for instance, are willing to pay premiums for household goods that are recycled, recyclable, and nondamaging to the environment; in France 50 percent of the consumers will pay more at the supermarket for products they perceive as environmentally friendly. This trend is growing elsewhere as well; according to a European study, consumers throughout the OECD area are willing to pay more for green goods (Vandermerwe and Oliff 1991).

Based on another research study, green markets are growing and transcending age and income groups (Vandermerwe and Oliff 1990). Young consumers and baby-boomers are becoming a "green-at-heart" market segment. They are aware of environmental issues, and it shows when they make buying decisions. Other green consumers are included in a lower income group that is considered a "swing" group. In the marketplace, they tend to be green followers as opposed to the more affluent green leaders. Half the time they are motivated by economic hardship or financial need and the other half by ecological concerns.

THE ROPER ORGANIZATION STUDY

A more recent study by the Roper Organization (1992) investigated environmental behavior of North American consumers. This study reports on three major surveys conducted in Canada, Mexico, and the United States. Although the national context of each country is unique, this study found distinct groups of green consumers within each market. Utilizing a segmentation model that characterizes similarities and differences in environmental behavior, five distinct clusters of consumers were profiled, and it was statistically determined that they transcend national boundaries. The following section is based on this study conducted by The Roper Organization and commissioned by S. C. Johnson & Son, Inc. It discusses briefly these five intermarket segments (see Figure 6-1):

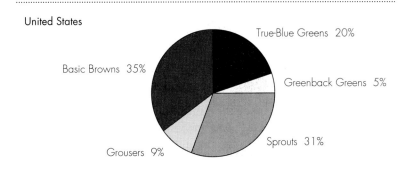

United States

True-Blue Greens 20%
Basic Browns 35%
Greenback Greens 5%
Grousers 9%
Sprouts 31%

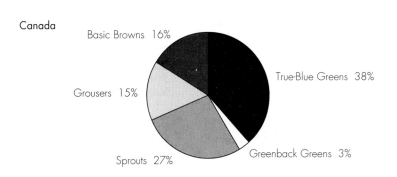

Canada

Basic Browns 16%
Grousers 15%
True-Blue Greens 38%
Sprouts 27%
Greenback Greens 3%

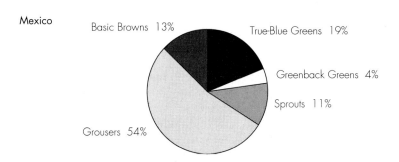

Mexico

Basic Browns 13%
True-Blue Greens 19%
Greenback Greens 4%
Sprouts 11%
Grousers 54%

FIGURE 6-1
INTERMARKET SEGMENTATION PROFILE BASED ON ENVIRONMENTAL BEHAVIOR OF NORTH AMERICAN CONSUMERS
SOURCE: ADAPTED FROM THE ROPER ORGANIZATION, INC. (1992). "ENVIRONMENTAL BEHAVIOR, NORTH AMERICA: CANADA, MEXICO, UNITED STATES," A STUDY COMMISSIONED BY S. C. JOHNSON & SON, INC., JULY.

Two Segments of Environmental Leaders

- *The "True-Blue Greens."*   They are characterized as forward thinkers with a very strong environmental commitment. They believe that their proenvironmental actions will make a difference in protecting the environment. Figure 6-1 illustrates the percentage of this segment in each of the three countries. In all three countries, this segment represents consumers with above average income, education, and occupational status. The True-Blue Green consumer tends to be married and tends to be outspoken regarding environmental issues.
- *The "Greenback Greens."*   This is a much smaller segment, representing an average of 5 percent of the North American market. The greenback greens express their environmental commitment by being willing to pay more for greener products. However, they are not willing to take the time to be actively involved in proenvironmental causes. The Greenback Green consumers tend to be highly educated with high incomes. However, they are considered the youngest of the five consumer groups.

Market Followers as the Middle of the Spectrum

- *The "Sprouts."*   They are individualistic in their behavior toward environmental marketing issues. The Sprouts tend not to work with proenvironmental groups. Their profile represents the middle of the market. However, the Sprouts in Mexico are the segment with the highest level of education, above the national average.

Nonenvironmentalists

- *The "Grousers."*   They rationalize their lack of involvement to factors beyond their control, such as high prices of green products, misleading advertising, and false green labels. They tend to be less than average in their levels of education and income.
- *The "Basic Browns."*   They don't feel the need to get involved because they believe that they can't make a difference. They are the most economically disadvantaged group.

This study by the Roper Organization reveals key differences in consumer awareness and behavior among the five segments, within each country, and among the three countries. Figure 6-2(a) illustrates the differences among the three countries regarding exposure to green advertising and labels. Canadian consumers are highly exposed to environmental information, followed by the United States and Mexico. Figure 6-2(b) points out that this pattern is true when it comes to buying green prod-

(a) Recall Seeing Label/Advertisement Saying Product Is
     Environmentally Safe

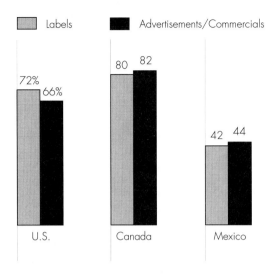

(b) Bought Product Because Ad/Label Said It Was
     Environmentally Safe

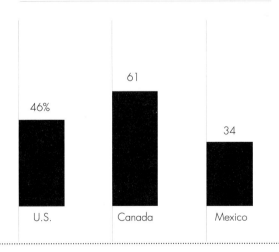

FIGURE 6-2

CROSS-NATIONAL
CONSUMER
DIFFERENCES IN
ENVIRONMENTAL
AWARENESS AND
BEHAVIOR
*SOURCE: ADAPTED
FROM THE ROPER
ORGANIZATION, INC.
(1992).
"ENVIRONMENTAL
BEHAVIOR, NORTH
AMERICA: CANADA,
MEXICO, UNITED
STATES," A STUDY
COMMISSIONED BY
S. C. JOHNSON & SON,
INC., JULY.*

ucts. Canadians are greener in making product buying decisions. Further, the Roper study reveals that in all three nations, the more educated and affluent the consumers, the more likely they will buy green products.

How Green Is "Green" Marketing?

Dramatic technological changes in product development, manufacturing, and packaging have provided consumers with great conveniences. Today's consumers are demanding these conveniences, regarding them as necessities. Some of these "necessities" are oriented toward saving time and effort. Because of major demographic changes (more single and working women, for example), growing demand for leisure activities, and increasing awareness of health and safety, more and more companies are closely monitoring these and other consumer trends. As consumers become accustomed to convenience, will they consider giving up packaging geared for microwaves and conventional ovens? If a company undertakes the development of green packaging, will consumers pay more for it? How far can a company go without having to develop green products that are inconvenient or expensive?

From this perspective, marketers have to monitor and react to key trends pertaining to target markets. For example, Procter & Gamble (P&G) launched a laundry detergent named Ariel Ultra in Europe. This product was packaged in a small box and only half the usual amount was required for a load of laundry, but it was reported that the product was tested on animals during the research-and-development (R&D) phase. Consequently, the detergent failed to appeal to the target market. On this market blunder, David Vietch, the public affairs manager for P&G in Europe, observed: "You have to approach environmental products from cradle to grave" (Rolfes 1990).

Vietch's statement means that management cannot afford to be myopic in looking at the finished product without considering the manufacturing and R&D phases as they relate to consumers' perceptions of what constitutes a green product. Nor can a company use traditional marketing principles to gain product acceptance. Put differently, both the input and output activities associated with the design, manufacture, and delivery of products must be considered, and each step within the value-creating process must be weighed in the light of its overall environmental impact and consequences. Figure 6-3 illustrates this issue.

In addition to considering and attracting green consumers, companies must still take mainstream consumers into account. For example, Ecover, a Belgian manufacturer of household cleaning products, won

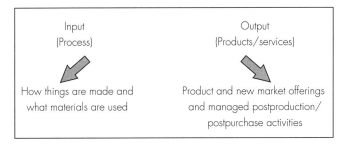

Input (Process)	Output (Products/services)
How things are made and what materials are used	Product and new market offerings and managed postproduction/ postpurchase activities

FIGURE 6-3
INPUT AND OUTPUT
ACTIVITIES
ASSOCIATED WITH
GREEN PRODUCTS/
SERVICES
*SOURCE: ADAPTED
FROM SANDRA
VANDERMERWE AND
MICHAEL OLIFF
(1990). "CUSTOMERS
DRIVE CORPORATIONS
GREEN,"* LONG RANGE
PLANNING, *23, 6,
10–16.*

acceptance from green consumers but not from mainstream consumers because of unattractive packaging and poor brand name recognition (Stuller 1990).

FRAMEWORK FOR GREEN THINKING

In making green decisions, managers must adopt an integrated framework. Such a framework takes into consideration the development of green products from research and development to manufacturing and marketing. An integrated approach to green thinking and decision making will help a firm avoid marketing blunders. Figure 6-4 depicts the integrated process that starts by understanding green consumer wants, needs, and expectations. It is the responsibility of management to integrate consumers' expectations in the marketing, manufacturing, and R&D functions.

As proenvironmental thinkers and decision makers, effective marketers must become increasingly responsive to green consumerism and position their products as green in order to thrive in a fiercely competitive marketplace. What might have once been viewed by some managers as a mere green fad can now be labeled as anything but a passing trend. The green phenomenon will not be gone tomorrow; it is here to stay. Corporate managements have responded to the growing green movement with varying degrees of response. The following section discusses the ways companies have chosen to respond.

IGNORE THE GREEN

As is the case with all businesses, many companies' policies and decisions are ultimately driven by the bottom line. Companies choosing to ignore the green movement may save money in the short run. However, these companies may face the loss of market share in the long run.

Pass as Green

Some companies are responding by adjusting their marketing messages for existing products (only if applicable) so the products can pass as green. Procter & Gamble, for example, has added one statement to its Fairy Dish Washing Liquid bottle: "Only biodegradable surface active agents are used in this product" (Wells 1990).

The interesting thing is that the statement has been true of Fairy Dish Washing Liquid since 1963, and P&G only recently decided to add it to the package label in response to the green movement.

Genuine Green

Some companies have gone to considerable expense and have committed major resources to research and develop green alternatives; some have introduced new eco-friendly products to the marketplace. American Environ Products, for example, has developed the Nappies Disposable Diaper,

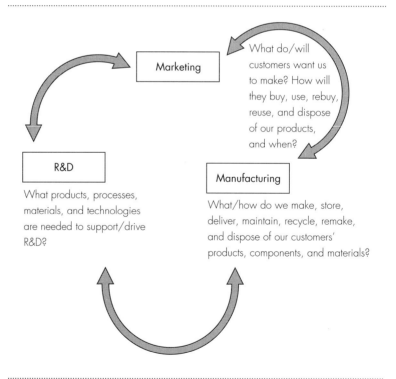

FIGURE 6-4
AN INTEGRATED
APPROACH TO MAKING
GREEN DECISIONS

Marketing

What do/will customers want us to make? How will they buy, use, rebuy, reuse, and dispose of our products, and when?

R&D

What products, processes, materials, and technologies are needed to support/drive R&D?

Manufacturing

What/how do we make, store, deliver, maintain, recycle, remake, and dispose of our customers' products, components, and materials?

which they claim is biodegradable because it is made from cornstarch rather than plastic.

Pro-Green

Pro-green companies have a sincere and "socially conscious" attitude. They donate money to environmental causes, sponsor environmental events, and react immediately and responsibly to major ecological issues. Amoco adopted this stance by initiating a campaign for collecting and recycling used motor oil. Amoco's campaign educates consumers about improper and environmentally dangerous ways to dispose of motor oil.

Some companies have become even more genuinely and proactively green by conscientiously anticipating future environmental obligations. Such obligations could range from having to locate alternative raw materials to realizing that their responsibilities extend well beyond the so called "end of pipe," or even "cradle to grave." The obligations might encompass several product transformations over multiple time frames. Here the ultimate objective is to use and reuse resources over and over again, as opposed to continuously disposing of products and using new ingredients, some of which are nonrenewable. Several European auto manufacturers, BMW and Opel for instance, are working closely with their suppliers; they have initiated new modular product designs with parts and components that can be used longer and then disassembled (demanufactured) and remade (remanufactured) at the end of their useful lives into new models (Vandermerwe and Oliff 1991).

This kind of long-term corporate commitment is in line with contemporary green consumption that is based on the following four R's:

- The RETHINKING of consumption life-styles to conserve natural resources, including energy.
- The REFUSAL to buy products that overuse/misuse scarce resources.
- The need to be able to REUSE products and packaging.
- The need to RECYCLE packaging.

What many companies now appreciate is that green issues cannot be solved by slick advertising and promotion alone. They must be integrated into overall corporate strategy—driven not just by communications but by everyone within the company. Initially, this realization often takes the form of a corporate environmental policy. Procter & Gamble states in its so-called Environmental Quality Policy, for example, that it is continually striving to "improve the environmental quality of its products, packaging and operations around the world." For the moment, moves like these tend to be curative, or "after-the-fact." In the future, however, we anticipate that environmentally proactive companies will think more in preventative terms as they build environmental criteria into their product and packaging designs.

The Making of Green Products

Green consumerism is making companies aware of environmental concerns, but it will take research and development to bring green policies to reality. Thus leading manufacturers of consumer products must blaze the way in their R&D efforts. Not only is it the ethical responsibility of companies like P&G and Mobil to find green solutions but also market reality will not give them much choice because of growing consumer concerns.

It would be hard to discuss recyclable packaging without mentioning Procter & Gamble, which initiated plastic packaging with the Ivory Liquid bottle in 1959. Because of this unique claim to fame, P&G now wants to be among the leaders in dealing with this problem. In doing so, they were innovative in marketing super concentrated detergents requiring 15 percent less packaging, and they offer Downy refills so consumers can use the same plastic container repeatedly (Schiller 1990).

In the computer industry, where the weight of user and technical documentation frequently far exceeds the weight of the mainframe and peripheral products themselves, new packaging initiatives are intended to eliminate waste. Similarly, computers themselves are being redesigned to allow the eventual gutting of components that rapidly become obsolete so they can be replaced with state-of-the-art versions and the casings will not add bulk to the already mounting disposal heaps.

Although consumers, responsible firms, and environmentalists are mostly concerned with solid waste, which takes up landfill space, there are also strong sentiments about cosmetics, shampoos, and hair sprays and how these products affect the environment. For example, Clairol is showing concern about the environment by introducing its new ClairMist hair spray, which they claim does not harm the ozone layer; "Preserve the earth's ozone—as well as your own beauty" the ad claims. Companies such as IBM and Wendy's are removing fluorocarbons, which are believed to destroy the ozone layer, from their packaging. DuPont, the world's largest producer of CFCs, plans to phase out the production of the substances entirely by the end of the century. The company is presently investing more than a billion dollars to find suitable alternatives for them. Some of the largest users of CFCs, the automobile and white goods industries, are taking steps to avoid their emission. Several American and European manufacturers are installing new air-conditioning devices in their cars so that CFCs are not dispersed into the atmosphere but constantly reused. Electrolux, the Swedish home appliances giant, is making a determined effort to use CFC substitutes in its refrigerators. This is just one part of its integrated plan to support the environment. For example, the company's washing machines need considerably less water and electricity to work as efficiently as standard models, and they are modularly designed to allow easy revamping with new technology rather than having to be thrown away and replaced every time an innovation occurs.

In developing environmentally safe products, companies are faced with the difficult task of creating products with an optimal mix of price, quality, and convenience and which are aesthetically and ecologically appealing. Because green is the new wave, companies will have to follow the lead of manufacturers such as P&G to maintain growth and profitability in the long run.

Green Labeling

Stemming from the popularity of green consumerism is the need to monitor consumer products and packages. Green labeling, also known as eco-labeling, is an attempt by private agencies, retailers, and manufacturers to monitor the environmental integrity of consumer products and packaging. Generally speaking, eco-labeling is a certification process that awards a symbol or seal to a manufacturer once a product has been deemed ecologically safe. The following eco-labeling topics are covered in this section: private "watch-dog" agencies in the United States, Germany, and Canada; whistle-blowing; green labeling by manufacturers and retailers; and green labeling in the service sector.

Watch-Dog Agencies in the United States

In the United States there are two private watch-dog agencies that are currently involved or will soon be involved in green labeling: Green Seal and Green Cross. These two groups are taking slightly different green-labeling strategies. Green Seal lacks a product category approach, and Green Cross takes a manufacturer/retailer approach. Initially Green Seal will evaluate light bulbs, laundry cleaners, house paint, toilet paper, and facial tissue, but it will eventually evaluate other product categories based on consumer demand. Green Cross works with supermarket chains and manufacturers rather than on a product-by-product basis (*Time Magazine* 1990).

Since the federal government has not yet regulated green labeling, consumers do not have to pay directly for it. Instead, manufacturers provide funding for the certification process as they compete for the honor of being recognized as environmentally safe. Manufacturers seeking the eco-logical seal of approval have to pay fees to cover the costs of analyzing their products.

WATCH-DOG AGENCIES IN GERMANY

The idea of green labeling started in West Germany more than 12 years ago when the "Blue Angel" symbol started appearing on consumer prod-ucts (Powell 1989). Consumers rely on the Blue Angel label as a basis for making purchasing decisions. The Blue Angel stamps some 3,000 prod-ucts ranging from batteries to shampoo (Tully 1989).

Involvement in the Blue Angel program is not limited to any one sector; it draws from the government to manage the program, from citi-zens and businesses to make suggestions, and from an independent com-mission (Bonn's Institute for quality Assurance and Labeling) for the Blue Angel symbol (Powell 1989). Once a product is awarded the Blue Angel symbol, the manufacturer pays a fee for the right to display the symbol. Due to consumer preference for Blue Angel products, both domestic and foreign manufacturers vie for the opportunity to participate in the pro-gram. Despite the popularity of Blue Angel, Germany may eventually be forced into accepting lower environmental standards from the European Commission (*The Economist* 1989). At the time of publication, the Euro-pean Commission had not implemented an eco-labeling program for Europe.

As is frequently the case in the European environmental arena, the German labeling scheme prompted other countries to design their own versions. The Scandinavian countries, for example, award the Nordic Council Environment Mark to products and packaging that are environ-mentally sound. In the summer of 1991 the United Kingdom, through its British Standards Institution, launched its official environmental seal of approval, which will be awarded to companies whose products and pack-aging comply with total "cradle-to-grave" environmental criteria. In order to bring standardization to the single European market, the European Community is drafting its own version of a labeling scheme. The new scheme will obligate all companies operating in the region and wishing to prove their "environmental worthiness" to follow strict guidelines, from design through disposal.

WATCH-DOG AGENCIES IN CANADA

In addition to European and U.S. eco-labeling programs, Canada has a certification program called Environmental Choice. The program is at-tempting to educate Canadians about products carrying the Environmen-tal Choice Logo.

These watch-dog agencies discussed here are not the only organizations concerned about environmental issues related to product labeling. Other organizations around the world are blowing the whistle on environmental scams. Britain's Friends of the Earth has launched a program that gives the worst environmental offenders a "Green Con of the Year" award (*The Economist* 1989). Whistle-blowing seems to be effective because it tends to make companies more cautious in their assertions about the environmental soundness of products.

Eco-labeling activities are not limited to the watch-dog agencies. Many retailers and manufacturers have taken the initiative to implement their own green label programs. On a global scale, grocers have started testing green label programs on their own. Britain's Sainsbury and Cooperative Wholesale Society (CWS), Canada's Loblaw, the United States' Big Bear chains are some of the green label pioneers. For example, Canada's largest supermarket chain, Loblaw, promotes its private-label line called "President's Choice Green" of more than 100 green items.

Since labels appear on products and packages, most consumers associate eco-labeling with consumer goods. However, the concept of green labeling reaches consumer services as well. Tourism, entertainment, financial services, and health care are examples of industries that offer services of environmental integrity. In the entertainment industry, for example, several concerts and celebrities have supported environmental organizations such as Friends of the Earth. While probably very few concertgoers specifically select concerts for the charities they benefit, environmental causes probably play a favorable role in post-purchase satisfaction.

GREEN ISSUES IN EUROPE AND CANADA

Europe and Canada have taken leadership in the commitment to preserve the environment. In these markets, consumers' attitudes are changing constantly across social classes and age groups. For example, the mature market of 50 plus in Great Britain is starting to change the buying habits of a lifetime. Now these consumers are beginning to appreciate unbleached lavatory paper according to BSB Dorland, a British advertising agency (*The Economist* 1989).

Changes in consumer attitudes and behaviors are influencing companies to make environmentally responsible decisions in order to be more competitive in an increasingly green marketplace. Consumer pressure is felt not only at the corporate level but also at the government level. The 12 countries of the European Community are beginning to develop environmental policies with higher standards that will not interfere with international trade. The Single European Act of 1992 gives EC firms equal legal footing in adhering to policies that protect the environment.

Bitter disputes over the strict standards that the EC has proposed are never ending. What is good for one country can severely hinder business operations in other countries. For example, the commission proposes to put stricter standards on car exhaust. The French oppose moves by the Dutch to increase restrictions on American-made cars because these moves will drive up the price of small cars, which the French make in large quantities (*The Economist* 1989). Another example involves Denmark where there is a mandatory deposit on beverage bottles in order to promote recycling. Importers claim that these moves are protectionist in nature and will indirectly restrict imports because of the high costs to comply with Danish regulations.

European and Canadian governments were the first to take major steps toward the development of policies that regulate the manufacturing and marketing of environmentally responsible products. In the near future, more countries are expected to legislate environmental regulations that will affect the corporate world. Consumers are in the driving seat of this movement, and companies have to be more responsive.

GREEN MARKETING: A CORPORATE RESPONSE

Many corporations now understand that the green phenomenon is not a fad but a serious marketing trend—generic to many industries and consumer groups. They recognize that they cannot afford to make environmental issues mere afterthoughts and that a proactive green company policy is one of the best long-term corporate image builders of the 1990s and beyond.

Marketers are therefore beginning to incorporate the new values and consumers' buying criteria into their strategies across a variety of industries. Those who have been successful have achieved not only top environmental performance but also healthy market share. Specifically, a green marketing mix has to consider the following factors:

- *Position:* Companies must devise strategies that reprofile corporations and brands to reflect new consumer values and corporate efforts and commitments.
- *Product:* Companies must design new products that prevent damage to individuals, communities, and the environment, allow the reuse and longer use of products and packaging, and allow the use of natural and nutritional ingredients.

- *Packaging:* Companies need to use *environmental packaging,* which includes minimal packaging as well as increased and reuse solutions.
- *Price:* Companies must make decisions as to how to keep prices competitive and who carries any extra costs. Environmentalists and opinion leaders are supporting the move toward standardized green production in order to get economies of scale that bring prices to more competitive levels. New pricing metrics will reflect longer-term objectives and concepts.
- *Place:* Companies need to rethink logistics and distribution to incorporate long-term responsibility in the packaging of used goods. They need to reappraise retail outlets sites in terms of their proximity to recycling centers.
- *Promotion:* Companies need to offer more education and information with long-term objectives and strategies to facilitate and promote new values and behaviors.

FINAL WORDS

The focus of this chapter is on the emergence of green consumers and how this is leading to corporate change, particularly in marketing. Nevertheless, marketing is only one part of the overall corporate strategy that is affected.

Research and development will play a crucial role as new concepts are built into product and packaging design. Manufacturers must find ways to adjust their tools and techniques to incorporate new, so-called clean production methods and demanufacturing and remanufacturing techniques. Logistics must incorporate collection schemes that are not only efficient but also cost effective.

It is undeniable that in most parts of the world consumers are increasingly concerned about the environmental features of the products they buy and about the environmental profiles of the companies they do business with. A growing proportion are willing to pay the price. Corporations and industries have to be more conscientious about the information they provide because promotional and scientific data that are used arbitrarily to support environmental claims can lead to confusion and misconceptions.

The consumer pressure that forced McDonald's to revert to paper packaging despite the lack of scientific evidence to support this switch from plastic is symptomatic of consumer ignorance stemming as much from excessive communication as from a lack of valuable information and communication. Taking a short-term view based on what consumers think they know can solve one environmental problem but lead to yet another.

What this means is that despite the increasing numbers of consumers demanding more environmentally friendly products and packaging, there is still an *educational* role that marketers have to fulfill. In general, marketing must become more informative. Consumers will continue to identify with strong images that well-positioned brands offer, but they will also want more *information* to help them make better decisions. Marketing's role should be geared more toward long-term values—making consumers aware of what is environmentally sound in terms of the products firms make and their buying and use behavior. New *performance criteria* and *evaluation tools* must match these long-term goals.

REFERENCES

The Economist (1989). "Greening Europe," October 14, 21.

The Economist (1989). "The Perils of Greening Business," October 14, 75.

Elkington, J. L., J. Hailes, and J. Makower (1990). *The Green Consumer.* New York: Penguin Books.

Ivey, M. (1990). "The Greening of Corporate America," *Business Week,* April 23, 17.

Powell, J. (1989). "The Eco-Labelers Are Coming," *Beverage World* (November), 88.

Rolfes, R. (1990). "How Green Is Your Market Basket?" *Across the Board,* (January/February), 50.

The Roper Organization, Inc. (1990). "The Environment: Public Attitudes and Individual Behavior," A study commissioned by S. C. Johnson & Son, Inc., July.

The Roper Organization, Inc. (1992). "Environmental Behavior, North America: Canada, Mexico, United States," A study commissioned by S. C. Johnson & Son, Inc., July.

Schiller, Z. (1990). "P&G Tries Hauling Itself Out of America's Trash Heap," *Business Week,* April 23, 101.

Time Magazine (1990). "How Green Is My Label," June 25, 44.

Tully, S. (1989). "What the 'Greens' Mean for Business," *Fortune,* October 14, 75.

Vandermerwe, S., and M. D. Oliff (1990). "Customers Drive Corporations Green," *Long Range Planning,* vol. 23, no. 6, 10–16.

———, (1991). "Corporate Challenges for an Age of Reconsumption," *Columbia Journal of World Business,* vol. 26, no. 3, 6–25.

Wells, R. P. (1990). "Environmental Performance Will Count in the 1990s," *Marketing News,* March 19, 22.

Chapter 7
Marketing to Women Around the World*

Rena Bartos

I t is a truism that effective marketing and advertising must be built on understanding the consumer. Yet sometimes preconceptions and assumptions about people and about countries prevent marketers from responding to the opportunities inherent in social change.

There are two subjects about which everyone in the marketing and advertising communities has strong opinions and preconceptions. One of them is women. The other is international marketing.

It wasn't too many years ago that markets in the United States were clearly separated by gender.

- The assumption was that men were the targets for all the expensive, big-ticket products and services such as cars, travel, and financial services.
- On the other hand, women were sold food, household products, fashions, and cosmetics.

It is remarkable to recall that working women were truly invisible in marketing and advertising plans at that time. Most advertisers thought of women consumers as housewives. The usual target definition was "any housewife, 18 to 49." Occasionally, advertisers would recognize young, single women, who in those days were described as "girls," as natural targets for cosmetic and fashion products. These two perceptions of women dominated marketing approaches to women in those days.

The surge of women entering the work force has revolutionized the way we define the consumer marketplace.

---

*This chapter is based on material from Rena Bartos, *Marketing to Women Around the World*. Boston: Harvard Business School Press, 1989. Copyright © 1989 by Rena Bartos.

- We find that men are crossing over into the supermarket and shopping for food and household products that used to be the exclusive responsibility of housewives.
- We find that women are crossing over into the big-ticket product categories. They have become good customers for financial services, travel, and cars.
- We find that not all working women are young, single girls and that not all housewives are married.

In short, our perception of the total consumer marketplace has been turned upside down as a result of this one simple demographic fact.

The concept that effective advertising and marketing must be built on understanding the consumer is particularly relevant to the international marketplace. The stereotypes and assumptions that marketers in the United States used to hold about consumers in their own country are compounded when they move overseas.

- Some believe that consumers are fundamentally the same around the world and that strategies that work in one market can be transported to others.
- Some concede that rapid change has occurred in the United States, but they believe that consumers in other parts of the world are still motivated by traditional values.
- Still others think that there are such strong cultural differences among countries and regions that every marketing effort should be based on indigenous cultural patterns and life-styles.

The Changing Women's Market

The changes in the women's market in the United States have been documented extensively. The question is: Have these changes occurred in other parts of the world or is this a uniquely American phenomenon? Do the traditional assumptions about the women's market hold up in Europe? In Latin America? In the Far East? In Canada?

- Even if some women in these other countries have, in fact, entered the work force, is it because they are so driven by economic necessity that they are not good customers for advertised products and services?
- Or, even if the surface manifestations of demography are similar to those in the United States, are the underlying attitudes and percep-

tions of women in those countries markedly different from those of American women?

The answers to these questions are essential if marketing and advertising in different parts of the world are to remain relevant to their target consumers. Therefore, we decided to examine the status of the women's market in a number of countries around the world. In the study, the countries represented in each region are:

- North American: Canada and the United States
- Latin America: Brazil, Mexico, and Venezuela
- Europe: Great Britain, Italy, and West Germany
- The Far East: Australia and Japan

The Demographic Realities

A number of basic demographic factors such as occupation, marital status, presence of children, and age help us to define the consumer marketplace and understand the dynamics of how both working women and nonworking women use products and services and respond to media. This basic demography is intertwined with attitudes and social values that are clues to their aspirations and motivations.

The first simple demographic fact is, of course, the presence of women in the work force. But in looking at demography around the world, we find there is no such thing as a simple demographic fact in international research! We observe wildly conflicting estimates of the number of women working in each country. For example, the estimate for the United States ranges from 54 to 63 percent and for Canada from 46 to 62 percent!*

Thus so, while the demography is not simple and may not be precisely parallel, anywhere from 27 to 55 percent of women in the ten countries studied go to work (see Figure 7-1). Although there are more working women in the United States than in the other countries, there are places

---

*Limitations of space preclude a discussion of the nature of the data sources and the reasons for their diversity. However, I have discussed this problem at some length in an article entitled "International demographic data? Incomparable!" published in the November 1989 issue of *Marketing and Research Today*. I decided to use the most recent population census of each country as the basis for this study.

in the world that have higher levels of working women. Relatively more women in the former Eastern Bloc and Scandinavia are in the work force than in any of the countries I'm reporting on here.

- The highest proportion of working women is in North America. Fifty-five percent of all women in the United States and 52 percent of women in Canada go to work.
- The level of working women in Japan, Great Britain, and Australia is also high. From 49 to 46 percent of women in those countries are working women.
- West Germany is in the middle at 39 percent.
- Relatively fewer women in Italy and the three Latin American countries are in the work force.

How does this compare with the past?

- Between 1960 and the 1980s the most dramatic increase occurred in North America—in Canada and the United States—followed by Australia.
- While there are currently more British than Italian women in the work force, the relative gain was more intense in Italy than in Great Britain.

FIGURE 7-1   PERCENT OF WOMEN IN THE WORK FORCE
SOURCE: CENSUS

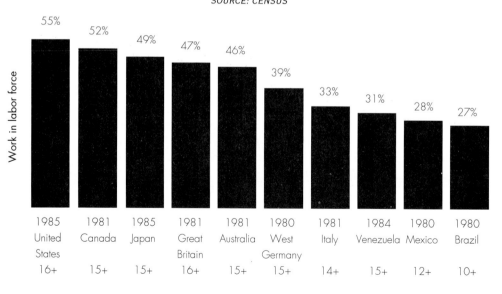

- Although slightly fewer women in the three Latin American countries go to work, there has been real change in that region. The proportion of working women almost doubled in Venezuela, and it rose sharply in Mexico and Brazil.
- On the other hand, there were minor declines in Japan and West Germany. In each of these countries the population is becoming older, and each country has a retirement age of sixty. Thus there are relatively fewer women of working age available to go to work. However, there have been major structural changes in the nature and quality of the women's work force in Japan and in West Germany.

Not All Nonworking Women Are Housewives

We might assume that in each of these countries the women who don't work must be at home keeping house. Therefore, they must be our traditional target consumers, the homemakers. However, when we consider the occupational profiles of all women in these countries, we see that some women are neither keeping house nor going to work. These "others" include schoolgirls who are too young to work or be married as well as the retired/disabled women who are out of the mainstream.

It is frustrating that we don't have precise occupational profiles for all the countries in our study, but I will report on those for which we do have these data.

- The highest proportion of nonactive women or "others" is in West Germany, where 25 percent of women are out of the mainstream. The majority of these are past working age.
- The second highest level of "others" is in Italy, and here they are mostly retirees.
- In Australia 22 percent of women are out of the mainstream; again they are mostly retirees.
- Nineteen percent of Japanese women are either retired, disabled, or still in school (see Figure 7-2).
- Sixteen percent of women in Venezuela are neither at work nor keeping house. The majority of these are still in school.
- Fifteen percent of women in the United States are neither keeping house nor in the work force.
- A smaller proportion of women in Canada are labeled "others." Only 10 percent of women in that country are either retired or still in school.

- Great Britain reported the lowest level of women who are out of the mainstream—neither at home keeping house nor going to work outside of the home.

Regrettably, we do not have this kind of information for the other two Latin American countries.

The Ratio of Working Women to Housewives

Once we remove the schoolgirls and grandmothers from consideration and confine our attention to active women, that is those who are either full-time homemakers or in the work force, we get a truer picture of the ratio of working women to housewives.

- This proportion has shifted rapidly in the United States. In the early 1970s slightly more women were keeping house than going to work. Currently, the ratio of working women to housewives is 65 percent to 35 percent.
- Japan, Australia, Canada, and West Germany have more working

FIGURE 7-2
OCCUPATIONAL
PROFILE OF WOMEN:
JAPAN
*SOURCES: ANNUAL
REPORT ON THE
LABOR FORCE SURVEY,
CENSUS 1985.*

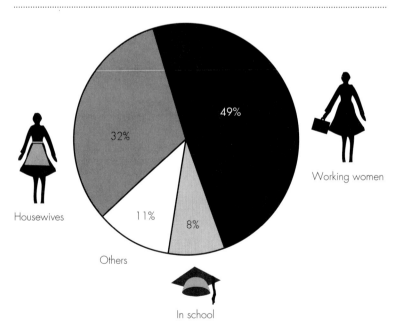

women than housewives. In Canada the ratio is 58 percent working women to 42 percent housewives.

- There are slightly more full-time homemakers than working women in Great Britain, but the difference is extremely slight. The ratio of housewives to working women is 50.5 percent to 49.5 percent!
- Italy is the only country with relatively more housewives than working women, with a ratio of 57 percent to 43 percent.

WILL THIS TREND CONTINUE?

Will this trend toward women working continue? Or is it a temporary blip? There are four reasons why I think it will continue.

First, there is a clear correlation between women's education and their presence in the work force. The more education a woman has, the more likely she is to go to work (see Figure 7-3). This refutes the notion that

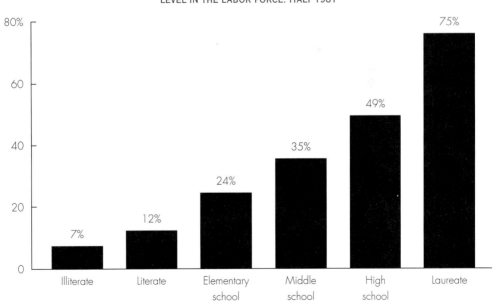

FIGURE 7-3   THE PROPORTION OF WOMEN AT EACH EDUCATIONAL
LEVEL IN THE LABOR FORCE: ITALY 1981

SOURCE: I STAT/CENSUS 1981

economic necessity is the only reason that women work. Clearly, better-educated women come from more affluent households, and those who are married tend to be married to the most achieving men. Conversely, women with the lowest levels of education are probably most in need of income and, yet, they are least likely to be in the work force. There was an amazing consistency in this pattern from country to country.

We do not have information on this matter for every country. As you know, the educational systems and educational terminology vary from country to country. Nonetheless, the pattern is remarkably consistent.

Because of the dramatic finding that the more education a woman has the more likely she is to work, I speculated as to whether the level of women's educational achievements in each country would correlate with their participation in the labor force. I have limited this analysis to the top two categories of educational achievement, "completed secondary school" and "completed post-secondary."

While there is not a direct correlation between women's educational achievements and their presence in the work force, the patterns are intriguing. The three countries with the highest proportion of working women—the United States, Canada, and Japan—also have the highest proportion of women who have graduated from college or gone beyond. And in those countries where women have the lowest levels of education, they are least likely to go to work (see Figure 7-4).

The second reason I believe the trend will continue is that in recent years there has been an increase in women seeking advanced education and in the extent to which they have studied professions that used to be exclusive bastions of men. This is also true for the five countries for which we do have such trend data.

The third reason is that in the United States more than half of the students currently enrolled in colleges and universities are women. This percentage is up substantially from a generation ago. In the eight countries for which we have such data, some comparisons are based on 1960 and others on the 1970s. In spite of these variations in the time span, the direction of the trend is clear. In every one of these countries there were more women enrolled in colleges and universities in the 1980s than there were in the 1960s or early '70s.

The most striking change occurred in Canada where in twenty years women moved from 33 percent of college students to a dramatic 55 percent! This is a bigger gain than that of the United States, which moved from 39 percent to 51 percent in the same time period. Although the level of women's college enrollment appears somewhat lower in Japan, the report from that country excluded junior colleges and graduate schools from its definition of college enrollment.

The fourth reason I believe this trend will continue is women's changing aspirations. The surge of women into the work force is an indicator of

FIGURE 7-4 HOW THE EDUCATION OF WOMEN RELATES TO WORK

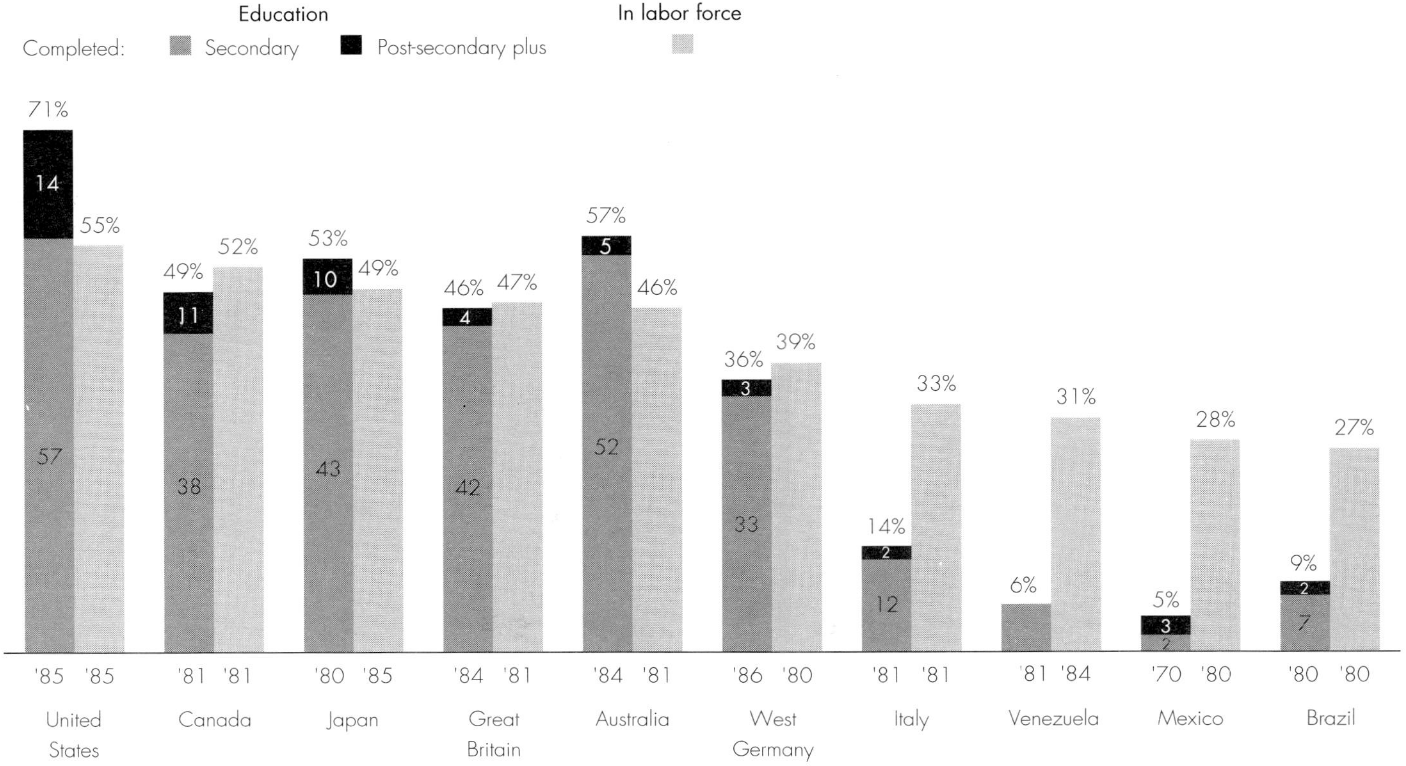

Education
■ Secondary   ■ Post-secondary plus

In labor force

Completed:

United States '85 '85: 71%, 55%, 14, 57

Canada '81 '81: 52%, 49%, 11, 38

Japan '80 '85: 53%, 49%, 10, 43

Great Britain '84 '81: 46% 47%, 4, 42

Australia '84 '81: 57%, 46%, 5, 52

West Germany '86 '80: 39%, 36% 3, 33

Italy '81 '81: 33%, 14% 2, 12

Venezuela '81 '84: 31%, 6%

Mexico '70 '80: 28%, 5% 3, 2

Brazil '80 '80: 27%, 9% 2, 7

change. However, I believe that it is a manifestation of a more fundamental change in women's aspirations and feelings about themselves and their roles in life.

WHY WOMEN WORK

Women's aspirations are revealed, in part, when we consider the reasons why they work. The obvious answer is economic—that they work because they need the money. It is true that there are strong economic reasons why women go to work.

- *Necessity*: Some women work for reasons of sheer economic necessity. These are women who must work if they or their families are to survive. They include unmarried women with no husbands or fathers to support them. Some have never married and have always had to work for a living. Others had their marriages interrupted by death or divorce and were suddenly thrust into the working world. Still others are married to men whose incomes simply cannot support their families.
- *The Second Paycheck*: There is another economic motivation—the "second paycheck." While many married women may not absolutely need the money, a second paycheck enables them to maintain or improve their families' standard of living. This reason for working tends to be far more universal than that of sheer economic necessity.

There are, however, motivations beyond the paycheck that attract women into the work force. The emotional and psychological rewards of work are intertwined with women's economic reasons for going to work.

- *Broader Horizons*: For many women, particularly those who are working for a second paycheck, the attraction of work is more a matter of what they are getting away from than what they are going to. The sense that the life of a housewife is a very narrow one is an attitude that transcends national boundaries. Women feel that there must be "something more to life than the kitchen sink." Even though many of these women don't have highly stimulating or responsible jobs or professions, they share the sense that going out to work is far more satisfying than staying at home. The social stimulation that occurs in the workplace and the enhanced sense of self that comes with working explains why many of these women say that they would rather work than stay at home.
- *Achievement*: Finally, a small number of women work for the same reasons that have always motivated ambitious men. They work be-

cause their work gives them a sense of achievement and for the stimulation of the work itself. These fortunate women have found work that gives them psychic rewards as well as economic ones. The real difference between these women and those who are motivated by a combination of economic and broader horizons is that they actually enjoy the work they do.

The Aspirations of Housewives

Some young housewives also want to be involved in the larger world outside the parameters of the home and hearth. While the traditional notion was that a woman's occupational goal in life was to become a wife and mother, there is increasing evidence that women, particularly younger women, seek to combine marriage, work, and children.

This yearning for "something more" is quite universal. It occurs in every one of the ten countries. The attitude was summed up by one young Japanese housewife who said: "I feel that I want to get involved in society. Get out there. It would be a good opportunity for me to learn about things in the everyday world . . . and, besides, the working mothers I see look so alive. I feel that working would give me a chance to use the energy that has been bottled up in me."

Why Women Don't Work

Not all housewives share these aspirations. The reason these women don't go to work is a direct reflection of their belief that women's proper role or function is to be at home caring for their husbands and children. Some say their husbands would not allow them to work or that their husbands can afford to have them stay at home. Such statements implicitly endorse the traditional perception of the male/female role, that the husband should work to support the family and the wife should stay at home and care for the house and children. Others say they are unable to work for reasons of health or reasons of age. These women have put themselves out of the running, so to speak.

Attitudes Toward the Role of Women

The reasons why some women aspire to a role outside the home and why others have no desire to work are linked to the way they feel about the basic role of women. Women's role has usually been defined in terms of marriage and children. The traditional assumption was that raising a family was the main reason why people marry and that children are essential to a happy marriage.

The Importance of Children

- Men and women in the three Latin American countries are strongly committed to the importance of children.
- While Australian women tend to say that every woman should have a child, their endorsement of motherhood is far less intense.
- With the exception of Italian men, men *and* women in the three European countries are likely to say that children are not necessary for a woman's personal fulfillment. Women in Great Britain particularly reject the idea that children are necessary to a woman's fulfillment.
- A majority of Canadian women believe that a woman can have a perfectly satisfactory life without having children.

Children and Marriage

A different picture emerges when children are considered in the context of marriage. Men and women in the three European countries are far more likely to say that children are very important for a happy marriage than they are to believe that a woman needs children in order to be fulfilled.

- The attitudes of Italians are most consonant on the issue of children and marriage. The degree to which they believe children are necessary to a woman's fulfillment is similar to their belief that children are important to a marriage.
- While British men and women were least likely to say that a woman needs children for her personal fulfillment, they believe strongly that children are very important to marriage.
- On the other hand, German people were slightly more likely than the British to say that a woman needs children to be fulfilled, and they are less likely than men and women in the other two European countries to link children to a happy marriage.

North Americans are less likely to believe children are necessary for a happy marriage.

- Three out of four Canadian women say a couple should not stay together because of the children if a marriage is unhappy.
- Large majorities of men and women in the United States say that a couple without children can be happily married.

Attitudes Toward Women's Place

The traditional perception of the proper roles of men and women is that the man goes to work and supports the family while the woman stays home and takes care of the house and children (see Figure 7-5).

- People in Latin America are most likely to feel this way. However, men and women in the three Latin American countries are less intense in saying woman's place is in the home than they are in stressing the importance of children.
- Women in Japan are almost evenly split on whether or not a man's place is at work and a woman's place is in the home.
- Slightly more German women reject than subscribe to the traditional view of the role of women.

FIGURE 7-5   ATTITUDES TOWARD WOMEN'S PLACE

Traditional   Nontraditional

Brazil
75% ███████████████████ 22%
72% ███████████████████ 24%

Mexico
63% ████████████████ 16%
57% ██████████████ 22%

Venezuela
62% ████████████████ 17%
59% ███████████████ 26%

Japan
40% ██████████████████████ 39%

West Germany
45% ████████████████████████████ 55%

Canada
22% ████████████████████████████████ 59%

Women ███
Men ░░░

Australia
23% ██████████████████████████████████████ 76%

- By more than two to one, Canadian women reject the traditional definition of a woman's place.
- Australian women have particularly strong feelings on this subject. Fewer than one in four believe that "a woman's only responsibility is to her home and family."

TRADITIONAL MARRIAGE VERSUS TWO-PAYCHECK MARRIAGE

A more tangible way of defining woman's place is the choice between traditional marriage, where the woman stays home and keeps house while the man supports the household, and the two-paycheck marriage where both the husband and the wife go to work. This issue was explored in the United States, Great Britain, Italy, West Germany, and Australia.

- In every one of the five countries, more people favored the nontraditional two-paycheck marriage over the traditional form.
- Women were slightly more likely than men to vote for two-paycheck marriages in the United Kingdom, Italy, and the United States.
- Although the predominant choice of people in West Germany was for two-paycheck marriages, men were slightly more likely than women in that country to take the nontraditional view.
- In Australia this question was asked only of women. By better than five to one, two-paycheck marriage was the overwhelming choice of Australian women.

TRADITIONAL MARRIAGE VERSUS PARTNERSHIP MARRIAGE

In the United States men and women were given a clear choice between traditional and partnership marriage, where husbands and wives shared in household responsibilities as well as in earning a living. In Australia women were asked whether they agreed or disagreed that husbands and wives should share in earning a living.

In the three European countries, however, men and women were given three choices: traditional marriage where the husband goes to work and the wife keeps house; a transitional form of the two-paycheck marriage where both work but the wife has a less demanding job and takes more responsibility for household tasks; and partnership marriage where husbands and wives share equally in earning a living as well as in household responsibilities.

The transitional form might be perceived as a bow to economic necessity, where the wife's paycheck is needed to maintain the family's standard of living, but both husbands and wives agree that the wife should continue to take primary responsibility for the household.

We have seen that men and women in the three European countries are far more likely to select two-paycheck marriages over traditional marriages. However, when the transitional option is removed, their selection of partnership versus traditional marriage reveals their true choices.

- Men and women in West Germany are slightly more likely to vote for traditional marriage over the partnership form. While German men were more likely than German women to favor two-paycheck marriages overall, they are less likely to endorse partnership marriages with its connotations of equality in the workplace and at home.
- English men and women are more likely to choose partnership marriage over the traditional form. However, English men are somewhat more likely than English women to favor the equality of the partnership arrangement.
- The greatest difference between the sexes occurs in Italy. More Italian men vote for traditional marriage than endorse partnership between husbands and wives. On the other hand, Italian women are almost twice as likely to select partnership as the ideal form of marriage as they are to say they prefer to live in the traditional marital relationship.

THE ROLE OF LIFE CYCLE

The role of the life cycle helps to keep our perspective on women in the context of reality. After all, neither working women nor housewives are cut out of a single dimension. All of us change as consumers as we move in and out of different stages of life. This affects both working women and full-time homemakers.

One way to assess the consumer potential of women in any country is to consider their situation in the life cycle. Are they married or not? Do they have young children or not? These two simple demographic facts define the way they live and have an impact on their needs as consumers, the way they buy and use products, the way they spend their time, and the way they spend their money.

WOMEN AND MARRIAGE

First, let's consider the simple demographic fact of marriage. Although we tend to think of all women consumers as being wives, the reality is that not all women are married.

- Among the ten countries we studied, women in Venezuela and Mexico are least likely to be married. Just half of all women in Venezuela and just over half (54 percent) of women in Mexico are married. (It should be noted that this is based on 1974 and 1970 census data. Mexico bases its reports on women twelve years of age and over, while Venezuela reports on women fifteen years and over.)
- In the United States only 55 percent of all women, sixteen years and over, are currently married. The unmarried, of course, include those who have not married, as yet, whom we designate as "single," as well as those whose marriages were terminated by divorce or those who were widowed.
- West Germany and Brazil are similar. Only 57 percent of women in those countries are married.
- In Italy, Great Britain, and Australia there are three married women to every two who are not presently married.
- The marital status of Canadian women is very similar to that of their counterparts in Great Britain and Australia. Sixty-two percent of Canadian women are married and 38 percent are either still single or had their marriages dissolved by death or divorce.
- In Japan there are two married women for every one who is not married.

Women and Children

The other basic demographic fact is the presence of children. How many women have children under the age of eighteen in their homes?

- Women in Great Britain and Japan are least likely to have children at home. Only one in three (35 percent) in each of those countries has at least one child under the age of eighteen, while 65 percent have no children at all in their homes.
- Women in the United States and West Germany are very similar to their British and Japanese counterparts. In each of these countries, 36 percent of women are mothers.
- Thirty-seven percent of the women in Australia are mothers of at least one child.
- Women in Canada are more likely to have children than women in Great Britain, the United States, West Germany, Japan, or Australia. Forty-one percent of Canadian women have at least one child at home.
- Motherhood predominates in Italy. There is at least one child in 60 percent of Italian households, while 40 percent of households are childless.

WOMEN AND THE LIFE CYCLE

When we combine the two basic demographic facts of marriage and motherhood, we create four life cycle groups:

- Married women with children.
- Married women without children at home.
- Women who are not married and have no children at home.
- Women who are not married but do have at least one child at home.

It has been customary to think of the women's market in terms of the traditional image of the woman living in a full-family group, complete with husband and at least one child at each side holding onto her apron strings.

It has been dramatic to observe that if we remove women living in this traditional life-style from our consideration, that 73 percent of all women in the United States do not belong in the traditional women's market. In other words, 73 percent of all women in the United States are either childless married women or not married.

We might assume that the situation in the United States is somewhat extreme and that women living in more traditional cultures might also live in more traditional life-styles.

- Actually, the pattern is slightly more intense in West Germany. Seventy-five percent of all women in that country are either childless married women or unmarried women with and without children in their homes.
- The situation in Great Britain is not dissimilar. There some 71 percent of all women live in nontraditional life-styles.
- The pattern is somewhat less intense in Australia, Japan, and Canada. Sixty-seven percent of Australian women are either unmarried or are childless wives. In Japan 66 percent of all women live outside the traditional full-family life-style. Sixty-six percent of Canadian women live outside traditional life-styles.

THE DYNAMICS OF THE LIFE CYCLE

Just as women's consumer needs change as they move in and out of different stages in life, their responsiveness to or rejection of work also changes. Women's options no longer seem to be an either-or choice between work and homemaking but rather a continuous interaction between the two.

Most nonworking wives in Europe and Canada have worked in the past. Unmarried women, young childless wives, and married women with older children are most likely to work.

There is a discontinuity in women's working lives. Many stop working when children are born. Mothers of young children are most likely to feel the pull between family and work, and they respond by seeking part-time jobs, temporary work, and yearn for flexible working arrangements.

Work takes on a different meaning for some women in the empty-nest stage. Rather than feeling that the "meaningful part of my life is over," some see this phase as an opportunity to spread their wings and "reach for something more."

The New Demographics

There is a way of segmenting the women's market that goes beyond occupation to the *attitudes* of housewives and working women toward work. I call this typology the New Demographics. It is based on a pair of questions that originated in the Yankelovich Monitor some years ago.

How Housewives Feel About Going to Work

The question asked of housewives was if they ever planned to go to work: near term, in the next five years, sometime in the future, or not at all. We designate those housewives who say they do not ever plan to work as "stay-at-home housewives," and those who answer yes to any of the other questions as "plan-to-work housewives."

This expression of a desire to work is not necessarily a prediction that women will do so, but it is a very sensitive indicator of different attitudes and predispositions which, in turn, translate into differences in the marketplace.

The New Demographics typology of the stay-at-home housewife reflects the traditional homemaker's perception of her role, while the plan-to-work housewife reflects the aspirations of some young housewives to move beyond the narrow confines of their domestic roles.

- Almost three out of four housewives in Great Britain (73 percent) opt to stay at home.
- Housewives in West Germany and Japan are also far more likely to say they would prefer to stay at home than go to work (69 percent and 68 percent, respectively).

- Approximately two out of three housewives in Mexico, Venezuela, and the United States say they would rather stay at home than go to work (65 percent, 64 percent, and 63 percent, respectively).
- While more housewives in Italy choose to stay at home (54 percent), a sizable proportion of Italian housewives yearn to enter the work force (46 percent). As a matter of fact, there are relatively more plan-to-work housewives in Italy than in the other European countries, Mexico, Venezuela, the United States, or Japan.
- The pattern is sharply reversed in Brazil, where 77 percent of housewives say they want to go to work.
- Housewives in Canada are far more likely to want to work than stay at home. Some 60 percent of Canadian housewives say they plan to go to work.
- We have two sources of data about the New Demographics in Australia. Just over half of the housewives in Sydney and Melbourne (51 percent) say they plan to go to work. On the other hand, if we consider housewives in the five mainland capital cities, almost three opt to stay at home (73 percent) for every one who says she plans to go to work (27 percent).

How Working Women Feel About the Work They Do

Working women were asked whether they consider the work that they do "just a job" or a career. This question does not relate to their occupations but rather to their attitudes toward their work. The differentiation between just-a-job working women and career women reflects the achievement orientation and ambition of career women. This is a very discriminating reflection of different values and life-styles which, in turn, translate into real differences in the ways they buy and use products.

- When we consider the working women side of the equation, we see that the highest level of career perception occurs in Venezuela. Fifty-seven percent of working women in that country are career oriented.
- Working women in Canada are also highly career oriented. Fifty-six percent say their work is a career, while only 44 percent think it is just a job.
- Australian women in Sydney and Melbourne show a somewhat similar picture. Just over half of working women (52.5 percent) in those cities are career oriented. On the other hand, when we consider working women in the five mainland cities, just over a third (36 percent) consider themselves career women, while 64 percent think their work is just a job.

- In the United States more women who work consider the work they do just a job than perceive their work as a career. Nonetheless, two out of five designate themselves as career oriented.
- Great Britain, Brazil, and Mexico have fairly similar proportions of career-minded women. Almost two in five women in these countries see their work as a career.
- In Japan there are two working women who think their work is just a job for every one who considers it a career.
- By more than two to one, working women in Italy see their work as just a job rather than a career.
- The lowest level of career orientation occurs in West Germany, where only one working woman considers her work a career for every three who say that it is just a job.

The size of the New Demographic segments is defined by setting the attitudes of housewives and working women toward work in proportion with the actual ratio of housewives and working women in the population of each country (see Figure 7-6).

- If we consider career orientation among working women and the desire to work among housewives as evidence of ambition and aspiration, it is striking to note that both Canada and Sydney and Melbourne in Australia have the highest proportions of career-oriented working women and plan-to-work housewives. This suggests that the quiet revolution is boiling up in each of these countries and has not as yet reached its full expression (see Figure 7-7).
- The high proportion of plan-to-work intentions among housewives in Brazil points to potential for change in that country.
- By the same token, women in Venezuela rank next in this level of ambition and aspiration.
- While the United States has the highest ratio of working women to housewives, the combined proportions of career women and plan-to-work housewives is 40 percent.
- Although there are relatively fewer working women in Italy than in the United States, there are almost identical proportions of "outward-bound" women in Italy (39 percent). This is due to the strong presence of plan-to-work housewives who yearn to enter the work force.
- There are very similar proportions of outward-bound women in Mexico, Japan, Great Britain, and the five mainland cities of Australia, but the emphasis differs. Plan-to-work housewives in Mexico are the source of aspiration potential in that country. In Japan, Great Britain, and the five mainland cities of Australia, there are relatively more career-oriented working women than plan-to-work housewives.

FIGURE 7-6 THE NEW DEMOGRAPHICS
** *CLEMENGER/REARK STUDY*

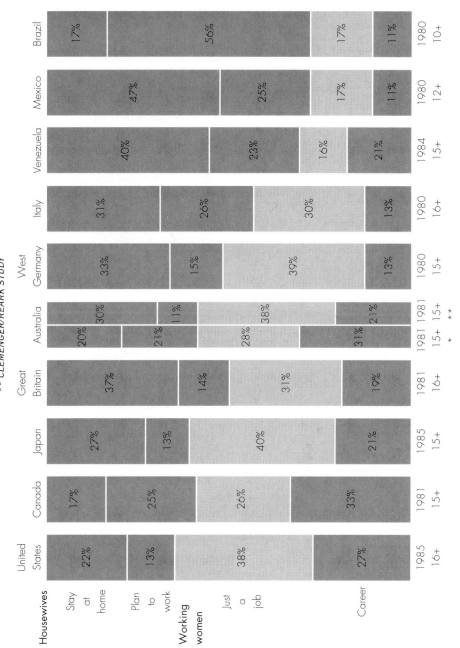

FIGURE 7-7 OUTWARD-BOUND WOMEN
** CLEMENGER/REARK STUDY

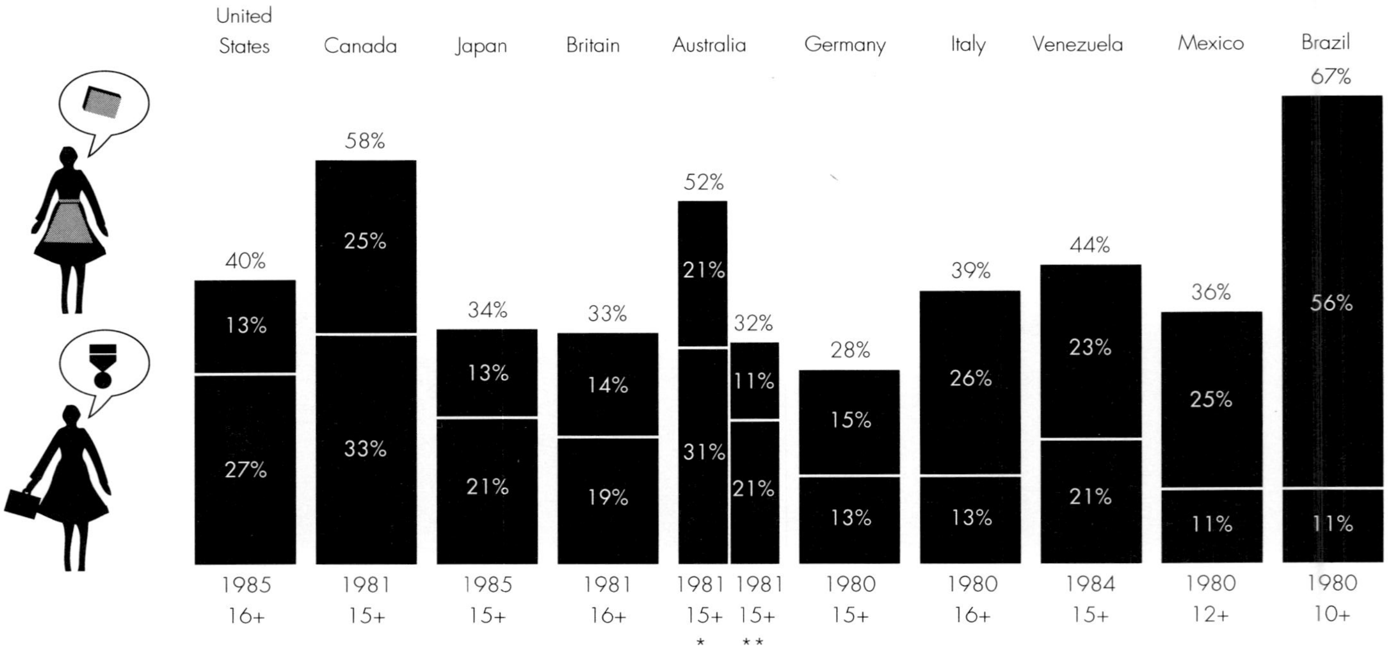

- Women in West Germany are the least likely to express this combination of aspiration and ambition. There are slightly more plan-to-work housewives than career-oriented working women in West Germany.

In the United States we have fifteen years' worth of evidence that the four New Demographic segments really differ from each other demographically, attitudinally, and the ways in which they behave in the marketplace. The two key demographic characteristics that differentiate them seem to be age and education. Stay-at-homes are the oldest and least well educated of all women, plan-to-work housewives are the youngest, and career women are the best educated and most affluent.

An examination of the demographic profiles of the segments in these countries parallels the observations we have made about the New Demographics in the United States. Although the proportions of the New Demographic segments vary from country to country, they reflect a spectrum of values ranging from the most traditional attitudes held by stay-at-home housewives to the most nontraditional perspectives expressed by career women. In many cases the plan-to-work housewives are far more like the two segments of working women than their stay-at-home counterparts.

This has been a brief glimpse into the fascinating subject of women around the world. Even this surface examination shows that there is enormous diversity in their levels of participation in the work force and the extent of their ambition and aspirations.

How Can Marketers Link This Perspective on Women to Real-World Marketing Applications?

I believe that the conceptual framework of women's place in the life cycle and their positions in the New Demographic spectrum presents an actionable way to link marketing programs to the changing realities of women's lives. At the beginning of this chapter I said that the most effective marketing and advertising is built on understanding consumers. Yet, if marketers' assumptions about consumers are out of step with reality, they may miss out on real marketing opportunities.

I have selected two case history examples from very different categories to illustrate this point. The products are gold jewelry and cars. In each case outmoded assumptions colored traditional approaches to the women's market.

- Conventional wisdom assumed that men were the targets for all the expensive, big-ticket products and services such as cars, travel, and financial services.
- On the other hand, women were sold food, household products, fashions, and cosmetics.

LET'S CONSIDER THE MARKETING OF GOLD JEWELRY

According to the traditional scenario, no woman bought luxuries for herself. If she wore furs or fine jewelry, it was because the man in her life bought them for her. Therefore, gold jewelry was marketed to men to give to their ladies.

How does the New Demographic/life cycle perspective apply to the marketing of gold jewelry?

- *Stay-at-home housewives* are the oldest and least well educated group of women in each of the ten countries. For the most part they live in the least affluent households. The exceptions to this are in Japan and Brazil, where stay-at-homes are second to career women in affluence.

  These women support the traditional view of women's role. Therefore, it is most appropriate to target them as receiving gifts of gold jewelry from their husbands.

  There are also real cultural differences among them. Affluent stay-at-home housewives in Great Britain and Italy are fashion conscious and no doubt responsive to owning jewelry. Stay-at-home housewives in Japan are very conservative and concerned about appearing too showy or conspicuous. Therefore they might be less responsive to gold jewelry as gifts.
- *Plan-to-work housewives* in all countries are the youngest segment. They are better educated than the stay-at-homes. They are interested in the world outside. Although they can't afford to spend as much as working women on fashion and grooming, they aspire to keep up with fashion. To the extent that their husbands can afford to do so, they would be excellent targets for gold jewelry as gifts. And as some of the wives move out into the working world, they have future potential as customers in their own right.
- *Just-a-job working women* represent two kinds of opportunities. Those who are married frankly admit that the second paycheck enables them to indulge in luxuries that they couldn't afford on their husbands' incomes. They are particularly interested in keeping up with fashion. They are responsive to owning fine jewelry, whether as gifts from their husbands, or whether they buy it themselves.

Unmarried just-a-job women are jewelry customers in their own right. Until recently this was an uncultivated market. I believe it represents future potential for marketers of gold jewelry.

- *Career women* represent the strongest opportunity of all. They are the best educated and most affluent group of women in each of the ten countries. They reject the traditional definition of the role of women. They have a strong sense of self-worth and of independence. They are very discriminating and valuable customers.

They lead the way in the world of fashion and cosmetics and have broken new ground by participating in big-ticket categories of cars, financial products, and travel. The career wives among them no doubt welcome gifts of gold jewelry from their husbands. However, both married and unmarried career women can afford to and do buy fine jewelry for themselves. In view of their attitudes toward partnership marriage, they also have strong potential as purchasers of gold jewelry as gifts for the men in their lives.

What about the car market?

Since the country-to-country data are not directly comparable, I have limited this example to the United States. However, the patterns described here appear to be occurring in other countries as well.

Is the conventional wisdom that the car market is a man's market really true? The current reality is that women constitute 47 percent of the principal drivers of new cars. Their value to the car market is almost equal to that of men.

For many years, when the industry studied new car buyers, it attributed all cars owned or driven by married women as belonging to their husbands. So the only women drivers acknowledged in those days were the unmarried women who bought and drove their own cars. This is an example of how assumptions can color the way data are gathered and interpreted.

The current ratio of working women to housewives in the United States is 68 to 32 percent.* The ratio among women drivers is even more dramatic; 87 percent of active women drivers are working women, whereas only 13 percent are full-time homemakers.

Remember the days when people in the industry thought of women drivers as housewives in station wagons taking the kiddies to cub scout meetings and meeting their husbands' trains? Well, that marketer would

---

*This ratio is higher than that quoted earlier. The international comparisons in the book *Marketing to Women Around the World* are based on 1985 census data. This is based on the 1988 census.

be missing out on the dramatic 87 percent of women who are principal drivers of cars but who are *not* at home keeping house.

The major difference between total active women and active women drivers is the proportion of women drivers who are career oriented. While 30 percent of total women are career women, career women account for exactly one-half of all women principal drivers.

When we consider both their situation in the life cycle and their place in the New Demographic spectrum, we can identify exactly which women are valuable to the car market.

- Among housewives, the childless stay-at-homes are more likely to drive cars. Conversely, the married plan-to-work mothers are more active in the car market than their childless counterparts.
- The only single mothers who are principal drivers of cars are working, and they are equally divided between those who think their work is just a job and those who are career oriented.
- Two-paycheck working wives, both just-a-job and career oriented, account for 44 percent of active women car drivers.
- Finally, the largest life cycle group of women in the car market are unmarried working women without children. A higher proportion are career oriented rather than job oriented.

Any marketer who is willing to challenge the conventional wisdom about women and cars has a real opportunity to cultivate this relatively untapped market of potential prospects.

ACTION IMPLICATIONS

I have tried to demonstrate that there are specific ways that global marketers can harness these changes to their marketing procedures. To link an understanding of the changing women's market to marketing applications, we need to learn what impact women's position in the life cycle and their situation in the New Demographics typology has on how they buy and use products and how they respond to media.

There are several concrete actions that global marketers can take to create this linkage.

I. BUILD AN ANALYTIC FRAMEWORK

The most basic step is for marketers to build an analytic framework that will enable them to track the consumer behavior of the life cycle/New Demographic segments within countries and across international borders.

In some cases this will require adding one or two demographic questions to ongoing studies.

- When the information is available, I recommend that past studies of the marketplace be reanalyzed from the life cycle/New Demographic perspective.
- Where the information is not available I recommend that the necessary items be added to current and future studies of the marketplace.

Specific elements in building the framework are:

1. *Clarify the definition of full-time homemaker.* Since many marketing and advertising efforts are aimed at housewives, it is imperative to isolate full-time homemakers from other nonworking women. I recommend that existing studies of the marketplace be reanalyzed to compare the market behavior of working women to that of full-time homemakers, rather than lumping all nonworking women together. If necessary, add a complete occupational question to future studies so that full-time homemakers can be differentiated from retired women and schoolgirls.

2. *Build the life cycle framework into marketing analysis.* Past studies of the marketplace can be reanalyzed from this perspective by creating a simple cross-tabulation of marital status and presence of children. This results in the four life-cycle groups: married with children, childless wives, unmarried with no children, and single mothers. This framework, in turn, should be extended to compare working women and housewives at each stage of the life cycle.

3. *Add the New Demographic definitions to analysis of the women's market.* Since these are new questions that were not included in past marketing studies, I recommend that they be added to ongoing and future studies and that the analytic framework of the women's market be expanded to include the New Demographics. This creates a sixteen-cell analytic model, which combines the four life-cycle groups and the four New Demographic segments. The New Demographic questions are currently incorporated in a number of databases around the world.*

---

*In the United States they are included in the two basic market and media sources, Simmons Market Research Bureau and Mediamark Research Inc., as well as by the Roper Organization and the Gallup Poll. In the United Kingdom, the questions are built into the Target Group Index conducted by the British Market Research Bureau, as well as the Gallup Poll conducted by Social Surveys Limited. In West Germany, the questions are incorporated in the Trendmonitor Omnibus Surveys conducted by Basisresearch. In Japan the JMRB National Survey conducted by the Japan Market Research Bureau, Inc., also asks the New Demographic questions.

4. *Evaluate the market potential of the New Demographic and life cycle segments.* An objective appraisal of their marketing behavior can tell whether women buy or use products differently or whether their media behavior is distinctive. An equally objective appraisal of their incidence or volume of product use can identify the potential each group represents for a product category or brand.

II. Request That Future Census Surveys of the Population Include Basic Demographic Data

The limitations and gaps in official demographic data in many countries present a serious obstacle to any marketer's attempts to conduct a definitive analysis of the marketplace from country to country. I am concerned about these gaps in basic demographic information because official census data describe the realities of the country's population. In turn, the census provides a factual base for sampling projections and sets realistic parameters for the study of consumer attitudes and consumer behavior. Without this kind of foundation, marketing research studies may present a distorted picture of the size and nature of particular consumer segments that could lead to erroneous decisions and misallocations of marketing resources.

Therefore, I urge marketers in those countries where data are lacking to strongly request that future censuses of the population in their countries include these kinds of basic demographic data.

The only constant in the world of international marketing is change. Consumers are changing. Markets are changing. And the cultural context is changing. On the other hand, the flip side of change is opportunity for the marketer with the courage and vision to seize the challenge.

CHAPTER 8

GLOBAL MARKETING
TO UPSCALE CONSUMERS

Lyn S. Amine

I n most countries there exist groups of upscale consumers who demand the best and are willing to pay high prices. Global brand names
signifying luxury, quality, style, and status are the focus of their attention, along with country-of-origin labels that offer assurances of prestige products. Variously defined as the "jet set" and the "luxury market,"
these consumers share many similarities from one nation to another. As a
result, marketers may be tempted to assume a homogeneity of demand
and consumption. This assumption may then lead to the formulation of
strategies offering standardized products and services on a global basis.

In this chapter we argue that it is inaccurate to view the upscale market as a homogeneous market. Indeed, a close inspection reveals remarkable differences between upscale consumers who ostensibly buy the same
expensive items. Questions are therefore posed as to whether a standardized marketing approach to world markets is appropriate and, if it is not,
how the upscale market might be effectively segmented.

Levitt (1983, 1988) has argued strongly in favor of globalizing market
offerings. He speaks of a "pluralization of consumption," according to
which "customers are now segment migrants, possessed of multiple segment preferences at the same time" (1988, p. 7). "Suddenly everybody
everywhere simultaneously occupies each of these product-market segments—often several on a given day . . ." (1988, p. 7). Levitt characterizes
consumers as "heteroconsumers . . . living lives of seemingly idiosyncratic
consumption" (1988, p. 7). Thus our attention is drawn to the fragmen-
tation and miniaturization of segments whereby consumers can "pick and
choose" the products and services that constitute a given life-style. Levitt
concludes that "additively, similar small preferences in many places cu-
mulate into global bigness in all places" (1988, p. 8). Thus global market-

ing will in many instances be appropriate in serving upscale consumers, but this strategy will be based on what is now known as "intermarket segmentation." This strategy can bind together similar small segments across a number of world markets in a way that produces economies of scale and improved marketing efficiency.

The approach followed in this chapter seeks to maximize opportunities for global marketing wherever possible. The myth of "one product fits all," based on an early misinterpretation of Levitt's (1983) exposition of globalization, is addressed by showing that luxury products cannot be marketed in the same way to a group of consumers worldwide whose only common characteristic is a willingness to spend.

This chapter is divided into three parts. Part I presents an analysis of upscale consumers, highlighting similarities and differences along three dimensions: income, social class, and use of status symbols. From this analysis, three distinct new market segments are identified: the truly affluent, conspicuous consumers, and indulgers. Part II explores the consumption styles of these three segments. Part III addresses issues relating to global marketing strategy, segmentation, and marketing mix decisions. Throughout the paper, examples are provided from markets in North America, the European Community (EC), and the Far East.

UPSCALE CONSUMERS: NOT ALL ALIKE

Definitions of upscale consumers usually focus on *income* as a differentiating factor. *Social class* is also relevant, along with *social status* and *consumption style.* In the following discussion, these three variables are explored to show how differences exist among upscale consumers. These differences can then be used as a basis for demographic and psychographic segmentation of upscale consumers.

INCOME

A decade ago there were already more than half a million millionaires in the United States (Stanley and Moschis 1984). In 1987, Lazer defined "super affluents" in the United States as those having annual incomes of more than $50,000, $75,000, or even $100,000. Engel et al. (1990) note that the wealthiest 20 percent of U.S. families now command 50 percent of after-tax family income. Moreover, the top 1 percent of U.S. families had an average 1988 after-tax family income of almost $304,000, up 74 percent over the 1977 level. These authors note that the "up market" is generally defined as the upper income quartile of the population. As they state, "the Up Market is likely to be dual-income households, time-constrained, and emphasizing quality in their product preferences" (Engel et al. 1990, p. 232).

Those figures demonstrate the lack of consensus that exists in the definition of the upscale market in just one country on the basis of just one factor: income. The question is rendered much more complex when one attempts to compare income levels across national boundaries. For example, in Asian markets there is a growing class of young professionals and entrepreneurs whose affluence is considerable in local terms but comparatively modest in Western markets. Table 8-1 presents 1990 income data for young urban professionals (yuppies) in five Asian markets. Income levels for Asian yuppies have been rising at an annual rate of 15–20 percent in recent years, and the number of young people aged 20–30 in these five markets is estimated at about one million. The importance of this demographic and life-style group lies in their propensity to spend, particularly on expensive designer products. Because of the difficulty of achieving home ownership, most people in this age group live at home, even after marriage. Thus resources normally allocated to buying and equipping a first home are being channeled into products and services designed to enhance the self (*Fortune* 1990). With regard to Japanese consumers, similar constraints on home ownership exist. One result is that young people, particularly young, single women, have gained a reputation for extravagant spending in recent years.

Similar conspicuous spending on high-tech and high-touch items is seen in EC markets. Beatson (1990) identifies two European segments of upscale consumers that he characterizes as pan-European "tribes": the "Gucci-Vuitton-Cartier" tribe and the "socially elite" tribe. Presumably the difference between these two "tribes" lies in their social backgrounds, which may be masked by similar extravagant spending and consumption

TABLE 8-1   INCOME COMPARISONS FOR YOUNG, URBAN PROFESSIONALS IN SELECTED ASIAN MARKETS (1990)

Earnings	Hong Kong	Singapore	Seoul	Taipei	Bangkok
Annual income: 32-year-old banker,	$35,000	$32,000	$31,000	$18,000	$12,000
per capita gross domestic product	$10,900	$11,000	$5,000[a]	$7,300[a]	$1,200[a]

Note [a]Figures are for South Korea, Taiwan, and Thailand.

SOURCE: FORTUNE *(1990). "ASIA'S NEW YUPPIES," JUNE 4, 230.*

TABLE 8-2

HOUSEHOLD INCOME
LEVELS FOR THE
"GET$ET" AND THE
GENERAL U.S.
POPULATION

SOURCE: BOWLES, T.
(1988). "DOES
CLASSIFYING PEOPLE
BY LIFESTYLE REALLY
HELP THE
ADVERTISER?"
EUROPEAN RESEARCH,
(FEBRUARY), 20.

Annual Household Income	Population (%)	Get$et (%)
Less than $35,000	70	0
$35,000–$39,999	7	19
$40,000–$49,999	11	33
$50,000 or more	12	48
	100	100

habits. Many of these wealthy consumers are located in a fairly concentrated geographic area. D'Arcy Masius Benton and Bowles, a leading advertising agency, has shown that the wealthiest EC consumers live mainly within a 250-mile radius around Cologne, Germany (*The Economist* 1990). Thus, while a marketer might be tempted to focus on the geographic concentration of upscale EC consumers, there is some indication that they should not be treated as a homogeneous group. Similarly, the level of income and spending priorities of upscale EC consumers and those in Asian markets may be found to differ significantly, which would again argue in favor of a close analysis of the varying characteristics of upscale consumers in world markets.

The propensity to spend lavishly exists even among consumers who do not have incomes indicative of traditional affluence, as defined above. Bowles (1988) describes a segmentation system used by Simmons Market Research Bureau which identifies those consumers who really dominate the U.S. market for premium products and services. According to this system, gross household income was not found to be the best indicator of spending behavior for a variety of reasons. Instead, the "high-spender" group was best identified in terms of ownership or purchase of a range of high-ticket consumer goods and services beyond a threshold level. Named the "Get$et," in 1988 these consumers all had annual incomes of more than $35,000, but only half had incomes over $50,000. Thus it is evident that high levels of spending are demonstrated not only by upper-class, high-income groups but also by middle-class, middle-income groups. (See Fierman 1987 for further discussion of the "high-living middle class.")

Table 8-2 shows the income distribution in 1988 for members of the Get$et compared to the general U.S. population. These figures support the two general findings in this section. First, upscale consumers cannot be reliably identified on the basis of income alone. Second, there is little agreement among researchers on an income cutoff level which effectively identifies upscale consumers.

SOCIAL CLASS

It is well known that measurement of social class using income alone results in anomalies and inaccuracies. Gilbert and Kahl (1987) identified nine key variables that are necessary to any accurate assessment of social class. These include economic variables—occupation, income, and wealth; interaction variables—personal prestige, association, and socialization; and political variables—power, class consciousness, and mobility. This classification schema draws attention to the fact that social class is not merely a label attached to an income but rather is experienced as a complex set of values and relationships that are determined by specific reference groups. Sociologists who consider group membership and interactions as primary determinants of class are sometimes referred to as the "who-invited-whom-to-dinner" school (Engel et al. 1990).

In addition, measurement of social class varies from country to country. This makes it difficult for a marketer to develop a standardized marketing program targeted simply to a specific social class. Figure 8-1 demonstrates the problem by presenting social class profiles for seven of the twelve EC member nations. It should be noted that five of the seven use alphabetical identifications of class strata in place of the more descriptive "upper/middle/lower" categories used in the United States. Figure 8-2 presents comparable data for the United States, seen from two points of view, those of Gilbert and Kahl (1982) and Coleman and Rainwater (1978).

Although social class divisions tend to be stable over time, during the 1980s in Britain policies of the conservative Thatcher government resulted in some notable class shifts as more people became homeowners and shareholders for the first time. Thus the 40 percent of the British population in classes ABC1 in 1990 (see Figure 8.1) reflects a 7 percent increase over the 1978 level (Worcester 1989). Similar changes in class structure due to increasing affluence are being noted across the EC. It would be unwise to equate growing prosperity across markets with similarity in tastes or values. "Patches of cross-border affluence in Europe do not necessarily mean that wealthy French, West German, Belgian and Swiss consumers will want to spend their cash the same way" (*The Economist* 1990).

Three important implications arise from the foregoing discussion. First, not only do consumers differ in their social styles of consumption between classes, but also the definitions of those classes vary among nations. Second, reliance on elite social class as a descriptor of the market for upscale items may result in neglect of the high-spender, "Get$et" type

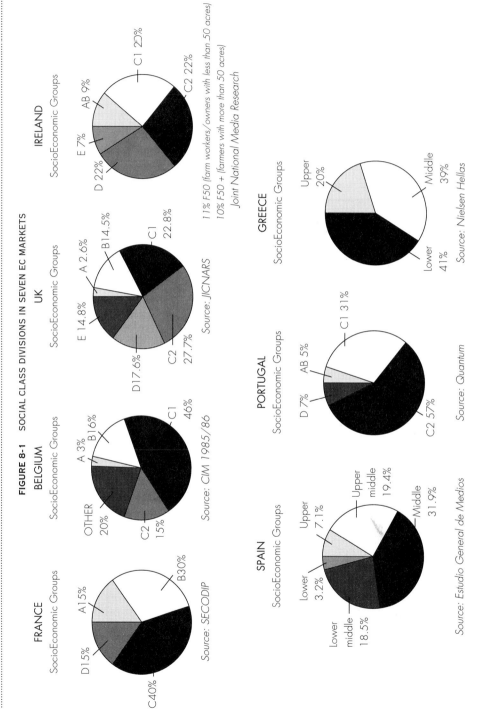

FIGURE 8-1 SOCIAL CLASS DIVISIONS IN SEVEN EC MARKETS

FRANCE
SocioEconomic Groups

A 15%
B 30%
C 40%
D 15%

Source: SECODIP

BELGIUM
SocioEconomic Groups

A 3%
B 16%
C1 46%
C2 15%
OTHER 20%

Source: CIM 1985/86

UK
SocioEconomic Groups

A 2.6%
B 14.5%
C1 22.8%
C2 27.7%
D 17.6%
E 14.8%

Source: JICNARS

IRELAND
SocioEconomic Groups

AB 9%
C1 22%
C2 22%
D 22%
E 7%

11% F50 (farm workers/owners with less than 50 acres)
10% F50 + (farmers with more than 50 acres)
Joint National Media Research

SPAIN
SocioEconomic Groups

Upper 7.1%
Upper middle 19.4%
Middle 31.9%
Lower middle 18.5%
Lower 3.2%

Source: Estudio General de Medios

PORTUGAL
SocioEconomic Groups

AB 5%
C1 31%
C2 57%
D 7%

Source: Quantum

GREECE
SocioEconomic Groups

Upper 20%
Middle 39%
Lower 41%

Source: Nielsen Hellas

SOURCE: ADAPTED FROM CENTAUR COMMUNICATIONS LTD. (1989). 1992 MARKETING IN EUROPE. LONDON: CENTAUR.

FIGURE 8-2   SOCIAL CLASS DIVISIONS IN THE UNITED STATES: TWO POINTS OF VIEW

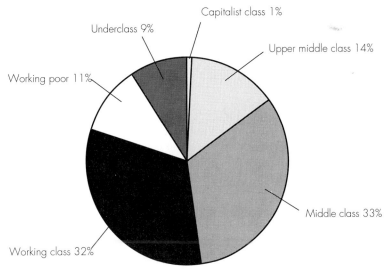

The Gilbert and Kahl
New Synthesis Class Structure

Capitalist class 1%

Underclass 9%

Upper middle class 14%

Working poor 11%

Middle class 33%

Working class 32%

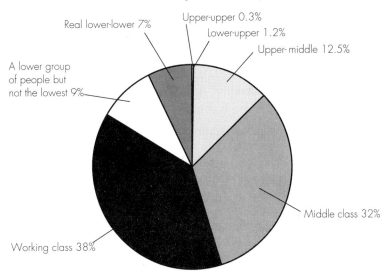

The Coleman-Rainwater
Social Standing Class Hierarchy

Real lower-lower 7%

Upper-upper 0.3%

Lower-upper 1.2%

Upper-middle 12.5%

A lower group
of people but
not the lowest 9%

Middle class 32%

Working class 38%

SOURCE: D. GILBERT, AND J. A. KAHL (1982). THE AMERICAN CLASS STRUCTURE: A SYNTHESIS. *HOMEWOOD, IL: THE DORSEY PRESS. R. P. COLEMAN, AND L. P. RAINWATER (1978).* SOCIAL STANDING IN AMERICA: NEW DIMENSIONS OF CLASS, *NEW YORK: BASIC BOOKS.*

of consumer. Third, and this point is the converse of the second point, focus on product purchase alone may result in the creation of a heterogeneous market that includes upper-upper, lower-upper, upper-middle, and even some middle-class consumers. Thus the risks of improper market definition are either (1) to miss the target, (2) to define too narrow a market, or (3) to define too large a market. The conclusion here is that social class and income are insufficient variables on their own or even in combination upon which to base a global marketing program for upscale products and services.

Status Symbols

Table 8-3 lists some examples of luxury brand names that are typically associated with the most elegant consumers in world markets.

As Goffman (1951) explained, "Status symbols visibly divide the social world into categories of persons, thereby helping to maintain solidarity within a category and hostility between different categories" (p. 294). Status symbols carry *categorical* significance that identifies the social status of the owner. They also carry an *expressive* significance that conveys something about the point of view, the style of life, and the cultural values of the owner. The second point is important in the context of international marketing because ownership of a globally recognized brand confers a cosmopolitan image upon the owner. In other words, if the particular brand were not known worldwide, ownership would lose much of its value for many upscale consumers. This may explain the origin of the term "jet set" to describe those consumers who have the means to shop anywhere in the world and buy brands that will be immediately recognizable, yet inaccessible, to most people.

The notions of inaccessibility and exclusivity are fundamental to a status symbol. Devices that restrict access to status symbols go beyond mere high price. Goffman (1951) identifies six sources of restrictions:

1. Moral: a self-imposed refusal to copy the consumption style of the upper classes
2. Intrinsic: the effective scarcity of "originals"
3. Natural: the natural scarcity caused by limited supply
4. Social: a selectivity reflected in an un-self-conscious social style
5. Cultural: the element of sophistication
6. Organic: the long-range physical effects of a superior diet, occupation, and environment

These devices work together to preserve the integrity of a social class. As Goffman states, ". . . In this way, the group avoids the danger, as it were, of putting all their symbols in one basket" (1951, p. 302). Using Goffman's schema of devices restricting the misrepresentation of status symbols by nonclass members, it is possible to create a three-part segmentation of upscale consumers, namely:

1. The truly affluent
2. Conspicuous consumers
3. Indulgers

The "truly affluent" segment includes those consumers who are not only wealthy but portray the long-term beneficial effects of three of the sources

Clothes and Shoes	Jewelry and Stores	Automobiles	Accessories	TABLE 8-3
Yves Saint Laurent	Bulgari	Rolls Royce	Beluga	A SELECT LISTING OF LUXURY BRAND NAMES[a]
Christian Dior	Tissot	Cadillac	Godiva	
Givenchy	Cartier	Range Rover	Montblanc	
Giorgio Armani	Rolex	Jaguar	Mark Cross	
Guy Laroche	Piaget	Mercedes-Benz	Parker Pen	
Charles Jourdan	Christian Dior	Porsche	Louis Vuitton	
Ermenegildo Zegna	Tiffany	Lamborghini	Hermes	
Hugo Boss	Harrods	Maserati	Architectural Digest	
Pierre Cardin	Van Cleef and Arpels	Ferrari	The New Yorker	
Emanuel Ungaro	Saks Fifth Avenue	BMW	Vogue	
Burberry	Lord and Taylor	Aston Martin	Dom Perignon	
Aquascutum	Neiman-Marcus		Moet et Chandon	
Jaeger			Bang and Olufsen	
Gucci			American Express	
Timberland			(Platinum Card)	
Allen Edmonds				
Bruno Magli				

[a]Numerous brands have been licensed across product categories, particularly perfumes and colognes. Duplicates are not listed.

of status restriction mentioned earlier, i.e., socialization, cultivation, and organic effects. "Conspicuous consumers" demonstrate a less innate level of sophistication and are noticeably more self-conscious, whereas "indulgers" are easily recognizable by their piecemeal approach to the purchase of luxury items and lack of true sophistication. Each segment demonstrates different values and shopping styles, although people from each segment may buy identical products. These differences are discussed in Part II.

Consumption Styles in the Upscale Market

Three themes are addressed in this part of the chapter: conspicuous consumption; reference groups, values, and life-styles; and purchasing patterns. The objective here is to show how these three segments of upscale consumers differ, further reinforcing the argument in favor of segmenting the upscale market.

Conspicuous Consumption

Engel el al (1990) illustrate vividly the link between income, social class, and consumption style with the following quotation by a 14-year-old student attending a private high school in an upper middle-class suburb:

> "There are three types of kids in our school. The rich kids wear Guess jeans or Forenza from The Limited. They have their parents' credit cards or their own, so they are used to getting what they want. They have to go to the bathroom after lunch to put on their makeup. They have seven Swatch watches, one for each day of the week. Their hair is curly or bobbed in a wave. At home they have waterbeds. The lower class kids don't dress as well. They don't hang around the cooler groups. They get made fun of a lot. They may have styles from The Limited but you know they bought them at T. J. Max. The lower class (at this school) have more money than the kids at public schools, but they don't dress well or act right. The middle class kids have money and dress nice but they are not really cool and they don't talk about themselves as much as the upper class kids" (Engel et al. 1990, p. 134).

Sheth et al. (1991) state that conspicuous consumption occurs when individuals buy or use products with the express intent of communicating socially significant meanings to others. Veblen (1953) defined the concept of conspicuous consumption as follows: "... the members of each stratum accept as their ideal of decency the scheme of life in vogue in the next higher stratum, and bend their energies to live up to the ideal" (p. 70). The upper-upper class, being socially secure, may not find it necessary or desirable to buy the most expensive brands to impress other people. In fact there may be a tendency to understate, rather than accentuate, consumption styles. Moreover, security in one's own class status may result in a consumption style that goes beyond understatement to "parody display" (Brooks 1981). This is the deliberate mockery of status symbols and elitist behavior. Coleman (1983) commented on the breakdown of behavioral styles between social classes in the United States, asserting that:

> ". . . The lifestyle variations that have emerged exist vertically within Upper America, crossing the substrata and combining people from several status layers into one consumer group with common goals that are differentiated internally mainly by income. . . . The result is that Upper America is now a vibrant mix of many lifestyles, which may be labeled post-preppy, sybaritic, counter-cultural, conventional, intellectual, political, and so on" (Coleman 1983, p. 270).

The same phenomenon of understated class membership is found in markets outside the United States. For example, Tang's of Singapore has created a new specialty clothing store dedicated to a subgroup of yuppies, termed NOPEs—not outwardly prosperous or educated. The key is the *subtle* display of wealth (*Fortune* 1990). Russel (1983) explored in detail the various aspects of what he calls the upper class's "process of rejection—of the current, the showy, the superfluous." Thus we infer from this discussion that a key difference between the truly wealthy and the two other segments, conspicuous consumers and indulgers, is a matter of style, where the discreet is preferred over the flamboyant and self-proclaiming. The ramifications of this finding are discussed in Part III with regard to promotional strategies suitable for each segment.

REFERENCE GROUPS, VALUES, AND LIFESTYLES

Conceptually, the differences between upscale consumers can be portrayed graphically as shown in Figure 8-3. The "truly affluent" of the upper-upper class constitute the membership group that serves as the pole of attraction for the second segment, the conspicuous consumers. "Conspicuous consumers" include the lower-upper and upper-middle classes. Those conspicuous consumers for whom the future holds promise of greater wealth may belong to an anticipatory aspirational group. Anticipation of membership of the truly affluent group may not be pertinent to the present generation of conspicuous consumers, but it may be possible for their children who will enjoy inherited wealth rather than earned wealth—the critical point of difference between the upper-upper and lower-upper classes. (See Coleman and Rainwater 1978 for a further discussion of class differences.) "Indulgers" also belong to the aspirational group. In contrast to conspicuous consumers, their aspirations are purely symbolic. There is no expectation of ever joining the truly affluent group, but purchase of identical products and services confers on indulgers a feeling of "living like" and "being as good as" the highest social class.

A further conceptualization can be used to differentiate the three upscale segments using the VALS and VALS-2 classification systems, as shown in Figure 8-4. (See Mitchell 1983 and Riche 1989 for further details about VALS and VALS-2.) The different life-styles and values of each of these groups are characterized by Riche (1989) as follows. "Actualizers" consider image important ". . . as an expression of their taste, independence, and character. Their consumer choices are directed toward the finer things in life." "Achievers" are "successful, work-oriented people who get their satisfaction from their jobs and families. . . . They favor

FIGURE 8-3   CLASSIFICATION OF AFFLUENT CONSUMERS BY TYPE OF REFERENCE GROUP

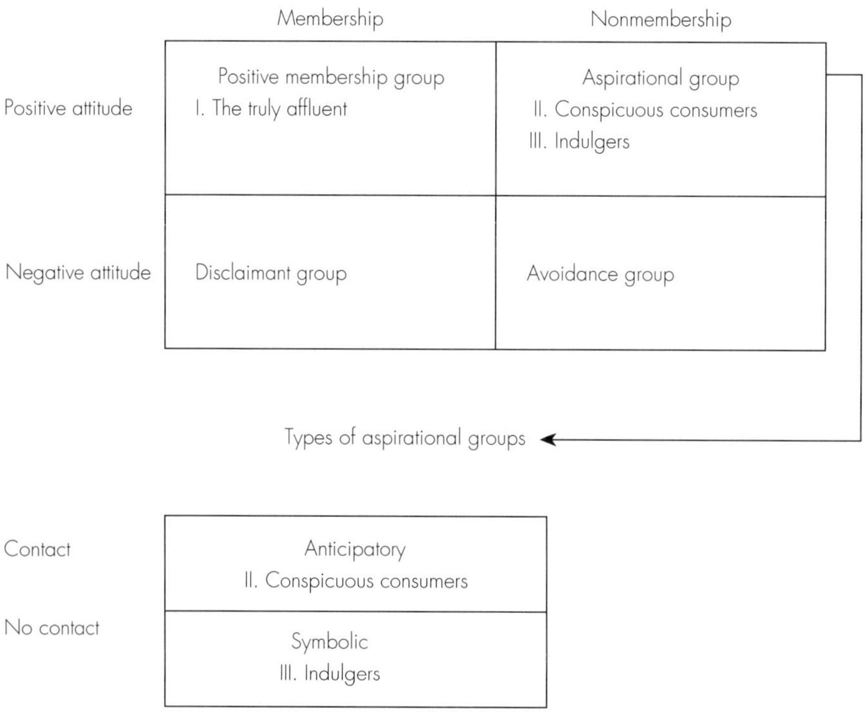

	Membership	Nonmembership
Positive attitude	Positive membership group I. The truly affluent	Aspirational group II. Conspicuous consumers III. Indulgers
Negative attitude	Disclaimant group	Avoidance group

Types of aspirational groups ◄─────────

Contact	Anticipatory II. Conspicuous consumers
No contact	Symbolic III. Indulgers

established products and services that show off their success to their peers." "Strivers" have "values very similar to achievers but have fewer economic, social, and psychological resources. Style is extremely important to them as they strive to emulate people they admire and wish to be like" (Riche 1989, pp. 24–26). The outer-directedness (VALS) and status orientation (VALS-2) that typify conspicuous consumers and indulgers underline once more their need for an external point of reference to fully enjoy ownership of luxury items.

Johansson (1986) discusses how Japanese consumers might be classified using a type of categorization reminiscent of the VALS/VALS-2 typologies. Building on work by Shainwald (1984), Johansson identifies two "non-conformist" groups described as "style-oriented" and "confident theoreticians." The style-oriented group, representing 15 percent of the population, is composed of ambitious, single women who are leisure oriented and for whom travel is a number one priority. These modern, university trained women tend to be office workers. The 5 percent of the population who are "confident theoreticians" are notable as trendsetters. They are the best educated consumers, have the smallest families, and live in large cities (Johansson 1986, p. 40). It would be reasonable to assume that these two life-style groups can be included in the conspicuous consumer group because of their interest in style and fashion.

Purchasing Patterns

Each of the three segments varies according to the consistency and continuity of their product purchases and brand choices. In other words, the

FIGURE 8-4   AFFLUENT CONSUMERS CLASSIFIED ACCORDING TO THE
VALS AND VALS-2 SYSTEMS[a]

Affluent segment	Lifestyle group	
	VALS	VALS-2
I. The truly affluent	Integrateds	Actualizers
II. Conspicuous consumers	Outer-directed achievers	Status-oriented achievers
III. Indulgers	Outer-directed emulators (some inner-directed experientials)	Status-oriented strivers

[a] See Mitchell (1983) for details about VALS and Riche (1989) for details about VALS-2.

truly affluent are able to create a life-style that is not subject to the vagaries of income fluctuations that are experienced to a greater or lesser degree by the other two segments. To illustrate, conspicuous consumers who belong to the upper-middle class have shown themselves willing to compromise on brand preferences and trade down in times of financial difficulty. They show a "disconcerting willingness to substitute sparkling wine for champagne, off-the-rack imitations for pricey designer clothes . . . (and) a most unsnoblike taste for "replica" brands—illegal copies of perfumes and bags that smell or look like originals but cost a fraction of the price" (*The Economist* 1991). American conspicuous consumers are also subject to the effects of the new 1991 luxury tax. Their EC counterparts may be affected by the probable phasing-out of duty-free sales for travelers within the newly integrated EC market. Wherever possible, though, conspicuous consumers will try to purchase the "right" brand, given its signal value as a symbol of class membership and achievement.

Because household incomes among conspicuous consumers are usually based on two earners, time is a valuable commodity and affects the type of products purchased. The truly affluent do not experience this constraint and are able to pay for all the support services they need. Lazer (1984) identified a list of products that offer conspicuous consumers both convenience and time savings. Lazer also identified those categories of products and services that complement a time-pressured life-style. These include products and services that are designed to enhance the physical and psychological self (such as spas and stress management courses) and to support mobility and immediate gratification (such as mobile telephones, laptop computers, and fax machines). The nature of these products and services reflects the fact that conspicuous consumers earn their wealth through hard work, in contrast to the leisurely lives of the truly affluent.

Two other categories identified by Lazer (1984) have a common appeal to both conspicuous consumers and the truly affluent. It is these categories that essentially constitute what is known as the "luxury" market. These two categories include entertainment and leisure services, and snob-appeal products and services. The second group includes gourmet foods, wines, decorator and designer products and services, paintings, sculpture, and performing arts such as ballet, opera, symphony concerts, and drama (Lazer 1984). It is evident from this discussion that these two segments of upscale consumers have different needs and priorities arising from their different sources of income and life-styles. But they also have much in common, particularly in regard to certain types of luxury products and services.

Indulgers are constrained in their purchasing habits by the various financial commitments associated with passage through the different life-stages. This means that the composition of this segment is fluid. Consumers move in and out of this segment as income is variously allocated to changing household commitments (such as education and health maintenance) or discretionary purchases (such as entertainment and leisure services and snob-appeal items). The general attitude of indulgers is summed up as "I want it, and I want it now." Their focus is not on creation or maintenance of a particular life-style but rather on instant gratification of inner drives through the purchase of highly visible and symbolic products and services. Indulgers are particularly prone to spend on travel, financial services, new cars (both domestic and imported), high-tech consumer electronics, and magazine subscriptions. According to Bowles' (1988) data on the "Get$et," indulgers include consumers in professional, managerial, technical, clerical, and skilled manual occupations, along with retirees. The socio-demographic characteristics of this group contrast sharply with those of the two other segments, and this is further evidence to support the need for segmentation of the upscale market.

From this discussion it is clear that substantial differences exist between the three segments with regard to the continuity of spending on high-ticket items. The truly affluent maintain a consistent purchasing pattern over time and over a wide range of product/service categories. Conspicuous consumers try to achieve similar goals but may be obliged periodically to trade down, make substitutions, rent or lease, or defer purchases. Indulgers pick and choose their luxury items, which constitute islands of self-indulgence in what are otherwise "mass-market" life-styles. Also, the truly affluent enjoy a range of services that the other two segments may perform themselves in order to have the means available to purchase high-visibility items.

In conclusion to this section on consumption styles, it has been shown that the upscale market is composed of three segments whose members do not buy in the same way or for the same reasons, even though the objects they purchase may be identical. It is this uniformity in the objects of purchase that may lead marketers to consider upscale consumers as homogeneous, when in fact there are three distinct segments. Part III of this chapter discusses the implications for marketing strategy and tactics.

MARKETING UPSCALE PRODUCTS AND SERVICES WORLDWIDE

In this section, three themes are addressed: global marketing strategy; a segmentation procedure using social class as a segmentation base; and marketing-mix decisions.

GLOBAL MARKETING STRATEGY

The homogeneity of products and services bought by upscale consumers may prompt one to argue in favor of a standardized marketing strategy targeted to all upscale consumers around the world. This strategy would allow important economies of scale across the production and marketing functions. However, in the foregoing discussion ample evidence has been provided that consumers in the world's upscale market are not homogeneous. Thus it would be prudent to consider other strategic options. Four alternatives may be considered.

First, intermarket segmentation is a means of identifying marketing opportunities in similar segments around the world, and these segments can be served using standardized policies for product and promotion. This type of segmentation is based on a method of country clustering.

Second, as Takeuchi and Porter (1986) have proposed, a policy of product standardization can be maintained by *targeting different segments in different markets with the same product*. In the context of the three upscale market segments, standardized products and services can feasibly be targeted across national segments in the following manner:

1. To North American upper-upper and lower-upper classes and to some upper-middle-class consumers with high and stable levels of discretionary income
2. To consumers in class A in the twelve EC markets
3. To yuppies across the more modern Asian markets

A third alternative would be a strategy of concentration on key markets, targeting only the truly affluent segment worldwide. The implications of this option that affect marketing-mix decisions, particularly promotion and distribution decisions, are discussed in a later section.

A fourth strategic option might be to create a "cash-cow" product that is positioned to be accessible to as many aspirational consumers as possible. This strategy can be applied either to an older, less popular or less successful brand name or, alternatively, to new brand names created especially for the purpose of appealing to aspirational consumers. Examples of this strategy are seen in the recent introduction by couture houses of new lines priced from $100 to $900. Givenchy has launched "Life"; Escada "A Priori"; Ungaro "Emanuel"; Yves Saint Laurent "Variation"; and Christian Dior "Coordonnees" (*Business Week* 1991). In the past, this strategy was inappropriately applied to highly successful brands with disastrous results. For example, extensive licensing of brand names such as Pierre Cardin, Louis Vuitton, Halston, and Yves Saint Laurent resulted in market saturation. In the case of the Yves Saint Laurent name, a buy-back from licensees became necessary to protect the brand.

The goal of a global "cash-cow" strategy is to generate revenues that can be used to support continued niche marketing of exclusive and established brand names. These are destined uniquely for the truly affluent global segment of some 2,000 women who are willing to pay more than $30,000 for one-of-a-kind "originals" (*Business Week* 1991). The rationale for combined use of a cash-cow strategy with a niche strategy derives from the need for protection of the exclusivity of status symbols and the continuing search for new symbols by elite consumers. Theoretically, this strategy is supported by Goffman's (1951) discussion of the circulation and restriction of the use of symbols. "The systematic circumvention of modes of restriction leads to downward and upward circulation of symbols" (Goffman 1951, p. 303). One consequence of this phenomenon is that "those with whom a symbol originates must turn from that which is familiar to them and seek out, again and again, something which is not yet contaminated" (p. 304). Illustrations of how other upscale brand names are currently being traded down to appeal to broader world markets are given in the discussion of promotional decisions.

Segmentation Procedure Using Social Class

The argument for segmentation of upscale consumers has been amply supported in this chapter. A segmentation procedure using social class as the segmentation base has been developed by Engel et al. (1990). This procedure has four steps:

1. Identification of social class usage of the product or service
2. Comparison of social class variables for segmentation with other variables (such as income, life-stage, etc.)
3. Description of social class characteristics identified in the target market
4. Development of marketing program(s) to maximize the effectiveness of the marketing mix(es) based on consistency with social class attributes (adapted from Engel et al. 1990, p. 129).

Use of this procedure will allow marketers to incorporate the key ideas presented here into a coherent strategy that combines the best features of standardized global product marketing and target marketing.

Marketing-Mix Decisions

The four P's of the marketing mix are discussed next, and examples of specific actions appropriate for marketing upscale products are presented.

PRODUCT   Figure 8-5 presents an analysis of the luxury market by product type. French brand names account for almost half of luxury sales, with German, British, Italian, Swiss, and a few Japanese and American brands making up the rest. The share of sales in 1989 by Japanese and American producers was only 11 percent (as shown in Figure 8-5). The 89 percent

FIGURE 8-5   SALES OF LUXURY GOODS BY PRODUCT TYPE

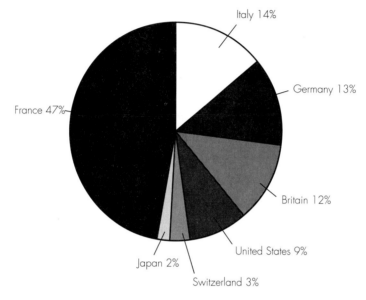

By National Origin
Total value: $52bn

Italy 14%

Germany 13%

France 47%

Britain 12%

United States 9%

Japan 2%

Switzerland 3%

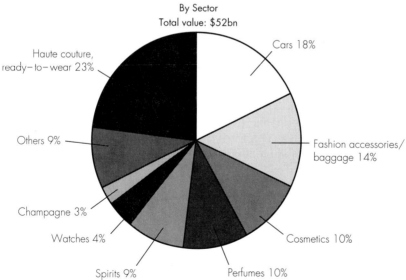

By Sector
Total value: $52bn

Cars 18%

Haute couture,
ready-to-wear 23%

Others 9%

Fashion accessories/
baggage 14%

Champagne 3%

Watches 4%

Cosmetics 10%

Spirits 9%

Perfumes 10%

SOURCE: THE ECONOMIST *(1990). "THE MYTH OF THE EURO-CONSUMER," NOVEMBER 4, 50.*

market share of European producers is heavily concentrated geographically, with about half of all their luxury goods being sold in the United
States and Japan.

Two points should be noted here. First, both producers and consumers of luxury goods are concentrated in the triad markets (Ohmae 1985),
which are fiercely competitive. Second, country-of-origin is a fundamental feature of the attractiveness of luxury products. The "Made in ———"
label is an assurance of authenticity that justifies the high price. Table 8-4
indicates those countries that a 1987 sample of affluent U.S. consumers
typically associated with luxury products.

It is striking to note the divergence in Figure 8-5 and Table 8-4 between actual sales volume by country-of-origin and U.S. consumers' perceptions of the importance of U.S.-made luxury products. Also noticeable
is the omission of Switzerland from the U.S. consumers' list. One might
infer that consumer perceptions of what constitutes a luxury product, in
terms of country-of-origin, vary substantially among markets. It is also
well-known that the Japanese believe "Made in Japan" to be a signal of
high quality if not necessarily of luxury status (Johansson 1986).

PRICE   Recently, producers for the luxury market have suffered from the
combined effects of recession, crisis in the American retailing sector, and

Country	Percentage
France	52.9
United States	49.5
Italy	43.4
Germany	31.5
Great Britain	22.0
Japan	16.3
Sweden	14.8
Belgium	11.3
Spain	9.3
Denmark	9.1
Norway	3.8

Note: Affluence is defined as a household income of $75,000 or more.

TABLE 8.4

COUNTRIES ASSOCIATED WITH LUXURY PRODUCTS BY AFFLUENT U.S. CONSUMERS

SOURCE: L. KESLER (1988). "$2,300 SCOTCH SETS TONE FOR GLENFIDDICH," ADVERTISING AGE, MARCH 21, S-12.

the tarnishing of some brands through overuse of licensing. To solve some of these problems, there is a need to refocus on those consumers who are sufficiently insulated financially to maintain their traditional high level of spending. The goal for producers is to achieve a balance between volume and scarcity. The careful protection of Ralph Lauren's Polo brand illustrates this point. A further goal is to protect profit margins by maintaining price skimming policies and introducing price increases. The Moet Index measures the cost of a market basket of a dozen luxury products—such as a Rolls Royce, Dom Perignon champagne, and beluga caviar. When the U.S. consumer price index increased by 4.4 percent in 1989, the Moet Index rose by 9 percent (*American Marketplace* 1989). The relative demand inelasticity associated with the truly affluent market segment argues in favor of a focused global marketing strategy using a price skimming policy.

As mentioned earlier, price is a source of unpredictability of purchase among conspicuous consumers and indulgers. Price rises may discourage or delay purchase, or they may encourage acquisition through rental or lease rather than purchase. If the marketer's goal is to broaden the market for a particular brand-name item, then attention to the consumer's cost of acquisition (through financing arrangements) may become an important element of pricing policy.

DISTRIBUTION   Pricing decisions are directly affected by distribution decisions. Prices of luxury items will vary depending on whether they are purchased at exclusive boutiques, chain specialty stores, department stores, off-price retailers, or through upscale catalogs. To indulgers, the place and means of purchase is unimportant because their goal is simply product ownership. Indulgers can therefore be expected to "shop around" for the best price, wherever it may be encountered. In contrast, for conspicuous consumers, the manner of purchase requires as much thought as product and brand selection because of the issues of purchase visibility and ability to pay high retail prices. In an earlier section of this chapter, the quotation by a 14-year-old student highlighted the subtle interactions of both product ownership, price, and place of purchase in the minds of consumers in this segment. (See *American Demographics* 1988 for a description of the frequencies of visits to different types of stores by various consumer income groups.) Thus conspicuous consumers want not only to own luxury products but also to be seen shopping for them in upscale retail stores.

If a decision is made to focus on the truly affluent segment, then the exclusivity of the brand name must be maintained through exclusive distribution policies. Licensing of the brand name must be strictly controlled, and every effort should be made to fight low-price product counterfeiting. (See Czinkota and Ronkainen 1990, pp. 548–552 for a full discussion of the impact of counterfeiting in world markets.)

PROMOTION In view of the differences in reference group membership and values among the truly affluent, conspicuous consumers, and indulgers, the types of persuasive and positioning messages vary notably. To illustrate this point, Figures 8-6 to 8-8 show examples of advertisements for a range of upscale products and services. The ad in Figure 8-6 for Ermenegildo Zegna is targeted to the membership group, i.e., the truly affluent. The ad in Figure 8-7 for Stouffer Hotels and Resorts is targeted to the aspirational group, i.e., conspicuous consumers and indulgers who want to enjoy luxuries and "live a cut above" the rest of the population but are constrained by the high price of such items. Figure 8-8 presents an ad for Jaguar where price concerns are also addressed, this time by means of convenient payment arrangements. It is notable that in ads directed to the truly affluent, messages are based on an affirmation of elite character. In contrast, ads directed to aspirational consumers convey the not-so-subtle notion that "you too can enjoy the pleasures of. . . ." The legitimacy of these approaches to advertising to conspicuous consumers and indulgers has been endorsed by Russell and LeMasters (1975). Middle-class consumers respond to the "pull" of wanting upward mobility more than do the lower or working classes because the lower classes do not revere the upper class as much as the middle class does.

Figure 8-9 is an outstanding example of the intricate use of class symbolism. The ad for Chivas effectively speaks to both the affluent membership group and the aspirational group of consumers by conveying two different messages. Thus, when the truly affluent tire of extravagantly toasting their successes with champagne, perhaps using a "heroine's" shoe, they can "settle for" Chivas. In contrast, when the "rags to riches," upwardly mobile Cinderella consumers finally find their glass slipper, they can also celebrate with Chivas. This is an example of a campaign that is designed to stretch the market for an expensive product by linking it to values held by segments that might not otherwise buy the product. Thus indulgers may choose to spoil themselves with Chivas in place of the less expensive Cutty Sark, which is trying to confer upon itself an elitist image.

A further example of a campaign that tries to stretch demand for a traditionally elitist product is the one for the Range Rover. The image of a product designed for the world's aristocracy is reformulated into the image of a product for the affluent, energetic, and adventurous. Two of the recent ads make explicit mention of cosmopolitan fashion centers "from St. Moritz to Milan" and exciting destinations such as the Serengeti and the Outback. "Breathe easier under water" uses the metaphor of "cabin pressure," a message pertinent to time-constrained, fast-track and high-income young urban professionals, the heart of the conspicuous consumer segment. The headline in a third ad directly addresses "upwardly mobile" conspicuous consumers. Prices range from "just north of $30,000" to "an investment of around $43,000," echoing the business jargon of yuppies. Finally, the symbols of appointment to members of

FIGURE 8-6

TARGETS TRULY AFFLUENT

FIGURE 8-7

ASPIRATIONAL GROUP: "CONSPICUOUS FUNS & INDULGERS"

The most fitting conclusion to a work week is a weekend of luxury.

Weekend *Breakations.*
For those who find luxury a necessity.

Which is why we offer Weekend Breakations.® Plush surroundings for relaxation and romance. Gracious personal services, like complimentary coffee and a newspaper delivered with your wake-up call, at what-

ever time you choose. It's this attention to service that has placed us among the top luxury hotel companies,

according to a national consumer report.

When luxury is a necessity, take a Weekend Breakation. Call your travel agent or 1•800•HOTELS•1.

COLUMBUS, OH	CLEVELAND, OH
STOUFFER DUBLIN HOTEL	STOUFFER TOWER CITY PLAZA HOTEL
$69	$89
DAYTON, OH	
STOUFFER CENTER PLAZA HOTEL	CHICAGO, IL
$69	STOUFFER HAMILTON HOTEL (Itasca)
CHICAGO, IL	$79
STOUFFER OAK BROOK HOTEL	ST. LOUIS, MO
$69	STOUFFER CONCOURSE HOTEL*
BATTLE CREEK, MI	ST. LOUIS-LAMBERT INTERNATIONAL AIRPORT
STOUFFER BATTLE CREEK HOTEL	$69
$69	

Available Friday or Saturday nights. Limited number of rooms available at these rates. Rates for two persons per night, good through 12/28/91, unless otherwise noted. Taxes not included.

STOUFFER HOTELS & RESORTS

YOU CAN DEPEND ON OUR GOOD NAME

FIGURE 8-8

There's One Way To Make A Jaguar Look Even More Beautiful. Lease It For Only $595 A Month.

Jaguar introduces an offer as gracious as its legendary motor-cars: The Jaguar Royal Charter Lease.

For only $595 a month, you can lease the 1991 Sovereign, an automobile with the style, elegance and grace that typifies Jaguar's classic beauty.

To experience a Sovereign first-hand, simply ask your Jaguar dealer for a test drive. He can also tell you about leasing plans for the Vanden Plas, the XJ-S and XJ-S Convertible.

Of course, while the beauty of a Jaguar is timeless, this offer, unfortunately, is not. It ends March 31, 1991. For the name of your nearest Jaguar dealer, call 1-800-4-JAGUAR.

J A G U A R

Lease offered by participating Jaguar dealers to qualified lessees. Must take retail delivery out of dealer stock by March 31, 1991. Example based on 1991 Jaguar Sovereign: $45,425 MSRP, includes all costs to be paid by customer except for licensing, registration, taxes and insurance. Price based on 48 month closed end lease requiring 48 payments of $595, totalling $28,560. Mileage charge of 14¢ per mile over 60,000 miles. A $595 down payment is required from customer at lease inception plus an acquisition fee of $595, a security deposit of $600 and first month's lease payment for a total of $2,785 due at lease signing. Option to purchase at end of lease for vehicle's published residual value. Lessee is liable for maintenance, repairs and excess wear and tear. All amounts shown and lessee obligations described are subject to applicable taxes which are extra. Dealer contribution may affect final cost. See your dealer for details on special terms and information on other available leases.

the British royal family are included as a visual reminder of quality and status.

In summary of this discussion of the marketing mix, we have identified a range of polices that allow the marketer to tailor a market offering to each or all of the three upscale market segments. Peter and Olson (1987) comment that differences in the three upper American social class groups

TARGET BOTH MEMBERSHIP & ASPIRATIONAL GROUPS

FIGURE 8-9

Why settle for champagne?

(upper-upper, lower-upper, and upper-middle) are likely to be relatively unimportant for most mass-marketed products. However, for luxury goods and services, the differences may be critical. On the basis of the ideas presented in this chapter, we infer that this criticality will affect the ways in which products are designed (showy versus classic); how they are promoted (flamboyantly versus discreetly); how they are distributed (exclusively versus selectively); and how they are priced (high price versus rental and lease arrangements).

Conclusion

In this chapter we have analyzed the upscale market according to a number of criteria to assess the appropriateness of applying a standardized marketing strategy. We have shown that consumers in the upscale market differ from one another in many respects even though they buy identical products. We have identified three distinct market segments that reflect these between-group differences. These segments are the truly affluent, conspicuous consumers, and indulgers. We have proposed a number of marketing strategies that show how marketers can choose to focus on a particular segment or combine several segments into a larger market. We have discussed the importance of decisions relating to brand-name usage and preservation.

This chapter has provided examples from the three major markets of North America, the EC, and the Far East. Once a clear understanding of the characteristics of consumers in the global upscale market has been established, it should be relatively straightforward for marketers to decide how best to target, position, and promote their products and services in world markets. Use of intermarket segmentation methods allows standardized global strategies to be used wherever possible to gain the greatest benefits from economies of scope and scale. The key danger is the assumption that consumers who are willing to spend lavishly are all the same. The evidence provided here proves that assumption to be false.

References

American Demographics (1988). "Blue-Blood Buyers," 10 (May), 20.

American Marketplace (1989). "Cost of the 'Good Life' Again Outpaces the CPI," 10, March 16, 47.

Beatson, R. (1990). "The Americanization of Europe?" *Advertising Age,* April 2, 16.

Bowles, T. (1988). "Does Classifying People by Lifestyle Really Help the Advertiser?" *European Research,* February, 17–24.

Brooks, J. (1981). "*Showing Off in America: From Conspicuous Consumption to Parody Display,*" Boston: Little, Brown.

Business Week (1991). "Haute Couture That's Not So Haute," April 22, 108.

Centaur Communications Ltd. (1989). *1992: Marketing in Europe.* London: Centaur.

Coleman, R. P. (1983). "The Continuing Significance of Social Class in Marketing," *Journal of Consumer Research,* 10 (December), 263–280.

Coleman, R. P., and L. P. Rainwater (1978). *Social Standing in America: New Dimensions of Class.* New York: Basic Books.

Czinkota, M. R., and I. A. Ronkainen (1990). *International Marketing,* 2nd.ed. Chicago: The Dryden Press.

Engel, J. F., R. D. Blackwell, and P. W. Miniard (1990). *Consumer Behavior,* 6th.ed. Chicago: The Dryden Press.

Fierman, J. (1987). "The High-Living Middle Class," *Fortune,* 115, April 13, 27.

Fortune (1990). "Asia's New Yuppies," June 4, 225 ff.

Gilbert, D., and J. A. Kahl (1982). *The American Class Structure: A Synthesis.* Homewood, IL: The Dorsey Press.

——— (1987). *The American Class Structure: A New Synthesis.* New York: Wadsworth Press.

Goffman, E. (1951). "Symbols of Class Status," *British Journal of Sociology,* 2, 294–304.

Johansson, J. (1986). "Japanese Consumers: What Foreign Marketers Should Know," *International Marketing Review,* (Summer), 37–43.

Kesler, L. (1988). "$2,300 Scotch Sets Tone for Glenfiddich," *Advertising Age,* March 21, S-12.

Lazer, W. (1984). "How Rising Affluence Will Reshape Markets," *American Demographics,* 6 (February), 7–8.

——— (1987). *Handbook of Demographics for Marketing and Advertising.* Lexington, MA: Lexington Books.

Levitt, T. (1983). "The Globalization of Markets," *Harvard Business Review* (May–June), 92–102.

——— (1988). "The Pluralization of Consumption," *Harvard Business Review* (May–June), 7–8.

Mitchell, A. (1983). *The Nine American Lifestyles.* New York: MacMillan.

Ohmae, K. (1985). *Triad Power.* New York: Free Press.

Peter, J. P., and J. C. Olson (1987). *Consumer Behavior.* Homewood, IL: Irwin.

Riche, M. F. (1989). "Psychographics for the 1990s," *American Demographics* (July), 25ff.

Russel, P. (1983). *Class.* New York: Ballantine Books.

Russell, F., and F. LeMasters (1975). "*Blue-Collar Aristocrats: Life Style at a Working Class Tavern,*" Madison, WI: University of Wisconsin Press.

Shainwald, R. (1984). "A Marketing Profile of the Japanese Consumer," Paper presented at the annual meeting of the Academy of International Business, Cleveland, Ohio, October 17–20.

Sheth, J. N., B. I. Newman, and B. L. Gross (1991). *Consumption Values and Market Choices: Theory and Applications.* Cincinnati, OH: South-Western Publishing Co.

Stanley, T. J., and G. P. Moschis (1984). "America's Affluent," *American Demographics,* 6 (March), 28–33.

Takeuchi, H., and M. E. Porter (1986). "Three Roles of International Marketing in Global Strategy," in M. E. Porter (ed.) *Competition in Global Industries.* Boston: Harvard Business School Press, 111–146.

The Economist (1990). "The Myth of the Euro-Consumer," November 4, 79–80.

The Economist (1991). "The Lapse of Luxury," January 5, 49–50.

Veblen, T. (1953). *The Theory of the Leisure Class.* New York: Mentor.

Worcester, R. M. (1989). "The Thatcher Revolution—Radical Policies in a Changing Society," *Long Range Planning,* 22, 4, 72–78.

PART III

CONSUMER BEHAVIOR IN THE GLOBAL MARKETPLACE

CHAPTER 9
TEMPORAL DIMENSIONS OF CONSUMING BEHAVIOR ACROSS CULTURES

Beverlee B. Anderson

M. Venkatesan

Many business people recognize that if you want to be successful in a foreign market today you must invest time and effort in learning about the culture and customs of that market. The benefits of this understanding are more likely to be indirect—through improved decision making and enhanced goodwill among customers and other foreign stakeholders. Unfortunately, it is not always easy to see a direct relationship between the level of cultural understanding and sales (Iverson 1991), which leads some people to question the value of this investment.

Even when they can't measure the impact on the bottom line directly, most firms perform basic environmental and market analyses before deciding to enter a foreign market. Preliminary analysis and screening are used to determine whether there is a potential match between the foreign market's needs and the firm's offerings. However, even when the unmet needs and the firm's market offering appear match, success is not assured. Many of the best laid marketing plans have been sabotaged by ignorance about the nuances and more subtle aspects of a culture and its customs.

THE CULTURAL CONTEXT OF TIME

International trade experts recommend that firms perform some type of cultural assessment as part of the more general environmental and market analyses. Cultural assessment examines aspects of an environment that interact to define and describe the design for living in a society. This information helps a firm determine whether a standardized market offering will blend with the living pattern of the culture. The assessment may also provide insights concerning potential problems the firm may encounter in its marketing efforts. Assessments can also help a firm identify aspects of its marketing effort that may require localized modification to be more compatible with the "mosaic of human life" (Wertsch 1985) in a culture.

Culture, itself, includes both abstract and material components that are intertwined to form a dynamic design that sets the tone and pattern for living. Cateora (1987) cautions firms to not lose sight of the total design presented by a culture, but at the same time he acknowledges that some individual elements of a culture may have a more direct influence on specific marketing efforts and, therefore, should be studied individually (p. 106). For example, language is one element that is salient to many marketing efforts.

Knowing the spoken and/or written language of a culture is essential for effective communication. However, people use many different forms of communication. In addition to using a formal verbal language, people communicate through several "silent languages" (Hall 1960). Hall identified the use of five different silent languages: time, space, material possessions, friendship patterns, and agreements across cultures. He concluded his comments on the language of time by saying, "The principle to be remembered is that time has different meaning in each country." A firm that does not recognize or consider differences is unlikely to examine the temporal aspects in its cultural assessment. As a result, many firms are never aware that a culture's time system may have played an instrumental role in determining the success/failure of a marketing effort.

SOCIAL TIME SYSTEMS

Social time has been referred to as the "heartbeat of culture" (Levine and Wolff 1985). It is that aspect of culture that sets the pace, the timing, the tempo of how time is lived. It also reflects how people think and feel about time. A social time system is a comprehensive framework that encompasses the rules, standards, practices, and customs of human behavior and interaction with respect to temporality.

Social time systems are influenced by natural time (nature's patterns) and mechanical time (man-created time segments and patterns). The relative prominence of natural time or mechanical time in a social time system varies across cultures (Gronmo 1989). For example, more agrarian, less industrialized cultures are more likely to have a time system that is closely related to aspects of natural time, whereas more developed industrialized societies appear to have time systems that are closely associated with mechanical time.

The shift to a greater use of mechanical time-based systems has become more pronounced as geographically dispersed cultures desire to increase their interactions and communications with one another. The need to synchronize movements, events, and behaviors leads to the need for standardized ways in which to measure and identify time. Man-made time units (hours, minutes, weeks, etc.), clocks, watches, and calendars serve this purpose. They provide an objective, though arbitrary, agreed-upon temporal standard that is used to communicate and coordinate activities (Zerubavel 1982).

Multiple Social Time Systems

The need to communicate and interact on an international or intercultural level through a mechanical time-based system has led, in some cases, to the adoption of multiple time systems within a given culture. This duality, unfortunately, has led some U.S. business people and travelers to assume that an entire culture operates on what may be termed "tiempo americano" because the local hosts and guides with whom they interact appear to be operating with an American view of time (Hall 1983).

Tiempo americano is a monochronic concept because time is thought of as linear and separable, a resource that can be bought, sold, exchanged, or saved. It is a scheduling approach to living one's life. Americans want not only to schedule time but to organize and manage it. This view is rather well integrated throughout U.S. culture to the point where many of the individuals managing our firms and organizations see it as "the only natural and logical way of organizing life" (Hall 1983, p. 49)

Individuals who have been socialized in a different time system may selectively adopt aspects of *tiempo americano* to facilitate more effective interaction with Americans while maintaining their own social time system for intracultural situations. When aspects of different time systems are operating simultaneously in a given society, there are many opportunities for misunderstandings and annoyances. In some cultures where two or more time systems are used, one may specify the system he or she is using. For example, in Mexico it is not uncommon for one to specify *hora ingles* as a technique for avoiding confusion.

Most cultures have a predominant social time system. However, there may be substantive variations in the time system found among different subcultures or regions within a culture (Levine 1988). For example Henry (1965) has written on "colored people's time," and Horton (1972) has written about social time of the "sporadically unemployed young Black street corner population" in the United States, which he has labeled "cool time." Whenever there are heterogeneous subgroupings of people found within cultures, there are likely to exist different social time systems within each subgrouping.

Regional differences within the United States were profiled in a series called "Beating the Clock," published in the *Wall Street Journal* (1991). Regional differences between the West and East Coasts cited included time priorities and punctuality. Westerners are reported to be more likely to make time for ideal weekends, hobbies, and vacations; easterners do not have the same priorities. It is also the westerners who are more likely to consider exchanging pay for more free time. The East Coast "insistence on punctuality, come hell or high water" (*Wall Street Journal* Aug. 14, p. B1), is contrasted with the belief by many westerners that being only five minutes late is being on time.

Time Classifications

Social time also recognizes that each form—viz., individual, group, and culture—has its own temporal rules, procedures, and perspectives. At the individual level, it is labeled "self-time" or "personal time," which is time as it appears immediately in the experience of the individual. Self-time is not homogeneous—rather it is spatial time that manipulates events in time in our memories. Thus each person's sense of self-time is unique and has significant effects on temporal perception and interaction with others (Lewis and Weigert 1981, p. 436).

When two or more individuals are interacting directly, a different time frame, namely "interaction time," is used. The rules and procedures of interaction time are socially determined and greatly influenced by cultural conditioning. For example, Levine (1987) outlined nine rules of waiting and interaction and considers waiting to be a power game played by two or more individuals.

When groups are formed or organized, part of the organizing process concerns rules and procedures related to temporal aspects, i.e., when the group will meet, what hours a firm will operate, etc. This is known as "organizational time." The temporal rules and practices are usually more rigid and inflexible in organizational time. Organizational time, like *tiempo americano*, generally expects everything to adhere to strict schedules and timetables. For example, if a bank posts its hours as 9:00 A.M. to 1:00 P.M., it is expected to open on the dot of 9:00, not 9:05 or 9:10.

The hours a firm is open for business and the expected work schedule for employees and executives may vary considerably across regions and cultures. The practice of using breakfast, lunch, and dinner meetings for conducting business, for instance, is more prevalent on the East Coast of the United States. One former West Coast executive suggested that those on the East Coast have little reverence for sleep or family meals (Rigdon

1991). The hours of retail operations also vary among cultures. Many retail stores and services still close for a midday siesta in Latin American countries, and limited weekend hours are common in many cultures. For example, in Denmark most retailers close at midday on Saturday and are closed all day Sunday. Very few stores have evening hours throughout all of Scandinavia.

Firms entering a foreign market must consider all three time forms. For example, in a service encounter, all three come into play. The organization delivering the service is operating on the rules of organizational time; the individual consumer is operating on the basis of self-time; and when the consumer interacts with the person representing the organization, they are operating on interaction time. Because the perspective of time is different for these three time classifications, the successful delivery of service must recognize and accommodate these differences.

FRAMEWORK FOR ASSESSING SOCIAL TIME AND MARKETING PROGRAM IMPLICATIONS

A social time system has several dimensions, all of which may be relevant to a venture. A framework for assessing a social time system has been proposed by Venkatesan and Anderson (1985a and 1985b) and Hornik (1990). This framework, based on a conceptual model presented by Lauer (1981), consists of (1) temporal pattern, (2) temporal orientation and perspective, and (3) temporal perception.

The framework is also useful in assessing some possible implications for elements of a marketing program. A complete listing of all possible implications would be extensive and some may relate to only one or two particular marketing offerings, but some important, more general implications are outlined in Table 9-1. The rows represent the major dimensions and elements of a social time system. The columns address different elements of a firm's marketing program that may be affected by temporality.

TEMPORAL PATTERN

Temporal pattern refers to the temporal aspects of behavior within a society and includes five elements: (1) periodicity, (2) tempo, (3) timing, (4) duration, and (5) sequence—all of which should be of interest to firms in planning their marketing efforts.

Information on the first element of temporal pattern, *periodicity*, details the frequency or regularity of specified activities. For example, sup-

TABLE 9-1   TEMPORAL DIMENSIONS AND SELECTED MARKETING
PROGRAM IMPLICATIONS

Consumer Temporal Dimensions	Product/Service	Price	Promotion	Distribution
Temporal pattern				
Periodicity	Frequency of use	Cumulative discounts	Choice of media	Scheduling of capacity
Tempo	Pace of product usage	—	Pace of advertisement	Stocking levels Distribution outlet types
Timing	When product is consumed or purchased	Demand-oriented pricing to even demand	Scheduling of promotion	Stocking patterns
Duration	Time spent consuming or purchasing product	Discounts	Media choices	Packaging
Sequence	Order of use among other activities and associated activities	Price bundling and discounts for advanced purchase	Demonstrate use in sequence	Order policies
Temporal orientation				
Past	Resistance to "new" products	—	Nostalgia appeal	—
Present	Want immediate benefits	Low monthly payments	Stress immediate benefits	Stocking
Future	Futuristic styling	Cash discounts	Stress future benefits	Advanced ordering
Selected temporal/perceptions				
Time pressure	Time saving goods	Premium price for speed	Save time appeal	Home/office delivery 24-hour ordering
Much leisure time	Time using goods	Discounts	Enjoyment appeal	Choice of retail outlets and locations

pose a marketer of shampoo learns that in one culture women wash their hair daily, whereas in another culture, women wash their hair monthly. The firm may be more successful if it makes modifications in its basic formula as well as in its advertising message. Or learning the frequency and regularity of engaging in various health care activities may be of relevance to a supplier of health care supplies and equipment.

2) *Tempo*, the second element, is concerned with the pace of life. Based on the accuracy of bank clocks, walking speed, and speed of service in post offices, Levine and Wolff (1985) ranked the pace of life in six countries. On all three factors examined, Japan ranked number one. The United States ranked second in accuracy of clock and post office speed, but was third in walking speed. The U.S. tempo was followed by England, Italy, Taiwan, and Indonesia. This study was prompted by an informal survey that found "Brazilian students defined 'being late' as anything over 33 minutes, while American students considered 19 minutes to be late" (Levine and Wolff as cited in Harrell 1986, p. 459).

The tempo of a culture, for the most part, falls within a certain range, and a pace that is either too fast or too slow may be evaluated as negative. This is particularly true in service encounters where a fast pace may be interpreted as "being rushed" and not being given appropriate consideration. This type of negative evaluation has been made about encounters with health care providers and restaurant personnel. On the other end of the spectrum, a slow pace may also lead to dissatisfaction; being kept waiting when one is in a hurry has caused many Americans to become extremely agitated when traveling in foreign cultures as well as when visiting parts of the United States that operate at a slower pace.

3) *Timing* concerns when individuals are most likely to engage in an activity. For example, in many cultures people have a strong preference for the time, day, or date for engaging in certain activities. Knowing when consumers are likely to eat a sandwich for a meal is useful information for any fast food provider, just as knowing when people are most likely to engage in purchasing and using certain products would be of interest to others. Being able to anticipate the timing of demand throughout the day, week, and month would help in better scheduling of services and inventory.

4) Knowing how people allocate and spend their time among various activities includes information on *duration*. For example, learning how much leisure time people have is important to the marketers of a variety of "time using" goods and services. On the other hand, marketers of "time saving" goods and services will be more successful in cultures where there is a perception of limited time and a feeling of time pressure. Knowing the expected and acceptable duration for activities and events is another aspect that may be of major interest to firms. For example, learning the usual

duration of a given type of meal or festivity may help a restaurant plan its seating and scheduling.

Sequence, or ordering, is closely related to planning. It is based on the idea that consumers have a preferred order for performing a series of activities. For example, in some cultures people wash their hands before eating, whereas in other cultures people wash their hands after eating. This observation is useful to international airlines in providing passengers with hot towels before and after serving meals. Also, related to this element of sequence is the notion of making reservations or appointments. In the North American culture, for example, most people make appointments with providers of medical services, but this practice is not common across all cultures. In some cultures, future planning is more general, lacking the specificity associated with making advanced reservations or appointments at designated times.

The five elements of temporal patterns are the basic dimensions of how time is lived by a group of people. It appears that while the emphasis may vary, almost all firms and organizations would benefit from temporal pattern information with respect to their own marketing efforts.

Temporal Orientation and Perspective

An awareness of past, present, and future is held by all individuals. J. T. Fraser states ". . . mature people, in their waking state, are aware of a 'now' or 'present' with respect to which they recognize a 'future' and a 'past'" (Fraser 1988). However, the *temporal orientation* of a culture may be so strongly tied to the present, as was the case with the Navajo view of time, that for all practical purposes, ". . . the only real time . . . is that which is here and now" (Lauer 1981, p. 36). The absence of a perceived reality in the future would make planning for or anticipating rewards in a future time unnecessary. Therefore, in such a culture any product or service that had as its major benefit a payoff or reward in the future would probably fail.

Temporal perspective—the view people have of the past, present, and future—may help to explain the reason for a particular temporal orientation as well as help to explain other temporal related behaviors. Cultures that have a past orientation, for example, may hold this orientation because of the perspective that in the past the nation was "great, powerful, etc.," whereas now there are only corruption and problems.

The presence of a dominant past orientation may manifest itself in a rejection of or resistance to "new," "improved," "modern" appeals, designs, and approaches. An adherence to the traditional way of solving consumer problems may make it difficult for firms offering new approaches and new technology to gain consumer acceptance.

TEMPORAL PERCEPTIONS

Investigation of the third component of a social time system—*temporal perception*—can provide useful information on the way people think and feel about time. An excellent example that helps to illustrate the importance of this type of information is Polaroid's experiences when it initially attempted to penetrate the French camera market (Buzzell and Lecocq 1977). Several issues emerge when the actions of Polaroid are analyzed in retrospect. However, one major impediment to the adoption of the "instant developing" camera was the low level of importance French consumers placed on speed in this situation. At that time (1960s), French consumers were more concerned with the quality of photographs than with how fast they could see a developed picture.

Another more recent example was reported by *The New York Times* news service. Marketers of products such as microwave ovens, VCRs, and automatic teller machines had concluded that because older Americans didn't buy/use these products, this segment of the population was resistant to new technology. However, a study by Daniel Yankelovich, Inc. found that there was no resistance to new technology; the products were marketed as "time saving," which is of little value to most retired Americans. In fact, the study found that less than a third of older Americans say they are looking for new ways to save time. Most are looking for things with which to fill or use their time, such as hobbies, cooking, or going to the store. The assumption that all consumers desire to save time or are a potential market for time saving goods and services can lead to incorrect decisions about target markets and promotional mix decisions.

Stalk and Hout (1990) of the Boston Consulting Group view time as a "strategic weapon" that firms can use to their competitive advantage. While it is accepted that time can be used to a firm's advantage, strategies should not be based solely on the American view of time because all consumers do not look for a trade-off between time and money. Therefore, before adopting a time-based strategy, it is to a firm's advantage to determine a match between the strategy and the social time system of the target market.

Robert Graham (1981) identified three very different perceptions of time that influence many aspects of consumer behavior and economic activity. In addition to the commonly held European and North American perception of time as something which is linear-separable, he identified circular-traditional and procedural-traditional as two alternative perceptions of time. In the circular-traditional view, time is viewed as a circle and follows a cyclical pattern; the past and future are one, a never-ending cycle in which the future will be like or similar to the past. The procedural-traditional time model, however, places time in the background with the activity being the primary focus. Activities take as long as necessary and are followed by other activities; time itself does not play a prominent role.

Temporal perception may include many dimensions in addition to the basic time models presented. Numerous studies of time have found that temporal perceptions, as with any process of perception, are influenced by both internal and external factors.

Social Time System Study of Three Countries

A study of social time systems was designed to collect information on temporal patterns, temporal orientation and perspectives, and temporal perceptions in three countries. The countries selected include the United States, Mexico, and New Zealand, which appear to have many cultural differences as well as similarities.

Countries and Cultures Studied

The choice of countries studied was greatly influenced by the backgrounds and experiences of the researchers, for whom the mainstream U.S. social time system was the most prominent. The choice of the United States as a base with which to compare and contrast other cultures was both practical and relevant for U.S.-dominant marketers.

United States   The United States is composed of many different groupings, and 77 percent of Americans are from an Anglo-European cultural base. The north central region of the United States was the area of the United States that was included in the reported research. The area is somewhat homogeneous in values and beliefs; it includes relatively representative employment in agriculture, manufacturing, and service industries.

As compared with the other countries studied, life expectancy in the United States is the longest, approximately 71 years for males and 78 for females. And while most adults are in the labor force, the vast majority of the people do not work after the age of 60.

The sampling frame used for the United States was a panel of households maintained by a midwestern university. From this panel, 160 households were randomly selected. This sample was supplemented by responses from 75 university students enrolled in graduate and undergraduate business classes.

Mexico   The location of Mexico, which shares a border with the United States, might lead people to think that the cultures are similar. However, it is Spanish speaking (90 percent), Latin American, and Roman Catholic (96 percent), and its cultural heritage is vastly different from that of the United States. Life expectancy in Mexico averages about 10 years less than in the United States. Men have a life expectancy of 61 years and women can expect to live to the age of 66.

Data on economic activity show that a relatively high percentage of individuals work throughout their entire lives. As the country moves toward a more industrial-based society, a growing middle class composed of small business owners, managers, and professionals is developing. Education is seen as the key to literacy and upward social mobility for many residents. It is from this educated, expanding middle class that the majority of respondents for this study was drawn.

The actual respondents were selected from individuals residing in a major urban area in eastern Mexico. The city of Mérida is approximately the same size and has many characteristics in common with the urban areas selected in the other countries. The 360 respondents represented a cross section of households in different parts of the city and had a variety of demographic profiles. Several students who attend the major state-supported University were also included in the sample.

New Zealand   Located on the other side of the world are the two principal islands of the Dominion of New Zealand. The 3.5 million inhabitants are of mostly English and northern European heritage. The indigenous Maori comprise about 12 percent of the population. Life expectancy in New Zealand is approximately the same as for residents of the United States; 71 for males and 77 for females. A former British colony, New Zealand became fully independent in 1947, and English is the official language.

New Zealand has a diversified industrial and commercial base. More than 80 percent of the population lives in urban areas, and it is from the urban area of Christchurch that the sample for this study was drawn. The 163 New Zealand respondents were a quota sample designed to represent a cross section of the 300,000 urban residents in Christchurch. Table 9-2 shows selected demographic characteristics of the three subsamples.

Discussion and Analysis of Findings

Temporal Patterns

Temporal patterns were examined with respect to consumer transactions, primarily in the service sector. The research focused on service transactions because in these encounters the customer must interact with the service provider and, therefore, time and time use were thought to be salient.

The findings confirmed that there are differences in temporal patterns of consumers across the three cultures. For example, in the periodicity or frequency of engaging in transactions, it was found that consumers from the United States use laundry/dry cleaning services with the greatest frequency, whereas Mexican consumers used them least frequently. This ordering of service transaction patterns, however, was different when other service transactions were examined (see Table 9-3).

TABLE 9-2 CHARACTERISTICS OF SAMPLE RESPONDENTS

Characteristic	United States	Mexico	New Zealand
Gender			
Male	46.4%	52.1%	52.5%
Female	53.6	47.9	47.5
Marital status			
Married	60.7	40.7	46.6
Single	24.3	54.2	47.8
Divorced	5.9	2.8	1.9
Separated	.8	.6	3.1
Widowed	8.4	1.7	.6
Educational level			
Grade school or less	2.4	14.5	2.0
Some high school	3.6	3.5	12.4
High school graduate	16.3	13.3	14.4
Some college	48.4	29.4	29.9
College graduate	15.4	25.1	10.3
Some post graduate work	14.0	14.1	30.9
Employment			
Employed	58.6	67.5	69.1
Not employed	41.4	32.5	30.9
Age			
Under 20	15.3	15.9	11.7
21–30	35.3	34.6	44.7
31–40	18.3	18.4	16.2
41–50	10.6	10.6	9.5
51–60	7.7	15.6	11.1
Over 60	12.7	4.7	6.7

New Zealanders appear to be the most frequent users of banking services. Almost three-quarters of the New Zealand respondents indicated they go to a bank on a weekly or more frequent basis. U.S. consumers tend to use banking services about every week or two, and Mexican usage of banking services is less frequent. In fact, almost one-third of the Mexicans use a bank less than once a year. But, whereas the Mexicans are not frequent users of banking services, they are the most frequent users of personal and health care services. More than 75 percent of the Mexicans studied visit a medical doctor at least once a year, and many go on a weekly or semiweekly schedule. In health care, it is U.S. consumers who indicated the least frequent visits. More than one-quarter of the U.S. consumers said they visit a medical doctor only about once a year; however, dental care visits are likely to be semiannual. In New Zealand, it appears that most consumers go to the dentist once a year.

The duration of service transactions also varies among the three countries. Mexicans appear to spend the most time in banking and medical service transactions. New Zealanders, however, appear to spend the least time engaging in these transactions. For New Zealanders, the average

TABLE 9-3   FREQUENCY OF USE OF SELECTED SERVICES

	Laundry/Dry Cleaner*			Banking*			Dentist*		
	U.S.	Mex.	N.Z.	U.S.	Mex.	N.Z.	U.S.	Mex.	N.Z.
Once a week or more	6.2%	5.3%	1.8%	62.0%	11.9%	74.9%	— %	1.7%	— %
About every 1–2 weeks	3.7	3.3	3.7	20.2	16.9	15.3	—	.8	—
About every 3–4 weeks	10.3	2.8	9.2	9.5	13.0	4.3	—	1.7	—
About every 1–3 months	16.9	2.8	12.3	5.4	16.1	3.1	2.9	7.8	1.2
About every 4–6 months	20.7	0.3	16.6	1.7	5.0	1.2	44.6	18.3	16.0
At least once a year	15.7	3.0	15.3	.4	5.8	—	30.2	32.4	45.4
Less than once a year	26.4	82.5	41.1	.8	31.3	1.2	22.3	37.4	37.4

*Chi square significance 0.000.

visit to a medical doctor takes just under one-half hour, whereas both U.S. and Mexican consumers spend approximately one hour when visiting a medical doctor. The waiting time at services also varies, with New Zealanders waiting the least amount of time and Mexicans waiting the longest. Table 9-4 compares the duration of selected services in average (mean) minutes.

It was interesting to find that not only did Mexicans indicate the longest waiting times for services and consider the long waiting times to be "reasonable," they also indicated the highest level of annoyance at being forced to wait. So just because Mexicans may expect to wait for service does not mean that they are happy about it. And further, significantly more Mexicans said they were likely to switch service providers if they were kept waiting for an unreasonable time period. It was not surprising to find that New Zealanders, who wait the shortest times, were also the least annoyed about waiting.

The regularity of timing of when people are likely to engage in an activity also proved to be different among the three countries. For example, New Zealanders tend to engage in banking activities with little regularity of day, date, or time of day. However, the American pattern of regularity proved itself in personal care service. U.S. consumers are more likely to go to personal care providers on the same day and time on each visit. This may indicate the use of standing appointments.

In relation to sequence, Americans are more likely to make appointments for most services, with the exception of banking. Only the Mexicans showed a tendency to make appointments for banking activities; however, Mexicans were unlikely to make appointments with health care providers. In many cases, health care providers are visited only when one is ill—and since one does not know when this will occur, the idea of making appointments with physicians did not seem necessary or appropriate.

TABLE 9-4 AVERAGE DURATION OF SELECTED SERVICE TRANSACTIONS	Country Mean (Minutes)				
Service	United States	Mexico	New Zealand	F Ratio	F Prob.
Laundry/dry cleaner	13.48	20.81	6.59	8.12	.0004
Barber/beauty shop	57.59	70.06	45.35	13.16	.0000
Bank	12.36	47.75	10.49	89.63	.0000
Dentist	49.51	71.69	30.22	39.30	.0000
Doctor	59.22	72.96	30.33	50.85	.0000

TEMPORAL ORIENTATION AND PERSPECTIVE

Differences were found among the three cultures in temporal orientation and perspective. Americans and New Zealanders demonstrated more similarities than differences in their orientations. However, New Zealanders were most optimistic about the future. All respondents, regardless of culture, thought the best time in their individual lives was the "present," which contrasted with their perception of what they believed to be true for others. Both Mexicans and New Zealanders believe that most people prefer the "past," even though they themselves prefer the present.

Both the Americans and New Zealanders were found to fantasize about the past, and this was particularly apparent in the preferred temporal settings of stories, books, movies, etc. The Mexicans, on the other hand, showed some preference for the present and future time settings for stories and movies.

Mexicans daydream about the present, unlike the U.S. and New Zealand respondents who are more likely to daydream about the future. The Mexican pattern of present → future → past held for story and movie preferences, and this pattern was consistent with the perspective of when things in general were/are/will be "best."

Table 9-5 shows findings on selected aspects of temporal orientation and perspective. The temporal orderings show that of the three groups,

Dimension	Country	Ordering	Pearson value	Signifi- cance	TABLE 9-5 SELECTED TEMPORAL ORIENTATION ORDERINGS
Talk about	U.S.	Present → Past → Future	37.57	.0000	
	Mexico	Present → Past → Future			
	N.Z.	Present → Past → Future			
Story preference	U.S.	Past → Present → Future	122.69	.0000	
	Mexico	Present → Future → Past			
	N.Z.	Past → Present → Future			
Daydream	U.S.	Future → Past → Present	68.00	.0000	
	Mexico	Present → Future → Past			
	N.Z.	Future → Past → Present			
Best time in life	U.S.	Present → Future → Past	23.74	.0001	
	Mexico	Present → Past → Future			
	N.Z.	Present → Future → Past			

Mexicans are more likely to talk about the past, which is one indicator of orientation. As in the findings on temporal patterns, the overall orientation and perspectives of Mexicans show a pattern that is unique and significantly different from the U.S. and New Zealand pattern.

TEMPORAL PERCEPTIONS

Differences among the countries were found on a vast majority of the temporal perceptions examined; however, these differences were not always in the direction anticipated. For example, Mexicans appear to engage in the most scheduling of activities. They are very concerned with managing their time and see managing one's time as an important key to success. It was the Mexican respondents who were also most likely to want to know the duration and ending time of any activity before committing themselves. They also like to stay with a task until it is finished, regardless of how long it takes. The Mexicans were less likely to spend time thinking about the past or the future, suggesting a very present-oriented existence.

While these perceptions may not be how many non-Mexicans would think of the Mexicans, these findings are not surprising when one considers the effort and time it takes to accomplish even small tasks in this culture. For example, for many Mexicans grocery shopping involves going to a meat market early in the morning, going to another location for fruits and vegetables, and finally going to a bakery. This process requires the Mexican housewife to schedule her activities; if she doesn't she may arrive too late to get meat or fresh produce. Many other activities, such as arranging trucking or other types of services, also require personal presence. For many people in the area of the study, transportation meant walking or riding on a crowded bus. Waiting is a part of most service encounters, and therefore it takes a considerable amount of scheduling and planning to accomplish the essential tasks of living.

The New Zealanders appear to feel the greatest amount of time pressure. They are most likely to feel that they never have enough time to do the things they want, and they also feel they have little control over their time. It is the New Zealanders who are more likely to see time as a straight line and treat it as a scarce resource. They exhibited the greatest frustration when they were unable to complete all they wanted in a given day (see Table 9-6).

Salient dimensions of the U.S. social time system that surfaced tended to be somewhat of a surprise. For example, it is the U.S. respondents who were most likely to agree that "What I don't get done today, I can always do tomorrow"—a phrase that is more likely to be associated with a Latin American culture. Other interesting aspects of the U.S. perceptions include the presence of a task orientation in which one may lose track of time. The U.S. respondents were also the people who were most bothered by "interruptions" to their planned routine and would like the pace of their lives to be a bit slower. One expected finding was that of the three cultures studied, Americans were most likely to consider themselves to be "very punctual."

TABLE 9-6   SELECTED TEMPORAL PERCEPTIONS AMONG CULTURES

Perception	Country Means			F Ratio	F Prob.
	U.S.	Mex.	N.Z.		
Never enough time to do the things I enjoy.	2.41	3.76	2.27	185.40	.0000
Interruptions to planned routine bother me.	2.75	2.16	2.633	30.84	.0000
People should not waste their time.	2.37	1.89	2.43	30.61	.0000
I plan each and every day.	3.25	2.86	3.19	11.11	.0000
Managing one's time is important to success.	2.05	1.76	2.07	13.3206	.0000
I always schedule shopping activities.	2.99	2.23	2.80	51.74	.0000
Always want to know how long task will take.	2.93	2.19	2.76	54.69	.0000
Rarely look at clock or watch.	3.67	3.14	3.78	27.71	.0000
I am a very punctual person.	2.21	2.48	2.28	5.91	.0028
Feel frustrated if don't complete all activities.	2.89	2.77	2.48	7.08	.0009
Feel great amount of time pressure.	2.92	3.00	2.75	3.07	.0472
Like to stay with task until completed.	2.49	2.25	2.62	11.88	.0000
People used to have more time than today.	2.96	2.70	3.06	7.53	.0006
I think of time as a straight line.	3.05	2.91	2.78	3.47	.0317
What's not done today, I can always do tomorrow.	2.45	2.69	2.57	4.31	.0137
Feel I have little control over time.	2.59	2.91	2.55	11.06	.0000
Try to group activities to save time.	2.38	2.80	2.28	22.27	.0000
Treat time as scarce resource.	2.82	2.93	2.66	4.11	.0169
Would like pace of my life to be slower.	2.75	3.07	3.11	8.59	.0002

Note: 1 = strongly agree; 5 = strongly disagree.

Summary and Conclusion

The studies conducted in these three countries demonstrate the existence of three very different social time systems. It was found that people in different cultures exhibit different temporal patterns, temporal orientations and perspectives, and temporal perceptions. *Assuming* one understands these dimensions of a social time system in another culture, without an assessment, may lead to incorrect assessments regarding wants, needs, and desires. This, in turn, can lead a firm to ignore local temporal differences and use a more standardized approach in marketing programs. An analysis of the social time system as part of a cultural assessment may help a firm to identify temporal dimensions of consumers that will require a localized adaptation of marketing plans to assure that the marketing effort will blend with the cultural environment.

As interactions among cultures increase through global media, other communication networks, diplomacy, trade, and tourism, there appears to be some convergence in the different social time systems. But appearances can be deceptive. As the reported study shows, even when two countries appear to have a similar cultural heritage and language, such as the United States and New Zealand, very different temporal patterns emerge. The mere fact that significant cultural differences were found on three-quarters of the temporal elements examined in the reported study makes it apparent that convergence is not complete.

While many elements of a social time system do not have a direct bearing on an individual organization's marketing efforts, consideration of how temporal elements will influence consumer behavior may lead a firm to include selected temporal elements in all cultural assessment studies. The knowledge gained may lead to local adaptations in marketing efforts that can tip the balance in favor of success.

References

Buzzell, R. D., and J.-L. Lecocq (1977). "Polaroid France (S.A.)," in S. H. Star, N. J. Davis, C. H. Lovelock, and B. P. Shapiro, *Problems in Marketing*, 5th Ed. New York: McGraw-Hill. 191–213.

Cateora, P. R. (1987). *International Marketing*, 6th Ed. Homewood, IL: Irwin.

Fraser, J. T. (1988). *Time: The Familiar Stranger.* Redmond, WA: Tempus Books of Microsoft Press.

Graham, R. J. (1981). "The Role of Perception of Time in Consumer Research," *Journal of Consumer Research*, 7(4), 335–342.

Gronmo, S. (1989). "Concepts of Time: Some Implications for Consumer

Research," in T. Srull (ed.), *Advances in Consumer Research,* vol. 16, Provo, UT: Association for Consumer Research.

Hall, E. T. (1960). "The Silent Language in Overseas Business," *Harvard Business Review,* May–June, 87–96.

Harrell, G. D. (1986). *Consumer Behavior.* Orlando, FL: Harcourt Brace Jovanovich, Inc.

Henry, J. (1965). "White People's Time—Colored People's Time," *Trans-Action,* 2, 31–34.

Hornik, J. (1990). "Contextual Issues in Time Perception and Orientation," Paper presented at the ACR Conference, New York, October, 5–7.

Horton, J. (1972). "Time and Cool People," in T. Kochman, ed., *Rappin' and Stylin' Out,* Urbana: University of Illinois Press, 19–31.

Iverson, S. (1991). "Using Language and Culture to Your Business Advantage," *Corporate Report: Wisconsin* (August), 8–9.

Lauer, R. H. (1981). *Temporal Man: The Meaning and Uses of Social Time.* New York: Praeger Press.

Levine, R. (1987). "Waiting Is a Power Game," *Psychology Today* (April), 25–33.

Levine, R. (1988). "The Pace of Life Across Cultures," in J. E. McGrath (ed.), *The Social Psychology of Time: New Perspectives.* Newbury Park, CA: Sage Publications.

Levine, R., and E. Wolff (1985). "Social Time: The Heartbeat of Culture," *Psychology Today* (March), 35.

Lewis, J. D., and A. J. Weigert (1981). "The Structures and Meanings of Social Time," *Social Forces,* 60(2) (December), 432–462.

Rigdon, J. E. (1991). "Managers Who Switch Coasts Must Adapt to Different Approaches to Use of Time," *Wall Street Journal,* August 14.

Stalk, G. Jr., and T. M. Hout (1990). *Competing Against Time.* New York: The Free Press.

Venkatesan, M., and B. B. Anderson (1985a). "Time and Consumer Behavior: A Historical Perspective," in Chin Tiong Tan and J. N. Sheth (eds.), *Historical Perspective in Consumer Research: National and International Perspectives.* Provo, UT: Association for Consumer Research.

——— (1985b). "Time Budgets and Consumer Services," in T. Bloch, G. D. Upah, and V. A. Zeithaml (eds.), *Services Marketing in a Changing Environment.* Chicago: American Marketing Association.

Wall Street Journal (1991). "Beating the Clock," a series. August 5–14.

Wertsch, J. V., ed. (1985). *Culture, Communication and Cognition.* New York: Cambridge University Press, 2.

Zerubavel, E. (1982). "The Standardization of Time: A Sociohistorical Perspective," *American Journal of Sociology,* 88(1), 1–23.

CHAPTER 10

COUNTRY-OF-ORIGIN ISSUES

Murray A. Young

Paul L. Sauer

H. Rao Unnava

Increasing domestic competition and saturated local markets are forcing several companies to consider marketing their products in foreign countries. Political changes taking place in the world, such as the triumph of capitalism over communism in Eastern Europe and the single market initiative of 1992 in Western Europe, are contributing to the necessity of and urgency for companies to become global in their perspective. As companies eagerly expand outward and attempt to sell their products overseas, their success depends on the acceptance of those goods by consumers in different countries. Even though some marketers would prefer that consumers make their choices based on objective product attributes, evidence indicates that the country-of-origin of the product has a significant effect on people's purchases (Johansson, Douglas, and Nonaka 1985; Han and Terpstra 1988; Hong and Wyer 1989; Thorelli, Lim, and Ye 1989; Eroglu and Machleit 1989). The objective of this chapter is to examine how consumers appear to be affected by country-of-origin information about a product. Specifically, we outline the psychological mechanisms that may explain how country-of-origin information is processed and used by consumers as they evaluate various products. Such an understanding should help global marketers to design better communications that would take advantage of positive country stereotypes and avoid the problems that emerge from negative country stereotypes.

PRIOR RESEARCH ON COUNTRY-OF-ORIGIN EFFECTS

There is now a substantial amount of evidence to indicate that consumers are indeed swayed by country-of-origin information as they make their evaluations of products. Bilkey and Nes (1982), in an excellent review of the literature pertaining to country-of-origin effects, discuss the problems faced by a West German manufacturer whose customers were reluctant to buy products assembled in Brazil. Similarly, White and Cundiff (1978) and Khanna (1986) describe the prevalence of country-of-origin effects in industrial buying situations. For example, in Khanna's (1986) study, it was found that Indian manufacturers suffered from the negative stereotypes in the minds of other Asian buyers. Several new buyers were found to shy away from Indian sellers based on the country-of-origin of the products.

Despite more than twenty years of research in this area, it appears that very few generalizations can be made about country-of-origin effects beyond the understanding that such effects exist. A significant source of this confusion is the diversity in this stream of research that seems to have progressed without an agenda and without much commonality between research designs and procedures (Bilkey and Nes 1982; Ozsomer and Cavusgil 1991). The result is a body of literature with the following attributes.

USE OF CUE CHARACTERISTICS

SINGLE-CUE PARADIGM   Respondents are given only information concerning the country-of-origin (e.g., Nagashima 1970; Schooler 1965; Wang and Lamb 1980). In such an informationally impoverished environment, presenting only the country-of-origin cue may lead subjects to establish a stronger connection between country-of-origin and the dependent measure, such as an attitude than would occur in a more realistic purchase setting. The results obtained in these studies might exaggerate the effect compared with those observed in more realistic and informationally enriched multiple-cue environments. Asking subjects to respond to a single cue has the potential of generating results caused more by demand artifacts than by the treatment itself (Monroe and Krishnan 1985).

MULTIPLE-CUE PARADIGM   Criticism of early country-of-origin research focused on the use of the country-of-origin as the sole treatment variable. Later research has employed country-of-origin in a multiple-cue environment. Interactions with both extrinsic (e.g., Cordell 1991; Wall, Liefeld, and Heslop 1991) and intrinsic (e.g., Hong and Wyer 1989, 1990) product cues have been documented.

Within the multiple-cue environment, increasing attention has been given to more complex relationships and the derivation of a theoretically appealing framework for describing country-of-origin effects. One such effort is the study of country-of-origin effects on price elasticity (Cordell 1991; Schooler and Wildt 1968). Another stream involves an attempt to apply a more extensive theoretical structure to the country-of-origin effect. Hong and Wyer (1989, 1990), Ozsomer and Cavusgil (1991), and

Obermiller and Spangenberg (1988) have proposed different possible frameworks derived from attitude theories. Of the three sets of authors, only Hong and Wyer (1989, 1990) empirically tested their proposed models.

USE OF NONVALIDATED MEASUREMENT INSTRUMENTS   Most studies have not used validated scales to measure dependent variables. Furthermore, for the most part, the dependent variables used in various studies have ranged from beliefs to choice, in part because little attention has been paid to theoretical structure. This diversity renders generalization across studies difficult. Exceptions include Erickson et al. (1984) and Johansson et al. (1985), where cognitive structure theory (Fishbein and Ajzen 1975) was used to develop both the process and measurement properties.

LACK OF DEFINITIONAL CLARITY   Only recently have efforts begun to be made in the literature to clarify what the term *country-of-origin* actually means to a consumer (Han and Terpstra 1988, Ozsomer and Cavusgil 1991). Specifically, does country-of-origin imply the country where the product was designed or the country where the product was assembled? Complex products are more likely to be bi- or multinational in origin, where *origin* refers to all countries that contribute to the design, manufacture, and sale of a product. Multinational origin raises concerns in consumers' minds about the quality and value of product design and assembly related factors.

FINDINGS WITH LITTLE GENERALIZABILITY   As Ozsomer and Cavusgil (1991) point out, country-of-origin effects have been found to be *product dimension-specific* (Erickson, Johansson, and Chao 1984; Han and Terpstra 1988; Johansson, Douglas, and Nonaka 1985; Kaynak and Cavusgil 1983), but the degree to which individual dimensions (e.g., *economy, serviceability,* and *workmanship*) are subject to effects varies. Further, different country cues are not uniform in effect size across product dimensions: Serviceability and workmanship are more sensitive to country-of-origin effects than brand name cues.

VARIABLE HALO EFFECTS   Certain countries seem to have positive or negative quality associations. For example, consumers in several North American and European countries seem to have positive attitudes toward Japanese products (Han and Terpstra 1988; Papadopoulos, Heslop, and Beracs 1990; Darling and Wood 1989; Wall and Heslop 1986). But products from other countries do not enjoy such favorable stereotyping, and there may be little an individual producer can do to offset or alleviate such bias. The seemingly piecemeal and sometimes contradictory findings of

prior work raise the question as to just how country-of-origin effects occur. The next section addresses this question by proposing an alternative
process based on existing theory.

Psychological Processes Behind the Country-of-Origin Effect

We propose that the country-of-origin information about a product
should affect a consumer's evaluation of the product in one of three ways:

1. By affecting attitudes directly through the halo process. This is the
    affect transfer process.
2. By affecting a consumer's beliefs about the product's attributes,
    which then affect attitudes and purchase intentions. This is called
    the cognitive mediation process.
3. By affecting the purchase intention directly.

Affect Transfer Process

Though consumers may react positively to a product's features, they may
lower their evaluation if it originates from a country that is negatively
evaluated by them. This affective theory holds that the feelings consumers
have about the country of the product's origin are transferred directly to
their overall evaluation of the product. That is, consumers' beliefs about
the product's attributes do not change because of the country-of-origin
information; only their overall product evaluations are affected. Figure 10-1 depicts this type of an effect of country-of-origin information on
consumers' evaluations of products.

This is a type of "mere exposure effect" mechanism (Obermiller
1985, Zajonc and Markus 1985) in which the name of the country is the
cue that triggers positive or negative feelings. This differs from Han's
(1989) summary construct model in that the country-of-origin cue is not
modeled as mediating the effect of beliefs on attitude, but rather as an
alternative construct to attribute beliefs that effect a change in attitude
toward the product. The country name acts as a triggering cue which,
when encountered, creates positive or negative affect without the person
recalling the specific cognitive beliefs which at one time created this negative or positive attitude. These latent feelings that are generalized affective
reactions to a country endure beyond the time when the underlying beliefs
about the product are recallable or perhaps even recognizable. These attitudes, driven by country-specific feelings, are more stable than attribute

information which has an impact on product beliefs and hence may override the belief effect on attitude.

COGNITIVE MEDIATION PROCESS

Other researchers have argued that the effect of country-of-origin information on attitudes is not due to "affect transfer" as just described but is
cognitively mediated (Erickson, Johansson, and Chao 1984; Johansson,
Douglas, and Nonaka 1985; Han 1989; Hong and Toner 1988; Hong and
Wyer 1989, 1990; Obermiller and Spangenberg 1988). According to the
cognitive mediation argument, beliefs about a product's features or attri-

FIGURE 10-1
AFFECT TRANSFER
PROCESS

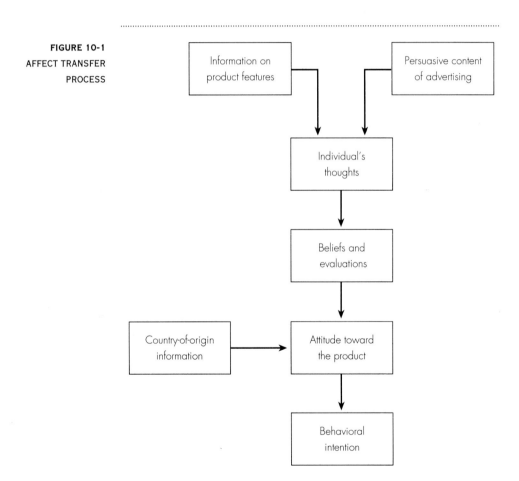

butes are directly affected by the product's country-of-origin information. These affected beliefs mediate changes in attitudes toward the product. Changes in product attribute beliefs occur when consumers encode information about a product (Greenwald 1968) in response to the content of advertisements concerning the product. Figure 10-2 depicts this process suggested by the cognitive mediation process.

Support for this process comes from recent studies. Erickson et al. (1984), using measures of beliefs about and attitudes toward automobiles made in different countries, found that the country-of-origin effect on attitudes was mediated by country-of-origin effects on subjects' beliefs about the various brand attributes. Similarly Han (1989) found that the

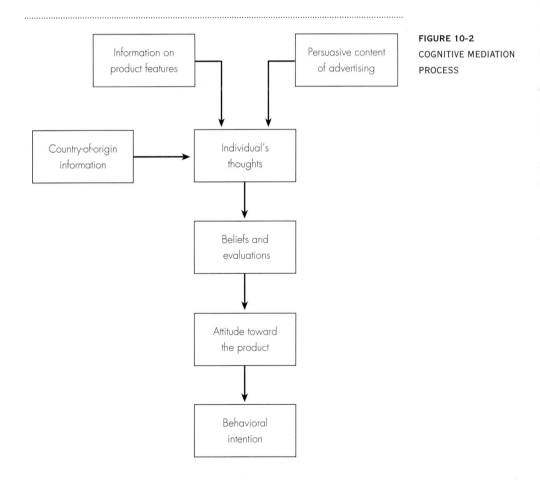

FIGURE 10-2

COGNITIVE MEDIATION PROCESS

cognitive mediation process held for both automobiles and television sets, but that the effect applied to Korean and U.S. products—not Japanese products.

A critical issue is whether this is an advertisement-specific halo effect that applies only to attributes contained in a target advertisement for a brand or whether it is a more global halo effect in which inferential beliefs about attributes not specifically addressed in the ad would be affected by the country-of-origin cue. Han's (1989) study does not test this halo effect distinction as telephone interviews were used and no treatment advertisements were employed.

Another concern with both the Han (1989) and Erickson et al. (1984) studies is the use of existing brands. Specifically, when existing brands are used in research, confounds related to experience with and prior knowledge about the brands can affect the results. Han (1989) attempts to resolve this by using ownership, past and present, to assess familiarity. Erickson et al. (1984), on the other hand, incorporated two familiarity measures. However, in their regression model, Erickson et al. hypothesized an effect of familiarity (or experience) directly on attitudes and not through beliefs (see their discussion on p. 695).

Fishbein and Ajzen (1975), in contrast, argue that experience with an attitude object results in strongly held beliefs about the object. More recent research by Fazio and his colleagues (Fazio 1985; Fazio and Zanna 1981) also supports the claim that information in the form of direct experience results in beliefs that are held more confidently compared to other forms of information. However, because Erickson et al. (1984) did not test for the direct effect of familiarity on beliefs and because Han (1989) used it as a moderating variable that was confounded with country, it is not clear what proportion of the country-of-origin effects they found in their research are attributable to the past experience of subjects. Despite this limitation, both studies are of considerable value because they demonstrate that the country-of-origin impact on attitude was effected through beliefs about the attributes of the product.

Hong and Wyer (1989) propose four models of country-of-origin effects. An important phenomenon incorporated into their modeling effort is the distinction between assimilation and contrast effects. In addition, a positive or negative response may be evoked by concepts activated by exposure to the country cue.

Four hypothetical models are proposed: encoding hypothesis; heuristic hypothesis; primacy-recency (P-R) hypothesis; and cognitive elaboration (CE) hypothesis. Of these four hypotheses, only the cognitive elaboration hypothesis is empirically supported. The CE hypothesis implies that a cognitive process precedes attitude formation. This is supported in results of an earlier study by Johansson, Douglas, and Nonaka (1985) in which country-of-origin beliefs mediated the evaluation process.

In a subsequent study (Hong and Wyer 1990) both a direct and an indirect country-of-origin effect on product evaluation were observed. This was achieved by incorporating a one day time buffer in the presentation of the country and noncountry treatment cues. The direct effect supports a large portion of past research, in which such a direct or main effect of the country cue was observed. The indirect effect involves a moderating effect of the country cue on the effect of other attribute cues on the product evaluation measure. This process is depicted in Figure 10-3.

Further insight into the alternative processes by which country-of-origin information affects attitudes toward and intentions to purchase a product were provided by Sauer, Young, and Unnava (1991). Their results support a cognitive process in which beliefs about ad-derived attributes are affected by country-of-origin cues. Belief effects mediate the effect on attitudes. Halo effects on inferential beliefs are not observed. Though an interaction between countries in the binational test was not significant, a simple main effect was observed which supports separate country-of-design and country-of-assembly effects.

Direct Behavioral Process

A third possible process by which country-of-origin information makes an impact on behavior is through the direct effect on behavior without mediating effects of product attributes or attitudes (Obermiller and Spangenberg 1988). An example of such a process is when an individual holds positive *product attribute* beliefs and a subsequent positive attitude toward a Japanese car but ends up buying an American car because of "buy-American" pressure that stems from his/her reference group. For example,

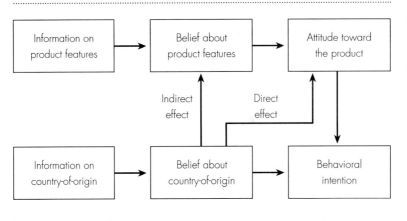

FIGURE 10-3
DIRECT AND INDIRECT
EFFECTS OF COUNTRY-
OF-ORIGIN CUE

peer pressure among unionized blue collar workers who may face loss of jobs from superior, competitive foreign products may override *product attribute* beliefs and attitudes that acknowledge superior Japanese quality automobiles. In this case, the effect of the country-of-origin on behavior is direct and is depicted in Figure 10-4.

It is possible that country-of-origin labels affect consumer response through each of the three processes just described. Han (1989), for example, finds that both his halo model and summary construct model hold for the same product, but which is valid depends on the country from which the product originates.

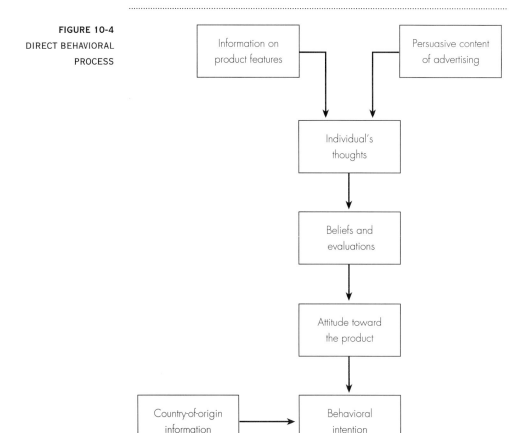

FIGURE 10-4
DIRECT BEHAVIORAL
PROCESS

The Country-of-Origin Effect
and Marketing Strategies

An important question that a marketer faces as s/he expands into a foreign country is how to counter potential biases that consumers may exhibit toward the product based on its country-of-origin. We believe that the strategies used by marketers should be designed according to the type of bias that is exhibited by consumers.

The most idiosyncratic of the three types of effects that we have reviewed is the direct behavior effect where consumers do not buy products from foreign countries because they are foreign. Obviously, the marketer is faced with a consumer who is swayed more by emotion than by reason. This type of bias should be evident against countries that are viewed as foes of the home country, whether political, religious, or ideological. Anecdotal evidence abounds on the resentment French people have toward Americans just because they are Americans (there is evidence for the reverse too!).

Marketers facing such negative bias should resort to image-building tactics. For quite some time, Japan was negatively perceived by Detroit because of all the jobs that were lost as American car manufacturers struggled to compete with Japanese manufacturers. The vivid television depiction of the plight of jobless Americans who were hurt in this competition helped to further the emotional reaction that most Americans already had toward the Japanese people. The positive reaction of Japanese car manufacturers to this situation is a classic example of how marketers should respond to emotional reactions that are directed toward a country.

The major suppliers—Toyota, Honda, and Nissan—started manufacturing and assembling cars in the United States. Their advertisements showed how their car operations in the United States were creating jobs. Honda managed to garner substantial publicity by exporting U.S.-made Accords to Japan. In addition to this, the car manufacturers started contributing to athletic scholarship funds at the college level. These actions definitely lessened the emotional negativity toward Japanese products.

The second process by which country-of-origin information was hypothesized to affect consumer evaluations was by a direct affect transfer process. Han (1989) found this effect to be particularly relevant to those people who are not familiar with a country's products. Such people appear to generalize their image of the country to the products from that country. While the image-building strategy just outlined is equally appropriate in this situation, it might be beneficial to the foreign marketer, in the long term, if s/he can enhance consumers' knowledge of the products from that country. Such knowledge enhancement should cause consumers to switch over from an affect transfer process to a cognitive mediation process. Since the affect transfer process does not discriminate between products from a given country, a negative affect toward a country should act to the detriment of all products from the country. Therefore, a marketer might benefit more by changing people's level of knowledge rather than working on the image of the country.

Some advertising campaigns illustrate these notions. The campaign undertaken by Chinese companies is one example of this strategy. Possibly to combat negative stereotypes about Chinese products, television commercials showed various products that Americans were already using in their daily lives that were manufactured in China. A similar example is that of Hyundai corporation, which advertises about all the sophisticated products that are manufactured by the company, from satellite communications equipment to automobiles. It is possible that the stereotype of low-quality products that is attached to South Korea (Khanna 1986) is combated by the ad that shows the technological might and sophistication of Hyundai.

Finally, if the mechanism by which country-of-origin information affects product attitudes is through cognitive mediation, then marketers should devise promotion strategies to affect the beliefs of consumers about the product. A classic example is that of Japanese automobiles, which have gained a solid reputation for being durable and reliable. When Honda, Toyota, and Nissan began to launch luxury automobiles, they were faced with the problem of countering a well-entrenched belief that Japanese automobiles were low-cost, basic machines and not comparable to the Cadillacs and BMW's in the market. All three manufacturers promoted their luxury automobiles on different names—Acura, Lexus, and Infiniti, respectively—and their success is well-documented. The success of the Lexus division of Toyota is particularly interesting when juxtaposed with the ailing Toyota Cressida, which was at one time the flagship of the Toyota brand.

Another strategy that relies on changing people's beliefs is employing distribution channels that provide a high-quality image to the product. Schooler (1971) reports a study in which college students viewed Italian goblets as less desirable than American goblets. However, when the same goblets were presented through a Neiman Marcus display, the students no longer viewed the American goblets as more desirable. The positive image of the retailer in this case appears to have been transferred to the product and overwhelmed any negative country-of-origin stereotypes.

An additional way to combat negative beliefs about a product's quality based on its country-of-origin is by having people experience the product. Such experience may persuade a consumer to insulate product attitudes from attitudes toward its country-of-origin. In one study, Young, Sauer, and Unnava (1991) found that consumers expressed less positive attitudes toward a Mexican brand of orange juice than toward an American brand of orange juice after reading an identical ad for both brands. Some subjects were then allowed to taste the juice and care was taken to ensure that the juice was very tasty. Subsequently, subjects expressed their attitude toward the brand of orange juice. It was found that the Mexican and American brands were rated equally after subjects tasted the juice. Thus product sampling eliminated country-of-origin effects.

This finding is consistent with Hong and Wyer's (1989, 1990) results in that country-of-origin information that is presented at the same time as product attribute information can reduce the positive attitude toward a brand. This finding, however, extends findings on country-of-origin effects in a significant way: *Actual product sampling* is incorporated as part of the experimental treatment. Other country-of-origin studies have merely introduced additional product information *after* the country-of-origin was revealed (e.g., Hong and Wyer 1989).

CONCLUSION

A number of the forces shaping markets and marketing during the 1990s may reduce the impact of country-of-origin information. At the macro level, the unification of Europe may lead to products being viewed more homogeneously because it will be less apparent in which country a good was produced. The "home nationality" of firms may be less known or obvious as companies increase their use of pan-European brands and as package and label information less frequently identifies a product's national origin. At the micro level, consumers may realize that an increasing number of products contain components, design, and workmanship from numerous countries and regions.

Other forces, though, will off-set those just identified. Nations with balance-of-trade inequities and balance-of-payment difficulties will continue to exhort their citizens to buy from national suppliers, just as the government gives preference to local producers. Ethnic and regional groups with strong reputations for craftsmanship and quality (e.g., French vintners and Swiss confectioners and watch makers to name but a few) will seek to maintain whatever competitive advantage accrues through such perceptions. And, to the extent that consumers seek to reduce the difficulty of choosing between product variations that are similar by using a simple heuristic such as the nationality of the producer, country-of-origin effects will still be observed.

For the marketer, one conclusion is clear: Further study of the process by which industrial and household decision makers select products is needed. To accomplish this task, increased cooperation among businesses, government units, and academic institutions is needed.

References

Bilkey, W., and E. Nes (1982). "Country-of-Origin Effects on Product Evaluations," *Journal of International Business Studies*, (Spring/Summer), 89–99.

Cordell, V. V. (1991). "Competitive Context and Price as Moderators of Country of Origin Preferences," *Journal of the Academy of Marketing Science*, 19(2)(Spring), 123–128.

Darling, J. R., and V. R. Wood (1989). "A Longitudinal Study Comparing Perceptions of U.S. and Japanese Consumers in a Third/Neutral Country: Finland 1975 to 1985," *Journal of International Business Studies*, 19 (Fall), 427–450.

Erickson, G., J. Johansson, and P. Chao (1984). "Image Variables in Multi-Attribute Product Evaluations: Country-of-Origin Effects," *Journal of Consumer Research*, (September), 11, 694–699.

Eroglu, S., and K. A. Machleit (1989). "Effects of Individual and Product Specific Variables on Utilizing Country of Origin as a Product Quality Cue," *International Marketing Review*, 6(6), 27–41.

Fazio, R. H. (1985). "How Do Attitudes Guide Behavior?" R. M. Sorrentino, and E. T. Higgins, (eds.), *The Handbook of Motivation and Cognition: Foundations of Social Behavior.* New York: Guilford.

—— and M. P. Zanna (1981). "Direct Experience and Attitude Behavior Consistency," in L. Berkowitz (ed.), *Advances in Experimental Social Psychology*, 14, New York: Academic Press, 14.

Fishbein, M., and I. Ajzen (1975). *Belief, Attitude, Intention and Behavior: An Introduction to Theory and Research.* Reading, MA: Addison-Wesley.

Greenwald, A. G. (1968). "Cognitive Learning, Cognitive Response to Persuasion, and Attitude Change," in A. Greenwald, T. Brock, and T. Ostrom, (eds.), *Psychological Foundations of Attitudes*, New York: Academic Press, 148–170.

Han, C. M. (1989). "Country Image: Halo or Summary Construct?" *Journal of Marketing Research*, (May) 26, 222–229.

——, and V. Terpstra (1988). "Country-of-Origin Effects for Uni-National and Bi-National Products," *Journal of International Business Studies*, (Summer), 19, 235–255.

Hong, S., and J. Toner (1988). "Are There Gender Differences in the Use of Country-of-Origin Information in the Evaluation of Products?" in T. K. Skrull, ed., *Advances in Consumer Research*, XVI, Provo, UT.: Association for Consumer Research, 468–472.

Hong, Sung-Tai, and R. S. Wyer, Jr. (1989). "Effects of Country-of-Origin and Product-Attribute Information on Product Evaluation: An Information Processing Perspectives," *Journal of Consumer Research,* 16(2) (September), 175–187.

———— (1990). "Determinants of Product Evaluation: Effects of the Time Interval Between Knowledge of a Product's Country of Origin and Information About Its Specific Attributes," *Journal of Consumer Research,* 17(3) (December), 277–288.

Johansson, J., S. Douglas, and I. Nonaka (1985). "Assessing the Impact of Country of Origin on Product Evaluations: A New Methodological Perspective," *Journal of Marketing Research,* (November) 22, 388–396.

Kaynak, E., and T. Cavusgil (1983). "Consumer Attitudes Towards Products of Foreign Origin: Do They Vary Across Product Classes?" *International Journal of Advertising,* 2, 147–157.

Khanna, S. (1986). "Asian Companies and the Country Stereotype Paradox: An Empirical Study," *Columbia Journal of World Business,* (Summer), 29–38.

Monroe, K. B., and R. Krishnan (1985). "The Effect of Price on Subjective Product Evaluations," in J. Jacoby and J. C. Olson (eds.), *Perceived Quality: How Consumers View Stores and Merchandise.* Lexington, MA: Lexington Books.

Nagashima, A. (1970). "Comparison of Japanese and U.S. Attitudes Toward Foreign Products," *Journal of Marketing,* (January), 34, 68–74.

Obermiller, C. (1985). "Varieties of Mere Exposure: The Effects of Processing Style and Repetition on Affective Response," *Journal of Consumer Research,* (June) 17–30.

———— and E. Spangenberg (1988). "Exploring the Effects of Country of Origin Labels: An Information Processing Framework," in T. K. Skrull (ed.), *Advances in Consumer Research,* XVI Provo, UT: Association for Consumer Research, 454–459.

Ozsomer, A., and S. T. Cavusgil (1991). "Country-of-Origin Effects on Product Evaluations: A Sequel to Bilkey and Nes Review," *1991 American Marketing Educator Proceedings,* 2 (Summer) 269–277.

Papadopoulos, N., L. A. Heslop, and J. Beracs (1990). "National Stereotypes and Product Evaluations in a Socialist Country," *International Marketing Review,* 7(1), 32–47.

Sauer, P. L., M. A. Young, and H. R. Unnava (1991). "An Experimental Investigation of the Process Behind the Country of Origin Effect," *Journal of International Consumer Marketing,* 3(2), 29–59.

Schooler, R. (1965). "Product Bias in the Central American Common Market," *Journal of Marketing Research,* (November) 2, 394–397.

———— (1971). "Bias Phenomena Attendant to the Marketing of Foreign Goods In the U.S.," *Journal of International Business Studies,* (Spring) 2, 71–80.

————, and A. Wildt (1968). "Elasticity of Product Bias," *Journal of Marketing Research* (February), 5, 78–81.

Thorelli, H. B., J. Lim, and J. Ye (1989). "Relative Importance of Country of Origin, Warranty, and Retail Store Image on Product Evaluations," *International Marketing Review*, 6(1), 35–46.

Wall, M., and L. Heslop (1986). "Consumer Attitudes Toward Canadian-Made Versus Imported Products," *Journal of the Academy of Marketing Science* (Summer), 14, 27–36.

Wall, M., J. Liefeld, and L. A. Heslop (1991). "Impact of Country-of-Origin Cues on Consumer Judgements in Multi-Cue Situations: A Covariance Analysis," *Journal of the Academy of Marketing Science,* 19(2)(Spring), 105–114.

Wang, Chih-Kang, and C. W. Lamb, Jr. (1980). "Foreign Environmental Factors Influencing American Consumers' Predispositions Toward European Products," *Journal of the Academy of Marketing Science,* 8 (Fall), 345–356.

White, P. D., and E. Cundiff (1978). "Assessing the Quality of Industrial Products," *Journal of Marketing* (January), 42, 80–86.

Young, M. A., P. L. Sauer, and H. R. Unnava (1991). "Insights on the 'Country of Origin' Effect: The Role Experience," Working Paper, University of Denver College of Business (Department of Marketing).

Zajonc, R. B., and H. Markus (1985). "Must All Affect Be Mediated by Cognition," *Journal of Consumer Research* (December), 12, 363–364.

CHAPTER 11

A STUDY OF CANADIANS'
COUNTRY-OF-ORIGIN
PREFERENCES

C. L. Hung

The rapid advances in global trade, transportation, and communication technology in the last two decades have transformed today's national markets into segments of integrated world markets. Market competition, especially for manufactured consumer goods, is now almost always international in dimension and scope no matter where the producers sell their products. Now consumers are exposed to a wide variety of competing products from different countries. Today's consumers are processing information cues related to the product country-of-origin as part of their product evaluation and selection. Through what they have heard, seen, or experienced in their daily activities, consumers often have in their subconscious minds stereotypes about things foreign—foreign people as well as foreign products. Consequently, while some consumers may make purchase decisions based on their expert knowledge of the physical and concrete product features—such as the type of materials, style, versatility, and the packaging—in relation to the price, irrespective of where the product is made or assembled, the informed or less confident consumers may use a product's country-of-origin to judge the quality of its other attributes. In other words, a product's nationality is not simply a piece of information attached to the product. Instead, it is an information cue by which the quality of other product attributes such as dependability and durability may be judged.

A product's country-of-origin as an information cue and its influence on purchase decisions have lately received considerable attention from business academicians. Studies on product nationality images first appeared in 1965 (Schooler 1965), and in the twenty-five years since then, there have been more than a hundred pieces of work on the subject. These studies are variously concerned with the effect of the country-of-origin on perceived product quality (e.g., Reierson 1966; Nagashima 1970 and 1977; Bilkey and Nes 1982; Kaynak and Cavusgil 1983; Johansson, Douglas, and Nonaka 1985; Barker and Robinson 1987; Heslop, Liefeld, and Wall, 1987), how the perceptions are formed (e.g., Halfhill 1980; Narayana 1981), how important the perceptions are in product evaluations (e.g., Khera, Anderson, and Kim 1982; Johansson and Spich 1982; Erickson, Johansson, and Chao 1984; Papadopoulos et al. 1987; Hung 1989), and how these perceptions vary with the shoppers' economic, social, and demographic backgrounds (e.g., Schooler 1971; Bannister and Saunders 1978; Heslop and Wall 1985, 1986; Barker 1987; Han and Terpstra 1988; Wall, Heslop, and Hofstra 1988; Howard 1989). More recently, attention has also been placed on the research design and analytical methods and how the sample frame, rating scales, questioning techniques, and number of cues might have influenced the findings (e.g., Bamossy and Papadopoulos 1987; Ettenson, Wagner, and Gaeth 1988; Barker and Kaciak 1989; Han 1989; Hong and Wyer 1989; Shellinck 1989; Sauer, Young, and Unnava 1991). These studies tend to confirm, in varying degrees of confidence, the general belief that the "made-in —" label connotes certain quality images and influences a shopper's perceptions of other product attributes and the overall value of the product.

A comprehensive literature survey of country-of-origin studies is beyond the scope of this chapter. (See Chapter 10 for a comprehensive view of the literature.) However, it is interesting to note that up to this date there has been no study on how strong the consumers' preferences are in terms of how much more they are willing to pay for a preferred country-of-origin. Whereas the attribute "price" is sometimes used together with the country-of-origin as an information cue for purchase decisions (e.g., Wall, Liefeld, and Heslop 1991), practically all existing studies on the impact of a product's country-of-origin have been on the direction of impact—not on the strength of impact.

OBJECTIVES AND RESEARCH DESIGN

This chapter presents the results of a survey on the direction and strength of Canadians' preferences on five manufactured consumer products from ten foreign countries. The central proposition underlying this study is that in selecting from among competing products in the same shopping environment (hence, with the nonproduct attribute variations removed), a consumer's decision will be based on an evaluation of the price in relation to all the visible and known product features such as the brand, the packaging, the type of materials, style, and country-of-origin. If all the outward appearances and features for two products are the same, except the country-of-origin, any difference in the price which the consumer is willing to pay for the two products reflects the relative money value of the product's country-of-origin.

The data in this study were obtained in a survey conducted in March–April 1990 in Calgary, the fifth largest city in Canada with a population of around 700,000. The survey covered five products from ten foreign countries and Canada. The five products chosen were all manufactured consumer goods that have wide open international competition in Canada, and the ten foreign countries were among the most important exporters of these products to Canada—dress shoes from Brazil and Italy; dress coats from Britain and Hong Kong; cordless telephones from Japan and Mexico; ski sets from South Korea and the United States; and hi-fi sets from Japan and the United States.

In the survey, shoppers were approached in a mall-intercept situation, and they were interviewed after they were ascertained to be Canadian residents. The interviewer first asked the shoppers to indicate their preferences on a foreign-made product versus a Canadian-made product with the same price and outward appearances and features. After they had stated their preferences, they were then presented a price for the Canadian-made product and asked to give a price for the foreign-made product at which they would be indifferent in their choice. Inevitably, there was a certain degree of artificiality in the experimental treatment, but the indifference prices suggested by the respondents should collectively provide a reasonably good indication of the relative money value of a product's country-of-origin in their minds.

Three hundred shoppers in major shopping malls across the city of Calgary were interviewed on different weekdays over a period of three weeks. After discarding those responses that were incomplete or biased to the extreme (e.g., from respondents who claim that "I am not going to buy (product) made in (country) at any price" or "I always buy Canadian at any price"), 249 useable responses were obtained. Table 11-1 gives a breakdown of the respondents by sex, by age ("age under 30" and "age

Annual Family Income	Age Under 30		Age 30 and Above			
	Female	*Male*	*Female*	*Male*	*Total*	TABLE 11-1 BREAKDOWN OF SAMPLE RESPONDENTS
Below C$30,000	29	20	18	8	75	
C$30,000–C$60,000	21	33	17	26	97	
Over C$60,000	21	28	9	19	77	
Total	71	81	44	53	249	

30 and above") and by annual household income (under C$30,000, C$30–60,000, and over C$60,000, categories which correspond roughly to the lower-, middle-, and upper-income groups in Canada).

······

Data Analysis and Findings

In this section, all the 249 responses are analyzed in terms of their nationality preferences for the products and the price premiums or discounts they put on a product's country-of-origin.

Direction of Preference

Table 11-2 summarizes the respondents' product nationality preferences for the five products.

- *Dress shoes:* In choosing between dress shoes with the same price and physical features from Canada and Italy, the respondents prefer the latter by a margin of about three to two. The preference for

TABLE 11-2 RESPONDENTS' PRODUCT NATIONALITY PREFERENCES[a]				
Preference for dress shoes				
Made in Canada	95 (38.2%)	vs.	made in Italy	154 (61.8%)
Made in Canada	207 (83.1%)	vs.	made in Brazil	42 (16.9%)
Preference for dress coats				
Made in Canada	144 (57.8%)	vs.	made in Britain	105 (42.2%)
Made in Canada	226 (90.8%)	vs.	made in Hong Kong	23 (9.2%)
Preference for cordless telephones				
Made in Canada	106 (42.6%)	vs.	made in Japan	143 (57.4%)
Made in Canada	247 (99.2%)	vs.	made in Mexico	2 (0.8%)
Preference for ski sets				
Made in Canada	166 (66.7%)	vs.	made in United States	83 (33.3%)
Made in Canada	244 (98.0%)	vs.	made in South Korea	5 (2.0%)
Preference for hi-fi sets				
Made in Canada	139 (55.8%)	vs.	made in United States	110 (44.2%)
Made in Canada	47 (18.9%)	vs.	made in Japan	202 (81.1%)

[a] *Total number of respondents: 249*

Canadian-made dress shoes over those made in Brazil is over-whelmingly in favor of Canada by more than a four to one margin.

- *Dress coats:* The respondents prefer dress coats made in Canada over those made in either Britain or Hong Kong. In the former case, the proportion of preference is slightly less than 3 to 2; in the latter case, it is as high as 9 to 1.
- *Cordless telephones:* Whereas the respondents on the whole show a moderate preference for Japanese cordless telephones, the rejection of those made in Mexico is practically unanimous.
- *Ski sets:* Canadians prefer ski sets made in Canada over those made in the United States by a 3-to-2 margin, and only 5 out of the 249 respondents would have picked South Korean-made ski sets with the same price and physical features.
- *Hi-fi sets:* The respondents are almost equally divided in their choice between Canadian-made and U.S.-made hi-fi sets, but there is a strong preference for those made in Japan.

Summing up, there is almost unanimity in that Canadian-made dress shoes, dress coats, cordless telephones, and ski sets will be preferred over those made in Brazil, Hong Kong, South Korea, and Mexico. This finding is not unexpected since it is comparable to those of related studies that show that shoppers in developed countries generally favor products made locally or made in other first-world countries (e.g., Heslop, Liefeld, and Wall 1987; Hung 1989). Since none of these four countries is an OECD member country, it is evident that Canadians are on the whole still suspicious of the quality of manufactured products made in newly industrialized countries.

When choosing between Canadian-made products and those made in other first-world countries, Canadians are not so sure, yet they still prefer Canadian-made ones over foreign-made ones such as dress coats from Britain and ski sets from the United States. However, Japanese electronics evidently have such a good reputation in the minds of Canadians that they are preferred over Canadian-made ones. Furthermore, judging by the significant difference in the proportion of preferences (81.1 percent vs. 57.4 percent), the more expensive Japanese consumer electronics (hi-fi sets) are considered to be better in value than the less expensive ones (cordless telephones).

STRENGTH OF PREFERENCE

More interesting than the direction of preference is the strength of preference indicated by the price premiums or discounts the respondents assign to the country-of-origin. The results in Table 11-3 reveal that quite extreme opinions exist with regard to how much a product's country-of-origin is worth. On the whole, a substantial value is attached when there is a clear-cut preference by the respondents. For example, the average price premium for dress shoes made in Italy is 20.8 percent, and for hi-fi sets made in Japan it is 17.1 percent. The price discounts for made-in-Mexico cordless telephones and made-in-South-Korea ski sets are even greater, at 32.9 percent and 28.2 percent, respectively. At the same time, when preferences are divided, the average price premiums/discounts are minimal; e.g., Japanese-made cordless telephones (+2.7 percent) and U.S.-made ski sets (−3.0 percent) and hi-fi sets (−1.1 percent). Also, whereas more respondents prefer Canadian-made dress coats over British-made dress coats, there are greater price premiums given to the made-in-Britain label by the latter group than the price discounts by the former group. Consequently, the price for British dress coats at which the average respondent would be indifferent in his/her choice is higher instead of lower than the Canadian price (by 5.5 percent). Finally, the standardized price premiums and discounts (given by the price indices in Figure 11-1) for the products indicate that the value given to the country-of-origin in percentage terms is not related to the original price of the product.

FIGURE 11-1
COMPARATIVE
INDIFFERENCE
PRICES[a]

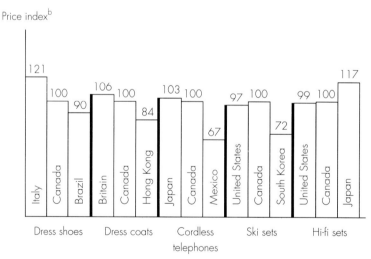

[a] The indifference price is the price at which the respondent would be indifferent in choosing between the Canadian-made product and the foreign-made product.
[b] Canadian-made product price index = 100.

Segregating the respondents into groups that have different country-of-origin preferences, the price premiums and discounts given in Table 11-4 provide further insight on how different the respondents value a product's nationality. When there is a notably greater proportion of respondents preferring the foreign-made products (e.g., Italian shoes and Japanese hi-fi sets), the price premiums put on the foreign country-of-origin are also significantly greater in percentage terms than the suggested price discounts when Canadian origin is preferred. For example, when we look at dress shoes from Italy and from Canada, those preferring the former on average gave it a price premium of 42 percent. By comparison, the average price discount given to Italian dress shoes by those who prefer Canadian is only 13.8 percent. In the case of Japanese hi-fi sets, the price premium is 23.9 percent compared to the price discount of 12.0 percent.

	Mean Price[b] in C$	Percentage Price Premium/Discount	Standard Deviation	TABLE 11.3 PRODUCT NATIONALITY PRICE PREMIUMS/ DISCOUNTS (ALL RESPONDENTS)[a]
Dress shoes ($50)				
Made in Italy	60.4	+20.8%	21.7	
Made in Brazil	45.0	−10.0%	14.8	
Dress coats ($100)				
Made in Britain	105.5	+ 5.5%	32.0	
Made in Hong Kong	84.1	−15.9%	24.2	
Cordless telephones ($150)				
Made in Japan	154.0	+ 2.7%	37.0	
Made in Mexico	100.6	−32.9%	31.6	
Ski sets ($300)				
Made in United States	291.0	− 3.0%	64.3	
Made in South Korea	215.5	−28.2%	61.5	
Hi-fi sets ($500)				
Made in United States	494.5	− 1.1%	118.3	
Made in Japan	585.5	+17.1%	146.9	

[a]Total number of respondents: 249

[b]The mean price is the average of the respondents' suggested foreign-made product prices at which they would be indifferent to choosing between the foreign-made product and the Canadian-made product. The price of the Canadian-made product is given in parentheses.

This clearly indicates that the strength in the preference for Italian dress shoes and Japanese hi-fi sets over Canadian dress shoes and hi-fi sets is much greater than when the preference is in the opposite direction.

On the other hand, when the proportion of preferences is closer (e.g., Japanese cordless telephones and U.S. ski sets), the average suggested price premiums and discounts are also much more comparable in absolute percentage terms. For Japanese cordless telephones, they are +16.6 percent and −16.2 percent; for U.S. ski sets, +14.9 percent and −11.9 percent. These percentage price premiums and discounts are consistent with the proportions of preferences and suggest that the respondents on the whole do assess the value of the country-of-origin rationally.

TABLE 11-4 PRODUCT NATIONALITY PRICE PREMIUMS/ DISCOUNTS (SEGREGATED BY PREFERENCES)	Respondents[a] Preferring					
	Canadian-made			Foreign-made		
	Mean Price[b] in C$	Price Discount	S.D.[c]	Mean Price[b] in C$	Price Premium	S.D.[c]
Dress shoes ($50)						
Made in Italy	43.1	−13.8%	8.8	71.0	+42.0%	19.9
Made in Brazil	40.6	−18.8%	9.3	66.5	+33.0%	16.7
Dress coats ($100)						
Made in Britain	88.0	−12.0%	17.2	129.5	+29.5%	30.7
Made in Hong Kong	80.5	−19.5%	17.8	119.6	+19.6%	40.7
Cordless telephones ($150)						
Made in Japan	125.7	−16.2%	26.8	174.9	+16.6%	26.1
Made in Mexico	100.7	−32.9%	29.3	155.0	+ 3.3%	n.a.
Ski sets ($300)						
Made in United States	264.2	−11.9%	46.2	344.6	+14.9%	54.0
Made in South Korea	213.8	−28.7%	59.2	304.0	+ 1.3%	n.a.[d]
Hi-fi sets ($500)						
Made in United States	426.7	−14.7%	79.3	580.3	+16.1%	92.8
Made in Japan	440.2	−12.0%	68.9	619.3	+23.9%	134.1

[a]Total number of respondents: 249
[b]Mean price. See note in Table 11-3.
[c]S.D.: Standard deviation
[d]n.a.: Not applicable (because of the small number of respondents)

However rational the respondents may be, their value assessments are quite extreme as can be seen in Figure 11-2, which shows the comparative indifference price indices of the respondents aggregated by the direction of preference. Take dress shoes for example. Respondents who prefer Canadian-made dress shoes give Italian dress shoes on average a price discount of 14 percentage points and Brazilian dress shoes 19 percentage points. On the other hand, the price premiums given to these foreign imports by those respondents who prefer them are 42 and 33 percentage points, respectively. The range, in both cases, is in excess of 50 percentage points, which is nothing short of dramatic given that the products' outward appearances and physical features are identical. Though the ranges for the other products are not as wide, they are all in the neighborhood of 30 or 40 percentage points.

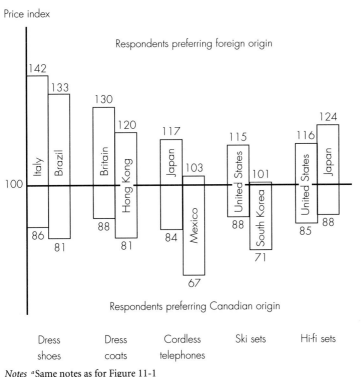

Price index

FIGURE 11-2
COMPARATIVE
INDIFFERENCE PRICE[a]
(SEGREGATED BY
PREFERENCES)

Notes [a]Same notes as for Figure 11-1

....

Comparison Between Respondent Groups

In this section, the responses are compared across sex, age, and household income groups.

Direction of Preference

Table 11-5 gives a break down of the respondents' country-of-origin preferences by sex, age, and income groups. Evidently, country-of-origin preferences have very little to do with the sex of the respondents. Out of the ten pairs of products, only the selection of hi-fi sets from Canada and the United States shows a significant difference between the two groups. Whereas close to two-thirds of the female respondents prefer hi-fi sets from Canada to those from the United States, the male respondents are split evenly in their preferences.

Compared to sex, the age of the respondents has a much greater influence on the country-of-origin preferences. There is a significant difference in the preferences in five out of ten product pairs by respondents who are under age 30 and by those who are age 30 and above—dress shoes from Italy, cordless telephones from Japan, ski sets from the United States, and hi-fi sets from the United States and Japan. In addition, there is a very obvious direction of bias. Without exception, the older age group shows a more favorable inclination toward Canadian-made products than foreign-made products. In two instances—dress shoes from Canada and Italy and hi-fi sets from Canada and Japan—the proportions of respondents from the older age group preferring Canadian products are respectively two and three times greater than those of the younger age group.

Income of the respondents also has some effect on the respondents' country-of-origin preferences, but the impact is not as strong as age. Apparently, the upper-income group (with annual household incomes in excess of C$60,000) has a greater preference for foreign-made products than the other two income groups when these products come from other developed countries. This is because the proportions of the upper-income group choosing foreign imports from other developed countries over Canadian are without exception greater when compared to the other two income groups—dress shoes from Italy, dress coats from Britain, cordless telephones from Japan, ski sets from the United States, and hi-fi sets from the United States and Japan. Moreover, the differences in proportions for the first three of these six product pairs between the upper-income and lower-income groups are statistically significant.

TABLE 11-5   PRODUCT NATIONALITY PREFERENCES[a]
(IN PERCENTAGES BY SEX, AGE, AND INCOME GROUPS)

	Sex		Age		Income (C$,000)		
				30 and			
	Female	Male	Under 30	Above	Under 30	30 to 60	Over 60
Dress shoes							
Preferred Canada	33.9	41.8	25.6[b]	57.7	41.3[c]	47.4[c]	23.4
Preferred Italy	66.1	58.2	74.3[b]	42.3	58.7[c]	52.6[c]	76.6
Preferred Canada	79.1	86.6	81.6	85.6	77.3	90.7	79.2
Preferred Brazil	20.9	13.4	18.4	14.4	22.7	9.3	20.8
Dress coats							
Preferred Canada	61.7	54.5	53.9	63.9	62.7[c]	63.9[c]	45.5
Preferred Britain	38.3	45.5	46.1	36.1	37.4[c]	36.1[c]	54.5
Preferred Canada	91.3	90.3	88.8	93.8	88.0	91.8	92.2
Preferred Hong Kong	8.7	9.7	11.2	6.2	12.0	8.2	7.8
Cordless telephones							
Preferred Canada	44.3	41.0	34.9[b]	54.6	52.0[c]	41.2[c]	35.1
Preferred Japan	55.7	59.0	65.1[b]	45.4	48.0[c]	58.8[c]	64.9
Preferred Canada	99.1	99.3	99.3	99.0	98.7	100.0	98.7
Preferred Mexico	0.9	0.7	0.7	1.0	1.3	0.0	1.3
Ski sets							
Preferred Canada	67.0	66.4	61.8[b]	74.2	66.7	71.1	61.0
Preferred United States	33.0	33.6	38.2[b]	25.8	33.3	28.9	39.0
Preferred Canada	98.3	97.8	98.0	98.0	97.3	99.0	97.4
Preferred South Korea	1.7	2.2	2.0	2.0	2.7	1.0	2.6
Hi-fi sets							
Preferred Canada	62.6[b]	50.0	50.7[b]	63.9	56.0	57.7	53.2
Preferred United States	37.4[b]	50.0	49.3[b]	36.1	44.0	42.3	46.8
Preferred Canada	20.0	17.9	9.9[b]	33.0	20.0	22.7	13.0
Preferred Japan	80.0	82.1	90.1[b]	67.0	80.0	77.3	87.0

[a]Total number of respondents: 249
[b]Difference between sex/age groups statistically significant at 0.05 level
[c]Difference between upper and lower income groups statistically significant at 0.05 level

Strength of Preference

Table 11-6 presents the average price premiums or discounts given to the foreign-made products by female and male respondents. Out of the ten products, only one is significantly different between the two gender groups—hi-fi sets from the United States. In fact, the numbers indicate that overall the females and the males have different preferences—females for Canadian hi-fi sets and males for U.S. hi-fi sets. However, in both cases the average price premium or discount given is small—plus 2.6 percent and minus 5.3 percent respectively.

In contrast to the sex groups, the differences in preferences between the age groups are much more pronounced and interesting (see Table 11-7). Out of the ten products, eight receive significantly different price pre-

TABLE 11-6   PRODUCT NATIONALITY PRICE PREMIUMS/DISCOUNTS
(BY SEX GROUPS)[a]

	Female			Male		
	Mean Price[b]	Percent	S.D.	Mean Price[b]	Percent	S.D.
Dress shoes ($50)						
Made in Italy	60.6	+21.2%	18.8	60.2	+20.4%	23.6
Made in Brazil	46.5	− 7.0%	14.9	43.6	−12.8%	14.2
Dress coats ($100)						
Made in Britain	106.3	+ 6.3%	33.3	104.8	+ 4.8%	29.8
Made in Hong Kong	84.8	−15.2%	25.7	83.5	−16.5%	21.9
Cordless telephone ($150)						
Made in Japan	151.7	+ 1.1%	34.6	155.9	+ 3.9%	37.0
Made in Mexico	103.4	−31.1%	33.1	100.0	−33.3%	29.1
Ski sets ($300)						
Made in United States	289.4	− 3.5%	62.0	292.4	− 2.5%	61.9
Made in South Korea	220.1	−26.6%	60.1	211.6	−29.5%	60.2
Hi-fi sets ($500)						
Made in United States[c]	473.5	− 5.3%	112.8	512.8	+ 2.6%	113.3
Made in Japan	584.3	+16.9%	152.0	586.6	+17.3%	134.8

[a]Number of respondents: Female—116; Male—133

[b]Mean price. See note in Table 11-3.

[c]Difference between groups statistically significant at 0.05 level

miums or discounts from the two age groups. On the whole, the younger respondents have a better value perception of all foreign-made products. Consequently, when the foreign-made products are preferred, they are willing to pay significantly higher price premiums for these products— Italian shoes and Japanese hi-fi sets. At the same time, when the Canadian products are preferred, the price discounts they give to the foreign products are significantly lower than the price discounts given by the older respondents—dress coats from Hong Kong and ski sets from the United States and South Korea. In fact, for cordless telephones from Japan and hi-fi sets from the United States, the younger respondents are willing to pay a price premium, whereas the older respondents on the whole believe that they should be priced lower than Canadian cordless telephones and hi-fi sets.

TABLE 11-7   PRODUCT NATIONALITY PRICE PREMIUMS/DISCOUNTS (BY AGE GROUPS)[a]

	Age Under 30			Age 30 and Above		
	Mean Price[b]	Percent	S.D.	Mean Price[b]	Percent	S.D.
Dress shoes ($50)						
Made in Italy[c]	62.8	+25.6%	17.4	56.5	+13.0%	26.0
Made in Brazil	45.8	− 8.4%	12.6	43.7	−12.6%	17.3
Dress coats ($100)						
Made in Britain	106.9	+ 6.9%	23.1	103.3	+ 3.3%	41.1
Made in Hong Kong[c]	88.6	−11.4%	19.5	77.2	−22.8%	27.8
Cordless telephones ($150)						
Made in Japan[c]	159.6	+ 6.4%	30.3	145.3	− 3.1%	41.8
Made in Mexico[c]	105.4	−29.7%	29.8	95.7	−36.5%	32.1
Ski sets ($300)						
Made in United States[c]	297.8	− 0.7%	52.2	280.6	− 6.5%	73.4
Made in South Korea[c]	223.4	−25.5%	61.6	203.5	−32.2%	56.2
Hi-fi sets ($500)						
Made in United States[c]	507.0	+ 1.4%	89.2	475.4	− 4.9%	143.7
Made in Japan[c]	599.4	+19.9%	132.0	564.0	+12.8%	156.3

[a]Number of respondents: Age under 30—151; age 30 and above—98
[b]Mean price. See note in Table 11-3.
[c]Difference between groups statistically significant at 0.05 level

There are also some notable and interesting differences when the preferences of the different household income groups are compared (see Table 11-8). Almost as a rule, the upper-income group gives greater price premiums on imports from other developed countries and greater price discounts on imports from the developing countries. To some extent, this suggests that a higher income leads one to place more emphasis on a product's country-of-origin.

TABLE 11-8   PRODUCT NATIONALITY PRICE PREMIUMS/DISCOUNTS
(BY INCOME GROUPS)[a]

Annual Household Income in C$,000

	Less Than 30			30–60			Over 60		
	Mean Price[b]	Percent	S.D.	Mean Price[b]	Percent	S.D.	Mean Price[b]	Percent	S.D.
Dress shoes ($50)									
Made in Italy[c]	58.7	+17.4%	19.5	57.2	+14.4%	19.9	65.9	+31.8%	24.4
Made in Brazil	45.4	− 9.2%	14.4	43.9	−12.2%	14.2	45.9	− 8.2%	15.4
Dress coats ($100)									
Made in Britain	103.7	+ 3.7%	26.7	102.9	+ 2.9%	30.1	110.5	+10.5%	36.6
Made in Hong Kong[c]	84.8	−15.2%	24.2	84.5	−15.5%	23.7	82.9	−17.1%	23.5
Cordless telephones ($150)									
Made in Japan[c]	148.4	− 1.1%	34.5	151.3	+ 0.9%	33.1	162.7	+ 8.5%	39.3
Made in Mexico	103.2	−31.2%	33.8	102.4	−31.7%	30.0	99.9	−33.4%	29.7
Ski sets ($300)									
Made in United States[c]	284.7	− 5.1%	61.2	285.7	− 4.8%	50.6	303.9	+ 1.3%	73.3
Made in South Korea	225.8	−24.7%	68.0	218.8	−27.1%	55.7	201.6	−32.8%	55.7
Hi-fi sets ($500)									
Made in United States	487.7	− 2.5%	118.0	486.5	− 2.7%	104.3	511.2	+ 2.2%	123.0
Made in Japan[c]	586.3	+17.3%	154.6	566.0	+13.2%	129.7	609.4	+21.9%	144.7

[a]Number of respondents: Income less than C$30,000—75; Income C$30–60,000—97; Income more than C$60,000—77

[b]Mean price. See note in Table 11-3.

[c]Difference between groups statistically significant at 0.05 level

Concluding Remarks

The survey on the direction and strength of Canadians' country-of-origin preferences has revealed several interesting findings. Not surprisingly, Canadians have country-of-origin preferences that influence their product selection when the products' outward appearances and features as well as the prices are the same. There is a very strong preference for locally made products over foreign imports when these imports come from the developing countries. However, when the imports come from other developed countries, preferences are divided, and nationalistic emotions may tip the balance in favor of Canadian-made products when Canadians feel the products offer them the same value. Yet, there is still some reliance on established reputation in their selections.

The price premiums or discounts that Canadians give to the country-of-origin indicate that they do put a significant value on a product's country-of-origin. When they prefer a particular country-of-origin, they may be willing to pay a price premium of as much as 30 to 40 percent. At the same time, they believe that products with a less desirable country-of-origin have to be priced much lower than Canadian products before they feel indifferent in their choice. This includes dress shoes from Brazil, dress coats from Hong Kong, and ski sets from South Korea, which may have better country-of-origin appeals than Canadian made ones in markets outside of North America. Apparently, Canadians are still prejudiced against products made in newly industrialized countries.

The direction and strength of country-of-origin preferences do not appear to be related to the sex of the respondents. By comparison, age is a much more important determining variable. The middle-aged and elderly Canadians, defined in this survey as those aged 30 and above, clearly show a greater preference for Canadian-made products than the younger Canadians. Income is also related to product nationality preferences and price perceptions. The upper-income group appears to favor imports from other first-world countries more than the middle- and lower-income groups, and it places a greater value on the country-of-origin as well. When the upper-income shoppers prefer a foreign product, they give it a greater price premium than the middle- and lower-income shoppers. At the same time, when they consider a foreign "made-in ———" label not as appealing as a made-in-Canada label, the price discount they assign to it is also much greater.

The findings have some important implications for marketing and investment strategies for Canadian marketers as well as foreign marketers. Because Canadian shoppers display biases in favor of imports from other developed countries and against imports from developing countries, and because they assign a significant value to a product's country-of-origin, marketers must take these into consideration when planning their logistics, pricing, and promotion strategies. For example, whereas imported products from other developed countries may be priced at or slightly above comparable Canadian product price levels, those from developing countries must be priced 20–30 percent lower. Hence, while locating production or assembly operations in developing countries may be a good idea from a cost perspective, it may not be a good idea from a marketing perspective. If a third-world country-of-origin means that the product has to be priced 20 percent lower than comparable products with a more appealing country-of-origin, then a developing country must offer at least a 20 percent cost savings for it to be worthwhile for foreign investors to locate their production facilities there.

The country-of-origin image also means that marketers have to be careful in making import decisions. For example, too many products imported from developing countries displayed in a store may adversely affect a store's quality image and turn away some shoppers. If a store's intention is to promote a high-quality image, it needs to procure its supplies from sources that will enhance or be compatible with the image of the store.

The survey results also provide a few helpful insights for Canadian marketers in planning their promotion strategies in the local market. For example, since the younger shoppers are more attracted to foreign products than are the older shoppers, nationalistic appeals should be more effective when they are targeted toward the latter group. At the same time, Canadian marketers can focus their promotion efforts more toward the young and use more international appeals when they are selling imported products. Finally, because the upper-income group has a better perception of imports from other developed countries and is prepared to pay a much higher price for a preferred country-of-origin, premium pricing along with prestige image promotion should be a workable strategy for quality imported products that cater to the upper-income class in Canada.

References

Bamossy, G. J., and N. Papadopoulos (1987). "An Assessment of Reliability for Product Evaluation Scales in Country of Origin Research," *World Marketing Congress International Conference Series*, III, Barcelona, Spain, 119–122.

Bannister, J. P., and J. A. Saunders (1978). "U.K. Consumers' Attitudes Towards Imports: The Measurement of National Stereotype Image," *European Journal of Marketing*, 12, 562–570.

Barker, A. T. (1987). "A Study of Attitudes Towards Products Made in Australia," *Journal of Global Marketing*, 1(1/2), 131–144.

————, and T. Robinson (1987). "Saskatchewan Consumers' Perception of Domestic and Imported Products," in R. E. Turner (ed.), *Marketing, Proceedings of the Annual Conference of the Administrative Sciences Association of Canada,* Toronto, Ontario: University of Toronto, 186–195.

Barker, T., and E. Kaciak (1989). "The Influence of Rating Scales in Country-of-Origin Research," in A. d'Astous (ed.), *Marketing, Proceedings of the Annual Conference of the Administrative Sciences Association of Canada.* Montreal, Quebec: 11–20.

Bilkey, W. J., and E. Nes (1982). "Country-of-Origin Effects on Product Evaluations," *Journal of International Business Studies,* 13 (Spring/Summer), 89–99.

Erickson, G. M., J. K. Johansson, and P. Chao (1984). "Image Variables in Multi-Attribute Product Evaluations: Country-of-Origin Effects," *Journal of Consumer Research,* 11 (September), 694–699.

Ettenson, R., J. Wagner, and G. Gaeth (1988). "Evaluating the Effect of Country of Origin and the 'Made in the USA' Campaign: A Conjoint Approach," *Journal of Retailing,* 64 (Spring), 85–100.

Han, C. M. (1989). "Country Image: Halo or Summary Construct?" *Journal of Marketing Research,* 26 (May), 222–229.

————, and V. Terpstra (1988). "Country-of-Origin Effects for Unational and Binational Products," *Journal of International Business Studies,* 19 (Summer), 235–255.

Halfhill, D. S. (1980). "Multinational Marketing Strategy: Implications of Attitude Toward Country of Origin," *Management International Review,* 20 (December), 26–32.

Heslop, L. A., J. Liefeld, and M. Wall (1987). "An Experimental Study of the Impact of Country-of-Origin Information," in R. E. Turner (ed.), *Marketing, Proceedings of the Annual Conference of the Administrative Sciences Association of Canada.* Toronto, Ontario: University of Toronto, 179–185.

Heslop, L. A., and M. Wall (1985). "Differences Between Men and Women in the Formation of Country-of-Origin Product Images," in J. C. Chebet (ed.), *Marketing, Proceedings of the Annual Conference of the Administrative Sciences Association of Canada.* Montreal, Quebec: University of Montreal, 148–158.

————, (1986). "Two Views of the World: Differences Between Men and Women on Perceptions of Countries as Producers of Consumer Goods," in T. E. Muller (ed.), *Marketing, Proceedings of the Annual Conference of the Administrative Sciences Association of Canada.* British Columbia: Whistler, 123–132.

Hong, S., and R. S. Wyer, Jr. (1989). "Effects of Country-of-Origin and Product-Attribute Information Processing Perspective," *Journal of Consumer Research,* 16 (September), 175–187.

Howard, D. G. (1989). "Understanding How American Consumers Formulate Their Attitudes About Foreign Products," *Journal of International Consumer Marketing*, 2(2), 7–24.

Hung, C. L. (1989). "A Country of Origin Image Study: The Canadian
Perception and Nationality Biases," *Journal of International Consumer
Marketing*, 1(3), 5–26.

Johansson, J. K., and R. S. Spich (1982). "Does Country-of-Origin Matter
in Multi-Attribute Product Evaluations?" in S. M. Dawson and J. R.
Wills (eds.), *Proceedings of the Academy of International Business Asia-
Pacific Conference*. Honolulu, Hawaii: University of Hawaii, 123–135.

Johansson, J. K., S. P. Douglas, and I. Nonaka (1985). "Assessing the Impact of Country of Origin on Product Evaluations: A New Methodological Perspective," *Journal of Marketing Research*, 22 (November),
388–396.

Kaynak, E., and S. T. Cavusgil (1983). "Consumer Attitudes Towards
Products of Foreign Origin: Do They Vary Across Product Classes?"
International Journal of Advertising, 2, 147–157.

Khera, I., B. Anderson, and Y. Kim (1982). "Consumer Attitudes Toward
Products from Selected Asia-Pacific Countries," in S. H. Dawson
and J. R. Wills (eds.), *Proceedings of the Academy of International Business Asia-Pacific Conference*. Honolulu, Hawaii: University of Hawaii,
110–122.

Nagashima, A. (1970). "A Comparison of Japanese and U.S. Attitudes Toward Foreign Products," *Journal of Marketing*, 34 (January), 68–77.

———, (1977). "A Comparative "Made-in" Product Image Survey
Among Japanese Businessmen," *Journal of Marketing*, 41 (July),
95–100.

Narayana, C. L. (1981). "Aggregate Images of American and Japanese
Products: Implications on International Marketing," *Columbia Journal of World Business*, 16 (Summer), 31–35.

Papadopoulos, N. et al. (1987). "Made in Canada, Eh?: A Cross-National
View of Canadian Products," in R. E. Turner (ed.), *Marketing, Proceedings of the Annual Conference of the Administrative Sciences Association of Canada*. Toronto, Ontario: University of Toronto, 196–205.

Reierson, C. (1966). "Are Foreign Products Seen as National Stereotypes?"
Journal of Retailing, 42 (Fall), 33–40.

Sauer, P. L., M. A. Young, and H. R. Unnava (1991). "An Experimental
Investigation of the Processes Behind the Country of Origin Effect,"
Journal of International Consumer Marketing, 3, 2, 29–60.

Schooler, R. D. (1965). "Product Bias in the Central American Common
Market," *Journal of Marketing Research*, 2 (November), 394–397.

———, (1971). "Bias Phenomenon Attendant to the Marketing of Foreign Goods in the U.S.," *Journal of International Business Studies*, 2
(Spring), 71–80.

Shellinck, D. A. (1989). "Determinants of Country of Origin Cue Usage," in A. d'Astous (ed.), *Marketing, Proceedings of the Annual Conference of the Administrative Sciences Association of Canada.* Montreal, Quebec: 268–275.

Wall, M., L. A. Heslop, and G. Hofstra (1988). "Male and Female Viewpoints of Countries as Producers of Consumer Goods," *Journal of International Consumer Marketing,* 1(1), 1–15.

Wall, M., J. Liefeld, and L. A. Heslop (1991). "Impact of Country-of-Origin Cues on Consumer Judgements in Multi-Cue Situations: A Covariance Analysis," *Journal of the Academy of Marketing Science,* 19(2), 105–114.

CHAPTER 12

IMPORTANCE OF PRODUCT INFORMATION CUES TO GLOBAL MARKETING

A. Coskun Samli

Dhruv Grewal

Mary K. Ericksen

I t has long been established in domestic marketing that consumer attitudes toward products are extremely important to purchasing behavior. According to Nagashima (1970), this concept can be usefully applied to products moving between national and international boundaries. Consumer behaviorists have stated that consumer attitudes toward the products of a particular nation are of major importance in determining international marketing strategies (e.g., Schooler 1965; Rierson 1966; Schooler and Sunoo 1969; Schooler 1971; Gaedeke 1973; Dornoff, Tankersley, and White 1974; Hampton 1977; Baumgartner and Jolibert 1981; Niffenegger, White, and Marmet 1982; Kaynak and Cavusgil 1983; Lumpkin, Crawford, and Kim 1985; Wall and Heslop 1986; Hung 1989; Lumpkin and Madden 1989). It is necessary for U.S. apparel manufacturers to develop international marketing strategies to fit the needs and wants of consumers.

Verhage and Henion (1986, p. 1) indicated that cross-cultural marketing can be successful only if management reacts to "specific cultural environments." They state that "knowledge, understanding, and acceptance of a different culture and its influence on behavior strengthens a marketer's position at home and abroad." The stereotypical image of U.S. apparel products is based on multiple information cues.

Olson and Jacoby (1972) classified product information cues into two categories: intrinsic and extrinsic cues. *Intrinsic cues* are product cues that cannot be changed without physically altering a product, whereas *extrinsic cues* can be changed without physically altering a product. A product's country-of-origin is one of the most important extrinsic cues. However, most country-of-origin studies deal with a product and a country in a general manner (Hugstad and Durr 1986; Nagashima 1970). They give the impression that country-of-origin is primarily country-specific and applicable to all the products produced in that country. Furthermore, most country-of-origin studies ignore the presence of other mediating variables (Cordell 1991). However, there is evidence that the effect of country-of-origin may be product-specific rather than country-specific (Kaynak and Cavusgil 1983).

In this chapter we propose that even if country-of-origin is highly important for a certain product (or product category), it cannot be operationalized as a marketing tool all by itself. A synergistic effect occurs only when a balance between intrinsic and extrinsic cues is attained. During the past fifteen years, much has been written on the country-of-origin concept, and numerous research projects have attempted to establish its importance in different product categories (Kaynak and Cavusgil 1983; Bilkey and Nes 1982; Bannister and Heyworth 1985). Although research has shown that country-of-origin is an important concept, very few attempts have been made to operationalize this concept to gain a competitive edge in global markets. However, operationalization of the country-of-origin concept is not only feasible but also necessary for future success in global marketing. Because the effect of country-of-origin may be product-specific, this chapter explicitly focuses on the apparel industry.

Industry Choice

Since World War II the impact of Western, and primarily American, apparel styles has become pervasive worldwide. The phenomenon can be observed in all European settings, as well as in the Far East, Africa, Latin America, India, and the Middle East. Thus the "global look" is that of the American. For most cultures traditional clothing is retained for special occasions and/or use by primitive indigenous people (Ericksen and Kaigler-Walker 1987). However, the U.S. apparel industry has been having a great deal of difficulty in global markets. Trade deficits continue to increase, whereas U.S. competitiveness, particularly in international markets, has not improved (Arpan, Torre, and Toyne 1981; Toyne et al. 1984; Czinkota and Ronkainen 1987; Hester 1987; Johnston and Yoon 1987;

Dickerson 1982). This fact suggests that U.S. global marketing strategies have not been very effective (Wills, Samli, and Jacobs 1991).

High labor costs in the United States make it extremely difficult for the U.S. apparel industry to compete effectively for low-price world market segments, and thus the global marketer needs to use existing strengths to focus on certain global consumer segments. This statement is the crux of this chapter. Conventional wisdom suggests segmentation of world markets primarily on the basis of countries (Goodnow and Hansz 1972; Jain 1984; Sethi 1971). However, the position taken in this chapter is that the U.S. apparel industry must segment its world markets on the basis of certain consumer characteristics. By using the inherent similarities among consumers in different countries, the industry can channel its efforts toward these varied world targets (Kale and Sudharshan 1987). Following this orientation, the industry can globally market its products to the Pro-American apparel segment.

In this chapter we address three specific questions. First, is country-of-origin important to the apparel product identified in this study? To address this question, we examine the effect of country-of-origin cues on consumers' product attitudes and purchase intentions through a review of the relevant literature. Second, are there desirable product information cues within the product group chosen for the study? In this case we present the results of two exploratory studies to identify key information cues for apparel products. Third, and finally, how can intrinsic and extrinsic product cues be combined to market a chosen product globally to specific international markets? In an attempt to answer this third question, we developed a marketing strategy using these information cues to facilitate the global marketing of apparel.

REVIEW OF COUNTRY-OF-ORIGIN EFFECTS

Consumers use certain information cues to hasten their product evaluation process (Scitovszky 1945). One such information cue that is important for understanding the position of U.S.-made apparel in world markets is the product's country-of-origin. Numerous studies have established that the product's country-of-origin influences consumers' likelihood of purchasing a product (e.g., Schooler 1965; Rierson 1966). In a major review, Bilkey and Nes (1982) discussed a number of issues pertaining to country-of-origin studies. Since then there have been a number of additional studies that examine country-of-origin effects on consumers' perceptions of certain products. However, only a few of these studies dealt directly with apparel. Building on Bilkey and Nes's (1982) review, we reviewed 21 country-of-origin articles dealing with apparel and related products. These articles were chosen from a total of 50 country-of-origin studies. A summary of these study characteristics is provided in Table 12-1.

A majority of the country-of-origin studies used adult subjects. In general, the studies we reviewed found significant country-of-origin cue effects. However, the results may actually be somewhat less significant than indicated because most of the studies dealt with only a single cue (the country-of-origin). If additional information cues (e.g., product attributes) had been provided, the results of country-of-origin effects on consumers' product evaluations might have differed. It must be pointed out that the vast majority of the studies assessed the perceptions of U.S. consumers (15 of 21 studies). The six studies that used non-U.S. respondents examined Guatemala (Schooler 1965), France (Baumgartner and Jolibert 1981; Niffenegger et al. 1982), Great Britain (Niffenegger et al. 1982), and Canada (Kaynak and Cavusgil 1983; Wall and Heslop 1986; Hung

TABLE 12-1   COUNTRY-OF-ORIGIN STUDIES
USING APPAREL PRODUCTS

Author (year)	Subject	Sample Size	Products	Cons. Country	Originating Country
Schooler (1965)	St[a]	$n = 200$	juice, fabric		Guatemala, El Salvador, Costa Rica, Mexico
Rierson (1966)	St	$n = 155$	general product classes (mechanical, food, fashion, and 26 specific products)	U.S.	U.S., Germany, Japan, France, Canada, Italy, Belgium, England, Sweden, Denmark
Schooler & Sunoo (1969)	A + St	$n = 320$	cloth, goblets	U.S.	Asia, Africa, South America, Western Europe
Schooler (1971)	A	$n = 866$	cloth, desk pens, goblets	U.S.	U.S., West Germany, Czechoslovakia, India, Chile, Nigeria

(continued)

TABLE 12-1   CONTINUED

Author (year)	Subject	Sample Size	Products	Cons. Country	Originating Country
Tongberg (1972)	A	$n = 83$	radios, men's dress shirts, cough syrup	U.S.	13 countries including U.S.
Gaedeke (1973)	St	$n = 200$	food, electronics, textiles, general	U.S.	U.S. and 11 developing countries
Dornoff, Tankersley, & White (1974)	A	$n = 216$	product classes: mechanical, food, fashion, electronics	U.S.	U.S., Japan, Germany, France
Hampton (1977)	A	$n = 176$	27 products	U.S.	(Based on Risk): Algeria, Pakistan, Turkey, Philippines, Hong Kong, Brazil, Canada, Japan, W. Germany
Baumgartner & Jolibert (1981)	A	$n = 108$	product classes: playing cards, life insurance, cough syrup, winter coats	France	U.S., France, Germany, England
Dickerson (1982)	A	$n = 408$	apparel	U.S.	U.S., imports (unspecified)
Khera, Anderson, & Kim (1982)	A	$n = 998$	product classes: clothing, shoes, toys, appliances, electronics	U.S.	Hong Kong, India, Korea, Taiwan
Niffenegger, White, & Marmet (1982)	A	$n = 163$	automobiles, electric appliances, textiles, cosmetics, food, pharmaceuticals	Great Britain, France	U.S., England, France

TABLE 12-1 CONTINUED

Author (year)	Subject	Sample Size	Products	Cons. Country	Originating Country
Samli, Tozier, & Alderson (1982)	A (women)	$n = 288$	clothing	U.S.	U.S., imports (unspecified)
Kaynak & Cavusgil (1983)	A	$n = 197$	electronic items, food, fashion, household goods	Canada	25 countries
Bannister & Heyworth (1985)	A	$n = 207$	clothing	U.K.	U.S., Korea, West Germany, United Kingdom, France, Italy
Lumpkin, Crawford, & Kim (1985)	A	$n = 1,462$	9 apparel categories	U.S.	U.S., Italy, Japan, Hong Kong, Mexico, Taiwan, Korea, Singapore, China, France
Hugstad & Durr (1986)	A	$n = 341$	autos, cameras, canned food, tires, shoes, sport shirts	U.S.	U.S., Japan, South Korea, People's Republic of China
McLean, Roper, & Smothers (1986)	A + St	$n = 218$	women's blouses	U.S.	varied by respondents' blouse ownership
Wall & Heslop (1986)	A	$n = 635$	cars, wine, footware, clothing, equipment	Canada	Canada and 18 trading electronic countries
Hung (1989)	A	$n = 120$	clothing, consumer electronics, dress shoes, sporting goods	Canada	U.S., Canada, Brazil, Italy, Japan, Mexico, South Korea, U.K.
Lumpkin & Madden (1989)	A	$n = 1,426$	apparel	U.S.	Brazil, Cuba, El Salvador, Haiti, Honduras, Mexico

[a]A = non-student respondents; St = student respondents

1989). Data from the review of the country-of-origin studies indicate that country-of-origin statements do affect consumer attitudes and purchase intentions.

Exploratory Studies

In order for the U.S. apparel industry to target international markets, marketers need to understand consumer attitudes toward U.S.-made apparel. Foreign students in the U.S. were used to represent international consumers. Two separate studies were conducted to determine what U.S. apparel product attributes are most desired by such consumers. Information also was collected about where subjects received their information about apparel—both in the United States and in their home countries. An attempt is made to show that such attitudinal information can be valuable for global marketing of apparel. It must be reiterated that the two studies are based on small samples and are exploratory in nature. In the future, similar studies need to be conducted in individual countries to provide marketers with critical guidelines for marketing products globally.

The samples were taken from international students at a major Southeastern university (Study 1) and a Western university (Study 2). A pretested instrument was used in both cases to measure their attitudes toward U.S.-made apparel. Nagashima's (1970) and Dickerson's (1982) instrument was used to develop the research instrument, which included:

1. Statements about U.S.-made apparel using a Likert-type scale ranging from (1) strongly disagree to (5) strongly agree.
2. Features of U.S.-made apparel that are most important to international consumers. The features selected for this section were size/fit, comfort, quality, design, price, and care. Each feature was paired against another feature, making a total of 15 paired comparisons. Respondents were asked to choose one feature in each pair.
3. Information on home-country apparel purchase behavior. This section included information on where the respondents received or sought information when purchasing garments, both in their home countries and in the United States.

Samples of 75 international students in Study 1 and 55 in Study 2 provided the data. The sample size was based on convenience and accessibility. Although the validity of using student subjects has been questioned, this sample was an appropriate source of information because these studies were conducted to provide an example as stated. Furthermore, foreign students are likely to reflect the values of young consumers in their home countries. The two studies yielded similar results, providing validity and reliability for each other.

In both studies, the samples represent a rich mixture of cultural and national backgrounds. The students understand the English language to the extent that research instruments can be completed successfully, yet each student is a good representative of his/her culture. Using immigrants or members of a racial/cultural subculture might not provide a clear picture of cultural/behavior/values/attitudes, etc., because a certain amount of acculturation in relation to the use of apparel is associated with the immigration process (Kaigler-Walker and Ericksen 1986).

Study Findings

Attitudes Toward U.S. Apparel   The data in Table 12-2 present the mean scores of attitude statements toward U.S.-made apparel. The statements were based on Likert-type scales ranging from strongly agree (5) to strongly disagree (1). The most favorable attitude toward U.S.-made apparel was that U.S. sportswear is comfortable to wear (mean = 3.69). Another favorable response was that U.S.-made garments are easy to care for (mean = 3.57). Features of U.S. apparel that were viewed as not favorable were style (mean = 2.61) and fabric quality (mean = 2.39). However, while the respondents indicated that they prefer European designs, they also stated that U.S. apparel is better made than European apparel.

Study 2 findings show similar mean scores for the various attitudinal statements. A comparison of the two studies, utilizing Spearman's coefficient of rank-order correlation, resulted in an $r_s = .78$, which is significant at the .01 level.* This comparison indicates that the two study findings are very similar.

Importance of Apparel Features   The subjects were asked to select certain apparel features that they considered important in making product evaluations. For Study 1, in descending level of importance, the subjects

---

*If n is greater than or equal to ten, the sampling distribution of Spearman's rank-order correlation is approximately normal, and a test of the null hypothesis of no relationship can be conducted (Blalock 1972, p. 417). In this case it results in a $Z = 3.26$, which is significant at the .01 level.

		Mean for Study 1	Mean for Study 2
TABLE 12-2 ATTITUDES TOWARD AMERICAN-MADE APPAREL	**Statement**		
	American sportswear is comfortable to wear.	3.69 (1)	3.67 (3)
	Care instructions on American-made garments are important to me as a consumer.	3.62 (2)	3.74 (2)
	American-made garments are easy to care for.	3.57 (3)	3.29 (5)
	Import duties in my country cause American apparel to be expensive to purchase.	3.28 (4)	3.38 (4)
	American-made apparel lasts for a long time.	3.09 (6)	3.09 (9)
	American apparel has good quality.	3.07 (7)	2.96 (13)
	It is hard for me to find the correct size in American-made apparel.	3.05 (8)	2.92 (15)
	American garments are well constructed.	3.01 (9)	3.20 (7)
	American-made garments are expensive.	3.00 (10)	3.78 (1)
	Clothing made in the United States fits very well.	2.96 (11)	2.96 (13)
	Fabrics used in American garments are fashionable.	2.84 (12)	3.12 (8)
	American-made apparel is stylish.	2.61 (13)	3.03 (11)
	American-made clothing is unusual.	2.59 (14)	2.70 (16)
	American apparel needs more high fashion design.[a]	2.50 (15)	2.96 (13)
	Fabrics used in American apparel are good quality.	2.39 (16)	3.05 (10)
	I would pay a higher price for a garment made in the United States.	2.35 (17)	2.56 (17)
	European apparel is constructed better than American-made apparel.[a]	2.18 (18)	2.18 (19)
	I prefer American designs to European designs.	2.14 (19)	2.20 (18)

[a]The lower score indicates a positive attitude to American-made apparel because of the reverse nature of the question. Numbers in parentheses are ranks. Scale Values: Strongly agree = 5; strongly disagree = 1.

selected quality, comfort, size, design, price, and ease of care (Table 12-3). A similar order was found in Study 2. Comparison of the results of the two studies, again using Spearman's coefficient of rank-order correlation, resulted in a $r_s = .77$, indicating a high association between the results of the two studies. Therefore, U.S.-apparel exporters can determine the relative importance of a number of product features and include these features in their product designs.

INFORMATION SOURCES   The majority of the subjects considered advertising the most important source of information for selecting apparel, both in the United States and in their home countries, while friends were also considered an important source of information in the subjects' home countries (see Table 12-4). With respect to home-country purchases, Study 2 findings indicated a greater importance of friends than did Study 1. This could indicate that there may be certain segments in which opinion leadership and communication networks are extremely important (Cosmas and Sheth 1980). This kind of information would enable U.S. apparel manufacturers to tailor their promotional decisions for global markets and help them promote their products.

On the basis of the findings of the two studies, it is observed that U.S. apparel products have certain positive product attributes or cues. Therefore, it may be possible to stimulate U.S. apparel exports by using these information cues to their full advantage in promotional efforts. Thus global marketers need to conduct their own studies to determine which

Feature	Mean for Study 1 $n = 75$	Mean for Study 2 $n = 55$	TABLE 12-3 RELATIVE IMPORTANCE OF FEATURES OF AMERICAN-MADE APPAREL[a]
Quality	4.00 (1)	3.00 (2)	
Comfort	3.91 (2)	3.20 (1)	
Size	3.61 (3)	1.78 (5)	
Design	3.25 (4)	2.76 (3)	
Price	3.01 (5)	2.55 (4)	
Care	2.16 (6)	1.33 (6)	

[a]Responses are based on the number of times the feature was selected. Numbers in parentheses are ranks.

features of their products are perceived as most important by specific international consumer target markets. This knowledge, along with country-of-origin information cues, will enable them to communicate a positive product image.

Strategic Implications

Wood et al. (1985) evaluated the competitive position of the U.S.-apparel industry and suggested that there was a need for companies to develop long-range strategic plans. Companies treating target markets as separate entities with particular needs and behaviors are most likely to be successful (Porter 1986). Figure 12-1 was developed to illustrate how U.S. apparel manufacturers can market their products globally to specific international consumer segments. The specific steps are discussed next.

TABLE 12-4 INFORMATION SOURCES FOR APPAREL PURCHASE	Percent[a] for Study 1	Percent[a] for Study 2
Purchase in United States		
Advertisements	46.67	30.9
Labels	26.67	23.6
Sales clerks	17.33	1.8
Other	16.00	3.6
American friends	12.00	16.4
Friends from homeland	10.67	21.8
Purchase in Home Country		
Advertisements	37.33	29.1
Friends	32.00	41.8
Sales clerks	25.33	10.9
Other	20.00	12.7

[a]Does not add to 100% because more than one response was given.

Entry Barriers

The first step is to consider possible entry barriers. There are two types of obstacles to the export of U.S. apparel: (1) traditional barriers such as quotas and customs duties and (2) competition from three groups (high-fashion and high-priced apparel from France and Italy, low-priced apparel from Southeast Asia, and the target country's own apparel industry). Despite these barriers, it is feasible for global marketers of U.S. apparel to enter selected international markets successfully.

Segmentation

The second step is to segment the markets by identifying highly receptive consumers. The specific market segments for U.S. apparel are likely to be out of the realm of standard segmentation procedures (Kale and Sudharshan 1987). A segmentation strategy that is based on socio-economic and

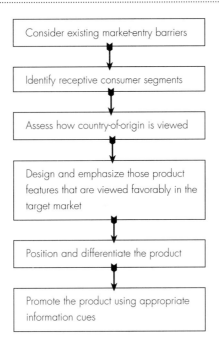

FIGURE 12-1

OUTLINE OF A GLOBAL
MARKETING STRATEGY

educational factors should be used to identify highly receptive consumers. Specific economic and educational levels existing within the populations of various countries are likely to have favorable attitudes toward American apparel. Recognizing the inherent similarities of these consumers across countries can help the global marketer to market a product that is adapted to meet these consumers' needs (Hill and Still 1984). At the same time, the manufacturer can operate more efficiently by ignoring superficial regional and national differences (Levitt 1983).

Pro-American apparel segments may exist. One such elite-consumer market would be international yuppies. Such international yuppies live in urban areas, are between the ages of 25 and 45, are well educated, have a Western orientation, are relatively wealthy, and have high personal aspirations. International yuppies exist in a number of countries (Armstrong and Buell 1987; Batutis 1987; Grotton 1986).

Country-of-Origin

The third step is to determine whether the country-of-origin (e.g., "Made in U.S.A.") information cue is viewed positively or negatively by consumers. If the country-of-origin cue is viewed positively, then the manufacturer should continue to pursue these markets. If it is viewed negatively, it may be difficult to get product adoption and acceptance, although certain steps such as price-promotions, warranties, guarantees, marketing through prestigious retail outlets, using well-known brands, and regional labeling may offset a negative country-of-origin bias (Schooler and Wildt 1968; Schooler, Wildt, and Jones 1987; Thorelli, Lim, and Ye 1989; Gaedeke 1973; Schooler and Sunoo 1969). Thus it is critical that apparel marketers target markets in which the perceived country-of-origin cue (i.e., "Made in U.S.A.") can be used to their advantage globally (Bannister and Heyworth 1985).

Product Features

The fourth step is to determine which product cues are considered desirable. Understanding the target market and appropriately positioning the product are critical for success. The emphasis of this strategy is that product features must be designed to fit the needs of the selected global consumers. It is important to find key product features that will help U.S. apparel exporters succeed in world apparel markets, thus enabling them to export *market-specific apparel*. In the studies reported in this chapter, certain product features of U.S.-made apparel surfaced as desirable characteristics. In addition, a study by Samli et al. (1982) indicated that U.S. apparel has many features that make it possible for them to be competitive in world markets. Similarly, Niffenegger et al. (1982) found that British and French respondents found U.S. products to be reliable. If studies conducted by global marketers indicate that their products have certain preferred features, then marketers can position the products by using those cues.

POSITIONING

The fifth step is to position the product to global consumer segments using appropriate information cues. In targeting global consumers, marketers of U.S. apparel must be very cautious when positioning their product vis-a-vis high-class competition, primarily from Western Europe. It is quite possible that one of the markets in which the U.S.-made apparel could compete most successfully is the high-quality leisure wear market rather than the high-fashion apparel market. Products need to be positioned in a manner that utilizes the psychological values associated with country-of-origin cues (Doeblin 1982). The products should be relatively high priced in order to convey a high-quality image (Rao and Monroe 1989). In addition, the products should be distributed through high-quality stores to consistently portray the products as being of high quality (Dodds, Monroe, and Grewal 1991). Marketers need to study gaps in the supply of apparel in other nations and then position their products to fill these gaps. Not all manufacturers have an exclusive product, but they can position themselves to fill certain niches of global consumer markets through specific product/service combinations (Porter 1980).

Amine and Cavusgil (1986), in a research study on the British clothing industry, suggest that a market segmentation strategy based on product benefits, such as product design and style (product cues), may improve the performance of global marketers. The strategy of focusing on positioning products based on their competitive attributes has been successfully used by European and East Asian firms.

PROMOTION

Finally, global marketers need to promote their products. It is particularly clear that promotion and personal influence are very important in the acceptance of U.S.-made apparel products overseas. The exploratory studies indicate that opinion leadership features exist in different cultures, and these need to be incorporated into promotional activity to increase consumer acceptance of the product being marketed. Thus advertising campaigns that are designed for specific global consumer target markets are crucial for the success of any marketing strategy. The effectiveness of these advertising campaigns depends on how successfully the industry can communicate its product features that are considered desirable. Global marketers need to take advantage of positive country-of-origin effects in their promotion (Dornoff, Tankersley, and White 1974). Rierson's (1967) findings indicate that promotional campaigns can improve consumer attitudes as long as the consumers are not intensely prejudiced against a nation's products.

It is important to point out that a few U.S. firms do compete effectively by using global marketing strategies somewhat similar to the ones suggested in this chapter. It has been reported that at the higher end of the market, the sales of U.S. apparel products, particularly children's wear, have grown substantially in the Middle East (Dawson 1986). Amine and Cavusgil (1986) suggest that the Middle East shows a strong potential for creating new markets for clothing exporters. Various U.S. apparel products (e.g., lingerie and Western wear) are well-liked in different parts of the Middle East (Dawson 1986), while similar findings have been reported for certain parts of Europe (U.S. Department of Commerce 1986). Support for the thesis of this chapter is provided by the Levi Strauss Company. U.S.-made Levis are sold in approximately 70 countries using different positioning and promotional campaigns (International Advertiser 1981). Levi's success reinforces Schleifer and Dunn's (1968) finding that advertisers need to select the reference group portrayed in the advertisement carefully. Because consumer perceptions may differ significantly between national-product stereotypes and product-specific attitudes (Etzel and Walker 1974), apparel exporters need to conduct research to determine consumers' perceptions.

Conclusion

This chapter emphasizes four key conclusions. First, a number of U.S. industries, including the apparel industry, are facing troubled times and need to improve their competitiveness to perform more effectively in global markets. Second, country-of-origin statements are critical in influencing consumer attitudes. The product claims made should be consistent with the country-of-origin perceptions of prospective consumers. Third, global marketers need to conduct studies to determine the specific product features that are critical for the targeted markets. Fourth, global marketers need to improve their competitive position by paying special attention to identifying pro-American consumer markets. In addition, they should determine the relative importance of information cues in these markets. Identifying global consumer markets and determining their respective sizes and specific idiosyncracies is vital for the long-term success of the U.S. apparel industry. Such information is essential if the U.S. apparel industry is to market its product successfully on a global scale. Ultimately, the product should be positioned and promoted to these markets, taking advantage of positive country-of-origin perceptions.

REFERENCES

Amine, L. S., and S. T. Cavusgil (1986). "Export Marketing Strategies in British Clothing Industry," *European Journal of Marketing,* 20(7), 21–33.

Armstrong, L., and B. Buell (1987). "The Rise and Rise of the Japanese Yuppie," *Business Week,* February 16, 54–6.

Arpan, J. S., J. DeLa Torre, and B. Toyne (1981). "International Developments and the U.S. Apparel Industry," *Journal of International Business Studies,* 12 (Winter), 49–64.

Bannister, J. P., and A. L. Heyworth (1985). "An Empirical Study of the Attitudes of United Kingdom Consumers Toward Clothing Made in Various Other Countries," *Journal of Textile Institute,* 76 (November–December), 434–41.

Batutis, M. (1987). "Northeast Yuppies," *American Demographics* (May), 52.

Baumgartner, G., and A. Jolibert (1981). "The Foreign Products in France," in H. Keith Hunt (ed.), *Advances in Consumer Research,* vol. 5, Ann Arbor, MI: Association for Consumer Research, 603–5.

Bilkey, W. J., and E. Nes (1982). "Country-of-Origin Effects on Product Evaluation," *Journal of International Business Studies,* 13 (Spring/Summer), 89–99.

Blalock, H. M., Jr. (1972). *Social Statistics,* Second Edition, New York: McGraw-Hill.

Cosmas, S. C., and J. N. Sheth (1980). "Identification of Opinion Leaders Across Cultures: An Assessment for Use in the Diffusion of Innovations and Ideas," *Journal of International Business Studies,* 11 (Spring/Summer), 66–72.

Cordell, V. V. (1991). "Competitive Context and Price as Moderators of Country of Origin Preferences," *Journal of the Academy of Marketing Science,* 19 (Spring), 123–8.

Czinkota, M. R., and I. A. Ronkainen (1987). "From the Guest Editors," *International Marketing Review,* 4 (Spring), 5–7.

Dawson, W. (1986). "U.S. Exhibitors Find That Apparel Continues to Show Well to Customers in Middle East," *Business America,* February 3, 19–20.

Dickerson, K. G. (1982). "Imported Versus U.S. Produced Apparel: Consumer Views and Buying Patterns," *Home Economics Research Journal,* 10 (March), 241–52.

Dodds, W. B., K. B. Monroe, and D. Grewal (1991). "The Effects of Price, Brand, and Store Information on Buyers' Product Evaluations," *Journal of Marketing Research,* 28 (August), 307–19.

Doeblin, J. (1982). "The Image of 'Made In . . .' Labels in Japan as a Criterion for Market Segmentation," in *Past, Present and Future,* 25th Annual Conference, London: The Market Research Society, 367–76.

Dornoff, R. J., C. B. Tankersley, and G. P. White (1974). "Consumers' Perceptions of Imports," *Akron Business and Economic Review,* 5 (Summer), 26–9.

Ericksen, M. K., and K. Kaigler-Walker (1987). "Standard Measurement Criteria: Methodology for Cross-Cultural Research on Appearance," S. P. Douglas et al. (eds.), *AMA Educators' Conference,* Vol. 53, Chicago: American Marketing Association, 11–14.

Etzel, M. J., and B. J. Walker (1974). "Advertising Strategy for Foreign Products," *Journal of Advertising Research,* 14 (June), 41–44.

Gaedeke, R. (1973). "Consumer Attitudes Toward Products Made in Developing Countries," *Journal of Retailing,* 49 (Summer), 13–24.

Goodnow, J. D., and J. E. Hansz (1972). "Environmental Determinants of Overseas Market Entry Strategies," *Journal of International Business Studies,* 3 (Spring), 33–50.

Grotton, K. (1986). "On the Trail of the Yuppies," *Marketing,* June 12, 20–23.

Hampton, G. M. (1977). "Perceived Risk in Buying Products Made Abroad by American Firms," *Baylor Business Studies,* 8 (October), 53–64.

Hester, S. B. (1987). "The Impact of International Textile Trade Agreements," *International Marketing Review,* 4 (Spring), 31–41.

Hill, J. S., and R. R. Still (1984). "Adapting Products to LDC-Tastes," *Harvard Business Review,* 62 (March–April), 92–101.

Hugstad, P. S., and M. Durr (1986). "A Study of Country of Manufacturer Impact on Consumer Perceptions," in *Proceedings of the Tenth Annual Conference of Marketing Science,* 115–7.

Hung, C. L. (1989). "A Country-of-Origin Product Image Study: The Canadian Perception and Nationality Biases," *Journal of International Consumer Marketing,* 1(3), 5–26.

International Advertiser (1981). "Exporting a Legend," *International Advertiser* (November/December), 2–3.

Jain, S. (1984). *International Marketing Management,* Boston: Kent.

Johnston, W. J., and H. D. Yoon (1987). "Reacting to a Textile and Apparel Trade Enforcement Act," *International Marketing Review,* 4 (Spring), 42–51.

Kaigler-Walker, K., and M. K. Ericksen (1986). "Acculturation of Hispanic-American Women: The Impact of Clothing Consumption," *Proceedings of the Workshop of Cultural and Subcultural Influence in*

Consumer Behavior in Marketing, Chicago: American Marketing Association.

Kale, S. H., and D. Sudharshan (1987). "A Strategic Approach to International Segmentation," *International Marketing Review,* 4 (Summer), 60–70.

Kaynak, E., and S. T. Cavusgil (1983). "Consumer Attitudes Towards Products of Foreign Origin: Do They Vary Across Product Classes," *International Journal of Advertising,* 2 (April–June), 147–57.

Khera, I., B. Anderson, and Y. Kim (1982). "Consumer Attitudes Toward Products from Selected Asia-Pacific Countries," in the *Proceedings of the Academy of International Business,* Honolulu: University of Hawaii, 110–12.

Levitt, T. (1983). "The Globalization of Markets," *Harvard Business Review,* 61 (May–June), 92–102.

Lumpkin, J. R., J. C. Crawford, and G. Kim (1985). "Perceived Risk as a Factor in Buying Foreign Clothes," *International Journal of Advertising,* 4(2), 157–69.

Lumpkin, J. R., and C. S. Madden (1989). "Profiling the U.S. Consumer Market for Apparel in Selected Latin American Countries," *Journal of International Consumer Marketing,* 1(3), 65–86.

McClean, F. P., L. L. Roper, and R. Smothers (1986). "Imported Versus Domestic Blouses: Women's Preferences and Purchase Motives," *Home Economics Research Journal,* 14 (March), 306–13.

Nagashima, A. (1970). "A Comparison of Japanese and U.S. Attitudes Toward Foreign Products," *Journal of Marketing,* 34 (January), 68–74.

Niffenegger, P., J. White, and G. Marmet (1982). "How European Retailers View American Imported Products: Results of a Product Image Survey," *Journal of the Academy of Marketing Science,* 10 (Summer), 281–91.

Olson, J. C., and J. Jacoby (1972). "Cue Utilization in the Quality Perception Process," in M. Venkatesan (ed.), *Proceedings,* Ann Arbor, MI: Association for Consumer Research, 167–79.

Porter, M. E. (1980). *Competitive Strategy: Techniques for Analyzing Industries and Competitors,* New York: The Free Press.

——, (1986). "Changing Patterns of International Competition," *California Management Review,* 28 (Winter), 9–40.

Rao, A., and K. B. Monroe (1989). "The Effect of Price, Brand and Store Name on Buyers' Subjective Product Assessments: An Integrative Review, *Journal of Marketing Research,* 26 (August), 351–56.

Rierson, C. (1966). "Are Foreign Products Seen as National Stereotypes?," *Journal of Retailing,* 42 (Fall), 33–40.

——, (1967). "Attitude Changes Toward Foreign Products," *Journal of Marketing Research,* 4 (November), 385–87.

Samli, A. C., E. F. Tozier, and D. H. Alderson (1982). "Attitude of American Women Towards Importing Clothing: A Major Export Line from Pacific Basin to the American Market," in the *Proceeding,* of the Academy of International Business, Honolulu: University of Hawaii, 136–47.

Schooler, R. D. (1965). "Product Bias in the Central American Common Market," *Journal of Marketing,* 11 (November), 394–97.

———, (1971). "Bias Phenomena Attendant to the Marketing of Foreign Goods in the U.S.," *Journal of International Business Studies,* 2 (Spring), 71–80.

———, and D. H. Sunoo (1969). "Consumer Perceptions of International Labeling," *Social Science Quarterly,* 49(4), 886–90.

———, and A. R. Wildt (1968). "Elasticity of Bias," *Journal of Marketing Research,* 5 (February), 78–81.

———, A. R. Wildt, and J. M. Jones (1987). "Strategy Development for Manufactured Exports of Third World Countries to Developed Countries," *Journal of Global Marketing,* 1 (Fall/Winter), 53–68.

Scitovszky, T. (1945). "Some Consequences of the Habit of Judging Quality by Price," *The Review of Economic Studies,* 12 (Winter), 100–5.

Schleifer, S., and S. W. Dunn (1968). "Relative Effectiveness of Advertisements of Foreign and Domestic Origin," *Journal of Marketing Research,* 5 (August), 296–9.

Sethi, S. P. (1971). "Comparative Cluster Analysis for World Markets," *Journal of Marketing Research,* 8 (August), 348–54.

Thorelli, H. B., J. S. Lim, and J. Ye (1989). "Relative Importance of Country of Origin, Warranty and Retail Store Image on Product Evaluations," *International Marketing Review,* 6(1), 35–46.

Tongberg, R. C. (1972). "An Empirical Study of Relationships Between Dogmatism and Consumer Attitudes Toward Foreign Products," Ph.D. dissertation, The Pennsylvania State University.

Toyne, B., J. S. Arpan, A. H. Barnett, D. A. Ricks, and T. A. Shimp (1984). "The International Competitiveness of the U.S. Textile Mill Products Industry: Corporate Strategies for the Future," *Journal of International Business Studies,* 15 (Winter), 145–65.

U.S. Department of Commerce (1986). "Memorandum for U.S. Textile and Exporters," *U.S. Department of Commerce* (July).

Verhage, B. J., and K. Henion, II (1986). "International Marketers Should Consider the Ecological Aspects of a Culture When Going Abroad," *Proceedings of the Workshop of Cultural and Subcultural Influence in Consumer Behavior in Marketing,* Chicago: American Marketing Association.

Wall, M., and L. A. Heslop (1986). "Consumer Attitudes Toward Canadian-Made versus Imported Products," *Journal of the Academy of Marketing Science,* 14 (Summer), 27–36.

Wills, J., A. C. Samli, and L. Jacobs (1991). "Developing Global Products and Marketing Strategies: A Construct and a Research Agenda," *Journal of the Academy of Marketing Science,* 19 (Winter), 1–10.

Wood, V. R., C. M. Nelson, and T. R. Gillpatrick (1985). "The Competitive Standing of the U.S. Textile Industry: Current Situations and Future Directions," in D. M. Klein and A. E. Smith (eds.), *Marketing Comes of Age.* Boca Raton, FL: Southern Marketing Association, 251–4.

PART IV

GLOBAL ADVERTISING PROGRAMS

CHAPTER 13

COMMUNICATIONS IN GLOBAL MARKETS

H. Rao Unnava

Roger D. Blackwell

Curtis P. Haugtvedt

Amy S. Mobley

I n the 1990s, the globe is becoming the marketplace for many corporations. Although the trend of moving beyond one's own country for growth opportunities has been in place for some time, the pace of such activity is increasing dramatically. Fast-paced political changes in Europe and elsewhere, increases in international communications and travel, and the increasing standard of living in many countries are but a few of the factors behind the growth of global marketing.

Because the focus on global markets is relatively new, many companies aren't sure what kinds of marketing strategies they should follow. Some companies have chosen a *globalization strategy* and have assumed that the similarities among consumers across different countries outweigh any differences that may exist. Companies like Coca-Cola and Levi Strauss seem to have been successful in using such an approach (Dichter 1962; Elinder 1961; Levitt 1983).

On the other hand, Procter & Gamble found that U.S. and Japanese consumers hold different beliefs about the relationship between the thickness and the absorbency of diapers. Whereas U.S. consumers react very positively to the concept of thin diapers, Japanese consumers are not convinced that thin diapers are as effective as their bulky counterparts. Companies choose a *localization strategy* and focus on the geopolitical and cultural differences that characterize the consumers in various countries. Successes of firms like Nestlé and Volvo (Huszagh 1986; Wind 1986) suggest that these differences should be nurtured and catered to. However, the problems that Ford Motor Company will face in the near future in their attempts to integrate the diverse brand images they have established across various European countries will surely make marketers think twice before blindly pursuing a localization strategy.

The successes or failures of companies that either maintained or varied marketing strategies in foreign countries have spurred an active debate on the relative advantages and disadvantages of globalization versus localization strategies (e.g., Britt 1974; Buzzell 1968; Levitt 1983; Onkvisit and Shaw 1987; Sorenson and Weichman 1975). Playing an important role in this debate is whether and how companies should devise advertising for global markets (Meffert and Althans 1986; Moriarty and Duncan 1991; Onkvisit and Shaw 1987). While some frameworks have been offered to guide global advertising strategy decisions (e.g., Douglas and Wind 1987; Onkvisit and Shaw 1987), we suggest that an appreciation for basic consumer behavior principles is necessary for the effective use of such frameworks.

Drawing on the research findings in consumer research, we identify potential areas for standardization of marketing communications across countries and cultures. Before presenting the basic consumer behavior principles, we briefly examine developments in international trade that have made global marketing such an important consideration.

Recent Developments in International Markets

Businesses are currently experiencing a transition from international marketing to global marketing. *International marketing* represents the actions of firms domiciled in one country and developing methods to market the same or similar products in additional countries. Most often, in the past, such firms sought additional markets in countries that were close in proximity or structure to the markets of the home country. For example, a German firm could sell its products in Switzerland or Italy with minor adaptation. U.S.-based firms could expand into Canada or England with relative ease, concerning themselves mostly with overcoming exchange and tariff obstacles and perhaps transportation and distribution problems.

Global marketing views the entire globe as the marketplace. The 1992 Single Market Initiative (SMI) of the European Community (EC) was an important catalyst to the development of this new view. As the reduction of trade and physical barriers became more likely, companies in Europe and some foresighted Japanese and U.S. firms realized that the world can now be treated as an enormous marketplace that can be approached using techniques that have been employed in domestic markets for more than a century.

The critical need for global marketing programs is exacerbated by the saturation of domestic markets in major industrialized countries and by changes in the distribution of the world's population. The population of affluent, industrialized countries (North America, Europe, Japan, Australia), for example, is projected to decline from 15 percent of the world's population in 1985 to barely 5 percent in the year 2100 (Wattenberg 1987). Faced with a declining rate of population growth, many international firms are now seeking to grow by reaching the same market segments they have dominated in the past, but now they must find the segments in other countries.

Other factors that contribute to global marketing strategies include increases in GNP per capita in many countries, steady rises in life expectancy, rapid increases in literacy and education levels, increases in share of manufactured exports by newly industrialized countries, advances in transportation and communications, and expansion of world travel.

Under these conditions that appear to facilitate international trade, companies peering beyond the frontiers of their own countries for new markets frequently find themselves grappling with the fundamental issue of whether they should tailor-make products and strategies for each country or whether they should continue to use the same products and strategies (with minor modifications) in various countries.

The benefits of standardizing **products** across countries are many. Standardization simplifies decision making, reduces costs because of economies of scale, results in operational and executional efficiency because of transferability of experience from one country to the other, and, finally, gives a company a uniform worldwide image of consistency (Onkvisit and Shaw 1987).

Supporters of standardization focus on the general convergence of consumption patterns and styles across several countries. The general trend toward aging populations, falling birth rates, and increased female employment—common to large segments of the modern industrialized world—seems to increase the similarities among peoples (Saatchi and Saatchi annual report 1983). Such convergence is viewed as an attractive climate for the launch of global products that have uniform positioning across several countries.

Proponents of localization strategies see things differently. They focus on cultural differences among people in various countries. Kahler (1983, cited in Onkvisit and Shaw 1987), for example, recognizes the critical nature of cultural similarity in determining the success of global products. However, given the vast cultural differences among peoples, Kahler believes that globalization is viable only for culture-free products such as industrial goods and some consumer durables. Culture-bound products, according to him, require adaptation. Wind (1986), however, argues against globalization of products for very different reasons. According to him, standardized products are underdesigned for some countries and overdesigned for others. Wind (1986) also believes that standardization stunts entrepreneurial activities.

Supporters of globalization are not blind to the differences among cultures. They appear to believe in an aggressive role for marketers in addressing these differences. For example, Levitt (1983), a strong proponent of globalization, admits the existence of cultural differences among countries. These differences may be so strongly entrenched in a country that they resist a manufacturer's attempts at homogenization of markets. However, Levitt (1983) believes that global marketers can modify the demand functions of consumers—that is, they can change the salience consumers attach to various attributes as they evaluate products. (For a good discussion on demand function modification, see Dickson and Ginter 1987.) "But the global corporation accepts and adjusts to these (cultural) differences only after reluctantly testing their immutability, after trying in various ways to circumvent and reshape them" (Levitt 1983).

The critics of globalization and localization, therefore, center their arguments on the differences among consumers in various countries and the ability of marketers to surmount those differences. Interestingly, though, the effect these differences may have on the decision-making processes of consumers in various countries has not been addressed in academic literature. The effects of differences among people in their exposure to and processing of advertising information, which are most pertinent to this chapter, have also not been given much attention. For example, one critical question is whether cultural differences are associated with preferences for different types of products, with different types of decision making and product choice strategies. That is, do different nationalities suggest that consumers process advertising information differently? A better understanding of the possible answers to these questions follows from a good understanding of the interaction between advertising and the decision-making process. Thus we first examine the typical decision-making process of consumers and then turn to global advertising considerations surrounding this process.

The Consumers' Decision-Making Process

The aim of advertising is to influence consumers to buy the advertised brand. Therefore, an understanding of the decision-making process of consumers is a precursor to the planning of advertising strategies that seek to influence that process. In this chapter, we use the consumer decision-making process framework proposed by Engel, Blackwell, and Miniard

(1993) to identify the various stages in the planning, purchasing, and the consumption of products.

According to Engel, Blackwell, and Miniard (1993), consumers first go through a problem recognition stage, where they feel the need for a product that would solve the problem. This need may be detected by the individual him/herself, as in the feeling of hunger. Alternatively, the social network of which the consumer is a part may prompt the consumer to consider buying a product. For example, the purchase of microwave ovens by several friends may cause a consumer to desire a microwave oven for him/herself. Finally, marketers themselves can stimulate a latent need in consumers through aggressive marketing practices. The manufacturing and marketing of several varieties of shoes, specialized by the activity the shoes are used for (e.g., tennis, basketball), is one example of a latent need that has been successfully triggered by marketers.

Assuming rational consumers who would actively seek information about the available alternatives before making a choice, Engel et al. (1993) propose the second stage in the consumer decision-making process to be that of information search. Several variables affect the extent of search activity. Consumer knowledge of the product class (Brucks 1985; Johnson and Russo 1984), the level of involvement (Beatty and Smith 1987; Bloch, Sherrell, and Ridgway 1986; Punj and Staelin 1983), individual differences (Haugtvedt, Unnava, and Talarzyk 1991; Kiel and Layton 1981), and consumers' uncertainty about the marketplace (Urbany 1986; Urbany, Dickson, and Wilkie 1989) have all been shown to moderate the nature and scope of information search. Generally speaking, higher knowledge, involvement, and uncertainty are expected to lead to greater search activity.

A common outcome of the search process is an abundance of information about the product class and the various brands that constitute the product category. Consumers are expected, in the third stage of decision making, to evaluate the information that they have gathered. Several rules that consumers may use to simplify the choice set to a manageable set of brands have been proposed and examined by consumer behavior researchers (e.g., Bettman 1979; Payne 1976; Wright 1975). Consumers do not always carefully examine all aspects of products. In some instances, they use simple heuristics to decide between brands (Hoyer 1984; Johnson, Meyer, and Ghose 1989; Sauer, Young, and Unnava 1991). For example, Hoyer's research revealed that consumers shopping for detergents used very simplistic decision rules (e.g., because I like the brand) in arriving at their brand choice. Finally, the relative dominance of affective processes, where decisions are driven not by brand cognitions but by the consumers' feelings about the product, have also been discussed (e.g., Batra and Ray 1986; Gardner 1985; Holbrook and Batra 1987; Miniard, Bhatla, and Rose 1990). In the Batra and Ray (1986) research, for example, the feelings evoked by emotional television commercials were found to affect people's attitudes toward the advertised brand.

Even though a brand may be perceived to be the best with respect to its features, consumers' decisions may not be in favor of the brand. The fourth stage of the decision-making process, therefore, deals with the factors that influence consumers' purchase decisions and purchases after an evaluation of alternative features has taken place. Several factors that are peculiar to a given situation or consumer might affect the outcome of this stage. For example, situational variables have been shown to explain deviation from planned behavior (Cote, McCullough, and Reilly 1985). Similarly, point-of-purchase sales or advertising materials have been shown to affect consumer choice (Inman, McAlister, and Hoyer 1990; Keller 1991). It has been argued that the use of advertisements on shopping carts influences choice (Rublin 1984; but see Schumann et al. 1991). Thus several marketing influences at the point-of-purchase may effectively change consumers' minds to the advantage of the marketer.

Finally, the results of a purchase, according to Engel et al. (1993), become important determinants of the future behavior of consumers with respect to a purchased brand. When a consumer is satisfied with a purchase, there is a good chance that the consumer will purchase the brand again. Dissatisfaction with a purchase may cause a consumer to complain about the product or simply not buy the product in the future (Folkes 1988).

The five stages just described are meant to be exhaustive to provide us with a thorough understanding of the various points that consumers may go through before making purchase decisions. Obviously, not all consumers go through these stages for every product they consume. It is conceivable, however, for consumers to be at one or the other stage of this process from time to time. For example, satisfied consumers of a brand of detergent may find themselves in the alternative evaluation stage when a new brand arrives on the market amidst much fanfare. Similarly, satisfied consumers may alter their purchase decisions when a slightly inferior brand offers a substantial price reduction that makes the brand more price competitive with respect to the preferred brand. It is important, therefore, to look at advertising as a means to draw people into one of the five stages of the decision-making process and then influence them to act in favor of the advertised brand.

ADVERTISING AND THE DECISION-MAKING PROCESS

The role of advertising in promoting and maintaining consumer loyalty can be understood by examining what advertising is expected to achieve at each stage of the consumers' decision-making process. Advertising can be used to stimulate a latent need in people (e.g., light beer) or to simply

inform people of the brand so that it can be part of the consumers' consideration set (Hauser and Wernerfelt 1990; Unnava and Burnkrant 1991).
For products where consumers tend to use advertisements as sources of
information (e.g., personal computers and vacation resorts), advertising
usually serves the function of informing and persuading consumers to buy
the advertised brand. The positioning of the product is one of the primary
functions fulfilled by advertising at this stage. Finally, by developing and
maintaining an image for a brand, advertising helps in reminding and
assuring consumers that the advertised brand is a good choice (Haugtvedt,
Leavitt, and Schneier 1991).

If advertising is aimed at influencing the decision-making process of
individuals, then a philosophy that espouses standardization of advertising across countries and cultures may rest on the assumption that the
decision-making process of individuals is culture invariant. Further, given
that advertising, as any other component of the marketing mix, is targeted
toward a specific segment (with the exception of companies pursuing a
mass-market strategy), standardization of advertising also assumes the existence of global segments. These two assumptions, the culture invariance
of consumers' decision-making process and the existence of global segments, are now examined in greater detail.

For exposition purposes, we consider those situations in which firms
have identified specific market segments to target rather than treating the
market as a uniform mass. This segmentation, it is assumed, is based on
consumer needs that are used to design the product. For example, the
need and desire of people to have fresh breath should have led the Lever
Company to design Close-up toothpaste. As part of an integrated marketing strategy, we assume that the firm will communicate its unique selling
proposition to its target audience. In the preceding example, this assumption translates to the communication of the benefit of fresh breath by
Close-up in all its advertising. The discussion that follows is based on this
assumption that every ad promotes the product's unique selling proposition, which was built into the product based on a need identified in the
marketplace.

ARE CONSUMER DECISION-MAKING PROCESSES CULTURE INVARIANT?

The decision-making process of consumers was discussed earlier in terms
of the stages consumers go through from planning to purchase to consumption of products. One of these stages is the problem recognition
stage, where consumers are made aware of a latent need, either by facing

the undesirable consequences of that unmet need or through exposure to social networks and marketer communications. The case of Gatorade, a product of Quaker Oats Company, is a good example of the way a marketer can ignite a latent need. Cashing in on the health consciousness of people in the United States, Gatorade was positioned as a drink that does not just quench post-exercise thirst; it also replenishes minerals lost during exercise. Feeling that the U.S. market is saturated, Quaker Oats is now moving Gatorade into European markets. Interestingly, Gatorade is being launched in the European market with advertisements and sports promotions similar to those that have helped the drink to succeed in the U.S. market (Erickson 1989). The company feels that the same life-style trends and health consciousness that propelled Gatorade in the United States are evident in the European market. That is, Gatorade promotions and products that stimulate and serve the needs for Americans are also seen as appropriate and effective for present-day Europeans.

Several companies have recognized the similarity of needs across cultures in various countries and have formulated communication campaigns that promote their products in a favorable light. Victor Kiam, the maker of the highly successful Remington powered shaving systems, uses the same television commercials in different countries after making the appropriate language translations. This does not mean that the products sold in various countries are identical. For example, battery-powered shavers are very popular in England. Kiam considered pushing the rechargeable cordless shaver in England because it appeared to be an attractive and cheaper alternative to the battery-powered shaver without sacrificing convenience. This decision was not implemented when market research found that English bathrooms do not have electric outlets, which would have made the rechargeable shaver unattractive to the English customers. However, because the shaver was promoted on the promise that it shaves as close as a blade, the company could continue to promote it exactly the same way in England as it had in the United States. Differences between people's evaluative criteria that emerged from country-specific variables did not affect Remington's advertising strategy because those differences were irrelevant to the unique selling proposition of the product. In other words, the basic need of Remington's customers, irrespective of their country of origin, appears to have stemmed from a concern about the product's performance. A promise to refund a dissatisfied customer's money successfully mollified this concern. The Remington experience thus exemplifies the commonality of consumers, across cultures, in terms of the importance attached to post-purchase evaluation and activities. More importantly, it also suggests that consumers the world over go through the post-purchase stage of the decision-making process in a similar manner.

Cultural differences among consumers are sometimes used inappropriately to explain fundamental differences in purchase behavior. For example, some researchers have suggested that Hispanic consumers are less prone to use coupons than their American counterparts (Hernandez 1988). Coupon use, as described in the decision-making process, falls in the decision stage where the price inducement offered by the coupon can alter the brand preference of the consumer. A lack of sensitivity to the financial gains associated with coupons does not agree with the fundamental principles of economics that portray the consumer as a utility maximizer. In line with this, Hernandez (1988) found that there is virtually no cultural basis for the nonuse of coupons by Puerto Ricans. A large majority of these consumers do not use coupons because of the institutional barriers (e.g., some stores did not accept coupons). Thus it would be a mistake to suggest that cultural differences between North Americans and Puerto Ricans affect their coupon proneness, or, more generally, their susceptibility to marketer influences at the decision stage of the consumption process. Marketers should not be too quick to think that culture per se is the cause of basic marketing problems.

Finally, as an example of the benefits that can be derived from using consumer behavior principles in planning global products, Wills, Samli, and Jacobs (1991) examined the role of consumer involvement and learning in product choice. A marketer interested in crossing the geographical boundaries of his/her country should realize that the effects of involvement and learning are the same, irrespective of the cultural setting of the consumer. The differences among cultures, according to Wills et al. (1991), are in the *levels* of involvement with a product or in the ability to learn about the product quickly. The marketer's job, then, is to understand the involvement of his/her audiences with the product and design his/her marketing programs to suit that level of involvement. For example, whereas soup is a relatively low involvement product in the United States, Swiss consumers may be more involved in purchasing soup. This suggests that Swiss consumers would spend more time making soup because it is important to them. Therefore, soup sold in Switzerland should be made so that consumers can make modifications to the product. In contrast, soup sold in the United States, where convenience is of paramount importance, should be ready-to-eat.

In sum, cultural differences among consumers do not seem to affect the fundamental decision-making process that they go through as they purchase and consume products. However, this does not mean that cultural differences among consumers do not affect the types of products that are consumed or the evaluative criteria that are employed by consumers as they choose among products.

Local customs, beliefs, values, and norms should affect the consumption activities of all consumers because it is well known that behavior is guided both by personal predispositions and social influences. We do not intend to convey the notion that cultural differences do not affect consumption. In fact, we believe that they strongly influence the types of products consumed. Often, these cultural differences necessitate changes in the product design by global marketers.

For example, shampoo sold in Japan must be gentle because most Japanese women wash their hair daily. Similarly, because clothes are washed in cold, hard water in Japan, detergents must be formulated for such conditions to be successful (Darlin 1989). One study showed that when college students from the United States, France, India, and Brazil viewed two common consumer products, they used different evaluative criteria because they emphasized different product attributes that were important to them (Green, Cunningham, and Cunningham 1975).

Such examples abound because the cultural differences among countries can be permuted for all countries in the world. Focusing on these differences would only add to the desperation of marketers because the concepts of global products and global advertising would appear remote and hopeless. The key is to realize that several of the differences that marketers seem to focus on in ruling out the viability of globalization are generally superficial. Marketing strategies that are built around the basic needs of consumers should ameliorate the effects of these surface differences and help in the realization of global segments.

THE REALITY OF GLOBAL SEGMENTS

In our view, the practice of global advertising is based on two assumptions: (1) that consumers all over the world use similar decision-making processes in choosing among products and (2) that the products appeal to a segment of people in every country whose basic need is met by the attributes of the global products. This second assumption of the existence of global segments is discussed now.

The philosophy of segmentation rests on the fundamental notion that differences exist among people in terms of the benefits they desire from various products and that people can be grouped together in terms of the similarity of the benefits desired. After identifying a basic need and finding a product that will satisfy this need, marketers need to find the segments to which they can successfully sell the product.

The possibility of detecting a global segment is enhanced when one addresses a basic need. As the need that is addressed in a segment becomes more and more localized, the segment that is catered to will also become equally localized. For example, it was mentioned earlier that Japanese women wash their hair daily, and therefore a shampoo must be gentle to appeal to Japanese women. The segment of women who wash their hair daily is localized predominantly to Japan. Thus, the possibility of making a global segment for a brand of shampoo that touts gentleness as its unique selling proposition and addresses those people who wash their hair daily is remote.

If the same shampoo manufacturer examines more basic needs that cut across countries and culture (e.g., dandruff control, conditioning formula), then, because of the prevalence of people in various countries who experience the basic need for a shampoo that controls dandruff or conditions their hair, the chances of realizing a global segment are maximized. That is, the idea of global segments is realized when one addresses needs that are basic and are experienced by people irrespective of their cultures.

One of the basic segments that seems to exist all over the world is the price conscious segment. For various reasons, which include general income level, education, and cultural norms, there always exist some consumers who are price sensitive and make product choices based on the prices charged by various brands. For example, in 1987 Brown and Williamson Tobacco Corporation dropped the price of Kent cigarettes in Japan, where it was generally believed that foreign brands must charge higher prices to succeed (Darlin 1989). Confounding analysts, Kent became one of the fastest selling cigarette brands in Japan, which made other companies drop their prices. The share of foreign companies in the Japanese cigarette market rose from 3 percent to more than 12 percent.

A similar experience is reported by Gold Star Company, a large South Korean manufacturer of home electronics products (Darlin 1989). According to Kim Young Jun, the managing director of Gold Star's overseas business operations, the price sensitive segment in Japan used to be virtually nonexistent, but it has come alive now, enabling low-cost producers to position their products on price as their unique selling proposition.

Revlon, the giant cosmetics manufacturer, strives to present a uniform image in the world market. The management at Revlon considered the preferences of more than 130 local markets and developed a campaign that would come closest to pleasing them all (Schroeder 1986b). While there are differences among local markets, Revlon does not believe that they are extreme enough to prioritize these markets differently.

Thus, as long as a basic need is identified, and a product is developed to address that need, the possibility of realizing a global segment is high. Mike Dowdall, Unilever's London-based detergents coordinator, identified two requirements for a product to succeed across countries: First, the brand's core position must be relevant in each country, and second, the expression of the core position must work in each market (Wentz 1989). He uses the example of Snuggle Fabric Softener to illustrate his point. Snuggle may have different names in different countries, but to convey a soft, cuddly feeling, a teddy bear is used in the United States, Europe, and Japan.

Most times, minor modifications are required in products to address country-specific needs. Gatorade, for example, uses natural colors in its drinks because Brazilians are averse to artificial colors. The popular children's toy "pound puppy" is named differently in different countries because most countries do not have dog pounds as we do in the United States. For example, the puppies with sorrowful eyes are called "Snif-Snif" in Brazil, which means that the dog is crying. The positioning of these products, however, remains the same across these countries because the segments that are being addressed are the same. Therefore the advertising message that is conveyed also remains the same among countries. Only the surface details of the advertisements change.

Problems in Global Advertising

The validity of global advertising is predicated on the existence of global segments. The existence of global segments has been questioned and criticized by some researchers (Douglas and Wind 1987, Wind 1986). According to Wind, standardized advertising requires that (1) the world's wants are homogenized; (2) the buyers are willing to sacrifice desired features to obtain higher quality or lower price; (3) the companies practicing global advertising should realize economies of scale; (4) there are minimal constraints, both external and internal, that would preclude a company from practicing global advertising; and (5) synergistic advantages of globalization are evident. Wind (1986) doubts that these conditions can ever be satisfied altogether, and therefore he advocates a "think globally but act locally" strategy.

While this argument appears valid, there are at least two problems with the logic employed. First, it is possible for individual consumers to be very different from each other and still form a uniform *pattern* of segments across countries. For example, the existence of a price conscious segment in every country cannot be disputed. The individual consumers constituting the segment in each country may be different from one another, demographically or otherwise. However, in their choice of the product in question, these consumers may find price-based claims more appealing than feature-based claims. Similarly there is in all countries a feature-oriented segment that is comprised of those consumers who attach great importance to the advanced features of the product, no matter what it costs. Insofar as such segments exist and are substantial enough to make their pursuit profitable, we do not see any reason to change advertising between countries.

AT&T, for example, wants to convince people all over the world that long-distance calling is not as expensive as people perceive it to be. AT&T attempts to achieve this objective by portraying the emotional aspects of voice-to-voice communication and then convincing people that it is not as expensive as they think it is (Cowherd 1986). The company realizes that price-based claims have a wide appeal and pursues this theme even though "very few countries around the world get the detailed billing statements we get in the U.S. With charges lumped together in bills that come out quarterly (overseas), the message of affordability can be difficult to put across" (Cowherd 1986, p. 10).

Some people, on the other hand, value the features of a product with little consideration for the price. Coleco, the maker of the popular Cabbage Patch dolls, discovered that their product was not selling well in Italy. Research revealed that Italians prefer beautiful dolls, which the Cabbage Patch dolls were not. Coleco changed the positioning of its dolls and made its appeal based on the doll's vulnerability—not its looks (Schroeder 1986a). It is possible that there was a very small segment in Italy that valued the attributes of the doll, but this segment might have been too small to make its pursuit profitable. Beautiful dolls, however, have a large and willing Italian consumer segment. There are several countries where one can identify segments of people who attach more importance to the beauty of a doll than to anything else. In other words, the *pattern of segments* remains the same among countries; only the sizes of those segments vary. When a country is found to lack the segment a company is pursuing, the company can change the position of the product to suit the country's needs, and with the change in positioning will come a change in the advertising.

Second, the argument that adaptation is necessary because consumers are different assumes that consumers do not change. Conventional wisdom, however, tells us that this is not the case. Several global brand names have achieved their success either by entering foreign markets that were becoming similar to their domestic markets (e.g., growth in two-income families and the need for fast food) or by modifying the demand functions of the markets that appeared different (see Dickson and Ginter 1987). In other words, as technology diffuses from the developed countries to the developing countries, the differences among consumers should diminish (Beatson 1987). The growth in communications and transportation should facilitate the exchange of ideas among cultures. This exchange should slowly lead to the homogenization of the world's population. In addition, marketers play an active and significant catalytic role in affecting these changes. The success of Colgate toothpaste in India, where only twenty years ago the dominant product used to brush teeth was locally made toothpowder, should exemplify the active role of marketers in changing the demand patterns of consumers. Similarly, Quaker Oats, which markets Gatorade, has pushed its product into European markets with ads and promotions similar to those employed in the United States. The Quaker Oats managers believe that the life-style trends in Europe are similar to the ones in the United States that made Gatorade successful there. Therefore, through similar advertising practices, they managed to create a need in the consumers' minds for a replenishing drink like Gatorade.

Finally, the term *global advertising* appears to be misconstrued to mean that the same advertisement is used in all countries. We take the view that as long as the positioning of a product is maintained, then the advertising that is used for that product is global. The execution of advertisements sometimes varies among countries because of local regulations and tastes. For example, no references to dieting are allowed in Belgium, and commercials that discuss weight loss are therefore prohibited (Wentz 1989). Child endorsements are not permitted in France, and comparative advertising is disallowed in Germany. Snickers candy bars will have problems in the U.K. where sweets are allowed to be positioned as occasional snacks only—not as lunch food. Thus there are problems in execution that one faces when one wants to use the same advertisement across all countries. But to expect to use the same advertisement all over the world is stretching the concept of global advertising too far. Advertising is just a vehicle used to convey a product's positioning. The positioning of a product is based on segmentation studies. Thus, as long as global segments exist and the same positioning is used for a product across the globe, we argue that global advertising is being practiced.

Conclusions

The concept of standardized advertising has seen its share of supporters and critics. The supporters believe that global segments exist and that the economies of scale and other synergistic benefits which result from global advertising justify its use. The critics of global advertising believe that the differences among local regions are large enough to require different types of advertising. They rely on the requirements of global segments for global advertising to exist, and they highlight differences among various cultures that cause people to use different evaluative criteria in choosing products to demonstrate the infeasibility of global advertising.

 We take the position that global advertising is based on the simple notion that global segments exist when the segments are based on a fundamental need in the customer population. Further, it is the pattern of segments that is relatively invariant across cultures, not the characteristics of people constituting the segment. We also believe that advertising is used to influence the decision-making process of consumers, and this process is relatively constant across cultures. What transpires in the process, in terms of the various evaluative criteria used, may be different among cultures.

Differences among people in various countries, the regulations that guide advertising in those countries, and the media habits of people in various countries are relatively superficial. These differences cannot be used as an argument against global advertising because they do not affect the positioning that is taken by a product. Their effects are in terms of the execution of advertisements. Different executions in different countries do not qualify to be called localized advertising strategy just as different packaging of a product in various countries does not suggest a localized product strategy. If the core benefit offered by a product is the same in each country, and if this core benefit has been incorporated into the product based on segmentation research that has identified a basic need in people, then it follows that a global segment has been identified.

For a marketer, our position suggests that the critical variable that determines the viability of global advertising is whether the product has been designed to address a basic need in people. If the answer to this question is in the affirmative, then the segment that is catered to by the product should be a global segment. Global segments should be addressable using global advertising. The advantages of global advertising will then be reaped by the marketer.

Note that the foregoing assumption of the existence of global segments does not ignore individual differences among consumers from various cultures. Such differences, after appropriate grouping (i.e., segmentation by desired benefits), are expected to form a pattern. It is this pattern that is assumed to be relatively similar across various countries. In other words, for every product, there exists a group of people in each country that values a particular benefit from that product more than anything else.

The emphasis we place on benefit segmentation does not imply that segmentation based on other variables is unimportant. We believe that demographic and psychographic descriptors pertaining to a consumer group will help us make distribution and communication decisions (e.g., media choice). Too, we do not dispute intercultural differences on demographics and psychographics; we think that such differences do exist on an intra- or intermarket basis. The development of global advertising is dependent on the identification of similar benefit clusters across countries, not only on the existence of similar media habits within national boundaries. If we expect consumers in a segment to have similar media habits for successful segmentation, then the issue of segmentation within a country is as open to question as the issue of global segmentation. Arguments that oppose global advertising because media consumption habits are different among cultures are open to question because they assume that media habits are homogeneous within a given country. Also, opponents of global advertising assume that media habits are the main determinants of global advertising. In reality, the choice of a medium is closely related only to the type of execution of a message and its associated costs. The expertise gained by advertisers in planning and executing coordinated mixed-media campaigns (e.g., Edell and Keller 1989) would make it relatively easy to translate a campaign from one medium to another. Therefore, differences in media consumption habits, or in the availability of various media in different countries, do not pose a serious threat to the concept of global advertising.

In sum, we propose that despite differences in cultural milieu, the patterns of benefits desired from products should be relatively similar across countries. Marketers who use the benefit segmentation approach to identify important attributes in the design of a product are expected to promote the product on those attributes. Given that the existence of benefit segments is universal, advertising that concentrates on those benefits should have global appeal too. Differences among people in terms of tastes, or in terms of the media facilities available in various countries, should affect only the execution strategy. In our opinion, advertising is global in spite of differences in execution if a constant appeal or theme is maintained.

References

Batra, R., and M. L. Ray (1986). "Affective Responses Mediating Acceptance of Advertising," *Journal of Consumer Research,* 13 (September), 234–249.

Beatson, R. (1987). "The Americanization of Europe," *International Advertiser,* 3(2), 5–9.

Beatty, S. E., and S. M. Smith (1987). "External Search Effort: An Investigation Across Several Product Categories," *Journal of Consumer Research,* 14 (June).

Bettman, J. R. (1979). *An Information Processing Theory of Consumer Choice,* Reading, MA: Addison-Wesley.

Bloch, P. H., D. L. Sherrell, and N. M. Ridgway (1986). "Consumer Search: An Extended Framework," *Journal of Consumer Research,* 13 (June), 119–128.

Britt, S. H. (1974). "Standardizing Marketing for the International Market," *Columbia Journal of World Business* (Winter), 39–45.

Brucks, M. (1985). "The Effects of Product Class Knowledge on Information Search Behavior," *Journal of Consumer Research,* 12 (June), 1–16.

Buzzell, R. D. (1968). "Can You Standardize Multinational Marketing?" *Harvard Business Review* (November/December), 102–113.

Cote, J. A., J. McCullough, and M. Reilly (1985). "Effects of Unexpected

Situations on Behavior Intention Differences: A Garbology Analysis," *Journal of Consumer Research,* 12 (September), 188–194.

Cowherd, S. (1986). "AT&T's Low Profile International Campaign," *International Advertiser,* December, 8–10.

Darlin, D. (1989). "Myth and Marketing in Japan," *Wall Street Journal,* April 6, B1.

Dichter, E. (1962). "The World Consumer," *Harvard Business Review,* 40 (July/August), 113–122.

Dickson, P. R., and J. L. Ginter (1987). "Market Segmentation, Product Differentiation and Marketing Strategy," *Journal of Marketing,* 51 (April), 1–10.

Douglas, S. P., and Y. Wind (1987). "The Myth of Globalization," *Columbia Journal of World Business* (Winter), 19–29.

Edell, J. A., and K. L. Keller (1989). "The Information Processing of Coordinated Media Campaigns," *Journal of Marketing Research,* 25 (May), 149–164.

Elinder, E. (1961). "International Advertisers Must Devise Universal Ads, Dump Separate National Ones, Swedish Adman Avers," *Advertising Age,* November 27, 91.

Engel, J. F., R. D. Blackwell, and P. W. Miniard (1993). *Consumer Behavior,* VII Edition, Dryden Press.

Erickson, J. L. (1989). "Gatorade Gusher Set: Quaker Prepares for Big International Expansion," *Advertising Age,* April 17, 10.

Folkes, V. S. (1988). "Recent Attribution Research in Consumer Behavior: A Review and New Directions," *Journal of Consumer Research,* 14 (March), 548–565.

Gardner, M. P. (1985). "Mood States and Consumer Behavior: A Critical Review," *Journal of Consumer Research,* 12 (December), 281–300.

Green, R. T., W. H. Cunningham, and I. C. M. Cunningham (1975). "The Effectiveness of Standardized Global Advertising," *Journal of Advertising,* 4 (Summer), 25–30.

Haugtvedt, C. P., C. Leavitt, and W. Schneier (1991). "Cognitive Strength of Established Brands: Memory, Attitudinal and Structural Approaches," in D. Aaker and A. Biel (eds.), *Advertising and Building Strong Brands,* Hillsdale, NJ: Lawrence Erlbaum Associates.

Haugtvedt, C. P., H. R. Unnava, and W. W. Talarzyk (1991). "Individual Differences in Pre-Purchase Search: The Interactive Effect of Cognitive Motivation and Attribute Variability on Extent of Search." Unpublished manuscript, College of Business, The Ohio State University.

Hauser, J. R., and B. Wernerfelt (1990). "An Evaluation Cost Model of Consideration Sets," *Journal of Consumer Research,* 16 (March), 393–408.

Hernandez, S. A. (1988). "An Exploratory Study of Coupon Use in Puerto

Rico: Cultural vs. Institutional Barriers to Coupon Use," *Journal of Advertising Research* (October/November), 40–46.

Holbrook, M. B., and R. Batra (1987). "Assessing the Role of Emotions as Mediators of Consumer Responses to Advertising," *Journal of Consumer Research*, 14 (December), 404–420.

Hoyer, W. D. (1984). "An Examination of Consumer Decision Making for a Common Repeat Purchase Product," *Journal of Consumer Research*, 11 (December), 822–829.

Huszagh, S. M. (1986). "Global Marketing: An Empirical Investigation," *Columbia Journal of World Business*, November, 31–43.

Inman, J. J., L. McAlister, and W. D. Hoyer (1990). "Promotion Signal: Proxy for a Price Cut?" *Journal of Consumer Research*, 17 (June), 74–81.

Johnson, E. J., and J. E. Russo (1984). "Product Familiarity and Learning New Information," *Journal of Consumer Research*, 11 (June), 542–550.

————, R. J. Meyer, and S. Ghose (1989). "When Choice Models Fail: Compensatory Models in Negatively Correlated Environments," *Journal of Marketing Research*, 26 (August), 255–270.

Keller, K. L. (1991). "Cue Compatibility and Framing in Advertising," *Journal of Marketing Research*, 28 (February), 42–57.

Kiel, G. C., and R. A. Layton (1981). "Dimensions of Consumer Information Seeking," *Journal of Marketing Research*, 18 (May), 233–239.

Levitt, T. (1983). "The Globalization of Markets," *Harvard Business Review*, 61 (May/June), 91–201.

Meffert, H., and J. Althans (1986). "Global Advertising: Multinational vs. International, Pros and Cons," *International Advertiser* (February), 34–37.

Miniard, P. W., S. Bhatla, and R. L. Rose (1990). "On the Formation and Relationship of Ad and Brand Attitudes: An Experimental and Causal Analysis," *Journal of Marketing Research*, 27 (August), 290–303.

Moriarty, S. E., and T. R. Duncan (1991). "Global Advertising: Issues and Practices," in James H. Leigh and Claude R. Martin Jr. (eds.), *Current Issues and Research in Advertising*, 13(2), 313–342.

Onkvisit, S., and J. J. Shaw (1987). "Standardized International Advertising: A Review and Critical Evaluation of the Theoretical and Empirical Evidence," *Columbia Journal of World Business* (Fall), 43–55.

Payne, J. W. (1976). "Task Complexity and Contingent Processing in Decision Making: An Information Search and Protocol Analysis," *Organizational Behavior and Human Performance*, 16 (August), 366–387.

Punj, G. N., and R. Staelin (1983). "A Model of Consumer Information Search Behavior for New Automobiles," *Journal of Consumer Research*, 9 (March), 366–380.

Rublin, L. R. (1984). "Dancing in the Aisles: Are Investors Too Bullish on ACTMEDIA?" *Barrons,* May 28.

Sauer, P. E., M. A. Young, and H. R. Unnava (1991). "An Experimental Investigation of the Country of Origin Effect," *Journal of International Consumer Marketing,* 3(2), 29–60.

Schroeder, M. (1986a). "Toys 'R' Going Global," *International Advertiser* (December), 38–39.

———— (1986b). "Revlon Strives for One Look," *International Advertiser* (April), 28–29, 39.

Schumann, D. W., J. Grayson, J. Ault, K. Hargrove, L. Hollingsworth, R. Ruelle, and S. Seguin (1991). "The Effectiveness of Shopping Cart Signage: Perceptual Measures Tell a Different Story," *Journal of Advertising Research,* 31 (February/March), 17–22.

Sorenson, R. Z., and U. E. Weichman (1975). "How Multinationals View Marketing Standardization," *Harvard Business Review,* 53(3), 38–44, 48–50, 54, 166–167.

Unnava, H. R., and R. E. Burnkrant (1991). "The Effect of Varying Ad Executions on Brand Name Memory," *Journal of Marketing Research,* 28 (November).

Urbany, J. E. (1986). "An Experimental Examination of the Economics of Information," *Journal of Consumer Research,* 13 (September), 257–271.

————, P. R. Dickson, and W. L. Wilkie (1989). "Buyer Uncertainty and Information Search," *Journal of Consumer Research,* 16 (September), 208–215.

Wattenberg, B. J. (1987). *Birth Dearth,* New York: Pharos Books.

Wentz, L. (1989). "1992 to Breed Global Brands," *Advertising Age,* April 24, 44.

Wills, J., A. C. Samli, and L. Jacobs (1991). "Developing Global Products and Marketing Strategies: A Construct and Research Agenda," *Journal of the Academy of Marketing Science,* 19 (Winter), 1–10.

Wind, Y. (1986). "The Myth of Globalization," *Journal of Consumer Marketing,* 3 (Spring), 23–36.

Wright, P. L. (1975). "Consumer Choice Strategies: Simplifying vs. Optimizing," *Journal of Marketing Research,* 60–67.

CHAPTER 14

THE IMPACT OF THE EUROPEAN COMMUNITY'S 1992 INITIATIVES ON GLOBAL ADVERTISING

Julian W. Vincze

Jane S. McNeill

Marketing to the post-1992 European Community (EC) may be viewed as focusing on commonalities and the power that comes from sharing regional information. The notion of organizing a firm's marketing efforts by global geographic regions is replacing the older country-by-country approach to marketing planning. The basis for marketing by global regions is the belief that basic consumer wants are universal or at least transcend national boundaries. This chapter discusses the impact of the EC 1992 initiatives on marketing planning with special concerns for advertising. The issues to keep in mind are: (1) will all 300 EC initiatives be operational and (2) will a standard advertising program be feasible for this single EC market?

GLOBALIZATION OF EC MARKETING

Major changes in EC political and economic structures continue to pave the way for the geographic regionalization of EC marketing with the most visible impact on advertising activities. In addition, pressures for EC regional marketing result from EC social trends that are converging in a number of important ways: birthrates are declining, the nuclear family is weakening, productivity is rising, and the workweek is becoming shorter while leisure time is becoming longer. Also, technological developments such as satellite television systems that cross national borders are enabling advertisers to utilize "cross-border" or "pan-European" media deals. Some observers believe that these changes are prompting governments to loosen restrictions on commercial media, thus creating additional advertising opportunities. Consequently U.S. publishers of magazines, trade journals, and other printed media are moving to fill a perceived advertising void in the EC marketplace. Although no specific figures on the number of publications that have entered the EC or gone global are available, Schleier (1989) senses that the pace is accelerating. These factors—the expansion of publications, the availability of satellite TV systems, and the single EC market—are pressuring advertisers toward more standardized advertising. The EC advertising arena is large and growing, and soon it may supersede the United States in total advertising expenditures.

The Importance of Advertising

Advertising as a global industry is believed by some to be the companion of individualism and a modern form of democracy. For example, John Dollisson, vice president of corporate affairs at Philip Morris International, said, "If there is one lesson to be learned from the great historical drama that has just taken place in Eastern Europe, it's that freedom is indivisible, that an open society can operate only in a free economic environment. Our system is the only system . . . that actually produces the goods. Advertising is part and parcel of that noble system" (Giges 1990).

Advertising is an important factor in stimulating trade and economic cooperation among nations. Fifteen countries account for 90 percent of worldwide advertising expenditures. To put their importance into perspective, these same fifteen countries comprise 20 percent of the world's population and 61 percent of global gross national product (Link 1988).

The Advantages of Large International Advertising Agencies

When compared to unaffiliated local agencies, large international advertising agencies offer their clients the advantages of integrated networks with worldwide information systems, coordinated planning, consistent disciplines, and sharing of learning on an international scale. These existing international agencies have realized that multinational firms demand global expertise, and they have realized the importance of the emerging trends to global products, global consumer tastes, needs, and converging purchasing patterns. Thus they see consumers as becoming more homogeneous. "Saatchi & Saatchi claimed that worldwide brands would soon become the norm and that such an advertising challenge could only be handled by worldwide agencies" (Jeannet and Hennessey 1988). However, many marketing professionals remain skeptical about global advertising claims.

Pan-European Advertising Examples

3M is an example of an established U.S. company which has used global advertising and which is reorganizing its marketing operations to respond to the emerging EC market. In the past, 3M's international subsidiaries were responsible for all products marketed within each country. This required separate strategies and different advertising agencies for each country. "It was just getting too expensive," stressed Don Lineman, 3M's marketing communications manager for Europe. So, in the summer of 1988, 3M consolidated all pan-European advertising for 3M's Scotchgard products in one agency (Cote 1988). Another example of pan-European advertising is an antacid ad that portrays harried people experiencing stressful, common everyday problems. The ad was aired in several languages, and it was successful because the situation is universal (Teinowitz 1990). Even advertising of more culturally sensitive subject matter is possible. Johnson & Johnson's new o.b. with applicator tampon uses the slogan "o.k., o.b." in print and in TV commercials. The o.b. compaign was initially introduced in Austria, Belgium, France, Germany, Italy, and Spain (Wentz 1989). Numerous other well-known firms are involved in pan-European advertising such as Xerox, IBM, Apple, Nissan, Benson & Hedges, Avis, Buitoni, Air New Zealand, and Panasonic (Jordan and Light 1987).

The European Community

General Information

The EC, now also referred to as the Euromarket, was originally a customs union established in 1958 as the European Common Market. Initially comprised of six countries, it has expanded to twelve: Belgium, Denmark, France, Germany, Greece, Ireland, Italy, Luxembourg, the Netherlands, Portugal, Spain, and the United Kingdom. The EC has increased its role over time through the establishment of the EC Commission, the Council of Ministers, the European Parliament, the Court of Justice, and the creation of the European currency unit (ECU), utilized in trade as a bookkeeping entry but envisioned to eventually be a circulating currency in general use. Because of its increased economic power, the EC has preferential trade agreements with the European Free Trade Association (EFTA), which includes Austria, Switzerland, and the Scandinavian countries of Finland, Iceland, Norway, and Sweden. However, the EC has not yet reached the stage of cooperation some leaders envision as a "United States of Europe," similar yet different from the United States of America.

EC 1992 Initiatives

The target date of December 31 of 1992 was established by the twelve member-nations of the EC as the time to have removed most of their internal trade barriers, eliminating restrictions on the movement of goods, services, financial resources, and people within member-nations. Standardized customs and tariff systems would result in creating a single Euromarket, and concurrently the competitive environment would change. This meant that any product or service that met EC "essential requirements" for health, safety, and environmental protection could be marketed throughout the Euromarket. Advertising would play an important role in the development of this vibrant marketplace.

The 1992 initiatives were a set of nearly 300 separate initiatives designed to remove the physical, technical, and fiscal barriers to trade within the EC. In place of the former myriad of country-specific restrictions would be a single set of regulations and directives, coordinated by the EC Commission headquartered in Brussels. These uniform EC standards would streamline the marketplace, and many observers believed that when all these measures were taken, a barrier-free Europe would save the economies of member-states some $200 billion. Size alone is important in terms of economic impact. After the barriers dissolve, there will be about 320 million consumers in the EC, making it one of the largest consumer markets in the world (Cote 1988). John Perriss, worldwide media director of Saatchi & Saatchi, noted, "It will create in Europe a market . . . that's substantially larger than the domestic U.S. market" (Mandese 1988). And if one includes the recently emerging economies of Eastern Europe, this market becomes significantly larger with tremendous long-term potential for growth. The people of Europe are facing a period of significant change; however, the general public appears to accept the idea that the EC's emergence as an economic superpower will bring benefits to all, and that the promise of the European logotype, "Europe for a Better Life," is real (Beatson 1990).

Differences in Promotion and Advertising Practices

Although Europe is on the verge of becoming a more cohesive market, it is not yet a single market. Euromarket is likely to remain heterogeneous in many respects even after the 1992 initiatives define what are legal advertising activities. Thus marketers planning to treat Europe as a single market will be disappointed. Many regional disparities in tastes, customs, and expectations will remain. Moreover, what is acceptable promotional activity in one country may still be inappropriate in another. The current situation is far from uniform as the following examples illustrate. Money-off-next-purchase is permitted in the United Kingdom and Ireland, where promotional law is the most liberal, but promotional law is very rigid in Germany and Luxembourg. And even though free mail-ins are allowed in Spain, John Hooper, group chairman of Clarke Hooper Consultancies, mentioned, "You wouldn't think of doing it because it would never get there" (Beatson 1990). Figure 14-1 briefly summarizes some of these differences in promotion.

Advertising practices currently vary greatly from country to country throughout the EC. This creates problems for global agencies. Synodinos et al. (1989) surveyed leading brand advertisers in fifteen countries around the world and identified some of these advertising practices. The EC

FIGURE 14-1
EUROPEAN
COUNTRIES SALES
PROMOTION
DIFFERENCES
SOURCE: ADAPTED
FROM DAHRINGER,
L. D., AND H.
MUHLBACHER.
(1991).
INTERNATIONAL
MARKETING: A GLOBAL
PERSPECTIVE,
READING, MA:
ADDISON-WESLEY,
505.

Promotion	U.K.	Spain	Germany	France	Italy
In-pack premiums	■	■	□	◆	■
Multiple-purchase offers	■	■	◆	■	■
Extra product	■	■	◆	■	■
Free product	■	■	■	■	■
Mail-in offers	■	■	□	■	■
Purchase-with-purchase	■	■	□	■	■
Cross-promotions	■	■	□	■	■
Contests	■	■	◆	■	■
Self-liquidating premiums	■	■	■	■	■
Sweepstakes	◆	◆	□	◆	◆
Money-off coupons	■	■	□	■	◆
Next-purchase coupons	■	■	□	■	◆
Cash rebates	■	■	◆	■	□
In-store demos	■	■	■	■	■

■ Permitted   □ Not permitted   ◆ May be permitted

countries involved were Denmark, Germany, and the United Kingdom. Some of the study's more interesting findings relate that advertising budget setting methods differ by country. Danish and British advertisers used executive judgment more frequently than the sample average. Advertisers in Germany and the United Kingdom used the all-you-can-afford and match-the-competition methods more often than the average; most non-EC countries preferred the objective-and-task method. Advertisers also vary in the timing of expenditures. British advertisers used the timing-for-sales-promotion strategy less frequently, whereas Danish advertisers used this strategy more often (Synodinos, Keown, and Jacobs 1989).

Use of different media and appeal was also evident. The British spent more money in television advertising than other EC countries, whereas Denmark spent more than the average for newspapers and magazines. The Swedish and Danish were similar; as a creative approach they used product identification more frequently than those in other countries. They were dissimilar, though, in that the benefit-awareness creative approach was used most frequently in Denmark; however, it was never used in Sweden. Testimonials and slice-of-life advertisements were especially popular in Denmark. Humorous approaches were used more often in Great Britain (Synodinos, Keown, and Jacobs 1989). In summary, although the study found some degree of commonality, it also revealed many differences.

Synodinos's (1989) findings were reasonably consistent with those of Sorenson and Weichmann (1975), who obtained empirical data from executives of major multinational firms regarding the degree of marketing standardization used by their companies. They found that there was generally a high level of product standardization. However, Sorenson and Weichmann also found that although the basic advertising message was somewhat standardized, other aspects such as budget allocations and media choices were not highly standardized (Synodinos, Keown, and Jacobs 1989).

Advertising Difficulties

Although common needs, wants, desires, and attitudes may exist within the EC, advertisers must recognize that there are also very divergent cultures, climates, religions, political structures, eating habits, family structures, and wealth distributions. Consequently, advertising styles and their relative effectiveness are similarly diverse. What is common practice in one country may be taboo in another. Teinowitz (1990) quotes the executive chairman of BSB Europe, as saying: "All French ads seem to end up in bed. All Italian ads always seem to revolve around a meal. The English ads all use humor." This diversity is illustrated by Compaq Computer Company, which planned its advertisements in Europe around a theme related to its rapid growth. The campaign was executed several ways. The print advertisement in the United Kingdom, executed via the agency's London office, reprinted a news account headlined "Compaq beats Apple record for fastest entry to *Fortune 500*." The humor showed up at the bottom of the announcement with the line, "Sorry, old fruit." But in Germany, the fastest growing computer concept was rejected as a theme. "Our German guys looked at it and said it was out of the question," said Kirk Walden, Ogilvy & Mather senior vice president and client service director in Houston. "The idea was seen as arrogant and perhaps an indication that the company grew so fast because it was too high-priced" (Lawrence 1989).

Even though different people from different cultures may purchase the same product, their priorities of product attributes may be very disparate. Thus the problem becomes how to develop a single campaign that overcomes these culturally based differences. For example, in marketing expensive automobiles in the EC, a marketer must know that in the United Kingdom, until recently 70 percent of new cars were company cars; thus advertisements dealt with drivers' views of themselves within their companies. In France, a car's elegance may be the important selling point. In Germany, engineering efficiency seems most important. Italian drivers seem to be more concerned about acceleration. Thus it appears that in just four of the EC countries, marketers of automobiles must utilize four different appeals (Teinowitz 1990).

This same problem is evident in the marketing of soap products. For example, using the same ad across Europe for a product like laundry detergent would run the risk of alienating some customers. In Spain, where more women stay home to take care of families, washing clothes is viewed as a good wife's duty. But in France, where far more women work, the attitude is much more casual (Foltz 1990b). Thus there will be some products that will be perceived differently by consumers in specific countries, and utilizing a single campaign could be disastrous. Effective ads must consider cultural differences in people's reactions.

The Importance of Regional Advertising

Because the EC countries have distinctive cultural, political, and competitive industry situations, they probably require tailor-made advertising applications rather than inflexible applications of an EC-wide strategy. Relevant local differences do matter, and opportunities vary by market. Thus, despite pan-European commonalities, every sale remains a local sale. Pan-European marketing will not be easy. Local competitive conditions, problems, and cultural biases must be recognized and dealt with in order for pan-European advertising to be effective; thus marketers may still need to act locally while thinking globally.

Thinking globally while acting locally means that commonalities are important but differences, when they exist, are acknowledged and acted upon. There seems to be a consensus among advertisers on the importance of this strategy. "Global brands are few and far between—Coke, Pepsi, Martini, and Levi's," commented Neil Kennedy. "For most other international brands, it makes enormous sense to have a global strategy, but local creative executions are vital" (Teinowitz 1990). Instead of a single pan-European campaign translated by country, media and creative strategies are tailored to the particular country. "We learn constantly that there are major differences between countries that make up Europe and you're bound to be more successful if you have creative authority at the country level," said Martin Hingley, research director at International Data Corp., Europa, a subsidiary of market researcher IDC (Lawrence 1989). Kirk Walden has similar opinions: "There's lots of talk about global advertising. Ogilvy's point of view is that we believe in ideas crossing borders, not necessarily execution. We see that advertising has to be different in tone in the U.K., but that doesn't usually mean that the idea is different" (Lawrence 1989). Making the same brand highly relevant to a lot of different people who speak different languages and dialects is the main challenge that all pan-European advertisers face in the single EC market. "There will be greater use of European brands. Yet, local markets and their special consumer needs can't be ignored. It will be a question of seeking the right balance," declared Michael Angus, chairman of Unilever, one of Europe's largest advertisers (Beatson 1990).

THINK GLOBAL, ACT LOCAL: AN EXAMPLE

Compaq Computer Corporation planned to launch its first pan-European campaign in a "think global act local" manner. They planned to position Compaq as the high-performance PC leader. The pan-European ads would provide "an umbrella overlay" to develop Compaq's brand across borders, reported James D'Arezzo, Compaq's vice president of international marketing. The "umbrella" would reach out to Europeans, rather than specifically to the French or the Germans. Kirk Walden revealed that this was possible because Compaq products—from desktop models to portables to the new laptop—were used in the same way in all countries. He also commented that relying on one marketing strategy for product or brand efforts is essential because it provides consistency, accuracy, and direction for all executions (Lawrence 1989).

However, Mr. D'Arezzo also said, "Individual executions allow you to take advantage of a country's culture, mores, history, and point of view, whereas a single worldwide approach can become meaningful for no one. The individual approach becomes meaningful for that country." Therefore, Compaq solved the dilemma: "You do what's right for the country,"

Mr. Walden added. "We [Compaq] have a clear direction with the ability to execute it to fit local mores" (Lawrence 1989). Ultimately, marketers must remember that 1992's end to trade barriers within Europe does not necessarily mean an end to separate advertising campaigns tailored to each market.

EC Advertising Industry Changes

As different competitors fight for larger shares of the Euromarket, their advertising agents are being drawn into battle with them. Advertising agencies eager to tap the huge EC consumer base are restructuring their strategies to keep pace with their clients' Euromarket expansion. Even those agencies previously opposed to internationalization are making moves to serve clients in other markets (Murrow and Wentz 1989).

Advertising Agency Strategies for Expansion

Establishing an effective network may be extremely important for an agency interested in globalization. In theory, a worldwide agency network can pool its savvy on the client's behalf and execute pan-European marketing or media plans for brands that wish to position themselves in this manner (Papazian 1988). Many agencies feel pressure from expansion-minded clients in need of advertising agencies able to handle pan-European accounts. When a client is very happy on a local basis, that client tends to want the same success across several markets. Also, agencies with strong international connections are more attractive to multinational clients.

The Network Strategy.   Without a European network, an agency may be less effective. Thus multinational alliances are forming and some smaller firms are merging. For example, Collett Dickenson Pearce, the United Kingdom's number thirteen agency with 1988 billing of $216 million, entered major European markets, buying a minority interest in agencies such as Alice in France and Canard Advertising in Italy. Also, Yellowhammer Advertising, the United Kingdom's number twenty-six agency with billings of $116 million, started its own agency in Paris called Yellowhammer Delafosse. A similar startup in Spain is also predicted for them (Murrow and Wentz 1989).

Expansion into Europe can be a lengthy process. Even European agencies with strong roots have expanded slowly and with care. Roger Swann, executive vice president of KLP International in London, stated,

"It took KLP five years to build a network of agencies in France, Holland, Spain, Ireland, and Scandinavia. It's a major effort for companies like Coke to send people around the world, let alone a promotion agency." (Fahey and Bowes 1990). Thus agencies interested in pan-European accounts are realizing that they may need to move quickly to find affiliations and keep up with the competition.

THE AUTONOMOUS STRATEGY.　An alternate strategy to expanding in order to solidify a network is for an agency to become autonomous; this is exemplified by Eurocom S.A., the largest French advertising, promotion, and public relations group, which is a 43 percent controlled affiliate of the French media and publishing giant Havas S.A. Eurocom has recently broken up a joint venture with Young & Rubicam of the United States and Japan's Dentsu Inc. in order to take total control and ownership of HDM, a lucrative international agency. This action by Eurocom is part of an international expansion program attempting to rival British giants Saatchi & Saatchi Co. and WP Group PLC. Eurocom desires to be an international power on its own instead of an allied entity (Browning and Lublin 1990).

McCann-Erickson followed a similar strategy and suggested that it had the best network in Europe because most of its agencies abroad were wholly owned subsidiaries. Other multinational agencies have usually taken less than 100 percent of local operation and hence may not possess the control necessary to harmonize cross-border advertising. McCann-Erickson claimed it had unrivalled and essential experience in "building brands across European borders." Its claim is backed by clients like Esso (which has been with the agency since 1911), Coca-Cola (advertised in a uniform style in fifty countries), and Martini (*The Economist* 1988).

Foltz notes that other agencies have restructured in order to remain competitive in a unified Europe. Grey Advertising, for example, has created a European board of executives to manage clients' advertising across Europe. The J. Walter Thompson agency has also set up a special pan-European management unit. The group, based at Thompson's London office, formulates media, marketing, and research strategies for clients to give them extra clout throughout Europe (Foltz 1990).

AMERICAN AGENCIES INCREASING INTEREST IN THE EC

The post-1992 Euromarket may become an increasingly important source of revenue for multinational U.S. agencies. Traditionally, advertising spending growth in the EC lagged behind the United States, and agencies maintained many unprofitable foreign offices primarily to serve clients—not to make money. However, revenues from EC operations have recently often exceeded those from the United States. For example, in 1989 Young & Rubicam's business in Europe represented about 40 percent of their total billing, compared to the 1974 figure of only 10 percent (Foltz 1990b). In 1987, McCann's billings (the amount its clients spent on advertising) were 33 percent higher in Europe than in the United States (*The Economist* 1988). And Grey Advertising's European operation is the fastest growing part of the agency (Foltz 1990b). It seems that an EC presence allows U.S. agencies to stay in close contact with their clients. Some industry observers perceive that the EC will become so important in the next ten years that the headquarters of some U.S. agencies may be moved overseas (Foltz 1990b).

DIFFICULTIES FOR NON-EC AGENCIES.   Non-EC based agencies desiring to be effective and prosper in the EC may need to recognize that generally consistent advertising styles that span most of Europe do exist. These styles are dissimilar from U.S. styles, but they are at the same time disparate due to regional preferences. For example, Jones observed that EC ads are thought to employ more original techniques than U.S. ads. Also, there is often a distinct difference in tone; for example, EC ads seem to consider consumers as intelligent people with minds of their own. Ads are more entertaining and less hard-selling than in U.S. campaigns (Jones 1990). In the crowded highly competitive U.S. marketplace, ads must be brand-specific, and they are often more factual. However, in the EC there have been more wide-selling brands that did not have too many competitors. Thus a different kind of advertising was required. Advertising frequently relies on motivating arguments but is also entertaining, amusing, intelligent, stylish, and relaxed. This advertising can be soft, generic, and emotional and is regarded as causing more potent impressions in Europe (Jones 1990). Thus agencies not familiar with EC styles may have difficulty adjusting.

CHANGING EC STYLES

In the post-1992 EC, as pan-European advertising campaigns become more prevalent, Fahey predicts that advertising styles will change significantly. Since ad messages will transcend national frontiers, they will also transcend languages. There are nine different official EC languages: Danish, Dutch, English, French, German, Greek, Italian, Portuguese, and Spanish. To communicate with people speaking different languages, ads must emphasize visual and musical content to be more effective. Fahey quotes Nick Beck, managing director of Outdoor Advertising International (OAI), as predicting that "major international advertisers are going to move increasingly into trans-frontier outdoor advertising in Europe because outdoor is the only medium that presents no translation problems when the creative treatment is right" (Fahey 1989). As agencies develop expertise in nonverbal communication, print media may also reconcentrate on graphics rather than on copy. Broadcasting via satellite will probably perpetuate these forms of communication, and in this manner the use of visual symbols and pictorial portrayals will provide clearer communications.

EC Ad Industry Growth

Beatson believes that EC 1992 will bring economies of scale that will produce an increase in the EC's gross domestic product of between 4.5 percent and 7 percent, or about $200 billion ECU at 1988 price levels. He foresees a drop in consumer prices of up to 6 percent (Beatson 1990). The EC Commission estimates that new jobs will be created for two million to five million people. As the total market expands, services will be the fastest growing sector.

Growth Factors.   Advertising spending in the EC is escalating as marketers prepare to take advantage of Euromarket 1992. Ad expenditures, expressed as a percentage of the EC GNP, are expected to double the spending rates of the mature U.S. market as technological and regulatory changes expand media opportunities. McCann-Erickson believes the non-U.S. expenditures will grow at a sharp rate for the rest of this century for three reasons (Link 1988):

1. Sales growth for many mature packaged-goods manufacturers will have to come from new markets. Recognizing this, advertisers will increase their marketing expenditures to build share.
2. The process of Euromarketization has created a heightened sense of competition. This will put pressure on the supply of advertising time and space.
3. The expansion of commercial TV availability, especially in strongly regulated TV markets, will be met by the pent-up demand for time.

TV will have a strong impact on advertising growth in the EC. This impact will be especially prevalent in Italy and France because of the development of private TV broadcasters and the availability of increased TV advertising time. In 1990, McCann-Erickson Worldwide predicted that Italian advertising spending would increase 9.2 percent combined with a 6.1 percent inflation rate. For France, they predicted an 11 percent growth and a 3.3 percent inflation rate (Hill 1990). Also partly due to the deregulation of TV throughout the EC, Link predicted that major media advertising spending would increase by 10.8 percent to $47 billion in 1988, by 9.8 percent in 1989, and by 9.3 percent in 1990 (Wentz 1988a). Because East Germany was absorbed, the total German advertising expenditures for the next few years are also likely to expand considerably.

DIRECTION OF EC ADVERTISING GROWTH.   Foltz noted that Veronis, Suhler, & Associates, a consulting and investment banking company, forecast that advertising expenditures in key European countries will increase by close to 10 percent or more annually during the next four years. They predicted a 9.2 percent compound annual growth rate for Germany and a 10 percent annual increase for both France and Italy. The biggest increase was predicted for Spain, where the media are now being deregulated. Spending there is expected to rise by 25.2 percent a year (Foltz 1990b). These statistics are fairly consistent with others' predictions. Phillips & Drew, a British stockbrokerage owned by the Union Bank of Switzerland, believes that advertising expenditures in Western Europe will grow by 12 percent a year for the next few years (*The Economist* 1988). Growth rates are already well above that in many parts of continental Europe. Phillips & Drew claim the increase is mainly due to the onset of pan-European brands and the growth of commercial television.

EC REGULATIONS

THE EC REGULATORY PROCESS

Like the Federal Trade Commission (FTC), the U.S. government agency that regulates advertising, the EC Commission proposes and enforces EC regulations. However, these regulations must first be approved by the European Parliament. Specific directives exist for many industries; for example, Foltz notes that the EC is considering restrictions on television advertising of toys or banning all advertising aimed at children (Foltz 1990a). Directives such as these set EC-wide rules and standards that will allow the free movement of goods, services, people, and capital while promoting a socially conscious multinational and cohesive market. It takes time for a directive to become a formal regulation. For instance, it took two years to get EC approval for the important directive concerning transnational TV broadcasts, which set up uniform guidelines for inserting commercials into programs (Cote 1989).

The EC Commission also ensures that competition is fair and not distorted in favor of any one entity. McCarter (1990) notes the example (under a provision of the 1956 Treaty of Rome) of the Finivest holding company, owned by Italian TV magnate Silvio Berlusconi, which was charged with violating limits on the level of ownership of available advertising space and time. Finivest was viewed as obstructing competition, and the EC Commission enforced its rulings. The EC is currently considering hundreds of proposed regulations to determine, among other things, what can be advertised and exactly what kind of claims can be made in the ads for some products. EC rules are supposed to take precedence in member countries, but a nation may maintain its own rules if they are more restrictive. For instance, advertising for alcohol and tobacco are already restricted in many European countries, and the EC regulations being considered could further restrict or even ban such advertisements.

HARMONIZING REGULATIONS

There are opportunities as well as problems associated with the standardization of EC regulations. With the member countries bringing varied economic, social, and philosophical backgrounds to a single market, it may be that not all will welcome free and open use of advertising. A consensus in advertising regulations among member-nations has presented much conflict, and although the EC is attempting to "harmonize" regulations, currently they differ markedly from country to country. In Greece, for example, toys cannot be advertised on television, and in Denmark magazines cannot carry ads for pharmaceutical products (Foltz 1990a).

A staff writer for *The Economist* noted that many complain that the European Parliament is increasingly hostile to marketing and advertising within the EC and that the commission's harmonization is favoring strict regulations. The commission is currently concerned with regulatory proposals that span both industries as a whole and specific segments within industries: TV directives forbid subliminal advertising, ban all forms of tobacco advertising, prohibit advertising for alcoholic beverages that promise sexual or social success, and regulate nutritional and health claims (Giges 1990). Thus advertisers conclude that the commission is unfriendly toward advertising and that the parliament, made up of "health-obsessed, anti-materialist children of the 1960's," is even worse (*The Economist* 1990).

RESISTANCE TO REGULATIONS

Marketers insist that the current maze of individual national regulations is stunting the growth of pan-European promotions. Many advertisers feel that the potential anti-advertising laws and rulings could completely undermine the ideal of one common market in which all companies can market their goods and services without suffocating restrictions. If advertising is so restricted, then it will not be as advantageous to ship products freely throughout the EC (*Advertising Age* 1990). Many marketers fear that Europe may become more tightly restricted than the United States. Foltz notes that Debra Miller, an international economist with the office of industrial trade at the Commerce Department, has said, "European countries have a tradition of more state intervention in the marketplace"

(Foltz 1990b). Thus advertisers are concerned that rigid legislation will be set that will span across other laws that are already less restrictive. Moreover, many observers speculate that the commission will introduce rules product-by-product and that the ban on tobacco advertising is just the beginning.

The International Advertising Association (IAA), a New York-based organization that holds the World Advertising Congress to discuss current issues, states that one of its main jobs is fighting for commercial freedom of speech (Giges 1990). This is the essential reason why advertisers feel compelled to speak out against strict and unfair restrictions against advertising. Some advertisers also feel that many advertising restrictions are simply back-door ways to protect locals and discourage new competition (*Advertising Age* 1990). For example, the French cabinet recommended approval of a measure to ban most tobacco and some alcohol advertising by January 1, 1993, and many advertising executives maintain that this ban is an effort to protect a state-owned tobacco monopoly under the pretense of a health issue. Some conclude that if tobacco advertising is banned in the United States, imports will not be able to compete (Giges 1990). There is general agreement that once the rules are written, they will be almost impossible to change (Foltz 1990a). Hence many profess that the entire advertising community must work together to see that the industry is unfettered.

LOBBYING ORGANIZATIONS.   A number of organizations have been formed to protect the interests of advertisers. A few of these that can influence regulations within the EC are the British Advertising Association, the European Advertising Tripartite, the European Association of Advertising Agencies, the World Federation of Advertisers, the Point of Purchase Advertising Institute Europe, the United State Leadership Council on Advertising, and the previously mentioned International Advertising Association and European Association of Advertising Agencies.

The British Advertising Association mainly strives to lessen restrictions. It brings together the advertisers, the agencies, and the media. The association has geared up to defend the products they believe are the most vulnerable: tobacco, alcohol, food, pharmaceuticals, and financial services (*The Economist* 1990). The European Advertising Tripartite, a pan-European group, is affiliated with the European Association of Advertising Agencies, but it is expected to become independent soon. The tripartite is a Brussels-based organization that represents agencies, clients, and the media (Giges 1990). Philip H. Geier Jr., chairman and chief executive officer of Interpublic Group of Companies, stresses that the European Advertising Tripartite is the right group to fight EC proposals to regulate advertising because he believes that existing pan-European organizations are too weak to effectively lobby the EC. The Tripartite is the major body through which other groups such as the World Federation of Advertisers and local groups can work to combat EC advertising restrictions (Hill, 1990b). Angela Mills, director of special issues and European affairs, has indicated that the industry is already working together to fight regulations. For example, the British Advertising Association funded a group of consultants that created the plans for the Tripartite's pan-European lobbying efforts. The most recent objective is "to alter the political environment in which advertising is perceived." Many advertising executives believe that advertising has a bad image, that advertising is seen by many EC politicians as the most visible symbol of capitalism, and that there's something inherently wrong with it (Hill 1990b). Thus, the Tripartite plans to deal directly with EC members to explain how advertising helps consumers, the economy, and the media. The Tripartite also acts as an adviser to national groups, lobbying their own legislators and boosting awareness of the problems of stricter regulations.

Other organizations focus on other effective methods. The Point of Purchase Advertising Institute Europe serves as an information exchange providing networking opportunities and keeps abreast of EC legislation (Bowes 1990). The Leadership Council, an ad hoc lobbying group, is a group of chief executive officers from major media, agency, and advertising companies that concentrate on lobbying but have no formal structure to their efforts (Hill 1990b). The most commercially significant and publicized categories being considered for advertising regulations (often more restrictive than current regulations) are television, tobacco, alcohol, food, and pharmaceuticals.

Changes in EC TV

Television is acknowledged to be the most intrusive medium for advertising. In most parts of the EC, advertiser demand for TV ad time dramatically exceeds supply. The trend for TV in Europe is toward channels financed by advertising that deliver programs capable of attracting mass-market audiences. Consequently, there is an increase in private channels, satellite systems, and TV advertising.

PRIVATIZATION AND SATELLITE SYSTEMS.   Most countries now allow private TV channels to compete with state-owned channels. Advertising executives cite increasing privatization as a major factor in ad growth in the EC. John Eger, president of Worldwide Media Group of New York, predicted "There will be increased experimentation with private TV channels, and nations are opening up state-run channels" (Downer et al. 1988).

There has also been a liberalization of the EC's satellite communications market and, consequently, satellite TV systems have been proliferating. TV in Europe has been shaken by the arrival of pan-European satellite channels like Sky Channel and Super Channel. These channels, broadcasting in English, were among the first in Europe to be planned from start-up as an advertising medium (Cote 1988). Saatchi & Saatchi Compton Worldwide projected that TV advertising revenues in Europe would increase from $5 billion in 1986 to nearly $7.5 billion by 1990 (Tully 1987). Over the next few years, the growth of TV in Europe could cause a marketing revolution. The advent of multinational TV networks has sparked a potentially powerful new trend—advertising that treats Europe like a single mass market instead of a patchwork of national markets. Long stymied by advertising bans and quotas on state-owned TV, advertisers foresee vast opportunities in EC satellite TV channels. Companies such as Coca-Cola, McDonald's, and Mattel can successfully advertise their uniform brand products on pan-European TV. They can dub in different languages and reap big savings (Tully 1987). The same ads could run in different countries, differing only in voice-overs. And companies could use the same packaging, allowing for various translations of instruction, etc. (Cote 1988).

DIFFICULTIES.   There are, however, problem areas. Advertisers planning TV campaigns for a mass European market are faced with audience measurement techniques that differ for each country even though they have been pushing for universally accepted research parameters to compare audiences in one country to those in another (Cote 1988). Moreover, agencies often must produce several separate versions of the same commercial to comply with disparate national regulations.

TV advertising in many EC countries is severely restricted. As late as 1988, television commanded a low share of advertising expenditures: West Germany—9 percent; Netherlands—5 percent; and France—17 percent. Some of the reasons for this are limited commercial TV availability, restricted TV commercialization policies, stringent television time-buying guidelines, and an extensive and well-established magazine and newspaper industry (i.e., a high literacy rate) (Link 1988). For instance, in terms of buying television time, the national TV outlets in Germany and France sell their time on an up-front, noncancelable basis. Options do not exist; scatter does not exist. It is a "first come, first served" business (Link 1988).

There has been difficulty in gaining an EC consensus for rules of satellite communications. Growth in the satellite market has been constrained by a maze of protectionist national regulations. National telecommunications monopolies are not allowing the satellite market to develop quickly enough. A few EC countries remain zealous in protecting their state telecommunications monopolies (Wall Street Journal 1990).

GERMANY.   In 1987, the three state-owned German stations banned commercials in prime time, all day Sunday, and on public holidays (Tully

1987). Deregulation in Germany has moved slowly, with three state-owned networks limited to airing only 20 minutes of advertising a day and 82 percent of the advertising expenditure still going to print (Wentz 1988a). TV regulations included restricting spots to four 5-minute blocks. However, Germany's two privately owned TV stations, transmitted largely to cable TV homes, are permitted to devote up to 20 percent of their air-time to commercials (Wentz 1988b).

THE NETHERLANDS.   Advertisers complain of strict regulations in the Netherlands. TV spots on Dutch networks are limited to 5 percent of air-time and must be booked up to a year in advance. Dutch programs do not have fixed time slots, making it impossible to plan commercial buys around desired programs. Thus advertisers have been pressuring the government for more commercial time on the three state-owned channels. In June 1988 the European Court ruled that the Dutch government cannot stop advertisers on pan-European satellite TV channels from aiming their spots specifically at Dutch viewers by subtitling or dubbing them in Dutch (Wentz 1988b).

DENMARK.   Advertising had been banned, but beginning in 1987 TV advertising began to be phased in (Tully 1987). Denmark had been Europe's most limited TV market with only one government-owned national station, but on October 1, 1987 several Danish channels formed a second national network called TV2 (Bartal and Wentz 1987). Kai Hansen, chairman of Young & Rubicam, believes that it is still too early to tell how much TV advertising will elevate total advertising spending in Denmark. However, total advertising expenditures increased by 40 percent in Austria and 20 percent in Holland after those two countries allowed TV advertising (Bartal and Wentz 1987).

THE UNITED KINGDOM.   The TV market in the U.K. has been growing rapidly. Anthony Simonds-Gooding, former top Saatchi & Saatchi Co. executive and chief executive officer of British Satellite Broadcasting (BSB), commented that commercial time was expected to more than double when the United Kingdom's three-channel direct broadcast by satellite service was launched at the end of 1989. BSB had a business plan calling for two and a half million of the nation's twenty million TV homes to acquire satellite dishes to receive BSB transmissions by 1992 and five million by 1995 (Wentz 1988b). Moreover, the anticipated addition of a fifth British TV channel in 1993 should also help keep the TV market growing (Wentz 1988a). In the United Kingdom, advertisers are actively lobbying the government for more TV commercial time. They have backed a study documenting the adverse economic impact of the current system and have tried to influence government examinations of the future of British broadcasting (Wentz 1988b).

FRANCE.   France has been lessening advertising restrictions for TV. In 1986, TV commercials were restricted to 7 hours a week, but by 1987 this number was increased to 20 hours a week when two new channels started and TF-1, France's largest channel, was deregulated and sold by the government (Wentz 1988a).

OTHER EC COUNTRIES.   Increased advertising spending in Italy, Europe's most deregulated TV market, can be attributed to continued developments in commercial TV and the comeback of the press with the recent launch of more than seventy magazines. Spain and Portugal are also expected to experience tremendous TV advertising growth due to TV privatization (Downer et al. 1988). Spain, Portugal, and Greece were all expected to increase spending in 1988 by more than 25 percent (Wentz 1988a).

ADVERTISING REGULATIONS OF OTHER INDUSTRIES AND THEIR PRODUCTS

EC TOBACCO REGULATIONS.   Tobacco advertising in the EC has been a controversial issue. A proposal restricts the use of people and realistic settings in tobacco advertisements and bans the use of tobacco-product brand names for nontobacco products such as lighters or fashion collections (Cote 1989). Britain already bans cigarette advertising on television, but from 1991 cigar and pipe-tobacco advertising will also be banned (*The Economist* 1990).

Laws that the EC has already passed are much stiffer. A total ban on tobacco advertising was expected to be in effect by 1992, but at the time of writing this ban had been postponed. The EC has a proposal to ban all tobacco advertising and sponsorship. If approved, the law would prohibit tobacco marketers from advertising their products in any medium or using any tobacco product logo in sporting or cultural events (Rosenbaum 1990).

ALCOHOL.   The European Commission is still working on an alcohol advertising directive, while individual EC countries (Spain, Italy, and France) are increasingly restricting alcohol advertising. For instance, France doesn't allow commercials for alcohol on television (Rosenbaum 1990).

FOOD.   As in the United States where the FTC has been cracking down on misleading food advertising, the EC is taking similar action. A proposed directive suggests that manufacturers should not be allowed to refer to helpful recommendations by health institutions, such as "The Intestines Inspectorate says fibre is good for you. Frizzo is 79.3 percent fibre"

(Rosenbaum, 1990). It would also ban the distinction between natural and artificial ingredients. Thus these regulations would restrict All-Bran's claim of aiding digestion and Diet 7Up's claim of being saccharin-free.

Marketers have many concerns about this type of directive, especially for advertising. They insist that the regulations need to be specific and leave no room for varying interpretations. For example, when foods are identified as "fresh," marketers need clear directions on what comprises a fresh food (Cote 1989).

··

CONCLUSIONS

Once EC advertising regulations are established, they will be used by the twelve member countries and possibly by Eastern European countries that want to harmonize their laws with those of the EC (Beatson 1990). The EC 1992 initiatives will undoubtedly modify business patterns within the Euromarket. For instance, new products and brands could be launched in the EC rather than in the United States. This could mean a diminution in the United States of high-impact, saturation media advertising that often follows the introduction of new products and brands in the marketplace (Chandran 1989). Also, the EC's regulations may prompt a restructuring of U.S. advertising rules. Mike Bowman, the director of multinational clients for Lintas International, deduced, "As the European market becomes more powerful, it is bound to influence the American market in terms of regulation" (Foltz 1990a).

One reason the Euromarket of 1992 has attracted so much attention is the feeling that, however it develops, Europe's mass market will be drastically different from the U.S. mass market. The Euromarket will be a multilingual, multicultural phenomenon of the next century. Some conclude that it will be more affluent and better educated than the American mass market. One EC official described 1992 as "a new religion sweeping Europe" (Cote 1988).

Walter Serwatka, president of McGraw-Hill Information Services, emphasizes that it is still too early to tell the impact of Euromarket 1992, but "The world is getting smaller and smaller, and the need for information is growing" (Schleier 1989). Whatever form Europe takes in the future, its new marketplace will provide a vital and unique challenge for the power of advertising. All 300 EC initiatives were not operational by December 31, 1992. EC-wide ad regulations also were not in force by that time. Thus a standard advertising program is still not feasible for the Euromarket 1992. Given the EC situation just discussed, this should not be surprising. As *Fortune* noted " . . . much of the blame lies with some national governments that are painfully slow at translating Community directives into national law. At the end of March 1991, member states were supposed to have implemented 122 EC measures. Italy, the worst offender, had managed just 45" (*The Economist* 1991). What this means for pan-European advertisers is that within the foreseeable future, a standardized advertising plan that meets a single set of EC regulations will not be possible. It will not be possible because a single set of EC advertising regulations that has been adopted by all twelve member countries and is thus operational does not seem probable for several more years. In addition, once such EC advertising regulations are operational, it seems unlikely that a single plan will be functionally effective because of the existing diversity of Euro customers. The Euromarket post-1992 will still be a heterogeneous market—not a single market—because of the continuing diversity of Euro customers. And, if Eastern European countries are allowed quick entry into the EC, then the reality of a single Euromarket will probably not exist until well after the turn of the century. But does this mean that pan-European marketing programs will not exist? The answer is that there will be a need for pan-European marketing planning and pan-European marketing programs, but there will still be a need to adapt to consumer diversity. The "think global act local" strategic adaptation noted earlier will be required for effectiveness in the Euromarket emerging after 1992.

REFERENCES

Advertising Age (1990). "How to Undermine '1992'," 15 June, 20.

Bartal, D., and Wentz, L. (1987). "Danes Phase in TV Spots: First Allowed in Scandinavia," *Advertising Age*, 23 November, 42.

Beatson, R. (1990). "Reaching United Europe Won't Be a Simple Task," *Advertising Age*, 9 April, 31, 41.

Bowes, E. (1990). "Targeting the Continent?" *Advertising Age*, 30 April, S11.

Browning, E. S., and J. S. Lublin (1990). "Eurocom Set to Break Up Venture with Two Partners," *Wall Street Journal*, 11 December, B6.

Chandran, R. (1989). "Home Is Where R&D Should Be," *Marketing & Media Decisions*, June, 128.

Cote, K. (1989). "Uncertain Future Plagues Marketers Planning for 1992," *Advertising Age*, 5 June, 1, 42.

——— (1988). "The New Shape of Europe," *Advertising Age*, 9 November, 98–100, 148.

Downer, S. et al. (1988). "Strong Spending: Foreign Ad Budgets Again Beat U.S.," *Advertising Age*, 28 March, 33.

The Economist (1991). "A Survey of Businesses in Europe," 8 June, 10.

The Economist (1990). "Single Marketing: As the Community Juggles with New Rules on Advertising, the Advertising Business Is Gearing Up to Do Battle in Brussels and Strasbourg," 24 March, 64.

The Economist (1988). "Avenue Madison," 22 July, 58–59.

Fahey, A. (1989). "Building for 1992: OAI Putting Together Net to Make Buying Overseas Easier," *Advertising Age*, 9 October, S16.

———, and E. Bowes (1990). "The European Scramble Is On," *Advertising Age*, 30 April, S9.

Foltz, K. (1990a). "Lobbying Is Recommended to Prepare for Europe 1992," *The New York Times*, 3 October, D21.

——— (1990b). "Agencies Set Sights on Europe," *The New York Times*, 21 August, D19.

Giges, N. (1990). "Int'l Split on Fighting Ad Rules," *Advertising Age*, 18 June, 84.

Hill, J. S. (1990a). "World Ad Spending: Outlook Dim," *Advertising Age*, 10 September, 81.

——— (1990b). "Ad Leaders Pick EC Lobbying Group," *Advertising Age*, 30 July, 30.

Jeannet, J.-P., and H. D. Hennessey (1988). *International Marketing Management: Strategies and Cases*. Boston: Houghton Mifflin, 475.

Jones, J. P. (1990). "Why European Ads Are More Amusing," *The New York Times*, 7 October, F13.

Jordan, R. O., and L. Light (1987). "The Worldly View: Thinking Global, Acting Local," *Marketing & Media Decisions*, June, 147.

Lawrence, J. (1989). "Compaq Prepares for European Push," *Advertising Age*, 12 June, 38.

Link, G. (1988). "Our Global Marketplace," *Marketing & Media Decisions*, May, 108–110, 112.

Mandese, J. (1988). "They've Got the Whole World in Their Hands," *Marketing & Media Decisions*, June, 56.

McCarter, M. (1990). "Berlusconi's Ad Strength Called into Questions by EC," *Advertising Age*, 26 March, 30.

Murrow, D., and L. Wentz (1989). "U.K. Shops Face 1992 Pressures," *Advertising Age*, 8 May, 48.

Papazian, E. (1988). "Global's Tall Order," *Marketing and Media Decisions*, September, 83.

Rosenbaum, A. (1990). "Tobacco Ad Ban for EC Members Clears First Hurdle," *Advertising Age*, 19 March, 3.

Schleier, C. (1989). "Europe Maze Befuddles U.S. Players," *Advertising Age*, 12 June, S9.

Sorenson, R. Z., and U. E. Weichmann (1975). "How Multinationals View Marketing Standardization," *Harvard Business Review*, 53,3, 38–54, 166–167.

Synodinos, N. E., C. F. Keown, and L. W. Jacobs (1989). "Transnational Advertisers in Fifteen Countries," *Journal of Advertising Research*, April/May, 43–47.

Teinowitz, I. (1990). "Diversity Still Factor in Euro Ads," *Advertising Age*, 13 August, 54.

Tully, S. (1987). "U.S.-Style TV Turns on Europe," *Fortune*, 13 April, 97–98.

Wall Street Journal (1990). "EC Commission Is Seeking to Open Satellite Market," 15 November, B7.

Wentz, L. (1989). "J & J Plans European Tampon Blitz," *Advertising Age*, 25 September, 14.

———— (1988a). "Europe Opens Wallet: Saatchi," *Advertising Age*, 4 July, 26.

———— (1988b). "All Eyes on European TV Time: WFA Focuses on Easing Limits," *Advertising Age*, 23 May, 71.

CHAPTER 15

AN ANALYSIS OF
ADVERTISING THEMES IN
VARIOUS COUNTRIES*

Michael Minor

T he issue of standardized versus adapted marketing strategy remains an important area of research and discussion in international marketing (Buzzell 1968; Domzal and Unger 1987; Hamel
and Prahalad 1985; Kotler 1985; Levitt 1983; Porter 1986; Quelch and Hoff
1986; Sheth and Eshghi 1989; Sorenson and Weichmann 1975; Walters
1986; and Wind 1985). Notably, much of the discussion centers on advertising and promotional strategy. According to Jain (1989), advertising is
the leading concern in the debate over whether a standardized or adaptive
marketing strategy is preferable for global marketers.

Perhaps promotion, and particularly advertising, is a leading concern
because advertising is reflective of the culture of a particular country. Indeed, a rather large amount of literature has developed which infers consumption and cultural values in foreign countries by studying its advertising. Concerning Asian countries, for example, Hong, Muderrisoglu, and
Zinkhan (1987) used this strategy to investigate Japanese cultural values,
whereas Madden, Caballero, and Matsukubo (1986) compared Japanese
and American cultures on this basis. Miracle, Chang, and Taylor (1989)
employed a similar approach to compare television advertising in the
United States and Japan, and Tse, Belk, and Zhou (1989) examined Hong
Kong, the People's Republic of China, and Taiwan.

Perhaps surprisingly, relatively little has been done to research cultural themes as reflected in Latin American advertising. Among the few

*The author thanks David L. Sturges for comments on an earlier version of the
manuscript and DeWayne Hodges for help with methodology.

examples are the Tansey, Hyman, and Zinkhan (1990) comparison of cultural themes in U.S. and Brazilian print advertising. Latin America, however, is not a monolithic entity, and there is little reason to assume that cultural themes in Brazilian advertising are reflective of the rest of Latin America.

The purpose of this research is to investigate advertising expression across cultures. Cross-cultural studies of this nature are important for both researchers and practitioners. On a theoretical level, comparisons serve to highlight differences and similarities among cultures. On a more practical plane, cultural differences constrain the degree to which advertising can be standardized.

U.S. and Mexican magazine advertisements were chosen for comparison here for two reasons. First, the two countries are important trading partners, and this partnership link may grow should a Canadian-U.S.-Mexican free trade agreement come into effect. Second, the U.S.-Mexican comparison is particularly apt because much of the prior cross-cultural advertising research has been done between countries at roughly the same level of economic development, such as the United States and Japan (Hong et al. 1987; Madden et al. 1986; Miracle et al, 1989) or the United States and Germany (Robbins and Paksoy, 1989). Like Tse et al. (1989), this study compares countries at different levels of development. Although Tansey et al. also studied a less-developed country, their examination of advertising was limited to media addressed to business people in both countries. Here we look at advertising themes directed toward consumers who possess less wealth and status.

The approach utilized here is content analysis of advertising in U.S. and Mexican magazines. The use of content analysis in advertising research has been supported by Kassarjian (1977). To assure comparability, the magazines in both countries must address the same general demographic/psychographic audience and must span the same period of time (the period of the 1980s is used here). The themes to be researched are urban versus wilderness themes and work versus leisure themes.

COMPARING MEXICO AND THE UNITED STATES

We chose two widely circulated magazines for study: *Popular Mechanics*, a U.S. monthly magazine for the "mechanically gifted," and *Mechanico Popular*, a similarly oriented Mexican monthly magazine. We examined issues between 1986 and 1990 for *Popular Mechanics* and between 1984 and 1990 for *Mechanico Popular*. This longer time frame for the Mexican

magazine was necessary to collect enough data for a meaningful comparison; in each case, 57 issues were used. We examined only automobile ads
in both magazines. The total U.S.-Mexican sample was 383 automobile
ads: 320 of these appeared in the U.S. magazine and 63 appeared in the
Mexican publication.

Following the methodology of Tansey et al. (1990), we studied two
sets of themes in Mexican and U.S. advertising: urban and wilderness
themes, and work and leisure themes.

Urban Versus Wilderness Themes

Before 1970 Mexico had a rural society. However, the predominant trend
in the spatial distribution of Mexico's population is toward urbanization.
Between 1930 and 1970 the country changed from 33 percent to 50 percent urban (Rengert 1978). By the early 1980s there were 73 cities in Mexico with populations over 50,000 (Selby and Murphy 1982). Mexico's annual mean increment in the proportion of population that was urban was
one of the highest in the world. The mean increment from 1940 to 1960
was 3.07, a rate exceeded only by Peru (3.41) and Venezuela (4.46). The
U.S. rate for the same period was 0.49 (Rengert 1978). While the trend
toward urbanization has slowed slightly, Mexico is still urbanizing rapidly.
From 1965 to 1973 the average annual rate of urbanization in Mexico was
4.8 percent, which slowed only slightly to 4.1 percent in the 1973–1983
period (World Bank 1985). Comparing Mexican and U.S. urbanization
rates for more recent periods, we find the following:

	1965–1973[a]	1973–1983[a]	1980–1989[b]
Mexico	4.8%	4.1%	3.0%
United States	1.6	1.2	1.2

[a] World Bank 1985, p. 217
[b] World Bank 1991, p. 265

Mexicans surveyed in the 1960s responded positively to questions about a
preference for an urban lifestyle (Kahl 1968).

In the United States city dwellers began to report a dislike of the urban
environment as early as the 1820s. Further, many Americans prefer to
spend time in nonurban surroundings (Tansey et al. 1990). However, in
the late 1980s this trend may have been reversed. In 1972, less than half of
city dwellers questioned said they preferred urban life. When asked the

same question in 1988, a slight majority (six out of ten) preferred urban life (Otten 1991). Thus the following null hypothesis is suggested:

H1   *Urban themes are used in the same percentage of consumer ads in Mexico and in the United States.*

There is no scholarly work that suggests what the attitudes of Mexicans toward the wilderness are. However, it is reasonable to assume that more urbanized Americans have a more pro-wilderness attitude than do Mexicans. This discussion suggests the following hypothesis:

H2   *Wilderness settings are used in a lower percentage of consumer ads in Mexico than in the United States.*

Work Versus Leisure Themes

A major influence on the development of U.S. culture was the Puritan ethic with its strong emphasis on the value of work (Belk and Pollay 1985). Mexican culture was not exposed to this Puritan ethic. Further, a survey of Mexicans in the 1960s found little support for occupational primacy (Kahl 1968). Therefore, we would expect that traditional values place a higher value on work in the United States than they do in Mexico.

H3   *Work themes are used in a smaller percentage of consumer ads in Mexico than in the United States.*

In traditional Mexico, leisure was primarily social, including biweekly walkarounds and religious festivals. As early as the 1960s, however, the Mexican government began promoting athletics (Hayner 1966). As early as 1948 *Excelsior*, the Mexico City newspaper, devoted most of three pages to the life of Babe Ruth following his death. This suggests that attitudes toward leisure are probably about the same in Mexico and in the United States. Thus we investigate the null hypothesis, H4.

H4   *Leisure themes are used in the same percentage of consumer ads in Mexico as in the United States.*

Testing the Standardization Argument

If the standardization argument is correct, the results should identify a similar percentage of themes in print ads from both countries, across both the urban-wilderness dimension and the work-leisure dimension. However, a review of the literature suggests that while we will find a similar percentage of themes in the print ads of both countries for urban and leisure themes, we will find significantly different percentages of themes for wilderness and leisure themes. As another way of describing the same thing, we would expect the results shown in Table 15-1.

	Hypothesized Relationship		
Theme	Standardization Argument	Literature Review	
Urban	M = U.S.	M = U.S.	**TABLE 15-1**
Wilderness	M = U.S.	M < U.S.	HYPOTHESES BASED ON STANDARDIZATION ARGUMENT VERSUS HYPOTHESES BASED ON LITERATURE REVIEW
Work	M = U.S.	M < U.S.	
Total leisure	M = U.S.	M = U.S.	
Physical leisure	M = U.S.	M = U.S.	
Social leisure	M = U.S.	M = U.S.	

M = U.S. indicates test of the hypothesis that the percentage of Mexican ads with this theme equals the percentage of U.S. ads with this theme (two-tailed test of significance).

M > U.S. or M < U.S. indicates test of hypothesis that the percentage of Mexican ads with this theme is greater or lesser than the percentage of U.S. ads with this theme (one-tailed test of significance).

CODING

Operationalization of the urban-wilderness and work-leisure concepts follows the scheme devised by Tansey et al. (1990) (see Table 15-2). It should be noted that "leisure" is a two-dimensional construct, composed of physical leisure and social leisure. Total leisure is a sum of the two dimensions.

RESULTS

The results of the analysis, shown in Table 15-3, can be described as follows.

H1   Urban themes. The hypothesis is supported. Urban themes are used in a similar percentage of consumer ads in Mexico and in the United States.

TABLE 15-2   DEFINITIONS FOR CODING SCHEME

Category	Definitions	Key Properties	Examples of ads that fit the categories	Examples of ads that do not fit the categories
Urban	Of, relating to, characteristic of, or constituting a city. (A city is an inhabited place of greater size, population, or importance than a town or village.)	1. Highly populated 2. Technologically sophisticated 3. A regional or national center of commerce or culture	1. A city-scape 2. A scene of heavy traffic	1. A picture of a single building 2. A street scene without enough information to show whether it is an urban, suburban, rural, or small town setting 3. An airport scene
Wilderness	A tract or region uncultivated and uninhabited by human beings	1. Pristine 2. Beginning at the frontier	1. A scene featuring a mountain chain in the background 2. A scene of underdeveloped beach	1. A view of some mountain cabins 2. A scene at a yacht club 3. A restaurant scene 4. An auto showroom
Work	The labor, task, or duty that is one's accustomed means of livelihood	1. Directed to the fulfillment of professional obligations 2. Outside the home	1. A scene in which executives at the foot of an office building are talking 2. A picture of engineers describing the technological features of a car	1. A picture of someone driving children to school 2. People in business suits, shown outside of a work setting
Total Leisure	Freedom provided by the cessation of activities, especially: time free from work or duties (also defined here as physical leisure plus social leisure)	1. Pleasurable or self-fulfilling 2. Can be pursued alone or in a group	1. Physical leisure (see below) 2. Social leisure (see below)	1. Physical leisure (see below) 2. Social leisure (see below)

SOURCE: TANSEY, R., M. R. HYMAN, AND G. M. ZINKHAN (1990). CULTURAL THEMES IN BRAZILIAN AND U.S. AUTO ADS: A CROSS-CULTURAL COMPARISON, JOURNAL OF ADVERTISING, 19(2), 30–39.

TABLE 15-2   CONTINUED

Category	Definitions	Key Properties	Examples of ads that fit the categories	Examples of ads that do not fit the categories
Physical Leisure	Time free from work or duties spent doing a strenuous physical activity	Same as above	1. A picture of a man jogging on a mountain road	1. A scene of a professional athlete in training 2. A scene of someone repairing his or her automobile
Social Leisure	Time free from work or duties spent doing a social activity	1. Can be pursued only in a group 2. Emphasizes culture or conversation	1. A scene at an art show	1. A picture of a grandmother baby-sitting her grandchildren

Theme	Percentage Present in U.S. Ads ($N = 320$)	Percentage Present in Mexican Ads ($N = 63$)	Actual Relationship	Z Score	TABLE 15-3 CULTURAL DIFFERENCES BETWEEN U.S. AND MEXICAN AUTOMOBILE ADVERTISEMENTS (CROSS-SECTIONAL DATA 1984–1990)
Urban	12.20	12.70	M = U.S.	−0.11	
Wilderness	51.90	28.60	M < U.S.	3.38[a]	
Work	12.20	9.50	M = U.S.	0.62	
Total Leisure	30.30	31.70	M = U.S.	−0.23	
Physical Leisure	17.20	7.90	M < U.S.	1.86[b]	
Social Leisure	13.10	23.80	M > U.S.	−2.20[b]	

[a] Significant at $p < .05$ (one-tailed test)
[b] Significant at $p < .10$ (two-tailed test)

H2   *Wilderness themes.* The hypothesis is supported. Wilderness themes are used in a much higher proportion of U.S. ads (51.9 percent) than in Mexican ads (28.6 percent).

H3   *Work themes.* The hypothesis is not supported. Work themes are used in an insignificantly higher proportion of U.S. ads than in Mexican ads.

H4   *Leisure themes.* The hypothesis was that leisure themes are used in the same percentage of consumer ads in Mexico and the United States. This hypothesis was supported for total leisure themes. However, there are very strong between-country differences in the types of leisure that appear in advertisements. Physical leisure themes are used much more in the United States than they are in Mexico. On the other hand, social leisure themes are used much more in Mexican than in U.S. ads. The U.S. ads were about equally likely to feature either physical or social leisure themes in ads (17.2 percent versus 13.1 percent). However, Mexican ads were much more likely to feature social leisure themes (23.8 percent) than physical leisure themes (7.9 percent).

Thus the research does not entirely support either the relationships suggested by the standardization argument or those suggested by the literature review. The standardization argument and the literature review both indicated the null hypothesis for urban themes, which was supported. The standardization argument suggested the null hypothesis for wilderness themes, whereas the literature review suggested that U.S. print ads would feature more emphasis on wilderness themes than Mexican ads. The literature review hypothesis was supported. The standardization argument suggested the null hypothesis for work themes, whereas the literature review suggested that U.S. print ads would feature more emphasis on work themes than Mexican ads. Here the standardization argument was supported.

Results for the leisure themes deserve careful attention. Both the standardization argument and the literature review suggest that leisure themes will appear with roughly equal frequency in both countries, and the results support this hypothesis. However, it is clear that this result obfuscates as much as it clarifies the situation. Leisure must be analyzed in terms of the physical leisure and social leisure dimensions. Physical leisure themes were significantly more likely to appear in U.S. ads than in Mexican ads. Contrarily, social leisure themes were significantly more likely to appear in Mexican ads than in U.S. ads. U.S. ads reflect a high affect for physical leisure activities, whereas Mexican ads reflect a high affect for social leisure activities. Thus, while the difference between the two countries in mentions of total leisure as a summary construct is not statistically significant, the difference between ads featuring physical leisure and social leisure is quite significant for advertising managers. The differential affect they create for Mexican and U.S. consumers appears to be significant as well.

Brazil and Mexico: A Rough Comparison

It may also be useful to compare the themes across two Latin American countries, using the data for Brazil generated by Tansey et al. (1990). There are several limitations to be noted. First, the time frame is different (the 1970s for Brazilian ads and the late 1980s for Mexican ads). Second, the media are not comparable. The Brazilian medium is a magazine directed to business executives (*Visão*, which is roughly comparable to *Business Week* in the United States), which is by no means similar to *Mechanico Popular* in Mexico.

Thus the comparison is potentially misleading. Nonetheless, the data are available and the results prove interesting as long as they are regarded as tentative at best. The formulation of formal hypotheses concerning differences between Brazil and Mexico is not justified because of the limitations of the data. Therefore, a general description of the results is presented. Generation of hypotheses will be appropriate in a future study on this subject. The results of a Mexican-Brazilian comparison are shown in Table 15-4.

Theme	Percentage Present in Mexican Ads	Percentage Present in Brazilian Ads	Relationship
Urban	12.70	7.14	M > B[a]
Wilderness	28.60	22.96	M > B
Work	9.50	16.33	M < B[b]
Total Leisure	66.60	9.69	M > B
Physical Leisure	7.90	4.08	M > B
Social Leisure	23.80	5.61	M > B

TABLE 15-4
CULTURAL DIFFERENCES BETWEEN MEXICAN AND BRAZILIAN AUTOMOBILE ADVERTISEMENTS

[a]M > B indicates that the percentage of Mexican ads with this theme is greater than the percentage of Brazilian ads with this theme.
[b]M < B indicates that the percentage of Mexican ads with this theme is less than the percentage of Brazilian ads with this theme.

Urban themes   Urban themes were somewhat more likely to appear in Mexican than Brazilian ads (12.7 percent versus 7.1 percent). At first glance this appears to be inconsistent with the demographic data. In 1983 71 percent of Brazilians and 69 percent of Mexicans, a roughly equivalent percentage of the population, lived in an urban environment (World Bank 1985).

Wilderness themes   Wilderness themes were about as likely to appear in Mexican ads as in Brazilian ads (28.6 percent and 22.9 percent, respectively).

Work themes   Work themes were a good deal more likely to appear in Brazilian ads than in Mexican ads (16.3 percent for Brazil versus 9.5 percent for Mexico).

Leisure themes   Total leisure themes were much more likely to appear in Mexican ads than in Brazilian ads (31.7 percent versus 9.7 percent, respectively). However, the differences for physical leisure themes are probably not significant (4.1 percent Brazilian versus 7.9 percent Mexican). The difference in the appearance of leisure themes can be accounted for almost entirely in terms of social leisure themes (23.8 percent for Mexico versus 5.6 percent for Brazil).

Overall, there appear to be differences between Mexican and Brazilian ads in terms of these four themes, although the extent of these differences must await comparable data. There are at least two methods of accounting for the differences between Mexico and Brazil. On the one hand, Mexico and Brazil are obviously different countries. Brazil is larger in terms of population (147.3 million versus 84.6 million for Mexico). Brazil is also a somewhat richer country: The 1989 per capita GNP of Brazil was $2,540, whereas that of Mexico was $2,010 (World Bank 1991). Mexico is poorer and therefore further behind on the transition to modernity than Brazil; thus the trappings of modernity (e. g., urbanization) may be more preferred by Mexican consumers than by Brazilian consumers. This does not account for the large difference in the presence of ads with work themes, although one can perhaps speculate that Mexico is not far enough into the transition to modernity for work themes to have as high a positive affect as in Brazil. On the other hand, these differences may be a function of the different time frame (the decade of the 1970s versus the mid- to late-1980s) from which the advertisements were taken.

Thus, while differences in the appearances of themes in Mexican and Brazilian ads were not consistently large, there do appear to be intriguing differences between Mexico and Brazil. These differences warrant hypothesis development and testing with comparable data at some future point.

....

STANDARDIZED MARKETING

We are now in a position to speculate about the possible implications of this study and the Tansey et al. (1990) research for standardized marketing and, in particular, standardized advertising. As Tansey et al. (1990) note, their study suggests that a single monolithic culture is not emerging: Brazilian ads were more likely to feature urban settings than U.S. ads, whereas leisure settings were more likely to be featured in U.S. ads than in Brazilian ads. On the other hand, both work and wilderness themes appeared with roughly equal frequency in U.S. and Brazilian ads. Thus their study does not offer a firm indication that standardized advertising should or should not be employed. Their conclusion was that caution should be exercised in the adoption of standardized advertising programs.

In the U.S.-Mexico study, urban themes were not significantly more likely to appear in Mexican ads than in U.S. ads. Wilderness themes were much more likely to be used in U.S. ads than in Mexican ads. Differences in the appearance of work themes were not significant. Leisure themes appeared with roughly equal frequency, but it is important to note that the nature of the leisure activity depicted was significantly divergent.

Thus the evidence of the U.S.-Mexico study is somewhat more conclusive than that of the U.S.-Brazil study. The study of U.S. and Mexican advertisements reported here strongly supports the conclusion that a single, monolithic culture is not emerging. Thus the standardization argument is not supported.

One additional comment can be made. It has been suggested that between the poles of standardization (Levitt 1983) and country-by-country adaptation (Hamel and Prahalad 1985; Quelch and Hoff 1986) there lies a middle ground, where two possibilities present themselves. On the one hand, marketers could develop regional products, appealing to the "European" or "Latin American" customer (Ohmae 1985; Sheth and Eshghi 1989). On the other hand, Peebles and Ryans (1984) described a "programmed management" approach, which they earlier called "coordinated decentralization" of advertising (Peebles, Ryans, and Vernon 1978). Under programmed management, common global advertising themes are devised, but these common themes are implemented in a fashion that reflects the characteristics of the local market.

The results of these two studies do not support the possibility of employing either a regional or a programmed management approach to advertising themes. It appears that the United States, Mexico, and Brazil are separate markets with sufficiently different characteristics to nullify the economies of scale generated by either standardized approaches or regional/programmed management approaches. Given the fact that standardization rather than adaptation has been the thrust of multinational corporate strategy in the recent past (Keegan, Still, and Hill 1987), this evidence is well worth noting.

For example, it appears that physical leisure themes are inappropriate in Mexico and Brazil, whereas social leisure themes are most appropriate in Mexico, and least appropriate in Brazil, with the United States holding the middle ground. Urban themes are not equally appropriate in Brazil and Mexico, although wilderness themes are about equally employed in both countries. Further, work themes are more appropriate in Brazil than in Mexico.

CONCLUSIONS

This study both complements and extends the conclusions of the Tansey et al. (1990) study. First, Tansey et al. studied one product, two magazines, and two subcultures, and therefore (as they note) their study may suffer from a lack of generalizable results. They suggest that other researchers could extend their study by (1) sampling ads for other types of products, (2) comparing the business subcultures of other Latin American countries to the business subcultures of the United States, and (3) studying subcultures other than the business subculture. This study helps to generalize their results by performing the same task on two other magazines and a different subculture, while holding the product type constant.

The use of standardized advertising themes is not supported by Tansey et al. This study confirms that conclusion, for both a different subculture and for a different country. Further—and this is a concern which could not be dealt with based on the U.S.-Brazil research—it does not seem advisable to attempt to standardize advertising based on either assumed regional commonalities nor on a programmed management approach.

The present study still leaves much to be desired. In particular, other subcultures remain to be explored. For example, the youth subculture comes to mind, since that subculture may signal future cultural trends for the United States and Mexico. Further, it is essential to add other Latin American cultures to future studies if we are to come to conclusions about Latin America as a whole.

REFERENCES

Belk, R. W., and R. W. Pollay (1985). "Materialism and Magazine Advertising During the Twentieth Century," *Advances in Consumer Research*, Vol. 12. Provo, UT: Association for Consumer Research.

Buzzell, R. (1968). "Can You Standardize Global Marketing?" *Harvard Business Review*, 46, 102–113.

Domzal, T., and L. Unger (1987). "Emerging Positioning Strategies in Global Marketing," *Journal of Consumer Marketing*, 4, 23–28.

Hamel, G., and C. K. Prahalad (1985). "Do You Really Have a Global Strategy?" *Harvard Business Review*, 63, 139–148.

Hayner, N. S. (1966). *New Patterns in Old Mexico: A Study of Town and Metropolis.* New Haven, CT: College and University Press.

Hong, J. W., A. Muderrisoglu, and G. M. Zinkhan (1987). "Cultural Differences and Advertising Expression: A Comparative Content Analysis of Japanese and U.S. Advertising," *Journal of Advertising*, 16, 55–69.

Jain, S. C. (1989). "Standardization of International Marketing Strategy: Some Research Hypotheses," *Journal of Marketing*, 53, 70–79.

Kahl, J. A. (1968). *The Measurement of Modernism: A Study of Values in Brazil and Mexico.* Austin: University of Texas Press.

Kassarjian, H. H. (1977). "Content Analysis in Consumer Research," *Journal of Consumer Research*, 4, 8–18.

Keegan, W. J., R. R. Still, and J. S. Hill (1987). "Transferability and Adaptability of Products and Promotion Themes in Multinational Marketing—MNCs in LDCs," *Journal of Global Marketing*, 1, 85–103.

Kotler, P. (1985). "Global Standardization—Courting Danger," *Journal of Consumer Marketing*, 3, 13–15.

Levitt, T. (1983). "The Globalization of Markets," *Harvard Business Review*, 61, 92–102.

Madden, C. S., M. J. Caballero, and S. Matsukubo (1986). "Analysis of Information Content in U.S. and Japanese Magazine Advertising," *Journal of Advertising*, 15, 38–45.

Miracle, G. E., K. Y. Chang, and C. R. Taylor (1989). "Relationships Between Cultural Variation and Differences in Japanese and U.S. Television Advertising," *Marketing: Positioning for the 1990s.* Charleston, SC: Southern Marketing Association.

Ohmae, K. (1985). *Triad Power: The Coming Shape of Global Competition.* New York: The Free Press.

Otten, A. L. (1991). "Street Where They Live Is Pleasing More People," *The Wall Street Journal*, January 14, B1.

Peebles, D. M., and J. K. Ryans, Jr. (1984). *Management of International Advertising: A Marketing Approach.* Boston: Allyn and Bacon.

Peebles, D. M., J. K. Ryans, Jr., and I. R. Vernon (1978). "Coordinating International Advertising," *Journal of Marketing*, 42, 28–34.

Porter, M. E. (1986). "The Strategic Role of International Marketing," *Journal of Consumer Marketing*, 3, 17–21.

Quelch, J. A., and R. J. Hoff (1986). "Customizing Global Marketing," *Harvard Business Review*, 64, 59–68.

Rengert, A. C. (1978). *The Process of Cityward Migration for Women and Men in Mexico: Implications for Social Development.* Ann Arbor: University Microfilms.

Robbins, S., and C. H. Paksoy (1989). "A Comparative Study of German and U.S. Magazine Advertisements: Has Global Standardization Been Achieved?" *Marketing: Positioning for the 1990s.* Charleston, SC: Southern Marketing Association.

Selby, H. A., and A. D. Murphy (1982). "The Mexican Urban Household and the Decision to Migrate to the United States." Philadelphia: *ISHI Occasional Papers in Social Change,* 4.

Sheth, J., and A. Eshghi (1989). *Global Marketing Perspectives.* Cincinnati: South-Western Publishing.

Sorenson, R. A., and U. E. Weichmann (1975). "How Multinationals View Marketing Standardization," *Harvard Business Review,* 53, 38–56.

Tansey, R., M. R. Hyman, and G. M. Zinkhan (1990). "Cultural Themes in Brazilian and U.S. Auto Ads: A Cross-Cultural Comparison," *Journal of Advertising,* 19(2), 30–39.

Tse, D. K., R. W. Belk, and N. Zhou (1989). "Becoming a Consumer Society: A Longitudinal and Cross-Cultural Content Analysis of Print Ads from Hong Kong, the People's Republic of China, and Taiwan," *Journal of Consumer Research,* 15, 457–472.

Walters, P. G. P. (1986). "International Marketing Policy: A Discussion of the Standardization Construct and Its Relevance for Corporate Policy," *Journal of International Business Studies,* 17, 55–69.

Wind, Y. (1985). "The Myth of Globalization," *Journal of Consumer Marketing,* 3, 23–26.

World Bank (1985). *World Development Report 1985.* New York: Oxford University Press.

World Bank (1991). *World Development Report 1991.* Oxford: Oxford University Press.

CHAPTER 16

MULTILINGUAL ADVERTISING: DOES IT HAVE THE INTENDED EFFECT?

Mary Ellen Ryder

Nina M. Ray

Gary McCain

Stanley V. Scott

This chapter presents preliminary attempts to explain the probable effects on different populations of foreign language expressions in advertisements, and it discusses the potential repercussions that these effects can have on product evaluations. We investigate possible connections among the types of country-of-origin stereotypes already shown to exist and some linguistic stereotypes found in both bilingual and monolingual populations. We have two main purposes for exploring probable marketing and linguistic explanations for the effects of foreign language expressions in advertisements. First, we hope to narrow the range of plausible factors in multilingual advertising to suggest profitable areas for future research. Second, we hope to provide information that advertising strategists and copywriters can use to develop more effective multi-language advertisements.

With consumer markets changing so rapidly in the world marketplace, global opportunities are on the increase. Given this situation, it is crucial that marketers have a clear idea of what stereotypes foreign consumers may have about their products and their means of advertising those products, and that marketers develop the most effective ways to elicit those stereotypes when they are positive. More and more, marketers are investigating the best way to reach these varied markets. A great deal of past discussion has centered on whether standardized or customized advertising approaches are best. Certainly one factor that could influence the choice between these approaches is whether the same perceptions or stereotypes of the products and advertising styles from the originating country are held among various targeted consumer groups.

The Use of Foreign Words in Advertising

One interesting and potentially influential characteristic of advertising copy is the use of words from more than one language within the same ad. Over the past couple of years we have been investigating possible rationales for the inclusion of foreign words in advertising (Ray, Ryder, and Scott 1991) and the specific phenomenon of dual-language words (words that can be interpreted as having different meanings in different languages) (Ray, Ryder, and Steele 1991).

English terms, both as slogans and as names of products and businesses, appear to be quite common in ads throughout Europe, Latin America, and Japan (Harris, Sturm, Klassen, and Bechtold 1986; Haarmann 1984; Haarmann 1986). One can find analogous cases where languages other than English are used in the United States and the United Kingdom (Ray, Ryder, and McCain 1991). We present many examples of these ads from English-language publications.

Two aspects that pose interesting questions for linguists and advertisers alike are often found in these multilingual ads. One is that the foreign expressions are often **ungrammatical**. Harris et al. (1986) report on examples such as Le Tigré shirts (correct spelling is *le tigre*, without an accent). There was also a U.S. fashion advertisement that read: "Go ahead. We derrière you to try the chic French look of our famous N'est ce pas French fit jeans . . ." (Hughes 1988), where the noun "derrière" is used as a verb, presumably capitalizing on its similarity to the English verb "dare."

Ungrammatical use of English is equally common. For example, English words and phrases used as product and store names in foreign countries often have misspellings and incorrect punctuation. Ball (1989) cites names in France such as "Sixteen Canddels," "Pippermint," "Rapid'Lab," and "New Master-Sweat Boutic" (the last including a misspelling of an English word, *boutique,* that exists in French with the same spelling).

The second interesting aspect of the use of foreign terms in ads concerns **the incomprehensibility of foreign expressions chosen**: It is extremely unlikely that consumers understand the meaning of many of the foreign terms used. For example, Haarmann (1984, 1986) reports seeing ads in Japan where the text was entirely or mostly in French or English, even though most Japanese consumers are monolingual. Dunlop (1989, p. 33) mentions an interesting example of a mixture of two languages in a lingerie shop window in Parma, Italy.

> *Printed decoratively across the front of the nightie was the apparently nonsense legend: 'Happiness in estate.' The perpetrator had no*

idea that estate *is an English word, but was using the Italian word* estate *(three syllables), meaning 'summer'.*

Another example of uncomprehended foreign terms is found in the recent campaigns of Mazda making claims about *Kansei* engineering and of Volkswagen extolling *Fahrvergnügen. Kansei* is the pronunciation of a set of different words, so there will be no single translation; Kojima and Takebayashi (1984) give the definitions 'to finish,' 'to complete,' 'perfection,' 'shout of joy,' and 'nice, quiet.' Because of this variety of meanings, it may not be surprising that Mazda makes little attempt to translate *Kansei* in its promotional literature. Volkswagen, in its promotional brochures, does describe *Fahrvergnügen* as "Description of a pleasurable sensation experienced when a car and its driver are in mutual harmony; A unique driving experience; Pleasure: Satisfaction; A feeling experienced by Volkswagen drivers." This definition is certainly close to official translations of the German words involved. *Fahren* means 'to operate a car or train,' and *vergnügen* means 'pleasure, enjoyment, and entertainment' (Langenscheidt 1969). However, recent Volkswagen commercials depict consumers asking "What does Fahrvergnügen look like?" The viewer is shown the mechanisms of the inside of a car. In other words, in this case the company does not attempt a translation, even though *Fahrvergnügen* does translate well.

There has been some theorizing about the reasons for the use of foreign terms, especially English ones, in advertisements around the world (Dunlop 1989; Haarmann 1984 and 1986; Mewshaw 1988). For example, Haarmann (1984, 1986) has suggested that the use of foreign languages in Japanese ads is intended to evoke certain cultural stereotypes. However, none of these authors gives a satisfactory explanation of why languages should carry the particular stereotypes they do, or how effective advertisements that call to mind these stereotypes may be.

O'Shaughnessy and Holbrook (1988, p. 197) report a "linguistic turn" in social science, which has forced "thinkers in a wide range of disciplines to recognize the manner in which language shapes the course and meaning of the human condition." If language plays such an important role in behavior, the linguistic analysis of marketing, and in particular advertising, should not be overlooked.

THEORETICAL BACKGROUND

By drawing on both the advertising and linguistic literature, we are able to provide some insight into the possible effects of multilingual ads.

Marketing Background

Past research has shown that the misunderstanding of monolingual consumer print ads is widespread; in some cases up to 40 percent of print and television ads are misunderstood (Jacoby and Hoyer 1987). It seems likely that using two languages in the same ad would increase the rate of misunderstanding. While two-language ads may attract the attention that the sponsor desires, they may be very confusing, cause readers to wonder which language they are reading, and lead them to misunderstand the intended meaning of the ad. As Simmons Marketing reports indicate, the average reader spends only 5–7 seconds scanning a given print ad. It is only those ads that attract additional interest (or break the "boredom barrier") that are read in greater detail. Interest can be attracted by something unusual, something very attractive, or by the activation of the perceptual vigilance mechanism. Given the fact that the average ad is viewed such a short time, the consumers' confusion may simply be exacerbated by a multilanguage technique. If it is true that reading a monolingual text is a "psycholinguistic guessing game" (Suhor 1984, p. 249), how much more uncertain will the interpretation of these multilanguage ads be? How much effort is the consumer ready to exert in deciphering the text? On the other hand, if he or she does exert the effort, the ad could attract just enough attention to allow the reader to remember the sponsor later (Schachter 1989).

Because several languages appear to have international prestige, they may elicit an emotional response in the minds of the consumers. Stout and Leckenby (1988) recently reaffirmed the belief that consumers who have an emotional response to an ad have more favorable attitudes toward the ad and the brand. In their study consumers with these emotional responses also indicated that they were more likely to purchase the product than those who showed no emotional response.

PSYCHOLINGUISTICS AND ADVERTISING MESSAGE COMPREHENSION.   A rather substantial body of literature in the area of psycholinguistics can aid in understanding the effects of multilingual message comprehension (e.g., Gough 1966; Harris et al. 1986; Postman 1970; Stern 1988). One theory in favor of the use of multilingual ads is that of script interruption. In both linguistic and advertising literature (Harris et al. 1986), many examples show that when various scenarios are interrupted by an unrelated set of events, the interruptions are remembered better than the main scenario itself. They report that advertisers may improve consumers' memories for key points in advertisements by inserting these points as interruptions. With these interruptions, an entirely new meaning or implication can be attached to the ad, and this new information may be the most memorable. While studies concerning script interruption have not involved foreign languages in advertising, the insertion of a foreign word should force a mental interruption in processing, especially for a target market accustomed only to monolingual advertising, such as the Americans or the British.

Introduction of words from one language into a text written in another language is a strong violation of grammatical norms. Stern (1988) found that ads which violate the audience's grammatical expectations are thought to attract attention, perhaps by breaking through the advertising clutter.

On the other hand, Postman (1970) found that words that are used frequently in everyday language are more easily comprehended and remembered. Clearly, the foreign words that are used in a print ad are not the same as those usually found in everyday language. Thus, while a foreign word may break the attention barrier and attract interest, its unusual nature and unexpected appearance in the text may cause a discrepancy between the meaning intended by the sender and the meaning attributed by the receiver.

COUNTRY-OF-ORIGIN.   A great deal of country-of-origin research investigating consumer stereotypes has already been done (Bilkey and Ness 1982; Cordell 1991; Hong and Wyer 1989; Kaynak and Cavusgil 1983; Nagashima 1970, 1977; Narayana 1981; Rierson 1966). It has been shown that while there is somewhat of a predisposition to favor the products of one's own country (Bilkey and Ness 1982; Kaynak and Cavusgil 1983; Narayana 1981), significant variations exist in attitudes toward the products of various other countries, and stereotyping occurs in evaluating attributes of those products (Rierson 1966).

Product evaluations have been found to differ according to the perceived country-of-origin for all products in general (Anderson and Cunningham 1972; Nagashima 1970, 1977; Rierson 1966), major classes of products (Etzel and Walker 1974; Han 1989; Kaynak and Cavusgil 1983; Nagashima 1970, 1977; Rierson 1966), and even for specific brands (Gaedeke 1973). Country-of-origin effects have been found to influence consumers' beliefs about specific product attributes (Johansson, Douglas, and Nonaka 1985) such as technical advancement, prestige, workmanship, price, and serviceability (Han and Terpstra 1988).

The evaluation of images held for products from different countries varies by both the nationality of those doing the evaluations (Cattin, Jolibert, and Lohnes 1982) and the country-of-origin of the products being evaluated. Evaluations of products also relate to the preconceptions regarding people of the country-of-origin. For example, there appears to be a positive relationship between the degree of development of the country-of-origin and the evaluation of its products; the more developed nations enjoy a more favorable image than the less developed nations (Schooler 1971).

The **cognitive elaboration hypothesis** may hold the key to the effect of country-of-origin stereotypes in advertising. This hypothesis suggests:

> . . . a product's country of origin stimulates subjects' interest in the product and consequently leads them to think more extensively about product information and its evaluative implications. . . . When subjects are extrinsically motivated to form an impression of a product, they may assess the implications of information about the product regardless of whether the country-of-origin is known (Hong and Wyer 1989).

The researchers found:

> When subjects had no particular interest in evaluating a product at the time they received information about it, conveying the product's country of origin before describing its specific attributes increased the influence of these attributes on product evaluations (Hong and Wyer 1989).

Clearly, the most direct way of eliciting a country-of-origin stereotype is to use the phrase "Made in _____." Some research has already been done using this strategy (Nagashima 1970 and 1977). However, such an approach is not always possible. For example, many products, such as Toyotas in the United States or McDonald's food products in Russia, are produced in the foreign market area in which they are sold. In addition, it may be advantageous to elicit the stereotype of a particular country-of-origin for a product that fits that stereotype, even when the product is not actually from that country. Haarmann (1984) states that this is being done in Japanese advertising. Obviously in such a case the phrase "Made in _____" cannot be used. We believe we have discovered a way that such stereotypes are elicited in U.S. and European advertising, a way that does not require the use of such a direct claim: Borrowed foreign language terms used in advertising may serve as immediately perceivable cues to elicit country-of-origin stereotypes without making specific claims about where a product was produced (Ray, Ryder, and McCain 1991). An examination of linguistic evidence shows how this can be done.

LINGUISTIC BACKGROUND

CODE-SWITCHING.   At first glance, it seems possible that ads containing two languages are intended to be understood as examples of **code-switching**. Bilingual speakers often code-switch, that is, they use two languages within a single utterance or discourse (Grosjean 1982). While anyone learning a second language will occasionally resort to his or her first language when at a loss for a word, this is not true in code-switching (Jacobson 1982). Code-switching usually occurs in the conversation of **balanced bilinguals**, people who speak both languages equally fluently (Hakuta 1986).

Some characteristics of code-switching may be relevant for use in advertising. Most code-switching occurs in informal, even intimate, situations, in conversations between friends and close relatives (Jacobson 1982). Such an impression of intimacy could be exploited by marketers in selling a product. Speakers may switch a word or phrase because that element carries different social or affective meanings in the two languages. Thus, a Mexican-American may choose to use the Spanish phrase *en Mexico* rather than *in Mexico* because the connotations and set of associations for the *Mexico* in Spanish are quite different from those in English, in terms of affection and respect for the country (Jacobson 1982). In the same way, advertisers could use the associations of a word or phrase in a particular language to enhance their product.

Bilingual speakers may use extensive code-switching to identify themselves, and those who can understand them, as different and (in this context) superior to others who cannot understand such discourse or who understand it only poorly. This function of code-switching was employed by some members of a Chicano student organization on the University of Texas campus whenever they wanted their ideas to be adopted. The implication was that those using it were in some sense more truly Chicano than those whose Spanish was not as good, and therefore they had more right to dictate the activities of the organization (Limón 1982). Thus code-switching can be used to create solidarity between speaker and listener and influence the listener to take the speaker's views. Use of two languages in an ad could conceivably create a similar feeling of solidarity between the producers of a product and the targeted consumer.

However, if these ads are intended for a bilingual audience, they may suffer from some disadvantages. While it is still an open question as to whether code-switching always makes language processing more difficult (Grosjean 1982), some research seems to show that bilinguals take longer to read passages with code-switching than equivalent monolingual passages (Grosjean and Soares 1986). One reason for this may be a priming effect created by the first language used (Simpson, Peterson, Casteel, and Burgess 1989). In the Grosjean and Soares (1986) study, they found that more stimuli were categorized as French when the first phrase was French, and more were categorized as English when the first phrase was English. Given the short amount of time generally used to process ads, this could be a serious disadvantage in an advertisement unless the ad is perfectly constructed and the longer time needed to read the ad results in better understanding.

Code-switching can have another negative connotation. Many monolinguals and some bilinguals as well consider code-switching to be a substandard use of language. For example, Gibbons (1987) found that in Hong Kong, switching between Cantonese and English among university students is quite common. However, even student subjects who frequently used a mixed code rated code-switching speakers to be less well mannered, more aggressive, and more inclined to show off than monolingual speakers. Therefore, advertisers do risk some negative consumer reactions when they use mixed language advertising. If part of the purpose of the ad is to produce negative reactions (say to a competitor's products), then negative consumer reactions may be a valid goal. However, if only positive consumer reactions are desired, then multilingual advertising should be approached cautiously.

In short, the use of two or more languages in an advertisement may create positive feelings in bilingual speakers through the affective aspects of the meanings of some of the words used and through the creation of a feeling of solidarity between the presumably bilingual creator of the ad and the bilingual reader. However, such positive effects may be partially or completely negated by a greater processing time, a chance of misidentification of words that is apparently inherent in multilingual texts, and a possible negative emotional reaction to code-switching.

If multilingual ads are meant for bilingual audiences, however, they are going to have more serious problems than those just mentioned. While it may be true that 26 percent of Italians and 21 percent of Spaniards, for example, read at least a little English (Mitchell 1984), it is very unlikely that many of them are balanced bilinguals. Since only 1 percent of Italians and 3 percent of Spaniards claim to read English fluently (Mitchell 1984), it seems unlikely that these consumers will understand any of the English words in these ads because the advertisers have made no effort to stick to a **basic vocabulary** (words that would have a high probability of being in the low-level English speaker's repertoire) (Carter and McCarthy 1988). The same can be said of Japanese consumers since 98 percent of them are monolingual (Haarmann 1986). If few of the ad's readers are going to recognize the message as code-switching, or be able to interpret the foreign language portion, why are the advertisers using this format? The most probable answer is that the foreign words and phrases in an ad have a value that is independent of their meaning.

BORROWING.   Linguists have long known that languages have varying degrees of prestige. Lambert's (1960) classic experiments with English and French in Canada showed this. He taped French/English bilinguals reading equivalent texts in each language. The tapes were then played for French and English speakers, who were asked to rate the speakers on such dimensions as good/bad or educated/uneducated. Even though the same speaker was used for both the English and the French texts, the ratings of that speaker differed with the language used. Both English and French speaking subjects rated the speaker more positively when English was used rather than French.

While Lambert's experiment dealt with bilinguals, there is also evidence that a foreign language can have an effect on a speech community even when that community is essentially monolingual. This evidence comes from a study of **borrowing**, the permanent adoption of words or phrases from one language or dialect into another. One of the basic reasons for borrowing to take place is **prestige** (Hock 1986). By adopting terms from an appropriate foreign language into their own speech, people can show that they are cosmopolitan, educated, or up-to-date. What language is appropriate has depended in part on the period of history in which borrowing took place. Latin and secondarily Greek were the prestigious foreign languages throughout the Middle Ages, and to a certain extent they have stayed prestigious through modern times. French and Italian achieved ascendancy during the late Middle Ages and the Renaissance as languages of culture and commerce, and then French became the language of court and nobility, and later of diplomacy, during the eighteenth and nineteenth centuries (Kahane 1982). After World War II, English began to supersede French as the major prestige foreign language in Europe (Fishman 1982; Hock 1986).

Partly due to their historical roles, different languages have contributed to different semantic areas in the vocabularies of borrowing groups. Since Latin and Greek were for centuries the languages of scholarship and government, words from these languages have been borrowed into most modern European languages as educational, technological, scientific, and political terminology.

The economic preeminence of Italy during the Renaissance caused a number of Italian financial terms to be borrowed (de Bruijn-Van der Helm 1986). An enduring admiration for Italy's art, architecture, and music has caused many Italian aesthetic terms to be borrowed by other countries over several centuries. For example, both English and French have borrowed the Italian words for piano, mandolin, piccolo, and madrigal, as well as balcony and cornice (Low 1985). As the language of the political and social center of Europe, French has contributed words to government and legal domains as well as those dealing with fashion and the arts (Pyles and Algeo 1982).

Since World War II, the United States has played many of the roles just mentioned: military conqueror, technical innovator, economic force, and exporter of culture, at least the culture of U.S. popular music, film, and clothing styles. As a result, it is not surprising that words from English and especially American English are being borrowed into many European languages, even in the face of official discouragement (Kahane 1982). Nor is the influence of English limited to Western Europe. Japan has probably borrowed more words from English than any other language during the twentieth century; it has been estimated that 5 to 10 percent of the vocabulary used by the Japanese in everyday life are borrowed from English (Stanlaw 1987). The most common subject areas in which English words are borrowed into Japanese are advertising and other business functions, engineering, computer science, journalism and broadcasting, and sports (Loveday 1990; Morrow 1987). For example, based on the listings in dictionaries of specialized fields, words borrowed from English make up 75 percent of marketing terms, 75 percent of journalistic terms, 67 percent of engineering terms, and 99 percent of computer terms (Loveday 1990). One finds similar types of borrowing from English in all the countries of Western Europe despite official and unofficial pressure to exclude them in many countries.

Spanish has borrowed a number of English words dealing with business and commerce, economy, electronics, telecommunications, information, publicity, transportation, and sports (Labrada 1989; Trup 1982). In fact, 60 percent of the entries in a Spanish dictionary of marketing terms are of English origin (Meunier-Crespo 1987). Recently, while visiting Spain, one of us saw advertisements for "The Madrid Business School: Master *en* Business Administration." Even though this school was attempting to appeal to Spaniards, every word in this title is written in English except for the preposition *en*.

In short, both borrowing and code-switching convey certain affective values and possibly create a sort of solidarity, that of cosmopolitanism. However, unlike code-switching, borrowing is a phenomenon found among all speakers, both bilingual and monolingual, although the small bilingual population may supply the "bridge" by which the words pass into the vocabularies of the rest of the population.

Relevance of Borrowing in Multilingual Ads

What does this phenomenon of borrowing have to do with the use of foreign words in advertising? People often have strong stereotypes about other cultures. For example, many Americans view Germans as scientifically minded, industrious, and efficient as well as aggressive and extremely nationalistic. Italians are seen as artistic, passionate, quick-tempered, and talkative. The Japanese appear to Americans to be industrious and ambitious (Karlins, Coffman, and Walters 1969).

Given that people have stereotypes about cultures, do they stereotype languages as well? Lambert's (1960) experiments, which we have already discussed, show that different languages may have different levels of prestige. The evidence from borrowing suggests not only that different languages have different *amounts* of prestige but also that the prestige is of different *kinds*. Because so many Latin and Greek words in modern languages refer to philosophy, scholarship, and science, one might expect the languages themselves to epitomize these fields. The abundance of Italian borrowings found in many languages in the areas of art, music, and architecture might give Italian an artistic stereotype. A stereotype for French as cultured and elegant might be created from the hundreds of words that refer to fashion, diplomacy, and the arts borrowed from French into other languages. The flood of American English words concerning technology, fashion, popular arts and life-styles, and recreation borrowed into so many foreign languages should give English an almost universal stereotype as representing technological advances: cultural and social modernity, and carefree youthfulness.

The development of such stereotypes depends of course on the ability of speakers to identity the origins of their borrowed words. There is some evidence that people often recognize the linguistic source of borrowed words, especially those words that were introduced fairly recently, whose spelling and pronunciation may not be completely integrated into the borrowing language's system (Hock 1986).

If such language stereotypes exist, the mere appearance of words or phrases from a particular foreign language should evoke its stereotype, even if the words themselves are unfamiliar, just as meeting a person from another culture evokes a cultural stereotype even when the individual is a stranger. Haarmann (1984, 1986) proposes a similar hypothesis for the use of foreign languages in Japanese advertisements.

If the evoking of a language stereotype is the main purpose of foreign terms in advertising, then we might expect to find certain patterns and characteristics in these ads. *First, since each language will have its own stereotype, the use of any language will be limited to products that are clearly connected to that stereotype.* For example, English will be used in ads for computers and other high-tech products, fashion, sports and recreation, and objects connected with the life-styles of the young. German will also be used to emphasize a product's technological quality. French will be used, not to imply technological quality, but to promote items such as clothing, cosmetics, and possibly food. Italian will have similar functions; its stereotype will be based partly on art, which is easily transferred to fashion and fashion accessories, product identifications that are probably reinforced by stereotypes of the Italian culture as well.

Second, since the meaning of the actual words used is not important, there will be no effort to use commonly understood expressions, nor will the expressions be translated. Third, since the meanings of the foreign words are probably unknown, the words will not appear as part of the informative text in ads. Instead, foreign words will be used only as attention-getting phrases, names of products or companies, or peripheral information about a company, such as its foreign origin or the year it was founded.

4   *Fourth, since the consumers aren't fluent in the language from which the foreign terms are taken, and often the advertisers or producers of the product aren't either, ungrammaticality will be acceptable and, in fact, usually unnoticed.* As long as the foreign expressions have some characteristic identifiable as "French," "German," "Italian," "Spanish," and so on, the expression will have served its purpose.

Based on our admittedly preliminary sampling of advertisements containing foreign terms, it appears that all these expectations are fulfilled. Throughout our discussion, we attempt to illustrate these principles using various ads collected over the period of the past two years. The example ads are gathered from periodicals published in the United States and Europe. In order to observe as many instances of multilingual use as possible, we considered any ad that contained copy written in more than one language to be a potential example. While ads were not collected in a systematic fashion, we took care to find examples from publications aimed at a high socioeconomic reader (e.g., *Vanity Fair, Architectural Digest*) as well as those aimed at not quite as high a socioeconomic level (e.g., *Good Housekeeping, Car and Driver*). Foreign publications in our collection include *Panorama*, an Italian news magazine, *El Europeo*, a Spanish news source, and the Spanish language version of *Marie Claire*, a traditional women's magazine.

1   Let us begin with our first expectation concerning the use of particular languages to promote particular products. The connection of Latin and Greek with science and medicine has long been exploited by English-speaking advertisers. In Victorian times, pseudo-Latin and Greek terms appeared in hundreds of advertisements to impress a public who held the classical languages in high regard, even, or perhaps especially, when the readers were not familiar enough with them to understand the meanings of the invented terms. "Teeth were stopped with 'mineral marmoratum'; raincoats were 'siphonias'; hair cream was an 'aromatic regenerator'; hair dye was an 'atrapilatory'" (Hughes 1988). Some modern brand names take the same linguistic advantage; consider the names of health and medical products such as *NeoSynephrine, Acutrim Diet Formula*, and *Neosporin*, which contains *Polymixin B-Sulfate*. Another example is a computer translator called *Hexaglot*.

Because of their modern connotations, both German and Japanese can also be used to convey an impression of scientific or engineering excellence, as in the Mazda campaign promising *Kansei* engineering or the Volkswagen campaigns using *Fahrvergnügen*. The Mont Blanc ad (Figure 16-1) for its *Meisterstück* pens is another example; few people know that *meisterstück* means 'masterpiece,' but its identification as a German word, based in part on the umlauted *ü*, ensures an evocation of fine engineering. The Shiseido ad (Figure 16-2) for skin moisturizer uses an interesting combination of language stereotypes. The brand name appears to

FIGURE 16-1

FIGURE 16-2

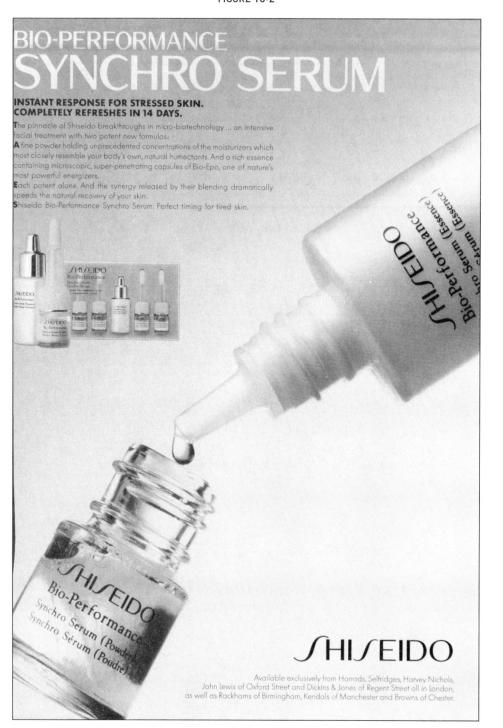

be Japanese. Since Japanese should have a scientific/engineering connotation, it seems at first to be inappropriate for a cosmetic product. However, the text of the ad indicates that it *is* the scientific image that is being used. The text is full of words based on Latin and Greek roots, such as *formula, bio-performance, synchro serum, microbiotechnology, synergy,* and *humectants,* thus reinforcing the scientific image evoked by the Japanese name. Perhaps as a safeguard, the advertisers also included French (written on both bottles in the ad), thus evoking in addition the more traditional stereotype of elegance usually connected with cosmetics.

We found ads for cosmetic products, interior decor, fashion, and cooking that had French names which would probably not be understood by consumers, who would know only that French-sounding terms are associated with the best in fashion, cuisine, and the arts. The use of French in the American ads for *N'est ce pas* jeans (mentioned in the introduction) are examples of the use of *identification* rather than *comprehension* of French as an advertising device for fashion and food. Mont Blanc not only has a pen called *Meisterstück,* but another, promoted in an extremely similar ad (Figure 16-3) called *Solitaire.* The two styles of pen seem very similar, but with the use of French rather than German in this ad, it is elegance that is being promoted, not fine engineering. *Courrèges Homme,* a clothing company that, according to the ad, is based in New York, not only has a French name but also uses the French phrase "*Courrèges est arrivé*" ('Courrèges has arrived') as its slogan (Figure 16-4). English acquired the word *cognac,* along with the liquor it names, from the French. Because of its spelling and its pronunciation, this is a word that many people both understand and recognize as being French. Thus the French language forms a bridge in an ad for French cognac, promoting Remy Martin. Almost the entire Remy Martin ad is in French: the slogan, "*Remy Martin est l'eau de vie*" ('Remy Martin is the water of life') as well as most of the small print in the ad, which in this case provides no vital information. Whether or not one understands any of the ad, however, is clearly not important; it is the recognizable French that conveys the message. Cacharel also produced an American ad for their *Anaïs Anaïs* perfume in which almost the entire ad is in French. The complete text reads: "*Anaïs Anaïs, le plus tendre des parfums, Cacharel, available at Macy's*" ('*Anaïs Anaïs,* the tenderest/most delicate of perfumes . . .'). English is used only for the important information about where the product can be bought.

Perhaps the exclusive or near exclusive use of French is a general policy of Cacharel. Haarmann (1984) describes a Japanese commercial for Cacharel de Paris cosmetics showing a Japanese woman elegantly dressed, but where the entire text is in French. Although this is a French company, Haarmann emphasizes that both French and English are often, even primarily, used to promote products made in Japan. For example, many of the larger, more elegant Japanese-made cars or limousines are given

FIGURE 16-3

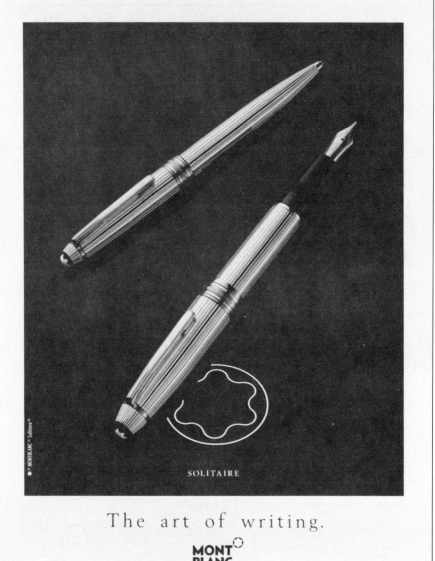

FIGURE 16-4

French names. French names are also given to most types of products for women, including cosmetic articles, high-quality biscuits and chocolates, and fashion accessories, whether these products are imported or domestic (Haarmann 1986).

We found a number of ads for Italian clothing, cologne, and fashion accessories marketed in the United States. Several of the ads have little or no English. It is interesting to note that two of them, a Maska ad and an Armani cologne ad, also include French words.

While "Americanisms" borrowed into other languages belong to many different fields (Kahane 1982), technology and the youth culture are probably the areas most relevant to advertising. Thus, like German and Japanese, English can be used to promote high-tech products, especially ones that are state-of-the-art. Like French and Italian, English can be used with fashion and cosmetic products. However, where French-promoted fashion and cosmetics are trying for an image of restrained elegance and high culture, English-promoted ones will be attempting to evoke a young, sexy, perhaps "tough" image. Many ads are for high-tech products, such as the Sony handycam (see Figure 16-5) or for clothes, fashion, and other products aimed at the youth culture (see Figure 16-6). The same is true of a Venezuelan ad for a magazine about alcoholic drinks, which uses the English word *barman*, as well as the borrowed but still "Englishy" word *cocteles* ('cocktails'). Ball (1989) lists among the types of French retail shops that have English names clothiers, travel agents, hair dressers, florists, motorcycle shops, pet shops, record shops, discotheques, bars and cafes, adding "in short, the purveyors of leisure, luxuries and entertainment rather than those who provide the basic necessities of life" (p. 196).

It is also instructive to consider the kinds of ads that do *not* contain words from various foreign languages. We cannot consider this at length here, so we will let one example suffice. Interestingly enough, aside from occasional place and resort names, travel ads do not generally make use of foreign expressions. We suggest that this is because a place plays only a minor role, if any, in the stereotypes people have about the language spoken there.

Our second expectation was that the foreign words used are not necessarily familiar to the consumer and will seldom, if ever, be translated. Translations were extremely rare among the ads we found. Our third expectation was that the foreign terms would not be used in the informative parts of the ad. An examination of all the ads already cited shows that this is the case. For example, in the *Courrèges Homme* ad (Figure 16-4), the French phrase is in large print, clearly intended to catch the eye. The informative text (in small print) providing information about outlets and about the fact that the clothing is made of pure wool is all in English. An additional ad, one for *Compagnie Internationale Express*, not only has the French name of the company in large print but also the company's Paris

FIGURE 16-5

FIGURE 16-6

address. Yet it is clear that the buyer is not expected to contact them there because at the bottom of the page there are instructions in English for getting more information about the product by calling an 800 number.

4. There is abundant evidence supporting our prediction about the occurrence of ungrammatical, or at the least extremely odd, usage in the foreign expressions employed. For example, a British interior decorating company advertises "The Faience Collection: fabrics—wallpapers—borders." This is an odd name for such a collection, because *faience* means 'pottery' or 'china.'

Another example of **semantically inappropriate** use of English is the name for a brand of Italian leisure-wear, Honky. The company even sponsors a professional basketball team, and neither the team members nor Italian shoppers appear to know or care that *honky* is a derogatory racial term (Mewshaw 1988). Probably some of these are simply names or labels that are chosen with no regard as to how they will translate in other languages. Haarmann (1984) reports a number of slogans and product names used in Japan that strike American ears as either odd or ungrammatical, including *New Sunny* (name of a car), *New Jog* (name of a scooter), and slogans like *new unique body object.*

As for **pronunciation distortions**, we find a bar in France called *Arys's Bar*, the first word of which probably derives from a mispronunciation of *Harry's* (Ball 1989). An ad for Disney World depended for its effect on a mispronunciation of the French word *bon*, meaning 'good.' In this ad, which featured the dog Pluto, the French phrase *bon voyage* was spelled as many Americans pronounce it, *bone voyage*, allowing a play on words that is impossible if the phrase is pronounced correctly. Japanese pronunciations of English words, both for borrowed words and terms used in advertising, are also quite different from the accepted pronunciations of native English speakers. For example, among the borrowed words, we find *ekusaito supotsu* for the expression *exciting sports, chokoreto keki* for *chocolate cake,* and *foku rifuto* for *fork lift* (Haarmann 1984). As Stanlaw (1987) says, "Much of the 'Japanese English' commonly found in conversations, in advertising, or on personal artifacts often is not transparent, or is even meaningless, to native English speakers. But meanings *vis-à-vis* English speakers is irrelevant" (p. 104). What matters is that the Japanese recognize it as English.

Standard spelling is usually preserved in the words used in advertising because it often provides the main clues for identifying a word as belonging to a particular foreign language. For example, while Japanese ads usually spell English words using their own syllabic script, they sometimes write them using English spelling (Haarmann 1986). However, it is necessary to realize that bizarre spellings may help consumers identify the foreign language used. Probably the most extreme example we found of use of ungrammatical spelling diacritics to indicate "foreignness" is in the *Modules* ad (Figure 16-7), which includes what appears to be a circumflex

FIGURE 16-7

over the *o* (which would indicate that the word once had an *s* between the *o* and the *d*), an umlaut incorrectly placed *under* rather than *over* the *u*, and an unidentifiable accent over the *e*, which would cause the *e* to be interpreted as a third syllable, all of which would produce an extremely unlikely pronunciation.

In conclusion, we claim that the use of foreign terms in advertising is intended to evoke a language stereotype in the consumer, based on largely unconscious evaluations of the origins of borrowed words in the native language. These evaluations are combined with present stereotypes he or she may have about the speakers of those languages. As a result, the words are neither intended to be informative nor expected to be used correctly. The mere presence of the individual foreign language chosen is enough to serve the purpose of the ad.

Preliminary Empirical Work

As we have shown thus far, the basic premise is that use of a foreign language with a particular positive linguistic stereotype will enhance the impact of the ad. This claim can be supported by evidence in small part from code-switching and in much greater part from linguistic borrowing using these expressions. Clearly, the advertisers who are using the foreign words believe that such enhancement takes place. However, controlled research into the effects on both monolingual and bilingual audiences from ads with and without foreign words would strengthen this claim. Are the English elements in Italian ads easily understood by the bilingual consumer and, if so, do they create a good affect or a feeling of solidarity? Likewise, if the often rather trite foreign words and phrases were translated into the native language, would the ads' effectiveness decrease, as predicted by the literature on borrowing?

Foster, Sullivan, and Perea (1989) performed a study involving both monolingual and bilingual (Spanish/English) Hispanics in the United States; they were presented with advertisements completely in Spanish. No significant differences existed between the monolingual and bilingual groups on overall comprehension, fact comprehension, or inference comprehension. This suggests that both monolinguals and bilinguals interpret ads written in the native language in similar ways. However, this research sheds no light on their interpretations of multilingual ads.

In Ray, Ryder, and McCain (1991), we investigated whether U.S. consumers hold certain perceptions of foreign products and their languages that could affect the interpretation and evaluation of advertising messages. Subjects were asked to list which languages come to mind when presented with certain cues such as "the language of science" and "the language of business." The top three responses in order of popularity are given below:

> the language of science: English, Japanese, German
> the language of medicine: English, German, Latin
> the language of engineering: English, German, Japanese
> the language of business: English, Japanese, German
> the language of advertising: English, Japanese, French
> the language of art: French, Italian, English
> the language of fashion: French, English, Italian
> the language of romance: French, Italian, Spanish
> the language of food: Italian, French, Spanish

Subjects were asked also to evaluate German, French, English, and Italian on eighteen semantic differential dimensions such as good–bad, colorful–colorless, and severe–lenient. This exact set of dimensions was used by Osgood, Suci, and Tannenbaum (1957) in some of their investigations.

Of eighteen adjective pairs, only two (rash–prudent and humble–proud) were not found to have significant differences among the four languages (nonparametric Kendall test, .05 level of significance). French is perceived as good, soft, feminine, sensitive, colorful, and interesting. German is hard, masculine, and severe. Italian is thought to be excitable and proud and English, active and changeable. French is perceived as the most colorful, good, and interesting. German is the most aggressive, pessimistic, and boring of the four languages; English is the most changeable. Italian is the most excitable and insane.

In short, at least in this small sample of U.S. students ($n = 30$), we found some preliminary evidence that different languages are in fact perceived differently, mostly in line with the perceptions predicted by distributions of borrowed words and previous cultural stereotype research.

IMPLICATIONS FOR FURTHER RESEARCH

An advertisement has many purposes, two of which are to attract the buyer's attention and to inform him or her of the product attributes. If foreign words and phrases are intended to catch the attention and create a receptive mood rather than to be understood, they will not carry the informative part of the ad. Instead, the important information will be in the native language, while the foreign words will mean relatively little. In the ads collected by the authors, this is the case; aside from the product name, the only other words in the foreign language contribute nothing significant to the meaning of the ad. For example, in the Spanish ad given in Figure 16-8, the phrase *high performance* could be deleted without creating a gap in the ad's text. In fact, the text would be more coherent without it because the phrase's meaning seems somewhat irrelevant to the rest of the text: "*un traje ligero, fresco y con tanta personalidad como el hombre que lo lleva*" ('a light suit, fresh and with as much personality as the man who wears it'). *More examples of such advertising from a wide variety of countries would either strengthen or disconfirm the prediction that the more effective ads do not place important information in the foreign language.*

2 If the function of the use of English is to suggest the young, cosmopolitan, conspicuous consumer, the types of products in which it is used should be those designed for this kind of market. The products represented in our collection certainly support this. Many of them are luxury items: They are for men's cologne, jeans, quality leather products, watches, expensive suits, and video equipment. Two that are not luxury products are cigarettes and sun screen, both of which are connected in advertising primarily with the life-style of the young. The ads appearing in U.S. and British publications tend to support the stereotypes of foreign languages when non-English words are used. German words are used to show high technology; Italian and French words are used with fashion.

In some of our collected ads, the only use of a foreign term is in the brand name. This use of foreign words seems to be a subject of some disagreement. While Sony keeps its *Handycam* name across cultures (Figure 16-5 shows a *Handycam* ad in Spanish), Unilever has a reputation for marketing its product under a variety of names. In the Netherlands, the brand is known as *Radion,* in Spain it is *Luzil,* and in Germany it is *Omo.* Its fabric softener is *Cajoline* in France, *Coccolino* in Italy, *Kuschelweich* in Germany, *Mimosin* in Spain, and *Snuggle* in the United States (Fraser 1990). This change in name may be done in part to create a word that conforms to the sound patterns of the native language of the country, since English includes a number of sounds and sound combinations not found in other European languages. There are more motivations for the change than this, however. The intent in the various names for the fabric softener is to convey the feeling of "cuddly softness" in each language. *There appears to be a possible trade-off between native brand names, which can convey emotional meaning directly, and foreign brand names, which must do it indirectly with the affective value the language itself has. Further research is needed on which of these methods is more effective, and on whether relative effectiveness changes depending on the nature of the product.*

Since it is clear that the value of borrowed words is often *solely* in their prestige, as the borrowing language already has adequate terms for items covered by the borrowings, *the introduction of words from a prestige language should enhance an advertisement, but it may not do so for all socioeconomic groups.* It is often the middle and lower classes that are most

FIGURE 16-8

receptive to foreign words in borrowing. French words from the Middle Ages survived in the rustic Middle-Low German dialects; fashionable Italianisms spread from Venice's empire to Greek fishermen and farmers (Kahane 1982). The greater adoption of foreign words by the least educated class may seem surprising at first, but there are at least two possible reasons for this phenomenon. First, there is the desire on the part of lower socioeconomic groups to appear to be higher in the social strata than they are. This is evidenced by such phenomena as the upgrading of dialect characteristics to a more prestigious variety under conditions that allow monitoring of speech (Fasold 1984). If the lower socioeconomic groups perceive use of foreign words as a sign of education, as they do the use of more prestigious dialectal forms, they are eager to adopt them for that reason. A cause for distaste of foreign words by some of the upper socioeconomic groups is suggested by Hock (1986, p. 416):

> Linguistic nationalism has been embraced mainly by (a subset of) the elite, traditionally defined as the educated and those in political power. On the other hand, the general populace, as well as many sections of the elite, are less concerned with linguistic nationalism and more with the prestige of foreign, often international, culture and vocabulary.

In other words, some of the elite may see use of foreign words as implying that the native language, and therefore the native culture and society, are inferior to the foreign one, and therefore they fear and resent the intrusion of foreign words into the native language. This is clearly the case in the official, if not the unofficial, stance of France on the use of English words (Kahane 1982). Similar views are often expressed by Spanish speakers (e.g., Labrada 1989). This suggests that, whereas the lower and middle classes might find the use of English words in an ad attractive, some of the upper class would be offended. Yet almost all the ads we collected come from magazines like *Vanity Fair*, *Mirabella*, *British House and Gardens*, *Architectural Digest*, and *Gentleman's Quarterly* whose readership is clearly the economic elite. Magazines aimed at other markets, such as *Good Housekeeping*, *US: The Entertainment Magazine*, and *Car and Driver*, have little if any foreign term usage. Somewhat surprisingly, neither do magazines aiming at an intellectual elite, such as *Smithsonian*, *Discover*, or *Scientific American*. Since it is generally the intellectual elite that object most to the introduction of foreign terms into native vocabulary, this last limitation appears logical. However, if it is the middle and lower economic groups that are most receptive to foreign words, why are these words not used in advertising aimed at that market? Clearly, more research needs to be done in this area.

There are linguistic problems we have touched on only briefly in borrowing words, even on a temporary basis, from one language into another.

One of the most obvious is that the sounds and sound combinations in the words may be sufficiently different from those in the borrowing language that the words are difficult to pronounce. In the ads we have found, no concession was made to the pronunciation differences between English and Italian. Certainly *Solares Waterproof* is not a headline that would easily flow from the lips of a Spanish speaker. Is this because the words were never intended to be pronounced in the first place, but merely recognized as English? Do English words also appear in *spoken* ads and, if so, do the kinds of words chosen differ because of this problem? The evidence we have collected, especially from Japanese advertising, suggests that lack of ease in pronunciation is not perceived as a problem for either written or oral ads. It is interesting to note in this connection that of the two foreign slogans being used in the United States, *Fahrvergnügen* and *Kansei*, the second is more in accord with English pronunciation than the first. In fact, the former word when used in the television ads is pronounced without the umlauted *ü*, making it sound somewhat more "English" without causing it to lose its German "flavor." *More work needs to be done on the trade-offs involved to discover how much and in what ways the pronunciation of a word can be changed to make it easy to say without losing the recognition by a consumer of its "foreign" quality.*

Additional issues that have yet to be addressed are the use of various dialects and **argots** within a language (different varieties spoken by different geographical, social, or professional groups). For example, is the difference among standard American English, BBC English, Cockney, Brooklynese, and others a factor in consumers' interpretations of messages, and does the influence of such factors depend on the market for which the ad is intended? In the United States, we see marketers attempting more and more to reach the Hispanic population in Spanish, and we also see commercials using Black English that target Afro-Americans.

In short, much more research needs to be done on the interacting variables involved in the introduction of foreign words into ads if we are to have a complete understanding of their positive or negative impact on the consumer. To summarize, we believe that some linguistic variables that could potentially affect attention, recall, and comprehension of print advertising are:

1. The consumer's perception of the country/language-of-origin/the product advertised and the foreign phrase used in the ad.
2. Whether or not the phrase to be interpreted is written in the consumer's native language.
3. Whether or not the phrase is translated for the consumer.
4. Whether or not the phrase has a dual meaning.
5. Whether or not the word or phrase conforms to the linguistic patterns of the native language.

Other important variables that could interact with the language issues are the type of product advertised (luxury versus everyday), the socioeconomic status of the target market, and whether that target market is mostly monolingual. Research must begin to measure the impact of the language issues discussed in this chapter.

Warnings and Suggestions for Multilingual Advertising

We have investigated the possible linguistic rationales for the use of foreign language words and phrases in print advertisements aimed primarily at monolingual audiences. We conclude that the use of the foreign language is mostly for prestige purposes; it attracts attention and penetrates consumers' perceptual defenses. If advertisers succeed in eliciting feelings of eliteness and sophistication, then the ad has had the intended effect. However, some general cautions are necessary. First, multilingual ads can easily be misinterpreted. If important information that is crucial to the success of the product is contained in the foreign language, consumers may not perceive the information correctly. Using two or more languages in a text can make comprehension more difficult and can cause negative emotional responses. For instance, various groups of consumers may be insulted by the foreign "intrusions" or by the "substandard" use of code-switching.

Second, while the borrowing of words is sometimes done for prestige purposes, the perceived stereotype of the borrowed language needs to be considered. Simple studies investigating the perceived characteristics of various languages and what they are known for in the consumer's mind could indicate whether the use of the foreign phrase will have the intended advertising effect.

Until further research is conducted in this area, we recommend that advertisers proceed cautiously with multilingual advertising. If a foreign word or phrase is used, care should be taken that there is no evident "dual meaning" (such as the "happiness in estate" example). The important, information-loaded part of the ad should appear in the native language with the foreign phrases used only to attract attention and to indicate prestige. If the ad is intended for a monolingual audience, advertisers should make sure that the target consumers can correctly identify the source language for the foreign expressions.

Naturally, speculation should not replace valid testing of proposed ads with representative monolingual and bilingual consumers. Only they can shed light on the question of whether the multilingual ads are having their intended effect.

References

Anderson, W. T., and W. H. Cunningham (1972). "Gauging Foreign Promotion," *Journal of Advertising Research*, 12 (February), 29–34.

Ball, R. (1989). "The French Retail Trade versus the English Language," *Modern Languages*, 70(4), 196–201.

Bilkey, W. J., and E. Ness (1982). "Country-of-Origin Effects on Product Evaluations," *Journal of International Business Studies* (Spring/Summer), 89–99.

Carter, R., and M. McCarthy (1988). *Vocabulary and Language Teaching*. London: Longman.

Cattin, P., A. Jolibert, and C. Lohnes (1982). "A Cross-Cultural Study of 'Made In' Concepts, *Journal of International Studies* (Winter), 131–141.

Cordell, V. (1991). "Competitive Context and Price as Moderators of Country of Origin Preferences," *Journal of the Academy of Marketing Science* (Spring), 123–128.

de Bruijn-Van der Helm, J. (1986). "'Netto' and 'Brutto': A Note on Early Attestations in Dutch of Two Commercial Terms of Italian Origin," *Neuphilologische Mitterlungen*, 87(3), 428–30.

Dunlop, A. (1989). "Parliamo Itangliano," *English Today*, 5(2), 32–35.

Etzel, M. J., and B. J. Walker (1974). "Advertising Strategy for Foreign Products," *Journal of Advertising Research*, 14 (June), 41–44.

Fasold, R. (1984). *The Sociolinguistics of Society*. Oxford, England: Basil Blackwell, Ltd.

Fishman, J. A. (1982). "Sociology of English as an Additional Language," in *The Other Tongue: English Across Cultures*, ed. by B. B. Kachru. New York: Pergamon Press.

Foster, J. R., G. L. Sullivan, and V. Perea (1989). "Comprehension of Spanish Language Ad Claims by Hispanic Consumers: A Comparison of Bilingual and Monolingual Performance," *Southwest Journal of Business and Economics*, 6(2–3), 13–18.

Fraser, I. (1990). "Now Only the Name's Not the Same," *Eurobusiness*, 2(7), 22–25.

Gaedeke, R. (1973). "Consumer Attitudes Toward Products 'Made In' Developing Countries," *Journal of Retailing*, 49 (Summer), 26–29.

Gibbons, J. (1987). *Code-Mixing and Code Choice: A Hong Kong Case Study*. Clevedon, England: Multilingual Matters.

Gough, P. (1966). "The Verification of Sentences: The Effect of Delay on Evidence and Sentence Length," *Journal of Verbal Learning and Verbal Behavior* (October), 492–496.

Grosjean, F. (1982). *Life with Two Languages: An Introduction to Bilingualism*. Cambridge, MA: Harvard University Press, 129–332.

Grosjean, F., and C. Soares (1986). "Processing Mixed Language: Some Preliminary Findings," in Vaid, J., ed. *Language Processing in Bilinguals: Psycholinguistic and Neuropsychological Perspectives.* Hillsdale, NJ: Lawrence Erlbaum Associates, 145–176.

Haarman, H. (1984). "The Role of Ethnocultural Stereotypes and Foreign Languages in Japanese Commercials," *International Journal of the Sociology of Language,* 50, 101–121.

——— (1986). "Verbal Strategies in Japanese Fashion Magazines—A Study in Impersonal Bilingualism and Ethnosymbolism," *International Journal of the Sociology of Language,* 58, 107–121.

Hakuta, K. (1986). *Mirror of Language: The Debate on Bilingualism.* New York: Basic Books.

Han, C. M. (1989). "Country Image: Halo or Summary Construct?" *Journal of Marketing Research,* 26 (May), 222–229.

Han, C. M., and V. Terpstra (1988). "Country-of-Origin Effects for Uni-National and Bi-National Products," *Journal of International Business Studies,* 16 (Summer), 235–256.

Harris, R. J., R. E. Sturm, M. L. Klassen, and J. I. Bechtold (1986). "Language in Advertising: A Psycholinguistic Approach," *Current Issues and Research in Advertising,* 9(1 & 2), 1–26.

Hock, H. H. (1986). *Principles of Historical Linguistics.* Berlin: Mouton de Gruyter.

Hong, S.-T., and R. S. Wyer, Jr. (1989). "Effects of Country-of-Origin and Product-Attribute Information on Product Evaluation: An Information Processing Perspective," *Journal of Consumer Research,* 16 (September), 175–187.

Hughes, G. (1988). *Words in Time: A Social History of the English Vocabulary.* Oxford, England: Basil Blackwell.

Jacobson, R. (1982). "The Social Implications of Intra-sentential Code-switching," in *Spanish in the United States: Sociolinguistic Aspects,* ed. by J. Amastae and L. Elías-Olivares. Cambridge, England: Cambridge University Press.

Jacoby, J., and W. D. Hoyer (1987). *The Comprehension and Miscomprehension of Print Communications.* Hillsdale, NJ: Lawrence Erlbaum Associates.

Johansson, J. K., S. P. Douglas, and I. Nonaka (1985). "Assessing the Impact of Country of Origin on Product Evaluations: A New Methodological Perspective," *Journal of Marketing Research,* 22 (November), 388–396.

Kahane, H. (1982). "American English: From a Colonial Substandard to a Prestige Language," in *The Other Tongue: English Across Cultures,* ed. by B. B. Kachru. New York: Pergamon Press.

Karlins, M., T. L. Coffman, and G. Walters (1969). "On the Fading of

Social Stereotypes: Studies in Three Generations of College Students," *Journal of Personality and Social Psychology*, 13, 4–5.

Kaynak, E., and S. T. Cavusgil (1983). "Consumer Attitudes Towards Products of Foreign Origin: Do They Vary Across Producer Classes?" *International Journal of Advertising*, 2, 147–157.

Kojima, Y., and Y. Takebayashi (1984). *Light House Japanese-English Dictionary*. Tokyo: Kenkyusha Publishers.

Labrada, E. B. (1989). "Influencias Anglicanizantes en el Español Contemporaneo," *Boletín de la Academia Columbiana*, 39, 139–146.

Lambert, W. E. (1960). "Evaluational Reactions to Spoken Languages," *Journal of Abnormal and Social Psychology*, 60, 44–51.

Langenscheidt's German-English, English-German Dictionary (1969). Berlin and Munich: Langenscheidt KG.

Limón, J. E. (1982). "El Meeting: History, Folk Spanish, and Ethnic Nationalism in a Chicano Student Community," in *Spanish in the United States: Sociolinguistic Aspects*, ed. by J. Amastae and L. Elías-Olivares. Cambridge, England: Cambridge University Press.

Loveday, L. (1990). "Lexical Transfer as Westernization? The Sociocultural Semantics of Contemporary Japanese Loanwords," *Doshisha Daigaku Eigo Eibungaka Kenkyu*, 51, 68–89.

Low, C. (1985). "Categories of Foreign Loan-Words in Modern French," *Geolinguistics*, 7, 105–118.

Meunier-Crespo, M. (1987). "Les Anglicismes dans la Presse d'Information Économique Espagnole," *Meta*, 32(3), 273–277.

Mewshaw, M. (1988). "For Only in Italy, Where People Think 'Go' Whenever They See 'Stop,' *European Travel & Life*, 4(10) (December): Murdock Magazines, 12–13.

Mitchell, D. (1984). "A European Researcher's View of European Business Marketing: Some Observations and Tips," *Business Marketing* (April), 70–76.

Morrow, P. R. (1987). "The Users and Uses of English in Japan," *World Englishes*, 6(1), 49–62.

Nagashima, A. (1970). "A Comparison of Japanese and U.S. Attitudes Toward Foreign Products," *Journal of Marketing*, 34 (January), 68–74.

——— (1977). "A Comparative 'Made In' Product Image Survey Among Japanese Businessmen," *Journal of Marketing*, 41 (July), 95–100.

Narayana, C. L. (1981). "Aggregate Images of American and Japanese Products: Implications on International Marketing," *Columbia Journal of World Business* (September), 31–35.

O'Shaughnessy, J., and M. B. Holbrook (1988). "Understanding Consumer Behavior: The Linguistic Turn in Marketing Research," *Journal of the Market Research Society*, 30(2), 197–223.

Osgood, C. E., G. J. Suci, and P. H. Tannenbaum (1957). *The Measurement of Meaning.* Urbana: University of Illinois Press.

Postman, L. (1970). "Effects of Word Frequency on Acquisition and Retention Under Conditions of Free-Recall Learning," *Quarterly Journal of Experimental Psychology,* (May), 185–195.

Pyles, T., and J. Algeo (1982). *The Origins and Development of the English Language,* 3rd edition. New York: Harcourt Brace Jovanovich, Inc.

Ray, N. M., M. E. Ryder, and G. McCain (1991). "Language Influences and Country-of-Origin Perceptions," in *Marketing in a Changing World,* Proceedings of the 18th International Research Seminar in Marketing, Institut d'Administration des Entreprises, Université d'Aix-Marseille, France, 235–256.

Ray, N. M., M. E. Ryder, and S. V. Scott (1991). "Toward an Understanding of the Use of Foreign Words in Print Advertising," *Journal of International Consumer Marketing,* 3(4), forthcoming.

Ray, N. M., M. E. Ryder, and T. J. Steele (1991). "Should Dual-Language Messages Concern Advertisers? A Pilot Study," in *Challenges of a New Decade in Marketing Education,* Proceedings of the Western Marketing Educators' Association Conference, San Diego, CA, April. 49–53.

Rierson, C. (1966). "Are Foreign Products Seen as Traditional Stereotypes?" *Journal of Retailing,* 42 (Fall), 33–40.

Schachter, D. L. (1989). "Memory," in *Foundations of Cognitive Science,* ed. by M. I. Posner. Cambridge, MA: The MIT Press.

Schooler, R. D. (1971). "Bias Phenomena Attendant to the Marketing of Foreign Goods in the U.S.," *Journal of International Studies,* 2 (Spring), 71–80.

Simpson, G. B., R. R. Peterson, M. A. Casteel, and C. Burgess (1989). "Lexical and Sentence Context Effects in Word Recognition," *Journal of Experimental Psychology,* 15(1), 88–97.

Stanlaw, J. (1987). "Japanese and English: Borrowing and Contact," *World Englishes,* 6(2), 93–109.

Stern, B. B. (1988). "How Does an Ad Mean? Language in Services Advertising," *Journal of Advertising,* 17(2), 3–14.

Stout, P. A., and J. D. Leckenby (1988). "The Nature of Emotional Response to Advertising: A Further Examination," *Journal of Advertising,* 17(4), 53–57.

Suhor, C. (1984). "Towards a Semiotics-Based Curriculum," *Journal of Curriculum Studies,* 16(3), 247–257.

Trup, L. (1982). "La características del lenguaje deportivo de la prensa cubana actual," *Yelmo,* 52–53 (April–September), 35–37.

PART V
....

WORLDWIDE CONSUMPTION
PATTERNS AND ISSUES

CHAPTER 17

CONSUMERISM IN CHINA

Youngho Lee

Ann C. Brown

C onsumerism concerns the movement that seeks to protect the rights of consumers by requiring such practices as honest packaging, labeling, and advertising; fair pricing; and improved safety standards. It also seeks to change social values relating to affluence and to create a political force responding to conservation and consumption. David Swankin, of the Consumers Union of the United States, Inc., defines consumerism as both the best use of productive resources and the distribution of these resources (Feldman 1976).

In defining consumerism, it is important to realize that while cultural and national differences affect consumerism in different settings, the universality of humanity provides an element of standardization of consumer behavior in all societies. Most consumers, faced with the duality of financial means and a bountiful market, will purchase accordingly (Miller 1984).

Consumerism in the developing countries has been given a considerable amount of attention. In Taiwan, this movement dates back to the 1950s. At that time, the government stressed the unpatriotic aspect of conspicuous consumption while supporting the consumer movement. Consumerism continued to make its way through Taiwan, and consumers there were characterized as volatile—their reactions harder to predict than those of the Chinese in Hong Kong or Singapore (Van Roo 1987). In India the Consumer Protection Act of 1986, passed by the Indian Parliament, constituted a step toward establishing consumerism as a part of public policy. This act clearly defines the consumers' rights as the following:

1. Protection against hazardous goods
2. Information about goods

3. Assurance of access to a variety of competitively priced goods
4. The right to be heard and receive consideration
5. The right to seek redress in cases of unscrupulous exploitation
6. Consumer education (Nayack 1987).

In a study undertaken to assess consumerism in New Zealand, New Zealanders appeared to be concerned about product quality, deceptive advertising, and high prices (Barker 1987). The overall concern in India, Taiwan, and New Zealand is the consumers' basic rights of freedom to choose, to be heard and be informed, to be safe, and to be represented. In other words, consumerism entails (1) a recognition of the need to protect consumers from deception, monopolistic pricing, dangerous products, and other undesirable marketing practices, (2) changing social values relating to affluence and consumption, and (3) a political force responding to the first two dimensions (Webster 1974).

Specifically, in consumerism, the focus is on basic issues between marketers (manufacturers and/or retailers) and consumers. From the consumers' point of view, consumer emancipation (liberating the consumer from being at the mercy of manufacturers) through consumer rights protection is mandatory because consumer rights should represent elementary human rights. Such emancipation is also a necessary (if not sufficient) prerequisite for the private sector to work like an open market. An open market can function only when there is some semblance of equality of status between buyers and sellers (Thorelli 1987). In the People's Republic of China (PRC), as in most developing countries, consumerism is a recent social phenomenon, characterized by the people's burning desire for reliable and safe products. (Throughout this chapter, when we refer to China, we mean the People's Republic of China.)

China's largest cities are experiencing unprecedented prosperity, which was lacking in the past forty years. This economic progress is manifested by the growth of businesses and bustling activities in the stores. Streets are being transformed into true shopping malls with queues forming in the predawn hours before the stores open. This amalgam in China's marketplace has given birth to consumerism in that country. Consumerism has gained prominence in China because of environmental factors, consumers' behaviors, and consumers' demands for protection.

In a commitment to economic reform (according to a politburo member in charge of ideology in September 1988), China's objective is "to create a market-oriented economy from that of government-controlled central planning (Soviet style economy)" (Southerland 1988). In this open market setting, the issue of consumerism is a vital one. Building on the assumption that an open economy encourages a certain degree of consumerism, this chapter focuses on the development of consumerism in the PRC and consumers' views of their rights.

History of Consumerism in China

Current Developments

Consumerism in China is very recent. It first appeared in 1979 when Deng Xiaoping took over leadership of China and began to adopt an "open door policy." He implemented drastic economic reforms through the modernization of agriculture, industry, national defense, and science and technology with the goal of enhancing production, productivity, and efficiency. These reforms led to increased incentives for workers (guaranteeing them more income) as well as for manufacturers and shop owners (providing them more income for their goods). The state's national income was increased through taxation. A race for foreign technology and trade was enhanced because foreign countries were required to bid competitively for a chance to provide both services and merchandise.

Before the 1979 reforms, as Hans B. Thorelli observed (Thorelli 1987), the PRC placed the consumers' welfare at the low end of national priorities. Traditional socialism regards marketing with a "jaundiced eye," seeing it as a tool of monopolistic manipulators and bourgeois profiteers. Socialist doctrine stresses the physical circulation of goods produced at the behest of planners and managers who presumably know better than the consumers themselves what is good for them. By contrast, modern China is embracing marketing with enthusiasm, realizing that it plays a dual and important role: (1) implementing the division of labor and specializations to create jobs for the people and (2) providing the stimulus of freedom of choice and value for money. The leadership soon realized that to be motivated as producers, most citizens had to be motivated first as consumers.

Through four decades of Communist Party rule, demand always outstripped supply, guaranteeing a market for even the shoddiest of goods, without advertising or promotion. The need for advertising or promotion is not always well understood by the majority of Chinese business executives because of the lack of an advertising tradition in Maoist China (The National Council 1987). Products were sold because there was a need for them and because they were available. As workers began making more money, a greater demand was created and the opportunity to purchase was greater. This demand was fostered by the initiation of the "responsibility system."

The "responsibility system," which related a person's pay to his/her performance, not only assured higher wages but also created differentiation in wages. Under this new dispensation system, individual households, groups of families, and production teams or brigades may contract with collectives, state enterprises, and other agencies for a certain minimum output, which is often more modest than previous quotas. In the agricultural sector, for example, the system is referred to as "household responsibility," and it replaced the commune with the family household as the basic unit of production. A farmer has a contractual right to farm a given amount of land. The contract further provides that a farmer must sell a specific amount of produce to the state each year. But a farmer may keep the proceeds from a sale, and in addition he may sell any surplus he produces for higher prices in the free market. Typically, farmers have considerable freedom in specifying what they want to grow, husband, or produce.

The differentiation in wages allowed in the responsibility system introduced competition, which in turn resulted in more income and more productivity for employers. The state-run population control program also affords consumers more disposable income. People have fewer children; only one is allowed under such a program. Thus people have fewer dependents to feed, clothe, and educate. As shown in Table 17.1, the number of persons supported by each worker was reduced by almost half from 3.4 in 1964–65 to 1.71 in 1984 in the urban areas, and from 2.14 to 1.87 in the rural areas.

"Free markets" were established so peasants could set their own prices to sell high-quality produce and handicrafts directly to urban consumers. Formerly, peasants were required to sell only to the bureaucratic

TABLE 17-1	Item	1957	1964/1965[a]	1984
SIZE AND EMPLOYMENT CHARACTERISTICS OF CHINA'S HOUSEHOLDS, FOR SELECTED SURVEY YEARS: 1957 TO 1984	Rural			
	Persons per household	4.85	5.03	5.37
	Workers per household	2.33	2.35	2.87
	Persons supported by each worker	2.08	2.14	1.87
	Urban			
SOURCE: J. R. TAYLOR AND K. A. HARDEE (1986). CONSUMER DEMAND IN CHINA, BOULDER, CO: WESTVIEW PRESS.	Persons per household	4.73	5.30	4.04
	Workers per household	1.44	1.60	2.36
	Persons supported by each worker	3.29	3.40	1.71

[a]Data shown under 1964/1965 for rural households are for 1965; data for urban households are for 1964. All figures are from income and expenditure surveys of rural peasant households and urban staff and worker families.

state distribution machinery. Total planning was typically associated with seller markets. To move in the direction of the freedom of choice and value for money associated with buyers' markets, China found it necessary to create a sizeable open market sector, which is characterized by decentralized initiative and competition. The "free markets" contributed greatly to the growth of durable goods in the marketplace, as well as to the increase in China's national income.

For a further explanation of the climate in China's major cities and the growing consumer buying power, Bronfenbrenner (1984) gave the following rationale:

1. People were exercising their buying power, making purchases of clothes, textiles, food, sewing machines, watches, radios, etc.
2. "Hoarding" and "panic-buying" were on the rise.
3. Quality of merchandise was deteriorating as some items were mass produced.
4. The black market was flourishing as hawkers filled the streets.
5. The "free market" system was becoming an important force in the economic arena, creating more income and incentives to buy.
6. State control was seemingly waning.

This situation led to the formation of consumer councils to address the problems of graft, price gouging, and shoddy merchandise, as well as the rudeness of sellers. The first consumer council was established in Canton in September of 1983. Its members were drawn from various government departments. The opening of Canton's council was attended by representatives from fifteen provinces, indicating that other areas might be interested in following Canton's example. The number of councils did in fact grow until there was a need to form a body to set policy and to oversee their activities. This body was formed and known as the China Consumer Association.

In 1985 the statutes of the China Consumer Association were formally accepted. The association consisted of consumer representatives from various organizations and their related departments, provinces, municipalities, and autonomous regions. The association was comprised of several hundred councils and was headquartered in Beijing. The following excerpt is from the statutes of the China Consumer Association.

GENERAL PROVISIONS OF THE CHINA CONSUMER ASSOCIATION

1. The purposes of the China Consumer Association are to supervise, through the public, the goods and services offered, with a view to protect consumers' interests; to guide the broad masses in their consumption; and to promote the development of a socialist economy.

2. In accordance with national laws and regulations as well as the policies, the association shall take drastic actions to safeguard consumers' rights, including the following:

    a. The right to get information on goods and services.
    b. The right to select goods and services.
    c. The right to acquire goods and services in safe and hygienic conditions.
    d. The right to supervise the price and quality of goods and services.
    e. The right to suggestions and comments on goods and services.
    f. The right to claim compensation for damages caused by poor quality goods and services offered.

3. In carrying out its tasks, the association shall keep close contact with the administrative authorities for industry and commerce and the various departments in charge of commodity inspection, standardization, measurements, prices, public health, etc., and shall, at the same time, get their help and support. The tasks of the association are the following:

    a. To publicize economic policies as they relate to consumption.
    b. To assist government in legislating for consumers' rights.
    c. To study and aid the dissemination of information concerning consumption and consumer protection.
    d. To conduct market research to ascertain consumers' desires.
    e. To hear consumers' complaints and refer the same to relevant agencies for timely handling.
    f. To produce/distribute journals and other publications of interest to consumers.
    g. To develop international contact; to take part in related activities in international and regional groups.

Moreover, the association is funded by private sources and subsidized by the state. The association is a member of the International Organization of Consumers Unions, whose headquarters is in The Hague, Netherlands. By the end of 1987, 703 consumer councils were in existence throughout China, representing one-third of the total number of cities and one-fifth of its provinces.

Pre-Tiananmen Developments

Prior to the Tiananmen Square demonstrations of 1989, China's citizens were able to purchase more consumer goods than ever before. The people's real income had increased substantially, thus raising per capita income and providing more disposable income for shopping and specialty goods. This situation not only created activity in the marketplace but also set the stage for a miasma of greed. In other words, marketers attempted to take advantage of consumers by assuming that they would buy anything and accept any kind of behavior or treatment (Sing Foo 1984).

In the major cities of China, the atmosphere was one of constant movement. During the day, Chinese citizens could be observed shopping in crowded stores. The hustle and bustle of the marketplace and the exchange of money was proof that China was indeed being transformed. This activity represented consumption not only by the Chinese but also by Westerners who shopped in the Friendship Stores. Standing in the center of the floor, one could hear the snap of the abacus throughout the building. An abacus consists of beads and balls strung on wires or rods set in a frame and is used to calculate prices.

This renewed activity in the marketplace has been perpetuated because people's value expectations have been raised. The people believe that they are entitled to certain goods and life conditions as manifested by the prevailing norms set by the immediate economic, social, cultural, and political environment. Television and newspaper advertisements and billboards in the streets conspicuously tantalize the senses with visions of mass-produced consumable goods. Western television programs (those cleared by the State) were instrumental in focusing on items such as cars, clothes, books, and high fashion designers' items (such as jeans and dresses) that were quickly becoming available to the Chinese people.

In May 1985 the government lifted price controls and thereby created free markets. The prices are higher in the free markets than in government- or state-run shops. According to a report (Sterba 1988):

> *Since the government lifted price controls on some 1800 food items in May 1985, free markets have burgeoned. China now has more than 61,000 free markets, which look much more like bazaars and flea markets held elsewhere. In addition, it has some 11.7 million registered private enterprises, exceeding the 7.2 million private businessmen around 1949, when communists took power. . . . Today's pioneers are relatively pikers, and it is not clear how large the government will let them grow.*

For the first time since 1949 and the Communist takeover, profiteers were enriching themselves through exploitation and inflation of prices, creating widespread graft and generating consumer complaints. A "pseudo-capitalist" mentality was spreading throughout China; "free enterprise" was growing. There was "more" of everything but at higher prices. The increase in prices was caused not only by the free enterprise system but also by an increase in the amount of the consumers' disposable income. Chinese citizens experienced increased economic freedom because they had more money and there was a proliferation of goods in the stores.

The strains of an orderly transition from a central economy, where one's basic needs are provided by the government, to an economy that is predominantly regulated by market forces have surfaced in today's China. The supply of consumable items, including food, is still one of the basic yardsticks for measuring the effectiveness of a government that takes responsibility for supplying the needs of the people.

CONSUMER BEHAVIOR AND PROTECTION OF CONSUMER RIGHTS

Consumers have greatly increased activity in the marketplace. In 1988, the State Statistical Bureau reported that retail sales of consumer goods for the first quarter of the year was 152.2 billion yuan (U.S.$15.4 billion), nearly one-quarter higher than that of the previous year. Sales of foods amounted to 87.8 billion yuan (U.S.$2.4 billion), 23.6 percent higher than that of the previous year. Average per capita consumption of food in China is 400 kg a year according to the latest statistics. Sales of canned food were up to 43.1 percent and sales of dairy products were up to 12.3 percent more than the first three months of the previous year. In the first three months, consumers purchased 9.47 million bicycles and 1.33 million refrigerators. Chinese consumers bought 23 billion yuan worth of clothing and spent 41.4 billion yuan for daily goods (*China Daily* 1988a). According to the State Economic Commission, sales of electronic goods remained strong throughout the year 1988. The supply of color television sets barely kept up with the demand, even with a production increase to 5 million sets for the year. Meanwhile, approximately 11.7 million black-and-white sets were produced.

"Free markets" have become quite popular, have contributed to the increase in the national economy, and threaten to outsell state-run shops in everything but grain and edible oil. To the average citizen, free markets represent the full scope of supply and demand. Consumers are happy with the supply but are apprehensive about the increase in demand and prices. In addition to the state-run shops and the free markets, there are private shops, individual peddlers (hawkers) who roam the streets, on foot or on bicycles, selling everything they can carry, and curbside hawkers, often unlicensed and untaxed, who continue in the black market tradition, selling watches, belts, jewelry, and live turtles. The latter also make large profits in the money exchange black market. These unauthorized peddlers, according to the more conservative authorities, represent a breakdown of law and order. They may become a problem in the future because they provide an avenue in which organized crime can operate. They may siphon off income from the government and flood the market with inferior merchandise. This operation may spread throughout China and even across its boundaries to Hong Kong and Taiwan.

The challenge in this atmosphere of free markets and sidewalk peddlers is to differentiate between inventive marketing (or the honest salesperson) and the con man. To remedy some of the dishonesty in the marketplace, several steps are being taken. In the larger stores some prices may be checked over a consumer hotline, while in some larger markets prices are posted on a chalk board for comparison with other stores (including the state-run stores) (*China Daily* 1988b). These practices help consumers make wise choices.

Regulations and limitations are not easy to enforce. It would seem that shoddy goods should eventually be replaced by good merchandise. In some instances, managers in the state-run stores can order what consumers want to buy, but managers must order goods as the state allocates them. Consumers are willing to pay for good, reliable merchandise. However, in order to get the asking price for shoddy or second-rate merchandise, some managers of state-run stores make piggyback sales. Piggyback sales consist of selling a consumer what he/she orders only if he/she also purchases a shoddy item. For example, good beer is sold only with a pack of cheap (shoddy) cigarettes.

Piggyback sales were banned by the government, mainly because they are a violation of the consumers' right to choose. The practice of piggyback sales bordered on fraud, and at best it was manipulation by the state. At this point in its transition, with the markets relatively open, the state decided it should not perpetuate the very practices from which it was supposed to protect its citizens.

Consumers' rights are constantly being infringed upon in the marketplace in China as elsewhere. It was for their protection that the consumer councils were initiated. Consumers around the country organized to fight for their rights and interests in the marketplace against market profiteers and speculators who drove up prices and dealt in shoddy merchandise. The council in Beijing handled 13,300 complaints in 1987 and even more the following year. It was reported that local councils around the country investigated in excess of 48,000 cases. More than 80 percent of the cases heard were resolved at a savings to consumers of 16 million yuan. The councils not only hear complaints and resolve cases but also administer market inspections and conduct sample surveys in an effort to "curb illegal trading and ensure quality products." The results of these surveys are published in the press with an admonition to government agencies to take appropriate action to ensure consumers' rights (Sterba 1988).

To further encourage and shame merchants into improving their merchandise, the Ministry of Light Industry threatened to display the country's shoddiest products: washing machines that eat clothes, dead and leaking batteries, "color" televisions without the color, refrigerators that do not keep food cool, shoes that fall apart in five days, and so forth. Though the public display of shoddy merchandise was canceled, some of the items were shown on television. As a result, about eighty repairmen came to Beijing to repair or replace merchandise.

In support of consumer protection, consumer groups from developing countries met at a conference held in the Bronx in New York during the week of May 31, 1986. This conference was organized by the International Organization of Consumers Unions and attracted delegates from 35 nations, including China and Taiwan (Greer 1986). It was the first time that China had been involved in such an effort. The conference provided a unique opportunity for exchanges of ideas and procedures for attacking problems in providing for consumer protection.

Since that time, China has continued to pursue ideas and suggestions from other areas in the matter of consumer protection. In September 1988 a delegation of four Chinese officials from the China Consumers Association visited consumer organizations, businesses, and a government agency in the United States. The primary objective of the visit was to gather information about consumer laws and codes here in the United States. These laws and codes were to be taken back to China to be revised and considered for adoption. The association has worked tirelessly from 1985 to the present to bring about some parity in the marketplace; to make merchants accountable for their merchandise, and to give the Chinese people confidence that the products they purchased will be of good quality and perform as promised.

Up to 1989 the China Consumers Association and its twenty-three provincial and regional councils handled 80,002 complaints and resolved 83 percent of those cases. The association has recovered more than 29 million yuan (U.S.$7.9 million) for consumers, and the government has imposed fines of about 2 million yuan (U.S.$540,000) on shops and/or factories, according to cases reported by nongovernmental consumer organizations. Statistics show a 79 percent increase in consumer complaints handled by the association over the previous year of 1988 (*China Daily* 1989).

POST-TIANANMEN DEVELOPMENT

What has been the state of the Chinese consumer movement since the Tiananmen Square incident in the summer of 1989? Although the government has projected an atmosphere of "business as usual" in China, it is apparent from the daily news that the government is not promoting the movement as vigorously as it did before. The China Consumers Association had been hearing complaints at a rate of about 280 cases per day. This number has dwindled to a fraction of what it used to be when the movement had the full support of the Communist Party. This apparent lack of government support leads one to ponder the future of the consumer movement in the larger cities of China.

It seems that at this time any criticism will not be viewed kindly. In fact, sources have revealed that the headquarters of the China Consumers Association has been moved from Beijing to an undisclosed location. This move does not indicate that the movement is continuing to experience success, at least in the Beijing area. In some of the other economic zones, the situation seems more favorable, especially in the southern areas of China. In these areas, the leaders seem to create less of a protectionist atmosphere and to exercise more moderate pragmatism. Its leaders and its youth seem to mutually agree that this area is to remain a model for economic change. The consumer councils in these areas also seem to enjoy a more liberal milieu in which to work. Their aim is to provide not only an atmosphere of economic progress but also protection for consumers.

Contrary to what many people expect, however, since early 1990 the market situation in China has been working for the benefit of consumers. Departing from the sellers' market where demand always exceeds supply, the PRC is now experiencing an unprecedented buyers' market, where consumers can pick and choose among mountainous stockpiles of inventory in the stores and factories. A recent report (Lawrence 1990) declares that, to everyone's bewilderment, there are now surpluses in China.

What happened is that consumer durables began piling up in early 1989, when individuals, who had done panic buying when an abortive attempt at price reform sent inflation soaring to nearly 30 percent in 1988, responded to newly stable prices by putting their money in banks. By that time, most Chinese citizens had bought all the big-ticket items that they planned to own. In addition, most state-run enterprises were still doing the same thing as they always did—concentrating on production quotas, paying little heed to quality or consumer preferences, and seeking new loans to keep turning out the same old goods that nobody wanted to buy. In addition, the economic slump starting in the summer of 1989 resulted in a nationwide inventory surplus of more than $24.2 billion worth of unsold merchandise. Two interest-rate reductions in 1990 did not lure much money out of individual savings accounts for purchases of refrigerators, washing machines, television sets, and other consumer durables. Loosening credit also had little effect on industrial stockpiles because many Chinese factories simply used new funds to pay for the production of more unwanted goods instead of making renovations so they could produce new or improved products (Lawrence 1990).

One can argue that big inventories of consumer durable goods can be reduced quickly by breaking down administrative barriers that prevent the goods from entering the huge rural market. For example, the state licenses only one or two stores in a county to sell color television sets. Increasing the number of retail outlets for consumer goods may help to reduce inventories, but it will not influence the factories to change the mix and quality of their products. For that, the state plans to authorize its wholesale and distributing agencies to buy from state-run enterprises only "marketable goods which meet standards." If this new program is implemented, however, it would mean potential bankruptcy of factories and unemployment of workers. The government has thus far not caused or encouraged unemployment, even when the factories in which people work are manufacturing goods that are outdated and substandard. It remains unclear whether the government is ready to accept the results and deal with the potential problems. If unemployment and bankruptcy are not government priorities, the factories have no more reason to be concerned about the new stockpiles the program will produce than they are about the stockpiles they already possess, as long as the government keeps paying subsidies for the financial losses of the factories and price subsidies to control inflation.

Some factory managers have listened to this *novel* idea of producing goods customers actually want to buy—refrigerators that keep food cool, shoes that don't fall apart in five days, and bicycles in a choice of colors and styles. The government's campaign to persuade state enterprises to begin courting consumers through trade shows, quality control, new products, and market research may appear ridiculous to Westerners because the ideas sound like sheer common sense. But they were novelties in China where such efforts were unnecessary because supplies had always been shorter than demands. Those factory managers who listened to consumers are gratified to find that the new marketing approach works. For example, the Flying Pigeon Bicycle Group now woos consumers with bikes painted in yellows and reds in addition to the traditional black. This simple innovation helped Flying Pigeon's sales take off. In fact, it took a stockpile of nearly 2 million bicycles to persuade one of China's leading consumer-goods companies to stop painting all its bicycles black (Lawrence 1990). This case speaks well for the current state of marketing in almost every government-owned industry and calls for further and continuous marketing development in Chinese enterprises.

CONCLUSION

As China moves toward an economy driven more by consumer demand than by central planners, its leaders have begun to recognize that greater consumer choice also requires greater consumer protection. To this end, it is evident that the government, working in conjunction with the people, has established a strong foundation for the consumer movement. From its inception in 1983, the movement has progressed rapidly. Privately funded but subsidized by the government, the China Consumers Association has grown from a few councils in 1985 to more than 865 regional offices. These offices have functioned well to protect China's billion plus consumers.

The Chinese people have developed a consumer consciousness although the movement has not reached its full potential. The Tiananmen Square incident in 1989 may have at first pushed the government to enforce stricter limitations on the consumer movement, but now it turns out to be working even better for the consumers' interests. At least in the search for solutions to the problem of stockpiles of unsold merchandise, the state has to encourage the factories and distributing agencies to be concerned about marketable goods that meet quality and product standards. Top Chinese officials are not yet in a position to yield to the calls for fundamental reforms of price decontrol and a complete free enterprise system.

With the changes in China's economic history coupled with the changes in attitudes and policies in recent years, China has become a vastly open market, floating like a balloon. There are many different views of the fate of Chinese consumerism in the future. As Lester Thurow (1989) mentioned, the student uprisings in the summer of 1989 were scary and cost a dear sacrifice, but they should be viewed as signs of success, not failure, of the vast country's policies.

The Party is attempting to create a market-oriented economy to provide good jobs and high-quality goods at reasonable prices to its 1.15 billion people. To aid in this endeavor, a property campaign—China's Long March to quality—was launched in February 1992 by state media outlets. Defective products were attacked by mixed media outlets. Nationwide television encouraged viewers to call special hotlines to expose substandard products during prime time (McGregor 1992).

Only time will tell how well and how soon China can manage further economic growth and development, including consumerism and consumer protection.

REFERENCES

Barker, A. T. (1987). "Consumerism in New Zealand," *International Marketing Review* (United Kingdom), Autumn 4:3, 63–74.

Bronfenbrenner, M. (1984). "China Since Mao: A Great Leap Backward?" *Atlantic Economic Journal.* XII-1 (March), 1–11.

China Daily. (1988a). "Consumption Patterns," July 26.

China Daily. (1988b). "Consumer Goods Output Increases over 1987 Level," April 7.

China Daily. (1989). September 2.

Feldman, L. P. (1976). *Consumer Protection: Problems and Prospects.* New York: West Publishing, 5.

Greer, W. R. (1986). "The Third World Looks at Consumerism," *The New York Times.* May 31.

Lawrence, S. V. (1990). "The Revolt of the Chinese Consumer," *U.S.News & World Report,* December 3, 62.

McGregan, J. (1992). "China's Cadres Bank on Consumerism," *The Wall Street Journal,* March 16, p. A10.

Miller, R. L. (1984). *Economic Issues for Consumers.* New York: West Publishing, 4–5.

Nayack, R. K. (1987). "Consumer Protection Act, 1986: Law and Policy in India," *Journal of Consumer Policy* (Netherlands), December, 10:4, 417–423.

Shao, M. (1988). "Laying the Foundation for the Great Mall of China," *Business Week,* January 25.

Sing Foo, and Jeh Pao. (1984). "As Consumers' Income Increases, China to Set up Association and Provide Advices on Spending," Associated Press. October 31.

Southerland, D. (1988). "Guangdon: The Golden Goose of China," *The Washington Post,* Washington, D.C. November 17.

Sterba, J. P. (1988). "China's Change: Peking Streets Teem with Merchants Again as State Loosens Reins," *The Wall Street Journal,* June 16.

Taylor, J. R., and K. A. Hardee. (1986). *Consumer Demand in China.* Boulder, CO.: Westview Press.

The National Council for US-China Trade (1987). *US Joint Ventures in China: A Progress Report,* March.

The Statutes of the China Consumer Association (1985). The Hague, Netherlands: International Organization of Consumer Unions.

Thorelli, H. B. (1987). "What Can Third World Countries Learn from China?" *Journal of Global Marketing,* Fall/Winter, 1:1/2, 69–83.

Thurow, L. (1989). "China's Economic Moves Make Sense," *Fortune,* June 5, 323–327.

Van Roo, M. (1987). "Researching the Taiwan Market: A Very Different Consumer," *Marketing Research Today* (Netherlands), Fall, 17:1, 54–57.

Webster, F. E. Jr. (1974). *Social Aspects of Marketing.* Englewood Cliffs, NJ: Prentice-Hall, 4.

CHAPTER 18

CONSUMPTION PATTERNS IN JAPAN AND THE NEWLY INDUSTRIALIZED COUNTRIES

Ahmed A. Soliman

T he remarkable boom in the economies of most nations in the Pacific rim, headed by Japan, has drawn the attention of observers and made this region attractive to many global marketers, including U.S. firms. The annual growth rate of the gross domestic product (GDP) of some countries in this region has reached an unprecedented level of 8 to 13 percent for several years. For instance, South Korea maintained a growth rate of 9 percent for the period 1962–1987 (Mittiga 1989). Other countries such as Malaysia, Indonesia, and Thailand are making economic progress in such a way that the region is expected to contain the fastest growing economies of the world for the foreseeable future (Jones 1988; Shale 1989).

In addition to Japan, the Pacific rim consists of eight countries that are united by their access to the Pacific Ocean. Four of these are known as the newly industrialized countries (NICs). They are Hong Kong, Singapore, South Korea, and Taiwan, and they are frequently referred to as the "Asian tigers." These countries along with Japan represent the focus of this chapter. The other four countries of the Pacific rim—Indonesia, Malaysia, the Philippines, and Thailand—are considered candidates for NIC status in the future if their economic growth continues at the current pace. For instance, the 1989 real growth in GDP is estimated at 8 percent in Malaysia, 9.2 percent in Thailand, and more than 5 percent in Indonesia (Shale 1989). This growth is fueled by Japan's direct investment and development aids to Southeast Asia. The last four countries, together with Singapore, form the Association of Southeast Asian Nations (ASEAN).

As economic growth continues in much of this region, both rising incomes and improved living standards motivate consumer spending which, in turn, is expected to convert their cultures from production cultures to consumption ones. As a major economic power, Japan continues to spur growth both through its own economy (by its domestic consumption) and through its foreign investment throughout the region (Jones 1988). While the economic health of the region helps expand local demand for foreign products, it also presents a challenge to U.S. products. The reason is simple: The NICs are substantially improving their product quality, and they are becoming seriously competitive in Japanese markets as well as in their own (*Tokyo Business Today* 1989).

As Japanese and NIC markets expand, U.S. firms targeting this region need a better understanding of the consumer behavior patterns and trends in order to ensure the development of effective marketing strategies.

In the following sections, we consider the characteristics, consumption habits, and buying patterns of consumers in Japan and the NICs. Several examples of the experiences of U.S. corporations in relation to these markets are discussed. Since gift giving plays a vital role in both family life and the business arena in Japan, this unique behavioral pattern is discussed in depth in a separate section. In the last section, we discuss the managerial implications of various buying behaviors. Lessons drawn from the U.S. experience in the Pacific rim are discussed, and directions for developing successful global marketing strategies are suggested.

Characteristics and Consumption Patterns of Japanese Consumers

With 125 million people and a per capita gross national product (GNP) of $25,430 a year (The World Bank 1992), Japan represents a huge market that is changing quickly toward a culture of consumption. As the second-wealthiest nation in the world after Switzerland in terms of per capita GNP (Smith et al. 1990), its citizens are becoming more and more status conscious.

Japan is undergoing an expansion in buying power led by a new breed of consumers called the *shinginrui*, or the "new mankind." This new generation is fashion conscious, upwardly mobile, and spends heavily on hobbies (Anderson and Wadkins 1991; Chipello 1987). Instant gratification is fulfilled through the escalating use of credit cards, which have been allowed only since the late 1970s (Borrus 1987).

The Japanese family is undergoing a structural change (Anderson and Wadkins 1991). The traditional emphasis on the extended family is being replaced by the nuclear family, which is prevalent in the West. The average size of a Japanese family is now three members, which opens the door for more individuality. Inspired by a climate of economic surplus and a proliferation of consumer goods and services, individuality results in diversity, which nurtures such values as novelty and variety.

③   The work values and life-styles of the Japanese are changing as well. Workers are becoming less concerned with group cohesiveness and more concerned with personal progress. A worker's identity is becoming a function of what he/she consumes, not what he/she produces. Thus the classical model of personal satisfaction that is derived from being a part of the corporate group is diminishing. As highly skilled positions are replaced by service jobs requiring less training, work is becoming less self-fulfilling. Traditional work values are changing in favor of seeking higher status through consumption (Anderson and Wadkins 1991).

The Japanese are quality conscious; they demand top-quality products in markets at home and abroad. Hutton (1988) reports that when the Japanese travel to the United States, they patronize upscale department stores such as Bloomingdale's in New York, Neiman Marcus in Houston, and Saks in San Francisco. The products they purchase range from expensive perfumes and cosmetics to designer-brand clothes.

In fact, the Japanese are encouraged to increase their spending abroad for several reasons. First, as part of fulfilling their social obligations toward their colleagues and friends, they must purchase souvenir gifts from the foreign country visited. Second, in July 1987 the Japanese government decided to double the value of goods that can be brought into the country duty-free to $1,600. Third, Japanese traveling abroad benefit from the high buying power of the yen relative to the U.S. dollar.

Although the Japanese appreciate product quality, a positive price-quality relationship doesn't always hold in their perception, at least among the frugal segment of the upscale population. For example, when Apex, Inc., an importer of Western luxury goods, started importing Hublot watches from Switzerland in 1984, it cut the price of one model to 1.2 million yen (nearly $9,600) from 1.8 million yen (nearly $14,400), the price that was charged by a previous importer. Many retailers of watches were furious, and some stopped carrying the watch because they believed that its image was hurt. Yet Apex's sales rose to 450 watches in the first year, exceeding the total sales of the previous three years by 150 watches (Darlin 1988).

This buying behavior is compatible with being thrifty and having a high propensity to save—a habit that reinforces the economic strength of the Japanese. While the Japanese save and invest their money in various portfolios, the government-owned postal system is a popular saving vehicle in Japan. One reason for this popularity is the fact that no taxes are charged on postal savings (Neff et al. 1991). Japanese consumers also tend to invest heavily in life insurance. One observer estimates that they invest more per capita in life insurance than consumers in any other nation (King et al. 1989).

While the Japanese are inherently thrifty—saving and investing heavily in the interest of securing their future—the consistent economic boom of their nation fosters a proclivity toward spending, which in turn leads to more economic boom. Some observers relate the tremendous increase in consumer spending in Japan to several factors. Among these factors are agricultural reform, import promotion, tax cuts, wage increases well above the inflation rate (which is less than 1 percent), and the rising number of individuals joining the work force (*The Economist* 1988). The increase in the size of the work force is caused by the baby-boom generation reaching working age as well as more women entering the labor market.

All indications suggest that the Japanese are inherently savers, but at the present time they are spending extravagantly—and this equation is difficult to balance. Nevertheless, this situation can be explained simply from both economic and behavioral points of view. As Japan undergoes several structural and social changes, both life-styles—thrifty and spendthrift—are likely to coexist in this unique nation with its peculiar cultural heritage and its tendency to preserve its culture. For instance, Darlin (1989) found that the rich Japanese, who make more than ¥ 10 million (approximately U.S. $80,000) a year and represent 10 percent of the population, can be divided into five distinct groups. These range from the "overts," who spend heavily, especially on foreign goods, art, and travel, to the "conservatives," who tend to save more or invest their money in their children's education. Furthermore, while the use of credit cards among young Japanese became fashionable during the last decade, the older generation is opposed to it; they feel that by using credit cards they are using up future money. In fact, personal bankruptcy rose sharply among young consumers in Japan as a result of the mismanagement of their credit privileges (Holden 1988; Stine 1990; *The Economist* 1992).

Accordingly, both savers and spenders exist among the Japanese. As the Japanese become more mobile and status conscious, saving and consumption habits are likely to change among some age groups and between social classes. On one hand, consumers who have been raised traditionally on conservative values and are likely to be older tend to be thrifty. On the other hand, younger individuals who enjoy higher wages and abundance of consumer goods and services and embrace Western consumption values tend to be big spenders.

The structural changes experienced by the Japanese society have also affected the status of women. Currently, Japanese women assume a more active role in the workplace, and the proportion of female employees is on the rise. However, the Japanese wife still manages the financial affairs of the household. Usually the husband turns the money over to his wife, takes an allowance, and leaves the rest for her to take care of (Marshall

1989). These social changes still make Japanese women a prime target for marketers when developing their marketing and advertising strategies.

Nonetheless, U.S. marketers must keep in mind that the Japanese culture strongly influences the buying patterns of women. In particular, this culture creates a status hierarchy among its citizens that lends more respect to its older employees, who usually enjoy more seniority in their companies. In Japan these norms regulate the buying behavior of corporate wives, who exercise extreme care in selecting products that reflect the status of their husbands in the company. This pattern is distinct from the Western model of consumption, which is competitive and attempts to alter the status quo (Anderson and Wadkins 1991).

Whereas Japanese culture sets strict rules concerning the hierarchy in society, it tolerates certain advertising practices that are considered sensitive in the United States, particularly when they involve bodily functions. Advertising agencies in Japan use lusty humor to advertise such delicate products as hemorrhoid formulas and toilet bowl cleaners. The Japanese consumers seem to accept it and think it is both fun and natural. One hemorrhoid preparation commercial features a man in a bizarre costume, his trousers around his ankles, sitting on a toilet whimpering about pain. Another ad for a toilet bowl cleaner is shot from inside the toilet showing a wife urging her husband to stick his head inside the bowl to see how good a job she did cleaning it (Darlin 1988).

In explaining Japanese openness about these matters, some observers believe the Japanese have always been relaxed about natural functions. Others attribute it to Japan's rejection of Christianity and the morality that comes with it. Still others believe that the lack of privacy in a crowded country forces the Japanese to be less self-conscious (Darlin 1988).

Another behavioral aspect of Japanese consumers is their adaptation to technology which makes their daily lives much easier. This is seen in the widespread use of personal bar codes. These codes identify the individual, who can use them to pay electric and gas bills at convenience stores, charge food and drinks at health clubs, track vehicle locations in amusement parks, program video cassette recorders, or activate microwave ovens to execute catalog recipes (*The Futurist* 1989).

The adaptation to bar-code technology is consistent with the tendency of the Japanese to avoid checks. The Japanese society is checkless, and businesses usually use promissory notes rather than checks in their transactions. Thus, instead of carrying a large amount of cash to pay for purchases, consumers use bar-code IDs almost everywhere.

Another source of convenience is the credit card, which has become popular only recently, especially among young consumers. The use of credit cards has accelerated since the government lifted curbs on foreign cards and bank-card operations in the late 1970s (Borrus 1987). It is worthy to note, however, that the Japanese government prohibits banks from offering revolving credit. Even though card balances must be paid off each month, card holders are happy with these cards because they provide convenience. This is evidenced by the tremendous rise in the number of credit cards in circulation, from 23.6 million in 1979 to 85 million in 1985.

Observers projected this number to jump to 150 million cards in 1990, but it actually soared to 166 million cards charging about $100 billion in that year. Interestingly, industry executives believe the Japanese conversion to revolving credit will be gradual, especially since the Japanese government intends to lift the 30-year ban on bank-owned credit card companies that offer consumer plastic cards with credit privileges (Borrus 1987; Libbey 1991; *The Economist* 1992).

Japan is emerging into a service society. Besides accepting credit cards and using bar codes to pay bills, consumers are beginning to use telephone information services very heavily. Telephone companies and all sorts of local organizations are expanding their services to accommodate a unique variety of consumers' requests for various types of information through telephone lines. In addition to seeking customary information such as financial news or horse and cycle racing results, callers can listen to the simulated voice of Genghis Khan or Shogun, who united Japan in the 16th century. Other peculiar services include sounds purportedly speaking from the grave, insect sounds and bird calls, the flattery line, the apology line, and the stress-reduction line. It is no wonder that the last two lines are very popular in the early evening (Kilburn 1988).

Other habits, preferences, and consumption patterns of the Japanese include the following:

- The Japanese prefer small products (Gelman 1988). U.S. manufacturers should incorporate this preference into the design of products aimed at Japan.
- The traditional breakfast in Japan is soybean soup, egg, rice, and fish. As a consequence, the Japanese resist buying cereals. This is complicated by the fact that the Japanese are tremendously suspicious of outsiders and slow to switch brands (Dreyfuss 1987).
- Unlike Latin Americans, Greeks, and Arabs, Japanese keep a distance of three feet or more when they speak to each other (Deigh 1988). This phenomenon has implications for personal selling when it is exercised by U.S. firms in Japan. Executives, salespeople, and other employees must keep their distance.
- The Japanese culture does not permit shaking the hand of a woman, but requires just bowing the head to her (Greene 1988). As for greeting men, both shaking hands and bowing are acceptable. The depth of bowing to another person reflects his social status and the degree of respect shown to him. Understanding this

cultural phenomenon is essential when dealing with Japanese businesses and customers.

- Japanese citizens are afraid of having the ends of their fingers cut off in accidents because they don't want to be mistaken for *yakuza*. Cutting off the last joint of a finger is a practice of the *yakuza*, or the Japanese Mafia (Greene 1988). Artificial limbs might find a good market in Japan.
- Japanese citizens are avid readers, but few speak or read English (Taylor and Adams 1988). The U.S. publishing industry should be active in preparing and selling Japanese translations of U.S. publications in various branches of knowledge.
- The Japanese like herbs in their cold medicines. U.S. pharmaceutical manufacturers might cater to this preference.
- Most Japanese girls wash their hair every day, so mild shampoos are preferred (Darlin 1989).
- Laundry is done in cold, hard water in Japan. This situation mandates the development of detergents that perform well in such conditions (Darlin 1989).
- Japanese consumers have a strong desire to be self-sufficient in food (Johnston 1988). U.S. fishery-equipment and farm-equipment manufacturers might capture this opportunity and target Japanese needs for these sorts of products.
- Gift giving is a ritual in Japan, and almost every occasion calls for a gift. Gift wrapping is as important as the gift itself, so gifts should always be wrapped, usually in subtly tinted rice paper, and they are never opened in front of the giver (Deigh 1988). Due to the importance of gift giving in Japan, this cultural phenomenon is discussed in detail in a subsequent section.

UNIQUENESS OF THE JAPANESE CULTURE

One can observe how extremes coexist amicably in Japanese society—from a strict cultural code that creates a hierarchy of social statuses of superiors and inferiors to a liberal cultural code that tolerates sensitive issues and scenes in advertising.

Japan seems to be a nation of antipodes: the savers versus the spenders, the ancient versus the modern, the traditional versus the novel, and the elderly versus the young. All appear to mix harmoniously in a fashion that advances the society to the future without losing its past. The Japanese society is developing into a nation of diversity, a nation of mingled culture, without losing or blemishing its identity. What seems to be the greatest strength of the Japanese people is their remarkable ability to adapt to the modern without abandoning the traditional.

Nevertheless, to achieve equilibrium between the demands of the traditional and the pressures or, if you will, the temptations of the modern, the Japanese must behave differently in their public and private lives. As Anderson and Wadkins (1991) put it, there is a striking gap between the public and private roles in Japan. Outside the home, the roles are rigidly prescribed; it is not considered appropriate to express one's true feelings publicly. This perhaps explains the overt respect the Japanese express to each other through bowing.

What are the implications of this to U.S. marketers? The emerging diversity in cultural values as well as consumption patterns among the Japanese offers more opportunities than threats to American corporations. First, the development and coexistence of several orientations and life-styles provide abundant opportunities for market niches in a country whose population is 125 million people with enormous buying power. Moreover, the adoption of new consumption values by many Japanese, combined with their high income, generates considerable demand for many goods and services including jeans; designer clothes; consumer electronics; cars; photography products; fast food; insurance; banking, financial, and investment services; travel services; and health and beauty products. Many of these goods and services are already produced in the U.S. and are targeted to service-oriented consumers—a segment that has been emerging in Japan. Indeed, the critical issue that faces manufacturers of goods and providers of services in the present time is how to compete for product quality on a global scale.

GIFT GIVING IN JAPAN

Gift giving in Japan is an extensive cultural activity that is practiced regularly by all Japanese like a ritual. It is governed by elaborate rules and represents an integral part of a larger system of social exchange (*Kodansha Encyclopedia of Japan* 1983). Almost every occasion calls for a gift: the New Year (*otoshidama*, when gifts are given to the children), the end of the year (*seibo*), midyear (*chugen*), birthdays, coming of age (*seijin*), marriage, friends traveling (for overseas or on long trips inside Japan), and even funerals. Gifts are also given to the sick and victims of fire or other disasters as encouragement (*mimai*). Moreover, travelers returning from even the shortest trips give gifts as souvenirs to friends, relatives, and others. In general, gifts are presented from families to families and from businesses to businesses rather than from individuals to individuals.

The average Japanese family gives or receives a gift at least once a week, and the Japanese find themselves obligated to spend substantial amounts of money on several occasions, almost all year, for gifts for superiors, teachers, customers, and friends to express appreciation and gratitude (Japan Travel Bureau 1991).

The big gift-exchange seasons in Japan are *chugen*, in July, and *seibo*, in December,* even though gifts are exchanged throughout the year. Some people exchange gifts during Christmas as well as at birthday parties, but this is not as common as it is in Western countries (Japan Travel Bureau 1991). An American citizen who lived in Japan for three years observes that the Japanese have recently adopted some U.S. holidays such as New Year's Day and Valentine's Day. Interestingly, on Valentine's Day only women give gifts to men, whereas on White Day (another Japanese holiday) only men give gifts to women.** Since the Japanese believe in the concept of social superiority, gifts are presented by persons in inferior positions to others in superior positions, such as a marriage mediator (*nakodo*), a family physician, or a teacher of traditional arts (e.g., flower arrangement or tea ceremony). Because of this, some people in the socially superior positions receive a disproportionate number of gifts (Befu 1983b).

---

*According to Befu (1983a), *chugen* is a term that denotes both the gifts and the custom of giving gifts at midsummer, particularly at the time of the Buddhist Bon festival, or all souls' day festival. "Traditionally, offerings to the souls of deceased family members made during Bon, in the 8th month of the lunar calendar, were distributed to relatives and others so as to share symbolically divine qualities among mortals. This custom (now carried out in July except in those areas where Bon is observed in August) has become secularized in recent years, so that even though gifts are given in coincidence with the Bon festival, they are no longer offerings to the souls of the deceased but are purchased at a store and delivered directly to a family" (p. 312).

Yamaguchi and Kojima (1986) explain that *chugen* is given to express appreciation of the special daily services received from others. They add that the custom is practiced on an individual as well as on a professional level, and among companies and organizations. The gratitude is expressed in the act of giving, not in the value of the gift.

Seibo, on the other hand, is a year-end gift given to superiors or good customers and also to a person to whom one feels a special obligation. *Seibo* gifts are given as an expression of appreciation for services and favors received in the past year. As with *chugen*, giving by itself is what matters, not the value of the gift (Befu 1983b; Yamaguchi and Kojima 1986).

**This information is based on the personal observations of Mr. Bruce Swenson. They are included here with his permission.

One of the Japanese cultural norms is bringing back a gift (*omiyage*) when returning from a trip, whether short or long, local or overseas. Since the Japanese consider their culture a "souvenir culture," or *omiyage bunka*, Japanese travel brochures usually emphasize shopping abroad and explain the various types of gifts that can be purchased.

From a Japanese point of view, gift buying is an important social custom that reinforces a group-oriented self-concept (Green and Alden 1988). For many Japanese, it is a source of pleasure on which they spend a lot of money. Gift giving is not a casual behavior; indeed, it is an old habit that is rooted in Japanese religious practices (Witcowski and Yamamoto 1991). It started with the offering of food and sake to supernatural beings and eventually led to a social obligation (*giri*) or an indebtedness within the circle of kin, friends, and acquaintances with whom one has reciprocity (*kosai*).

While the Japan Travel Bureau (1991) estimates that the average Japanese family gives or receives a gift at least once a week, other sources assess this figure at the level of twenty-three gifts every month (Witcowski and Yamamoto 1991). This gift exchange activity is taken so seriously that once involved in reciprocity, a family finds it difficult to quit. Although some educated Japanese consider this activity a vexation and an empty formality, the main stream of society still believes it matters.

Since the Japanese are group-oriented people, gift-giving behavior seems to be partly an egalitarian endeavor to share a travel experience with family and friends at home. In addition, giving *omiyage*, or souvenir gifts, enhances the social status of the giver among his group and shows that he/she has been abroad. Since the concepts of *kinen*, or souvenir, and *meibutsu*, or a specialty of the area visited, are very important in the Japanese culture, extreme care is exercised by Japanese travelers in obtaining gifts from the tourist site (Witcowski and Yamamoto 1991).

However, the actual contents of the gift are not as important as the act of giving itself. Gift giving is viewed as a symbol of thoughtfulness and appreciation of others. Furthermore, Japanese traditions dictate that when a traveler comes back to work, he/she apologizes to his/her co-workers for the long absence while presenting the gifts. Japanese norms almost mandate that the gifts should cost approximately half the price of farewell gifts (*senbetsu*) received by the traveler before his/her departure and be tailored to the age and sex of the giver (Witcowski and Yamamoto 1991).

The Japanese expend far more money, time, and effort in buying gifts than in purchasing items for personal use. Gifts are available everywhere in Japan: in train stations, gift shops, and department stores. Many stores devote whole sections for the display of gifts and are willing to process gift orders from customers and deliver them to gift receivers.

Cultural norms dictate that a gift receiver does not open the gift in front of the giver. They also mandate that gift packaging receives special attention. After studying gift buying behavior by Japanese travelers in the

United States, Witcowski and Yamamoto (1991) found that the place of manufacture and the appearance and packaging of the gift are more important criteria for gift buying than they are for items purchased for personal consumption.

The emphasis placed by the Japanese on gift packaging may be explained by what Anderson and Wadkins (1991) call "the sacred nothing" principle, which stresses form over substance and the boundaries over the core. According to this principle, which is rooted in the Japanese culture, the core is empty but the borders are important. This can be seen in Tokyo, Japan's capital. Whereas the heart of other cities in the world is replete with business activities, Tokyo's heart is empty where the Emperor's palace is located.

Another interesting aspect of Japanese culture can be summarized by the "synthetic ideal" principle (Anderson and Wadkins 1991). This principle explains gift-packaging behavior as well as a great deal of Japanese consumption behavior. This principle stipulates a dichotomy between reality and the ideal. Thus the Japanese are not interested in the real self; they place greater emphasis on artificiality. Artificiality is appreciated for its own sake and for its beauty, which can be created and idealized, because beauty is unattainable in reality. No attempt is made to conceal this behavior. Eventually, this behavior leads to a preoccupation with fantasy, which might foster a consumption ethic.

Anderson and Wadkins (1991) argue that these two principles simultaneously foster and inhibit consumption. On one hand, they reinforce consumption through the furthering of multiple identities and the emphasis on form over substance. The focus on the superficial aspects of the self and its preoccupation with fantasy tends to promote consumption. On the other hand, the principle of the sacred nothing involves the notion of hierarchy. But the traditional Japanese emphasis on hierarchy and group orientation runs counter to a consumer culture based on the belief that material welfare and consumption can enhance individualism. Also, fantasy is viewed in Japan as unattainable when projected in reality. This is manifested in the tragic drama of Japan, whose happy endings are rare.

However, as mentioned before, the Japanese have been able, in a unique way, to maintain a balance between the antipodes that characterize their existence, a quality that a few nations enjoy. Perhaps it is the tenacity of the Japanese people that placed Japan at the top of the list of developed nations.

THE EXPERIENCE OF U.S. FIRMS IN JAPAN

Many non-Japanese firms like Coca-Cola, IBM, NCR, and Nestlé have invested nearly $6.2 billion in Japan during the 36-year period ending

March 1986 (*The Economist* 1987). These firms achieved remarkable returns on their investments because they produced goods in Japan instead of exporting them from the United States and other countries. Basically, these firms manufacture and sell very similar products in their home countries. The factors attributed to their success in Japan are understanding the local culture, establishing joint ventures with Japanese entrepreneurs, hiring nationals for both lower and upper management positions, and slightly adapting their products to local tastes.

For some U.S. businesses, it was easy to penetrate the Japanese market and account for a substantial share of it. For instance, U.S. bank-card issuers have been extremely successful in penetrating this market since the Japanese government permitted bank-card operations in the 1970s. In 1987, U.S. card issuers had a 47.8 percent share of the $19 billion worth of products purchased with general-purpose credit cards (Borrus 1987). Visa, in particular, had an impressive growth record for its card circulation during the last ten years, not only in Japan but in the whole Asia-Pacific region (Stine 1990).

Campbell Soup Company was also able to penetrate the complex Japanese distribution system swiftly in the summer of 1987. This occurred when 7-Eleven, Japan signed an agreement with Campbell to stock its Pepperidge Farm cookies in their 3,300 chain stores throughout Japan (Holden 1988). Now the company has easy access to the market by delivering its cookies directly to one of 7-Eleven's wholesale suppliers.

However, for many U.S. firms, the road to success in Japan was not easy. For instance, it took twenty-five years for Kellogg's to penetrate the Japanese dry cereal market in which it holds an 80 percent share in the present time (Dreyfuss 1987). The Japanese habit of eating fish, rice, an egg, and soybean soup at breakfast caused astounding resistance to Kellogg's efforts, which were aimed at convincing consumers to switch to cereals. Still, Kellogg's is not very happy with its success because the average consumption per person in Japan is only 1.8 ounces of breakfast cereal a year compared to nine pounds per person in the United States.

In addition to Kellogg's cereals, many American products are now popular in Japan, including Coca-Cola, M&M candies, Kodak color films, Listerine mouthwash, and fast food from McDonald's and Kentucky Fried Chicken. These products are essentially the same as their American counterparts except for the packaging.

Nevertheless, because the Japanese are traditionally apprehensive about foreigners and foreign products, most of these products faced serious resistance during their introduction to the Japanese market. For instance, U.S. executives were afraid that cola's taste would be perceived as too medicinal, that pizza's taste would resemble soap, and that Oreo cookies, Nabisco's popular brand, would be considered "black food." At the present time, cola is the most popular soft drink, pizza is the most beloved fast food, and Oreo is now the number one brand of cookies in Japan (Darlin 1989).

Coping with business traditions (which are basically derived from the Japanese culture) is also one of the key factors for business success there. When Kentucky Fried Chicken (KFC) opened its first store in Japan, the local management team prepared a number of brown-bag gifts filled with KFC products. Then KFC employees marched in a line headed by their managers, carrying these gifts, and visited all businesses in the neighborhood. With traditional Japanese bowing, they offered these gifts to the managers and employees of area businesses as a gesture of goodwill and in the hope that these businesses would accept KFC as a new member in the locality.

Kentucky Fried Chicken is just one of many companies that are responding to an expanding service market in Japan. As Japan changes from an industrial society to a service one, the market for many consumer services is becoming lucrative. Many U.S. service firms have been successful in gaining a good share of this market. A good example is insurance companies. Some U.S. insurance firms have been able to achieve success in Japan by offering such unique plans as investment-oriented plans and life insurance plans that pay off only if the holder dies of cancer. These U.S. firms have been successful in competing against many Japanese rivals that are considered the largest insurance companies in the world (King et al. 1989). Other companies are attracted to this market and try to benefit from their experience in the field. For instance, building on their domestic experience with relationship marketing, i.e., establishing a personal relationship with customers, Equitable and Prudential insurance companies hope to succeed in Japan.

On the negative side, Procter & Gamble (P&G) seems to lose its battle with the Japanese market. Since 1973, P&G has lost an estimated quarter of a billion dollars in the land of the rising sun. Several reasons account for P&G's flop, among which are their failure to study Japanese marketing strategies and their use of hard-sell television advertisements (Tanzer 1986).

There is no doubt that cultural influences are strong in Japan. Nevertheless, the success of many U.S. products there provides evidence of the plausibility of globalization with minor adaptation. In order to be effective in a foreign market, global marketers should develop strategies that take into consideration local tastes. For example, as we mentioned earlier, most Japanese girls wash their hair every day, so they prefer mild shampoos. Also, because laundry is washed in cold, hard water in Japan, certain types of detergents that perform well in such conditions are required (Darlin 1989).

Even some services require minor adaptation. For instance, American International Group (AIG), a New York-based insurance conglomerate managing 375 offices in 130 countries, specializes in fine-tuning its products to meet local needs. In Japan, AIG sells health and accident insurance policies with a built-in saving feature (Nasar 1989) because the Japanese like to save money. These changes in product design, whether a good or service, are minor and can be accomplished without too much cost.

....

Consumers in the Newly Industrialized Countries: Their Characteristics and Consumption Behavior

VALUE
STRUCTURE

In most of East Asia, Confucianism forms the foundation of ethics and morality in business as well as in the social and personal lives of individuals. It emphasizes harmony between human relationships and nature and involves a system of subordination to enforce order. The major focus of Confucian thought, however, is on family relationships. The biological family is the single most important institution in the society, and corporations are usually owned and operated by biological families (Oh 1991).

Most consumers in the NICs are rapidly becoming more educated, and their household incomes are growing. For instance, the 1990 per capita GNP was US$11,160 in Singapore, US$7,970 in Taiwan, and US$5,400 in South Korea. The GDP per capita in Hong Kong was US$12,070 in the same year* (*Encyclopedia Britannica* 1992; The World Bank 1992). As more women enter the work force, the number of dual-income families is rising. In South Korea, the proportion of working women has reached 45 percent (*The Economist* 1989).

The population in these countries is relatively young, industrious, and shares a growing interest in foreign goods, especially U.S. products. In particular, the Taiwanese exhibit great interest in U.S.-made cars. As people become more educated, consumerism is on the rise as well (Hill, Fox, and Gadacz 1988).

In the NICs, the level of economic affluence accelerated in the 1980s such that consumer interests are beginning to move beyond the basic necessities of life. As the number of two-income families increases, demand is increasing for consumer appliances, electronic products, cars, convenience foods, cosmetics, designer clothes, and disposable diapers. In addition, because many Asian graduates live at home until their late twenties,

------

*The per capita GNP in Hong Kong is not available. The GDP stands for the gross domestic product.

their discretionary income is above average, boosting their buying power for many goods and services (*The Economist* 1991).

Like the Japanese, NIC consumers are becoming quality conscious. Consequently, firms conducting business in this region are taking appropriate measures to ensure the quality of their products. To protect their reputation, some NICs, such as Taiwan, have enacted legislation that precludes shipment of defective hardware. These countries have full government support in their quality development strategies (Kathawala and Nanda 1989).

NIC natives share saving and investment habits with the Japanese (*The Economist* 1991), but unlike the case in many developing countries, the national income is distributed relatively equally among NIC citizens* (Koretz 1989). This phenomenon has an important strategic implication for global marketers with a presence in the NICs because income equality permits steady buying power throughout market clusters over time. This situation is likely to increase repeat purchase rates once consumers establish confidence in the product.

Last, but not least, most Asians usually refuse to take tips and will chase a guest down the street to return a tip unless it is presented in a sealed envelope. Only in this case can a tip be considered a gift (Deigh 1988). Familiarity with this cultural phenomenon may save U.S. executives the embarrassment of rejection and smooth their relationships with natives of these countries.

The Experience of U.S. Firms in NICs

Citibank's venture in Asia provides a good example of a successful global strategy. When Citibank targeted affluent consumers, it outperformed local banks. The bank's strategy was simple, albeit costly: to provide its customers with innovative services, to use new banking technology, and to fulfill customer wants (Owens 1990). The quest for product quality seems to be a universal consumer desire.

This strategy was successful partly because the bank used new technology to better serve customers' needs. Opportunities to modernize industries worldwide seem to be great in the 1990s. Companies that specialize in equipment that uses modern electronic technology such as Nordson are expected to prosper as new and innovative applications are introduced

---

*In Peru, for instance, one percent of the population accounts for nearly half the national income (see Koretz 1989).

to a wide range of countries from Taiwan and Hong Kong in the Pacific rim to Brazil in South America (Winter 1988). Nordson, a medium-sized manufacturer of electronically controlled equipment used to apply adhesives, sealants, and coatings, derived more than half its 1988 sales of $240 million from overseas. In 1992 Nordson's overseas sales represented two-thirds of its total sales of $426 million. Sales to Japan alone were $63 million, representing 22.3 percent of the company's international sales (The Nordson Corporation 1993).

Until now, NICs used to export clothes, consumer electronics, and other products to the United States and compete stiffly with U.S. manufacturers in the latter's home market. As U.S. markets become saturated and consumer demand for more products accelerates in NIC markets, U.S. producers will find a better opportunity in expanding NIC markets. Some U.S. companies such as Mars, Levis, and Scott Paper have already made profits both in Taiwan and in South Korea. The experience they gained in these countries, especially in regard to packaging and advertising products for Asian consumers, should pay off when they target other Asian markets (*The Economist* 1991).

Nevertheless, U.S. producers may face tough competition in NIC markets, not only from their European and Japanese counterparts but also from NIC competitors. In order to survive and grow in these markets, they must be creative in product and marketing strategies. The Coca-Cola Company provides a good example of creativity; its global marketing strategy helped create a differential advantage and carved out a niche for the company in the Indonesian market. In Indonesia, the favorite national drinks are tea and tropical drinks. Well-known as an aggressive global marketer, the Coca-Cola Company introduced strawberry-, pineapple-, and banana-flavored soda pop and thus achieved high success in selling carbonated beverages in a country where soft drinks are not widely accepted. A trend toward a less sweet taste in Indonesia also helped Coca-Cola in its venture. Indeed, the potential growth in the global soft drink market is enormous because foreigners consume only 14 percent as many soft drinks as Americans do (McCarthy 1989), and creativity is needed to activate this potential.

Perhaps the major challenge facing global marketers is to understand local traditions and customs and adjust to them. United Airline's experience with the Pacific-rim countries is a resounding example. On February 11, 1986, United Airlines acquired the entire Pacific division of Pan American Airways. Rapidly, United began to serve thirteen cities in ten Pacific-rim countries, the fastest growing and probably one of the most competitive regions in the world. Most Chinese business travelers were shocked during the inauguration of United's concierge services for first-class passengers. To mark the occasion, each concierge proudly wore a white carnation—a well-known oriental symbol of death. For the same reason, the Ronald McDonald promotion of McDonald's failed in Japan because of his white face (Zeeman 1987).

Developing Successful
Global Marketing Strategies

Drawing on the experiences of U.S. firms in Southeast Asia, we suggest some guidelines for developing successful marketing strategies. First of all, global marketers who want to conduct business in East Asia need to show respect for and appreciation of the values prevailing in the host country. Attitudes of humility, formality, and reciprocity are requisites for success in these markets (Oh 1991).

Understanding the local code of conduct and coping with business norms and traditions help U.S. executives avoid embarrassment as well as loss of business. Being accepted by local businesses and customers in this region not only facilitates business transactions but also paves the road for fast growth.

U.S. business experience in this region suggests that producing American products abroad, especially in Japan, rather than exporting them from the United States, is effective in overcoming trade barriers. Moreover, visible activities involving the establishment of plants and hiring nationals provide evidence of commitment, which makes a difference in the business community (Covey 1988). Joint ventures with local entrepreneurs are preferred over direct investments in sole proprietorships for several reasons. First, a partnership with nationals in the host country encourages cooperation on the part of local suppliers, dealers, bankers, government officials, etc., and facilitates the acceptance of the foreign venture by the local business community. In addition, consumer resistance to U.S. products is minimized.

Establishing partnerships with locals also reduces the negative impact of the collusive network building up in Japan against U.S. and other foreign businesses* (Neff et al. 1991).

---

*For example, when considering a new bid, Japanese contractors meet secretly to decide whose turn it is and what price should be offered. Every contractor except the pre-agreed one bids higher. These meetings are, of course, closed to foreign contractors. Besides, a certain percentage goes to the ruling party as a favor. It is estimated that 2.8 percent of construction revenues are channeled to the ruling Liberal Democratic Party each year through its agents in the construction industry

Another effective method is to enter into a strategic alliance with another U.S. retail venture in Japan. As mentioned before, the strategic alliance between Campbell Soup Company and 7-Eleven, Japan helped the former to crack the intricate distribution system of Japan easily.

Currently, U.S. marketers can use the structural change experienced by the Japanese distribution system to their benefit. The 1.3 million neighborhood mom-and-pop stores (*sakays*) that once dominated retailing are losing their monopoly (Chipello 1987). Due to their small size and the costs associated with long channels of distribution, these stores have worked inefficiently and thus their prices are necessarily notoriously high. The growth of these stores is leveling off, whereas the number of corporate chain stores is increasing. Campbell's success story can be repeated.

To reduce the cost of entering a foreign market and ease organizational dealings, U.S. firms in Southeast Asia need to hire, train, and motivate the vast majority of its employees from the host country. One reason for the effective performance of Citibank Corp. in its global markets is that 98 percent of all branch managers and higher executives are host-country nationals (Guenther 1989).

Key requisites for success in global marketing strategies are thorough research of the foreign market, a study of prevailing social trends, and identification of local consumption habits, tastes, preferences, and shopping behavior. Only then can underserved markets be identified and targeted. Standard products can be tailored to local tastes through minor modifications, and advertising can be developed without violating cultural codes and taboos. If adapting a product to local tastes within the U.S. market and using different advertising copy through regional marketing are legitimate strategic options for U.S. manufacturers,* then adaptation to varying conditions in global markets makes even more sense.

The unique nature of gift giving in Japan provides an opportunity for U.S. manufacturers in both Japanese and U.S. markets. Because the Japanese now accept many U.S. products, gifts conforming to Japanese norms and tastes can be designed for export to Japan. Special attention should be given to packaging because the packaging is as important as the gift itself from a Japanese point of view. On the other hand, as the number of Japanese traveling to the United States is on the rise, more attention to gift preparation and packaging that targets Japanese tourists and business executives should pay off in high dividends.

(*zoku*), who watch out for different interest groups and intervene when necessary (see Neff et al. 1991).

*For example, the Campbell Soup Company is known for varying the types and amount of spices in their soup products to accommodate the local tastes of consumers in different geographic regions in the continental United States.

⑧ The use of latest technology in both manufacturing and marketing, as well as back-office technology in consumer services (such as banking), should help U.S. firms enjoy a distinctive advantage over the competition. It also improves product quality. Indeed, U.S. corporations should strive to maximize product quality to regain their leadership in the global market. Global consumers, especially in Japan and the NICs, are becoming more discriminating and quality conscious.

⑨ U.S. firms can use their reputation and established image to achieve a synergistic leverage based on the effective use of their resources worldwide. One way to accomplish this is to establish good social relationships with a local community in the host country and to serve community interests beyond the basic offering of the firm. This strategy will help establish rapport between the company and its local community and will enhance its credibility with its clientele. For instance, McDonald's gives away more than 10,000 sweatbands and posters to kids' basketball clinics around the world from Spain to Taiwan (Trachtenberg 1989). Entertaining children around the world using various means has earned the giant fast food provider the appreciation of its global customers.

While changing culturally rooted consumption habits is difficult, it is not impossible. It may take a long time to influence these habits, but eventually consumption patterns are likely to change because modern communication technology has converted the globe into a one-town community. Kellogg's cereal is a case in point.

Conclusion

Although each country in the world has its own idiosyncrasies and peculiarities, the latest developments in computer, telecommunications, and communication technologies are converting the world into a global market where consumer segments with similar life-styles and consumption patterns are emerging. This situation presents opportunities for aggressive marketing strategies and tactics on the part of shrewd marketers who desire to compete in the Southeast Asian market.

Differences in cultural orientations among nations should not be perceived as obstacles to global market strategies. By developing goods and services that meet global consumer needs, and by positioning them to capitalize on local preferences, firms can make inroads to new markets with good potential for growth (Koepfler 1989).

U.S. entrepreneurs have a high potential for success in Southeast Asia for several reasons (Covey 1988):

- English is the dominant language of the business community in the area.
- The social barriers against Americans are far fewer than in other parts of the world. Indeed there is a real admiration of U.S. business within the NICs.
- Business opportunities in the region are at their best. The area is characterized by affluent consumers, an educated work force, established financial and communications industries, government support of business, and rapidly improving copyright protection.

Other opportunities await U.S. global marketers in potential NICs in Southeast Asia, including Indonesia, Malaysia, Thailand, and the Philippines. Although political problems and decayed infrastructure obstacles plague some of these countries, they still enjoy several strengths. The major advantage is their huge supply of cheap and relatively well-educated workers. Trade within the region is highly active, and if it continues at the current pace, it will surpass that of the United States and Canada. This increasingly integrated and dynamic market offers major opportunities for U.S. companies.

REFERENCES

Anderson, L., and M. Wadkins (1991). "Japan—A Culture of Consumption?" in R. H. Holman and M. R. Solomon (eds.), *Advances in Consumer Research*, 18, 129–134.

Befu, H. (1983a). "*Chugen*," in *Kodansha Encyclopedia of Japan*, 2, New York: Harper & Row, 312.

———— (1983b). "*Seibo*," in *Kodansha Encyclopedia of Japan*, 7, New York: Harper & Row, 49.

Borrus, A. (1987). "The U.S. Is Getting Japan Hooked on Plastic," *Business Week* (May 25), 100–104.

Chipello, C. (1987). "Small Shopkeepers Losing Grip on Japanese Consumers," *The Wall Street Journal*, March 18, 26.

Covey, R. E. (1988). "The Four 'Tigers'—Opportunities and Challenges," *Industry Week* (September 5), 14.

Darlin, D. (1988). "Japanese Ads Take Earthiness to Level Out of This World," *The Wall Street Journal*, August 30, 1, 7.

———— (1989). "Myth and Marketing in Japan," *The Wall Street Journal*, April 6, B1.

Deigh, R. (1988). "How to Be a Gracious Guest Abroad," *U.S. News & World Report*, May 30, 71.

Dreyfuss, J. (1987). "How to Beat the Japanese at Home," *Fortune*, August 31, 80–83.

Gelman, J. (1988). "Capa Correspondent Brings It Back Home," *Modern Photography*, 52, 4 (April), 7.

Green, R. T., and D. L. Alden (1988). "Functional Equivalence in Cross-

Cultural Consumer Behavior: Gift Giving in Japan and the United States," *Psychology and Marketing*, 5 (Summer), 155–168.

Greene, B. (1988). "Japanese Beat," *Esquire*, 109, 3 (March), 51–55.

Guenther, R. (1989). "Global Reach: Citicorp Strives to Be McDonald's and Coke of Consumer Banking," *The Wall Street Journal*, August 8, A1.

Hill, J. S., M. Fox, and O. Gadacz (1988). "Asia's Little Dragons," *Advertising Age*, November 9, 104–106.

Holden, T. (1988). "Campbell's Taste of the Japanese Market Is Mm-mm Good," *Business Week*, March 28, 42.

Hutton, C. (1988). "Born to Shop," *Fortune*, June 6, 14.

Japan Travel Bureau (1991). *Japan in Your Pocket! Tokyo, 1991.*

Johnston, G. (1988). "Three Ways Japanese Farmers Are Better Off Than You," *Successful Farming (Iowa Edition)*, 86, 7 (April), 50-H.

Jones, S. (1988). "Asia's Success-Story Nations Learning How to Consume," *The Wall Street Journal*, November 1, A24.

Kathawala, Y., and V. Nanda (1989). "Quality in a Global Context: A Framework for Analysis," *International Journal of Quality and Reliability Management*, 6, 2, 31–39.

Kilburn, D. (1988). "In Japan, Voice of Authority, or Flattery, a Call Away," *Advertising Age*, February 1, 46.

King, R. W., L. Armstrong, S. J. Dryden, and J. Kapstein (1989). "Who's That Knocking on Foreign Doors? U.S. Insurance Salesmen," *Business Week*, March 6, 84–85.

Kodansha Encyclopedia of Japan, Vol. 3 (1983). New York: Harper & Row.

Koepfler, E. R. (1989). "Strategic Options for Global Market Players," *Journal of Business Strategy*, 10 (July–August), 46–50.

Koretz, G. (1989). "Why Asian Countries Blossomed While Latin America Wilted," *Business Week*, August 28, 16.

Libbey, M. B. (1991). "Japan Gets Set for Revolving Plastic," *Credit Card Management*, 4, 8 (November), 16–20.

Marshall, K. (1989). "The Land of the Volunteer Sun," *American Way*, February 1, 80–86, 100.

McCarthy, M. J. (1989). "The Real Thing: As a Global Marketer Coke Excels by Being Tough and Consistent," *The Wall Street Journal*, December 18, A1.

Mittiga, M. (1989). "The Emerging Tigers of Asia," *Benefits and Compensation International*, 18 (March), 2–7.

Nasar, S. (1989). "America Still Reigns in Services," *Fortune*, June 5, 64–68.

Neff, R., T. Holden, K. L. Miller, and J. Barnathan (1991). "Hidden Japan," *Business Week*, August 26, 34–38.

Oh, T. K. (1991). "Understanding Managerial Values and Behaviour Among the Gang of Four: South Korea, Taiwan, Singapore, and Hong Kong," *Journal of Management Development*, 10, 2, 46–56.

Owens, C. (1990). "Citibank Assumes a Starring Role in Asia," *The Wall Street Journal*, August 2, A8.

Shale, T. (1989). "South-East Asia: A New Crop of Tigers," *Euromoney*, (September), 91–92.

Smith, C., A. Rowley, D. Gibson, L. doRosario, C. Perry, and S. Awanohara (1990). "Japan 1990," *Far Eastern Economic Review*, 148, June 21, 37–66.

Stine, S. F. (1990). "Credit Card Sales War Heats Up," *Asian Finance*, 16, 3, March 15, 72–76.

Tanzer, A. (1986). "They Didn't Listen to Anybody," *Forbes*, December 15, 168–169.

Taylor, S., and P. S. Adams (1988). "Publishing in Japan," *Publishers Weekly*, June 3, 37–38.

The Economist (1987). "An Inside Job in Japan," April 11, 68–69.

——— (1988). "Japan: A Nation That Just Loves to Consume," July 2, 56–58.

——— (1989). "South Korea: A New Society," April 15, 23–26.

——— (1991). "Asia's New Consumers: Pamper Them," February 16, 56–57.

——— (1992). "Japanese Consumer Dept: Less Thrifty Than They Seemed," February 8, 80–82.

The Futurist (1989). "New Uses for Bar Codes," 23, 6 (November), 47.

The Nordson Corporation (1993). *The Nordson Corporation 1992 Annual Report*. Westlake, Ohio.

The World Bank (1992). *World Development Report, 1992: Development and the Environment-World Development Indicators*. Washington, DC.

Tokyo Business Today (1989). "Is the NIEs Product Boom Over?" (March), 36–39.

Trachtenberg, J. A. (1989) "Marketing: Playing the Global Game," *Forbes*, January 23, 90–91.

Winter, R. E. (1988). "Nordson Is Poised to Compete in the '90s," *The Wall Street Journal*, November 29, A8.

Witcowski, T. H., and Y. Yamamoto (1991). "*Omiyage* Gift Purchasing by Japanese Travelers in the U.S.," in R. H. Holman and M. R. Solomon (eds.), *Advances in Consumer Research*, 18, 123–128.

Yamaguchi, M., and S. Kojima (eds.) (1986). *A Cultural Dictionary of Japan*. Tokyo: Kenkyusha Publishing Co., 171.

Zeeman, J. R. (1987). "Service: The Cutting Edge of Global Competition." Speech given at *The Annual Meeting of the Academy of International Business*, November 14, Chicago, IL.

PART VI

CURRENT GLOBAL MARKETING CASES

CASE 1

REEBOK INTERNATIONAL, LIMITED *

I n January 1992, days before the launch of Reebok's new "World's Greatest Athlete" campaign, CEO Paul Fireman was reflecting on Reebok's position in the athletic footwear market and the challenge of implementing a global campaign. Reebok had spent the last three years trying to regain its U.S. market share lead, which it lost to Nike in 1989. A strategic meeting of top Reebok executives was held shortly after Nike took the lead to evaluate the future direction of Reebok. The primary areas of concern for Reebok were:

- The slowdown of a once "hot" U.S. market because of a recession, a saturated market, and intense competition.
- Implementing a global marketing campaign in areas of the world dominated by strong, established international competitors.

Reebok looked at the international market as an opportunity for growth. In 1989 the company made some changes in its marketing strategy to address the international opportunities. Other changes are still in progress. As Fireman analyzed the company's global position going into 1992, there was still cause for concern. Although international sales had grown dramatically in the past two years and there were ten times as many foreign distributors as there were two years ago, Reebok's market share followed Nike's share in Europe as well as in the United States. Fireman hired an outside consulting firm to evaluate Reebok's position and the movement of the athletic footwear industry over the past five years.

---

*This case was prepared by Leslie A. Anchor, Robert A. Cutting, Ernest Duncan, Jr., Scott Oser, Amy B. Kerner, and Indong Kang under the direction of Professor Salah S. Hassan at The George Washington University.

COMPANY BACKGROUND

Reebok was established in 1895 by Joseph William Foster, a young member of the British Bolton Primrose Harriers athletic club. Foster realized that several runners were faster than he was, so he set out to find new ways to improve his performance. He hammered a set of makeshift spikes through the soles of his shoes and discovered that his performance was indeed improved. He established the J. W. Foster Company to sell his revolutionary product, and soon thereafter all the Harrier athletes were wearing spiked shoes made by Foster's company. The J. W. Foster Company continued to revolutionize the athletic shoe industry by inventing other products, including the "Running Pump," which it introduced in 1909.

Foster's grandsons took over during the 1950s, and they established a new company named after a swift, agile African gazelle. Thus the Reebok corporation was born. Today, Reebok International, Ltd. is headquartered in Stoughton, Massachusetts, and it is a predominant designer and marketer of active life-style and performance products, including footwear (see Exhibit 1-1) and sports apparel. The company's goal is to produce the

EXHIBIT 1-1 REEBOK PRODUCTS	Sport	Shoe	Description
	Running	The Graphlite Trainer	Lightweight shoe with Hexalite heel and CMEVA midsole for cushioning and shock absorption.
	Volleyball	Pro Volley II	Lightweight shoe with die-cut EVA midsole for cushioning and shock dispersion.
	Aerobics	Aerostep Pro	Lightweight shoe with Graphweave overlays for stability and Meta-flex hinge for flexibility.
	Walking	Comfort I Ultra	Versatile shoe with Dynamic Cushioning system and removable sock insert for cushioning.
	Basketball	The Pump	High-top shoe containing inflatable chambers that the wearer can adjust for custom fit.
	Tennis	Center Court	Durable shoe with Indy 500 rubber forefront for durability and removable sockliner for cushioning.

best, most innovative, and most exciting sports and fitness brands in the world.

With its roots in nineteenth century England, Reebok was virtually unknown in the United States until 1979. Today Reebok has a portfolio of well-known brands with products distributed in approximately 120 countries through 41 exclusive distributors. Despite its UK heritage, Reebok International, Ltd. constitutes a U.S. success story—an entrepreneurial venture turned into a big business that has enjoyed phenomenal growth and has demonstrated a flexible yet assured sense of direction. Following public offerings in 1985, 1986, and 1987 that raised approximately $160 million in capital, Reebok diversified its product lines by acquiring footwear companies such as Rockport, Frye, and Avia. In 1988 Reebok acquired the Italian firm, Ellesse, a maker of expensive athletic footwear and apparel.[1] Paul Fireman, chairman and cofounder of Reebok, had ambitious plans for the firm; he wanted to diversify it into a $2-billion multinational by 1990. Fireman's three-pronged diversification strategy involved (1) acquisitions, (2) internal development, and (3) international expansion. The company planned acquisitions of firms with products that appeal to the 18–45-year-old age group. The acquisitions of Avia and the Rockport Co. gave Reebok a wider base in the shoe market. Since the type of distribution channel can influence consumers' perceptions, Reebok planned to sell its products only in upscale locations, such as department, specialty, and sporting goods stores. International sales, at only 10 percent of the company's total sales in 1987, were expected eventually to account for 50 percent.[2]

Reebok was able to increase its revenues from $1.5 million in 1981 to $919 million in 1986, even though the running fad was fading, by introducing fashion footwear for the neglected aerobics market. In anticipation of the next recreational fad, Reebok became increasingly market-driven with the acquisition of the Rockport Co. in 1986, maker of high-quality walking shoes.

In the first half of 1987, sales rose 64 percent to $640 million. In the same year, Reebok became a $1 billion business and one of the leading sports-shoe marketers in the United States.[3] By the end of 1991, as Exhibit 1-2 shows, Reebok's sales reached $2.7 billion. The company's international sales—45 percent of total business—jumped 75 percent from 1990 to 1991, with 55 percent growth projected for 1992.[4] Still, Reebok made some mistakes during this time. For example, in 1986, when Reebok diversified into apparel, the poor quality of sportswear caused the firm to hold back deliveries and miss out on the critical spring season, resulting in disappointing annual sales.

Chairman Paul Fireman moved to correct these mistakes through management changes and acquisitions. Douglas Arbetman, formerly of Calvin Klein Industries, Inc., was put in charge of the apparel unit in September 1986, and he promptly replaced most of the design and sales staff. Another weakness for Reebok in the 1980s was product performance; its designer shoes were made with soft leather, which fell apart when used for rigorous activities. As a result, sporting-goods analysts predicted that buyers would return to reliable brands of athletic shoes that would stand up to the rigors of sport. Therefore, Reebok brought in new management to focus on the development of the performance-oriented products.

In 1989 Reebok took a major step in establishing itself in the area of performance technology by introducing the Pump. The Pump technology system, a patented process, has inflatable chambers that allow the wearer to adjust for custom fit and support. The retail price for the Pump basketball shoe was $170. The Pump technology is also included in tennis, cross-training, and other footwear at retail prices ranging from $80 to $135. With the introduction and huge success of the Pump line of shoes, Reebok refocused its marketing around performance coupled with style, emphasizing the expensive new Pump line.

In 1992, Reebok introduced two additional technological break-throughs, the Insta-Pump and the Pump Custom Cushioning, which are extensions of the Pump technology. Other performance technologies developed by Reebok include: GraphLite, a graphite composite structure en-

EXHIBIT 1-2   REEBOK'S TOTAL U.S. AND INTERNATIONAL SALES

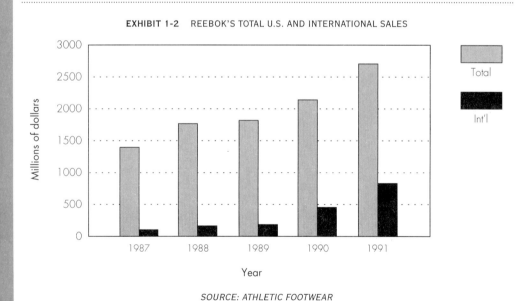

SOURCE: ATHLETIC FOOTWEAR
ASSOCIATION

gineered for lightweight arch support; Dynamic Cushioning, an outsole design that provides a unique cushioning feel for fitness walkers; and Hytrel foam, a material providing durable cushioning and added spring. Four of the technologies developed by Reebok are patented.

Marketing is critical for Reebok International, Ltd. The company does not actually manufacture its products; instead, it designs footwear that it believes Americans will buy and then contracts the manufacturing out to low-wage factories in places like Taiwan and the Republic of Korea. Reebok currently positions its products with a combination of performance and style, emphasizing individuality and freedom of expression.

Reebok tries to overcome the typical corporate culture through its social activism. It wants to expand its image to one that stands for more than sales and earnings power, as manifested by Reebok's sponsorship of the 1988 Amnesty International Human Rights Now! tour, its establishment of the annual Reebok Human Rights Award, and its efforts to improve the lives of inner-city dwellers through the renovation of city basketball and tennis courts, and the development of an urban scholarship program. The company is dedicated, through the Reebok Foundation, to promoting individual freedom and social change.[5]

Paul Fireman depends on savvy management to motivate workers, maintain high quality, protect the all-important brand image, and tune into marketplace needs. Keys to the company's success have been its access to capital, its effective marketing strategies, a risk-taking approach, a dedicated staff, product development through teamwork, and a focus on the customer. Fireman's emphasis on entrepreneurial management helps explain why *Fortune* magazine named him one of twenty-five American leaders making the United States a stronger competitor worldwide. Reebok's success is built on the business styles of managers like Reebok France SA's Jean Marc Gaucher—managers who strike a careful balance between a global brand and local cultures. Management styles have to be adapted to be effective in each culture. Two elements of Reebok's corporate culture transcend every local culture: sharing ideas for innovation and listening to customers.

The U.S. Athletic Footwear Market

The U.S. athletic footwear market has evolved to a $6.4 billion market (wholesale dollars), corresponding to a total of 381 million pairs of athletic shoes.[6] Athletic shoe sales had double-digit gains through the 1980s. As Exhibits 1-3 and 1-4 show, the number of athletic shoes sold (retail) has more than doubled in the past ten years and retail dollar sales have

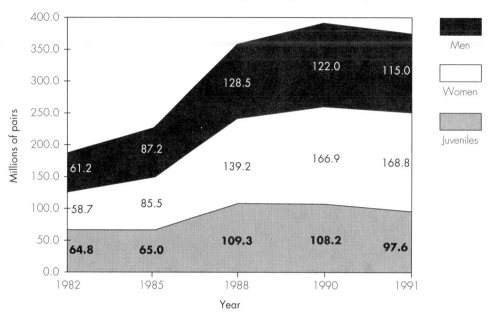

EXHIBIT 1-3 RETAIL PAIRS SOLD (ATHLETIC SHOES)

SOURCE: ATHLETIC FOOTWEAR ASSOCIATION

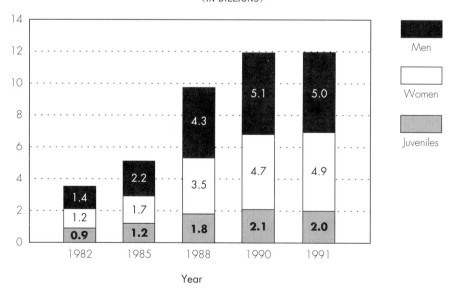

EXHIBIT 1-4 RETAIL DOLLAR SALES OF ATHLETIC SHOES
(IN BILLIONS)

SOURCE: ATHLETIC FOOTWEAR ASSOCIATION

more than tripled over the same time period. Despite this promising growth, overall market activity declined from 393 million pairs in 1990 to 381 million in 1991.[7] While unit sales declined, dollar sales in 1991 were level with 1990. This slow growth rate, which began in the late 1980s, is attributable to the recession and to a saturation in many of the niches that have been carved out over the past ten years.

Two decades ago, sneakers were known as "tennis shoes" with a rubber sole, a canvas upper, and not much else. At that time people wore "tennis shoes" to play tennis, basketball, volleyball, and almost every other imaginable sport. Today's market offers an athletic shoe for almost every occasion, characterized by "activity-specific" niches such as aerobics, tennis, running, basketball, racquetball, cross-training, walking, and many more. A 1991 national survey found that 84 percent of U.S. consumers from ages 13 to 75 wear athletic shoes, and 72 percent have bought at least one pair in the past year.[8] The average athletic shoe wearer owns about three pairs.

Sneakers have come a long way from the canvas topped, rubber-soled shoes two decades ago. Today's athletic footwear is characterized by technological features such as air-inflated pumps, foams, gels, carbon fibers, and catapults. Examples include Air Cushioning (Nike), the Pump technology (Reebok), the Propulsion Plate System (Brooks), the Catapult Power Feedback System (L.A. Gear), the GEL System (Asics), the Power Pak (Mizuno), and the Torsion system (Adidas). However, sales of high-tech performance shoes appear to be leveling off with a trend in the '90s toward sport casuals, active fashion, and outdoor looks. Manufacturers are introducing rugged hiking style shoes and active fashion shoes. These shoes are addressing a demand for soft, comfortable shoes that also make a fashion statement. Additionally, the recession has persuaded many athletic footwear companies to pay attention to the price sensitivity of consumers, focusing on the back-to-basics trend.

The industry initially evolved in the 1970s as a performance-oriented industry with shoes specifically designed to improve the performance of athletes, particularly runners. Prior to 1980, Nike was the dominant athletic footwear supplier, with a focus on performance-oriented product innovation and low-cost production. However, in the early to mid 1980s, the industry experienced a shift from a performance orientation to a market orientation, combining fashion and fitness with performance. This shift was primarily attributable to the introduction of the first aerobic shoe designed for women (Reebok's Freestyle) in 1982. Running gave way to aerobics as the fitness fad of the 1980s. Three major trends transformed the athletic footwear industry: (1) the aerobic exercise movement, (2) the influx of women into sports and exercise, and (3) the acceptance by adults of well-designed athletic footwear for street and casual wear.[9]

Due to the explosive growth in the athletic footwear industry which followed this transformation, product extensions and activity-specific brand segmentation flourished. At the same time, performance technologies continued to be developed to improve product function. The current market is characterized by expensive, brand name, technologically advanced athletic shoes designed for specific sports. After the introduction of the Air Jordan line of basketball shoes by Nike in 1985, basketball shoes in particular became fashion statements. From 1986 to 1989, the entire athletic footwear industry grew approximately 45 percent,[10] with athletic shoes representing more than one-third of all shoes sold in the United States. Basketball shoes are currently the largest segment within the athletic shoe industry, representing nearly 30 percent of all athletic shoe sales. As of 1990 basketball shoe sales had been growing at a 27 percent compounded growth rate for five years.[11] However, this growth started to decline in 1989 and 1990 because of the introduction of a cross-training shoe, which was portrayed as the shoe for multiple sports activities and streetwear. As Exhibit 1-5 indicates, basketball shoes and cross-training/fitness shoes combined make up approximately 44 percent of all athletic footwear sold.[12] This exhibit also shows the primary segments of the athletic footwear market based on sport-specific activities. However, only 10.5 percent of the athletic shoes purchased in 1991 were for sports/fitness participation. The remaining 90 percent were purchased for casual and general use.[13]

After the huge growth that resulted from the aerobics and fitness craze, athletic footwear suppliers realized that there was a pent-up demand for a shoe that not only performs but also fills a need for more style, comfort, fit, and fashion. Nine out of ten consumers place comfort, fit, and

EXHIBIT 1-5
SALES OF ATHLETIC
FOOTWEAR BY TYPE
(1991 WHOLESALE
DOLLARS—$6.4
BILLION)
*SOURCE: ATHLETIC
FOOTWEAR
ASSOCIATION*

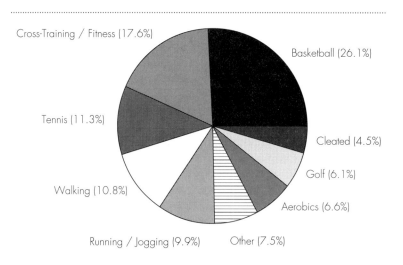

Cross-Training / Fitness (17.6%)
Basketball (26.1%)
Tennis (11.3%)
Cleated (4.5%)
Golf (6.1%)
Walking (10.8%)
Aerobics (6.6%)
Running / Jogging (9.9%)
Other (7.5%)

feel as the most important characteristics of athletic footwear.[14] Other characteristics important to the consumers, as shown in Exhibit 1-6, are that the shoe suits an active life style and has performance and fashion advantages.

In addition to a shift toward a marketing orientation and increasingly advanced technological product features, the current athletic footwear market is characterized by sophisticated advertising and marketing strategies as well as by big-name athlete sponsorships and endorsements. Until the late 1980s, magazines were the major advertising vehicle of the athletic footwear industry, with a heavy concentration in specialty periodicals and a lighter concentration in general interest magazines. The advertising structure of the industry then shifted its emphasis to intensive television advertising in the late 1980s, and it is currently characterized by TV advertising battles between the top market leaders. Although television advertising is the most visible portion of the marketing mix, athletic footwear wearers cite in-store displays as the most important in providing information about sneakers.[15] In addition, word of mouth and personal observation are nearly as important as television advertising to consumer purchase decisions. This is an indication that manufacturers and retailers should focus more on in-store displays and training of salespeople.

EXHIBIT 1-6   CONSUMERS' DECISION CRITERIA FOR BUYING
ATHLETIC FOOTWEAR
SOURCE: ATHLETIC FOOTWEAR ASSOCIATION

13%	Is "hot" with friends, celebrities
27%	Has good brand aura
29%	Has conservative appearance
41%	Good for everyday wear
50%	Meets basic needs
54%	Has fashion advantages
56%	Has performance advantages
63%	Suits active life style
83%	Comfort, fit, and feel

Adidas was the athletic footwear company that pioneered the concept of sponsorship of national sports federations and athletes. Through popular, media-exposed sports events, athletic footwear suppliers showed consumers that world-class athletes compete while wearing their products. The intense competition over signing world-class athletes to long-term contracts was evident between Nike and Reebok and the rest of the shoe industry throughout the 1980s and in today's market. Celebrities appear to play an important role in TV advertising toward influencing buyers to purchase athletic footwear. However, in actuality, more than 80 percent

EXHIBIT 1-7

AGES OF MALE AND FEMALE PURCHASERS

SOURCE: ATHLETIC FOOTWEAR ASSOCIATION

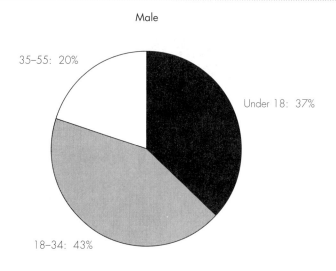

Male

35–55: 20%

Under 18: 37%

18–34: 43%

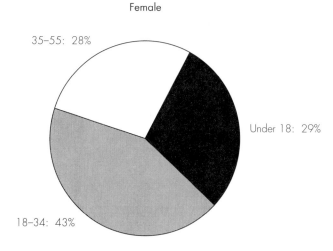

Female

35–55: 28%

Under 18: 29%

18–34: 43%

of adults and more than 60 percent of teens indicated that a celebrity endorsement does not affect their decision to purchase footwear.[16] Celebrity endorsements are viewed as being most effective in attracting attention to a new brand or style.

Initially, the general target audience for the athletic footwear industry was the 18–34-year-old male and female who were reached through a mix of sports and life-style programming and magazines. However, as product segmentation proliferated, this target demographic segment expanded drastically. Due to the heavy fashion orientation of athletic footwear in the mid to late 1980s, a younger, teen population became a large, very important target audience. Today, 15–22-year-olds make up only 15 percent of the entire U.S. population; however, they buy on average four pairs of athletic shoes a year, which represents approximately 40 percent of all athletic shoes sold.[17] Athletic shoe marketers are fighting off saturation in the U.S. market by offering shoes for every occasion, for every look, and for every age. The dramatic acceptance of athletic footwear as casual streetwear opened up the market with additional focus being placed on older customers who purchase athletic shoes strictly for walking and everyday use. As Exhibit 1-7 shows, female purchasers were, on average, somewhat older than males. More than 33 percent of males were under the age of 18, compared with only 25 percent of the females. Conversely, 25 percent of the female buyers in 1991 were 35–55, whereas 18 percent of males were in that age bracket.[18]

As depicted in Exhibit 1-8, 75 percent of athletic footwear is purchased at retail for less than $44.50.[19] The unit price of athletic shoes increased dramatically along with the explosive growth of the industry in the

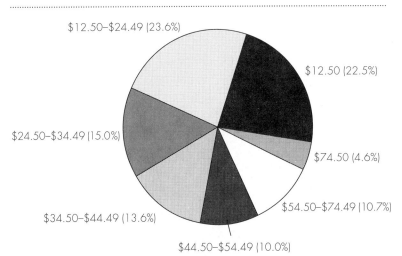

EXHIBIT 1-8
RETAIL PRICES PAID FOR ATHLETIC FOOTWEAR (1991)
SOURCE: ATHLETIC FOOTWEAR ASSOCIATION

1980s. The average price consumers paid in 1991 for a pair of sneakers was $42.50, a 42 percent increase over the average price paid in 1988.[20] Although females purchase substantially more pairs than males, men spend more per pair.[21] Exhibit 1-9 shows the average retail prices paid for athletic footwear in 1991 by market segment. Despite the significant increases in unit prices, all groups say they are willing to pay substantially more in the future than they paid in the past. Although the average price paid in 1991 was $42.50, most would be willing to spend up to $61.60[22] in the future based on Athletic Footwear Association national consumer surveys. This is an important implication for athletic footwear manufacturers and marketers, indicating that consumers perceive athletic footwear as a good value and are willing to pay more for increased value. Despite the growth in unit price, there has been a trend among athletic footwear manufacturers to focus on shoes in the middle price range. This trend is primarily due to increased price sensitivity among customers during the recession, combined with overall market saturation. The trend toward price sensitivity is also evidenced by the fact that discount outlets accounted for a 27 percent share of unit sales of all athletic footwear,[23] as shown in Exhibit 1-10.

The importance of brands when consumers purchase athletic footwear has been growing. Consumers who intended to buy a specific brand doubled between 1988 and 1991.[24] However, only 29 percent of consumers who purchased sneakers in 1991 intended to buy a specific brand.[25] More importantly, more than half of the consumers planning to purchase athletic footwear are undecided about the type of athletic shoe they intend to buy; 26 percent had no plans and decided to buy sneakers while shop-

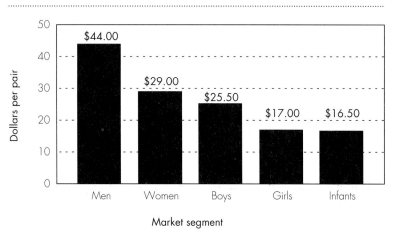

EXHIBIT 1-9
AVERAGE RETAIL
PRICES PAID FOR
ATHLETIC
FOOTWEAR—1991
SOURCE: ATHLETIC
FOOTWEAR
ASSOCIATION

Market segment

ping, and 30 percent were just planning to buy some type of sneakers.[26] This is a further indication that in-store displays and information provided by salespeople play an important role in influencing a consumer's purchase of sneakers.

DOMESTIC COMPETITORS

Competition among the companies in the athletic footwear industry is fierce. Performance and reliability of shoes, new product development, product identity through marketing and promotion, and customer service are important aspects of competition in this industry. Nike, Inc. is currently the leader in the U.S. market.

NIKE

Nike's principal business involves the design, development, and global merchandising of high-quality footwear and apparel products. Nike sells its products through a mix of independent distributors, licensees, and

EXHIBIT 1-10   RETAIL OUTLET MARKET SHARE: JAN.–DEC. 1991

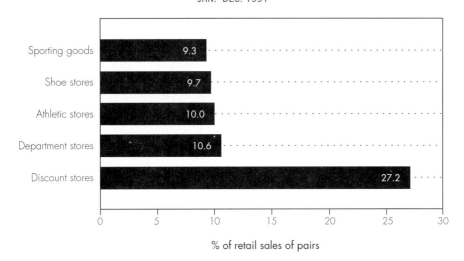

% of retail sales of pairs

SOURCE: ATHLETIC FOOTWEAR ASSOCIATION

subsidiaries in approximately eighty countries around the world. Virtually all of the corporation's products are manufactured by independent contractors. Most footwear products are produced outside the United States, whereas apparel products are produced both domestically and abroad.[27] International sales accounted for 33 percent of revenues in fiscal 1992, compared to 29 percent in fiscal 1991 and 21 percent in fiscal 1990.[28]

The Nike mystique is the reason that Nike is so successful. Early advertising and promotional efforts focused on the shoe, its features, and its benefits. "Just do it" and "There is no finish line" were more than advertising slogans. Endorsements by leading athletes helped establish Nike as an authentic athletic company. In the years since, corporate communication has broadened to make Nike one of the few global leaders with an actual personality. Nike creates an emotional tie with consumers, giving them an opportunity to believe in the products and motivations of Nike. The slogans reflect the shaping of a new way of life: a life where there is competition, determination, achievement, fun, and spirit.

Nike places considerable emphasis on quality construction and innovative design. Basketball, fitness, and running shoes are currently the top-selling product categories and are expected to continue to lead in product sales in the near future. However, Nike also markets shoes designed for tennis, golf, soccer, baseball, football, bicycling, volleyball, aquatic activities, wrestling, cheerleading, and general outdoor recreational use. Nike plans to make every category more accessible to consumers by placing its technology in lower price ranges.

Nike also sells active sports apparel and accessories covering each of the preceding categories. Its apparel and accessories are designed to complement Nike's athletic footwear products and are sold through the same marketing and distribution channels.

Its marketing strategy is based on diversification through niche marketing, focus on performance, and successful advertising campaigns. Nike competes on a segment-by-segment basis with specific products and advertising directed at that segment. Most of its advertisements depict serious athletes participating in sports.

The athletes who endorse Nike products must meet three requirements. The first requirement is that the athlete must be one of the best in the sport. Character is the second requirement; the athlete must be committed to the spirit of competition and must appeal to the public. The third requirement is that the athlete have a distinctive sense of style.[29] Without these requirements, it would be difficult to maintain the Nike image.

This approach to endorsements contrasts with Reebok's. Reebok has sought endorsements with the concept of "the more, the merrier." This approach allows the company to saturate various sports with athletes who wear its products. Critics, however, believe that this saturation blurs the Reebok image.

Nike lost and later regained the #1 position in the athletic shoe industry from Reebok. Reebok successfully anticipated aerobics as the next fitness craze and created a soft leather athletic shoe rather than using the traditional stiff shoe design. Nike did not aggressively enter the aerobics market until years later. It did so not by following Reebok's decision to emphasize the fashion side of shoes but by focusing on quality and performance.

Performance remains the cornerstone of every Nike product. The Air Jordan shoe has helped Nike become the undisputed leader in the basketball shoe market. Air Trainer High defines the cross-training segment. Constant innovation and refinement of Nike-Air cushioning have been at the core of these products. Most recently, Nike introduced the Air Huarache running shoe. The Huarache Fit stretches to hug the foot, enhancing both fit and comfort.

Nike believes that its research-and-development efforts form the foundation for its past and future success. Nike has done more than stick its trademark "swoosh" emblem all over its products; it has improved the comfort, durability, and performance of its footwear. Technical innovation in the design of footwear and apparel receive continued emphasis as Nike strives to produce products that reduce or eliminate injury, aid athletic performance, and maximize comfort. In fiscal 1992 Nike spent approximately $19.8 million on product research, development, and evaluation, compared to $16.8 million in 1991 and $12.8 million in 1990.[30]

Nike used the 1992 Olympics as a springboard to expand its worldwide reach. Nike outfitted the entire U.S. Olympic track and field team in a collection of red, white, and blue apparel. Several members of the U.S. Olympic basketball team endorse Nike products. In conjunction with the Olympics in Barcelona, Nike spent more than $30 million in Europe in the two months leading up to the Olympic Games.[31]

L.A. Gear

While Reebok is pursuing Nike, L.A. Gear is chasing Reebok. L.A. Gear is currently third in the U.S. market, behind Nike and Reebok. Since its inception, L.A. Gear has expanded its product line from its original concentration on fashionable women's footwear to diversified collections of footwear for men, women, and children. The company is organized into two primary marketing divisions: Athletic (including men's and women's basketball, fitness, walking, tennis, and aerobics) and Lifestyle (casual footwear styles intended for nonathletic use). L.A. Gear's new marketing strategy focuses on increasing brand awareness for its footwear products. All of its footwear products are manufactured by independent producers located primarily in the Far East.[32]

In 1987 L.A. Gear introduced a line of sports and casual apparel products and accessories. These products were designed and marketed by the company for approximately four years. Rather than allowing for growth, this approach resulted in L.A. Gear spreading itself too thin. In late November 1991, it decided to discontinue its in-house apparel design and marketing operations. L.A. Gear expected to complete the sale of all remaining apparel inventory during the first two quarters of fiscal 1992. Through its new Worldwide Properties division, the company intends to increase its efforts to *license* the L.A. Gear brand name for global use on a wide range of nonfootwear products, including apparel.[33]

Its marketing plan is to develop several products that will support L.A. Gear in the long run. A primary goal is to establish collections of footwear which are intended to survive the changing preferences of consumers and which are expected to form a foundation for sales. In order to focus its marketing efforts more directly on its reorganized Athletic and Lifestyle product lines, L.A. Gear plans to significantly reduce the number of product lines that it carries and to continue its efforts to lower existing inventory levels through price reductions.[34]

Advertising and promotion activities are key elements in L.A. Gear's selling and marketing strategies. It has recently hired Ogilvy & Mather, an international advertising agency, to assist in the creation of new advertising campaigns and marketing concepts. In February 1992 L.A. Gear introduced a new advertising campaign promoting its Athletic and Lifestyle product lines. The new "Get in Gear" campaign is aimed at showcasing the L.A. Gear brand. The overall brand is emphasized rather than individual product lines in order to build brand awareness, especially among its male audience.[35]

L.A. Gear has obtained endorsements of its products by a number of celebrities and athletes. Several of the promotional contracts with its celebrity and athlete endorsers provide for the payment of royalties based on sales of certain footwear styles. Both Karl "The Mailman" Malone and Hakeem "The Dream" Olajuwon introduced new lines of basketball footwear in 1992. L.A. Gear will continue to utilize Joe Montana and Paula Abdul to promote its Lifestyle collections. Participation in major sporting goods and trade shows is also critical to its future promotional activities.[36]

In an attempt to build on L.A. Gear's position in the domestic athletic footwear market, management initiated a new strategic direction for the balance of the 1990s: Provide consumers with products that will address their desire for a functional relationship between price and value. In order to accomplish this objective, L.A. Gear plans to create footwear "collections," in which the high end of each line will be used as the base from which each shoe in a particular family is designed. L.A. Gear believes this differentiates it within the brand footwear market and at the same time helps L.A. Gear's brand reach a much broader range of potential consumers.[37]

Just as L.A. Gear is restructuring its operations, Nike and Reebok must closely examine their operations. Even though athletic shoe sales are still rising approximately 3 percent a year, sales are growing at a much slower pace than in the past. It will take extra effort to reach new consumers. The 1990s will demand changes in order for Nike, Reebok, and L.A. Gear to prosper.

The International Athletic Footwear Market

The international athletic footwear market is a relatively new market for Reebok. Fortunately for Reebok, as well as for all of the other major athletic footwear companies, the international athletic footwear market is now considered by many to be in the same boom stage that the United States footwear market experienced in the 1980s.

In the past, the European market was dominated by two German-based companies, Puma and Adidas. However, Reebok and its main domestic competitor, Nike, are quickly gaining ground and overtaking market share from the already well established and highly recognizable Puma and Adidas.

For the past 10 years, Adidas and Puma controlled approximately 75 percent of the European athletic shoe and apparel market. As can be seen in Exhibit 1-11, at the end of 1990 Adidas was still considered to be #1 with approximately $870 million in European revenues. Puma, on the other hand, had fallen to fourth, with Nike and Reebok ranking second and third, earning European revenues of $500 million and $380 million, respectively.[38]

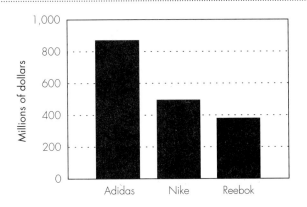

EXHIBIT 1-11
EUROPEAN ATHLETIC FOOTWEAR REVENUES (1990), TOP THREE COMPETITORS
SOURCE: ATHLETIC FOOTWEAR ASSOCIATION

The problems leading to the decline of Adidas and the much smaller Puma can be linked to both internal and external factors. The main internal factor that caused years of losses for Adidas was the excessive number of products offered. Adidas alone offered more than 1,200 different shoe variations and styles. Such a large range of products increased costs and made it very hard to produce a focused marketing plan, and it also angered many of their distributors.[39]

The fascination of Europeans with American products is an external factor on which both Nike and Reebok are capitalizing. Adidas and Puma are associated with Europe, whereas Reebok and Nike are associated with the United States. Nike and Reebok are therefore taking advantage of their American image and quickly overtaking market share from the other two.

To try to curb their declining market share, both Adidas and Puma have hired new management. Under its new management, Adidas has cut the number of products offered. It is currently launching a new shoe line called Equipment, which features no-frills shoes for soccer, tennis, and track. It is also introducing a highly acclaimed line of hiking and outdoors shoes. Puma's new management, which has brought strong financial resources to the company, is hoping to turn around its decline by investing more capital in the company. As shown in Exhibit 1-12, in 1992 Puma planned to increase its European advertising budget to $40 million.

EXHIBIT 1-12
EUROPEAN
MARKETING AND
ADVERTISING
EXPENDITURES
(1992), TOP FOUR
COMPETITORS
SOURCE: ATHLETIC
FOOTWEAR
ASSOCIATION

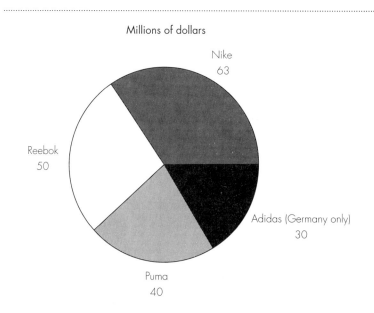

Millions of dollars

Nike 63

Reebok 50

Adidas (Germany only) 30

Puma 40

The new concepts and inputs of the new management at both Puma and Adidas have helped the companies to once again gain profits instead of accumulating losses. However, when it comes to advertising, which is essential in the shoe market, neither company currently has the finances to battle with Reebok or Nike.

In 1992 Nike planned to spend 7 percent of its European revenues on European advertising, which will amount to approximately $63 million (see Exhibit 1-12). With this $63 million, Nike will continue to sponsor such athletes as Olympic medalist and track star Katrin Krabbe and German soccer player Andreas Moller. In addition, Nike has recently signed an agreement to advertise on EuroSport, a pan-European cable channel. This large expenditure on advertising, coupled with the European population's interest in American fashion and sport, is what has allowed Nike to become the #2 seller of footwear in Europe.

Reebok's international sales increased 75 percent in 1991, bringing the yearly total up from $475 million in 1990 to $833 million in 1991.[40] These sales, which include $117 million from Reebok Italia and Reebok Japan, were due to the fact that Reebok footwear is sold in 120 countries.

Reebok currently has eight wholly owned subsidiaries in Spain, France, Germany, the United Kingdom, Italy, Chile, Canada, and Holland, and a majority-owned subsidiary in Japan.[41] The complete or partial ownership of these subsidiaries in various countries better enables Reebok to advertise and pursue the sponsorship of athletes in regard to marketplace trends in each of these markets. In Europe alone, Reebok plans to spend approximately $50 million on advertising (Exhibit 1-12). Some of the international athletes that Reebok is currently sponsoring include Australian track star Brad Bevin, Australian boxer Jeff Fenech, and kayaker Richard Fox of England.[42] Sponsoring athletes in various countries and having a presence in these countries is allowing Reebok to incorporate a more global approach to its product advertising. A more global approach helps increase profits and decrease costs due to economies of scale, with a wider distribution of more focused product lines.

In early 1991 the Reebok Italian distributor became a subsidiary as a result of an acquisition by Reebok. The Italian market had recently become a hotbed for international sales due to the rapidly growing popularity of sports such as basketball in the country. The basketball fans there have become a frenzied audience whose international league has grown stronger every year, partially due to the recruiting of popular American players, such as Danny Ferry. The control that Reebok gained from this acquisition allowed it to directly regulate the marketing process within this booming marketplace, thus enabling it to better coordinate Italian operations with its international goals.

Reebok's Japanese distributor became a subsidiary in April 1991 through a venture partnership that allowed Reebok to increase its share holdings in the distributor from 25 percent to 51 percent. This, too, is an example of Reebok not only assuming more profits from a growing market but also gaining majority control over a key international distribution area. This partnership with Japan was an exceptionally strong move due to evolving Japanese interest in U.S. products.

Among these geographic microenvironments, Reebok has established itself as the market leader in the United Kingdom, Australia, Spain, Sweden, France, Hong Kong, Singapore, Canada, Columbia, New Zealand, and Malaysia. Reebok also reports significant partial ownership in twelve of its forty distributors in areas that Reebok considers advantageous for future acquisition.

THE GLOBALIZATION OF REEBOK

Reebok's opportunities for international expansion were abundant in the late 1980s while its opportunities in the domestic market were diminishing. The saturation of the domestic athletic shoe market, which resulted from rapid growth and intense competition within the market, provided the stimulus toward a global movement for Reebok. Such a movement had considerable implications for Reebok because it was also confronted with two problems in the U.S. market:

1. The difficulty in gaining domestic market share occurred when Reebok wanted more than ever to revenge its drop to the #2 spot in the industry. The combined Nike/Reebok market share held steady over the past five years. Between the momentum of Nike and the increasing presence of other strong competitors, Reebok hoped to, at best, maintain its market share in the 1988–1989 season.
2. Reebok's push for high-tech and thus high-priced products in the market contradicted the cooldown in the market for pricy athletic shoes due to more conservative buying.[43]

Recently Reebok's philosophy has been to establish technological leadership for its products and thus gain high product image for the long-term success of the company. This apparent contradiction between the high cost of technological advancements and the buying patterns during the recession may be resolved by shifting sales emphasis toward international markets that are not as severely affected by recession. The international opportunities for Reebok were considered excellent vehicles that could carry this philosophy into the future and help Reebok regain its leadership in the athletic shoe market.

The Motivation

In 1988, when Nike overtook Reebok as the leader in U.S. market share, the overseas markets were as undeveloped as the U.S. markets were in the early 1980s when the "shoe-boom" took place in the United States.[44] The lack of thorough exploitation overseas by the American athletic shoe leaders, coupled with the extensive consumer base to be won, was an enticing motivator for Reebok to expand internationally in light of the maturing domestic market. This is not to say that Reebok had not yet recognized the potential of the international market. In 1987, while holding various operational interests in several foreign countries, Reebok experienced a 400 percent international sales growth.[45] This figure, perhaps misleading since it corresponds to a total international sales figure for Reebok of $81 million in an estimated $4.5 billion market, provided promise for the future if the proper focus were established and maintained.

Another motivation for globalization was the need to control recent inventory problems. Reebok's inventory turnover rate had dropped drastically from a healthy 7.5 times a year in 1986 to 5.8 times a year in 1987, and to a low of 2.5 times a year in 1988.[46] Reebok contracts almost all of its manufacturing overseas and is committed to buying an established annual amount from the producers, which prevents a flexible response to growing inventories. By quickly widening its international consumer base, Reebok would be able to counter its inability to cut production rates.

Obviously, these motivations were also being reviewed in the conference rooms of all Reebok's competitors, so Reebok had to move rapidly to engage an accurate international strategy. Since opportunities were available to everyone, Reebok needed to look at those opportunities that would offer it the most significant results.

International Opportunities and Execution

Reebok took a huge step toward international expansion in 1989 shortly after Nike replaced it as #1 in the United States. This move was coordinated within Paul Fireman's plan to revive his company, which was "getting stale."[47] After hiring John Duerden in 1987 to run the daily operations of the company, Reebok's international sales doubled to $212 million in just two years. Mr. Duerden placed an emphasis on customer service within every marketplace in which Reebok operated.[48] This appeared to be the proper method to begin a move toward international dominance, considering the yet-to-be-developed athletic shoe industry overseas. Many financial analysts believed Reebok could continue to have significant international market share gains and penetration that would establish a 20 percent bottom-line growth.[49] Recent figures show Reebok with a 26.6 percent worldwide sales increase in 1991, despite only a 2 percent sales growth in the United States. This strong growth is a result of Reebok's handling of many global opportunities that played to its strengths during the 1988–1990 timeframe. The most significant opportunities for Reebok were:

1. Use of its established global presence.
2. The decline of Adidas.
3. The opening of the Eastern European market.

GLOBAL PRESENCE   Beneficial to Reebok's position on global expansion in the late '80s was its already established position in the existing overseas market. This international presence, accented by its U.K. heritage, created the most advantageous opportunity for Reebok. At the time Nike overtook the market share, Reebok operated within foreign countries through individual contracts with a diverse group of worldwide distributors. This vast network of wholly owned subsidiaries, independent distributors, and joint ventures throughout the world was a functional framework for international expansion. However, the challenge for Reebok was to ensure that this international framework could easily be adapted to any economic change within any of its market centers. Such adaptation would provide the flexibility Reebok needed to reposition product lines efficiently within regions with respect to the financial capabilities of its consumers. Furthermore, Reebok was challenged not only to build within the existent channels but also to create new international channels.

During an interview in 1990, Paul Fireman acknowledged the future of overseas acquisitions with Reebok.[50] He recognized the international market as Reebok's biggest priority and concluded that acquisitions would be a major factor in achieving this global goal. Reebok has since demonstrated this interest by broadening and strengthening its marketing channels overseas, as witnessed by its recent acquisitions of the Italian (1991) and Spanish (1992) distributors and its venture partnership with its distributor in Japan (1991). During the 1980s many financial analysts were wary of the way Reebok planned to use its huge cash flow and therefore classified Reebok stock as a risky purchase. However, in 1991, Bob Doll of Oppenheimer Management Corporation noted that these international acquisitions were excellent ways for Reebok to maintain growth and to spend its cash flow.[51]

From 1988 to the end of 1991, Reebok widened its distribution to 129 countries. Although delighted with the extensiveness of its presence overseas and its international sales growth, Reebok's hurdle is coordinating its operations of its autonomous distributors and foreign manufacturers with its management headquartered in the United States.

THE FALL OF ADIDAS   Another overseas opportunity for Reebok was the decline of a major competitor—Adidas. Although holding the #1 market share in Europe, Adidas started to show signs of declining popularity during the late '80s because of unfocused marketing schemes and a glut of diverse products.[52] Since Adidas was forced to focus on these internal problems, Reebok had an opportunity to take advantage of the lowered defenses and attack the once impregnable European market. Once again, however, this opportunity was available to all competitors, and it created another power struggle between Reebok and Nike.

With respect to the European market, a market that over the years has been roughly the same size as that of the United States, Paul Fireman insisted that he would not be pleased until Reebok was #1.[53] According to Mr. Fireman, European dominance would be obtained by the firm that captured the most consumers who were once loyal to the now-diminishing Adidas. Both Nike and Reebok have profited from long-term problems at Adidas and Puma, once the #1 and #2 market share holders, respectively.[54] Adidas' poorly coordinated marketing in the late 1980s caused European distributors to desert to up-and-coming Reebok and Nike.[55] An example of this desertion is depicted by the recent five-year market figures in Germany. In 1987 Adidas and Puma, both German firms, controlled 85 percent of the German market. In 1991, however, their combined share was 56 percent, while Nike and Reebok generated a combined market share of 23 percent. Even more of a shift is expected by the end of 1992.[56]

Reebok reemphasized its heavy grass roots international marketing approach in 1989 through accurately targeted sponsorships and fewer media-based promotions. This approach has historically been the best way for Reebok to gain share efficiently in a new territory. In the 1970s Adidas had cornered practically all the major European athlete endorsements, not only making it tough on its closest competitor Puma, but also making it tough for any foreign athletic shoe companies who wanted to enter the market. Reebok, whose strength is creating a long line of top player endorsements, has been able to pick up a majority of the pieces. Currently, Adidas is still #1 in Europe, followed by Nike, Reebok, and Puma.

The disappointing lag behind Nike is only one of Reebok's worries. Adidas and Puma are heading toward resurgence. Puma's new management is pumping money into marketing. Adidas' new owner is cutting production lines and creating more efficient production and purchasing facilities in Asia.[57] In addition, both companies are heading to a "no-frills" product line that will again separate Reebok from its competitors, making Reebok appear an outsider in the international market.

EASTERN EUROPE   More recently, the opening of the Eastern European markets and their respective "sports machines" provided yet another opportunity for international growth. Reebok, which has historically favored player endorsements of its products, found this opportunity to be compatible with its practice of athletic sponsorships, as many high-quality athletes and past Olympic/international heroes stepped forward to get these lucrative contracts. More importantly, the freedom of Eastern Europe introduced 700 million people to the European market. This boost in market size, coupled with the continued "Americanization" of many foreign societies, provided a powerful cultural and social motive for American manufacturers to shift their marketing emphasis to this region.

Reebok found this opportunity especially inviting because athletic footwear is an image-oriented product in Europe. Paul Fireman considered the 700 million consumer addition to the European market as the best marketing news he'd heard of in years.[58] Reebok pushed its Pump technology into the region and established independent international design shops to help implement the new concept. Richard Litzel of Reebok Pump Deutschland reported that offering new products that are "all the rage in America" was key to approaching the Europeans who are drawn to U.S. street fashion.[59]

THE CURRENT INTERNATIONAL MOVEMENT

"LIFE IS SHORT."   Reebok remains concerned about its need for international growth. Recently, Reebok took a major step toward exerting itself as an international power by realizing its need for a coordinated advertising campaign. In the past, Reebok has been criticized for being unable to establish a coordinated, worldwide marketing plan. This is a direct reflection on the aforementioned decentralization of Reebok's global operations. Reebok addressed this problem with its most powerful advertising theme to date—"Life is short. Play hard."

Internationally, Reebok has emphasized promotional player endorsements and event sponsorships rather than consumer-directed advertising. Even though past U.S. umbrella campaigns have been short-lived and have never translated well overseas, this new effort was designed to be adapted for international use and as part of a $20 million summer Olympics campaign.[60] The campaign started with this concept in mind by using skysurfing in its premiere commercial. This commercial was obviously not directed at any one culture but provided an eye-opener for the adventurous while showing off the design of the footwear. Before any portion of the campaign aired, David Ropes claimed that the umbrella campaign has "the potential to go global."[61] With the help of international advertising powerhouse Chiat/Day/Mojo, its London-based office worked closely with

Reebok's international network to manage its individual needs for accepting this campaign.

"DAN AND DAVE."   In 1990 Reebok saw an opportunity to pursue its strategy of using well-known athletes as promoters of Reebok's products. The timing was ideal for Reebok to deploy this tactic. With the 1992 Olympics quickly approaching, the corporation realized that the Olympic Games represented a great opportunity for it to break into the international arena.

Reebok was a sponsor of the 1992 United States Olympic Team and had several successful campaigns produced to promote this connection. However, the sponsorship rights extended only to the United States, which eliminated any potential global promotional programs that Reebok might otherwise have coordinated. Therefore, the individual distributors were left to set up their own campaigns, promoting their own country's athletes and teams. Reebok's marketing theme, therefore, concentrated on using the Olympics to begin developing a global image for the organization, starting in the United States. Reebok successfully promoted its Olympic involvement to domestic consumers and viewed this as a preliminary step to developing a global campaign in the future.

One of the company's more famous ventures was a product of the New York advertising firm of Chiat/Day/Mojo, which had been hired to create an advertising campaign to promote Reebok's cross-trainer shoes. David Ropes worked with Chiat/Day on the $20 million campaign that would feature two previously unknown Americans who participated in the decathlon. Reebok chose this particular type of athlete because these athletes are considered by many to be the ultimate cross-trainers. In addition, the United States had not had a serious medal contender in the decathlon event since 1976, when Bruce Jenner and Fred Dixon won the gold and silver medals in the Montreal Olympics. By featuring decathletes, Reebok hoped to share the credit for returning the decathlon gold medal to the United States in the 1992 summer Olympic Games in Barcelona. At the same time, Reebok planned to link the success of the athletes to its products, particularly its cross-trainer shoes. According to Ford Ennals, Reebok's senior vice president of worldwide marketing, the ads demonstrated that the world's greatest athletes wear Reebok footwear and apparel.

The athletes that Reebok chose for this campaign were Dan O'Brien and Dave Johnson. Although they were two of the world's top athletes, they were also largely unknown. Therefore, Reebok took a tremendous risk when it signed these potential Olympic contenders to long-term contracts. In addition, it produced the "Dan and Dave" ads prior to the U.S. Olympic trials, where the 1992 United States Olympic decathletes would be determined.

The "Dan and Dave" campaign consisted of a totally integrated marketing effort involving promotions, public relations, point-of-purchase materials, direct marketing, and in-store videos. Television advertisements consisted of eleven different spots, with the first five making their debut during the highly visible Superbowl telecast on January 26, 1992. The spots were then shown throughout the year to generate interest and enthusiasm over the competition between the two decathletes and to link their successes with Reebok's cross-trainer shoes.

Although response to the advertisements was generally favorable, criticisms against the campaign surfaced soon after the spots aired during the Superbowl. For example, many critics stated that the Dan versus Dave promotion didn't put enough emphasis on the product being promoted, which had been a criticism of previous campaigns. However, Reebok refuted these claims by stating that the shoe was selling at a record pace throughout the summer. Others charged Reebok with taking a huge risk by putting all of its eggs in one basket.

As of mid-June, however, these concerns seemed insignificant as the company reported record first-quarter sales, which it attributed primarily to this campaign. Reebok had already enjoyed high name recognition. In addition, both Dan and Dave became a tremendous hit with the youth market. They became household names, and the Dan and Dave campaign seemed to take on a life of its own, with the well-known slogan, "Who is the world's greatest athlete? . . . to be settled in Barcelona." It was apparent that the campaign was already on track even before the Olympic games had actually begun.

According to John Gillis, Reebok's director of marketing communications, Reebok officials had plans to expand this rivalry beyond the Olympics. On June 27, 1992, however, all hopes for future marketing success from this project seemed to disappear. On that day, Dan O'Brien missed his attempt at the pole vault in the Olympic trials and failed to make the United States Olympic team. Reebok was suddenly left with expensive contracts with two athletes and no campaign to use them in.

After exploring several options, Reebok determined that the best strategy would be to come up with a new campaign—one that would successfully take advantage of Dan's failure and, at the same time, emphasize Dave's success. There were several drawbacks to this approach. For example, Reebok was concerned that this strategy would cause consumers to link Dan's failure with its product. And, if Dave Johnson also performed below expectations, the perception that Reebok supported unsuccessful athletes would be reinforced. This was also the most expensive option available to Reebok because it would have to produce new commercials quickly to be aired immediately.

However, it was apparent to Reebok that this was its only viable alternative. It believed that consumers would view a move to drop Dan O'Brien and/or Dave Johnson at that time as callous and unethical. So, within one week, Reebok invested an additional $25 million in the campaign and replaced the "To be settled in Barcelona" advertisements with new spots. These advertisements continued to feature both Dan and Dave and played on the emotions and disappointment of the American public. Fortunately for Reebok, its quick response generated positive results. As a matter of fact, while the initial ads were popular primarily with the younger generation, the follow-up campaign ignited a heartwarming reaction from adult viewers. And, most importantly, sales remained high.

The employment of these new worldwide campaigns appeared to show foresight and to create a means for deeper penetration of the global network Reebok already had in place. The "Life is short" campaign, however, never caught on overseas, and individual distributors stuck by their autonomy to create marketing packages they felt best accommodated their consumers. The "Life is short" campaign has been used in only about 5 percent of its foreign interests. Although the theme generated high brand awareness in the United States, marketing in individual countries overseas remained a country-by-country approach. Similarly, the "Dan and Dave" campaign was unable to be targeted worldwide, but it created excellent exposure for its new products in the United States. The Olympics, in general, provided the global awareness Reebok sought; Reebok was able to flood the international airwaves with famous athletes wearing its newest, high-tech designs.

Having received the consultants' analysis, Paul Fireman has assembled his senior management team to discuss the findings and the future direction of Reebok.

NOTES

[1] D. S. Haverson, "Reebok: Making Its Mark," *Perspective 1987*, v. 13 no. 2, 22–25, 36–37.

[2] A. L. Stern, and A. Hollyday, "Reebok: In for the Distance," *Business Month*, August 1987, 22–25.

[3] L. Helm, "Recent Blisters Seem to Be Healing," *Business Week*, August 3, 1987, 62.

[4] R. Soslow, "How Reebok Runs," *World Trade*, July 1992, pp. 44–50.

[5] Reebok International, Ltd., *Backgrounder*, February 1992, 14.

[6] Athletic Footwear Association, *The U.S. Athletic Footwear Market Today*, 1992, 3.

[7] *Ibid.*, 3.

[8] *Ibid.*, 4.

[9] *Backgrounder*, 3.

[10] B. Kanner, "Reebok on the Rebound," *New York*, October 1989, 26.

[11] P. Sloan, "Reebok Gets Pumped for 1990," *Advertising Age*, November 1989, 7.

[12] Athletic Footwear Association, *The U.S. Athletic Footwear Market Today*, 1992, 2.

[13] Sporting Goods Manufacturing Association, "Athletic Footwear Sales Growing at Discount Stores and Athletic Shoe Stores," Press Release, April 6, 1992, 2.

[14] Athletic Footwear Association, *The U.S. Athletic Footwear Market Today*, 1992, 4.

[15] Athletic Footwear Association, 4.

[16] *Ibid.*, 7.

[17] B. Kanner, "Reebok on the Rebound," *New York*, October 1989, 26.

[18] Sporting Goods Manufacturing Association, "Athletic Footwear Sales Growing at Discount Stores and Athletic Shoe Stores," Press Release, April 6, 1992, 1.

[19] Athletic Footwear Association, *The U.S. Athletic Footwear Market Today*, 1992, 5.

[20] *Ibid.*, 5.

[21] *Ibid.*, 5.

[22] *Ibid.*, 5.

[23] Sporting Goods Manufacturing Association, "Athletic Footwear Sales Growing at Discount Stores and Athletic Shoe Stores," Press Release, April 6, 1992, 1.

[24] Athletic Footwear Association, 6.

[25] Athletic Footwear Association, *The U.S. Athletic Footwear Market Today*, 1992, 6.

[26] *Ibid.*, 6.

[27] Form 10-K, 1991, Nike, Inc., 2.

[28] Form 10-K, 1991, Nike, Inc., 1.

[29] G. E. Willigan, "High-Performance Marketing: An Interview with Nike's Phil Knight," *Harvard Business Review*, July–August 1992, 95.

[30] Form 10-K, 1991, Nike, Inc., 3.

[31] M. Grimm, "'Unofficial' Sneaker Blitzes Europe," *Adweek's Marketing Week*, June 8, 1992, 6.

[32] Annual Report on Form 10-K, 1991, L.A. Gear, Inc., 2.

[33] *Ibid.*, 3.

[34] *Ibid.*, 6.

[35] *Ibid.*, 6.

[36] *Ibid.*, 6.

[37] Letter to Our Shareholders, 1991, L.A. Gear, Inc., 2.

[38] Igor Reichlin, DoriJones Yang, and Keith Hammonds, "Where Nike and Reebok Have Plenty of Running Room," *Business Week*, March 11, 1991, 56.

[39] *Ibid.*, 60.

[40] Annual Report, Reebok International Ltd., 1991, 22.

[41] *Backgrounder*, 5–6.

[42] Annual Report, Reebok International Ltd., 1991, 2–3.

[43] "Can Paul Fireman Put the Bounce Back in Reebok?" *Business Week*, June 18, 1990, 181.

[44] A. Zipser, "Pumping Up Profits," *Barron's*, October 21, 1991, 46.

[45] G. Morgensen, "Has the Runner Stumbled?" *Forbes*, September 19, 1988, 119.

[46] *Ibid.*

[47] D. S. Haverson, "Reebok: Making Its Mark," *Perspective 1987*, v. 13, no. 2, 181.

[48] *Ibid.*

[49] Zipser, 46.

[50] "Reebok Chief Looks Beyond Nike," *Advertising Age*, January 1990, 16.

[51] Zipser, 46.

[52] Reichlin, Yang, and Hammonds, 56, 60.

[53] "Reebok Chief Looks Beyond Nike," 57.

[54] Reichlin, Yang, and Hammonds, 56.

[55] Reichlin, Yang, and Hammonds, 60.

[56] L. Bannon, "Athletic Firms Slugging Toe-to-Toe in Germany," *Footwear News*, March 16, 1992, 30.

[57] Reichlin, Yang, and Hammonds, 60.

[58] "Reebok Chief Looks Beyond Nike," 57.

[59] Reichlin, Yang, and Hammonds, 56.

[60] P. Sloan, "Reebok's Global Leap—New 'Life Is Short' Ads Set for Int'l. Use," *Advertising Age*, August 1991, 33.

[61] *Ibid.*

XEROX: THE DOCUMENT COMPANY *

Xerox's CEO, Paul Allaire, believes his role is "to take the concept of quality and to make it a reality, with the customer as the focal point."[1] It is this philosophy that has made a world of difference to "The Document Company," as Xerox refers to itself.

Xerography, a term which literally means "dry writing," is a process that was invented on October 22, 1938 by Chester Carlson. Xerography is a process that combines light and a photoconductive material to produce an image. Carlson patented his idea and began to search for a manufacturing firm. In 1944 Battelle Memorial Institute, a nonprofit research firm, began to develop Carlson's process. In 1947 Battelle teamed up with a small photo-paper company named Haloid, which later became Xerox, to develop the first xerographic machine. In 1959, twenty-one years after Carlson's discovery, the 914 copier, which can make plain-paper copies at the touch of a button, was introduced. The rest is history (see Exhibit 2-1).

Between 1976 and 1982, Xerox's share of worldwide copier revenues dropped by half, from 82 percent to 41 percent.[2] Xerox's loss of market share was due to increased competition from Japanese manufacturing firms, such as Canon, Minolta, Ricoh, and Sharp. "Japanese competitors, offering higher quality and cheaper prices, were squeezing Xerox, which introduced the world's first plain-paper copier, out of the industry that it had created."[3] It was obvious to the managers of Xerox that changes had to be made. In 1981, under CEO David Kearns, company leaders implemented a ten-point program that put Xerox back on track and brought the corporation to its current success. The program included:

1. *Competitive benchmarking:* Sending investigative teams throughout the world to learn the best manufacturing and service methods.

---

*This case was prepared by Tina Arndt, Lesley Kearns, Hani Khoja, Tiffany Rogers, and Maysoune Ghobash under the direction of Professor Salah S. Hassan at The George Washington University.

2. *Pushing responsibility down*: Giving the responsibility of conceiving, developing, and manufacturing products to small teams of product designers.
3. *More emphasis on market research*: Observing what customers want.
4. *A rallying point*: Recreating a fighting spirit with a new line of copiers.
5. *Driving technology*: Developing a technology that would be complex, sophisticated, and difficult for others (e.g., the Japanese) to mass-produce.

1938	Chester Carlson invents xerography	**EXHIBIT 2-1**
1947	Haloid Corporation (later called Xerox) is formed	**XEROX TIME LINE**
1949	Haloid introduces its first xerographic machine–Xerox	
1959	914 copier introduced by Xerox: it could copy 9 × 14 sheets Net income = $2 million	
1960	Net income = $2.6 million	
1961	Net income = $5.3 million	
1962	10,000 914 copiers shipped to customers: Net income = $13.9 million	
1963	Net income = $22.6 million	
1964	Carlson receives "Inventor of the Year" Award	
1965	Carlson donates first machine and copy to Smithsonian	
1976–1982	Worldwide revenues drop from 82 percent to 41 percent	
1981	Management meets to discuss Japanese threat	
1983	Made-in-America strategy—Xerox gains 3 points Diversification into financial services	
1988	Xerox global account marketing strategy launched	
1989	Xerox reduces staff of 100,000 by 2,000 employees Xerox wins Malcolm Baldridge National Quality Award	
1990	Xerox discontinues real estate and financial operations Allaire becomes CEO Three-year "Total Satisfaction Guarantee" introduced DocuTech production publisher introduced Third-party financing and leasing business discontinued	

6. *Internationalization*:   Developing worldwide sourcing and global strategies.

7. *Just-in-time manufacturing*:   Reducing the number of parts vendors and inventory and introducing automated parts warehouses.

8. *Automation and computerization*:   Modernizing; tying vendors to computer-aided design (CAD) systems.

9. *Moving faster*:   Accelerating product development due to shorter product lives.

10. *Emphasis on quality*:   Defining quality as conformance to customer requirements. The idea is to design for quality, not to inspect for quality.[4]

Implementing this program was somewhat painful. The London-based overseas subsidiary, Rank Xerox, had to decrease its staff by 40 percent; the cost savings from this cut amounted to $200 million. Because of price competition from Japanese companies, Xerox also had to slash margins from approximately 18 percent to approximately 6 percent, resulting in flat equipment revenues through the '80s.[5] However, "since 1980, Xerox has closed the 50% cost gap that had existed with the Japanese."[6] The emphasis on quality was successful; at the main manufacturing plant in Rochester, NY, "defective incoming parts dropped from 100,000 per million to 300, as the number of suppliers was slashed from 5,000 to 350 to boost quality."[7] In addition to implementing new strategies, Xerox diversified into financial services by buying Crum & Forster, a property casualty insurer, and Van Kampen Merritt and Furman Selz Holding, investment banking firms.

Following the implementation of the program that stressed quality, Xerox introduced the 10 series products. According to Wayland Hicks, executive vice president for marketing, "The 10 Series products repositioned the company in terms of both product performance and price." Xerox beat the Japanese copier manufacturers at their own game; consequently, Xerox took a positive turn and once again became the leader in copier technology. The fact that the company's copier business rebounded and created impressive earnings was not enough (see Exhibit 2-2). Throughout the 1980s, Xerox spent more than $3 billion on research and development.[8] The firm was looking beyond copiers and into digital imaging.

Diversification did not come easily, however, and the electronic "light-lens" document processing business was faltering, as was the once highly profitable financial services division. Now CEO Paul Allaire hopes to overcome the diversification problems and "leapfrog IBM, the Japanese, and other competitors with a family of all-new, all-digital, 'image processing' machines."

EXHIBIT 2-2   INDUSTRY SEGMENT DATA

Industry Segment Data

(In millions)	Document Processing			Insurance and Other Financial Services			Consolidated Continuing Operations
	Business Equipment	Xerox Equipment Financing	Total	Insurance	Other Financial Services	Total	
1990 Revenues from unaffiliated customers	$12,692	$ 891	$13,583	$ 4,184	$ 206	$ 4,390	$17,973
Operating profit	$ 1,045	$ 307	$ 1,352	$ 129	$ 16	$ 145	$ 1,497
General expenses, net	(132)	–	(132)	(198)	(64)	(262)	(394)
Income (loss) before income taxes	913	307	1,220	(69)	(48)	(117)	1,103
Income (taxes) benefits	(328)	(106)	(434)	103	20	123	(311)
Minorities' interests	(164)	(23)	(187)	–	–	–	(187)
Income (loss) from continuing operations	$ 421	$ 178	$ 599	34	(28)	$ 6	$ 605
Interest and other IOFS costs, net of tax				124	40		
Legal entity income				$ 158	$ 12		
Assets	$ 8,018	$ 6,150	$14,168	$13,573	$ 643	$14,216	$28,384
Allocated short- and long-term debt	$ 956	$ 4,897	$ 5,853	$ 2,026	$ 420	$ 2,446	$ 8,299
Allocated acquisition and other debt				(2,026)	(395)		
Legal entity debt				$ –	$ 25		
1989 Revenues from unaffiliated customers	$11,720	$ 711	$12,431	$ 4,591	$ 207	$ 4,798	$17,229
Operating profit	$ 875	$ 258	$ 1,133	$ 331	$ 39	$ 370	$ 1,503
General expenses, net	(115)	–	(115)	(177)	(56)	(233)	(348)
Income (loss) before income taxes	760	258	1,018	154	(17)	137	1,155
Income (taxes) benefits	(299)	(79)	(378)	23	5	28	(350)
Minorities' interests	(128)	(24)	(152)	–	–	–	(152)
Income (loss) from continuing operations	$ 333	$ 155	$ 488	177	(12)	$ 165	$ 653
Interest and other IOFS costs, net of tax				131	35		
Legal entity income				$ 308	$ 23		
Assets	$ 7,710	$ 5,566	$13,276	$12,488	$ 575	$13,063	$26,339
Allocated short- and long-term debt	$ 1,334	$ 4,444	$ 5,778	$ 1,850	$ 345	$ 2,195	$ 7,973
Allocated acquisition and other debt				(1,850)	(320)		
Legal entity debt				$ –	$ 25		
1988 Revenues from unaffiliated customers	$11,152	$ 536	$11,688	$ 4,295	$ 194	$ 4,489	$16,177
Operating profit	$ 522	$ 198	$ 720	$ 318	$ 46	$ 364	$ 1,084
General expenses, net	(136)	–	(136)	(139)	(48)	(187)	(323)
Income (loss) before income taxes	386	198	584	179	(2)	177	761
Income (taxes) benefits	(220)	(69)	(289)	23	(1)	22	(267)
Minorities' interests	(130)	(17)	(147)	–	–	–	(147)
Income (loss) from continuing operations	$ 36	$ 112	$ 148	202	(3)	$ 199	$ 347
Interest and other IOFS costs, net of tax				89	30		
Legal entity income				$ 291	$ 27		
Assets	$ 7,780	$ 4,423	$12,203	$10,985	$ 474	$11,459	$23,662
Allocated short- and long-term debt	$ 712	$ 3,364	$ 4,076	$ 1,560	$ 306	$ 1,866	$ 5,942
Allocated acquisition and other debt				(1,560)	(281)		
Legal entity debt				$ –	$ 25		

About the Industry Segment Data: The industry segment data portray the contributions to operating results and selected balance sheet data for the Company's four industry segments. These data exclude, for all periods presented, financial information relating to operations discontinued during 1990. For 1990 and 1989, the Business Equipment industry segment includes (in millions) $756 and $785, respectively, of debt associated with the Company's Employee Stock Ownership Plan. For 1988, the Business Equipment industry segment includes the effect of the $275 million before-tax charge incurred in connection with the restructuring of certain Document Processing operations. This charge reduced Business Equipment income from continuing operations by $244 million.

INDUSTRY

Xerox and the rest of the copier/printing industry face a different type of competition than they have in the past. Customer needs are shifting, and Xerox will be greatly affected by these changes. Society is moving toward fully integrated systems and eventually a paper-free world; therefore, Xerox's competition includes computers. Today's consumers demand systems that can be incorporated with their existing investments in hardware and software. New document imaging and management systems allow users to create, publish, and manage documents. These systems enable users to store and retrieve documents from multiple applications and search for documents across a multiple-server network.[9]

COPIER INDUSTRY

The low end of the U.S. copier market was dominated by imports—mostly Japanese products. Some foreign producers have also begun to manufacture products in the United States to avoid high shipment costs and also to improve the company's public image with the U.S. government. The Computer and Business Equipment Manufacturing Association (CBEMA) projected that sales of low-speed copiers (up to 24 copies per minute) represented 60 percent of the $1.4 million total plain-paper copier unit shipments in the United States for 1990. The high-end light-lens copier industry remains crucial to the success of Xerox, and the Japanese are putting pressure on the U.S. domestic market. Japanese producers are gaining an edge with faster copiers (up to 70 copies per minute).

The copier/printing industry is currently focusing on integrated systems that will perform high-speed copying, printing, scanning, facsimile imaging, and computing. Currently, the industry is marketing stand-alone copiers and printers. Forecasts indicate a trend toward office systems, which will place Xerox in competition with the computer industry. Xerox realizes that society is moving toward "computerized documents," meaning that documents will exist primarily in computers, while paper will become a means of display.[10]

Industry members are investing hundreds of millions of dollars into electronic image-processing technology and color copying. Color copiers may be the determining factor in image-processing growth because of the need to reproduce the color graphics of computer laser printers quickly and cheaply.[11] The trend toward digital machines allows the integration of office equipment. Digital copiers cannot match the speed, quality, or productivity of optical copiers, but they offer more flexibility. As the technology evolves, digital machines are expected to share the market with optical machines.[12]

In 1990 IBM and Unisys Corporation announced systems designed with digital technology. Their systems were targeted at large-scale paper pushers, such as banks and government contractors. Eastman Kodak Company introduced a LionHeart high-speed printing system that can be connected to a wide range of desktop computers.

Japanese companies such as Ricoh Corporation, Canon Incorporated, and Sharp Corporation plan to introduce low-end machines that copy, print, scan, and fax based on the same multifunctional attributes as Xerox. National Semiconductor Corporation recently developed a microchip that will enable such machines to be made cheaply.[13]

COMPUTER INDUSTRY

The computer industry has developed document imaging and management systems that threaten the copier and printing industry. These systems will eliminate the paper load for sophisticated personal computer users. Low-cost imaging tools are now available, whereas a decade ago the imaging solutions required highly customized software and hardware that cost millions of dollars.[14]

Prime Computer, Inc.'s system is one that is fully integrated with its database. This system can store paper documents as electronic images so that they can be attached to any database record. Prime Computer enables users to access and manipulate a variety of data types. The system is particularly suited to large organizations that need on-line access to paper-based documents.[15]

PC Docs, Inc. allows users to store and retrieve documents from multiple applications and to search for documents across multiple servers. This makes it easier to move around and account for each document on a multiple-server network. For the first time a global network searching feature will permit users to search for documents on remote servers as if the files were stored locally.[16]

The Boeing Company has developed a system to improve time spent on searching, updating, and creating documents. A project called product standard data system provides "view only" capabilities for selected documents so that authorized users are able to search, retrieve, and view. In addition, users are able to create and publish documents using a desktop publishing package and on-line configuration management to manage various documents.[17]

Computer scanners allow information to be put into computers almost as quickly as it can be printed out. The scanner technology market is growing at a rate of 33 percent a year.

DOCUMENT IMAGING

Year	Units	Percent Growth
1990	420,000	—
1991	640,000	34%
1995	1,800,000	64

Scanners are similar to copying machines and work much the same way. A scanner takes an image of a sheet of paper like a copier, but instead of printing that image onto another sheet of paper, it places it into a computer. Until recently, the problem with scanning was that computers could do very little with the image unless it was part of a very large and expensive system. The development of new and inexpensive software is changing that, and personal computers can now use sophisticated scanners. Scanners can be used as an office automation tool, but their success depends on the degree to which consumers move toward document imaging. The drawbacks of using scanners with personal computers include inaccuracy (99 percent means an average of ten errors per 2,000 character page), and the difficulty of recognizing colored paper and tables of numbers. As these problems are corrected, more companies will move into this market. The market is growing, and it will continue to grow rapidly.[18]

XEROX EQUIPMENT

COPIERS AND DUPLICATORS

As of June, 1991 Canon USA was the industry forerunner in copiers;[19] however, Xerox plans to regain its dominance. The copier market is divided basically into four groups, and Xerox offers products for each of these groups:

1. Personal copying for the home/office.
2. Convenience copying in a center designed to meet the needs of a department within a specific company.
3. Copying in a center for moderate to large jobs.
4. Xerographic duplicating in an environment that supports entire businesses.

Xerox small copiers that are designed for the home/office include Xerox 5012, 5014, 5018, 5028, 5034, and 5042 from the 50 series. These copiers work at speeds ranging from 12 to 35 copies per minute, and they offer special options such as color kits, high-capacity feeders, and copying units. The features included depend on the particular model.

Mid-volume copiers offered by Xerox include the Xerox 5046, 5052, and 5065, along with the 1050 and 1075 models. These copiers offer a range of automatic features with the ease of use associated with low-volume desktop copiers. The Xerox 5065 copier is the first of the mid-volume copiers to offer remote interactive communications (RIC). This service acts as a "distant early warning" system that automatically alerts the Xerox service district of any potential problems within the system. The service department is then able to correct a problem before it occurs and thus save the customer and Xerox both time and money.

High-volume copiers include the Xerox 1090 and the 5100. Both models offer the RIC service and are perfect for high-volume copying, print shops, and central reproduction departments. The 5100 project was undertaken by a joint venture between Xerox and Fuji Xerox in Tokyo, and it was designed as a single version to be marketed internationally. The copier is controlled simply by touching symbols on an interactive video screen. The 5100 model's ability to adapt to different languages depends on the addition of a few electronic chips that can be easily installed at a foreign distribution point. The 5100 goes from 0 to 100 copies in 1 minute, making it both an easy and fast machine to use.

Xerox also offers four duplicator models: Xerox 9900, 9900/50, 9900/60+, and 5090. The 9900 model offers all of its features through a series of "menus" on a large CRT screen. Standard features on all four models include automatic document handling, variable reduction, image shift, and automatic duplexing. The Xerox 5090 is the premier duplicating system, featuring a touch control screen. This model also includes an estimated job completion time before and during a particular job.

LASER PRINTING SYSTEMS

Xerox is the world leader in providing electronic, laser printing systems and also in providing the largest number of physical connections linking printers to central processing units (CPUs). The 4030 II model emulates up to seven different data streams and is therefore capable of producing several different print formats. Print speed, however, is only 11 pages per minute. Other models offered by Xerox include the 4045 models, 3700, 4050, 4075, 4090, 4650, 8790, and the Xerox 9790 laser printing system.

Another printing system recently released is the Xerox 4850 highlight color laser printing system. This printer represents Xerox's long-awaited assault on the color-copier market, and it is a direct result of Xerox's huge investments in research and development. The 4850 is the first printer to produce color documents in one pass, rather than the several passes required by other color printers. Although the model prints only in black and one color, it is nevertheless twice as fast as the competing color laser copiers and priced considerably lower.

DocuTech Publishing Series

On October 8, 1990 Xerox unveiled one of its first "hydra" products: DocuTech publishing series, a combination printer, scanner, and copier aimed at electronic publishing applications in large companies. This "high-end of the market" machine is able to digitally scan up to twenty-three documents per minute and store the images in the unit's memory. Users can then make changes or manipulate images in memory and print out the desired document. This model was recently updated by a connection to local area networks (LANs), allowing compatibility with leading desktop publishing packages and page description languages. This network version allows users to create documents at their own workstations and to send them electronically to be printed.

DocuTech is aimed at companies with large in-house printing needs and, according to David H. Goodstein of Interconsult (a market research firm), there are 60,000 companies with in-house printing operations large enough to justify the purchase of DocuTech.[20] Some analysts believe, however, that the DocuTech multifunctional machine is too expensive (approximately $220,000) and wonder whether customers will spend so much money for a product that is basically a print server, even if it does offer better performance, quality, and new functions. Analysts also feel that DocuTech may erode Xerox's high-end copier sales, their main revenue producer.

Document Processing Systems

The compatibility of Xerox workstations, software, and networks with other products and systems allows users to access information from all available sources including PCs, workstations, minis, and mainframes. GlobalView software, including GlobalView Desktop and GlobalView for the PC, allow users to create, edit, and format documents with simple, easy-to-learn commands. Document processing software includes DocuTeam Software, which stores important tables in a "shared library book with database," DocuBuild Software, and Document Search and Retrieval, which gives users instant access to the precise information desired from among thousands of documents in a central database. Other software includes Xerox

FormBase 1.1, Publishing Illustrator's Software, and the Ventura Publisher Gold Series.

The UNIX-based Xerox 6500 series (6520 and 6540) represents the corporation's workstation line. The Xerox 6540 Workstation is a result of the technology agreement between Sun Microsystems and Xerox. It is equipped with Xerox GlobalView software, and it has enhanced graphics and power capabilities that are required by technical, scientific, financial, as well as government institutions. Other Xerox options, services, and software are shown in Exhibit 2-4.

Xerox Imaging Systems

Xerox Imaging Systems (XIS) offers products in desktop scanning, image processing, and text recognition for IBM PC and PS/2 and Apple Macintosh systems. The K5100 and K5200 are XIS high-end scanners for high-volume applications requiring intelligent systems. Other products within the Kurzweil series include the PC/KPR and the Personal Reader, which converts print into easily understood synthetic speech, a function especially valuable to blind, dyslexic, and other physically challenged individuals. Xerox also offers other XIS Graphic Systems, including the GS Plus Scanner, Gray F/X, and XIS MacImage. All such products are under the XIS satisfaction replacement feature guarantee, which is similar to the Xerox total satisfaction guarantee.

Telecopier Facsimile Terminals

Xerox introduced the first fax machine for business users more than 25 years ago, and today it offers the widest selection of plain-paper fax machines. There are currently three types of fax technology:[21]

1. Thermal fax, at the low end.
2. Direct thermal fax, an intermediate process to produce a plain bond output.
3. Laser technology, at the high end.

Plain-paper fax machines have some advantages over thermal; plain paper lasts longer, is readily available, is less expensive, and produces better print quality. In short, even though plain-paper fax machines are more expensive than thermal fax units, they are ideal for businesses where productivity is a priority. The industry believes that the public is leaning more toward plain-paper fax units because prices are declining and technology is being advanced at a rapid rate.[22]

Some of the units offered by Xerox include the 70 series (7009, 7012, 7017, 7017SF, 7020, 7021, 7032, and 7033) and the 72 series (7220, 7240,

7260). The 7220 Personal Fax was introduced on May 1, 1990, and it allows users to send and receive documents anywhere in the world instantly. It is a fax machine, a full-function telephone, and a convenience copier all in one unit, and it is affordably priced. It also has an automatic receive feature that allows users to receive and send faxes automatically without staying by the machine.

XEROX VOICE MESSAGE EXCHANGE

The Xerox Voice Message Exchange (XVMX) allows users to avoid the problems caused by "telephone tag" by sending, receiving, redirecting, storing, forwarding, and broadcasting voice messages to associates anytime and anywhere. The XVMX stores voice messages on a magnetic disk for retrieval at any time, and it uses any tone-generating telephone, making it useful for organizations whose employees travel a great deal.

ELECTRONIC TYPEWRITERS

The Xerox line of typewriters begins with the 6010 model, which works best on one-line revisions, and finishes with the Xerox 6420. The 60 series includes the 6010, 6020, 6025, 6040, and 6045 Memorywriters. A screen display is included on the latter model, and the model automatically adjusts the text to accommodate changes made by the user. Also included are an automatic spellcheck and "background printing," which allows the user to edit a document while simultaneously printing another. The 62 series includes the 6225 and the 6240 Typing Systems. This series offers a whisper-quiet impact printer that delivers exceptional print quality.

ENGINEERING SYSTEMS

Xerox Engineering Systems is the world's largest supplier of engineering copiers, printers, plotters, and other products for engineering document management. It provides engineers, drafters, and designers with products that help create, revise, store, print, and distribute engineering drawings and other large-scale documents.

A new product introduced by Xerox Engineering Systems is the Versatec CADcolor, a low-cost, high-resolution color plotter. Also introduced in the Versatec line are the Versatec 8600E series and PlotLinq. The Xerox 2520 ASF engineering copier, a mid-volume, plain-paper copier, was also introduced, as was the Xerox 8840-D electronic graphics printing system, the Xerox 2520 ASF engineering copier, the Xerox 7124 engineering facsimile/copier, and the Xerox 8810, a high-resolution, monochrome laser plotter. Xerox also offers a wide range of engineering supplies, including paper in both sheets and rolls and optimum toners.

Xerox Business Services

Xerox also offers a nationwide network of Xerox business service centers that offer a variety of document processing services. These offices, in fact, thrive on emergency requests, difficult jobs, and tight deadlines. They are equipped with the latest in document processing equipment and are fully staffed with professionals able to handle the needs of any business. Xerox also offers special events programming, reprographics, expert litigation copying, routine/emergency supplies, and teleservice facsimile networking.

Xerox Financial Services

Xerox diversified into the financial services business in 1982 and experienced almost immediate success. By the end of 1987, half of the company's profits were accounted for by insurance, leasing, and mutual funds businesses. Xerox was in fact producing, at one point of time, as much in the area of wholesale financial products, such as mutual funds and leverage leases, as in office equipment.

However, the recession of the late 1980s and early 1990s, along with several failed investments, hurt the once-profitable Xerox financial services area. Plunging real estate values and soft capital and investment markets hurt Xerox financial services, and the fact that the property/casualty insurance markets didn't emerge from the downturn in the insurance cycle didn't help matters.

Xerox Supplies

Xerox provides all the supplies necessary to complement its equipment. Copier supplies include toners, copy cartridges, and other products. With the creation of the 50 series, Xerox began to provide 50 series products and supplies including paper, stitcher wire, tabs, and other 50-series-unique supplies. They also offer paper/thruput, electronic typewriters, and other supplies—all supported by Xerox telemarketing.

Team Xerox

Xerox backs up its products with Team Xerox, an organization that provides the in-depth product knowledge, training, training materials, consulting, customized services, trouble-shooting, and any support that customers need. Courses held at Xerox training centers are available for a variety of document processing systems, including networks, printing systems, and workstations. Xerox was one of the first business equipment suppliers to offer financial assistance as a customer service as early as 1980. It has continued this policy and has also provided customers with the support they need after a purchase is made. Customer service also allows customers to monitor the performance of the corporation through the customer satisfaction measurement system (CSMS). The CSMS allows customers to tell Xerox how it's doing and how to improve certain areas.

Other services offered by Team Xerox include customized service, financial options, customer administration, and systems customer support centers.

LAUNCH

Document processing has replaced copying. Now Xerox is branching out into wave-of-the-future products, hoping to return to "double-digit growth days."[23]

In 1991, Xerox introduced software to tie the DocuTech multifunction machine to existing computer networks.[24] This new software, Network Publisher I, is compatible with personal computers and workstations, networks, publishing applications software, and page description languages. Xerox has learned from past mistakes not to insist on proprietary workstations to integrate with their printers.[25] In order to link DocuTech with computers, Xerox teamed up with NetFrame, Inc. to sell a file-server that will store document images.[26] Xerox plans to introduce low and mid-volume versions of DocuTech to reach customers in other market segments.

The Xerox customized applications service (CAS) group specializes in modifying copiers for special uses. "The CAS Group has made copiers 'talk' so that the equipment can be used by the blind; has designed controls that make the units operable by people who don't have use of their arms and hands, and even has altered copiers for use aboard government aircraft, including Air Force One."[27]

Xerox is branching out into computer networks with an office automation system that allows employees to work together on a new dimension. The system will "mimic real life as closely as possible" by using a variety of media.[28] The system, which is currently in the research stage, will equip each workstation with a computer terminal, television set, microphone, and video camera. Employees will wear special devices that will track their movements via infrared sensors. The result will be an environment in which employees can look at or talk to any fellow employee. The video/audio, location sensor, and computer networks will all be connected. If an employee is worried about invasion of privacy, he or she can prevent people from watching or listening. The innovators have not yet discovered all of the uses for this new system, but it is currently an effective tool for keeping managers informed about office activities.

Xerox's corporate research group provides the technology for future products. Currently, the major thrust of the group is color production. The company wants its customers not only to be able to copy in color but also to be able to create color images and place the images into documents.

DISTRIBUTION

Xerox distributes its equipment through distributors and carriers and pays them according to their performance. This policy is an attempt on the part of Xerox to improve its quality and lower its costs. It has implemented a performance incentive program to encourage its carriers to provide the best service. National carriers move Xerox products from three distribution centers to fifty local centers. Field transportation carriers are responsible for moving equipment from the local centers to customers and installing equipment for them.[29]

In order to maintain control and quality standards, Xerox has reduced the number of national carriers from twelve to five. At present, the on-time delivery rate is close to 100 percent. Xerox negotiates delivery plans that address the type of shipment, distance, length of time, how many drivers are used, origin, and destination. Carriers must pick up and deliver within 2 hours of the agreed time. The contracts are negotiated with most of the carriers for 5-year terms. The length of the terms has enabled Xerox to keep its costs down.[30]

The Xerox national dispatch center coordinates scheduling and routing for the carriers. New equipment is picked up from three distribution centers in Santa Fe Springs, California; Lewisville, Texas; and Webster, New York. National carriers also pick up used equipment that has been traded in for new products and transport it to remanufacturing centers that are located in West Mifflin, Pennsylvania and Sparks, Nevada.

Transportation is scheduled to ensure a continuous movement of Xerox products. Trucks drop off one load and immediately pick up another. The dispatch center controls the sequences. It successfully manages to move 250 million pounds of equipment in 12,000 shipments every year.

Xerox intends to use software to organize both routing and scheduling. This move will increase cost effectiveness and efficiency. (Lower costs and efficiency have already been achieved with traditional methods even without the new software.) The national carriers are equipped with computer software that calculates how many miles the carriers have driven. The data go into another computer, and it calculates billing automatically. Every quarter, audits are carried out and those drivers who meet targets receive bonuses. As a result, performance has improved considerably.

Xerox products are distributed through its sales or agents' offices. The agents' offices are essentially dealerships that serve both the general public and companies. Xerox also sells its systems to the federal government through its federal supply service, which has its headquarters in Arlington, Virginia. On an international scale, Xerox has direct sales offices around the world; all were chosen with care to ensure that quality and price standards are met.

Customers who are interested in a product contact the nearest sales office. Customer inquiries are first handled over the phone. Xerox does not have large showrooms where the public can browse and observe the merchandise. Instead, customers are allocated to a particular service representative according to which products they are inquiring about and which geographic area and zip code they are located in. The service representative initially agrees to send product information to the office or, in some cases, to the home. The next step in Xerox's distribution system is to invite the customer to Xerox for a product demonstration. Appointments are required so the customer can see the products.

Once products have been chosen, the dealer proposes several payment options. Companies can purchase the equipment they need outright, rent it, or lease it. The last two options allow the customer to exchange equipment as needs change and to protect the customer's company from owning obsolete equipment.

Xerox dealerships install the equipment and often arrange service contracts that include maintenance and quality checks. They provide training and training materials, consulting services, and workshops to teach customers to deal with document processing systems.

Before it made changes in its distribution system, Xerox had approximately 5,000 suppliers of its parts. In its restructuring, Xerox cut this figure down to 480. The 480 suppliers work closely with Xerox. The suppliers undergo "process qualification," whereby the suppliers' production and control processes are analyzed. The suppliers also receive training in various areas, such as quality techniques and statistical process control. The suppliers feel that Xerox has improved its products and operations as a result of the new strategies. By reducing the number of suppliers, Xerox regained control over the quality and image of its products. The number of defective parts that reach the production line has fallen by 73 percent in the last five years.[31] Xerox reduced its number of suppliers to benefit from profits from servicing agreements. In fact, this policy led to Xerox, Canada Inc. being sued by independent operators in Canada.[32]

Small copiers for personal use are distributed by Sears in addition to the Xerox dealerships. Xerox has attempted to broaden its distribution base while maintaining control. It also sells products through American Express, Diners Club, and warehouse sales.[33]

PRICE

Approximately 70 percent of Xerox's business product and systems revenues come from copiers and other duplicating equipment. The rest is divided among the sales of electronic printers, typing equipment, workstations, and software products.[34]

Xerox's pricing system is varied and flexible. The price is different for a copier that is sold commercially and one that is sold to the federal government. The government enjoys lower prices.

The flexible purchase options—outright purchase, rent, or lease—are negotiated by Xerox dealerships. Customers are able to trade in older models, even from other manufacturers, when they purchase new Xerox copiers.

Equipment prices vary from customer to customer to the degree that applicable laws permit. For large accounts, Xerox may have to bid against its competitors to gain new business. In these cases, it may charge less because it anticipates a large number of sales. Xerox also gives substantial discounts to fledgling companies that cannot afford higher prices in order to gain future business and brand loyalty. Sales representatives tend to choose such companies with care; they need to be confident that such companies have potential for growth.

Prices for the leasing and rental of Xerox products are also flexible, and a great deal of consideration is given to the company's strength and financial status. More favorable terms are given to those companies that are in more secure financial positions.[35]

The prices that are quoted to the federal government are significantly lower than prices offered at the retail level. Finally, the list prices of Xerox products, as well as their competitors' products, are substantially higher than retail prices. Dealers normally sell at a 15 percent to 20 percent discount from the list price. Prices for Xerox's document equipment range from $2,000 the $125,000 for the low- to high-volume machines. However, Xerox does sell its most expensive laser printer for $400,000.

Copiers for Commercial Use

Type	Lease to Own/Month	Own
Low-volume (3010)	$ 1,119.00	$ 7,995.00
Mid-volume (5034)	$ 1,820.00	$ 9,100.00
High-volume (9900)	$ 31,432.00	$104,775.00
Xerox Docutech	—	$220,000.00[36]

Copiers for Government Use

Type	Rent/month	Lease to Own/Month	Own
Low-volume (5028)	$ 140.00	$ 362.68	$ 4,050.00
Mid-volume (1050)	$ 268.00	$ 801.95	$ 8,955.00
High-volume (9900)	$ 1,839.00	$ 7,663.00	$ 85,570.00
Xerox Docutech	$ 1,800.00	$ 14,794.15	$165,200.00[37]

Product	Low-end	High-end
Laser printer	$140,500.00	$400,000.00
Facsimile	$ 1,325.00	$ 2,500.00
Electronic typewriter	$ 825.00	$ 2,685.00

COMPETITION

Xerox's products compete in about 40 percent of the $80 billion market for copying, faxing, printing, scanning, and document storage. It plans to be in about 60 percent of the market that is eventually projected to become a $100 billion market[38] (see Exhibit 2-3).

The photocopier market is gradually becoming one of a maturing technology. The expansion in unit volume is occurring at a rate of only 5 percent. Most of the growth is taking place at the lower price end. At present, color copiers make up 2 percent of market sales, but this percentage is expected to increase ten times to reach sales of $1.6 billion in 1992.[39]

In 1979 Xerox's unit share of the small-machine photocopier market—products capable of making 12 to 30 copies per minute—was 17 percent. Then the Japanese entered the market and pushed its share down to 8.6 percent. By 1988, Xerox took back enough to hold on to a 15 percent

EXHIBIT 2-3
COMPETITOR PRODUCT LINE MATRIX

Company / Product line	Plain copier	Color copier	Laser printer	Multifunction (Hydra)	Workstation	Engineering system	Facsimile	Plain paper facsimile
Xerox	■	■	■	■	■	■	■	■
Canon	■	■		■				■
Ricoh	■			■			■	■
Minolta	■						■	
Kodak	■							
Sharp				■			■	
Konica	■	■					■	
Lanier	■							
Mita	■							
AT&T							■	
Panasonic							■	
Toshiba	■						■	
3M Harris	■						■	
Brother	■						■	
Murata							■	
IBM				■	■			
Unisys				■	■			
Hewlett-Packard			■		■	■		
Calcomp						■		
Okidata			■					
Alps–America			■					
Sun Microsystems					■			
DEC					■			
Pitney Bowes							■	
Intergraph					■			
Silicon Graphics					■			

share of the market. In 1991, it had a 16 percent unit share of the copier market. In revenues this share is 38 percent of the copier market.[40]

The copier market is subdivided in three categories: low-, mid-, and high-volume copiers. Xerox is strongest in the high-volume segment of the market. It has yet to be surpassed, but it is facing stiff competition from Japanese companies that are focusing on the small but lucrative segment.

The Japanese are strongest in the low-volume market, with Canon, Inc. in the lead. In 1988 Canon had 23 percent of the unit sales of the 924,000 copiers that were sold that year. Xerox was second with 16 percent. Sharp followed with 11 percent. Together, these three made up more than half of the U.S. copier sales and rentals. Mita had 10 percent, Minolta had 7 percent, and Toshiba had 3.7 percent. Other competitors—Ricoh, 3M-Harris, Brother, and Konica—make up the rest of the sales in the low-volume segment.

Xerox found its market share eroding from the late 1970s to the mid 1980s. In comparison with its competitors' prices, Xerox's prices ranged 30 percent to 40 percent higher. Japanese competitors had lower manufacturing costs and were therefore able to offer lower prices. In the low-end market, Xerox is still at a cost disadvantage. Toshiba offers a desktop copier that retails for $1,695.00, whereas a similar product offered by Xerox typically sells for $6,000.00.

In the mid-volume copier market, Xerox's strongest competitor is Kodak, with several Japanese companies following. On a worldwide scale, Xerox holds a 35 percent share for mid-volume copiers. Xerox has 50 percent of the U.S. market for high-volume photocopiers. In the global market, Xerox has a 75 percent share in high-volume copiers. In this segment, its strongest competitor is Eastman Kodak Co., which in 1987 took over IBM's copier business.[41] Japanese competitors are attempting to edge into this market and may soon begin to meet success. Until recently, Xerox and Kodak were the only two contenders in this segment. However, in 1991 foreign manufacturers had a 25 percent share in the high-volume market. In 1989 Ricoh introduced a machine that produced 100 copies per minute and retailed for $63,000.00. It competed directly with Xerox Model 1090, which sells for $78,000.00, and a similar product from Kodak, the 250F, which sells for $89,000.00. Japanese companies are also entering the growing color copier segment as well as the digital imaging segment.[42]

Xerox's main competitive edge in the high-volume market is its software, which can handle large data flows, and its extensive sales force, which works with large corporate clients. Japanese companies currently lack these two advantages.

In the facsimile market, seven industry leaders make up 70 percent to 90 percent of the market's unit sales. By 1995 the size of the market is expected to grow to $12 billion. Sharp leads with 19 percent to 21 percent of the market. It has low-, middle-, and high-end machines. Murata is second with 15 percent to 17 percent of sales. Murata is moving from the low end of the market to the middle and higher end. Canon has 16 percent of the market. Canon differs slightly from the rest of its competitors because it focuses mainly on plain-paper machines rather than on thermal paper machines. Ricoh has 10 percent to 15 percent of sales. It targets thermal paper machines for the low and middle end of the segment and plain paper for the high end. Xerox has 5 percent to 10 percent of the market and has a full line of machines. Its strategy is to divide the market into home use and business use. In the latter segment, the emphasis is on plain-paper facsimile. PanaFax holds about 4 percent of the market with its full line. The last major competitor, Pitney Bowes, has about 4 percent to 6 percent of the market with a line that is targeted toward the high end of the market. Other competitors include 3M-Harris, Toshiba, Fujitsu, Minolta, Konica, Savin, Sanyo, NEC, and Brother.[43] The home office market is the fastest growing segment. By 1995 it is forecasted to be worth $780 million. Competition at the bottom of the market will become more frenzied. At present Japanese companies are in the lead, but South-Korean companies such as Daewoo, Lucky-Goldstar, and Samsung are expected to drive prices down to approximately $300.[44]

The market for workstations has seen prices fall rapidly. High-end prices run about $50,000 but are slowly falling below the $10,000 price barrier. Technical workstations have typically catered to scientists and engineers. Now they serve corporate departments and small businesses. In addition, pressure has built for companies to introduce machines that can communicate with one another.

In the workstation industry, Sun Microsystems is considered to be the strongest workstation manufacturer for the 1990s. Hewlett Packard, which acquired Apollo Computer in 1989, is also a strong competitor. Digital Equipment Corporation (DEC), which introduced workstations to the market, follows with IBM behind it.

The worldwide workstation market was worth $6.1 billion in 1989, and it continues to grow. In 1990 Sun Microsystems had 28.7 percent of the market, and Hewlett Packard had 26.4 percent. DEC held 15.9 percent of the market. Intergraph was in fourth place with 6 percent. Silicon Graphics had 5 percent, and IBM had 1.8 percent.[45]

Sun Microsystems has the Sparcstation and Digital Equipment has the Vaxstation, which are both popular workstations. IBM is effectively competing against these two with its Risc System 6000 that can run software developed by Next, but price erosion may harm IBM in the long run.

Hewlett Packard is in the forefront of the "open systems" movement that is attempting to join standard computers, software, and networking designs for the whole industry. Data General and Unisys are also competing with open systems. Xerox is marketing its workstations as being compatible with other products and systems. Xerox integrated systems are able to share information among different offices and different countries by using GlobalView Desktop and Xerox Network Services. The Xerox 6520 is a SPARC workstation that uses Xerox applications as well as non-Xerox applications. Xerox, however, is still a new competitor in this market.

Xerox developed the Xenith, which integrates office systems, computers, and software. It costs approximately $200,000. It will serve as a link between document processing and computers. With such a system, it is facing competition from IBM and Unisys, which are competing for the same target market, including insurance companies, banks, and government contractors that process a large number of documents. Xerox has attempted to emphasize the fact that its products will be able to use other companies' computers and software. However, it was beaten by Eastman Kodak, which came out with a product called LionHeart that prints large volumes at high speeds and works with desktop computers. In addition, Japanese companies such as Ricoh, Canon, and Sharp are also beginning to compete with multifunction machines that copy, print, scan, and fax and are aimed at the low end of the market.[46]

Xerox no longer manufactures electronic typewriters; however, many of its models are still being sold by dealers. Xerox's competitors in the electronic typewriter market are IBM, AT&T, Adler-Royal, Smith-Corona, Canon, Brother, Swintec, and Panasonic.

When IBM and Xerox introduced laser printers in the mid-1970s, the machines filled up half a room and they cost thousands of dollars. In 1979 Canon developed laser technology and designed a product that could be sold for $3,500.00. Hewlett Packard and Apple Computer took advantage of the technology and, along with Canon, benefitted from the growing desktop publishing business. They are the leaders in the laser printer market. However, Japanese companies may edge further into low-end printers as they have in other technological markets.

GLOBAL STRATEGY

Xerox serves a large number of Fortune 500 companies in the United States. Many of these companies, however, are multinational corporations. With the arrival of the European Common Market in 1992, Xerox realized the need to market their products directly across Europe by targeting and segmenting consumer groups. In order to meet the technology requirements of its clients abroad, Xerox introduced an international marketing strategy. Xerox initially focused on seven pilot accounts; the strategy grew and eventually became the Xerox global account marketing strategy. It aims to "provide comprehensive account support for customer document processing needs on a unified, worldwide basis."[47] Xerox strives to tailor itself to local markets under the umbrella of a single global positioning message. It hopes to do this by using a worldwide network, regional production bases, and national fulfillment points.[48] A global strategy gives the multinational corporation a single point of contact with a global account manager who will follow customers wherever the business leads. This strategy has led to the receipt of numerous awards—similar to the Malcolm Baldridge National Quality Award in the United States—in Canada, France, England, Japan, Brazil, Mexico, Australia, and Holland.

To better serve its clients, Xerox has established marketing and service groups around the world (see Exhibit 2-4). These groups include:

- *U.S. marketing group*:   This group markets and services major accounts and commercial customers.
- *Rank Xerox*:   This group markets and services Xerox products in Canada and more than 40 countries in North, South, and Central America; the Caribbean; the Middle East and North Africa; China and Hong Kong; and Europe.
- *Fuji Xerox*:   This group develops, manufactures, markets, and services Fuji Xerox document processing products in Japan, Australia, New Zealand, and other territories in the Pacific rim.

In September 1991 Xerox and Fuji Xerox joined to form a new company to market low-end printer products worldwide.[49] The joint company, called Xerox International Partners, will "focus on selling printer products to original equipment manufacturer customers as well as supplying those products to the Xerox operating companies."[50] According to CEO Paul Allaire and Fuji Xerox President Yotaro Kobayashi, "It brings into a partnership the quality and strength of product development, manufacturing, marketing and customer service of both Xerox and Fuji Xerox. We hope to link our customers seamlessly with Xerox and Fuji Xerox while enhancing the position of our customers and our position as key players in the important and expanding low end printer business."[51]

MANAGEMENT

LEADERSHIP THROUGH QUALITY

In late 1983 Xerox embarked on a major new journey in its quest for quality and called it leadership through quality. It was a long-term process aimed at fundamentally changing the way Xerox employees work and

EXHIBIT 2-4

Document Processing

U.S. Marketing Group
Markets and services Xerox document processing products to major accounts and commercial customers.

Rank Xerox
Markets and services Xerox document processing products in more than 80 Eastern Hemisphere countries.

Americas Operations
Markets and services Xerox document processing products in Canada and more than 40 countries in North, South and Central America; the Caribbean; the Middle East and North Africa; and China and Hong Kong.

Fuji Xerox
Develops, manufactures, markets and services Fuji Xerox document processing products in Japan and other territories in the Pacific Rim, Australia and New Zealand.

Xerox Engineering Systems
Develops, manufactures, markets and services wide-format plotters, printers, reprographic equipment and systems for the worldwide engineering community.

Xerox Equipment Financing
Finances customer purchases of Xerox document processing products worldwide.

Development and Manufacturing
Develops and manufactures Xerox document processing products, including copiers, duplicators, electronic printers, facsimile products, scanners, network systems, workstations, computer software and supplies.

Corporate Research Group
Performs research and exploratory development to enable the transfer of technologies to the Development and Manufacturing organization.

Insurance and Other Financial Services

Crum and Forster, Inc.
Provides primarily commercial property and casualty insurance protection.

Xerox Life
Provides market-sensitive life insurance and annuity products.

Van Kampen Merritt Inc.
Offers fixed-income investment products, such as mutual funds and unit investment trusts, and provides investment advisory and capital market services.

Furman Selz
Provides institutional brokerage, investment banking, money management and other institutional financial services.

1990 Financial Summary

(Dollars in millions, except per-share data)	1990	1989	% Change
Revenues			
Document Processing	$13,583	$12,431	+ 9%
Insurance and Other Financial Services	4,390	4,798	− 9%
Total	$17,973	$17,229	+ 4%
Income			
Document Processing	$599	$488	+23%
Insurance and Other Financial Services	6	165	−97%
Income from Continuing Operations	605	653	− 7%
Discontinued Operations	(362)	51	*
Net Income	$243	$704	−66%
Primary Earnings (Loss) Per Share			
Continuing Operations	$5.51	$6.05	− 9%
Discontinued Operations	(3.85)	.51	*
Primary Earnings Per Share	$1.66	$6.56	−75%
Shareholder Value			
Book Value per Common Share	$53.73	$53.59	−
Dividends Declared per Common Share	$3.00	$3.00	−
Employees			
Document Processing	99,000	99,000	−
Insurance and Other Financial Services	11,000	11,600	− 5%
Total	110,000	110,600	− 1%

Calculation not meaningful.

Revenues
(dollars in billions)

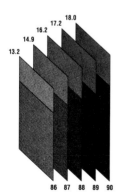

86 87 88 89 90

■ Insurance and Other Financial Services
■ Document Processing

**Primary Earnings Per Share:
Continuing Operations**
(dollars)

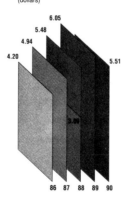

86 87 88 89 90

■ Before document
   processing restructuring

Return on Equity
(percent)

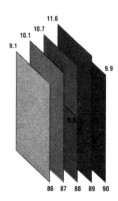

86 87 88 89 90

■ Before document
   processing restructuring

Total Company Revenue increased as a result of good growth in Document Processing, which more than offset a decline in Insurance and Other Financial Services revenue due primarily to lower capital gains. Earnings Per Share and Return on Equity declined as strong Document Processing income growth was offset by a reduction in Insurance and Other Financial Services income.

manage so they can continuously improve the way they meet the requirements of their customers.

According to then Chairman and CEO David T. Kearns, the largest single reason behind the leadership through quality initiative can be summarized in the words *cost* and *competition*. Kearns went on to say, "Today, more than 100 different companies make copying machines that compete directly with Xerox. And scores of companies—from industrial giants to small competitive entrepreneurs—make office systems one of the world's most competitive markets. Much the same situation exists in the office products and systems marketplace. Xerox market share dropped from a dominant position in the 1960s with high revenue and profit growth. By 1980, the trend began to exhibit itself in lower rates of revenue on assets: inadequate to maintain long-term business vitality." [52]

Xerox read the warning signals, and as a result major changes were put in place. Under the leadership of Mr. Kearns, Xerox began the long process of changing the way it managed its business. The turnaround Xerox has experienced since 1983 is attributed to the leadership through quality initiative. The top twenty-five senior operating executives from around the world, in a series of meetings spanning a 15-month period, developed the Xerox quality policy and the broad outlines of a quality strategy implementation plan, known as "the green book." [53]

The Xerox quality policy says: "Xerox is a quality company. Quality is the basic business principle for Xerox. Quality means providing our external and internal customers with innovative products and services that fully satisfy their requirements. Quality improvement is the job of every Xerox employee." [54]

The management team realized that implementing this view of quality into Xerox culture would require massive change. A strategy for change that was unique to Xerox was laid out for a five-year period, and it identified six mechanisms for change. The six mechanisms were: [55]

- *Management behavior and actions*:   Ensures that the management team—at all levels of the corporation—provides the necessary leadership, sets the right tone, and acts as an example for the successful implementation of leadership through quality. Managers must not only espouse the principles of leadership through quality but also practice them daily.
- *Transition teams*:   Guides the change process and supports line management in assuring consistent implementation.
- *Standards and measurements*:   Provides all Xerox employees with new ways of assessing and performing their work; solving problems; a nine-step quality improvement process; competitive benchmarking; an emphasis on error prevention and doing things right the first time; and techniques for determining the cost of quality.

- *Training*:   Provides every Xerox employee with an understanding of leadership through quality and a working knowledge of the tools and techniques for quality improvement. Training is delivered in "family groups," consisting of a manager and the employees who report to him/her, and includes the application of newly learned skills on a work group project.
- *Recognition and reward*:   Ensures that all employees are encouraged and motivated to practice the behaviors of leadership through quality. Both individuals and groups are recognized for their quality improvements.
- *Communications*:   Ensures that all Xerox employees are kept informed of the objectives and priorities of the corporation in general and their work group in particular. Communications include both formal media, such as magazines and films, and informal media, such as staff meetings.

Armed with quality policies and supporting mechanisms, Xerox in effect started an internal revolution in 1983. This revolution began Xerox's pursuit of the Baldridge award. Throughout this period, David Kearns, and later Paul Allaire, provided consistent leadership and guidance.

As a result of the implementation of leadership through quality, Xerox was able to shorten its production development cycle by 25 percent to 50 percent and improve the quality of incoming parts from 92 percent to 99.2 percent defect-free. This was achieved by implementing the quality program down to Xerox's vendors. Inventory was reduced from 5–6 months for production to 36–37 days for production. Also as a result of this new quality program, production costs were reduced by 40 percent.[56]

ADAPTIVE ORGANIZATION

In the past 4 years Xerox has slowly but surely led the way to a new mode of management—management by process. Instead of the old way of asking the boss for direction and waiting for weeks for upper management to make a decision, Xerox is forming a new mode of communication. Employees are placed in work teams and are trained to work closely with the work process and to come up with solutions for improvements even if it means temporarily leaving their regular jobs to join an ad hoc team to attack a problem. CEO Paul Allaire gave one reason for the move to a new adaptive organization. He said, "We're never going to outdiscipline the Japanese on quality. To win we need to innovate new ways to capture the creative and innovative spirit of the American worker."[57] Another problem that CEO Paul Allaire has recognized is that the competition has consistently beaten Xerox to the market with new innovative products.

In 1989 Xerox found out that it was not able to give its customers an exact date of delivery after receiving an order. This situation caused much embarrassment and led to customer dissatisfaction. As a new approach to the problem, Allaire assigned a seasoned middle manager to tackle the problem. Taking the initiative the manager pulled a group of people out of their regular jobs in functions such as distribution, accounting, and sales. The team developed a system that tracks each copier through the distribution process and makes sure that the computer and its accompanying paper work check out. Xerox boosted customer satisfaction, as measured by a company survey, from 70 percent to 90 percent. According to Xerox employee Sean Combs, "It is the challenge of constantly working on different projects and working with other areas of the company that makes my job here at Xerox very intriguing. I get to learn about other areas of the company and I feel that I am making a contribution to the total success of the organization."[58]

ADVERTISING

Over the years Xerox has come full circle with the themes and messages of its ads. Faced with improving the penetration of the office marketplace, Xerox wanted to decentralize copying and promote applications everywhere from engineering to the executive suite. In 1958 Haliod Xerox ran an ad depicting different situations at the office from executive meetings to idle gossip at the water cooler; the message was "every department of your business benefits from xerographic coping."

In 1971 the "owl" ads stressed the quality and value of Xerox copies. They implied that the copy quality equaled that of offset printing; Xerox copies were shown as having attained the stature of a Picasso original.[59]

In 1981 Xerox began selling the quality of convenience, such as easy two-sided reproduction, and since 1977 it has stressed the role of Xerox products in the office of the future. In 1991 the theme was "putting it all together." Through these ads Xerox is stressing the features of its new products, like DocuTech, which will bring together all the customers' existing hardware, software, and networks into an efficient data information management system. Through its ads Xerox has shown the company moving from a world of print and distribute to a world of distribute and print.[60]

Along with directly addressing the features and benefits in its ads, Xerox has also used environmental influences such as an appeal to a nation's cultural value to put its messages across. An example of this appeal was seen in a Xerox ad showing human hands of all different colors with the message, "A team that has no prejudice has no limits." In this ad Xerox expresses its support of egalitarianism, an important core value in American society.[61]

PUBLIC RELATIONS

Xerox executives are involved in various activities to help improve both society and Xerox's corporate image. Some of the areas in which they actively participate are environmental protection, U.S. education, nonprofit organizations, and customer relations.

SOCIAL SERVICES

The company has a twenty-year-old social service leave program that supports corporate involvement in the community. Xerox employees are loaned out to nonprofit organizations to contribute the skills they have obtained during their careers at Xerox. Typically, Xerox allocates 264 months of leave each year, and employees may apply for a one- to twelve-month leave of absence. A committee determines who is accepted and the length of the term. Regular Xerox salaries are paid to the employees during their leaves, and employees also retain their benefits and seniority. The factor that differentiates Xerox's community program from other companies' programs is that the ideas and activities originate with the employees. The range of social issues addressed are literacy, AIDS, child abuse, plight of the homeless, and chemical dependency. Xerox executives feel this program is a reflection of their commitment to the community.[62]

EDUCATION

A second public relations project on which Xerox is focusing is education in the United States. The emphasis on education began with David Kearns, who feels that the U.S. education system is a "national disaster."[63] His solution advocates a complete restructuring that will infuse education with competition and market principles. He feels that American business leadership is necessary to facilitate these changes. Knowledge concerning competition, the marketplace, quality processes, and management training are areas in which the corporate world can be of assistance.[64]

Xerox spends $260 million each year for vocational training for its workers. One of Xerox's top educators is currently on loan to the Washington, DC public school system for management training with principals, superintendents, and administrative staffs. A similar project is occurring in Rochester, NY.

Additionally, $5 million was contributed to the nonprofit Institute for Research on Learning to fund research of the use of computers in learning how people learn. The issue is efficiency in the American education system, not money. The U.S. spends twice as much per student as Japan, but is educating only 50 percent of the population compared to their 90 to 95 percent. Xerox is a member of the Business Roundtable, which consists of CEOs from the two hundred largest companies in the country. It is an organization committed to work with the education leaders in the states in which they are operating.[65]

ENVIRONMENTAL PROTECTION

Xerox is concerned about the planet earth and has integrated that concern into its business activities. The Xerox environment philosophy states, "Xerox is committed to leadership in environmental protection and has established a history of research and applied technology for environmental health and safety. Moreover, Xerox is committed to incorporating the latest advances in environmental technology into its products and operations worldwide."[66] The standards it sets go beyond government requirements for health, safety, and environmental protection. It created a corporate environmental health and safety organization to ensure integration across the corporation. Xerox is committed to environmental protection and conservation. These efforts focus on its facilities, product design, and operations. It intensified its efforts by establishing the environmental leadership program that focuses on resource conservation, recycling, and reuse.[67]

MINORITY PROGRAMS

Xerox participates actively in minority programs. It is dedicated to making the concept of equal opportunity a reality. Xerox developed programs in every phase of its structure, from pre-entry training up through the top of upper management. For its progress, it was awarded the Department of Labor Exemplary Voluntary Effort Award for affirmative action.[68]

CUSTOMER RELATIONS

Xerox began focusing on customer satisfaction in 1986 when Paul Allaire made it the company's number one priority, ahead of even market share and return on assets.[69] In the past three years, customer service ratings have improved by one-third. "Quality" is a chief corporate theme and cannot be dismissed as a public relations gimmick; it has improved customer relations dramatically. There has been a change in attitudes in the corporation because employees and management realize that by "doing it right the first time" they save money.[70] In 1990 Xerox introduced a three-year warranty with a "total satisfaction" plan to replace any machine at no extra cost with a comparable one if a customer is dissatisfied for any reason. This recent guarantee has further reinforced the customers' confidence in Xerox's product reliability and service.[71] It uses customer satisfaction and quality as a marketing tool and a competitive weapon. The strategy has paid off for Xerox; it was rated number one in its industry in product reliability and service by a Dataquest report.[72]

The Future

Chief executive officer Paul Allaire is betting on digital imaging for the future of Xerox. Digital imaging is a process that uses a fast, high-resolution electronic scanner and a high-speed printer rather than the traditional light-lens technology. Xerox's first entry was the DocuTech multifunctional machine. Its price is high; and because the current depressed market has dramatically decreased sales throughout the United States, the DocuTech entry has been less successful than anticipated. However, Allaire predicts that once the economy recovers, sales will pick up, and Xerox's entry into the digital imaging field will then reach its estimated sales.

Today digital systems represent only a fraction of Xerox's total sales. However, Allaire expects these systems to be the company's lifeblood within 10 years. In fact, Xerox recently released its first new color product in 5 years, the Xerox 4850 highlight color laser printing system, which is based on digital imaging technology. Xerox expects the new high-speed color copiers to compete directly with Canon's CLC line.

Japan's Canon targeted and quickly grabbed the lion's share of the low-volume copier market in the late 1980s; it has henceforth targeted Xerox's bread and butter, the high-margin, high-volume end of the market. Canon has also pursued digital imaging technology, which is a further indication that the trend in the market is toward this new technology. Xerox, however, has an edge over Canon because it has the direct sales and service forces needed to deal with large corporate customers. Xerox also possesses the software necessary to manage massive data flows crucial for this type of technology.

Through its total quality management philosophy, Xerox has regained market share from the Japanese. Xerox is continuing with the quality program and is working toward its goal of being *number 1* in the document processing industry. The industry is driven by customer needs; therefore, technology is driven by customer needs. Today's consumers are demanding digital imaging functionality combined with ease of use and service, and Xerox intends to compete successfully on a global basis based on its product quality and customer satisfaction.

NOTES

[1] Dumaine, B. "The Bureaucracy Busters," *Fortune,* June 17, 1991, 36.

[2] Jacobson, G., and J. Hillkirk. *Xerox, American Samurai,* New York: Macmillan, 1986.

[3] Dumaine, B., *Op. cit.,* 37.

[4] Jacobson, G., and J. Hillkirk, *Op. cit.,* 9.

[5] Norman, J. R. "Xerox Rethinks Itself—And This Could Be the Last Time," *Business Week,* February 13, 1989, 93.

[6] *Ibid.,* 92.

[7] *Ibid.,* 92.

[8] *Ibid.,* 91.

[9] Higgins, S. "PC Docs Adds Management Features to Delayed Upgrade," *PC Week,* May 27, 1991, 45.

[10] Hooper, L. "High-Tech Gamble: Xerox Tries to Shed Its Has-Been Image with Big New Machine," *The Wall Street Journal,* September 20, 1990, A8.

[11] "Electronic Imaging," *Fortune,* 158.

[12] Evans, S. "Copiers: A Mature Technology, Full of Innovation," *Industry Week,* May 21, 1990, 76.

[13] Hooper, L., *Op. cit.*

[14] Booker, E. "Low-Cost Imaging Tools Enter the PC Picture," *Computerworld,* May 27, 1991, 99.

[15] Moser, K. D. "Prime System to Ease Image Storage, Access," *PC Week,* July 1, 1991, 45.

[16] Higgins, S., *Op. cit.*

[17] Piyarali, A. "Product Standards Data System: For Online Document Management," *Industrial Engineering,* April 1991, 45.

[18] Belsie, L. "Makers of Computer Scanners Plan to Crack the Office Market," *The Christian Science Monitor,* August 16, 1991, 8.

[19] Vogel, T. "At Xerox, They're Shouting 'Once More into the Breach,'" *Business Week,* July 23, 1990, 62–63.

[20] Feder, B. J. "Xerox and DocuTech," *The New York Times,* October 3, 1990, C1, D1.

[21] Hewer, J. M. "What's New in Fax?" *CMA Magazine* (Canada), December 1990/January 1991, 21–22.

[22] Alvich-LoPinto, M. "The Plain Facts About Plain-Paper Fax," *Today's Office,* July 1991, 12–17.

[23] Norman, J. R. "Xerox on the Move," *Forbes,* June 10, 1991, 71.

[24] *Ibid.*, 71.

[25] Vogel, T., *Op. cit.*, 63.

[26] *Ibid.*, p. 63.

[27] Patalon, W. "Xerox's Made-to-Order Machines," *Democrat and Chronicle*, August 18, 1991.

[28] "Percolating," *The Economist*, May 18, 1991, 92.

[29] Cooke, J. A. "Xerox's Drive for Logistics Quality," *Traffic Management*, October 1990, 51.

[30] *Ibid.*, 52.

[31] "1989 Award Winner: Xerox," *Business America*, November 20, 1989, 11.

[32] "Court Issues Order to Xerox Canada Inc. in Competition Case," *The Wall Street Journal*, November 5, 1990, B5.

[33] Hetzer, B. "How Xerox Zapped the Japanese," *Business Month*, June 1989, 81.

[34] "1989 Award Winner: Xerox," *Op. cit.*, 10.

[35] Hirsch, J. S. "Salesforce: To One Xerox Man, Selling Photocopiers Is a Gambler's Game," *The Wall Street Journal*, September 24, 1991, A1.

[36] Xerox Copier/Duplicator and Accessory Sale Price List (Effective September 1, 1991).

[37] Xerox Federal Supply Schedule Price List (for the period of October 1, 1990 through September 30, 1993).

[38] Norman, J. R. "Xerox on the Move," *Forbes*, June 10, 1991, 71.

[39] Norman, J. R. "Xerox Rethinks Itself, and This Could Be the Last Time," *Business Week*, February 13, 1989, 91.

[40] Holusha, J. "Stress on Quality Raises Market Share at Xerox," *The New York Times*, November 9, 1989, D1.

[41] "Kodak Buys Out IBM Copier Business," *Purchasing*, June 16, 1988, 27.

[42] Norman, J. R. "Xerox Rethinks Itself, and This Could Be the Last Time," *Business Week*, February 13, 1989, 91.

[43] Bagot, B. "Fax Facts," *Marketing and Media Decisions*, December 1989, 129–140.

[44] Karayama, F. H. "Who's Fueling the Fax Frenzy?" *Fortune*, October 23, 1989, 151.

[45] Verity, J. W. "IBM Is Finally Saying: 'In UNIX We Trust,'" *Business Week*, February 12, 1990, 86.

[46] Hooper, L., *Op. cit.*, A1.

[47] "Xerox, The Document Company," *Annual Report*, March 8, 1991, 15.

[48] Barras-Hill, I. "EuroDirect," *Marketing (UK)*, November 3, 1988, 33–35.

[49] Gibson, F. "Xerox, Fuji Xerox Form U.S. Venture to Market Printers," *Financial World*, October 1, 1991.

[50] *Ibid.*

[51] *Ibid.*

[52] "The Xerox Quest for Quality," Xerox, 1990.

[53] *Ibid.*

[54] *Ibid.*

[55] *Ibid.*

[56] *Ibid.*

[57] Dumaine, B., *Op. cit.*, 38.

[58] *Ibid.*, 42.

[59] "Advertising Evolution," *Industry Week*, September 7, 1981, 98.

[60] Xerox, The Document Company," *Annual Report*, March 8, 1991, 6.

[61] Engel, J. F., R. D. Blackwell, and P. W. Miniard. *Consumer Behavior*, Chicago: The Dryden Press, 1990, 196–197.

[62] Halcrow, A. "Social Service at Xerox," *Personnel Journal*, March 1987, 10.

[63] Galagan, P. A. "David Kearns of Xerox: The Education Gap," *Institutional Investor*, December 1989, 47.

[64] Morrison, A. "Lessons for Xerox's Ex-Boss," *Fortune*, October 21, 1991, 133.

[65] Galagan, P. A., *Op. cit.*, 48.

[66] Xerox, The Document Company," *Annual Report*, March 8, 1991.

[67] Ibid., 23–26.

[68] *Best of Business*, "Xerox Wins Award," Summer 1990, 96.

[69] Norman, J. R., "Xerox Rethinks Itself, And This Could Be the Last Time," *Business Week*, February 13, 1989, 93.

[70] Samuelson, R. J. "Competition, Not Trade Restrictions, Will Protect U.S. Companies," *American Banker*, March 23, 1988, 6.

[71] Norman, J. R. "Xerox on the Move," *Forbes*, June 10, 1991, 71.

[72] Schlossberg, H. "Customer Satisfaction: Not a Fad, But a Way of Life," *Marketing News*, June 10, 1991, 18.

CASE 3

KINTETSU: A COMPANY AND ITS COMMUNITY *

Masahiro Katoh is a 30-year-old Osaka businessman working as a salesman in a medium-size manufacturing firm. He currently lives with his parents, as most single Japanese people do, and he commutes to work every Monday through Saturday by train, which takes a little more than an hour each way. In six months, Masahiro will be married. He is the oldest son in his family. The uniting of these two families will accomplish another in a long series of goals set down for him by his family when the doctor said, "Congratulations, it's a boy," some thirty years ago. He worked hard to pass tests, get into the right high school and university, find the right company, and now marry a woman with the right last name and proper upbringing who will hopefully be the mother of the next Katoh son.

Akiko Katsumi is a 26-year-old O.L., or "office lady," who lives with her parents and younger brother thirty minutes by train outside of Osaka, not far from the Katoh home. Although she attended a good university and is bilingual, she has been neither promoted nor given a decent raise in the four years she has been employed in the nation's third largest bank. The company has been slow to promote her because they know that the Katsumi family has been eagerly searching for a husband for Akiko, and as is the norm in most cases, the Japanese woman is expected to quit her job when she gets married so she can devote her time to having children and keeping a household. Since Akiko does not have a car and does not pay anything for room or board, all of her income can be considered discretionary. Since graduating from college, she has traveled extensively throughout North America and Hawaii and has never been shy about spending money on clothes and accessories. She wears the latest fashions

---

*This case was prepared by Robert Hurley under the direction of Professor Roger D. Blackwell at The Ohio State University.

445

from Tokyo, New York, and Paris, except, of course, for the green uniform she must wear to work five days a week. After all this, she has little in the way of savings, but she is far from worried about her financial stability.

Three months ago, a meeting was arranged between Akiko and Masahiro by a third party, or *omiai*. This was not a traditional date but rather a chance for the two families to find acceptable marriage partners for their children. Masahiro's parents, who knew that their son was approaching his thirties and was still single, felt that he needed to settle down and have a family. The Katoh name was in jeopardy of dying out, and his parents were quite concerned. For a fee, Akiko and Masahiro met and, although it was not love at first sight, each saw in the other a person who could fulfill respective needs and satisfy the families involved. Within ninety days of the couple's first meeting, a wedding date was set.

It is a Sunday morning and the future Mr. and Mrs. Katoh are going to spend the day making plans for the life they will spend married to each other. At 10:00 A.M. Masahiro arrives by taxi to pick up Akiko. Enter Kintetsu. Here the relationship is born. The taxi is owned by Kintetsu. The couple are driven to the nearest train station, a mere three minutes away. They board a Kintetsu train bound for Osaka. After a twenty-five minute ride, the train pulls into Kintetsu-Abeno station in south-central Osaka.

Less than two minutes later, the two have entered the Kintetsu Department Store, which is located above Kintetsu-Abeno station. They are immediately greeted at the door and escalator by a Kintetsu employee, who shouts "welcome" to the thousands of customers who visit the Abeno department store every Sunday. Most of the shoppers are overworked fathers, impatient mothers, and *genki*, or lively children who are happy not be studying.

The couple head straight to the eighth floor where the Kintetsu travel pavilion is located. They are eager to make their honeymoon plans. During Golden Week, the first full week in May, the couple will fly to Sydney, Australia for a five-day honeymoon. While Akiko is busy making the arrangements with the travel agent, Masahiro walks over to the Osaka Passport Agency to obtain a passport. He uses a cash machine so he can pay for the deposit on the honeymoon. Because most Japanese travel during Golden Week, prices are exceptionally high, and Masahiro has worked hard to save up for this trip.

After the itinerary is set, the couple go back down to the fourth floor and the Kintetsu bridal salon. Akiko has another fitting for her dress, and Masahiro looks over tuxedo choices. They also have to choose kimonos to go along with their Western-style wedding apparel. Most Japanese weddings have two ceremonies: a traditional Shinto wedding and a Western-style wedding. After that, the couple head to the ninth floor for lunch with both sets of parents. Plans and choices are discussed over French food.

After lunch, the men and women split up into two groups. The women head to floors one, two, and three to the European boutiques while the men head up to the roof to the Kintetsu golf school to hit some balls and momentarily escape the wedding hype. Fifty or so swings later, the six meet on the tenth floor to reserve a banquet room for the wedding reception. The group of six once again becomes two as Masahiro and Akiko head to one of the more than twenty coffee and dessert cafés that are a frequent sight in Japanese department stores.

After a short break, the couple head to the used car department to look at pictures of hundreds of used cars. Without having to move thirty feet, the couple then sit with a financial advisor who assists them with investing for a future house and family. Exhausted, Masahiro and Akiko head to "Kintetsu Studio 100" to watch the latest film from Hollywood.

At 6:00 P.M. the couple head to the basement and board a crowded Kintetsu express train and sleep the rest of the way home. They both know that in the weekends to come, they will be back at Kintetsu to look at kitchen appliances, wedding gifts, luggage, and even a new home.

Shinichi Katsumi is a 43-year-old engineer living in Nara city, about thirty minutes from downtown Osaka. He and his wife and two children are excited about the upcoming weekend. He and his family have a rare three-day weekend in which they will travel and take in a baseball game. Early Friday afternoon, the foursome board a Kintetsu train bound for Fujidera Stadium, located southeast of Osaka city in Osaka prefecture. The Seibu Lions baseball team is in town to play a weekend series with the hometown Kintetsu Buffaloes. Both teams have traditionally held the top two spots in the Pacific League for the past five years, and both teams are famous for their home-run-hitting American imports. Nine innings later the Kintetsu Buffaloes are triumphant, and an excited Katsumi family heads home on the Kintetsu express. Tired, they take a Kintetsu taxi home and head to bed early, knowing full well that the next forty-eight hours will be spent trying to cram a week's vacation into two days.

At 6:30 A.M. the family is already at the station ready to board the next express. Some thirty minutes later, they will board a second train, the Kintetsu Urban Liner for the ocean resort towns of Ise-Shima and Kashikojima in Mie prefecture. About 9:30 A.M. the train pulls into Kashikojima where a van is waiting for them. The driver is an employee of the Shima Kanko Hotel, which is owned by Kintetsu. From the train station he will personally take the family to the front door of the hotel and assist with their check-in. Now settled into their rooms, the Katsumis have no time to waste. *Otoosan* (meaning father) looks over the itinerary that was tailor-made by a travel agent at the Kinki Nippon Tourist Company, a member of the Kintetsu Group, located at the Uehonmachi Kintetsu Department Store in downtown Osaka:

Saturday	12:00	Lunch at the hotel (Japanese style)
"	1:15	Board Kintetsu bus for Ise Bay
"	1:45	Board Kintetsu hydrofoil cruise
"	1:50–3:50	Ise Bay cruise
"	4:00–5:00	Shopping/free time
"	5:15	Return to hotel
"	7:00	Dinner to be served in room
Sunday	7:00	Breakfast to be served in room
"	8:45	Check-out
"	9:00	Board Kintetsu sightseeing bus for Ise shrine
"	10:00–12:00	Sightseeing at Ise shrine
"	12:15–1:00	Lunch at shrine
"	1:15	Board bus for Toba aquarium
"	2:00–4:00	Toba aquarium tour
"	4:00–5:00	Shopping/free time
"	5:15	Board bus for Ise Bay sunset dinner cruise
"	6:00	Board Kintetsu cruise
"	6:15–7:45	Ise Bay sunset dinner cruise
"	6:30	Dinner (on ship)
"	8:00	Board bus for Ise station
"	8:30	Board Kintetsu Limited Express for Nara (change of trains at Yagi and Saidaiji stations)

Mr. Katsumi grimaces a bit at the regimented schedule because he knows he will need another vacation just to recover from this one.

Haru Ikeda is a 34-year-old housewife and mother of two young girls. She lives in a medium-sized bedroom community, a Kintetsu "new town" about 45 minutes by Kintetsu express from downtown Osaka. Her husband is a section chief at an insurance company in Osaka. They live in a new but small house and own a new car. The day officially starts early with Mr. Ikeda taking the 7:05 A.M. express into the big city. The train is already packed with commuters, but this is nothing compared to the nearly two-hour car ride where some of his neighbors spend more time sitting bumper-to-bumper on narrow expressways than they do driving.

By 8:00 A.M. Haru already has the older child off to school and the younger one fed and ready to hit the road. They too are off on a journey of sorts. Before 4:00 P.M. the two will take in a play, see an art exhibition, purchase and mail holiday gifts to family, friends, and company employees, ride a merry-go-round, buy a new purse, buy a flea collar for the family dog, eat lunch at an Italian restaurant, and buy enough fresh fish, beer, and sake for tonight's big dinner with the in-laws. They will come in contact with dozens of salespersons and clerks. In a short period of time, the two will have visited a theater, a gallery, an amusement park, a boutique, a catalogue and delivery service, a supermarket, and a liquor shop. Subtract the one hour commute, and Haru and her daughter will accomplish in less than five hours what would take most Americans days to complete. Is it possible?

The answer is yes. Kintetsu has put the world's most extensive and all-inclusive shopping mall under one roof and made it accessible and convenient to the more than sixteen million people living in the Kansai area. Not only is it possible, but similar scenarios are carried out by millions of Japanese each week. With several large and prestigious department stores competing within a few miles of Kintetsu, this giant conglomerate cannot afford to let up. From transportation to consumer goods, services, tourism, and entertainment, for more than eighty years Kintetsu has been building a relationship with the people of central Japan that not only goes beyond the front doors of traditional retailers but to the front doors of its customers as well.

The Japanese Zaibatsu

During the Meiji period, which began in 1868 and ended in 1912, Japan saw increases in growth that were matched only during the post World War II era. Out of this growth came changes that directly affect the Japan of today more than any other time in Japanese history. This era began when Commodore Perry and his American fleet of "black ships" pulled into Tokyo Bay, thus reinforcing Japan's long and deep-rooted fears of outsiders. Japan responded by building a military force that could not only protect it from "barbarians" but also enable Japan to capture foreign lands to create markets for its products and to gain access to resources that a developing and naturally unendowed Japan desperately needed, just as European nations had been doing centuries before.

Japan went on to establish itself as a military power with victories over China and Russia around the turn of the century. It also established itself as an economic power, first in the textiles industry, because Japan could be competitive due to its low labor costs and access to large yet poor Asian markets, and second, in a large ship-building industry, a result of Japan's growing military forces. In addition, unlike its Western counterparts, a strong bond was developing between government and big business in the form of government-guided mergers and cartels. Out of this relationship came the monolithic *zaibatsu*.[1]

EXHIBIT 3-1   THE NO-NONSENSE GUIDE TO DOING BUSINESS IN
JAPAN, P. 115.

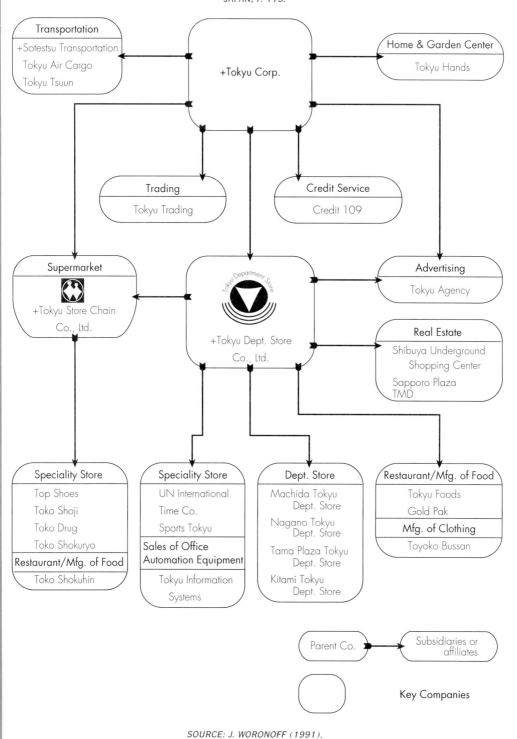

SOURCE: J. WORONOFF (1991).

Generally speaking, the *zaibatsu*, or financial clique, was a centrally run, family-owned holding company that usually controlled a large number of industrial companies, which in turn operated an even larger number of smaller companies. All of these companies, which routinely numbered well over a hundred (as they do today), centered around one financial institution. The original *zaibatsus* included Mitsui, Mitsubishi, Sumitomo, and Yasuda. Similar to the feudal lords of medieval Europe and Japan, these families developed strong ties among their upper-level managers and executives, mostly through the initiation of lifetime employment policies. These policies are still evident today since 15–20 percent of all Japanese workers stay with the same company from the time they leave school until retirement.[2] Instead of using profits for the purchase of material goods, these companies wisely reinvested profits in the expansion of their economic empires.

After World War II, occupation reforms called for the dissolution of the *zaibatsu's* wealth and power, dismantling the power of the individual families and spreading the wealth among Japan's citizens.[3]

Today, the spirit and the paternalistic attitudes of the *zaibatsus* are still alive although these conglomerates are commonly referred to as a *keiretsu*. Examples of today's *keiretsu* include the four previously mentioned companies plus Matsushita, the electronics giant (also known as Panasonic), Toyota, the auto company, Tokyu and Seibu, which are larger versions of Kintetsu, located in Tokyo. Within these groups, manufacturing, provision of raw materials, and financing are coordinated among the member companies.[4] Exhibit 3-1 presents an illustration of the structure of one such conglomerate, the Tokyu Retail and Distribution Group.

THE KANSAI

The Kansai area consists of seven prefectures covering 33,070 square kilometers, an area roughly the size of the state of Maryland. While Tokyo may be the brain of Japan, the Kansai is the soul. From A.D. 710 to 1185 the first capitals of ancient Japan were established in Nara city and Kyoto.[5] This area boasts the largest concentration of temples and monasteries, several of which are more than eight hundred years old, as well as the world's largest and oldest wooden structures. Many Japanese art forms, such as Kabuki and the tea ceremony, originated in the Kansai and are still a trademark of the area today. The Kansai is also famous for its unique dialect, which is centuries old and is still widely used today, especially among Osaka's merchants. Each prefecture also has its own unique variation of the dialect.

As of 1991, the population of the Kansai was about 21.8 million people, roughly one-sixth the country's total population. The second largest city in Japan after Tokyo is Osaka city, or the "cement jungle" as it is sometimes called, which has a population of about 2.6 million people who live in only 610 square kilometers, an area approximately the size of the city of Cleveland, which has a population of 500,000. It is both an industrial city and a port city lying on the Seto Inland Sea. It is surrounded by mountains to the east and north and the city of Kobe with its 1.4 million residents to the west. Osaka is an important city in Japanese history, yet little of ancient Osaka can be seen today. Most of the city burned down during the fire-bombings of World War II, and therefore most of the temples, shrines, and even the famous Osaka Castle were all destroyed. This destruction created the foundation for transforming one of Japan's oldest towns into Japan's most modern metropolis. While the neighboring prefectures and towns are steadily growing as overcrowding in the big cities worsens, much of the land still consists mostly of rolling green mountains, rice fields, picturesque villages, shrines, temples, and gardens beyond the bedroom communities. Exhibit 3-2 shows a map of Japan superimposed over the Eastern United States. Notice the size of the Kansai area, which stretches from Kobe to Nagoya, as compared to the United States.

THE KINTETSU GROUP

In an era of unprecedented industrial growth in Japan, the Kintetsu (pronounced "keen-teh-tsu") Corporation (Kintetsu, literally translated as "near" and "iron," is actually an abbreviation for the company's full name of Kinki Nippon Tetsudou Kabushiki Gaisha, or Kinki Nippon Railway Co., Ltd.) was founded as the Osaka Electric Railway Company, Ltd. in 1910. Eighty years and two world wars later, it has grown from a small, single-purpose railway company into an enormous international conglomerate consisting of more than 82,000 employees working in 157 companies operating in Asia, North America, Europe, and the Pacific. Net sales of Kintetsu Group members generated almost $25 billion from April of 1990 to March of 1991.[6] Exhibit 3-3 shows a profile of the Kintetsu Group as of March 1991. The figures are in U.S. dollars.

THE KINTETSU RAILWAY

With 370 miles of track and nearly 2,000 railway cars, the Kinki Nippon Railway Company not only is the largest private railway in all of Japan but also represents the largest holder of capital stock and the second largest employer in the Kintetsu group. On an average day, Kintetsu trains carry approximately 2.1 million passengers to and from Osaka city, Nagoya, Kyoto, Nara city, and nearly every town and tourist attraction in between.[7]

While the extent of the network is limited to a relatively small geographic region, Kintetsu's frequent express services to Osaka, Kyoto, and Nagoya help passengers hook up with the Japan Railway's *shinkansen* (bullet trains), which service most major metropolitan centers between Sendai

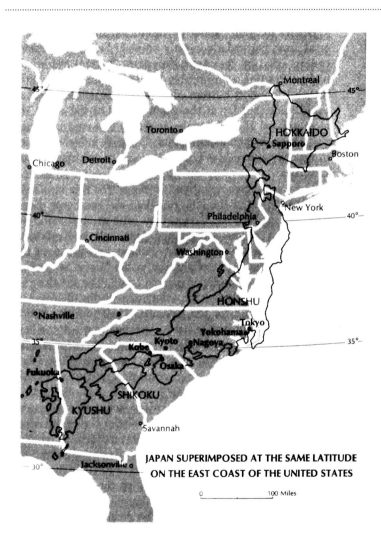

JAPAN SUPERIMPOSED AT THE SAME LATITUDE
ON THE EAST COAST OF THE UNITED STATES

0 ———————— 100 Miles

EXHIBIT 3-2

JAPAN: THE STORY OF A NATION, P. 5.

SOURCE:

E. REISCHAUER (1981).

EXHIBIT 3-3   PROFILE OF KINTETSU GROUP

SOURCE: THE KINTETSU CORPORATION, OSAKA

Type of business	No. of Com- panies	Capital Stock (in millions)	Net Sales (in millions)	No. of Employees	Remarks
Railroad transportation	1	755.0	2,140.0	12,030	Kinki Nippon Railway Co., Ltd. Length of railroad line: 370 miles (595.2km), 1,938 cars
Bus transportation	13	58.3	764.1	7,680	Mie Kotsu Co., Ltd. Nara Kotsu Bus Lines Co., Ltd., etc. Length of bus lines: 10,300 miles (16,573km), 4,274 Vehicles
Taxicabs and car rental	28	7.5	336.7	5,950	Kintetsu Taxi Co., Ltd. etc., 3,174 taxicabs, 3,264 car rentals
Trucking and air cargo	4	235.0	2,616.7	20,160	Fukuyama Transporting Co., Ltd. Kintetsu Freight & Trucking Ser. Co. Ltd. etc. Length of truck lines: 13,269 miles (21,350km), 15,444 trucks
Ferryboats and hydrofoils	5	10.8	65.8	410	Ise-wan Ferry Co., Ltd. etc. Length of lines: 437 miles (703km), 39 ships
Travel agencies	6	42.5	6,016.7	6,460	Kinki Nippon Tourist Co., Ltd. etc. 366 sales offices (348 in Japan/18 overseas)
Hotels and Japanese inns	28	135.0	833.3	5,500	Miyako Hotel, Ltd. Miyako Hotel Tokyo, Ltd. etc. 22 hotels, 5,606 rooms, 29 Japanese inns, 1,124 rooms

Department stores and supermarkets	9	61.7	4,551.7	8,870	Kintetsu Department Store Co., Ltd. etc. dept. stores: 318,540 sq. meters (18 stores), supermarkets: 72,198 sq. meters (98 stores)
Food service	9	10.0	507.5	2,640	Kintetsu Kanko Co., Ltd. etc. Highway services, restaurants, coffee shops: 322 shops and restaurants (28,207 seats), stalls: 368 shops
Recreation and entertainment	14	23.3	219.2	1,580	Kinki Eiga Gekijo Co., Ltd. Kintetsu Kogyo Co., Ltd. etc. 5 amusement parks, 8 golf courses, 4 bowling alleys, 4 movie theaters, playhouses, 1 baseball stadium
Automobile sales and service	10	7.5	569.2	1,340	Kintetsu Motors Co., Inc. etc. 18,540 new and used car sales per year
Real estate and development	12	70.8	1,438.3	1,710	Kintetsu Real Estate Co., Ltd. etc.
Manufacturing, construction, and other businesses	18	135.8	4,870.0	8,570	The Kinki Sharyo Co., Ltd. Dai Nippon Construction etc.
Total	157	1,553.3	24,929.2	82,900	

in northern Honshu and Fukuoka, located on the island of Kyushu in western Japan. This makes most of Japan accessible by train in less than eight hours for a huge majority of Kansai residents. While the Kinki Nippon Railway Company may be the largest private railway company in Japan, it faces competition on some lines from the Japan Railway Company, or JR. Kintetsu goes relatively unchallenged in most parts of the Kansai, especially in the smaller towns that dot the map in between the bigger cities. This is due to Kintetsu's larger investments in multiple track lines, which increase the number of trains per hour and decrease travel time because trains heading in different directions are not sharing the same tracks. Kintetsu's stiffest competition is in the battle for passengers between Osaka and Nagoya, Japan's two largest and most important centers of industry outside of Tokyo.

Three years ago Kintetsu carried only about one million limited express passengers a year to and from Osaka and Nagoya, or 2739 passengers a day. The limited express used in this case refers to those trains that run nonstop between the two cities. Several other less expensive yet slower trains run as well. Based on current prices, with the dollar equal to ¥120, Kintetsu's average daily gross profit was $79,888. In looking at four different factors in comparing the two companies (Kintetsu and JR), travel time was obviously shorter on the high-speed JR bullet trains. This was a definite advantage for those businessmen who needed to conduct business in both cities in less than a day.

The following factors were examined to determine competitive advantages:

- Fare
- Frequency—number of trains leaving one city at one time
- Accommodation—i.e., leg room, size of chairs, width of aisles
- Travel time—the time it takes by train from Osaka to Nagoya and vice versa

Along with the introduction of the Urban Liner and adjustments in the seating and capacity designs, Kintetsu was able to pull ahead of JR in the area of accommodation, which made the slower ride more comfortable and thus more enjoyable for passengers.

Table 3-1 examines the four factors in determining competitive advantages between the JR Shinkansen and the Kintetsu Urban Liner.

While JR has a definite advantage over Kintetsu in both travel time and frequency, Kintetsu can offer its riders 20 percent more room, which is a 30 percent increase over the last three years, at a price that is 47 percent lower than that of JR. While JR may currently have the majority share of business passengers, Kintetsu is making a profit on those riders who wish to save money and whose schedules are not as rigid as, say, those business passengers whose time commitments outweigh saving money. Families who had up until now taken very expensive train rides or ridiculously long car rides (considering the actual mileage and the lack of convenient road-ways) finally have an option that is more comfortable and cheaper than the *shinkansen* and much, much faster than the family car.

The location of each company's Osaka terminal was also an important factor. The Urban Liner departs daily from Kintetsu's Namba terminal. Namba is essentially the heart of Osaka, with numerous shopping malls, department stores, and Kabuki theaters all surrounding Namba station and, in some cases, on top of Namba station. Namba, along with Hon-machi and Umeda, form the business district of Osaka. Three subway lines (a fourth is only minutes away by foot) and one other private line in ad-dition to the Kintetsu line service Namba station, making it and Umeda station the two largest and most accessible stations in the Kansai area. To the north of these stations lie Shin-Osaka Station, where all of JR's bullet trains stop. Unlike Namba, this station is serviced by only one subway line. The point here is that while travel by *shinkansen* is currently much faster than travel by Urban Liner, the majority of business travelers find Namba station's location much more convenient than Shin-Osaka, and therefore much of the time saved traveling by the more expensive Shinkansen is lost on the way to the station.

Kintetsu is also proud of the relatively low number of strikes it has experienced in comparison to its competitors. Many of its railway workers are from small towns where their families are well known. In the words of Mr. Shigefuji, "If railway worker A is on strike and this strike causes complications for his neighbors in the way of lost wages or incon-venience, what kind of relationship would worker A have with his or her community?"

Kintetsu also hires a large number of men who are the second and third sons of farmers. These sons have few obligations and therefore have fewer expenses, as many of them live at home and receive compensation for work done on the family farm. This fact, along with the overall general concern Kintetsu has for the community it serves, account for fewer lost hours than other private railway companies in the region.

Since 1988's figures, Kintetsu has gained an additional 400,000 riders, many of whom are business travelers who, until now, had seen the JR

Company	Fare	Frequency	Accommodation	Travel Time	
JR	$54.00[b]	6–7/hour	100%[a]	1:10	**TABLE 3-1**
Kintetsu	$29.00[b]	1/hour	120%	2:00	KINTETSU VERSUS JR

[a] JR's accommodation is set equal to 100%
[b] These figures were based on 1991 statistics using $1 = ¥120

shinkansen as the only option. Once again, based on current prices, this increase translates into an additional $11.67 million a year in gross profits. Kintetsu successfully gained market share without increasing the speed or dramatically improving the technology of its Urban Liner.

KINTETSU TRANSPORTATION SERVICES

In addition to its railway service, Kintetsu also owns and operates a large number of cargo and passenger transportation companies. The trucking and air cargo companies alone represent Kintetsu's largest employers in the Kintetsu Group, more than 20,000 employees worldwide. Kintetsu World Express, Inc., or KWE, the largest and most experienced air cargo company in Japan, has offices and terminals in twenty-three cities nationwide plus several overseas offices operated by seven Kintetsu subsidiaries in the United States, Canada, Europe, Hong Kong, and Taiwan. The Kintetsu Freight & Trucking Service Co. and the Fukuyama Transportation Co., Ltd. are two of Kintetsu's bigger subsidiaries serving Japan's trucking industry. With almost 15,000 trucks and 13,000 miles of routes serving the four main islands, Kintetsu is the second largest trucking company in Japan.[8]

Kintetsu and fourteen of its subsidiaries provide bus service for Japan using a fleet of 4,300 buses covering 8,750 miles of scheduled routes. Kintetsu also operates 3,200 taxicabs through its twenty-eight subsidiaries in most of central and western Japan.[9]

In addition, there are thirty-eight Kintetsu car rental agencies located in metropolitan areas along the Kintetsu Railway network. Through an association with Nippon-Rent-a-Car Service Company, Kintetsu can service businesspeople and tourists alike nationwide.[10]

KINTETSU DEPARTMENT STORES AND SUPERMARKETS

In 1936, on the south side of Osaka city, Kintetsu's Abeno Department Store was opened. Today it claims to be the largest department store in Japan, covering 66,000 square meters over fourteen floors and employing 5,300 full- and part-time workers. Its eighteen stores are located in fifteen cities throughout the Kansai and Tokyo as well. Exhibit 3-4 shows Kintetsu's Abenobashi store, located on top of the Kintetsu Abenobashi train station.

These "multi-storied shopping centers" sell everything from women's lingerie to live shrimp. They house travel agencies, movie theaters, art galleries, amusement parks, driving ranges, passport agencies, banquet halls, wedding consultants, nurseries, and ticket outlets. Kintetsu's Nara store even has a television studio that broadcasts live over monitors located throughout the store. These centers also have shops that sell every food item imaginable, including a liquor store and a supermarket selling fresh meats, fish, fruits, and vegetables, as well as dozens of restaurants and coffee shops. Located on the basement floors of the Abenobashi store is the Coquelin Aine Boutique, a deluxe food gallery, Sweets Street with dozens of self-sufficient bakeries, and the Gourmet Food Avenue, which sells the finest wines, teas, coffees, and dried foods that are popular gift items during the holiday seasons.

After World War II, a train company president revolutionized the retail business in Japan. Ichizo Koyabashi, the founder of Hankyu Rail Lines, a similar but smaller version of the Kinki Nippon Railway Company that connects Kyoto, Osaka, and Kobe, began selling housing sites along his rail lines to create more passengers for his company. He went a step further and put a Hankyu Department Store at one end of his line. This development brought housewives into the city and created even more riders for his lines.[11] His Umeda Department Store, one of eight, is located

EXHIBIT 3-4

KINTETSU'S ABENO
DEPARTMENT STORE

on top of Hankyu's Umeda Station, which sits across the street from two rival department stores, Hanshin (famous for its baseball team) and Daimaru, considered to be one of the highest class department stores in Japan (see Exhibit 3-5). Both stores are located above train stations; the Hanshin Umeda terminal and the JR Osaka station, respectively.

Below each store is a series of shopping malls, and below them are three subway lines. These malls, which are lined with small restaurants, bars, clothing and electronic shops, all are connected to form a huge and congested underground shopping network.

Among Kintetsu's members, the department stores face perhaps the stiffest competition of any subsidiary. In Japan, a lot of consideration goes into deciding what gift to buy for a particular person. In Japan, the most important aspect of buying a gift is the image of the department store from which the item is purchased.

In Japan, there are three major types of retail outlet that sell consumer goods:

1. *Kouriten*: The smallest and most abundant, these shops sell everything from electronics to toys and umbrellas and are popularly known as "mom and pop" stores in the west.
2. *Suupaa*: These stores, which take their name from the word "supermarket," are found much less frequently. *Suupaas* usually

 EXHIBIT 3-5

cover more than one floor and are Japan's version of Meijer's, an American supermarket, although Japan's *suupaas* are never open 24 hours a day. The emphases are on selection, especially in perishable food items, and on price. These stores can be found in the big cities as well as in small towns.

3. *Depaato*: These are the enormous, multi-storied department stores that sell "everything and then some" under one roof; Kintetsu is a perfect example. They are found in every metropolitan center in Japan and in many bedroom communities as well. The emphases here are on elegance, store appearance, selection, and service, and thousands of workers are employed in each store. In some ways a typical Japanese department store resembles New York City's Macy's department store.

Other types of stores, including specialty stores and discount shops, are discussed later.

When examining the Japanese buying habits for goods such as clothing and food items, goods that are traditionally bought by housewives, we can make several assumptions: food and related items for personal consumption tend to be bought from *suupaas*, which offer the best selection and the lowest prices. Older housewives who may not live near a *suupaa* generally tend to buy from *kouritens*, whose owners are neighbors as well as shopkeepers, and therefore a certain obligation is felt by those who live near these small "mom and pop" stores. Depending on the item, housewives usually head to a department store for expensive goods, such as dresses or sweaters, while choosing to shop at a *suupaa* for cheaper items and children's clothes.

Now comes the difficult part. Deciding which department store to buy from is not easy, for each department store's name carries a certain image, and there are several opinions as to which stores are the best. The problems arise when one is buying an item, not for oneself, but as a gift for another person. When a gift is purchased in Japan, it is usually wrapped by a store employee in the store's own wrapping paper with the store's name and logo brightly displayed on top.

In many cases, what is inside the wrapping is not as important as what is written on top. In the case of a gift, it is considered in bad taste to buy the present from a *suupaa* and then have it wrapped in the store's personal wrapping paper. (It is important to note here that almost all goods purchased from a *suupaa* or *depaato* are wrapped in paper in order to cut down on shoplifting and to promote the company.) For example, if a gift is to be purchased for the husband's boss, then the housewife (or single man or woman) would go to Daimaru or Takashimaya, the two most expensive and glamorous department stores in downtown Osaka. Regardless of the purchase, the boss in this example would know that his (or her) employee has integrity and good taste as long as the gift came from one of these stores.

Kintetsu, which falls somewhere in the middle, competes with four other Kansai-based, nationally known department store chains and several other Tokyo-based stores in Osaka city alone. Each store is elegant in its own unique way. For example, at Sogo Department Stores, brass chandeliers adorn the ceilings. At Hankyu, "elevator girls" (Exhibit 3-6) greet customers at the elevators while other young and attractive female employees keep the escalator railings dust-free while saying *irasshaimase*, or welcome, to every customer who rides the escalators. In much the same manner, customers who leave a certain department at Kintetsu on a busy Sunday will hear *arigatoo gozaimashta*, or thank you, from every single employee in the vicinity, and often in unison.

These stores also have internationally known companies leasing space within the store itself. The Hankyu-Umeda store has a Sharper Image and a Cartier Boutique, while Kintetsu-Abeno has a Laura Ashley, a Crabtree & Evelyn, and a Polo department all inside its doors—a "store within a store." Kintetsu, as well as its competitors, cashes in on its "Westernness." It is no secret that the Japanese are entranced with everything Western, from Mickey Mouse to Elvis. In the Kintetsu department stores, pic-

EXHIBIT 3-6
ELEVATOR GIRLS AT
HANKYU DEPARTMENT
STORE

tures of Michael Jackson, America's Cup winner Dennis Conner, and James Dean are everywhere selling blue jeans, boat shoes, and stereos, while television monitors play clips from the Indy 500 Race and the latest Hollywood blockbusters.

Kintetsu competes with the nationally known *suupaas* as well, mostly in the supermarket business. Kintetsu must be able, day-in and day-out, to offer the freshest and most complete selection of fish, meats, produce, and pastries for demanding Japanese consumers. Kintetsu also competes, albeit to a lesser extent, with the "mom and pop" stores that rely entirely on service to sell their products.

In 1990, Kintetsu's 18 department stores, 98 supermarkets, and its nearly 8,900 employees generated more than $4.5 billion in net sales, the third highest among all of Kintetsu's group members.[12]

It is important to remember that which train line a customer lives on greatly determines which department store he or she patronizes. This statement does not take into account, however, the competition by group member real estate companies to sell next to and around their companies' train lines.

KINTETSU TRAVEL AGENCIES AND RELATED COMPANIES

With more than 348 offices nationwide, 18 offices overseas, and over 6,400 employees that generate a net sales figure in excess of $6 billion in 1991,[13] the Kinki Nippon Tourist Company, Ltd., is one of the largest travel agencies in Japan, second only to the Japan Travel Bureau, or JTB. Located throughout Japan and the world as well, with locations in the United States, Europe, Southeast Asia, Guam, and Saipan, Kintetsu can cover all of its customers' travel needs both at home and abroad.

Kintetsu, in association with Gray Line, Inc., an American bus company, is involved in Japan's most popular form of domestic travel, touring by bus. Kintetsu plans and manages sightseeing tours for Japanese and foreign tourists in Nara and Kyoto. Kintetsu also operates bus companies in Tokyo, Osaka, Nagoya, and in western Japan. Many of these buses use scenic toll roads that are constructed and operated by Kintetsu. In addition to bus companies, Kintetsu operates a number of aerial trams and sightseeing cruises in and around the Kansai area.

Kintetsu operates the well-known, Western-style Miyako hotels, with fifteen located in Tokyo, the Kansai, Kyushu, and Okinawa. Two Miyako hotels were recently opened in the United States; the first was opened in

San Francisco and the second was opened in Los Angeles in 1992. In addition to the hotels, Kintetsu also operates 30 *ryokans*, or Japanese-style inns, mostly in western Japan.[14]

When Kintetsu Group members are broken down by industry (tourism, transportation, retailing, manufacturing/construction, and real estate/development), companies that are involved in tourism accounted for 30 percent of Kintetsu's total revenues in 1990. Since 1980, Kintetsu's tourism-related companies increased their revenues from ¥372 billion to ¥909 billion in 1990, or a 144 percent increase over the last eleven years.[15] Since 1982, these companies have contributed the largest share of Kintetsu's revenue among its five industrial sectors.

KINTETSU REAL ESTATE

Founded in 1968, the Kintetsu Real Estate Co., Ltd., or KRE, is one of the largest real estate development companies in Japan, with net sales of over U.S. $1.4 billion in 1990 and some 1,700 employees nationwide in Tokyo, Nagoya, Hiroshima, Nara, and Osaka. KRE is involved in several businesses, including the construction, sale, and management of housing, buildings, and condominium complexes. KRE also is involved in the management of parking lots (big business in a densely populated industrial country) and golf courses. KRE, through a subsidiary, also engages in real estate brokerage activities and offers consultations to individual property owners.

KRE may be best known as one of Japan's leading private residential developers. In the hills between Osaka city and Nara city is the Gakuen-mae New Town, Kintetsu's most widely publicized project to date. This affluent bedroom community covers 860 acres and includes more than 6,000 homes housing more than 23,000 people. This community is all situated within Kintetsu's Gakuenmae train station. Nearing completion is a similar project in Nabari, between Osaka city and Nagoya. Soon it will provide housing for 30,000 people.[16]

In resort areas such as Ise-Shima National Park, located in the southwestern part of the Kansai, KRE is an active developer of vacation homes and properties. KRE properties are also found in the mountains of central Japan in Nagano prefecture and along the beaches of Wakayama prefecture, south of Osaka. Besides doing business in Japan, in 1968 Kintetsu opened the Japanese Cultural and Trade Center in San Francisco. It has also been active in opening hotels in San Francisco, Los Angeles, and Saipan, as well as a new 432-room property to be opened in the Little Tokyo area of Los Angeles in 1992. Kintetsu also currently owns and manages a shopping complex in San Francisco.[17]

ROLLING STOCK MANUFACTURING

Accounting for almost 20 percent of Kintetsu's 1990 net profit, the Kinki Sharyo Co., Ltd., the Dai Nippon Construction, and other smaller Kintetsu construction companies, along with their 8,570 employees, were some of Japan's leading manufacturers of rolling stock and prefabricated housing components.

The Kinki Sharyo Co., Ltd. builds a variety of passenger train cars, including the two-floor Kintetsu "Vista-Car." Ironically, Kintetsu also builds coaches for the Japan Railway's famous bullet trains, the *shinkansen*. Kintetsu is once again gaining international recognition from its exports of rolling stock to countries in Southeast Asia, South America, the Middle East, and Africa. In addition to its manufacturing firms, Kintetsu has a number of engineering, landscape architectural, building maintenance, and construction firms.[18]

FROM AUTOMOBILES TO BASEBALL

In addition to Kintetsu's manufacturing, retail, and service industries, it also has a stake in ten automobile sales and service companies. Kintetsu Motors Co., Inc., along with three other subsidiaries and affiliated companies, manages automobile dealerships in Tokyo, Shizuoka, Nagoya, Kyoto, Nara, Osaka, and Kobe. Together, they form the largest network of Ford dealerships in Japan. Volvo, Nissan, and Isuzu cars, Iveco-Magirus fire-fighting vehicles, and Winnebago motor homes are also sold through Kintetsu-operated companies.[19]

After its railway and department stores, Kintetsu may be most famous for its professional baseball team, the Kintetsu Buffaloes, which plays its home games in Fujidera on the southeast side of Osaka city. The Buffaloes (Exhibit 3-7) are consistently near the top of the Pacific League, winning three pennants between 1979 and 1989.

Kintetsu is also involved in the entertainment business, including the management of amusement parks, theaters, bowling alleys, tennis courts, and golf courses. Being located in the most culturally rich region of Japan, Kintetsu operates museums, galleries, and an aquarium in the Kansai area.

In 1988, Kintetsu entered the telecommunications industry with the introduction of the Kintetsu Cable Network, or KCN. Broadcasting news, music, and movies, KCN was the first urban cable TV station in the Kansai region.

With a history of more than 82 years of serving Japan, the 157 companies and nearly 83,000 employees of Kintetsu have grown, suffered, endured, and prospered along with their community of more than 120 million neighbors. Japan faces a new millennia, optimistic, strong, and proud—proud of its people and the relationships formed between communities and *its* companies. The recession of 1992–93 is affecting Kintetsu as well as the other companies of Japan. Today Kintetsu must evaluate its opportunities in the domestic market as well as opportunities for international expansion. This might be done by making strategic alliances with other global organizations for products and services that might be sold in Japan through Kintetsu's comprehensive distribution system or for expansion outside of Japan.

EXHIBIT 3-7   THE KINTETSU BUFFALOES STADIUM

NOTES

[1] Reischauer, E. (1981). *Japan: The Story of a Nation*, 130, 160–162.

[2] Woronoff, J. (1991). *The No-Nonsense Guide to Doing Business in Japan*, 44.

[3] Reischauer, E. (1981). *Japan: The Story of a Nation*, 232–233.

[4] Khambata, D., and R. Ajami (1992). *International Business, Theory and Practice*, 304.

[5] Reischauer, E. (1981). *Japan: The Story of a Nation*, 377–378.

[6] The Kintetsu Corporation. *Profile of Kintetsu Group*.

[7] The Kintetsu Corporation. *Kintetsu*, 5.

[8] The Kintetsu Corporation. *Kintetsu*, 7.

[9] *Ibid.*, 7.

[10] *Ibid.*, 7.

[11] Lu, D. (1987). *Inside Corporate Japan*, 12–13.

[12] The Kintetsu Corporation. *Profile of Kintetsu Group*.

[13] *Ibid.*

[14] The Kintetsu Corporation. *Kintetsu*, 11.

[15] The Kintetsu Corporation. *Profile of Kintetsu Group*.

[16] The Kintetsu Corporation. *Kintetsu*, 15.

[17] *Ibid.*, 15.

[18] The Kintetsu Corporation. *Kintetsu*, 25.

[19] *Ibid.*, 17.

SELECTED REFERENCES FOR FURTHER INFORMATION

Hirobayashi, B. (1989). *Age of Information Marketing*. Chicago: A. C. Nielson.

Khambata, D., and R. Ajami (1992). *International Business: Theory and Practice*. New York: Macmillan.

The Kintetsu Corporation (1991). *Kintetsu*. Osaka, Japan.

The Kintetsu Corporation (1991). *Profile of Kintetsu Group*. Osaka, Japan.

Lu, D. J. (1987). *Inside Corporate Japan*. Rutland, VT and Tokyo: Charles E. Tuttle.

Ono, S. (1962). *Shinto, the Kami Way*. Rutland, VT and Tokyo: Charles E. Tuttle.

Reischauer, E. O. (1981). *Japan: The Story of a Nation*, Third Edition. Tokyo: Charles E. Tuttle.

Woronoff, J. (1991). *The No-Nonsense Guide to Doing Business in Japan*, Tokyo: Yohan Publications.

CASE 4

CENTER PARCS

T he year 1968 was a significant time in Europe, especially in Holland. It was the date identified by Allan Fuff in his book *Holland
and the Ecological Landscapes* as the beginning of a new environmental movement. Holland in the late 1960s and 1970s became a mecca
for environmental planners and landscape architects worldwide. The new
landscapes, based on a philosophy of man's relationship to nature, established new images and new techniques, and set standards for landscape
design and management that are now the accepted norms in a far more
environmentally aware continent.

Land development and management needed a completely new outlook based on ecological principles. Recognizing this, it is no coincidence
that the Center Parcs concept was soon developed in Holland. It responded to and helped shape the philosophy that man needs contact with
nature for his well-being. Center Parcs was a unique concept in that it
offered vacations close to nature in a forest setting, in a manner that em-
bodied the very essence of these new principles. Often viewed as a concept
before its time, Center Parcs was, in fact, a generator of ideas, setting new
standards of environmental awareness and care in its approach and in its
day-to-day operations.

Now, the management of Center Parcs faces a new challenge: the potential of entering the U.S. market. The magic of Disney has been transferred from the U.S. culture to Japan and Europe. The management of
Center Parcs is studying how to bring the most successful vacation/resort
concept in Europe to the United States.

THE CENTER PARCS CONCEPT

The Center Parcs concept began by responding to the problems experienced by people planning a vacation in Northern Europe's unpredictable
climate. It recognized the changing patterns of vacations as leisure time

among Europeans increased. The market grew for short break holidays to complement the traditional summer vacation.

The concept started in Holland in 1967 with a "villa in the forest" and has expanded into a unique holiday destination. The Center Parcs formula begins with the combination of high quality accommodations and an extensive range of indoor and outdoor sports and leisure facilities. Then it adds a mix of restaurants, bars, and retail outlets, all set in a natural environment where woodland and water are considered essential elements. The aim is to create an escape from the hustle and bustle of everyday life and to be at one with nature, with its relaxing and restorative qualities.

Central to the Center Parcs concept is an extensive landscape setting of forest, glades, and water areas. It offers visitors the chance to enjoy contact with nature in a forest environment that absorbs people, buildings, and cars with minimal impact on the landscape.

The grounds include a large lake, forest, hotel with adjacent conference center, registration house, and central atrium. A layout of the grounds is shown in Exhibit 4-1. The atrium contains a tropical forest with

EXHIBIT 4-1   CENTER PARCS'S GRAPHICS LAYOUT

COURTESY OF CENTER PARCS

EXHIBIT 4-2   CENTER PARCS'S TROPICAL PARADISE

COURTESY OF CENTER PARCS

stream and live birds, fish, and turtles. It also contains numerous restaurants of many different styles, various retail shops, a supermarket, a disco and open entertainment areas. This open area is used for nightly family entertainment. Guests can also use the indoor tennis courts, badminton courts, and bowling alleys in the atrium. But the atrium's main attraction is the "Subtropical Swimming Paradise," shown in Exhibit 4-2. Guests enter the pool area and may use any of the amenities such as the wave pool, current pool, hot tubs, and water slides.

Guests stay in individual bungalows or in a small number of hotel rooms spread throughout the park area connected by roads and paths. Shuttle buses travel a frequent schedule throughout the park. Guests can rent bikes, which also allow people to travel throughout the grounds freely. Walking, however, is the preferred transportation mode for most guests.

Each bungalow has a kitchen, living room, dining area, fireplace, television, bathroom, shower room (separate from the room with the toilet, which is common in Europe), bedroom(s), and patio. There are no phones in the individual bungalows, but patrons can use public phones in the registration house.

The bungalows tend to have an open structural feel with modern decor. Depending on the size of the party, bungalows have between two and four bedrooms. The bedrooms feature single beds that can be pushed together to accommodate couples rather than queen or king size beds. This makes it easier to accommodate a larger number of people in the bungalow who wish to sleep separately. The kitchens are equipped with a stove, sink, and cooking and eating utensils. The shower room has a sink with a vanity and mirror and a large whirlpool bathtub with a shower head. The living area contains nice, not luxurious, furniture and opens out onto the patio overlooking the park or the lake. The patio comes equipped with lawn furniture and a grill for summer cookouts. A complete list of items furnished by Center Parcs is shown in Exhibit 4-3.

GUEST SERVICES AND FACILITIES

Center Parcs tries to have something to appeal to everyone. Regardless of age or degree of physical fitness, guests easily find things to keep them occupied and happy for weeks. A complete list of Center Parcs facilities is shown in Exhibit 4-4. Different parks offer different combinations of facilities to their guests.

INVENTORY - LIST

EXHIBIT 4-3   CENTER PARCS'S INVENTORY LIST

Living room	VM61	VM62	VM63
Armchair	2	2	1
Ashtray	2	2	2
Coffee table	1	1	1
Colour TV	1	1	1
Poker	1	1	1
Radio	1	1	1
Sofa	1	1	1
Vase	1	1	1

Kitchen	VM61	VM62	VM63
Bin	1	1	1
Gas cooker	1	1	1
Ice cube tray	2	2	2
Refrigerator	2	2	2

Dining area	VM61	VM62	VM63
Dining chairs	10	8	6
Dining table	1	1	1

Bedrooms	VM61	VM62	VM63
Beds	8	6	4
Bedside tables	6	5	4
Bible	1	1	1
Blankets	2	2	8
Coat hangers	16	12	8
Dressing table stool	20	16	12
Mattress cover	1	1	1
Mattresses	8	6	4
Pillows and pillow cases	10	8	6
Undersheets	8	6	4

Patio	VM61	VM62	VM63
Patio chairs	8	6	4
Patio table	1	1	1

Cutlery (Kitchen)	VM61	VM62	VM63
Bottle opener	1	1	1
Bread knife	1	1	1
Carving fork	1	1	1
Cheese slicer	1	1	1
Corkscrew	1	1	1
Cucumber slicer	1	1	1

	VM61	VM62	VM63
Dessert spoons	12	12	8
Forks	12	10	8
Knives	12	10	8
Potato serving spoon	1	1	1
Sauce ladle	1	1	1
Scissors	1	1	1
Soup ladle	1	1	1
Spatula	1	1	1
Spoons	12	10	8
Teaspoons	12	10	8
Vegetable spoon	1	1	1

Crockery (Kitchen)	VM61	VM62	VM63
Breakfast plates	12	10	8
Cups and saucers	12	10	8
Dinner plates	12	10	8
Plates/soup bowls	12	10	8

Glassware (Kitchen)	VM61	VM62	VM63
Aperitif glasses	12	10	8
Dessert dishes	12	10	8
Duralex dishes	3	3	3
Lemon squeezer	1	1	1
Sherry glasses	8	6	4

	VM61	VM62	VM63
Teapot	1	1	1
Tumblers	8	6	4
Wine glasses	8	6	4

Pans (Kitchen)	VM61	VM62	VM63
Casserole 24 cm	1	1	1
Casserole 28 cm	1	1	1
Frying pan 28 cm	1	1	1
Milk pan 14 cm	1	1	1
Milk pan	1	1	1
Saucepan 24 cm	1	1	1
Saucepan 22 cm	1	1	1
Saucepan 20 cm	1	1	1
Saucepan 18 cm	1	1	1

Children's furniture (in storage area)	VM61	VM62	VM63
Child's bed and mattress	1	1	1
High chair	1	1	1
Playpen	1	1	1

Miscellaneous (Kitchen)	VM61	VM62	VM63
Bread basket	1	1	1
Bread bin	1	1	1

	VM61	VM62	VM63
Bread board	1	1	1
Coffee pot	8	6	1
Coffee maker	8	6	1
Colander	1	1	1
Draining board	1	1	1
Egg cups	12	10	8
Kettle	1	1	1
Milk jug	1	1	1
Potato peeler	1	1	1
Potato masher	1	1	1
Simmer plate	1	1	1
Storage tins	3	3	3
Sugar bowl	3	3	3
Table mats	3	3	3
Tin opener	1	1	1
Tray	1	1	1
Washing-up bowl	1	1	1
Washing-up brush	1	1	1
Whisk	1	1	1
Wooden spoon with hole	1	1	1
Wooden spoon	1	1	1

Miscellaneous (Bathroom)	VM61	VM62	VM63
Bucket with lid	1	1	1
Drying rack	1	1	1
Potty	1	2	1
Toilet set	2	1	1
Waste bin	1	1	1

Miscellaneous (Storage room/Bathroom)	VM61	VM62	VM63
Broom	1	1	1
Carpet sweeper	1	1	1
Cleaning pack	1	1	1
Dustpan and brush	1	1	1
Feather duster + pole	1	1	1
Shopping trolley	1	1	1
Sponge	1	1	1
Vacuum cleaner	1	1	1
Window wiper	1	1	1

EXHIBIT 4-4   FACILITIES AT A GLANCE

FACILITIES AT A GLANCE

FACILITIES	EH	HB	HH	KV	LB	MD	VB	EP	VM	BF
SUBTROPICAL SWIMMING PARADISE										
Jacuzzi	•	•	•	•	•	•	•	•	•	•
Outdoor pool	•	•	•	•	•	•	•	•	•	•
Wave pool	•	•	•	•	•	•	•	•	•	•
Hot-Whirlpool	•	•	•	•	•	•	•	•	•	•
Jungle River						•				
Babies and toddlers pool		•								
Cold plunge pool	•		•	•	•	•	•	•	•	•
Herbal bath							•			
Rapid tanner	•	•	•	•	•	•		•	•	•
Solarium	•	•	•	•	•	•	•	•	•	•
Children's pool	•	•	•	•	•	•	•	•	•	•
Rippling rapids	•	•					•	•	•	•
Water slide	•	•		•	•	•	•	•	•	•
Water slide, indoor-outdoor		•		•	•	•		•	•	•
Water slope								•	•	•
Waterfall	•	•		•		•	•	•	•	•
Competition pool			•							
Cascade	•	•	•		•			•	•	•
Wild water cave			•	•	•					
Sun lounge	•	•				•	•			
Salt water pool	•									
Swimmers' snack bar	•	•	•	•		•	•	•	•	•
Swimmers' bar	•	•	•	•	•	•	•	•	•	•
Swimmers' bar in the water							•			
SAUNA AND FITNESS										
Hot whirlpool	•	•	•	•				•	•	•
Floatarium	•									•
Facial tanner	•		•				•	•	•	•
Karwendel	•							•	•	•
Roman sauna	•									
Sauna	•	•	•	•	•	•	•	•	•	•
Sauna bar	•								•	
Sauna garden	•			•		•	•	•		•
Sauna garden with jacuzzi		•	•	•				•		
Sauna log cabin			•						•	
Rapid tanner	•	•		•				•	•	•
Thalasso								•	•	•
Turkish bath	•	•	•	•	•	•	•	•	•	•
Solarium	•	•	•		•	•	•	•	•	•
SPORTS										
Badminton	•	•		•		•		•	•	•
Basketball			•	•	•	•				
Catamaran	•		•							
BMX track	•	•		•		•		•	•	•
Fitness room	•	•		•		•		•	•	
Golf										•
Archery	•	•		•	•	•		•	•	
Marina	○									
Canoeing	○	○	○	○			•	○		
Riding school	30km			5km	250m	5km	10km	5km	25km	
Horse riding		•								
Horse stables		•			250m		7km			•
Roller skating						•				
Snooker	•	•	•	•	•	•		•	•	
Sports café	•	•		•		•		•		
Sports hall	•	•		•		•		•	•	•
Sports field	•	•			•	•		•	•	
Squash	•	•		•		•		•	•	•
Windsurf storage	○	○		○		○			○	
Windsurf hire/Windsurf school	○	○		○		○			○	
Tennis (indoor)	•	•		•		•		•	•	•
Tennis (outdoor)	•	•	•	•	•	•	•	•	•	•
Tennis practice wall						•				
Tennis school	•	•								
Jogging track	•			•		•	•	•	•	•
Fitness training						•				
Football field	•					•		•	•	
Volleyball	•	•		•	•	•		•		
Waterskiing	○									
Watersports	•	•		•	•	•		•	•	
Sailing dinghy hire	○		○							
Sailing school	○									

FACILITIES	EH	HB	HH	KV	LB	MD	VB	EP	VM	BF
RESTAURANTS										
Bar/Bowling	•	•	•	•	•	•	•	•	•	•
Bar										
Bistro	•		•	•	•	•	•	•	•	•
Reception rooms	•		•	•	•	•	•		•	•
Café Chez Pierre	•	•		•	•		•	•	•	•
Conference centre		•	•	•			•	•	•	
Croissanterie	•		•			•			•	•
Gelateria			•							
Lagoon Bar			•							
Music bar/Disco	•	•		•		•		•	•	•
Pancake house	•	•	•	•	•	•	•	•	•	•
Pizzeria	•	•		•		•		•	•	•
Plaza/Family Restaurant	•	•	•	•	•	•	•	•	•	•
Rising Sun restaurant			•			•				
Sports café	•	•		•		•		•		
Grill (Steak Restaurant)		•						•		
Fish restaurant									•	•
Snacks and ices	•	•	•	•	•	•	•	•	•	•
Swimmers' bar	•	•	•	•	•	•	•	•	•	•
Swimmers' snack bar	•	•	•	•	•	•	•	•	•	•
SHOPS AND SERVICES										
Car wash	•						1km			
Chemist	•									
Bank/Change	★		•	•		•		•	•	•
Petrol	•	10km	2km	2km	3km	4km		1km	4km	7km
Bakery	•	•	•	•	•	•	•	•	★	•
Boutique	•									•
Bijouterie	•		•	•			•	•	•	•
Hairdresser									•	•
Post Office	•									
Safe deposit boxes	•	•	•	•	•	•	•	•	•	•
Butcher	•	•	•	•	•	•	•	•	•	•
Off-Licence	•	•	•	•	•	•	•	•	•	•
Sportique	•	•	•	•	•	•	•	•	•	•
Supermarket	•	•	•	•	•	•	•	•	•	•
Sweet shop	•	•	•	•	•	•	•	•	•	•
Launderette	•	•	•	•	•	•	•	•	•	•
Gift shop	•	•	•	•	•	•	•	•	•	•
RELAXATION										
Arcade games	•	•	•	•	•	•	•	•	•	•
Baby-sitting service	•	•	•	•	•	•	•	•	•	•
Billiards	•	•	•	•	•	•	•	•	•	•
Bingo	•	•	•	•	•	•	•	•	•	•
Woods	•	•	•	•	•	•	•	•	•	•
Tenpin bowling	•	•	•	•	•	•	•	•	•	•
Darts	•	•	•	•	•	•	•	•	•	•
Bicycle hire	•	•	•	•	•	•	•	•	•	•
Deer sanctuary	•	•		•		•		•	•	
Petanque	•	•		•		•		•	•	•
Children's zoo						•		★		
Kindergarten (3-12 years)	•	•	•	•	•	•	•	•	•	•
Mini-golf	•	•	•	•	•	•	•	•	•	•
Bar/Disco	•	•		•		•		•	•	•
Rowing boat hire			○	•						
Playground	•	•	•	•	•	•	•	•	•	•
Playing field	•	•		•	•	•		•	•	•
Game and toy hire	•	•	•	•	•	•		•		
Table tennis	•	★	•	•	•	•	•	•	•	•
Video network	•	•	•	•	•	•	•	•	•	•
Fishing	•	•	•		•	200m		3km	2km	•
Pedaloes	•	○	○	○		○	○	○	○	○
Beach (lakeside)	•	•	•	•	•	•	•	•	•	•
OTHER FACILITIES										
Garage								•		
Canine toilet	•	•	•	•	•	•	•	•	•	•
Hotel									•	•
Information desk	•	•		•	•	•	•	•	•	•
Chapel									•	•
Church	•	•	•	•	•	•	•	•	•	•
Parc Plaza	•	•	•	•	•	•	•	•	•	•
Conference facilities	•	•		•		•	•	•	•	•
Reception facilities	•	•		•	•	•	•	•	•	•

EH - DE EEMHOF (NL), **HB** - HET HEIJDERBOS (NL), **HH** - HET HUTTENHEUGTE (NL), **KV** - DE KEMPERVENNEN (NL),
LB - DE LOMMERBERGEN (NL), **MD** - HET MEERDAL (NL), **VB** - HET VENNENBOS (NL), **EP** - ERPERHEIDE (B), **VM** - DE VOSSEMEREN (B), **BF** - LES BOIS FRANCS (F).
● = AVAILABLE ○ = IN THE SEASON ★ = UNDER CONSTRUCTION

14

The European Center Parcs do not offer maid service during guests' visits; however, a cleaning service is provided before new guests occupy the bungalows. Guests are asked to complete some simple tasks to help in the cleaning process before they leave, including turning the refrigerator to the lowest setting, turning off the central heating, taking the trash out and placing it in the large containers, and stripping the beds and folding the blankets and sheets.

RESTAURANTS

Center Parcs offers its visitors a variety of restaurants and snack shops from which to choose. The atrium contains a higher priced, fancy restaurant where a couple can enjoy a romantic dinner; a few family-style restaurants, one full service and one buffet style; an Italian restaurant; a seafood restaurant; a Belgian waffle house; and a fast food restaurant with dining facilities. Most of these restaurants are casual to conform to the vacation mode of its guests. One restaurant is designated as an international theme restaurant, where dining gives guests an experience in a different country each night.

Center Parcs provides its guests with yet another food alternative. All guests are invited to shop in the park's grocery store. Guests are able to buy items to prepare in their bungalows for meals or snacks. It gives guests the option to dine in privacy, buy exactly what they want, prepare it as they like, and save on the dining costs of their vacation. The grocery store has its own bakery where many guests buy their breakfast rolls fresh from the oven.

Center Parcs must decide how to best service its U.S. location. It has two primary strategies from which to choose. It can contract with its European suppliers to service and supply its U.S. location, or it can contract with U.S. equivalents.

In the past Center Parcs has been very successful at establishing its own restaurants and retail shops on its park grounds. It manages its own restaurant and retail shops and operates them as profit centers for the parks. This includes hiring and training all employees. With this strategy, Center Parcs controls all of the activities of the profit centers and also keeps all of the profits.

Center Parcs might reduce risk related to entering the U.S. market, however, by forming strategic alliances with established and reputable suppliers of services and products. By contracting with restaurant and grocery chains and food service companies, compliance with local regulations and customs will be simplified. Strategic alliances might be formed with a variety of companies including family restaurants, fast food restaurants, snack shops, a grocery chain, and retail outlets.

Sport Facilities

Center Parcs offers its guests a wide variety of sports activities. The swimming pool equipped with water slides and wave pools is the most popular among guests of all ages. The current streams take daring swimmers on a ride through part of the indoor facility and then outside through part of the park. Swimmers are finally "deposited" back inside the tropical atrium. The indoor atrium also houses four tennis courts and numerous badminton courts, complete with changing rooms and shower facilities.

Nature provides the largest playground for Center Parcs guests. Walking, jogging, and biking on the many trails are the most popular activities. People of all ages can be found during most times of the day and early evenings enjoying the atmosphere of the park. In the summer, it is possible to rent rowboats and venture out onto the man-made lakes within the park grounds.

Center Parcs has reserved a park area for its younger guests. In addition to the traditional playgrounds found in most parks, Center Parcs has added a dirt bike trail for exclusive use by children. They can rent the dirt bikes and protective gear and ride up and down hills, and with parental permission, learn to jump small hills. Although some of these facilities might post potential harm to some of the abusers of the equipment or facilities, Center Parcs does not staff these areas with personnel. Parents are responsible for their children and are expected to watch them. This is accepted and preferred among European families.

A similar policy exists in the water areas. Very few staff persons are present in the pool area because guests and parents are expected to be responsible for their own safety rather than rely on lifeguards, starters, or others to "police" activities as is often done in the United States.

Green Roots

In contrast to other companies which have only recently realized that green issues are here to stay, Center Parcs's consistently fine environmental record stands alone. Its twelve established villages in the Netherlands, Belgium, France, and Britain provide proof of the standards it sets in environmental care, design innovation, and quality control. Pollution control, recycling of materials, and use of natural resources are important concepts in the design and management of the parks.

Center Parcs has revolutionized the European leisure market. With its introduction of short breaks in forest settings, it attracts discerning guests seeking quality, choice, and close contact with nature. Of paramount importance to Center Parcs is the quality of the forest environment provided—its visual beauty and wildlife diversity. Indeed, nature is the catalyst, the key element that makes the Center Parcs philosophy unique.

One goal of Center Parcs is to bring people and nature together. It manages forest environments that not only provide for a relaxing vacation experience but also protect and enrich the countryside. Through its role in creating new habitats, Center Parcs is widely recognized as a beneficial force for nature conservation. It prides itself on its obsession with environmental quality, landscape protection, and nature conservation.

Center Parcs wants to ensure that it maintains its leading position in the area of environmental awareness. The Board of Directors of Center Parcs International has appointed an in-house team, with representatives of each country and from each operational discipline, to coordinate research into new methods of design and construction, the use of environmentally sustainable materials, the continued improvement of habitat management, and the setting of energy conservation standards and quality of water supplies. The team is supported by a professional staff consisting of architects, landscape architects, interior designers, and energy, heating, and water specialists.

The environmental development team has direct responsibility for enhancing the design concept as suggested by research and incorporating new innovations into the village design, including major facilities such as the Subtropical Swimming Paradise, the Parc Plaza, and the sports complex. Funding environmental research that leads to product improvement and continued reinvestment in existing Center Parc villages has been and continues to be a priority for Center Parcs. This ensures that Center Parcs will stay ahead of the increasing demand for higher standards of quality of both the facilities and the environment in which they are set.

Entering the United States

Center Parcs has been very successful in its European locations in the last 25 years. With parks in the Netherlands, Belgium, France, and England, Center Parcs is planning to expand into other European countries and the United States.

Center Parcs is planning on entering the United States in 1993 with its first location in the upper regions of New York State. It has a number of options in adapting to its new environment, and there are many specific areas to consider modifying, such as the bungalows, the common park area, and the retail area. Center Parcs could choose to change its concept to be more American so that the attractions and facilities will be more familiar to American patrons. Or Center Parcs might choose to remain "European" to gain a unique position in the market.

There are many issues Center Parcs is considering before entering the U.S. market. It is through the development and implementation of a long-term strategy for the U.S. market that Center Parcs will achieve long-term success. Its strategic plan will address the competitive environment, differences between the U.S. and European markets, and positioning strategies.

Center Parcs's U.S. Competitors

In identifying potential competitors, Center Parcs is examining *similar* vacation destinations because there are no competitors at this time that offer the same mix of facilities and services that Center Parcs does. Broadly defined, Center Parcs will compete with many organizations for U.S. consumers' vacation dollars and time. A partial list of such competitive forms of vacations might include:

- Federal and state parks
- Amusement parks
- Weekends at hotels
- Aquatic parks such as Sea World
- Water parks such as Wet 'n Wild
- State fairs
- Camps for children

While all of these facilities and activities compete for consumers' time and money, many other such competitors exist. Some indirect competitors for these consumer resources include families choosing to stay home to spend time with family. Consumers may also choose to spend their dollars on products to enhance their leisure time, such as sports equipment, boats, or recreational vehicles.

Center parcs recognizes that there exist some parks that might enter this specific market and become direct competitors by expanding their current facilities. Potential entrants might include Disney, state parks, and various water park facilities. By adding lodging and other family sport facilities they would compete more directly with the Center Parcs concept.

Differences Between the United States and Europe

Center Parcs is currently identifying and understanding the similarities and differences between the European and U.S. markets in order to identify necessary modifications of the Center Parcs concept.

FAMILY AND CHILDREN   The U.S. family unit and the importance it places on children differs from its European counterpart. Americans go on vacation to escape from everyday life, including the problems and demands of their children; therefore, they often leave the children at home rather than take them along or enroll them in "Camp Hyatt" or programs offered by other hotels designed to relieve parents of the needs to be with their children most of the time.

The number of families that are including their children in their vacation plans may be increasing, as may be the importance of family among many consumers. Yet, many parents do not know what to do with their children if they do take them on family vacations.

WORKING WOMEN   There are more and more women entering the work force everyday and, consequently, the trend toward domesticity has declined rapidly. While there is a similar trend in Europe today, it is not as profound as in the United States. Vacation is a time when the woman of the house wants to be pampered, so she can relax and enjoy her family. Some of the women visiting Center Parcs, however, will not be working women, and their needs and desires may differ from those of working women.

ELDERLY   Members of this group tend to be less active than their European counterparts. On average they have relatively high disposable incomes and have the time to vacation. Because they tend to be more sedentary than other markets, they represent the market that might spend a whole week at the parks. While this market tends to be in good health and claims to be more interested in health than in the past, it is not as physically active as the European 65+ age group. While older Europeans are accustomed to walking or riding bikes to the store or for exercise, Americans are not.

....

POSITIONING

Center Parcs is considering two different positioning strategies for its U.S. parks: *price positioning* and *attitudinal positioning*. Price positioning is effective in creating a position of a product or service in the minds of various consumers based on price. In many ways, Center Parcs combines the "return to nature" appeal of camping or visiting parks with the creature comforts and facilities of good hotels. Prices are typically substantially less than resort hotels but more than would be paid for camping in federal or state parks. A major decision facing Center Parcs is how to position the park with respect to price.

Attitudinal positioning emphasizes activities and amenities of Center Parcs to create an image of the park in the mind of consumers, regardless of demographic profile. Regardless of positioning strategy, Center Parcs has focused on what consumers really buy when they visit the park—an *escape from urban reality*, which includes nature, convenience, and fun. Management faces decisions about how to position the park with respect to luxury, the environment, and values relating to family, nature, and perhaps even philosophical (conservational, spiritual) values.

Center Parcs hopes to appeal to many groups of U.S. consumers. They can traditionally be identified in terms of demographics, lifestyles, and psychographics. A study recently completed by Erdos & Morgen identified four distinct groups of frequent leisure travelers, those who have taken five or more leisure trips in the past 3 years and have an income over $35,000 per year. These groups are as follows.

ADVENTURE ENTHUSIASTS   With an average age of 43 and an average household income of $65,400, this group makes up 17 percent of the frequent leisure travelers. They averaged 19 trips in the last 3 years and prefer shorter, less expensive trips, often visiting country bed-and-breakfast inns.

COUNTRY CLUB SET   This group makes up 14 percent of frequent travelers and is the most affluent of all leisure travelers with an average income of $77,200 per year. They are only a few months older than the "Adventure Enthusiasts" but take longer and more expensive trips, often fly first class, and stay at first-rate hotels. They are most likely to stay at beach resorts, where many of them golf.

CITY SOPHISTICATES   With an average age of 54, this segment accounts for 15 percent of the total frequent leisure traveler market. Because many are retired, they have the time to enjoy longer trips than the younger groups and the money (an average of $65,300 per household) to enjoy overseas travel.

FAMILY FUN   This is the largest segment, 36 percent, of the total leisure traveler market. This group has the lowest household income of the identified groups ($56,900), is somewhat older than the enthusiasts (47), and spends less than half as much as the others on travel. They take fewer and shorter trips, often travel by car, stay in economy motels, and visit friends and family.

Center Parcs is able to segment its market in many ways, not restricted just to the groups listed. While these groups seem important to Center Parcs, it also targets more conventional markets based on age, interest, and other demographical and psychographical information. In Europe, some Center Parcs include excellent meeting facilities and attract small conventions and strategic planning "retreat" types of meetings by business firms and associations. Since some parks include a chapel and prices of accommodations are modest when bungalows are shared by several people, parks attract a number of religious organizations for group meetings and retreats.

MARKETING CONSIDERATIONS

Center Parcs is committed to a strong consumer orientation. It frequently conducts consumer research on how to improve its parks, its facilities, and its services. A typical questionnaire used for surveying current customers is shown in Exhibit 4-5.

Center Parcs believes it has the ability to build a strong business in the U.S. market with the proper marketing. It is considering the best location for the first parks in the United States and is committed to purchasing the first locations in Pennsylvania, New Jersey, or New York, probably within easy driving distance of New York City and Philadelphia.

Management is examining various marketing efforts to make the parks successful. Decisions must be made concerning advertising, pricing, and other sales and marketing elements in a total marketing program. These efforts might include cross bookings between European and U.S. Center Parcs locations. The company must also decide if it should use the same name and logo as used in Europe or whether adaptation is needed for the U.S. market.

Some of the most important decisions concern design of the parks to be most effective in the U.S. markets. What modifications, if any, will be needed in the bungalows? What price and attitudinal positioning strategies should be used to serve American lifestyles? What types of merchandising facilities and strategies should be employed? What strategies should be used with respect to food operations? These are just a few of the issues faced by Center Parcs's management in its attempts to translate a highly successful concept in Europe to the American market.

EXHIBIT 4-5   CENTER PARCS CUSTOMER SURVEY

Bungalow-Park / Nom du Parc / Bungalowpark:

Bungalow-Nummer / Numéro du bungalow / Bungalownumber:

Ankunftsdatum / Date d'arrivée / Date of arrival:

1. Wie oft waren Sie früher bereits in einem unserer Bungalowparke? / Combien de séjours avez-vous déjà faits dans un de nos Parcs? / How often have you already been to one of our bungalowparks?

0x	1x	2x	3x	4x	5x	6x	7x	8x	9x	10x oder mehr ou plus or more

2. Wenn ja, in welchem Jahr und in welchem Monat? / Si oui, quelle est l'année de votre dernier séjour et le mois? / If so, in what year was your last visit and in what month?

Monat / Mois / Month _____   Jahr / Année / Year 19____

*Bitte zutreffendes ankreuzen. *Cocher les bonnes cases. *Please mark what is applicable		sehr gut excellent excellent	gut bien good	mässig moyen moderate	schlecht mauvais bad
Rezeption / Réception / Reception	1				
Bungalow-Ausstattung / Confort du bungalow / Bungalow comfort	2				
Familien-Restaurant / Restaurant des familles / Family-Restaurant	3				
Bistro / Bistro · Restaurant à la carte / Bistro	4				
Café Chez Pierre / Café Chez Pierre / Café Chez Pierre	5				
Sportique / Magasin de Sport / Sportique	6				
Eis · Snackladen / Snack · Glacier / Icecream · Snackshop	7				
Pfannkuchenhäuschen / Crêperie / Pancake restaurant	8				
Bowling / Bar · Bowling / Ten pin-Bowling	9				
Schwimm-Paradies / Paradis Aquatique Tropical / Swimming paradise	10				
Supermarkt / Supermarché / Supermarket	11				
Allgem. Eindruck Personal / Accueil du personnel / General impression personnel	12				
Sauberkeit Park / Proprieté du parc / Tidiness of the park	13				

Bitte hier notieren, was Sie als "mäßig" oder "schlecht" empfunden haben. / Par quoi avez-vous été deçus. / Please give details of your moderate or bad experiences.

Was kann man noch verbesseren? Und Wie? / Avez-vous des suggestions? / Comments, wishes, suggestions?

Welche (Freizeit)-Angebote möchten Sie zusätzlich haben? / De quelles installations supplémentaires souhaiteriez-vous profiter? / Which facilities would you like to be added to our park?

	ja oui yes	nein non no

3. Kommen Sie noch einmal in diesen Park zurück? / Reviendrez-vous dans ce Parc? / Will you come to this park again?

4. In einen anderen Park? / Irez-vous dans un autre de nos Parcs? / Will you come again to one of the other parks?

5. Beabsichtigen Sie, im nächsten Jahr zurückzu-kommen? / Avez-vous l'intention de revenir l'année prochaine? / Do you intend to come back next year?

6. Welche (Freizeit)-Angebote haben Sie · oder einer der anderen Bungalow-bewohner genutzt? (sofern vorhanden) / De quelle installations avez-vous pro-fité? (si présent) / Did you or any of the other bungalowguests make use of? (if available)

a. Sporthalle / Halle des Sports / Sports Hall

b. Sauna · Türk. Dampfbad / Sauna · bain turc / Sauna · Turk. steambath

c. Tennis-, Squash / Tennis · squash / Tennis-, Squash

d. Fahrradverleih / Location de bicyclettes / Bicycle renting

e. Bowling / Bowling / Bowlingalley

f. Minigolf / Mini-golf / Crazy mini golf

g. Tretboot / Pédalo / Peddalos

h. Kindergarten / Jardin d'enfants / Childrens playsch.

i. Freizeitprogramm / Animation (spectacles, tour-nois...) / Entertainment programme

CASE 5

WENDY'S INTERNATIONAL

W endy's management believes the best way to succeed in creating shareholder value is to build customer value. Customer value is created when customers come to Wendy's and receive the superior quality and competitive prices they expect. There is a direct relationship between customer value and shareholder value, and Wendy's has developed four main points of its strategic plan to ensure both customer and shareholder value:

1. Exceed customer expectations
2. Build a performance-driven culture
3. Build brand equity plus value
4. Grow a healthy restaurant system

EXCEED CUSTOMER EXPECTATIONS

Wendy's main objective is to fulfill and surpass customer expectations by delivering total quality every day. Customers give Wendy's high marks for quality, variety, and atmosphere. They do not rank Wendy's as high on price/value, operational consistency, and convenience. Thus, in addition to building on its current strengths, Wendy's has aimed its strategies at improving customers' perceptions of the latter three, as well. All six characteristics together—quality, variety, atmosphere, price/value, operational consistency, and convenience—are referred to as the "total quality equation."

One key to operating a successful restaurant is balance—balance between satisfying the customer and satisfying sales and profitability goals. It means establishing priorities and doing many things well. Increased profitability in a restaurant comes from either higher sales or improved efficiency and productivity. Wendy's managers are trained to strike the balance to achieve both.

The Sparkle program, developed in 1989, is an incentive program designed to measure quality, service, and cleanliness in every restaurant. It is a concentrated effort to ensure consistent customer satisfaction. The result, when all is working well, is a sales increase that directly measures the delivery of customer satisfaction. More customers plus greater satisfaction equal higher sales and profits for Wendy's.

Wendy's achieves enhanced profitability by implementing the Total Quality Equation. Total Quality equals the retention of quality, variety, and atmosphere plus the building of the price/value relationship, consistency, and convenience.

BUILD A PERFORMANCE-DRIVEN CULTURE

Wendy's believes that building a performance-driven culture is essential to accomplishing the goals it sets for itself. This commitment to its employees means that Wendy's strives to articulate thoroughly the expectations of employees, give people the tools they need to perform well, reward them for excellence, and provide leadership with a focus on strategy. Wendy's wants to become the employer of choice by giving people the proper training and offering competitive wages, incentives, and benefits. Wendy's also feels it is important to give employees a sense of involvement and continuing recognition. On the management level, Wendy's compensation and incentive programs are also highly performance-oriented.

BUILD BRAND EQUITY PLUS VALUE

The year 1991 ended with America accompanying Wendy's founder, Dave Thomas, on his "world tour" in search of new product ideas—at least in the "anything is possible" world of advertising. The campaign topped off what was a banner year in terms of advertising awareness for Wendy's.

Wendy's marketing approach was developed with two objectives: first, reinforce Wendy's heritage of superior quality food (brand equity) while providing for specific price and product promotion (value); and second, increase Wendy's advertising awareness, thereby closing the gap on the competition. Given recent successes on both fronts, this strategy remains in place.

Wendy's, as a total system, spends in excess of $125 million in paid advertising. The Wendy's National Advertising Program (WNAP), the administrator of both company and franchise advertising dollars, will oversee a budget in excess of $60 million in 1992, representing the required 2 percent of domestic systemwide sales. Another 2 percent, at minimum, is spent at the local level on television, radio, newspaper, and direct mail.

Wendy's menu is known for the wide variety of fresh, nutritious choices. As the menu evolves throughout the 1990s, the key requirements set for new products respond to consumer desires: quality, value, and convenience, supported by nutritional merit and variety. Wendy's tries to balance new products that increase the average check and those geared toward increasing volume or transactions. Both build total sales. Chicken Cordon Bleu, for example, a premium chicken sandwich with a relatively higher price point, falls most directly into the check-building category, while a new product idea for the Super Value Menu is more clearly transaction building.

Grow a Healthy System

When Jim Near became Wendy's president in 1986, he quickly took steps to eliminate plans to build new company restaurants. He felt that it was not wise to open new restaurants until the existing ones were operating better. Today existing stores are operating extremely well. Following five years of earnings improvements and greatly improved quality, service, and cleanliness ratings, Wendy's is implementing a plan that anticipates aggressive company and franchise growth. Enormous opportunities exist to increase market penetration and enhance location convenience for customers. Yet the company recognizes it is just as important to grow responsibly as it is to grow aggressively. Targeting its strongest markets for growth and ensuring the buildings are cost effective and efficient are two ways it plans to grow responsibly. According to Jim Near, Wendy's goal of 5,000 restaurants by the mid-1990s is within reach.

Wendy's Goes Global

While the advertising of Wendy's in the United States featured founder Dave Thomas in his global visits, something more serious was occurring in the firm's strategy. Wendy's International was in an expansion phase of international development. It has just begun to tap into the vast opportunities offered by global expansion with a very profit-oriented strategy.

Its global expansion plan calls for 75 new international restaurants to be opened in 1992. Wendy's currently has 3,820 stores worldwide, 188 of those outside the United States and Canada. Wendy's operates in 28 countries outside the United States, with contracts signed or negotiated to develop in 15 more in 1992. Exhibit 5-1 lists the countries in which Wendy's is currently operating and those for which it has expansion plans.

Although Wendy's plans to enter new markets in 1992, its primary goal is to increase market penetration in existing foreign markets through 1993. A primary expansion period is planned for 1993 as Wendy's plans to open approximately sixty-seven new stores worldwide in countries including Japan, Mexico, Poland, Honduras, and Egypt. By the end of 1993, Wendy's plans to have well over 300 international operations, nearly twice its 1990 operations.

Wendy's sees much growth potential in the international market. Its goal, however, is not to see how rapidly it can build stores and how many different exotic locations it can find. It is looking for opportunities that make sense from a financial and economic standpoint both in the short and long term. Exhibit 5-2 shows the number of restaurants per region in its worldwide operations.

Wendy's largest market outside the United States and Canada is Korea. One of the challenges Wendy's faced when it entered Korea was name recognition. Dr. Y. I. Kim, owner of thirty-three Korean Wendy's, decided to locate his restaurants in high-traffic, prime visibility locations that kept Wendy's in the public eye constantly. Every morning when thousands of commuters pour from the subway into the main intersection of Seoul, South Korea, the first thing they see is a striking, seven-story Wendy's sign above an attractive restaurant. Another restaurant borders the largest women's university in Korea, while a third is in the Itaewon shopping district. There is even a Wendy's in the Korea World Trade Center. With a population of 40 million and an increasing per capita income, there is great continued potential to capitalize on Korea's growing appetite for American-style, quick food service.

Another challenge for companies entering foreign markets is adapting to cultural norms and tastes. Before Japanese cars were introduced into the U.S. market, the cars had to be redesigned so that the steering wheels were on the left side of the car. One of Wendy's products in the Pacific stores is spaghetti. It added this special item because of a recognized demand for spaghetti among Filipinos and other Asian consumers. Similarly, Wendy's has included items such as teriyaki hamburgers and shrimp cake sandwiches in Japan, bone-in-chicken in the Pacific and Caribbean markets, and corn soup in Taiwan.

Wendy's has experienced its fair share of growing pains during its international expansion efforts. The company is honest about some of the mistakes that were made in the past and intends to make its international

EXHIBIT 5-1
INTERNATIONAL
STORES OPEN AND
INTERNATIONAL
DEPARTMENT
PROJECTED 1993
OPENINGS

International Stores Open	
Country	*Total*
Aruba	2
Bahamas (Freeport 1; Nassau 1)	2
Dominican Republic	1
El Salvador	1
Grand Cayman	1
Greece	3
Guam	2
Guatemala	2
Honduras	1
Hong Kong	3
Iceland	1
Indonesia	4
Israel	6
Italy	9
Japan	30
Korea	39
Kuwait	1
Mexico	5
New Zealand	4
Philippines	20
Puerto Rico	19
Saudi Arabia	6
Spain	0
Switzerland	3
Taiwan	15
Turkey	2
United Kingdom	2
Virgin Islands (St. Croix 2; St. John 1; St. Thomas 1)	4
TOTAL	188

International Dept. Projected 1993 Openings		
Country	*Projected Openings*	
Egypt, Morocco, Tunisia	2	
Greece	5	
Gulf States	9	
Hungary	1	
Poland	1	
Switzerland (Weneco)	1	
Turkey	2	
U.K.	2	23
Antigua, Barbuda, Barbados, St. Lucia	1	
Argentina	1	
Aruba, Bonaire, Curacao	1	
Bahamas–Nassau	1	
Chile	2	
Colombia	2	
El Salvador	1	
Guatemala	1	
Honduras	1	
Mexico (Hamburg.)	4	
Mexico (Wend Jal)	2	
Mexico (Other)	2	
Panama	1	
Puerto Rico	3	23
Australia	1	
Hawaii	2	
Hong Kong	2	
Indonesia	4	
Japan	3	
New Zealand	2	
Philippines	4	
Thailand	3	21
TOTAL PROJECTED '93 OPENINGS		67

expansion as successful as the turnaround in domestic operations that has occurred in the past few years. Wendy's management recognizes that the international openings were not always done right the first time out but believes the present approach is much sounder.

The global expansion vision of Wendy's is built upon the premise that people may differ in specifics but that they are universally similar in the important attributes of quality and service. While Wendy's may not have as much recognition as some competitors, it has something more im-

EXHIBIT 5-2

AD OF WENDY'S

WORLDWIDE

portant. Wendy's can describe itself as having the best hamburgers in America. This premise is based upon the fact that in a highly competitive environment Wendy's has been named as having the "best hamburgers in America" for the past 13 years. Wendy's may not be the largest restaurant, but it intends to be number one in quality and service in whatever country it may be operating.

As part of its vision for excellence in global operations, Wendy's has closed stores in some countries in which it formerly operated. While Wendy's currently maintains an interest in operating or franchising restaurants in countries such as Germany and Belgium, it has closed stores formerly operated in these and some other countries. The reasons for closing operations varies between countries. In some cases, the stores were not operated in conformance with the quality expectations of Wendy's management. In other cases, political and social changes caused management to believe closings were necessary. In other countries, the company believed that cash available from selling the restaurants could be used more effectively in the restructuring process that occurred in Wendy's domestically during the late 1980s. Although the company closes stores in countries cautiously and sometimes regretfully, management believes that such moves are sometimes necessary to accomplish the mission of quality in products and service on a global basis.

FRANCHISING

Wendy's has expanded globally by concentrating on franchise operations. Of its 316 stores outside the United States, 82 are company-owned and 234 are owned by franchisees. Exhibit 5-3 shows how the number of company-owned Wendy's stores has decreased since 1986 and how the franchised stores have increased.

Wendy's is reviewing its policy on joint ventures with a view to assessing the advantages of joint ventures over franchising. Currently, Wendy's international operations award an exclusive franchise to an operator in each country. The franchisee has the right to operate within the

	1986	1987	1988	1989	1990	1991
Company	129	115	97	87	88	82
Franchise	102	119	144	178	203	234

EXHIBIT 5-3
COMPANY- VERSUS
FRANCHISE-OWNED
RESTAURANTS
*SOURCE: WENDY'S
INTERNATIONAL
ANNUAL REPORT 1991*

country in which the franchise has been awarded. Wendy's is looking for strong local businesspeople who understand the culture and the infrastructure. Franchisees often have other businesses and always have contacts and personnel in the foreign market. Finding these partners and conducting the required research for opening a new store in a new market often takes several years. Wendy's has been doing basic background research in Russia and the Eastern European countries for some time. Although the process has been time-consuming, this initial work helps ensure good business decisions.

The franchise operations have led to many countries having only one or two stores, which has hampered Wendy's ability to advertise effectively and to impact the market. In a few instances Wendy's has entered into joint ventures. The idea is to build several restaurants with a partner to test the market with limited financial exposure. It is an approach that will be used cautiously. Joint ventures are expected in the United Kingdom and Australia in 1992.

Wendy's has also utilized a third distribution system to expand internationally. It has joined the U.S. Navy. Wendy's restaurants can be found on the naval base in Naples, Italy, and the naval air station in Sigonella, Sicily. A third restaurant just opened at the Keflavik Naval Base in Iceland. Although only three restaurants have opened by means of this new expansion strategy, the potential for further expansion is great.

······························

EUROPEAN FAST FOOD MARKET

The European fast food market has developed substantially over the last decade. Because it is not as saturated as the American fast food market, there exist many opportunities for new entrants into the market. The European market is dominated by McDonald's, which has been there longer than any other American fast food company. After 20 years, McDonald's has assumed a lead in Europe. Its early entry into the market has helped McDonald's secure its premiere locations in most markets.

Even when all indicators seem positive, no organization is invincible, including Wendy's. It entered Germany in the late 1970s and early 1980s with thirty-seven restaurants and by 1989 had closed them all. Similarly, the four Belgian restaurants opened in the early 1980s were all closed within 2 years of operation. Yet, other European locations, such as those in Switzerland, Greece, and the United Kingdom, have remained open and have performed well. This leads Wendy's to believe that many opportunities exist to increase its profits, enhance its image, and compete with its competitors effectively.

Wendy's is looking to Europe and the United Kingdom for one area of expanded profits in the 1990s. McDonald's opened more than half of its new restaurants in 1991 in Europe, and Burger King has followed suit. Other American-format restaurants are also opening under both American and European ownership. One reason for growth in the European market is the fact that it has been underdeveloped in the fast food market in the past. The European Economic Community has a population of approximately 320 million people, many of whom are waiting for more fast food restaurants to open.

Another reason for expected growth is the increase in the number of working women in Europe. Many of the trends taking place in Europe are similar to what has happened in the last decade in the United States. The demographics are changing more toward food away from home. Home life is changing, and a meal at Taco Bell or Pizza Hut is becoming part of the daily expectations of families. This trend means profitability for European Wendy's. The three Wendy's restaurants in Greece had sales averages in 1991 of over $2 million per unit, and the Greek operations are regarded as highly successful and a good base for future expansion.

MARKET ANALYSES

Before entering any market, Wendy's conducts primary and secondary research to better understand the environmental conditions of its new potential market. Wendy's, once present in Germany, does not want to repeat unnecessary mistakes should it reenter Germany. To avoid such problems, Wendy's has conducted some limited research into the German fast food market. Some of the results are summarized below to serve as a guideline for the types of information needed to evaluate global opportunities. This information may also help evaluate why closings were necessary in some countries during the past few years and serve as a base for reopening these countries. Additional information about other European markets is outlined to provide insights into some of the differences and similarities among European fast food consumers.

GERMANY

COUNTRY DATA   The latest census taken in 1990 showed total German population to be the largest population base in Europe since reunification. The Eastern portion of Germany represents a large population that had been denied American fast food for many years.

Much of Germany has experienced a decline in expenditures on food and drink at home when compared to other types of expenditures on items such as clothing, education, and leisure activities. However, expenditures on eating out of the home have continued to grow, particularly in single-person households.

Wendy's is evaluating potential new restaurant openings in Germany, with four tentatively planned for 1993. All stores in the country were closed in the late 1980s for various reasons, including operational and service problems and a lack of adaptation to the German cultural climate. Wendy's international approach has been the same as McDonald's in the past. Thus, German consumers often do not differentiate the two restaurants. In order to achieve success in the new Germany, Wendy's believes it must develop a more thorough understanding of the decision processes of German restaurant patrons.

MOTIVATION AND NEED RECOGNITION   German consumers tend to eat fast food because it is convenient, quick, and inexpensive. Most of these fast food customers do not plan their purchases, which often occur while shopping, after an evening at the local discotheque, or when returning home from work. Very few German families eat at fast food restaurants as a family unit. They prefer to eat at home. The typical Wendy's customer is a teenager, who goes to meet friends after playing soccer or seeing a movie. More and more businesspeople are going to Wendy's for lunch rather than going home for the traditional large midday meal.

Some observations and conclusions drawn by German consumers about Wendy's and its appeal to the market include the following:

- The prices are low compared to the typical German restaurants and to European restaurants in general
- Wendy's is on the way (to work, etc.)
- Families never meet at fast food restaurants
- Wendy's gets the most business on weekends, when people come home from discotheques

SEARCH FOR INFORMATION   German consumers can find Wendy's conveniently located on busy city blocks. To this consumer group convenient location is very important in its fast food choice. They consider Wendy's to be the best American fast food restaurant, based on the quality of the food, citing the salad bar as the most preferred product sold. The purchases are generally done on impulse; thus, the most convenient source of food is chosen without a great deal of consideration of the alternatives available. Yet many Germans state they would not go to Wendy's, or any fast food restaurant, if they were concerned about nutrition.

Exterior signage is important when the consumer is interested in making a fast food purchase. Convenience, however, is the main focus of the search for Wendy's fast food, with taste and price of the menu items being the main product determinant characteristics.

ALTERNATIVE EVALUATIONS   The main criterion for selection is convenience. When asked which German fast food restaurants were most similar to Wendy's many Germans named two other American restaurants, McDonald's and Burger King. They consider these restaurants to be symbols of America and different from their European counterparts, but very similar to each other. German consumers do have various alternatives from which to choose, including convenience food from street vendors, cafes, beer gardens, pizza delivery services, and small, privately owned, inexpensive restaurants.

Several product attributes are used to evaluate these alternatives. The issue of packaging and waste is an important consideration for the majority of Germans. They tend to avoid American fast food restaurants because of the restaurants' lack of environmental concern and actions. Wendy's is preferable to the other American fast food restaurants, however, because of its more traditional restaurant atmosphere, which is very important since Germans enjoy meeting friends and acquaintances in restaurants. The quality of food in local restaurants is perceived as better, especially the meat dishes and the small details they associate with small, privately owned establishments.

Germans also value taste and nutritional quality of food. They feel that American fast food buns and bread are too soft and spongy. Consumers are accustomed to whole grain, chewy breads. Germans also insist on cleanliness, and they view McDonald's as cleaner. Several of these attributes are used when choosing fast food, with convenience and lack of excessive packaging being the most salient. While service is considered to be important, it is viewed differently according to the food source. In a fast food restaurant service is expected to be quick, but in local restaurants, it is expected to be personal.

PURCHASE BEHAVIOR   German consumers spend little energy choosing one fast food establishment over another, except for the packaging/ recycling issue. Germans prefer to eat at home when simply hungry and wish to spend time with their families at home over meals. Eating out is viewed as a social occasion and rarely a hurried activity. Drive-through restaurants, however, are seen as potentially useful, especially for commuters returning home after work.

DIFFERENT STROKES FOR DIFFERENT FOLKS

BELGIUM   Wendy's opened stores in Brussels and Antwerp in the early 1980s and closed them two years later. Belgian consumers apparently did not see Wendy's as representative of the typical American fast food restaurant because of the emphasis on the salad bar rather than on hamburgers. For Belgian consumers American fast food means hamburgers. In general most fast food is consumed on the premises rather than taken home and is consumed primarily by teenagers who buy from restaurants they perceive as American. As they grow older, the importance of American image diminishes, and they tend to frequent Pizza Huts or similar restaurants which have good seating and service and relatively inexpensive prices.

SPAIN   Spanish consumers perceive Wendy's as representative of a typical American fast food restaurant, although they tend to be somewhat suspicious of the ingredients of the various food items. Many consumers mention they would enjoy drinking beer with their meals at Wendy's and would be appreciative of the stores staying open longer because many Spanish people do not eat dinner until 10:00 P.M. and stay out until 5:00 A.M.

TURKEY   While the Turkish people are not yet as environmentally sensitive as the Germans, there is a sense that they will be soon. This is a country which embraces the American image, but Wendy's is not differentiated significantly in the minds of the Turkish consumer. It is viewed as just another American restaurant. Turkish consumers often make their fast food eating experiences a part of a larger occasion, such as getting a hamburger and fries before going to a movie or to a disco with friends rather than family. They usually spend at least 30 minutes at the restaurant and do not appear to be interested in drive-through service.

THE UNITED KINGDOM   Consumers in this country often turn to fast food restaurants for snacks rather than for meals and use the take-out services often. Speed of filling orders is not as important to this group; they would prefer to see more personal service at a slower pace. They also do not like having their orders announced over loudspeakers for cooks to fill. This system seems too impersonal.

How Different Consumers Evaluate Different Attributes

An American Image

An American image continues to attract many European consumers to Wendy's and the other American fast food chains. The European consumer views the fast food restaurant, particularly the hamburger restaurant, as very American. They go for the American "experience" first rather than primarily for the food. Therefore, they do not expect many local dishes to appear on the menus. Although some adaptations are wise, European consumers want the menus to remain American and not to focus too much on their countries' local flavors. They can go to local restaurants if they want that type of cuisine.

European consumers also want the American image to carry through to the actual restaurants. They expect the buildings to appear modern, clean, and nicely decorated, and they expect them to be consistent in appearance from one location to the next. Minor variations in details and appearance in business districts or central city areas are acceptable and often encouraged, with the American image remaining predominant.

Most Europeans, representing a variety of countries, like the American image of Wendy's and the other American fast food restaurants. However, the degree to which this image should be emphasized changes from country to country. For example, in Greece and Turkey, the American image was highly desired and played an important part in the purchase decision, but in Germany, while the American image was acceptable, it was not considered to be a highlight or strength of the restaurant. Wendy's is evaluating how to emphasize or de-emphasize the American image in different European countries.

CASE 6

JAPAN AIRLINES: WELCOME TO WASHINGTON, DC! *

"American Airlines to Cut Routes and Operations," "Delta Airlines, United Airlines, Airline Industry Face Tough Times." Headings such as these seem to suggest that the airline industry is slowing down, but in an industry and an economy where airlines are cutting back and consolidating their positions, Japanese Airlines (JAL) decided to enter the U.S. market. On 31 March 1991, JAL made its first Washington, DC–Tokyo nonstop flight using 747-200 series aircraft. This is JAL's ninth gateway to North America.

JAL is not only a late entrant into the U.S. market, but it faces competition in Washington, DC from two large American airlines, Northwest and United, and from its main rival, an already established Japanese competitor, All Nippon Airways (ANA). Of these airlines, ANA, Northwest (NW), and United Airlines (UA) offer Washington, DC–Tokyo flights, although these flights are not on the same days. ANA has been operating in the market for about 4 years now.

Until JAL was deregulated in 1987, its success was largely attributed to Japan's protectionist attitude and government financing, but these reasons no longer apply since the 1987 privatization. JAL has fared quite well in the international arena of "free" competition, and it now connects sixty-three cities in thirty-one countries and territories.

JAL celebrated its fortieth anniversary in 1991. In its forty year history, it has undergone increasing competition from domestic carriers and foreign carriers, privatization in 1987, image changes,[2] loss of customer

---

*This case was prepared by Huiyu Hsieh, Aseem Patel, Injae Shin, Yoshihiro Kawamura, Takao Sato, and Hisao Tomita under the direction of Professor Salah S. Hassan at The George Washington University.

traffic due to crashes (1985), the oil crisis, the Gulf War, and a host of other troubles. In spite of all these problems, JAL remains a vital airline to be reckoned with, as can be observed in Exhibit 6-1.

JAL's success is largely due to its long-term planning and investments, which allow it to take advantage of opportunities that other airlines might not be able to because these opportunities do not have immediate returns

EXHIBIT 6-1	Top 20 in Passengers	
THE WORLD'S TOP 20 AIRLINES		
	Airlines	*No. of Passengers (in thousands)*
SOURCE: "1990 WORLD AIRLINE REPORT," AIR TRANSPORT WORLD, JUNE 1991, P. 104	1. Aeroflot	137,742
	2. American	73,251
	3. Delta	65,789
	4. USAir	60,059
	5. United	57,612
	6. Northwest	41,046
	7. Continental	35,496
	8. All Nippon	33,048
	9. British Airways	25,172
	10. TWA	24,416
	11. JAL	**23,464**
	12. Lufthansa	22,400
	13. Eastern	21,505
	14. Southwest	19,831
	15. Alitalia	18,203
	16. Pan Am	17,930
	17. Air Inter	16,163
	18. Air France	15,731
	19. America West	15,624
	20. Iberia	15,500

Top 20 in RPKs (Revenue Passenger Kilometers)

EXHIBIT 6-1
CONTINUED

Airlines	No. of RPKs (in millions)
1. Aeroflot	234,847
2. American	123,891
3. United	122,528
4. Delta	94,996
5. Northwest	83,978
6. British Airways	65,906
7. Continental	63,030
8. USAir	57,202
9. TWA	55,744
10. JAL	**55,195**
11. Pan Am	50,827
12. Lufthansa	41,503
13. Air France	36,778
14. All Nippon	33,007
15. Singapore	31,270
16. Qantas	27,754
17. Eastern	26,950
18. KLM	26,739
19. Air Canada	26,672
20. Cathay Pacific	24,461

Top 20 in FTKs (Freight Ton Kilometers)

Airlines	No. of FTKs (in millions)
1. Federal Express	6,309
2. Lufthansa	4,104
3. JAL	**3,477**
4. Air France	3,440

EXHIBIT 6-1

CONTINUED

5. Aeroflot	2,675
6. Korean	2,526
7. UPS	2,397
8. KLM	2,138
9. Northwest	2,062
10. Singapore	1,697
11. United	1,552
12. El Al	1,543
13. Cathay Pacific	1,448
14. Cargolux	1,186
15. Atlanta	1,168
16. Quantas	1,123
17. American	1,117
18. China	1,116
19. Rossenbalm	1,041
20. Pan Am	1,007

Top 20 in Employees*

Airlines	*No. of Employees*
1. Aeroflot	400,000
2. American	82,655
3. United	75,025
4. Delta	55,000
5. USAir	52,000
6. British Airways	50,658
7. Lufthansa	47,619
8. Northwest	40,000
9. Air France	39,000
10. Continental	33,000

JAL is 23rd (20,498).

EXHIBIT 6-1

CONTINUED

11. *Eastern*	*30,000*
12. *TWA*	*29,815*
13. *Atlanta*	*29,641*
14. *Iberia*	*28,000*
15. *Varig*	*25,654*
16. *KLM*	*25,195*
17. *Pan Am*	*24,600*
18. *Saudi*	*23,787*
19. *Air Canada*	*23,109*
20. *SAS*	*22,179*

Top 20 in Fleet Size*

Airlines	No. of Aircraft
1. Aeroflot	1,379
2. American	552
3. United	462
4. USAir	452
5. Delta	444
6. Continental	339
7. Northwest	332
8. Federal Express	259
9. British Airways	227
10. TWA	210
11. Lufthansa	177
12. Pan Am	162
13. Eastern	142
14. UPS	135
15. Atlanta	133
16. SAS	128

*JAL is 21st (98).

EXHIBIT 6-1
CONTINUED

17. Metro Airlines	*115*
18. Air France	*113*
19. Air Canada	*106*
20. All Nippon	*106*
21. WestAir	*104*

Top 20 in Operating Profit

Airlines	*Operating Profits (in millions)*
1. Singapore	775
2. JAL	**468**
3. Cathay Pacific	464
4. Federal Express	424
5. Thai Int'l	268
6. SAS	264
7. Swissair	240
8. Korean	144
9. Southwest	82
10. ABX Air	69
11. American	68
12. Phillippine	67
13. Braathens	60
14. Malaysia	55
15. Britannia	47
16. Aviaco	46
17. Atlantic Southeast	40
18. TAT	31
19. Air India	31
20. Martinair	24

or they require large financial outlays. An example of such planning can be found in its fleet expansion. JAL's fleet consists of sixteen 767s, sixteen DC-10s, and sixty-three 747s of various models. It has placed an order for sixty-four more 747s and twenty MD-11s. Another example of its long-term planning is the study by JAL executives on meeting future transportation needs.

JAL's strategy for future planning has been summed up under four main headings: cost control, expansion of domestic and international services, fleet renewal, and diversification into new activities that are not necessarily related to the airline business.

The history of JAL reflects these strategic elements, shown in Exhibits 6-2 and 6-3.

Six months after starting the new Washington, DC–Tokyo route, JAL had 23 percent of the market. Although this share does not make this route profitable, JAL has fared quite well in a short time period. A description of what makes JAL tick and what helps it succeed where others are struggling may be due to some of the continual improvement process shown in Exhibit 6-4. This case describes only JAL's U.S.–Japan route and specifically the Washington, DC–Tokyo route. The competitors considered are ANA, JAL's closest Japanese competitor, and the others. The others include Northwest and United Airlines. JAL considers Japanese travelers as its primary customers because cultural bonding among the Japanese travelers is shown in their preference for Japan's airlines.

Name of Company/Activity	Year	Business
JAL	1951	Air transport established with a capital of 100 million yen
Airport Ground Service Co., Ltd.	1957	Ground handling services—freight, baggage, mail
JAL Trading, Inc.	1962	Wholesale, retail, agent for property, casualty, insurance
Southwest Air Lines Co., Ltd.	1967	Air transport—to cater exclusively to southern islands of Japan
Japan Creative Tours Co., Ltd.	1976	Planning and marketing of JALPAK and other package tours
JAL Development Co., Ltd.	1970	Hotel management for JAL and other related interests

EXHIBIT 6-2

DIVERSIFICATION PROFILE OF JAL

SOURCE: JAL ANNUAL REPORT, *1990–1991*

EXHIBIT 6-2
CONTINUED

Name of Company/Activity	Year	Business
Japan Asia Airways Co., Ltd.	1975	Air transport, exclusively for the Japan–Taiwan sector
JAL Construction Co., Ltd.	1976	Construction—all aspects of construction
Domestic Creative Tours Co., Ltd.	1976	Planning and marketing of "JAL Story" and other domestic package tours
JAL Data Communication & System Co., Ltd.	1978	Development, operation and maintenance of information-processing systems
Pacific Fuel Trading Corp.	1982	Sale and supply of aviation fuel
JAL Development (USA), Inc.	1983	Hotel and restaurant business in the United States
Hotel Nikko of New York, Inc.	1983	Hotel, restaurant and in-flight catering business in New York
JAL Card, Inc.	1984	Credit card services
JAL Finance Corp.	1988	Financial services
Pacific World Corporation	1989	Investments in hotels and other enterprises
JAL Finance Europe B.V.	1989	Financial services
JAL Leasing (Hong Kong) Co., Ltd.	1989	Leasing
JAL Leasing (USA) Inc.	1989	Leasing
JALCOS	1990	JAL Coordination Service Academy—An educational institution
JAL Foundation	1990	Research and education
Global Logistics Systems Worldwide	1991	Development of international cargo information and management systems
AXESS	1991	Computer information systems

Route	Year	Comments
Japan–Moscow–Paris	1970	First international airline to do so with DC-8-62 planes
Trans-Pacific routes	1970	747's introduced
Tokyo–Hong Kong	1971	747's introduced
Tokyo–San Francisco	1971	747's introduced
Tokyo–Anchorage–New York	1972	Route inaugurated
Tokyo–Amsterdam–Hamburg–Paris	1972	747's introduced on polar routes
Tokyo–Guam service	1974	747's introduced
Tokyo–London–Frankfurt	1973	747's introduced on polar routes
Japan–China	1974	Route opened
Tokyo–New York	1976	First nonstop flight
	1977	DC-10's introduced into JAL international service
Nagasaki–Shanghai	1979	First flight opened
	1980	B-747-SR, world's largest capacity airplane enters JAL service
	1983	JAL is official carrier to Tokyo Disneyland
Tokyo–London	1985	First nonstop flight operates
Japan–USA	1987	Japan–Atlanta route opened, sixth U.S. gateway
Japan–Frankfurt	1990	Flights increased to daily
Nagoya–Pusan	1991	New route opened
Nagoya–Honolulu	1991	Flights increased to daily
Tokyo–Washington, DC	1991	Route opened—nonstop flight
Osaka–Singapore	1991	Flights increased to daily
Tokyo–Chicago	1991	Flights increased to daily
Hiroshima–Seoul	1991	Route opened
Tokyo–Paris	1991	Flights increased to daily and service made 'direct'
Tokyo–London	1991	Flights increased to daily and service made 'direct'
Tokyo–Frankfurt–Berlin	1991	New route to be opened in November 1991

EXHIBIT 6-3
ROUTE EXPANSION—INTERNATIONAL

JAL's Background

Since its establishment in 1951, JAL has followed a strategy of diversification and expansion of services and flight routes. This strategy became more pronounced after the 1987 privatization. Although it is not always the case, most of its new ventures have complemented its basic business, the airline business. It has expanded its business into such areas as construction, ground services for airlines, hotels and restaurants, leasing, tourism, information systems, and trade (import–export). On the airline side it has established separate companies to deal with specific areas of the market; for example, Southwest Airline Co., Ltd. caters to the southern islands of Japan, Japan Asia Airways Co., Ltd. caters to the Japan–Taiwan sector, etc.

The 1987 privatization was a risky move for JAL, but it has managed to expand its operations at a faster pace and show increasing profits since that time.

EXHIBIT 6-4	Year	Service
COST CONTROL MEASURES AND INVESTMENTS BY JAL	1967	JALCOM: the computerized reservation system.
	1968	JAL jet training center established to foster the training of airline pilots.
	1970	JAL flight crew and cabin crew training center established at Haneda Airport to improve supportive activities for the airlines.
	1975	JAL successfully tests new magnetic levitation vehicle.
	1986	Kizuki Maintenance established to look after all aspects of aircraft maintenance.
	1990	JAL opens its sixth flight training center in Nagasaki.
	1991	JAL constructs new hangars for 747 maintenance.
	1991	JAL develops window polishing robots.
	1991	JAL introduces brake aligning robots.
	1991	JAL developing robots to speed maintenance and reduce labor costs.
	1991	JAL introduces new containers to keep fish alive while transporting them.

....

WORLD AIRLINE INDUSTRY

GENERAL TRENDS

In recent years, the international airline industry has been going through major structural and operational changes as a result of several factors:

- A rising global interest in the free enterprise system as a means of obtaining faster economic and social development.
- Deregulation of the U.S. airline industry and mounting pressure, directly or indirectly, for more liberalization in international markets.
- Automated systems, which are being used to reduce operating costs and the use of more effective yield management techniques.
- The privatization trend affecting many government-owned enterprises.
- Technical advances in aircraft, such as greater nonstop range, more cost-effective turboprops, etc.
- Limiting infrastructural constraints (such as insufficient airport capacity at a number of airports around the world), which may seriously undermine the establishment of a more competitive system.
- Steady growth of air travel, spurred in large part by globalization.
- Greater competition in international air markets.

Of the preceding factors, the deregulation of the U.S. airline industry brought about the most dramatic changes in the international airline industry. In October 1978 the U.S. Congress enacted the Airline Deregulation Act of 1978, which placed maximum reliance on competitive market forces to determine the quantity, quality, and price of air transportation services to be provided by the airlines.[2] Government control of entry, exit, fares, and service was phased out gradually over the years. The resulting changes include the expansion of the hub-and-spoke system, fare wars, consolidation, code sharing, and greater reliance on automation. Although most of these changes have taken place in U.S. domestic markets, they have had a profound effect not only on the North American international airline industry but also, to varying degrees, on the worldwide airline industry. Outside North America, pressure to follow the U.S. experience has come from the U.S. government, which has attempted to export its regulatory philosophy.

Although deregulation includes positive aspects such as fare wars, new entrants and broader price/service options, it has negative aspects such as increasing delays, fare subsidization, new barriers to entry, and poorer overall services.

Therefore, the most noticeable changes in the international airline industry were caused by less government control. The deregulated marketplace was a remarkable contrast to the regulated environment, in which routes, tariffs, service standards, and mergers were strictly controlled by government.

CURRENT STATUS AND FUTURE OPTIONS

RECENT CHANGES IN THE WORLD'S AIRLINE INDUSTRY   The world's airline industry suffered its worst period in the fourth quarter of 1990 because of a major economic downturn, particularly in the United States and the United Kingdom, the Gulf War, the resulting hike in fuel prices, and worldwide fears of terrorism. This situation created a special brand of "stagflation" for the airlines.[3] Even though this slowed growth of the international airline industry represents a temporary phase in the trend in air travel demand, from a long-run perspective, it is not expected to have great impact, and the airline industry was expected to recover after the perceived threat passed.

CURRENT STATUS   Exhibit 6-5 shows the ratio of the number of passengers, RPM, and FTK in each traffic area of the world.

EXHIBIT 6-5	Region	Passengers	RPK	FTK
PASSENGERS, RPK,[a] AND FTK[b] RATIO BY REGION	Africa	1.2%	0.9%	0.8%
	Asia/Pacific	14.8	16.8	25.2
SOURCE: "WORLD AIRLINE REPORT," AIR	Canada	2.0	2.6	2.3
TRANSPORT WORLD,	Europe	33.5	34.4	31.0
JUNE 1991, P. 99. INTERNATIONAL CIVIL AVIATION	Latin America/ Caribbean	4.5	4.0	4.3
ORGANIZATION, "CIVIL AVIATION STATISTICS	Middle East	1.0	2.5	4.6
OF THE YEAR,"	The United States	41.9	38.8	31.8

MONTREAL: ICAO, DECEMBER 1989.

[a]FTK represents freight tonne-kilometers; one tonne (2,205 lb) transported one kilometer; tonne-kilometers are computed by multiplying the aircraft kilometers flown on each inter-airport hop by the number of tonnes carried on that hop.

[b]RPK represents revenue passenger-kilometers; one revenue passenger transported one kilometer in revenue service. Revenue passenger-kilometers are computed by summation of the products of the revenue aircraft kilometers flown on each interairport hop multiplied by the number of revenue passengers carried on that hop.

The International Civil Aviation Organization (ICAO) estimated operating revenues increased up to 10.6 percent (excepting U.S.S.R.) in 1990 from 1989. But cost was the big problem as operating expenses climbed 17.1 percent to $200.5 billion. This figure indicates that the industry showed an operating loss of about $2.5 billion, the worst loss on record relative to the 1980–82 period when the world was in the grip of a severe economic downturn spurred by the oil crisis. Exhibit 6-6 shows that even though passengers continued to increase, profits eroded to a loss in 1990.

The world's airlines carried 1.16 billion passengers in their scheduled services, 4 percent more than in 1989. International passenger boardings were up 7 percent to 281 million, or 24.2 percent of the total.

Total scheduled RPKs were up only 6 percent for the year, with 1.89 trillion RPKs generated. International RPKs were up 8.3 percent to 897 billion, or 47.5 percent of the total.

Total scheduled FTKs gained only 3 percent in 1990, when 58.5 billion FTKs were generated. The total tonnage carried actually declined 1 percent to 18.1 million tonnes.

The overall ICAO figures show that 1990 losses came in a year in which relatively good traffic growth occurred. The 1980–1982 losses occurred when traffic actually declined.

FUTURE OPTIONS   It is obvious that the changing worldwide environment in which deregulation, globalization, automated systems, greater competition, and technical advances are prevailing has produced challenges for international airlines. For successful airline managers, the new environment contains substantial risks but it also presents enormous opportunities.

In particular, the consolidation of European countries, deregulation of the U.S. airline industry, and economic growth in Asia present many opportunities to world airlines to access those markets. To survive this changing environment, airlines must offer passengers—particularly business travelers—consistent, frequent service to all major cities in these regions.

THE JAPANESE AIRLINE INDUSTRY

Unlike the airline industry in other countries, Japanese airlines are planning for strong traffic growth through the year 2000 despite airport and airways capacity shortfalls and a dip in traffic resulting from the recent Persian Gulf war. A major part of the air transportation boom in Japan is the country's $3-trillion economy. Also, Japan is the third-largest domestic

EXHIBIT 6-6

SCHEDULED AIRLINE
PROFITS
*SOURCE:
INTERNATIONAL CIVIL
AVIATION
ORGANIZATION, "CIVIL
AVIATION STATISTICS
OF THE YEAR,"
MONTREAL: ICAO,
DECEMBER 1989.
"1990 WORLD AIRLINE
REPORT," AIR
TRANSPORT WORLD,
JUNE 1991.*

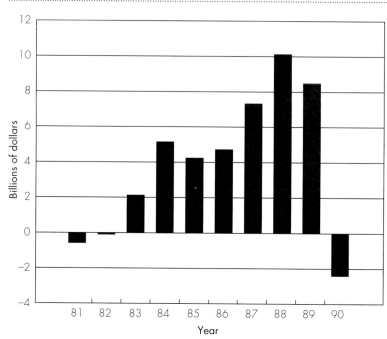

USSR international operation only.

PASSENGERS ON
SCHEDULED AIRLINES

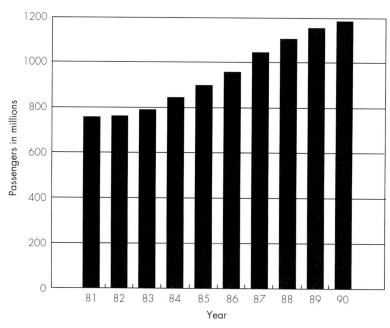

air transportation market in the world with 60 million passengers annually. However, only 7 percent of the Japanese have traveled overseas, compared to 17 percent of all Americans and 50 percent of all U.K. residents. Consequently, the Japanese government is encouraging overseas travel to help reduce Japan's trade surplus.

In 1985, no more than 5 million people in Japan traveled overseas. This number is forecasted to shift up to more than 20 million by the year 2000 because of the approaching high average incomes with an increase in leisure time. The three major airline companies in Japan have placed orders for $25-billion worth of large aircraft to accommodate the expected long-term demand increase.

PROBLEM 1 IN THE JAPANESE AIRLINE INDUSTRY

There is a shortage of airways and of airport space. Now there are more than 11,000 international routes between Japan and other countries. Surprisingly, only two major airports handle this large transportation business market. These two airports are always filled by international flights. Therefore, if Japan's three major airline companies expand into the global market, they will need other airports to accommodate additional flights. Basically there are two options to solve this difficulty. One is to build a new airport. The other one is to create a new international route from the existing domestic airports.

EXPECTED SOLUTION (1)

Although there is a lack of airport space and air routes in Japan, the new Kansai airport in Osaka and the expansion of Tokyo's Haneda airport will ease the structural problems created by these shortfalls. If the new Kansai airport in Osaka is built and if Haneda airport expands its capacity in 1995, more than 230,000 additional slots will be available between Japan and other countries.

ADVANTAGES OF A NEW AIRPORT   Since the proposed Kansai airport will be built offshore in Osaka Bay, it can avoid noise problems which are always controversial.

Also, because noise won't be a problem, the new Kansai airport can operate twenty-four hours a day.

PROBLEMS ASSOCIATED WITH AIRPORT CONSTRUCTION   Recently the New Kansai Airport Corp. postponed normal operations for about 15 months. There are two main environmental concerns.

1. Negotiations must be conducted with the fisherman's union to compensate them for lost jobs and destruction of their fisheries.

2.   Land must be reclaimed in order to build the new airport offshore. However, because the uneven terrain is sinking, construction will cost more than was originally expected.

Also, the government is trying to disperse service from Tokyo to secondary cities. The big two airline companies, JAL and ANA, responded by setting up charter subsidiaries to accommodate the demand for tourist flights.

PROBLEM 2 IN THE JAPANESE AIRLINE INDUSTRY

There is a shortage of aircraft and crew members. In addition to suffering from airport and airway shortages, the Japanese airline industry also suffers from a lack of assets and skilled labor. Since the three major airline companies in Japan are going to conduct their business both in domestic and international markets, they need an appropriate number of the aircraft and skilled crew members.

EXPECTED SOLUTION (2)

Japan's airlines are suffering from a lack of crew members. This problem is going to become more noticeable in the near future. Therefore, all three major carriers have ambitious pilot cadet recruitment and training programs. Presently a large number of experienced pilots are being hired from other countries such as Australia and the United States.

JAL recently established a joint business with other airline companies to supplement its lack of crew members. Japanese airline companies are purchasing aircraft aggressively for the expected increase in future demand. In addition, they are shifting from one type of aircraft to another.

JAPAN AIRLINES

Japan Airlines is capitalizing on its nation's overseas travel boom and its control of many slots at Japan's crowded airports to strengthen and expand its route networks and service. JAL invested in advanced technology to increase its productivity and improve service to help overcome the lower labor-cost carriers. JAL will continue to accomplish its long-term objectives to gain capacity in spite of the fact that travel plummeted during the Persian Gulf War.

JAL wants to increase its domestic capacity at a 6 percent annual rate, and it wants to increase seats on international flights at a 10 percent annual rate. Eventually, it wants all of its long-range flights to be nonstop. Consequently, JAL is trying to acquire new aircraft to adjust effectively between long flights and short flights. To support its acquisition of new air-craft, the airline is increasing the frequency of flights and adding new destinations to supplement its already extensive routes.

Recently JAL opened its international service with Tokyo–Washing-ton, DC flights (begun in March 1991). There are three flights a week, and this is JAL's ninth destination in the United States. By January 1992 JAL will be serving sixty-four international destinations and thirty-two coun-tries and territories.

....

COMPETITION IN THE WASHINGTON, DC–TOKYO ROUTE

CURRENT STATUS

In recent years Washington, DC has been considered one of the most popular proposed sites for many airlines' route expansion because of in-creasing tourism and investment in this area. It is also emerging as an important hub for connections to other major and smaller cities.

By bilateral agreement with the United States, Japanese airlines had restricted operations; the number of cities served and the number of flights were limited. Recent negotiations between the two countries re-sulted in JAL's expansion. As a result of these negotiations, JAL, ANA, and Japanese Air Systems (JAS) chose Washington, DC, New York, and Hono-lulu, respectively.

The first airline service link between Washington, DC and Tokyo was forged by ANA in 1986, and a couple of airlines began their service be-tween the District of Columbia and Tokyo. On January 8, 1991 United Airlines began offering a flight that originates in Washington, DC and stops in Chicago before proceeding to Tokyo; JAL began its nonstop ser-vice from DC to Tokyo on March 30, 1991.

COMPARISON OF COMPETING AIRLINES: ANA, UA, AND NW

JAL's competitors can be narrowed to three major airlines, All Nippon Airways (ANA), Northwest (NW), and United Airlines (UA). Of these three, ANA, another Japanese airline and an old rival in domestic markets, can be regarded as the most vigorous competitor.

GENERAL COMPARISON   See Exhibit 6-7 for a comparison of JAL's competitors.

CURRENT STATUS OF COMPETING AIRLINES

ANA: ANA, Japan's largest domestic carrier, began international operations in 1986 because it recognized that the big money was in overseas travel.[4] ANA's venture into scheduled international operations began in March 1986 with service between Tokyo and Guam. The following July, ANA became more aggressive in the international arena with nonstop operation between Tokyo and Los Angeles in direct competition with JAL and other airlines, and it also got an exclusive nonstop route between Tokyo and Washington, DC.[5] Its Tokyo–Washington route was the only nonstop service between the capitals of Japan and the United States.

Since those beginnings, ANA has been aggressively developing an international route structure and now, like other major airlines, it is battling for a piece of the hottest market in travel—the fast growing and highly profitable routes from Asia to the Americas and Europe.

Currently, ANA serves thirty-one stations in Japan plus ten foreign stations, including the new Tokyo–New York route. It operates sixty-seven international flights a week.[6] Recently ANA announced a 5-year plan calling for expansion. By the end of this period, ANA hopes its international services will account for 36 percent of its overall business, up from the current 19 percent.[7] ANA is ranked as the eighth largest airline in terms of the number of passengers. However, like many other airlines around the world, ANA is suffering from a lack of pilots and landing slots at Japan's major airport. These factors are limiting further expansion.

NW: As one of the big three U.S. airlines, along with Delta and American Airlines, NW has a pretty good reputation domestically and internationally. However, the 1989 leveraged buyout of Northwest by investor Alfred Checcni is continuing to drag down the company's financial position. NW's bond rating has been reduced to a point barely above the "junk" level, and Moody's expected NW to lose money again in 1991 and to suffer from a constrained cash flow because of capital expenditures and debt payments.[8] In addition, it had its worst time during the Gulf War, although it is recovering slowly.

EXHIBIT 6-7					
COMPARISON OF					No. of
COMPETING AIRLINES	Airline	Passengers	RPK	FTK	Employees	Aircraft

Airline	Passengers	RPK	FTK	Employees	No. of Aircraft
JAL	23,464	55,159	3,477,278	20,498	98
ANA	34,048	33,007	532,759	12,617	106
UA	57,612	122,528	1,552,291	75,025	462
NW	41,046	83,978	2,062,024	40,000	332

AS OF THE END OF 1990

SOURCE: "1990 WORLD AIRLINE REPORT," AIR TRANSPORT WORLD, JUNE 1991, PP. 114–121.

Despite its financial troubles, NW has been acquiring assets, among them Eastern's gates and slots at Washington's National Airport. In April 1991 it purchased a 25 percent stake in Hawaiian Airlines, along with some of that airline's routes.[9] Additionally, it is considering a hub in Atlanta.

Meanwhile, NW posted one of the better passenger traffic growth records among the major U.S. airlines in 1990, reporting gains of 5.6 percent to 41,046,000 passenger boardings and 10.7 percent to 84 million RPKs.

UA: Since UA has flights from Chicago to Tokyo, it is a strong competitor in terms of the flight market between Tokyo and Washington, DC. The total operating revenue of UA gained 12.7 percent relative to the increase of passenger boardings (4.8 percent), and it had a 9.3 percent RPK increase in 1990. Although its total operating profit and net income fluctuated downward, UA is in good shape in financial stability, fleet plans, and domestic hub strength. Recently, UAL, which is the parent company of UA, aggressively pursued airline acquisitions and buyout efforts. Because of this action, the company suffered a loss.

UA purchased the London route from Pan Am in 1991. Then UA started its service between London's Heathrow and several airports, including Washington, DC (Dulles Airport) in April 1991. UA also purchased the largest number of aircraft in aviation history plus a number of gates and slots at Chicago's O'Hare from defunct Eastern Airlines. Now UA is trying to promote itself as the biggest and fastest growing U.S. airline.

FLIGHT SERVICE FROM WASHINGTON, DC TO TOKYO

JAL: DC–Tokyo (nonstop), 3 flights a week, 13 hours, 747-200
ANA: DC–Tokyo (nonstop), 6 flights a week, 13 hours, 747-400
UA: DC–Chicago–Tokyo, 5 flights a week 16 hours and 30 minutes, 747-400
NW: NW has at least 3 flights a day between Washington, DC and Tokyo through various connections. Flight time depends on the route. (All are more than 17 hours.)

DIVERSIFICATION

ANA: Like JAL, which has ties to Nikko Hotels International, ANA aims to increase traffic by packaging flights with hotel rooms. Besides diversifying into travel-related businesses like JAL, ANA's expansion is coordinated with U.S. and other foreign-flag carriers through link-ups and other agreements. ANA will soon serve Orlando, Florida, via Washington, DC, through a code-sharing agreement with US Air.

NW: NW has one of the best-known service systems, so-called World Perks, which offers frequent-flyer miles and linked service with hotels and car rentals. NW actively provides expanded services such as car rentals in Europe and some areas in the United States, such as Florida,

California, and Nevada. However, NW doesn't have any expanded service in Asia and in the Washington, DC area.

UA: UA tried diversifying into travel-related businesses. It expanded into car rentals with Hertz and into the hotel business with the Westin chain. (It even changed the name of the parent company to Allegis for a brief period.) As a result, UA's core airline business suffered. Therefore the company quit the travel-related business and concentrated on the airline business and abandoned the short-lived name of Allegis.

Benefits

ANA: ANA's biggest advantage is its nonstop service. Nonstop service is convenient and time-saving for all travelers, and it is especially important for business travelers. Internationally, ANA's longest nonstop flight is the Tokyo–Washington, DC route.

ANA has better connecting flights in Japan to local destinations than JAL. In addition, ANA offers somewhat cheaper domestic fares than JAL.

One of the challenges faced by ANA is to attract non-Japanese travelers by promoting travel to Japan.

NW: Although NW does not offer nonstop service, it provides one of the most generous frequent-flyer programs—i.e., entitling a passenger to free trips after he/she flies a requisite number of miles—and believes that the program is a major attraction for trans-Pacific passengers.

In addition, NW benefits from a U.S. law that requires government employees to use U.S. airlines whenever possible.[10] Federal contractors are also often required to choose U.S. airlines for flights abroad.

UA: UA does not offer nonstop service to Japan from Washington, DC. But, like NW, UA provides an attractive frequent-flyer mileage program, and it too can take advantage of the U.S. law that requires federal and government employees to choose a U.S. airline.

Conclusion

JAL selected the Washington, DC route for several reasons.

DC as an Attractive Market with Growing Needs   The reason Washington, DC is attractive to Japanese airlines is that Washington has proved to be a popular destination for Japanese tourists. A year after ANA launched its service to Washington, DC, Japanese tourism in the region increased by 260 percent.[11] Increasing Japanese investments in this area prompted JAL's decision. According to an interview with an American businessman in *The Washington Post*, businesses from countries that are served nonstop from the Washington area are more likely to establish operations in the area. In 1988 and 1989, a total of forty Japanese-affiliated businesses invested more than $200 million in Virginia, creating more than 2,000 jobs.[12]

DC as an Important Hub to Other U.S. Cities   Another reason that makes Washington such an attractive area is its importance as a hub; it is expected to be used for a foothold for further expansion in the United States, using the hub-and-spoke system.

The General Trend of Deregulation of the U.S. Air Industry   As mentioned earlier, the deregulation of the U.S. airline industry and its effect on the whole international airline industry provided an opportunity for expansion in the United States by foreign competitors.

Bilateral Agreement Between Japan and the United States   JAL, along with other Japanese airlines, benefitted by bilateral aviation agreements between Japan and the United States. These agreements loosened up some restrictions on airline operations. (JAL originally considered Maui in Hawaii as a proposed site for expansion in the United States, but it changed its plans because of technical difficulties and the starting costs of developing additional airport capacity.)

JAL's Comparative Advantages   Most airlines, especially U.S. airlines, have suffered from poor financial management, and mergers with other airlines and leveraged buyouts by investors are the result. However, JAL has maintained its well-structured financial status. It has taken advantage of the strong economic climate in Japan, actively invested for the future, and supported its affiliates.

JAL'S Marketing Strategy

Target Market

JAL basically segmented its markets by national origin. National origin is related to the frequency of one's flights to Japan and his or her level of awareness of JAL.

Segmentation by usage—business trips, sightseeing, or other purposes—is of secondary importance to JAL. Business travelers are considered to be less sensitive to price differences and more sensitive to the comfort of flights or availability of flights at certain times and dates. On the other hand, sightseers are more sensitive to price and more influenced by promotions by airline companies and travel agencies.

JAL, the world's eleventh biggest airline in terms of number of passengers carried, did not limit its target market to one of those market segments. Instead it tried to appeal to each segment of the market. However, because each segment has different levels of market potential and unique characteristics, JAL assigns different degrees of importance to each segment and implements its strategies in accordance with the segments' characteristics.

THE JAPANESE MARKET   JAL sees Japanese travelers as its most important market because they fly to Japan most frequently. Japanese in the Washington, DC area are diplomats, businessmen, journalists, doctors at the National Institutes of Health, university students, and so on. The number of Japanese in the Washington area has been increasing and is expected to increase even more. The number of Japanese businesses in this area has been increasing because political decisions have affected their business strategies more than ever before. Some Japanese manufacturers, such as Canon and Mitsubishi Electronics, opened factories in this area. More and more high school and university students hope to study in the United States, so the number of Japanese students in this area has been increasing. Approximately 10,600 Japanese now live in the suburban DC area. These people fly to Japan to see their families, to conduct business, or for other various reasons.

The Japanese in this area have formed distinct communities. They live in certain areas (e.g., Potomac or Rockville) and maintain close relationships with each other. Because they live in a different culture, they are strongly influenced by the information they receive in these ethnic communities. The communities serve as a very influential reference group.

Because of its long history as the only Japanese airline that had international flights (now ANA and JAS have international flights as well), and because it is by far the largest Japanese airline company, JAL has become a household name for Japanese. It has successfully established a reliable image among the Japanese. Some Japanese have a negative image of JAL because they think it is bureaucratic and conservative, and these people prefer ANA over JAL. Although this perception is not widespread, it is a concern for JAL. In this market, JAL's major competitor is ANA.

THE ORIENTAL MARKET   Chinese, Koreans, Vietnamese, and Filippinos in the Washington, DC area are also an important market for JAL. In terms of population, this market is much larger than the Japanese market (total 101,000), and it is growing rapidly. (In the last decade, the Asian population in this area grew by 143 percent and was the fastest growing segment.) There is a demand to fly to Asian countries for business and family reasons. However, none of these country's airlines offers direct flights from Washington. By offering indirect flights (one stop in Tokyo) to their final destinations, JAL can be a competitive player in this market.

Chinese, Koreans, Vietnamese, and Filippinos also form their own communities, and these communities play a role similar to that of Japanese communities.

JAL expects that many Asians know about JAL because JAL has flown to their countries (except Vietnam) for a long time, although their knowledge about JAL may be limited. JAL is uncertain as to how well it has served this market, and it is still struggling to find its way. Nevertheless, JAL thinks it is a very important market.

In this market, competitors are considered to be United Airlines, Northwest, Korean Air, and Singapore Airlines.

THE AMERICAN MARKET   Basically, all the rest of the people living in this area form the American market. Of course, this population is the largest of the three, amounting to 3.7 million people. For JAL, this market is the most difficult one to serve. Even though this market is very large, the number of people who fly to Japan is very limited. Despite increasing economic ties between Japan and the United States, more business travelers fly to Europe than fly to Japan. And Japan is not perceived as a popular tourist destination compared with Europe, the Caribbean islands, Hawaii, and China.

In the American market, JAL has focused on such segments as diplomats and government agencies, IMF and the World Bank, exchange scholarship students, and big businesses such as Mobil. Many of these people do not know about JAL and have never used it. The major competitors in this market are United Airlines and Northwest.

BUSINESS TRAVELERS   As a market segment, business travelers are very attractive for airline companies because they pay higher prices (they are more likely to use business class or first class) and their travel isn't seasonal. On the other hand, it is hard to increase the number of business travelers by advertising and promotion. Tourists might consider travel to Japan attractive if it were cheaper to travel to Japan than to travel to Europe, but businesspeople don't change their destinations because of price. Business travelers are sensitive to time. Direct flights have a significant advantage over indirect flights, and availability of flights on certain dates and at certain times is often a decisive factor for business travelers. Business travelers prefer more spacious and relaxing seats, upgraded meals, and in-flight telephones.

TOURISTS   Tourists are more price sensitive and more influenced by promotions. Tourist travel is seasonal. As for the Tokyo–DC flight, winter is the slow season. In fact, summer is not a good season for tourists in both Tokyo and Washington. As a tourist destination, both cities have a secondary importance. China appeals to more Americans than Japan does, and New York City, Florida, and the Caribbean islands appeal to more Japanese. JAL needs to sell its Tokyo–DC flight by offering package tours using Tokyo or Washington as a gateway to these other popular destinations.

PRODUCT

Like other airlines, JAL offers travelers three kinds of classes—first class, executive class, and economy class. See Exhibit 6-8 for a comparison of JAL and ANA. To differentiate its product from ANA, JAL developed its product strategy as follows:

FIRST CLASS   JAL's first-class service begins with flight reservations when passengers can specify the seats they prefer. At the airport, first-class passengers can check in at exclusive counters, and in fifteen of the world's airports, first-class passengers can relax in the quiet surroundings of JAL's special Sakura Lounges. First-class comfort continues on board the aircraft itself.

1.   *Seats*   In the 747-200 there are thirty-two seats for first-class passengers. The sky recliner seat features the latest ergonomic developments for extra comfort. Each seat is 53.3 cm wide for plenty of

EXHIBIT 6-8		JAL		ANA	
THE COMPARISON OF PRODUCTS BETWEEN JAL AND ANA	Aircraft	747-200		747-400	(747-200)
	Flight frequency	3 flights per week		6 flights per week	
	Seat configuration	First—32		First—19	(F—24)
		Executive—124		Business—86	(B—80)
		Economy—112		Economy—260	(E—214)
		Total—268		Total—365	(T—318)
	Flight timing	Day		Day	
		Tu, Th, Sa, 12:40		M, F, Sa, 11:55	
				Th, Su, 10:55	
				Tu, 17:05	
	Mileage system	Applicable for only first class and executive class, tie-up with Delta		Applicable for only first class and business class, tie-up with USAir	
	Giveaway gifts	Travel kits		Travel kits or sake cup	
	Other in-flight services	Personal video service (Sony Video Walkman)		TV with seat, CD (as a source of audio service), language lesson program, TV games	

elbow room, and each seat stretches out to a maximum 60-degree angle, guaranteeing a restful flight.

2.   *Meals*   There are three menus—Western, Japanese, and quick service—for first-class passengers. One is a typical Western menu, including dishes such as fillet of beef, saurel and shrimp in wine sauce, or chicken fricassee. A Japanese menu might include grilled yellowtail, fan-shaped shrimp, and dried mullet roe. Soups, salads, cheeses, desserts, and fruit in season are also served. The quick service menu is new for passengers with light appetites, and it includes sushi and other light Japanese delicacies.

JAL also offers wines and liqueurs with a variety of choices, such as Dom Perignon champagne and great vintages from the vineyards of Bordeaux, Burgundy, and Mosel.

3.   *Video Systems*   JAL's first-class passengers can enjoy personal video service with Sony Video Walkman sets, and they can enjoy personalized video viewing on individual adjustable 5-inch liquid crystal screens mounted in the armrest.

4.   *Other Services*   JAL supplies other services to the first-class passengers, such as doorside baggage loading, toiletry sets, slippers, Happi coats (traditional clothes for attending festivals), and electric headphones.

EXECUTIVE CLASS   Executive class is also called business class.

1.   *Seats*   Of a total of 252 seats, JAL offers 108 seats to executive class travelers. Newly designed seats recline at a featured 43-degree angle and have a three-stage adjustable headrest, an adjustable legrest, and a two-stage adjustment for improved back support.

2.   *Meals*   For executive class passengers, JAL offers a special Japanese meal, Jubako, which is served in a set of lacquered containers, just as it is in a traditional teahouse. In addition, in executive class, JAL also offers healthy menus for calorie-watchers and high-quality wines from France and California.

3.   *Video Systems*   Like the passengers in first class, executive class passengers can enjoy JAL's personal video service.

4.   *Other Services*   Each passenger in executive class can get an executive class travel kit, which includes slippers, a shoehorn, a toothbrush and toothpaste, a comb, a clothes brush, and a sleeping mask.

ECONOMY CLASS

1.   *Seats*   In economy class there are 112 seats. Economy class passengers are also treated to JAL's world-renowned service from the

moment of boarding, including a choice of smoking or nonsmoking seats.

2. *Meals*   JAL offers full meal service with choices available, upon prior request, for special diets. Moreover, JAL offers special menus for those passengers who have special needs because of religion or health. Some examples are low cholesterol, no salt, low fat, light vegetarian, strict vegetarian, Hindu, Muslim, kosher, and children's and infants' menus. Passengers may choose cocktails or other beverages at no additional charge.

3. *Other Services*   Like other airlines, JAL offers a wide variety of international reading material, movies, and video and audio entertainment.

PRICE

In the airline industry, developing a pricing strategy is limited to international pricing and official pricing. Each strategy will be explained in detail.

INTERNATIONAL PRICES   First, every airline company has to negotiate prices within the international organization—International Air Transportation Association (IATA)—that controls air fares for all airlines with international routes.

OFFICIAL PRICES   After negotiating with IATA, JAL sets its prices under the official prices that are determined by both the American and Japanese governments. Basically, official prices are based on government issues.

REGIONAL PRICES   Under the restrictions of international and official prices, JAL's headquarters can set its own prices according to the needs in different regions. For example, for the Washington–Tokyo route, a round-trip ticket bought in Washington is cheaper than a round-trip ticket bought in Tokyo because more people have flights that originate in Tokyo than originate in Washington. Thus the need for round-trip tickets is greater in Tokyo. To stimulate need in Washington, DC, JAL set lower prices there.

Generally speaking, JAL develops its pricing strategy based on its competition; that is, if Japan's market is strong, JAL will not follow its competitors in reducing prices; if Japan's market is not strong, JAL will be a follower and lower its prices. JAL has not always followed its competitors, such as Northwest and United Airlines, in lowering prices.

If JAL itself wants to reduce prices, it may lower retail prices by paying kickbacks to travel agencies. It may also offer special commissions or fees to some large companies, and JAL also offers mileage systems for corporate clients.

Exhibit 6-9 shows JAL's prices in three classes.

Promotion

Since the inauguration of JAL's Washington, DC–Tokyo flight in March 1991, JAL has executed a number of promotional programs. However, the Washington branch of JAL is limited in terms of what it can do. It can target customers or prospects in the DC area, but JAL's headquarters in Tokyo makes the decisions that establish promotions for those who are bound for Washington, DC from Tokyo.

Promotion JAL's Headquarters

1. *Ad Campaigns*   JAL employed Richard Gere, an actor famous for the movie "Pretty Woman," for its ad campaign for the inauguration of the Washington to Tokyo route in Japan. Using actors/actresses, singers, and professional athletes is one of the most popular advertising strategies in Japan. JAL had a conservative image that originated when it was a semi-governmental corporation, and it changed its image after privatization in 1987. Also, JAL is trying to capture the youth market with this ad campaign.
2. *Gift Campaigns*   JAL offered gifts to the passengers who flew first class or executive class between Japan and Washington, DC from March 30th to June 29th, 1991. The gifts were (1) a silver fountain pen, (2) a luxury cup and saucer, (3) an Estee Lauder skin care set, (4) a world globe, (5) a Ping Putter Anser 2, which is a golf club, and (6) a Samsonite suitcase.
3. *Sushi Bar in the Air*   JAL provided a sushi bar for passengers who flew first class or executive class during the initial three months of

Class	JAL	ANA	EXHIBIT 6-9
First class		No difference	JAL'S AND ANA'S PRICES
Executive class		No difference	
Economy class	Weekday $760–770	Weekday $770–780	
	Weekend $825–870	Weekend $845–870	

service on this route. This original service was reported favorably by some Japanese newspapers and weekly magazines.

4. *Bonus Mileage* JAL gave both 3,000 and 5,000 bonus miles to those who became new members of JAL's Mileage Bank, and it gave 505 additional miles for flights within six months from the beginning of service to Washington, DC.

PROMOTION DONE BY THE DC BRANCH

1. *Promotions Targeting Americans and Other Foreigners*
   (a) *Ads in the* Washington Post: JAL ran ads in the *Washington Post* because it wanted to notify the start of its new route to both Japanese and Americans.
   (b) *Spot commercials in local radio programs*: JAL aired some commercials to inform Americans, particularly businesspeople in the metropolitan area, of its new route. These commercials were on the air early in the morning and in the evening so commuters would hear them in their cars.
   (c) *Promotions to travel agencies*: In most cases, customers purchase airplane tickets through travel agencies. Thus JAL's marketing efforts target travel agencies as well as travelers. JAL provides various kinds of support for the agencies. First, JAL takes agents to Japan and China so they can learn more about the destinations and hence give customers more information. Such trips are called "firm trips." JAL shows agents its check-in counter and its VIP room at Dulles Airport, and agents board an airplane to see how seats are arranged and to have samples of in-flight meals. All this is intended to let travel agencies know about the quality of JAL's service. In addition, JAL tries to respond to agents' requests that are out of the ordinary. For example, if an agency's customer applies for a package tour after JAL's deadline, it may arrange to include the customer anyway.
   (d) *Direct marketing*: Some international institutions in Washington, such as IMF and the World Bank, are good accounts for JAL because their employees fly to Asia often. As the competition in the U.S. market gets tougher, some American airlines will be weeded out, as were Pan Am and TWA. Although powerful American companies such as Northwest, United, and Delta are dominant in the market, JAL still thinks there is room for another carrier, especially in the ethnic Asian market.

2. *Promotions to the Japanese Market in the DC Area*

   (a) *"Nikko Meijin Kai"*:   JAL sponsored a *"Nikko Meijin Kai,"* an entertainment event where Japanese comedians entertained Japanese in the DC area.

   (b) *Series of lectures*:   JAL sponsored lectures that were given by famous Japanese scholars and journalists.

   (c) *Karaoke party*:   A *karaoke* party is a typical leisure activity for Japanese; it is a singing party with instrumental songs on laser disks. Such a party is usually held at a bar or pub that has a *karaoke* facility. There are few opportunities for Japanese to express themselves in a straightforward manner like Americans or other Westerners because Japanese are generally too shy to express their emotions. Thus most Japanese abroad really miss *karaoke*. For the Japanese community in the DC area, having an opportunity to go to a *karaoke* party offered by JAL was much appreciated.

   (d) *Cherry tree festival*:   JAL invited a professional team of Japanese drummers, *"ondeko-za,"* for the cherry tree festival, which is one of the biggest annual festivals in Washington, DC, at the end of March. JAL also sponsored a Japanese float with JAL's logo for the festival's parade.

   (e) *Ads in Japanese newspapers in the United States*:   JAL ran advertisements in the satellite versions of some Japanese newspapers, such as Asahi, Yomiuri, and Nikkei, to notify Japanese people here that it would start its new service.

   (f) *Sponsorship of Japanese TV programs*:   JAL sponsored some TV programs on channel 54, which covers the District of Columbia and part of northern Virginia.

   (g) *Direct marketing*:   JAL is trying to market directly to some branches of Japanese companies in the DC area, the Japanese Embassy, which has more than one hundred employees, and the National Institutes of Health, where many Japanese researchers work.

DISTRIBUTION

Tickets for JAL's Tokyo–DC flight are sold by JAL's offices and travel agencies all over the world. JAL has a computerized ticketing system called AXESS, which covers JAL's offices throughout the world and travel agencies in Japan. Tickets sold by travel agencies in the United States are recorded in JAL's computer through the Sabre or Apollo system. Upon selling a ticket, travel agencies get 8–10 percent of the ticket value as a commission. Although air tickets from Washington to Tokyo are sold all over the world, there is no doubt that a significant portion of them are sold in the DC area.

In the DC area, JAL has only one office, and it sells most of its tickets through travel agencies. Because JAL is a new entrant in this market, it needs to establish good relations with travel agencies to boost its ticket sales. For this reason JAL offers various kinds of support and special incentives for travel agencies.

Four Japanese travel agencies in the DC area are considered to be the most important distributors for JAL, but ANA has already established a strong relationship with them.

Status

Six months after inauguration of JAL's Washington, DC–Tokyo flight, JAL's market share (in terms of passengers carried from DC to Tokyo during July and August of 1991) reached approximately 23 percent (3,956 passengers) whereas ANA served 67 percent (11,524 passengers). United Airlines and Northwest combined served the remaining 10 percent (1,720 passengers). This means JAL has carried an average of 152 passengers per flight (3,956 ÷ 26 flights), whereas ANA has carried 222 per flight (11,524 ÷ 52 flights). By JAL's estimate, 70 percent of the seats, or 188, must be sold in order to break even.

Although JAL has underperformed ANA and has yet to reach the break-even point, it may not be a bad record for the first six months in operation. After all, JAL may need to allow more time for its strategy to work successfully.

Is it enough for JAL to pursue its present strategy to reach the break-even point and finally outperform ANA? Or does JAL need to take a different course of action? If JAL does need to change its strategy, what kind of strategy should it follow?

NOTES

[1] "Deregulation, Privatization Spur JAL to Diversify Operations," *Aviation Week & Space Technology*, May 8, 1989.

[2] Taneja, N. K., "The International Airline Industry," Lexington, MA: Lexington Books, 1988.

[3] "1990 World Airline Report," *Air Transport World*, June 1991, p. 98.

[4] "All Nippon Seeks New Routes to US, Australia & Europe," *Aviation & Space Technology*, June 22, 1987.

[5] Proctor, Paul, "All Nippon Expanding Fleet, Flight Crews in Move to Develop International Network," *Aviation Week and Technology*, May 13, 1991, pp. 64, 67.

[6] *Ibid.*

[7] Mathewson, William, "All Nippon's Expansion," *The Wall Street Journal*, September 20, 1990, p. A11.

[8] "1990 World Airline Report," *Air Transport World*, June 1991, pp. 178–180.

[9] *Ibid.*

[10] Hamilton, Martha M., "Japan Air Plans to Start Nonstop Flights to Tokyo," *The Washington Post*, December 28, 1990.

[11] *Ibid.*

[12] *Ibid.*

SELECTED REFERENCES FOR FURTHER INFORMATION

Air Transport World (1991). "World Airline Report 1990," June, 98–240.

Aviation Week & Space Technology (1991). "JAL Executives Complete Study on Meeting Future World Transportation Needs," May 13, 41–52.

Aviation Week & Space Technology (1991). "Japan Starts $23 Billion Program to Build New Airport, Expand Haneda and Narita," May 13, 77–78.

Borris, A. (1989). "Look! Up in the Sky. It's the Other Japanese Airline," *Business Week*, (Industrial/Technology Edition), April 17, 92A, 92D.

Danziger, C. (1989). "High Flying Airlines Compete for Business Class Passengers," *Tokyo Business Today*, (September), 46–47.

The Economist (1990). "Calm Before the Storms," August 18, 58.

Hamilton, M. M. (1990). "Japan Air Plans to Start Nonstop Flights to Tokyo," *The Washington Post*, December 28, C2.

International Civil Aviation Organization (1989). "Airlines Financial and Selected Operating Data, By Carrier," Montreal: ICAO.

——— (1989). "Airline Traffic," Montreal: ICAO.

——— (1989). "Airport Traffic and Flight Activity," Montreal: ICAO.

Jones, C. (1990). "Japan's Consumers Protest High Air Fare Costs," *The Christian Science Monitor*, August 22, 5.

Kurtenbach, E. (1988). "Can Japan Airlines Out-Compute Its Rivals?", *Business Week*, (Industrial/Technology Edition), July 11, 76B.

Mathewson, W. (1990). "All Nippon's Expansion," *The Wall Street Journal*, September 20, A11.

McDonald, H. (1991). "Japanese Airlines Look to International Route," *Far Eastern Economic Review*, January 31.

McKenna, J. T. (1990). "Airlines Will Compete for New International Route Authorities," *Aviation Week & Space Technology*, March 19, 113, 115.

Miyazaki, K. (1988). "Deregulation and a New Age of Aviation," *Tokyo Business Today*, (June), 18–22.

Nomani, A. Q., and R. Wartzman (1991). "AMR, in a Sharp Reversal, Curbs, Outlays, Jet Options," *The Wall Street Journal*, September 12.

Ott, J. (1990). "Northwest's New Owners Shed Old Policies, Forge New Image," *Aviation Week & Space Technology*, April 9, 64–68.

———— (1991). "Core U.S. Airlines Battling Hard to Survive International Competition," *Aviation Week & Space Technology*, June 17, 169, 171.

Pinsdorf, M. K. (1991). "Flying Different Skies: How Cultures Respond to Airline Disasters," *Public Relations Review*, Spring, 37–56.

Proctor, P. (1991). "Japan Air System Vies with JAL, ANA in Building Broader Route Network," *Aviation Week & Space Technology*, May 13, 72.

———— (1991). "Japan Capitalizes on Travel Boom, Control of Scarce Airport Slots," *Aviation Week & Space Technology*, May 13, 41–52.

———— (1991). "Japan's Airlines Anticipate Decade of Strong Growth," *Aviation Week & Space Technology*, May 13, 36–37.

———— (1991). "All Nippon Expanding Fleet, Flight Crews in Move to Develop International Network," *Aviation Week & Space Technology*, May 13, 64, 67.

———— (1991). "Strong Asian Economy Boosts Outlooks for Airlines, Industry," *Aviation Week & Space Technology*, May 27, 85–87.

Sanger, D. E. (1991). "A Japanese Airline Duel in the U.S. (All Nippon Airlines and Japan Air Lines Compete for U.S. Market)," *The New York Times*, March 26, C1(N), D1(L).

Shearson Lehman Brothers, Inc. (1991). "Airline International Focus," June 12.

Taneja, N. K. (1988). "The International Airline Industry," Lexington, MA: Lexington Books.

The Wall Street Journal (1991). "Japan Air Seeks Berlin Route," July 29, C4.

Woosely, J. P. (1989). "All Nippon's International Expansion Is on Schedule," *Air Transport World*, June, 38.

Yamaichi Research Institute of Securities and Economics (1991). "Japan Airlines—Company Report (Brief)," February 27.

CASE 7

SINGAPORE AIRLINES

Early in 1947 a twin-engine airspeed consul bearing the insignia "Malayan Airways" completed its first commercial flight linking Singapore, Kuala Lumpur, Ipoh, and Penang. Malayan Airways grew steadily during its first eight years of operation, and by 1955 a fleet of Douglas DC3s was operating flights throughout the region.

With the formation of the Federation of Malaysia in 1963, the airline was renamed Malaysian Airways. In 1966 the governments of Malaysia and Singapore acquired joint control of the airline, which was then renamed Malaysia-Singapore Airlines (MSA). Having developed a route system encompassing most of southeast Asia, MSA began to expand its intercontinental network. The airline's Boeing era began in 1968, when the company acquired three B707s and extended its northern route to Tokyo.

On October 1, 1972, MSA ceased operations and Singapore Airlines (SIA) took to the skies as its successor. The new airline continued to serve the entire international network of the previous company and retained all its B707 and B737 planes. Another B707 was added to the SIA fleet, and in 1973, SIA started to fly the wide-bodied B747s.

On May 10, 1978, SIA embarked on its fleet modernization program by signing a record $900 million order for thirteen B747s and six B727s. This was followed by a $1.8 billion order for eight 747-300s (dubbed BIG TOP) and six A300s in 1981; a $1.4 billion order for six more B747-300s, four B757s, and six A310s; a $3.3 billion order for twenty 747-400s (dubbed MEGATOP) in 1986; and a $5.5 billion order for thirty B747-400s in 1990.

By 1993, SIA's young and modern fleet will comprise twelve MEGA-TOP 747s, fourteen BIG TOP 747s, four B747-200s, two B747 freighters, and sixteen A310s. By the end of 1992, the SIA network stretched across sixty-seven cities in forty countries. The most recent additions to the network are Hanoi and New York.

....

Singapore—The Country

It is perhaps ironic that one of the world's larger airlines is located in one of the world's smaller countries. "No Crime. No Poverty. No Dirt." These are words used to describe the country by many visitors to Singapore. Even visitors from Switzerland and Germany, countries also renowned for their cleanliness, often marvel at the spotless perfection of Singapore. The tree and flower lined expressways are not only free of traffic jams; they are free of litter. Hardly ever will a scrap of paper, a cigarette butt, or a gum wrapper be found on Singapore's streets and expressways. This is accomplished not only by the well articulated values of the nation but by heavy fines for littering, smoking in nondesignated places, or failure to flush a public toilet. Visitors are clearly warned upon entry to the country that use of illegal drugs is punishable by death.

More than 24 million passengers pass through the Changi airport each year on over 1,900 flights a week. The airport is always spotless; even the restrooms are clean with flowers displayed on the tables in men's and women's facilities.

Singapore caters to everyone from businesspersons to "boat bums"—and prospers from them all. Over 250 ships enter the Singapore harbor each day to leave or pick up cargo from nearly every corner of the world. Around the clock, ships await their specific 4-hour unloading period and take their turn in one of the largest and most efficient cargo handling facilities in the world.

To say Singapore is no fun would be unfair. To say that it is "clean" fun is entirely justifiable. Dropping a gum wrapper on the street brings an automatic fine of about $250. But don't worry too much as a foreigner. The Singaporians are so friendly and concerned about other people that should a tourist drop paper on the street a local person will often pick it up and dispose of it properly so the foreigner will not be fined.

Not only the streets are clean in Singapore but so are most options for having fun. Prostitution, drugs, and excessive forms of activity are not part of the scene in Singapore. One of the best known forms of "clean" fun in Singapore is the Jurong Bird Park, featuring the Penguin Parade. Among other things it contains 100 penguins of various species waddling among a landscape of rocks, cliffs, nesting alcoves, and burrows. Jurong Bird Haven displays over 5,000 birds of more than 430 species. In Singapore, even the bird cages are clean!

Much credit for the "economic miracle" called Singapore can be attributed to Lee Kuan Yew, the nation's leader for many years. Lee is an urban planner by discipline, and his training shines through every part of the city, no place more so than the airport. Changi airport has all the normal restaurants, duty-free shops, car rental services, and so forth that you would expect but is run more efficiently than perhaps any other airport in the world. Beyond that, the airport boasts a supermarket, children's play area, cinema, hair dressing salons, nursery, pharmacy, hotel, and a business center complete with first-rate secretarial services. Perhaps the thing that impresses visitors most are the trees lining the road to the airport. With characteristic forethought, Singapore planners planted the trees years before the airport was opened so they would be just right when the airport was completed. Trees and flowers surround Changi airport.

Planning is a key to understanding Singapore. The freeways are not crowded. This is partly due to excellence in design, but also, the government does not allow more cars to use the freeway than it can safely and swiftly accommodate. Private cars must be sold, usually to people in other countries, before they are 10 years old in order to prevent breakdowns and other problems associated with driving old cars. An even shorter period is mandated for commercial vehicles.

A striking aspect of Singapore is the low frequency of crime. This situation is created partly by the condition of having few poor people. Few people are wealthy but most people have enough to live comfortably. Low crime rates are also partly due to strict observance of law and order. Absence of crime was not always the situation in Singapore, however. A Chinese underground controlled drugs, prostitution, gambling, and other assorted vices for centuries. Neither the British nor Japanese could control these practitioners of organized crime. But Lee did, by rounding up the criminals, getting rid of them, and then maintaining a strict system of swift and certain punishment for crime.

Former U.S. President Richard Nixon wrote in his book *1999* that in his 40 years of public service and travels throughout the world, no leader had impressed him more than Lee Kuan Yew. He has helped create not only a country of enormous economic success with some of the highest levels of educational excellence and computer literacy in the world, but also a society that incorporates cultural diversity. The country's official languages are Mandarin and English, but Cantonese and other languages are common. Singapore encompasses population groups of Chinese, Malaysian, English, and other racial and national backgrounds. Significant segments of the population are Buddhist, Christian, Hindu, Jewish, or Muslim in their religious beliefs. Lee explains that the achievements of Singapore are a function of its values. In one of his most famous statements, he is quoted as saying, "We are an immigrant nation. Our values are those required for survival, stability, and success."

SIA Markets and Routes

Singapore Airlines flies around the world. Although SIA serves North America, Europe, and Africa, it is a primary server of Asia and the Pacific Rim.

Pacific Rim Economies

The economies of the Asia-Pacific area have, for 3 decades, been growing two to three times the world average growth rate, and this growth advantage is continuing. Northeast Asia produces one-third of the world's vehicle output, one-quarter of world steel output, two-thirds of world consumer electronics production, and one-third of world computer output. The population and GDP (total and per capita) of key Asian countries are shown in Exhibit 7-1. Monthly wages of East Asian countries are shown in Exhibit 7-2.

Rapid growth is making for some unusual developments. The South Korean economy is now about the size of the economy of Australia. Tai-

EXHIBIT 7-1		Population (millions)	GDP (US$ million)	GNP per capita (US$)
POPULATION AND ECONOMIC SIZE OF KEY ASIAN ECONOMIES, 1990	Japan	123.5	$2,942,890	$25,430
	Hong Kong	5.8	59,670	11,490
SOURCE: THE WORLD BANK. WORLD	Singapore	3.0	34,600	11,160
DEVELOPMENT	Taiwan	20.2	161,600	7,992
REPORT 1992, P. 222– 3, AND NIHON BOEKI	S. Korea	42.8	236,400	5,400
	Malaysia	17.9	42,400	2,320
	Thailand	55.8	80,170	1,420
	Philippines	61.5	43,860	730
	Indonesia	178.2	107,290	570
	China	1,113.7	364,900	370

wan, with a population of 20 million, has an economy half the size of China's billion population. East Asia's share of world trade has been increasing very rapidly and much of the increase in Asian trade is within Asia. Savings and investment throughout the area are at very high levels, with the exception of the Philippines. The levels are high enough to provide self-sustaining growth without the critical need for foreign investment.

The powerhouse economy, of course, is Japan. Alone, it totals about three-quarters of the total economies of East Asia and is nearly the size of Britain, France, and Germany combined. If growth rates continue as they have for the past 10 years, Japan's economy will overtake the United States, making Japan's the largest in the world by the year 2000 and more than twice as large as the U.S. economy on a per capita basis. Japan's current investments are increasingly focusing on Asia because of the higher growth and profitability for Japan. Asia is now a larger export market for Japan than North America.

SIA ROUTES

SIA dominates many routes in the Asia-Pacific area. SIA routes are shown in Exhibit 7-3.

	General Workers
Singapore	$615–846 (8–10)
Hong Kong	769–1000 (10–15)
Taiwan	639–1231 (7–21)
S. Korea (starting salaries)	515 (17)
Malaysia	208 (8–12)
Thailand	162 (5–6
Philippines	123 (2.7)
Indonesia	54–77 (19)
China-Beijing	39 (12)
China-Shanghai	54–77 (10–15)

EXHIBIT 7-2

MONTHLY WAGES IN EAST ASIA (US$, PERCENT CHANGE FROM 1990 IN PARENTHESES)

SOURCE: NIKKEI WEEKLY, NOVEMBER 30, 1991, 3

EXHIBIT 7-3   SIA ROUTES

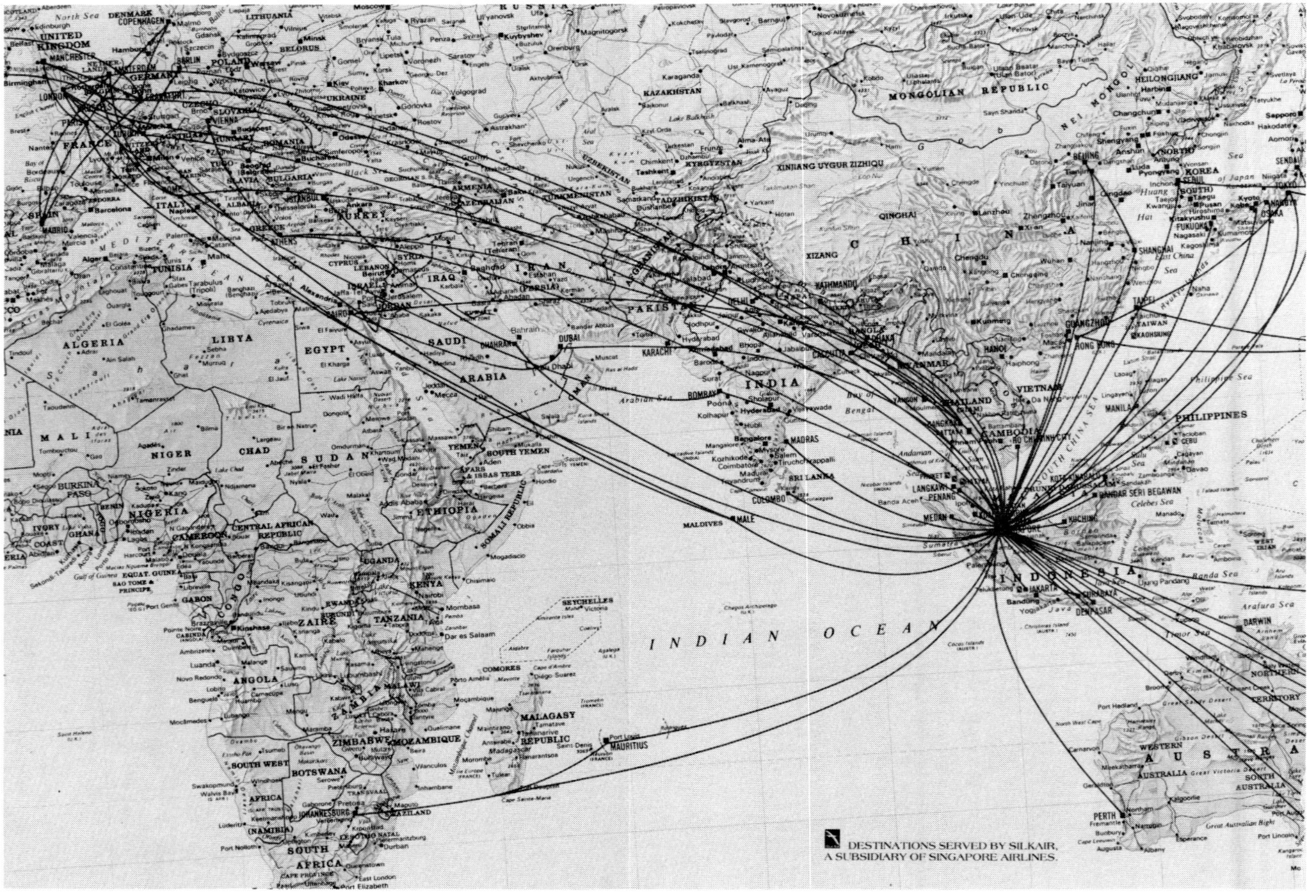

DESTINATIONS SERVED BY SILKAIR, A SUBSIDIARY OF SINGAPORE AIRLINES.

EXHIBIT 7-3   CONTINUED

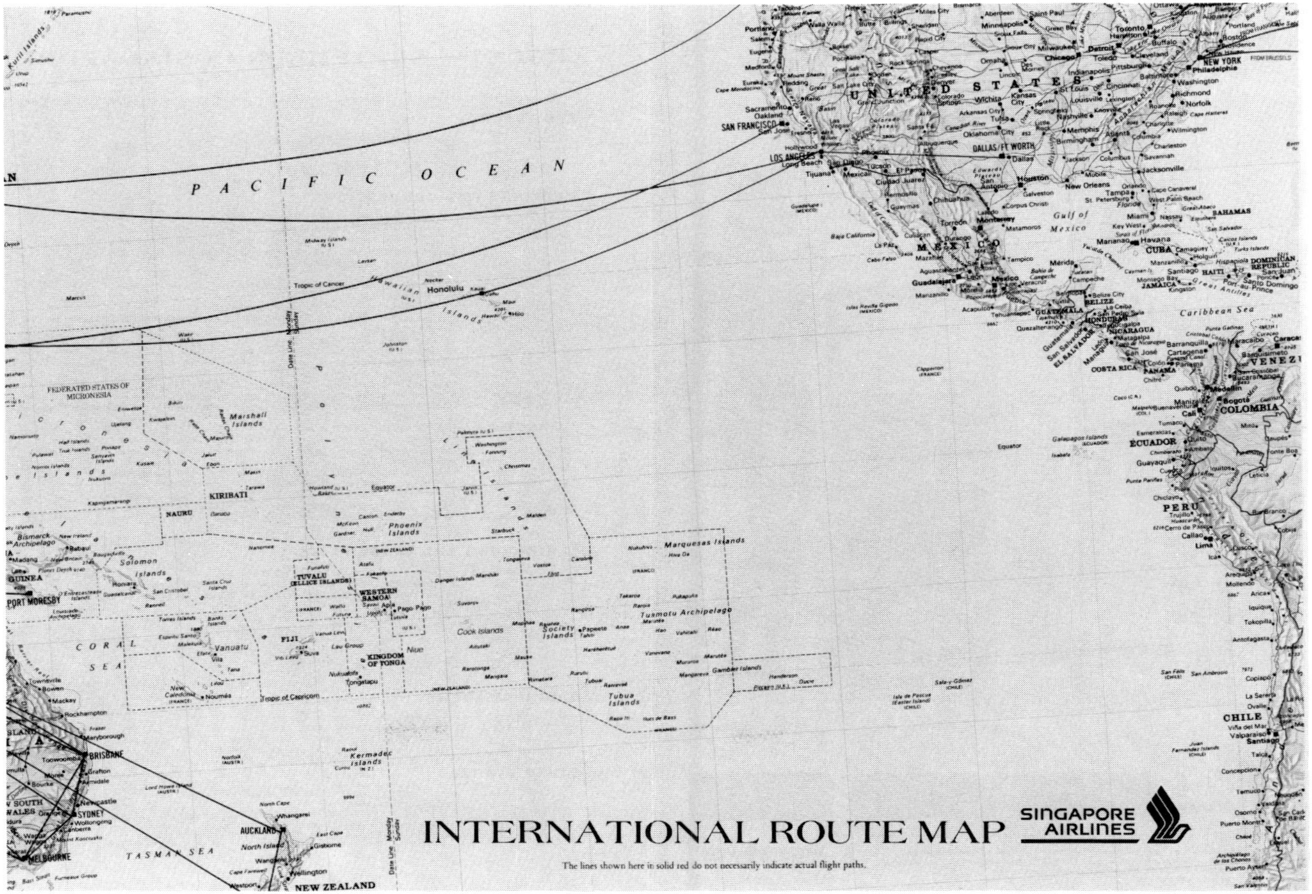

INTERNATIONAL ROUTE MAP

SINGAPORE AIRLINES

The lines shown here in solid red do not necessarily indicate actual flight paths.

In 1992, SIA added Madrid, Johannesburg, and Ho Chi Minh City to its fast growing international network. Madrid is served twice weekly, on Saturday and Wednesday, by B747-400 aircraft. The Saturday flight is via Amsterdam and beyond to Madrid and Paris. The Wednesday flight is via Paris and beyond Madrid to Frankfurt. As the Capital of Spain, Madrid is one of Europe's most interesting destinations with famous museums, art galleries, palaces, churches, shops, and restaurants.

The flight to Johannesburg is a bi-weekly turnaround service on a circular routing. One flight uses the B747-300 and the other, the B747 combi. Flights leave Singapore for Johannesburg via Mauritius on Thursday and return nonstop to Singapore. On Sunday SIA flies nonstop to Johannesburg and returns via Mauritius. Johannesburg is South Africa's largest industrial, financial, and cultural center as well as a gateway to Cape Town in the south, Pretoria and Krueger National Park in the north, and other cities and cultural attractions.

After a break of almost 17 years, SIA has resumed its service to Vietnam. Ho Chi Minh City is served four times weekly. There is also a Hanoi service with two flights each week.

In 1992, SIA also began direct service to New York, offered six times a week. The flights are routed through Frankfurt or Brussels and fly across the Atlantic rather than the Pacific, cutting down the flight time required for the trip between Singapore and New York.

An advertisement used to announce service to New York is shown in Exhibit 7-4. This ad indicates some of the specific details of the flight as well as attempts to capture an image of the city.

SIA Quality Service

Singapore Airline provides a quality of service that is the envy of nearly every other airline in the world. Year after year, Singapore Airline is rated as the number one or two airline in the world for quality of service in a variety of polls of airline passengers and travel agents.

SIA provides three classes of service: economy, business (named Raffles Class), and First Class. Unique among airlines, SIA passengers often describe economy service on a par with the business class of other airlines and rate the Raffles Class as equal to or better than the First Class service of other airlines.

Passengers comment most on the excellence of service provided by flight attendants. They are recruited from Singapore, Taiwan, Japan, and other Asian countries and achieve a level of attention to detail that is unparalleled. In First Class and Raffles Class, passengers find it difficult to finish a glass or dish without someone immediately inquiring about additional needs or removing the used item. Hot foods are very hot and cold foods are appropriately cold, in contrast to the serving practices of some airlines. Small details are obvious everywhere. Hot towels are larger and more frequent than in competitive airlines. Earphones are top quality. The variety of foods and beverages is large, providing greater choices than among most airlines. Toilets are kept clean during the flight and stocked with a large variety of amenities such as perfume, toothbrushes, and other items. Although most of these items are found on other airlines, the quantity and quality of such items is usually better on SIA.

Perhaps First Class best typifies SIA. First Class is normally quite good in most airlines but SIA's First Class reaches new heights of luxury, with the finest champagnes, vintage wines, international beers, gourmet teas, and a choice of meals and mealtimes.

Renowned Krug Grande Curvee champagne is served as an additional choice on flights of two and a half hours, or more. An "Easy Meal" has been introduced to give passengers on long-haul flights the flexibility to dine at the time they prefer. Before the meal, a wide variety of hot savouries is offered. These include hot canapes and satay. The main meal is comprised of hors d'oeuvres, a main course, and fresh fruit for dessert. On SIA's Orient and Trans-Pacific flights, Sheraton Cuisine is offered as a meal choice for lunch, dinner, and supper. This cuisine is a blend of Asian spices and traditional ingredients, with emphasis on fresh, natural ingredients to create lighter, healthier meals. As an elegant finishing touch, SIA offers the best and widest choice of teas—Earl Grey, Darjeeling, Lipton Yellow label, Camomile, and decaffeinated tea. To round off the meal, there's white or dark chocolate.

Entertainment has recently been upgraded with progressive installation of in-seat videos, enabling passengers to watch movies and short features from six channels. Even the cabin has been given a new look. SIA's B747-400 Megatops have been refitted with thicker carpets and seats that offer the highest level of comfort. The airline's most experienced stewards and stewardesses work First Class. Because of their extra years of service, they understand the needs of all types of passengers and attempt to meet every need.

Raffles Class, carrying the name of a famous hotel, street, and historical hero, provides a level of service that rivals First Class on most airlines. The seats provide less leg room than First Class and the foods and wines may not provide quite the level of luxury, but quality is just as high.

Female flight attendants wear a uniform that is as unique as the service level of SIA. The uniform is a traditional floor-length dress, including traditional sandals.

EXHIBIT 7-4   SIA NEW YORK SERVICE

Singapore Airlines now offers the first and only direct service from Singapore to New York. Our exclusive MEGATOP 747 departs daily except Wednesday and flies across the Atlantic (via either Frankfurt or Brussels)

EXHIBIT 7-4   CONTINUED

arriving in New York (JFK) in time for lunch. So now you can fly the fastest same-plane service to the Big Apple, whilst enjoying inflight service even other airlines talk about.   **SINGAPORE AIRLINES**

Promotional Programs

SIA engages in a wide variety of promotional programs. These include television ads in key markets such as Hong Kong, as well as print media and direct marketing in most other important markets.

A major theme or slogan in SIA advertising is "That Singapore Girl." The theme is extended to all media, including print and television, as well as to promotional and specialty items such as laminated cards to attach to luggage with the traveler's business card on one side and a picture and slogan "That Singapore Girl" on the other.

Singapore Airlines participates in the frequent flyer programs of American, Delta, and other U.S. airlines. In addition, it has special programs such as the SIA travel bonus, offered for a limited time to passengers flying the Raffles Class to the United States. Any passenger traveling the SIA Raffles Class from Hong Kong to San Francisco with SIA adult-fare tickets purchased in Hong Kong within the promotional period is entitled to an "Award MCO" (miscellaneous charges order) worth HK$700 for one way, and HK$1,400 for a round trip. The program also provides benefits to passengers heading for destinations beyond San Francisco as long as they travel Trans-Pacific on specified flights.

The Award MCOs are valid for one year from the date of issue and are good for payment of SIA tickets (including special fare tickets through agents) issued in Hong Kong, excess baggage charges, and the fare difference for upgrading. Passengers using Award MCOs for upgrading get an additional bonus. Only HK$4,200 worth of Award MCO is needed for one-way upgrading from the Raffles Class to First Class (and HK$8,400 for round trip), much less than the original fare difference between the two classes.

SIA also initiates other special promotions. Often these feature special events for travel agents, corporate travel planners, and other influential people. An example of such a promotion for the Hong Kong travel business community is shown in Exhibit 7-5.

Researching Decision Processes

A continual problem facing airline management is the question, "How do customers decide which airline to fly?" Is their decision based on schedules? Price? Service? Food and beverage? Equipment? Or some combination of these and other attributes?

EXHIBIT 7-5   SIA PROMOTIONAL MEETING FOR HONG KONG TRAVEL
PLANNERS

SQ TOPICS

1992 MAY ISSUE   SINGAPORE AIRLINES HONG KONG

SIA'S ANNUAL DINNER "THE ASEAN ROUNDABOUT" WAS AN ALL-ROUND SUCCESS.

The Asean Roundabout Hub display was the centre of attention.

First Prize Winner, Mr. Simon Yim, Air Goal International Ltd.

The Playboy Bunnies had the place hopping.

The reception area had many welcoming Asean touches.

Once again, SIA played host to its many friends in Hong Kong's travel industry with its annual dinner. The theme of "Asean Roundabout" was to highlight Singapore as a hub for travel to the Asean countries — Indonesia, Malaysia, Brunei, Philippines and Thailand. The spectacular dinner featured spicy sensations from around the region. This year the entertainment had even more bounce, with a team of Playboy Girls high-tailing it into town. The four beautiful bunnies sang and danced their way through a long line up of songs — "Money, Money, Money", "Hanky Panky", "Get Ready", and many other pop hits. There were two Lucky Draws. Table Prizes included name card holders and calculators. Grand Prizes were round trip tickets to Singapore on Singapore Airlines and tickets to any one Asean destination served by Silk Air.

Indeed, it was a night roundly applauded by everyone.

EXHIBIT 7-6   SIA MARKETING RESEARCH QUESTIONNAIRE

Dear Passenger

We are pleased to welcome you on board and hope that you have an enjoyable flight. We would like to ensure that we continue to provide you with the best possible service.

We therefore regularly monitor the quality of our services in order to determine areas where we can further improve our performance.

Please help us by taking a few minutes to complete this questionnaire. We are surveying only a scientifically selected sample of passengers on each flight. Your opinions are therefore of great importance to us.

One of our cabin crew will collect it prior to landing.

Thank you for your assistance.

Michael J. N. Tan
Deputy Managing Director
(Commercial)

Date: _____   Flight No. SQ _____

1. PLEASE RATE EACH OF THE FOLLOWING SERVICES, BASED ON THIS PRESENT TRIP.

Please check ☑ one of these 5 ratings, for each service listed:

	EXCELLENT 1	GOOD 2	AVERAGE 3	POOR 4	VERY POOR 5
INFLIGHT SERVICE:					
Friendly, helpful attitude	☐	☐	☐	☐	☐
Prompt, efficient service	☐	☐	☐	☐	☐
Clarity of PA (Public Address) system	☐	☐	☐	☐	☐
Announcements by cabin crew	☐	☐	☐	☐	☐
Announcements by captain or cockpit crew	☐	☐	☐	☐	☐
FOOD AND BEVERAGE:					
Eye appeal of food	☐	☐	☐	☐	☐
Taste of food	☐	☐	☐	☐	☐
Quality of food	☐	☐	☐	☐	☐
Did you get your choice of main meal? 1 ☐ Yes 2 ☐ No					
Taste/flavour of coffee/tea	☐	☐	☐	☐	☐
Quality of wines	☐	☐	☐	☐	☐
Variety of choice of wines	☐	☐	☐	☐	☐
INFLIGHT ENTERTAINMENT:					
Inflight music/audio programmes:					
• Music/audio programme selection	☐	☐	☐	☐	☐
• Sound quality	☐	☐	☐	☐	☐
Inflight movies:					
• Types of movies shown	☐	☐	☐	☐	☐
• Picture quality	☐	☐	☐	☐	☐
• Sound quality	☐	☐	☐	☐	☐
AIRCRAFT INTERIOR:					
Aircraft seating comfort	☐	☐	☐	☐	☐
Clean cabin and seats	☐	☐	☐	☐	☐
Clean washrooms/toilets	☐	☐	☐	☐	☐

2. DID YOU TELEPHONE AN SIA OFFICE TO MAKE RESERVATIONS?   1 ☐ Yes   2 ☐ No

IF SO, IN WHICH CITY IS THE SIA OFFICE? Please check ☑ one:

☐ 1 Adelaide	☐ 8 Brussels	☐ 15 Jakarta	☐ 22 Melbourne	☐ 29 Rome
☐ 2 Amsterdam	☐ 9 Colombo	☐ 16 Kuala Lumpur	☐ 23 Nagoya	☐ 30 San Francisco
☐ 3 Auckland	☐ 10 Copenhagen	☐ 17 London	☐ 24 New York	☐ 31 Seoul
☐ 4 Bandar Seri Begawan	☐ 11 Denpasar	☐ 18 Los Angeles	☐ 25 Osaka	☐ 32 Singapore
☐ 5 Bangkok	☐ 12 Frankfurt	☐ 19 Madras	☐ 26 Paris	☐ 33 Sydney
☐ 6 Bombay	☐ 13 Fukuoka	☐ 20 Male	☐ 27 Penang	☐ 34 Taipei
☐ 7 Brisbane	☐ 14 Hong Kong	☐ 21 Manila	☐ 28 Perth	☐ 35 Tokyo

Please check ☑ one of these 5 ratings, for each service listed:

	EXCELLENT 1	GOOD 2	AVERAGE 3	POOR 4	VERY POOR 5
Easy to reach office by phone	☐	☐	☐	☐	☐
Fast, efficient reservations	☐	☐	☐	☐	☐
Friendly, helpful attitude	☐	☐	☐	☐	☐

3. AT WHICH AIRPORT DID YOU BOARD THIS FLIGHT? Please check ☑ one:

☐ 1 Adelaide	☐ 8 Brussels	☐ 15 Jakarta	☐ 22 Melbourne	☐ 29 Rome
☐ 2 Amsterdam	☐ 9 Colombo	☐ 16 Kuala Lumpur	☐ 23 Nagoya	☐ 30 San Francisco
☐ 3 Auckland	☐ 10 Copenhagen	☐ 17 London	☐ 24 New York	☐ 31 Seoul
☐ 4 Bandar Seri Begawan	☐ 11 Denpasar	☐ 18 Los Angeles	☐ 25 Osaka	☐ 32 Singapore
☐ 5 Bangkok	☐ 12 Frankfurt	☐ 19 Madras	☐ 26 Paris	☐ 33 Sydney
☐ 6 Bombay	☐ 13 Fukuoka	☐ 20 Male	☐ 27 Penang	☐ 34 Taipei
☐ 7 Brisbane	☐ 14 Hong Kong	☐ 21 Manila	☐ 28 Perth	☐ 35 Tokyo

Please check ☑ one of these 5 ratings, for each service listed:

	EXCELLENT 1	GOOD 2	AVERAGE 3	POOR 4	VERY POOR 5
Fast, efficient check-in	☐	☐	☐	☐	☐
Friendly, courteous check-in	☐	☐	☐	☐	☐
Efficient seat assignment	☐	☐	☐	☐	☐
IF YOU TRANSFERRED FLIGHTS AT SINGAPORE:					
Efficient transfer handling at Changi Airport	☐	☐	☐	☐	☐

4. DID YOU VISIT AN SIA TICKET OFFICE? 1 ☐ Yes 2 ☐ No

IF SO, IN WHICH CITY? Please check ☑ one:

1 Adelaide	8 Brussels	15 Jakarta	22 Melbourne
2 Amsterdam	9 Colombo	16 Kuala Lumpur	23 Nagoya
3 Auckland	10 Copenhagen	17 London	24 New York
4 Bandar Seri Begawan	11 Denpasar	18 Los Angeles	25 Osaka
5 Bangkok	12 Frankfurt	19 Madrid	26 Paris
6 Bombay	13 Fukuoka	20 Male	27 Penang
7 Brisbane	14 Hong Kong	21 Manila	28 Perth

29 Rome	36 Vancouver	
30 San Francisco	37 Zurich	
31 Seoul	38 Others	
32 Singapore	(Please write)	
33 Sydney		
34 Taipei		
35 Tokyo		

Please check ☑ one of these 5 ratings, for each service listed:

	EXCELLENT 1	GOOD 2	AVERAGE 3	POOR 4	VERY POOR 5
Fast, efficient service	☐	☐	☐	☐	☐
Friendly, helpful attitude	☐	☐	☐	☐	☐

5. OVERALL RATING:

All things considered, how would you rate your experience with Singapore Airlines on this trip?

EXCELLENT 1	GOOD 2	AVERAGE 3	POOR 4	VERY POOR 5
☐	☐	☐	☐	☐

6. (i) Have you taken a flight of similar length as this, on another airline, in the past 12 months?

1 ☐ Yes   Continue to 6(ii)   No ☐   Go to Question 6(iv)

(ii) Which other airline did you most recently use on a flight of similar length? Please name the airline and the route travelled on that flight:

Airline : _____ *(Name one airline only – latest travelled)*

Route travelled : _____

(iii) How would you compare that airline with SIA in the following areas?

Please check ☑ one of these 5 ratings, for each service listed:

	WELL ABOVE SIA 1	SLIGHTLY ABOVE SIA 2	SAME AS SIA 3	SLIGHTLY BELOW SIA 4	WELL BELOW SIA 5
Inflight Service	☐	☐	☐	☐	☐
Food and Beverage	☐	☐	☐	☐	☐
Inflight Entertainment	☐	☐	☐	☐	☐
Aircraft Interior / Comfort	☐	☐	☐	☐	☐
Overall Rating	☐	☐	☐	☐	☐

(iv) Have you flown from the same city as this occasion, on another airline, in the past 12 months?

Yes ☐ Continue to 6(v)   No ☐   Go to Question 7

(v) Which other airline did you most recently use from the same city?

Airline : _____ *(Name one airline only – latest travelled)*

(vi) How would you compare that airline with SIA in the following areas?

Please check ☑ one for each service listed :

	WELL ABOVE SIA 1	SLIGHTLY ABOVE SIA 2	SAME AS SIA 3	SLIGHTLY BELOW SIA 4	WELL BELOW SIA 5
Telephone Service	☐	☐	☐	☐	☐
Ticket Office Service	☐	☐	☐	☐	☐
Airport Service	☐	☐	☐	☐	☐

7. STATISTICAL INFORMATION:

I am travelling by: 1 ☐ Economy Class   2 ☐ Business Class   3 ☐ First Class

My age is: 1 ☐ Under 20   2 ☐ 20 to 35   3 ☐ 36 to 49   4 ☐ 50 and over

I am 1 ☐ Male   2 ☐ Female

I am a national of

1 Brunei	8 Hong Kong	15 France	22 Turkey
2 China (PRC)	9 Japan	16 Greece	23 Germany
3 Indonesia	10 South Korea	17 Italy	24 United Kingdom
4 Malaysia	11 Taiwan	18 Netherlands	25 USSR
5 Philippines	12 Other Asia	19 Scandinavia	26 Other Europe
6 Singapore	13 Austria	20 Spain	27 United States
7 Thailand	14 Belgium	21 Switzerland	28 Canada

29 Latin America	36 Sri Lanka
30 Australia	37 Maldives
31 New Zealand	38 Mauritius
32 India	39 Egypt
33 Bangladesh	40 United Arab Emirates
34 Nepal	41 Saudi Arabia
35 Pakistan	42 Africa
	43 Others

The main purpose of my travel, on this trip, is:

1 ☐ Business   2 ☐ Pleasure/vacation   3 ☐ Business and pleasure   4 ☐ Other purpose

NUMBER OF TRIPS ABROAD IN PAST 3 YEARS:
Not counting this trip, the number of trips abroad which I have made by air in the past 3 years is (count each round trip as one trip):

1 ☐ None   2 ☐ 1 – 5   3 ☐ 6 – 20   4 ☐ 21 and above

Your name and address please (optional)

Name _____

Address _____

_____

OUR CREW WILL COLLECT THIS QUESTIONNAIRE BEFORE LANDING. THANK YOU.

SINGAPORE AIRLINES

EXHIBIT 7-6 CONTINUED

敬啟者：

我們很高興您加入航空公司家庭。航空旅途愉快，祝您旅途愉快。為感念您對本機的喜愛與支持，我們希望能將更好的服務提供給您。故此，我們將竭盡所能，以便我們能進一步改善我們的服務。我們誠摯的邀請您，提出寶貴的問卷意見。填完後交由本機客艙服務人員收回即可。

問卷：您的意見對我們十分重要。

謝謝。您的合作。

Michael J. N. Tan
副董事兼經理
（商業部）

日期：_____　班機號碼 SQ _____

1. 現在請對本機次的下列服務項目給予評估：

請就以下各項服務中，勾出您各項對服務的滿意度等級

機內服務	非常滿意	滿意	普通	欠佳	很差
友善服務的態度	☐	☐	☐	☐	☐
快速高效的服務	☐	☐	☐	☐	☐
播音器（PA）系統的清晰程度	☐	☐	☐	☐	☐
機艙服務機組人員的儀容	☐	☐	☐	☐	☐

食品與飲料					
食物的選擇	☐	☐	☐	☐	☐
食物的美味	☐	☐	☐	☐	☐
飲料種類					

您是否曾從選單上做過主菜選擇？　1 是　2 否　不是

咖啡和茶的味道	☐	☐	☐	☐	☐
酒的品質	☐	☐	☐	☐	☐
酒的多樣化	☐	☐	☐	☐	☐

機上的娛樂					
機上的音樂／音響節目					
・音樂／音響節目選擇	☐	☐	☐	☐	☐
・聲音素質	☐	☐	☐	☐	☐
機上的電影					
・播放電影的種類	☐	☐	☐	☐	☐
・聲音素質	☐	☐	☐	☐	☐
・畫面素質	☐	☐	☐	☐	☐

機艙					
座位的舒適	☐	☐	☐	☐	☐
機艙及座位的清潔	☐	☐	☐	☐	☐
洗手間之清潔	☐	☐	☐	☐	☐

お客様各位。

当機をご利用いただき誠にありがとうございます。皆様に快適なフライトをお楽しみいただくことをより願っております。これからも最高のサービスを皆様にお届けしたいと考えております。さて、このアンケートは、私共がお客様に対する一層のサービスの向上を図るために定期的に行っているものです。

お客様の意見は我々十分重要。下記の質問にお答えいただければ幸いです。なお、当調査は科学的な方法によりアトランダムにお客様をお選びし、実施いたしております。皆様のご意見は回収係りにとり大変貴重なものとなります。

キャビン・クルーの係の者がお手持前に回収に参ります。

ご協力ありがとうございます。

Michael J. N. Tan
常務取締役代理
（商業部）

年月日 _____　便名 SQ _____

1. 今ご利用の当機について各サービスごとに評価をお願い致します。

各サービスの項目につき五段階の中からひとつを選んで☑を記入して下さい。

機内サービス	満足している	やや満足	普通	やや不満	非常に不満
接客員・他の態度	☐	☐	☐	☐	☐
迅速で手際よいサービス	☐	☐	☐	☐	☐
機内放送の明瞭さ	☐	☐	☐	☐	☐
客室乗務員によるアナウンス	☐	☐	☐	☐	☐
キャビンアテンダントと客室員によるアナウンス	☐	☐	☐	☐	☐

食事と飲物					
食べ物	☐	☐	☐	☐	☐
味	☐	☐	☐	☐	☐
質	☐	☐	☐	☐	☐

お好みの料理をメニューより選べましたか？　1 はい　2 いいえ

コーヒー／紅茶の味、風味	☐	☐	☐	☐	☐
ワインの品質	☐	☐	☐	☐	☐
ワインの種類の豊富さ	☐	☐	☐	☐	☐

機内娯楽					
機内音楽／音声プログラム					
・音楽／音声プログラム選択	☐	☐	☐	☐	☐
・音質	☐	☐	☐	☐	☐
機内映画					
・上映映画の種類	☐	☐	☐	☐	☐
・映像の質	☐	☐	☐	☐	☐
・音質	☐	☐	☐	☐	☐

機内設備					
客室内及び座席の座り心地	☐	☐	☐	☐	☐
客室内及び座席の清潔さ	☐	☐	☐	☐	☐
トイレ内の清潔さ	☐	☐	☐	☐	☐

Cher Passager,

Nous vous souhaitons la bienvenue à bord et espérons que vous faites un vol agréable. Nous aimerions continuer à vous offrir le meilleur des services.

Ceci exige que nous contrôlions régulièrement la qualité de notre service afin de déterminer le secteur où nous pouvons l'améliorer.

Nous vous serions très reconnaissant si vous vouliez nous aider en remplissant ce questionnaire. Notre enquête est réalisée uniquement selon un échantillon de passagers choisis scientifiquement sur chaque vol.

Votre avis est très important pour le succès de cette étude.

Notre personnel de cabine ramassera les questionnaires avant l'atterrissage.

Merci de votre coopération.

Michael J.N. Tan
Directeur Général Adjoint
(Service Commercial)

Date: _____ Vol No. SQ _____

1. VEUILLEZ EVALUER CHACUN DES SERVICES SUIVANTS EN VOUS BASANT SUR LE PRESENT VOYAGE

Marquez l'une des cinq appréciations pour chaque service mentionné ☑

	EXCELLENT 1	BON 2	MOYEN 3	MAUVAIS 4	TRÈS MAUVAIS 5
SERVICE A BORD:					
Attitude amicale et prévenante	☐	☐	☐	☐	☐
Service rapide et efficace	☐	☐	☐	☐	☐
Clarté du système P.A. (sonorisation extérieure)	☐	☐	☐	☐	☐
Annonces par le personnel de cabine	☐	☐	☐	☐	☐
Annonces du pilote ou du personnel de cockpit	☐	☐	☐	☐	☐
BOISSONS ET REPAS:					
Aspect des plats	☐	☐	☐	☐	☐
Goût de la nourriture	☐	☐	☐	☐	☐
Qualité de la nourriture	☐	☐	☐	☐	☐
Avez-vous obtenu votre choix du repas principal?	1☐ Oui	2☐ Non			
Arôme/saveur du café/thé	☐	☐	☐	☐	☐
Qualité des vins	☐	☐	☐	☐	☐
Variété du choix des vins	☐	☐	☐	☐	☐
DIVERTISSEMENT A BORD:					
Musique/programmes d'écoute en cours de vol					
• Sélection musique/programme d'écoute	☐	☐	☐	☐	
• Qualité du son	☐	☐	☐	☐	
Films en cours de vol					
• Types de films projetés	☐	☐	☐	☐	
• Qualité de l'image	☐	☐	☐	☐	
• Qualité du son	☐	☐	☐	☐	
INTERIEUR DE L'AVION:					
Confort des sièges	☐	☐	☐	☐	
Propreté de la cabine et des sièges	☐	☐	☐	☐	
Propreté des toilettes	☐	☐	☐	☐	

Lieber Passagier!

Wir freuen uns, Sie an Bord begrüßen zu können, und hoffen, daß Sie einen angenehmen Flug haben werden. Wir möchten sicher gehen, daß wir Ihnen weiterhin den bestmöglichen Service bieten werden.

Aus diesem Grund müssen wir regelmäßig die Qualität unseres Services überprüfen, um Bereiche aufzudecken, in denen wir unsere Leistung verbessern können.

Bitte unterstützen Sie uns, indem Sie sich ein paar Minuten Zeit nehmen und diesen Fragebogen ausfüllen. Wir befragen lediglich eine statistisch ausgewählte Stichprobe von Passagieren auf jedem Flug.

Ihre Meinung ist daher äußerst wichtig für uns.

Ein Mitglied unserer Crew wird den Fragebogen vor der Landung einsammeln.

Vielen Dank für Ihre Unterstützung.

Michael J.N. Tan
Stellvertretender Geschäftsführer
(Kommerz-Abteilung)

Datum: _____ Flugnummer SQ _____

1. BEWERTEN SIE BITTE DIE FLUGGESELLSCHAFT AUF DIESER GEGENWÄRTIGEN REISE.

Kreuzen Sie bitte für jede der aufgezeichneten Dienstleistungen eine der 5 Spalten an ☑

	AUSGEZEICHNET 1	GUT 2	MITTELMÄSSIG 3	SCHLECHT 4	SEHR SCHLECHT 5
SERVICE AN BORD:					
Freundliches hilfreiches Verhalten	☐	☐	☐	☐	☐
Sofortige tüchtige Bedienung	☐	☐	☐	☐	☐
Deutlichkeit der Lautsprecheranlage	☐	☐	☐	☐	☐
Durchsagen des Kabinenpersonals	☐	☐	☐	☐	☐
Durchsagen des Flugkapitäns oder der Cockpitbesatzung	☐	☐	☐	☐	☐
SPEISEN UND GETRÄNKE:					
Appetitlichkeit/Aussehen der Speisen	☐	☐	☐	☐	☐
Geschmack der Speisen	☐	☐	☐	☐	☐
Qualität des Essens	☐	☐	☐	☐	☐
Haben Sie das Hauptgericht erhalten, das Sie gewählt haben?	1☐ Ja	2☐ Nein			
Geschmack/Aroma von Kaffee/Tee	☐	☐	☐	☐	☐
Qualität der Weine	☐	☐	☐	☐	☐
Auswahlmöglichkeiten an Weinen	☐	☐	☐	☐	☐
UNTERHALTUNG AN BORD:					
Inflight-Musik-/Audio-Aufzeichnungen:					
• Auswahl der Musik-/Audio-Aufzeichnungen	☐	☐	☐	☐	
• Tonqualität	☐	☐	☐	☐	
Inflight-Filme:					
• Art der gezeigten Filme	☐	☐	☐	☐	
• Bildqualität	☐	☐	☐	☐	
• Tonqualität	☐	☐	☐	☐	
FLUGZEUG-INNENRAUM:					
Sitzkomfort im Flugzeug	☐	☐	☐	☐	
Saubere Kabine und Sitze	☐	☐	☐	☐	
Saubere Waschräume/Toiletten	☐	☐	☐	☐	

Singapore Airlines maintains a marketing research group to provide information about decision processes on a continuing basis, as do other airlines. A variety of methods are employed but one of the most important is a passenger opinion survey. A copy of a recent form of this survey is shown in Exhibit 7-6. The complete form is presented in English, although the first page of the questionnaire is shown in the other languages most likely to be read by passengers.

One of the issues facing management is the question of whether or not this questionnaire contains the relevant attributes that should be measured concerning airline service. Another question facing management is how best to segment the market for airline service. The latter part of the questionnaire in Exhibit 7-6 offers many possibilities for analysis of demographic and other data.

THE WORLD WILDLIFE FUND *

T akao Shimizu is a prominent Japanese businessman who recently misplaced his *hanko*, a seal that has been used in Japan for centuries in place of handwritten signatures. In ancient times the seals were made from gold and used only by the elite. Now the seals are commonly used and may be purchased for less than $10. Mr. Shimizu, like many Japanese, prefers that his *hanko* be tooled from smooth, white elephant ivory, and therefore he will spend more than $200 to replace his *hanko*.

Sarah Hamilton is a wealthy Washington socialite. Because it is becoming fashionable to do so, she calls herself an environmentalist and has attended several black tie events in order to raise money for this worthy cause. Ms. Hamilton enjoys wearing black and drapes herself in ivory jewelry to provide contrast. This rare and expensive substance gives her a feeling of status and allure.

Mr. Shimizu and Ms. Hamilton have one thing in common. They purchased products that were manufactured from raw ivory poached in Africa and exported to Hong Kong. Their values and attitudes toward ivory products have helped to drive the African elephant population to near extinction.

*This case was prepared by Byoungman Ahn, Helen Burch, Paula Commodore, Douglas Houston, Elizabeth Jones, James Love, and Tom Taggart under the direction of Professor Salah S. Hassan at The George Washington University.

THE ELEPHANT POPULATION

In 1900, the African elephant population was approximately one million. Through controlled hunting and the creation of protected reserves, the elephant population gradually rose to approximately 1.5 million by 1970. Illegal hunting, known as poaching, has escalated over the past decade, causing a decline in the African elephant population from 1.3 million in 1979 to 609,000 in 1990 (see Exhibit 8-1).

The range land available to support the elephant has also diminished. At the beginning of the sixteenth century, Africa had an estimated 16 million people and 10 million elephants. Elephants roamed over virtually all of the sub-Saharan continent.[1] Today the human population of Africa has soared to 500 million, and it continues to grow at a rate of 3 to 4 percent

EXHIBIT 8-1   ELEPHANT POPULATION

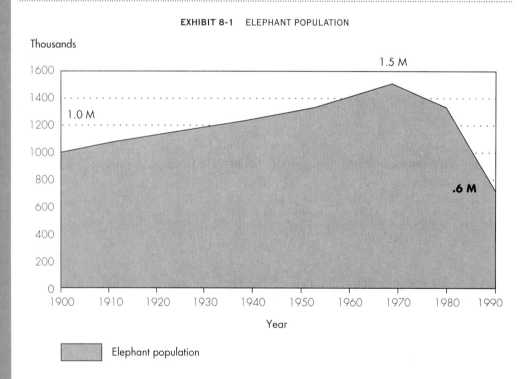

Elephant population

per year. The elephant now occupies less than one-fourth of Africa's area. Zoologists estimate that today Africa can support only two million elephants.

THE IVORY MARKET

As the demand for ivory increased, its price skyrocketed. As a result, poaching became rampant. Thirty years ago, the world market price for ivory was around $2.45 per pound. That price rose to approximately $27 per pound by 1983 and to $82 per pound by 1988. In the Far East, where ivory is a traditional symbol of status, the price rose from $12 per pound in 1970 to approximately $114 per pound by 1989 (see Exhibit 8-2).

Penalties are severe for ivory poachers in many African countries. In Kenya, officials have orders to "shoot on sight" any poachers. Additionally, Tanzania and Kenya have mandatory five-year prison terms for possession of ivory. But with the market price of ivory escalating, African

EXHIBIT 8-2   PRICE OF IVORY

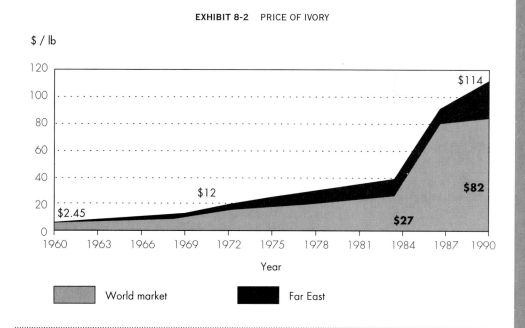

poachers are willing to accept the risk. An African villager might make $20 per month if he could find a legitimate job. One successful poaching expedition can yield 40 to 50 pounds of ivory. At better than $100 per pound and a 25 percent profit margin (after renting automatic weapons and purchasing ammunition), a team of poachers can make $250 to $300 in one outing.

The world market demanded about 825 tons of raw ivory per year, with the Far East as the primary source of demand. The mature elephants were the first ones targeted because they yield an average of 20 pounds per tusk. By 1990 the mature population had been destroyed and poachers had to settle for the juvenile population, which yields an average 10 pounds per tusk. Therefore, more elephants have to be killed to satisfy the market demand. As many as 80,000 elephants per year were slaughtered in 1989.

Compounding the population problem is the effect that illegal poaching is having on the elephant society. The lifespan of male elephants is typically 40 to 60 years. They do not begin to breed until they reach 30 years of age. Today, in many parts of Africa, it is rare to find male elephants older than 30.[2] The older females are disappearing also. Elephant society is matriarchal, and without the older females, the survival of the young is estimated at about 50 percent.[3] Therefore, although 600,000 elephants sounds like a large population, the problem runs much deeper. Ivory poaching strikes the center of elephant society and puts the ability of the herd to replinish itself at high risk.

GENERAL ENVIRONMENTAL CONCERN

Highly publicized environmental disasters, such as the Exxon Valdez oil spill in 1990, are increasingly focusing society's attention on the environment and important conservation issues, such as the plight of the African elephant. According to a recent Gallup poll, 78 percent of those surveyed consider themselves to be environmentalists.[4] In addition, about one-half (51 percent) of those polled have given money to an environmental cause. The same poll summarized consumer attitudes toward the seriousness of environmental problems as shown in Exhibit 8-3.

These concerns are listed in order of the level of consumers' concern, with "pollution of drinking water" topping the list and "acid rain" falling at the bottom. However, even more importantly, this survey demonstrates that very few people have no opinion.

While a majority of people call themselves environmentalists, only 28 percent have taken action, such as boycotting a company because of its environmental record. Boycotting is the most common and well known way in which consumers' attitudes and behaviors toward a product are changed. Boycotts have been employed as a coercive mechanism to promote change for centuries. *Black's Law Dictionary* defines a boycott as a "concerted refusal to do business with a particular person or business in order to obtain concessions or to express displeasure with certain acts or practices of a person or business."[5]

Boycotts are important for affecting change. However, they have not

Environmental Concern	Great Deal	Fair amount	Only a little	Not at all	No opinion
Pollution of drinking water	67%	19%	10%	3%	1%
Pollution of rivers, lakes, and reservoirs	67	21	8	3	1
Contamination of soil and water by toxic waste	62	21	11	5	1
Air pollution	59	27	10	4	*
Ocean and beach pollution	53	26	14	6	1
Loss of natural habitat for wildlife	53	27	15	5	*
Damage to the earth's ozone layer	49	24	15	8	4
Contamination of soil and water by radioactivity	44	25	20	10	1
Loss of tropical rain forests	42	25	21	10	2
"Greenhouse" effect or global warming	35	27	21	12	5
Acid rain	34	30	20	13	3

*Less than one percent

EXHIBIT 8-3
SERIOUSNESS OF ENVIRONMENTAL PROBLEMS
SOURCE: THE GALLUP POLL MONTHLY, APRIL 1991

been readily accepted as a marketing measure. This situation appears to be changing because of the following occurrences:

1. Boycotts are reaching epidemic proportions. This means that marketers should no longer dismiss boycotts as social quirks that were prevalent only in the late 1960s and early 1970s.
2. Boycott agents are becoming more sophisticated. Experienced boycott organizers have adopted high-technology techniques to improve the effectiveness of their cause.
3. Recent court decisions have supported boycotts as legal forms of protest. Recent rulings indicate that targets of boycotts have limited refuge from boycotts in the legal system.
4. Marketing strategists have neglected marketing policy boycotts as relevant environmental forces.
5. Marketing policy boycotts present a "double-barreled" challenge to marketing.

A study reported in the *Journal of Marketing* in 1987 found that a boycott will be most effective when the economic and image pressures on a target are high and the target's policy commitment is low.[6]

Boycotts can be implemented in several ways and in varying degrees. Below are some of the popular boycott mechanisms used:

1. *Attacking brand-name products.* Examples are the successful campaign to stop canners from selling tuna fish caught in nets that also trap and kill dolphins and the boycott of products of companies that experiment on animals. L'Oreal has been targeted by the People for the Ethical Treatment of Animals (PETA) with such slogans as "L'Oreal Sunscreen: First fry white mice in tin foil."[7]

   The success of these campaigns, which are directed at a single company, is contingent on their ability to persuade others to adopt the same tactics. For example, antiapartheid groups concentrated on a boycott of Shell gasoline although Shell is just one of many multinational companies that have done business in South Africa.
2. *Offering carrots and sticks.* This tactic is used when companies are singled out for either honorable or dishonorable corporate response to consumer concerns.
3. *Shaming shoppers.* Most notable in this category is the treatment of fur-wearing persons. People who wear furs are often barraged by animal-rights advocates who hold them indirectly responsible for the cruel deaths suffered by furry animals.
4. *Pressuring shareholders.* This tactic was demonstrated when AT&T announced that because of growing political sensitivity, it would no longer make charitable donations to the Planned Parenthood Federation of America. The chairman of the federation, Ms. Faye

Wattleton, countered with full-page advertisements in newspapers that appealed to Americans to oppose "this act of corporate cowardice" by donating AT&T shares or proxies to the federation so that it could exercise direct influence on AT&T.

5. *Scaring consumers.* Midwest dairy farmers were able to temporarily halt the use of a hormone protein, developed by Monsanto, by emphasizing health risks (which Monsanto claims are nonexistent).

Conservation groups have taken advantage of these changing attitudes to further their respective causes. Events such as Earth Day have motivated the consuming public to a new level of awareness and action. Consumer movements are no longer disorganized, ill-defined, ineffective, or disrespected. Gone from our society are the images of the 1960s: Nader's Raiders climbing the steps of the capitol and housewives boycotting iceberg lettuce. Instead, movements have taken on a corporate style of marketing and are becoming increasingly effective.

OVERVIEW OF THE WORLD WILDLIFE FUND

One effective group is the World Wildlife Fund (WWF), which recently celebrated its 30th anniversary. Founded in 1961, WWF began as a small grant-making organization dedicated to protecting endangered and biologically significant habitats in Latin America, Africa, and Asia. Its primary strengths were scientific research and field work in targeted countries.

In 1985, WWF merged with the Conservation Foundation (CF), whose primary strengths were policy analysis and implementation. The marriage of these two organizations and the resulting synthesis of their strengths created the largest not-for-profit conservation foundation in the world. In the 30 years since its inception, WWF has worked in more than 140 countries and has implemented more than 3,000 projects. In short, WWF works to change attitudes and behaviors that destroy natural resources for short-term gain.

As it exists today, WWF is an international organization with a global vision of conservation. Worldwide, it has more than three million members. The WWF network has organizations, associates, or representatives in more than 40 countries, including Brazil, the United Kingdom, Kenya, India, and Japan. The organization is headquartered in Gland, Switzerland, but its largest office is in Washington, DC.

Indeed, WWF's Washington office has become the largest single source of private support for conservation work. It now has a budget of

$30 million and a domestic membership of more than one million. This represents one-third of WWF's memberships worldwide. WWF memberships have increased from 200,000 to one million in the last three decades.[8]

MEMBERSHIPS AND FUNDRAISING

Like most not-for-profit organizations, WWF recognizes different membership levels and accompanying benefits. For contributions under $1,000, there are six types of memberships available:

$ 15   Member
$ 25   Friend
$ 50   Associate
$100   Contributor
$200   Sponsor
$500   Sustainer

These six membership levels receive a number of benefits.

- A membership card.
- A yearly subscription to WWF's bimonthly newsletter featuring articles, photographs, and field reports on projects.
- Invitations to WWF activities such as presentation lectures, and opportunities to visit WWF project sites.[9]

For more personal involvement with WWF, partners-in-conservation memberships are available. The partnership program consists of four levels of support:

$ 1,000   Partner
$ 2,500   Sponsoring partner
$ 5,000   Leadership partner
$10,000   President's circle

At the partner's level, members receive four additional benefits:

- The partner's letter, a quarterly publication featuring a behind-the-scenes look at WWF conservation programs and announcements of partner's activities.
- The partner's dinner, a yearly event where members meet WWF's scientists, board of directors, national council, and fellow partners.
- The partner's international conservation tour, which provides partners exceptional opportunities to visit priority conservation projects.
- Partner's briefings, scheduled around the country for members to meet conservation leaders and WWF staff.[10]

Corporate sponsorships are also a source of revenue for WWF. Ford Motor Company funds a portion of WWF's Eastern European program, providing support for local nongovernment organizations. Procter & Gamble Company makes grants toward WWF's global conservation projects, and the S. C. Johnson & Sons Company donates funds through a program called "We Care For America." [11]

The combined sources of revenue for WWF and CF for 1990 are as follows (see Exhibit 8-4): [12]

EXHIBIT 8-4

SOURCE: WORLD WILDLIFE FUND AND THE CONSERVATION FOUNDATION 1990: A COMBINED REPORT

World Wildlife Fund, Inc.
Source of Revenues
Fiscal Year Ending June 30, 1990

Individuals	$30,050,292
Corporations	387,739
Foundations	2,855,528
Investments	2,309,897
Government Grants and Contracts	3,350,020
Royalties	3,573,850
Contributed Advertising	1,330,004
Total Revenues	$43,857,330

Program Expenses

Latin America and Carribean	$6,662,777
Africa and Madagascar	4,043,907
Asia and Pacific	3,709,249
Conservation science and policy	5,151,128
Sustainable Development	1,284,270
Membership Outreach	5,514,865
Public Education	9,631,379
Total Program Expenses	$35,997,575

The Conservation Foundation, Inc.
Source of Revenues
Fiscal Year Ending June 30, 1990

Individuals	$286,321
Corporations	485,262
Foundations	2,085,974
Investment Revenue	404,914
Government Grants	1,606,861
Publication Sales	587,415
Total Revenues	$5,456,747

Program Expenses

Land and Wildlife	$1,542,612
Environmental Quality	1,248,936
RESOLVE	987,413
Sustainable Development	501,375
Crosscutting Programs	288,155
Public Education	317,130
Total Program Expenses	$4,885,621

Source	Percentage of Total Revenue	$ Amount
Individuals	62%	$30,336,613
Corporations	2	873,001
Foundations	10	4,941,502
Investments	6	2,714,793
Government	10	4,956,881
Other	10	5,491,287
Total	100%	$49,314,077

Purpose and Programs

WWF's core function is defined by its mission statement as follows:

> WWF's mission is the conservation of nature. Using the best available scientific knowledge and advancing that knowledge where we can, we work to preserve the diversity and abundance of life on earth and the health of ecological systems by:
>
> 1. Protecting natural areas and wild populations of plants and animals, including endangered species;
> 2. Promoting sustainable approaches to the use of renewable natural resources; and
> 3. Promoting more efficient use of resources and energy and the maximum reduction of pollution.
>
> We are committed to reversing the degradation of our planet's natural environment, and to building a future in which human needs are met in harmony with nature. We recognize the critical relevance of human numbers, poverty, and consumption patterns to meeting these goals.[13]

Currently, WWF has ongoing projects across five continents. Its four top priority areas are (1) rain forests, (2) endangered species, (3) global warming, and (4) wildlife trade. The programs of WWF are divided into two major groups: developed country programs and developing country programs. In turn, these two groups are divided by regions, usually continents. For example, there are vice presidents in charge of affairs in Africa, Asia, South America, etc. WWF's conservation, field, and policy expenses for 1990 by region were as follows:

Region	Percentage	$ Amount
Latin America	31%	$ 6,662,777
Asia & Pacific	15	3,709,249
Africa & Madagascar	16	4,043,907
United States	16	4,043,907
Multiregional	22	4,728,422
Total	100	23,188,262[14]

To give a sense of the breadth and diversity of WWF's activities, an overview of some of its major projects follows.

AFRICA
- Training for conservation, Madagascar
- Acoustic communication in African elephants
- Ivory trade and elephant conservation
- Utilization of rain forests by gorillas
- Zambia wildlands and human needs program
- Rhino horn trade and rhino conservation

SOUTH AMERICA
- Alternative timber harvest practices for tropical forests
- Exotic bird protection
- Creation of Rio Abisco
- Marine turtle nesting and feeding site protection, Brazil
- Conservation education curriculum, Argentina
- Golden Lion Tamarin Project, Poco da Antas, Brazil

ASIA
- Analysis of trade in bears and bear parts
- Buddhist perceptions of nature
- Debt for nature, Philippines
- Trust fund for environmental conservation, Bhutan
- Protection of large cats
- Giant panda conservation

NORTH AMERICA
- Support for owl rehabilitation research, Canada
- Large carnivore conservation, Canada
- Great Lakes ecosystem conservation
- Priorities for terrestrial arthropods, United States
- Energy strategies and global warming[15]

Development of the Issue

As with any marketing issue, the road to developing a conservation strategy begins with the identification of a need—the realization that a gap exists between a desired state and an actual state. To a conservationist, needs arise whenever goods are produced in an environmentally unsound manner so that species and habitats are threatened. For WWF, needs are identified by research scientists, volunteers, or other conservationists working in the field. From there, proposals flow through a lengthy review process before WWF will allocate money and effort to fund the conservation issue.

According to Mike Sutton, senior program officer with WWF, after WWF identifies a need or problem and justifies funding, it begins to formulate a campaign that most frequently focuses on new regulation. This has a direct impact on the injurious action. In the case of the African elephant, the imposition of new regulations and international trade bans dramatically reduced poaching activity. However, he claims, "We don't ever think it's good enough to just ban the trade and go home and declare victory. Because then what you're doing is slamming the door on the Third World. You have to work with them to close the loop, to complete the job. Banning the trade is only sort of a Band-Aid, treating the symptoms, not the underlying problems. The underlying problems are in Africa, not in the developed countries." [16] He continues to explain that for WWF, there are three aspects of every issue—species, habitat, and people.

The first step in a conservation campaign may focus on the threatened species, in this case the African elephant, and work to immediately halt the threat. But quickly after that, efforts widen to include an emphasis on habitat and native inhabitants. "People in developing countries, the poachers, the villagers and so forth, are causing the problem with the decline of the species," reasons Sutton.[17] For the ivory campaign, WWF developed a multipronged, economically based plan to suppress both the supply and the demand of ivory worldwide, as well as to replace the need for poaching in African villages.

Sutton believes that WWF is particularly effective in affecting legislation around conservation movements. A dichotomous staff helps the organization surround an issue and attack it from two sides. On the one hand, they have scientists and Peace Corps volunteers, whose experience and knowledge lends credibility to the movement. On the other hand, WWF's attorneys and employees with policy experience add strength to the tactical side of the movement.

Together, it's a winning combination. "When we go up to Capitol Hill, people listen because they know that we have field projects in 140 countries," claims Sutton.[18] WWF works with Congress, federal agencies, and international treaty organizations to affect policy changes, which is perhaps why regulations banning the trade in ivory were enacted so quickly after WWF became involved with the issue.

The ivory trade was first identified as a problem that threatened the existence of the African elephant late in the 1970s. WWF began supporting the conservation of elephants and advocating the ban on ivory trade in the late 1980s. The actual collapse of the ivory market began in October of 1988 when the United States Congress passed the African Elephant Conservation Act. This act gave the president authority to ban ivory imports, which he did on Samolian ivory in February of 1989 and on all ivory imports in June of 1989.

By 1989 the issue had garnered widespread international support that culminated in an international moratorium on the importation of ivory, an act that was signed into law at the Convention on International Trade in Endangered Species (CITES) that same year. The treaty listed the African elephant and prohibited all commercial trade in the species.

The primary focus of WWF is not to eliminate trade in wild animals but rather to maintain trade at sustainable levels, a goal anchored in consumer behavior and not in regulation. Unlike other issues, the trade in ivory lends itself nicely to behavior modification tactics. Ivory is a luxury item, and therefore it is not perceived as a necessity. Also, the ivory trade is easily challenged. Unlike the trade in exotic birds, where birds are taken from the wild and sold as pets, ivory products exist only as a result of the brutal and untimely death of an animal. It is natural to build a case by appealing to consumers' senses of compassion. And ultimately, elephants are compelling animals. Unlike certain species of endangered cockroaches, most people feel sympathy for elephants and are inclined to behave in a way to preserve this species.

Consequently, WWF began using communication techniques that appeal to compassionate consumers. Public service announcements proclaimed, "Stop the slaughter," and pictured blood-spattered, dying elephants. However, the organization quickly discovered that consumers around the world have less benevolent attitudes toward conservation of an animal species than Westerners have. In many Asian and African countries, these appeals fell on deaf ears. WWF was successful in stopping the ivory trade and the threat to elephants because the organization analyzed behavioral patterns in each country and developed different types of campaigns for different types of consumer attitudes.

Behavioral techniques were used to implement regulations as well. While ivory is not a necessity, many Asian consumers place more value on the commodity than do Westerners. Ivory is used in the Far East to make artifacts that are deeply rooted in tradition. Demand there was such that an abrupt halt in legalized trading would have created an opportunity for black market trading. Legislators in Great Britain knew this and took a six-month reservation for Hong Kong so that conservationists could discourage demand while supply simultaneously tapered.

WWF recognizes that different cultures have different values, and it strives to work within the framework of each country's value system. Remarks Sutton, "We have to be careful of charges of cultural imperialism. Sometimes we are accused of pushing our conservation ethics on other cultures." [19] But WWF is careful to tailor conservation so that, in the end, it becomes a common goal.

Conservation Campaign in the United States and Western Europe

In 1989 WWF had a clearly defined problem of a declining African elephant population due to an increasing international demand for finished ivory products. As an organization committed to preserving the world's endangered species and their habitats, WWF was responsible for putting a stop to the ivory trade to save the African elephant.

While most of WWF's efforts were focused on controlling the supply of ivory products through international regulations and diplomatic efforts, it was very important to examine consumers' attitudes toward ivory products and attempt to alter the demand for the product. By so doing, WWF could work to eliminate or sharply reduce the demand for ivory products and, therefore, the profit incentive for killing elephants.

To launch an effective campaign targeting demand for ivory products, it was necessary to examine consumers' attitudes not only toward ivory products but also toward the environment in general.

1. *Ivory*   The United States and Western Europe accounted for approximately 20 to 25 percent of the worldwide demand for finished ivory products before trade bans were enacted in 1989. In the West, ivory is primarily used for expensive, high-status jewelry or carvings.

2. *The environment*   As noted earlier, there is a growing concern for and awareness of the environment and its conservation in the United States and Western Europe. A close examination of the concerns that plague the public most, however, indicates that endangered species and their habitats are not a top priority. Given this fact, it was also necessary to examine the attitudes held toward the elephant to raise Westerners' level of consciousness about the ivory trade and its effect on the African elephant population.

3.   *The elephant*   Americans and Western Europeans seem to love
     elephants. As Mike Sutton says, "There's something special about
     [elephants] that people would be willing to give up their jewelry in
     favor of protecting [them]. People grew up reading Dumbo and
     Babar and they don't want to see elephants go extinct." [20]

It was WWF's challenge to run a campaign in the United States and
Western Europe that would target consumers' concern for the environment and love for the elephant. This was accomplished by an education
campaign, which showed that while ivory may be a beautiful status symbol, its trade is killing elephants.

WWF launched this campaign through a number of media, each designed to strike at a particular group.

FOCUS

Focus is the WWF newsletter that is sent to WWF's one million domestic
members bimonthly. *Focus* details information about WWF's projects and
provides members with opportunities to get involved in wildlife preservation. WWF published at least nine newsletters with reports on the ivory
trade. By targeting its membership, WWF was able to reach a large and
influential audience at minimal cost.

In the spring of 1989, *Focus* offered WWF members an opportunity
to take a tour of West Africa to see the National Parks of Tanzania and
Kenya. In this way members were able to view, first hand, WWF's work
and carry their experiences back to the United States to be relayed to
acquaintances and relatives. Additionally these tours helped WWF to
provide the ivory-producing nations with much needed income from
tourism.

In the summer of 1989, WWF launched its "Don't Buy Ivory" campaign through its newsletter. The president of the organization encouraged WWF's members to spread the word that ivory is not a "symbol of
elegance [but rather] parts of the stinking bodies of dead elephants." [21]

Members responded to WWF's call to action by displaying posters
and bumper stickers to stimulate conversation and education on the issue;
writing to their congressmen to lobby for additional support for elephant
conservation; and writing to local retailers to persuade them to pull ivory
off their shelves.

By focusing so much of its effort on educating children, WWF has
helped to rear environmentalists with a global vision of conservation. Even
though children would not be making the purchasing decision for ivory
products, studies have shown that families with children tend to be more
concerned with the environment because parents want to leave the world
a better place for their heirs.

"Suitcase for Survival"

In a cooperative effort with the U.S. Fish and Wildlife Service, the American Association of Zoological Parks and Aquariums, and the National Fish and Wildlife Foundation, WWF developed a hands-on project designed to acquaint young people with protected wildlife and how illegal trade in these species threatens them with extinction.

WWF received donated suitcases from American Tourister and packed them with products made from endangered species, which were donated by the Fish and Wildlife Service. The kits included such items as elephant ivory carvings and a purse made from a lizard skin where the head of the lizard served as the latch.

Also included in the packages were an assortment of background materials, slides, and other information for use in the classroom. Initially, the suitcases were distributed to major zoos, but they were later made available to schools and other educational institutions. By placing these materials in the classroom, WWF gave students an opportunity to see and handle wildlife products, to understand how trade can endanger certain vulnerable species, and to learn how to choose their purchases carefully.

For WWF, education is a key component of conservation. Tools like the "Suitcase for Survival" education kit provided a vivid, hands-on way to show young people that what they buy does make a difference in saving endangered species.

"Cargo to Extinction"

This display was similar to the "Suitcase for Survival." It consisted of four large display cases filled with actual animal products, photographs, and texts designed to educate the public about the evils of endangered species trade. The exhibit was available for the cost of shipping and appeared in a number of different zoos as well as the San Francisco International Airport.

Wildlife Trade Education Kit

An educational tool designed for school age children, the Wildlife Trade Education Kit included an 80-slide show with script, fact sheets, color posters, and an educator's guide to the kit, including suggested activities and a wildlife trade quiz.

Public Service Announcements

The ivory issue was highlighted in a powerful message developed by the Ogilvy and Mather advertising firm on a *pro bono* basis. The announcement tied the purchase and use of ivory jewelry to the death of innocent elephants in Africa.

According to the National Association of Broadcasters, the Federal Communications Commission has regulations requiring broadcast stations to address public issues, and public service announcements fulfill these requirements. Unfortunately, the decision of when to run the advertisements is left entirely to the station manager and the program director of local stations. This limits WWF's control over the target audience.

The Discovery Channel and "Ivory Wars"

The Discovery Channel is a cable channel committed to education on a wide range of topics. WWF teamed with the Discovery Channel to produce the "Ivory Wars," a documentary on the ivory trade and its effect on the elephant population.

WWF also solicited the efforts of the advertising agency W. B. Doner & Company to develop an advertising campaign to be aired on the Discovery Channel. Four different messages were produced. Their purpose, according to Valerie Sheppard, manager of the project, was to reinforce the "Don't Buy Ivory" public awareness message, to promote elephant conservation efforts on the African continent, and to enlist thousands of new members to help with WWF's international conservation efforts.[22]

WWF reaped enormous benefits from this campaign. Eleven thousand people responded to the advertisements and more than $240,000 was raised on the elephants' behalf.

Print Advertisements

With the help of the Wilder and Holden advertising firm, WWF developed an effective print advertisement focusing on the ivory trade and its effect on the African elephant population. A copy of the advertisement ran in WWF's newsletter, and members were asked to send copies of the advertisement to their favorite magazines to request that the advertisements be run as a public service. The headline read: "*You have to kill a whole elephant to get a little ivory.*"

Public Speaking Engagements

WWF makes its employees available for public speaking engagements for large, influential audiences. These engagements help WWF to spread its word to those present and to obtain media coverage of the event and the additional exposure provided by the people who do attend the presentations.

CONSERVATION CAMPAIGN IN THE FAR EAST

Altering the buying behavior of people with diverse cultural backgrounds is a special challenge for WWF. The basic approach of WWF has been to protect endangered species by implementing government laws, establishing boycotts, and removing consumer demand, but this approach has not always been successful worldwide.

WWF promotes wildlife conservation internationally by working through various institutions, including the United Nations, CITES, and the World Heritage Convention. WWF also helps to define the U.S. role in global conservation by working with Congress to enact legislation and to secure funding for international wildlife projects, and by working with the executive branch to strengthen its position in international policy.[23]

Because of cultural differences, WWF soon recognized that it would have to tailor its environmental campaigns to address the attitudes of each country. According to Mike Sutton, the countries most resistant to conservation efforts are those in the Far East and some African nations.

Over the past ten years, the primary demand for raw ivory has been in Hong Kong and Japan. Japan is the world's largest consumer of finished ivory products. Hong Kong is the center of the world ivory trade, but much of the ivory manufactured there is re-exported, primarily to Japan, the United States, and Europe.[24]

In Japan, ivory is considered a luxury item and is used to make *hankos*, small signature stamps bearing a family's name. Ivory *hankos* are rooted in Japanese tradition and have been used for centuries. The fact that ivory is such an integral part of Japanese culture poses a great barrier for the WWF.

The Japanese may not possess a strong propensity toward conservation. Their attitude is one of superiority, man over nature. Animal needs do not take precedence over human desires.

Approaching the Japanese with environmental, and sometimes unpopular, proposals has to be done with a very delicate touch. Culturally, the Japanese are accustomed to strict protocol and doing things in a very logical, well-structured manner. Therefore, the best way to reach them is through negotiation and not through emotional or confrontational tactics. As a result, intense diplomatic pressure has been WWF's method of dealing with Japan. Negotiations with warnings of trade sanctions and government boycotts are particularly successful. The Japanese sometimes regard trade sanctions as a public embarrassment, which they consider a political disaster. WWF successfully used this tactic when implementing worldwide trading regulations on whaling.

When the CITES ban on international trade in ivory was passed, it was feared that Japan would take a reservation on the treaty, a legal opposition that would allow importing and exporting of ivory. This would have proved disastrous for the WWF, as the vastness of the Japanese market would have encouraged ivory poaching. As it happened, China took a reservation (which it has since withdrawn), and the United Kingdom reserved the right to continue trade in Hong Kong for six months (which has since ended).

Since the CITES treaty, the WWF has investigated ways to make elephants a "valued" species worthy to the Japanese of preservation. Although illegal poaching still exists, Japan has supported the ban on the ivory trade. A Japanese manufacturer of *hankos* has now started producing the treasured items in gold and silver, rather than the traditional ivory, and donates 2 percent of the profits to WWF.[25]

CONSERVATION CAMPAIGN IN AFRICA

In Africa, the ivory trade was a prosperous business. Poaching was viewed in a strictly economic sense as a means to gain revenue for some of the poorest African countries. Five African nations—Botswana, Malawi, South Africa, Zambia, and Zimbabwe—all major exporters of ivory, took exception to the CITES ban on ivory. South Africa, because of its historic conservation attitude, has such an abundance of elephants that ivory is now piling up in huge excesses in warehouses, left over from the national harvesting of elephants that occurs in its national parks and wildlife preserves.

WWF is now concentrating its conservation efforts on local African villages. In an attempt to stop ivory poaching, local governments reward villagers who report poachers or other illegal forms of ivory trade. In addition, WWF is promoting tourism to provide villagers with alternative sources of income.

CONCLUSION

It is important to note that it is not illegal to buy ivory. It is illegal only to import ivory. In spite of this, few people are buying ivory products. There is no demand. Jewelry stores are taking ivory off their shelves because no one wants it. In fact, consumers are boycotting jewelry stores that continue to sell ivory. According to Sutton, "We get calls all the time from people saying, 'The jewelry store down the street is still selling ivory. Isn't that illegal?' Jewelry stores are saying they don't want the hassle. They're losing customers. It's almost gone too far."

On the agenda for future CITES meetings is the African elephant. Should it be downlisted so that the animals' skin and meat can be traded? Can there exist limited and regulated trading in ivory?

As for downlisting the African elephant, history has shown that elephants are not poached for skin or meat. And since the demand for ivory has diminished considerably, there is reduced threat of renewed poaching of elephants for their tusks. "That is the beauty of using economics to benefit wildlife," says Sutton. However, because the population of African elephants has rebounded, the animals are a threat to the crops and water supplies of villages in South Africa and Zimbabwe. Villagers inevitably kill some of the animals and could trade the skin and meat for other necessities.

As to whether or not the ivory trade should resume, Sutton believes that Asian nations would gladly fall back into their old ways. "History suggests that the ivory trade is so difficult to control that you probably would have leakage of illegal ivory into the legal stream." He concludes, "The danger is such that we will probably have to oppose reopening the ivory trade." [26]

NOTES

[1] Cohn, J. P. "Elephants: Remarkable and Endangered," *BioScience*, January 1990, p. 10.

[2] *Ibid.*, p. 11.

[3] Morell, V. "Running for Their Lives (African Elephants Target of Ivory Poachers)," *International Wildlife*, May/June 1990, p. 11.

[4] Hueber, G. *The Gallup Poll Monthly*, April 1991, p. 6.

[5] *Black's Law Dictionary*, 1983, p. 98.

[6] Garrett, D. E. "The Effectiveness of Marketing Policy Boycotts: Environmental Opposition to Marketing," *The Journal of Marketing*, April 1987, p. 46.

[7] *The Economist.* "Boycotting Corporate America," May 26, 1990, p. 69.

[8] *World Wildlife Fund and the Conservation Foundation 1990: A Combined Report*, 1990, pp. 4–10.

[9] World Wildlife Fund Contribution Brochure.

[10] World Wildlife Fund and the Conservation Foundation Brochure.

[11] "Your Guide to Green Groups: Where Top Advertisers Turn for Help," *Advertising Age*, October 28, 1991.

[12] *World Wildlife Fund and the Conservation Foundation 1990: A Combined Report*, pp. 10, 66.

[13] *Ibid.*, p. 1.

[14] *Ibid.*, p. 10.

[15] *Ibid.*, p. 50.

[16] Interview with Michael Sutton, senior program officer, The World Wildlife Fund, October 23, 1991.

[17] *Ibid.*

[18] *Ibid.*

[19] *Ibid.*

[20] *Ibid.*

[21] Train, R. "President's Message," *Focus*, Summer 1990, p. 2.

[22] "World Wildlife Fund Uses Television for Elephant Action Campaign," *Focus*, Special Report 1990, p. 1.

[23] World Wildlife Fund and the Conservation Foundation promotional brochure.

[24] "The Ivory Trade and the Future of the African Elephant," Interim Report, Ivory Trade Review Group, prepared for the second meeting of the CITES African Elephant Working Group, July 1989, p. 15.

[25] "Japanese Change Their Ways," *Focus*, Spring 1990, p. 1.

[26] Interview with Michael Sutton.

SELECTED REFERENCES FOR FURTHER INFORMATION

Time (1991). "A Grisly and Illicit Trade." (April 8), 67–68.

Bohlen, J. T. (1989). "Nightmare in Africa: Wanton Elephant Poaching Takes Huge Toll," *Focus* (March/April).

Burmeister, L. (1991). World Wildlife Fund, Washington, DC, Interview, 22 October.

The Economist (1990). "Boycotting Corporate America," May 26, 69–70.

Cohn, J. P. (1990). "Elephants: Remarkable and Endangered," *BioScience* (January), 10–14.

Garrett, D. E. (1987). "The Effectiveness of Marketing Policy Boycotts: Environmental Opposition to Marketing," *Journal of Marketing* (April), 46–55.

Graham, F. (1990). "Ban Bankrupts the Far East Ivory Carvers," *Audubon* (September), 64–65.

Hueber, G. (1991). "Americans Report High Levels of Environmental Concern," *The Gallop Monthly Poll* (April), 6–9.

Focus (1990). "Japanese Change Their Ways," (Spring).

Jones, R. (1990). "A Farewell to Africa." *Audubon*, (September), 51–65.

Jones, S. (1989). "Hong Kong Ivory Industry Seeks Buyers as International Ban on Trade Nears," *The Wall Street Journal*, 22 December.

Laser, W., and E. Kelley (1973). *Social Marketing: Perspectives and Viewpoints.* Homewood, IL: Richard D. Irwin.

McCune, J. G. (1990). "Consumer Activism Means Big Business," *Management Review* (December), 16–19.

Morell, V. (1990). "Running for Their Lives," *International Wildlife* (May/June), 4–13.

Newsweek (1986). "Peddling a Social Cause," September 1, 58–59.

The Economist (1989). "Saving the Elephant—Nature's Great Masterpiece," July 1, 15–17.

Simmons, R., and U. Kreuter (1989). "Save an Elephant—Buy Ivory," *The Washington Post*, 1 October.

Sutton, M. (1989). "Don't Let Them Buy Ivory," *The Washington Post*, 9 October, A21.

——— (1991). World Wildlife Fund, Washington, DC, Interview, 23 October.

The Ivory Trade and the Future of the African Elephant (1989). Ivory Trade Review Group (July).

World Wildlife Fund and the Conservation Foundation (1991). World Wildlife Fund.

Author Index

Company/Product Index